BIHAR AND MITHILA

Bihar and Mithila

The Historical Roots of Backwardness

J. ALBERT RORABACHER

MANOHAR
2016

First published 2016

ISBN 978-93-5098-000-2

Published by
Ajay Kumar Jain *for*
Manohar Publishers & Distributors
4753/23 Ansari Road, Daryaganj
New Delhi 110 002

Printed at
Salasar Imaging Systems
Delhi 110 035

This volume is dedicated to
the American Institute of Indian Studies, the AIIS,
through whose generosity I was permitted to visit
India as an aspiring Ph.D. candidate to undertake
my first research project in 1974-5. That grant opened
my eyes and mind to the unbelievable and beautiful
world of South Asia. Hopefully, this volume will
begin to repay some of the inestimable debt I owe you.

Contents

Illustrations and Tables

DIAGRAMS

FIGURES

GRAPHS

MAPS

PLATES

TABLES

Glossary

Abwab	:	Items of taxation, cesses, imposts, taxes. Usually illegal. A cess levied in addition to ordinary revenue or rent.
Adalat	:	Court of justice.
Adhvaryu	:	Those Brahmins who were in charge of the physical details of rituals and sacrifice.
Amil	:	Agent, manager, or retainer of a landlord.
Amla	:	Plural form of *amil*.
Anna	:	One-sixteenth (1/16th) of a rupee.
apauruseya	:	Not of human origin.
Ashab-u'l-amamah	:	Theologian.
Ashab-u'l-qalam	:	Masters of the pen.
Ashab-u's-saif	:	Masters of the sword.
BSP	:	Bahujan Samaj Party. Centre-left national party.
Bakast or *Bekast*	:	Self-cultivated lands.
Balan	:	River.
Bania	:	Hindu merchant or shopkeeper.
Barahils	:	Landlord's retainer or guard.
Batai	:	A rent system with rent paid in kind as a certain portion of the produce. A form of share-tenancy.
Bataidari	:	Sharecropper.
Batta	:	Allowance, especially for troops in the field.
BC	:	Backward Classes.
Begari	:	A system wherein a group of people are required to perform certain compulsory duties for the landlord and other village residents.
Bhuiyan or *Bhupati*	:	Pre-Mughal land tenure system.
Bigha or Begah	:	A unit of land measurement. Equal to 1.6 acres or 0.67 hectares. The size of a *bigha* varies by region.

Bils	:	Marshlands. Natural runoff retention areas.
Bindi	:	A bright dot of red colour applied in the centre of the forehead close to the eyebrows.
biradaris	:	A term meaning caste and creed.
BJP	:	Bharatiya Janata Party. Currently the ruling national political party in India. Right wing.
Boh	:	Sheet-flooding in Bihar.
BPL	:	Below Poverty Line.
BRGF	:	Backward Regions Grant Fund.
Bund	:	An embankment against flooding.
Cesses	:	A use tax.
Chaudhuri	:	A permanent superintendant and receiver of land revenue.
Chaurs	:	The name for natural drainage patterns in Bihar.
Chowkeedar or *chaukidar*	:	Watchman.
Circar	:	The state or government.
Crore	:	A numerical term meaning 10,000,000.
Dacoit or *dakait*	:	Gang member, robber.
Dacoity	:	Violent gang robberies.
Darshan or Darśana	:	A term meaning 'auspicious sight' in the sense of an instance of seeing or beholding and being seen or beheld at the same time; an event of consciousness—an interaction in presence between devotee and a god or guru. For the devotee, it represents a 'breakthrough' or heightening of one's consciousness.
Distraint	:	The seizure of someone's property in order to obtain payment of rent or other money owed, especially in common law countries.
Diwan	:	During the Mughal period, the term *diwan* stood for a person, the head of the revenue department, and the office was known as *diwani;* the head of the branches of the revenue department was also known as *diwan.* Also, Dewan.

Diwani adalat	:	Civil court.
Diwani sanad	:	A title-deed given by the finance ministry.
Diwani	:	The office or jurisdiction of a *diwan*.
Dole	:	Bucket.
Durbar	:	The court, hall of audience.
EBC	:	Extremely Backward Castes.
Ektha	:	Spoon-like water-lifting device.
Enam	:	Present, gift, favour, gratuity.
Farman or *Firman*	:	Imperial order.
Ghatwal	:	Guard.
Godown	:	Warehouse.
Gotra	:	A clan; people who are descendants in an unbroken male line from a common male ancestor.
Grama	:	One of several hierarchical divisions within the Maithil Brahmanas complicated system of lineages.
Grihasthas	:	Typically high-caste Hindus who do not cultivate the soil.
Hak zamindar	:	Zamindar's share/remuneration for services.
Haks	:	Service fees. Rights.
Hali	:	A method of assessment.
Hasili	:	Land subject to assessments.
Hastabood or *Hastobud*	:	A comparative account or rent-roll.
Hat or *Haut*	:	A village market, occurring at least once a week and more as the village increases in size.
Havildar	:	Revenue collectors.
HDI	:	Human Development Index.
Hijab	:	A veil that covers the head and chest, which is particularly worn by Muslim women.
Hindutva	:	Hindu nationalism.
Hotr	:	Those Brahmins in charge of the invocations and litanies.
IMD	:	Indian Meterological Department.
INC	:	Indian National Congress. Oldest political party in India, founded in 1885. National, modern, liberal platform.

Inqilab : Revolution.

Izzat : Self-respect.

Jagir : *Raikar* lands assigned to government employees and functionaries in lieu of salary.

Jagir, Jagheer or *jaghire* : A Persian term meaning land assigned. In medieval India, it meant the assignment of non-hereditary rights in land and its rent as an annuity to state functionaries. With the departure or death of the incumbent, the state normally resumed the *jagir* and settled it with the next incumbent.

Jagirdar : Beneficiary of a *jagir* land assignment.

Jagiri : Land resumed from a *jagirdar*.

Jajmani : A system of *jati* interdependence and exchanges.

Jama or *Jamma* : The total of a territorial assessment.

Jat : One of several cultivator groups/castes, especially in western and north-western India and Pakistan.

Jati : Caste or a local social substructure.

JD : Janata Dal party. Political party. Splinter parties include Rashtriya Janata Dal, Janata Dal United, and Janata Dal (Secular), among others.

JD(U) : Janata Dal United, was once the fifth largest political party in India, centre-left, primarily in Bihar and Jharkhand.

Jeth ryots : Rent collectors under the Darbhanga Raj system.

Jotedar : A very rich peasant.

Kanungo : The person who measures the land, a type of early surveyor, who prepared the land registers, the basis for the establishment of land-rents.

Karad raja : A rent paying king.

Karmakanda : Rules of proper conduct. That part of the *Śruti* (Vedic) writings which relate to ceremonial acts and sacrificial rites.

Karin : Manual, spoon-like water-lifting device.

Kas or *khas* : Private land.

Kartika : A month in the Hindu calendar. It begins with the new moon in November and is the eighth month of the year.

Khálsa : Referring to the Emperor or Crown, as is Crown Lands. Treasury Department.

Kharif : Refers to the planting, cultivation and harvesting of any domesticated plant sown in the rainy (monsoon) season for harvest in the autumn.

Khas lands : Land cultivated by a landowner's own draught animals or labourers or hired draught animals or labourers. See also, *bekast*.

Khichri : Technically, a dish made of rice, dal, and other ingredients. It is an easy dish to prepare and is provided by the government during relief efforts, especially during floods in Bihar. The term has become synonymous with welfare or charity in Bihar.

Kisan : Cultivator/peasant/farmer.

Kists : Monthly installments.

Kulachar : The system of inheritance, a modified form of primogeniture, that applied to both the ownership of the Darbhanga Raj and succession. Each raja had to be named by his predecessor and the family's lands were not subject to traditional Hindu inheritance laws and thus were impartible.

Kut : A system of sharecropping under which the landowner appropriated a specific quantity of produce or stated sum in cash as rent.

Kut System : Cultivator usually paid a stipulated sum in cash or kind. Assessment rates bore no relationship to actual field productivity.

Laïcité : A French term meaning/concept denoting the absence of religious involvement in government affairs as well as absence of government involvement in religious affairs – the strict separation of State from Church.

Lakh or *Lac* : A numerical term meaning 100,000.

Lathyals : Strongmen for a zamindar, enforcers.

Laukit : A new series of lineage titles created to overcome a marriage impasse for the Darbhanga Raj's family, since they were finding it difficult to find suitable mates.

LJP	:	Lok Janshakti Party. Secular/Socialist Party, primarily in Bihar.
Madhyasvatva	:	Literally 'subinfeudation'. An illegal landed intermediate class in Bengal. Their existence was not provided for in the Permanent Settlement regulations or statute books.
Maharaja	:	'Great king' or 'high king'.
Mal-wajibi	:	Revenue-paying but primarily revenue-collecting lesser zamindars.
Mamoridar	:	A Rajputana local rent/tax farmer.
Mandal	:	Of or relating to the Mandal Commission, a commission established in 1979 by prime minister Morarji Desai with a mandate to identify the socially or educationally backward in Indian Society.
Mandap	:	A covered, raised platform whose primary function is to protect the Vedic fire at its centre.
Mansabdar	:	Mughal officer/official.
Mansabdari	:	The Mansabdari System was a non-hereditary, non-feudal aristocracy instituted by Akbar and organized the nobility, army, and civil administration. Every official position was assigned a numeric value. The system classified the functionaries of the kingdom as fighters, *ashab-u's-saif* (masters of the sword); clerks, *ashab-u'l-qalam* (masters of the pen); theologians, *ashab-u'l-amamah*. The *mansab* denoted a rank of office, its obligations, precedence, and pay grade. Each rank included a *zat* and *sawar* responsibilities.
Mauza or *Mouza*	:	Revenue villages, the lowest-level revenue collection unit.
MGNREGA	:	Mahatma Gandhi National Rural Employment Guarantee Act, aka National Rural Employment Guarantee Act, 2005.
MLA	:	Member of the Legislative Assembly, state level.
Mocurrery	:	A lease for a specified period at a fixed rate.
Mofussil	:	A subordinate division of a district.

Mouzawar	:	Land enclosed within a village's boundary.
MPI or OPHI	:	Oxford Multidimensional Poverty Index.
Mukaduami	:	Collection fee.
Mula	:	A maximal lineage within the Srotriya marriage ranking system.
Mulagram	:	Permanent titles based on maximal and minimal (gram) lineages.
Naib diwan	:	Deputy Finance Minister.
Naib	:	Deputy.
Nawab	:	Governor.
Nawabzadas	:	Variation of the term nawab but typically referring to the son of a nawab or a title given to a 'lesser' nawab.
Naya Bihar	:	New Bihar.
Nazarana	:	Fee paid by a service provider.
Nazim	:	Governor of department of justice at provincial level.
Nazimat	:	Branch of government responsible for administration of justice.
NCP	:	National Congress Party. Centre-left political party, primarily in Maharashtra.
NDA	:	National Democratic Alliance. Coalition of several regional/state political parties. The BJP is the primary focus of this alliance.
NIC	:	National Informatics Centre.
NDA	:	National Democratic Alliance, a centre-right alliance of political parties, currently led by Narendra Modi of Gujarat.
OBC	:	Other Backward Castes.
Paddial	:	Agricultural labourers.
Pagri	:	Turban.
Pakho	:	Arable hillsides, which drained rapidly, and were used for the cultivation of millet and maize. Unirrigated.
Paliwals	:	Tax collector.
Panchayat	:	Village or village council.
Panial	:	Agricultural labourers.

Panjikars	:	Hereditary Maithil Brahmana genealogists.
Panjis	:	Originally detailed geneologies maintained on treated palm leaves. Later transferred to paper and, even later, becoming computer files.
Pargana nirikh	:	Established rent rate.
Parmangee	:	Formal permission to marry, once provided by the Maharaja of Darbhanga for Srotriya marriages.
Patel	:	Local village agent or headman.
Pathis	:	One-twentieth of a volumetric *muri*.
Patni	:	A subinfeudatory tenure, resulting from fictitious land purchases and transfers.
Patpar	:	Sand, gravel, and rock casted land. Usually results in loss of land for productive purposes.
Patta (1)	:	Villages subject to the payment of a fee called a *rakm*.
Patta (2)	:	A land allotment certificate in the Terai region.
Patta, Patam, or *Pottah* (3)	:	Lease.
Pattadari	:	Tenure. Cultivators kept land as long as they paid their revenue in a timely manner. This also applied to the series of sub-zamindars, who paid the zamindars a fixed annuity in exchange for a permanent intermediary position or status.
Pattidars	:	Those holding a *patta* tenure.
Patwari	:	Local village agent, accountant, record keeper, similar in function to the *kanungos*.
Pergunnah	:	A pre-Permanent Settlement revenue unit consisting of several *mouzas*. A small district consisting of several villages.
Peshkashi	:	Tribute-paying allies of the Mughal Emperor.
PIL	:	Public Interest Litigation or filing.
Pravara	:	Invocation at the beginning of sacrifice or to one's ancestors. Also, used to describe one's position within the Srotriya lineage hierarchy.
Pucca or *Pukka*	:	Finished, permanent.
Pulbandi	:	Embankment levies/charges.
Punyah	:	A ceremony during which the assessment was set and revenues collected. On the first day of the new

		year, the tenants paid taxes to the zamindars and in turn the *zamindars* paid their dues to the government.
Rabi	:	Refers to agricultural crops sown in winter and harvested in the summer season.
Rahat	:	Colloquial term for Persian wheel in northern Bihar.
Raikar	:	Lands on which taxes are collected from individual landowners, traditionally regarded as state-owned.
Rajanya	:	The noble or warrior category within the *Varna* system.
Rajputs	:	A member of one of the patrilineal clans of western, central, northern India and some parts of Pakistan.
Rakm (1)	:	A fee paid by *patta* villages.
Rakm (2)	:	Unpaid and compulsory labour service due to the government from peasants cultivating *Raikar*, *Kipat*, and *Raj Guthi* lands.
Rashtriya Barh Ayog	:	National Commission on Floods.
RJD	:	Rashtriya Janata Dal, a social conservative, secular political party, led by Lalu Prasad Yadav. Primarily in Bihar.
RLSP	:	Rashtriya Lok Samata Party, Socialist Party, primarily in Bihar.
Ryot or *Raiyat*	:	All people engaged in agricultural production and paying land tax to the state via landholders. *Ryots* under the Mughal constitution had rights in land, which were protected by custom and usage within the *parganas*. Sometimes spelled *raiyat*. In most current government documents, the term *raiyat* seems preferable to *ryot*.
Ryotwari	:	Settlement made directly with the *ryots*.
Sadhu	:	Priest or holy man.
Samskaras	:	Major life-cycle rites
Sanad	:	Mughal document conferring a privilege, to make a grant. All *jagirs* and zamindaris were granted by issuing *sanads*.
Sardar	:	Perso-Turkish term meaning prince, nobleman,

		aristocrat, chief or leader. Colloquially used to refer to Sikhs.
Sarkar or *Circar*	:	A territorial division of a *Subah* or province.
Sayer Mahals	:	Taxes on *hats* and bazaars.
Sawar	:	Indicated the number of cavalrymen a *Mansabdar* was required to maintain.
SCS	:	Special Category State.
Sena	:	Armed gang or private army.
Seer	:	Officially a unit of weight equivalent to 0.93310 kg (2.057131 lb). However there were many local variants throughout India.
Seristadar	:	Chief revenue accountant.
Shakha	:	Hindu theological school that specializes in learning certain Vedic texts. May also be used to refer to an adherent of a particular orthodox system.
Shreni	:	A set of additional lineage titles and classifications within the *laukit* classification, used to diversify and open the marriage pool of the Maharajas of Darbhanga.
Sicca rupee	:	Silver coin minted by the East India Company as the government of Bengal, becoming the legal tender in Bihar and Bengal. Also known as the 'Company's Rupee'.
Smrti	:	'That which is remembered'. Refers to a specific body of Hindu religious scripture, and is a codified component of Hindu customary law. *Smrti* also denotes non-*Śruti* texts.
Śrauta or *Shrauta*	:	Conservative ritualistic traditions of the historical Vedic religion in Hinduism, based on the body of *Śruti* literature.
Srotriya	:	The highest division of Maithil Brahmanas.
Śruti or Śhruti	:	The body of sacred texts comprising the central canons of Hinduism and is one of the three main sources of dharma.
Subah	:	A province.
Subahdar	:	Mughal provincial governor.

Tahsildar or *Tehsildars*	:	Government official at the *tahsil* level. Assistant managers at the circle level within the Darbhanga Raj system.
Talluqa	:	Synonymous with the term zamindari.
Taluka	:	A political subdivision.
Talukdars	:	Landlords not easily distinguished from zamindars. Sometimes subordinate to zamindars. Or, may refer to village-level revenue collection functionaries in Bengal.
Taluqdars	:	The term *taluqdar* has different meanings in different parts of India. In north India a *taluqdar* is a great landholder. But in Bengal, a *taluqdar* is next to a zamindar in extent of land control and social status.
Terai	:	Marshy grasslands, savannas, and forests located south of the outer foothills of the Himalaya, the Siwalik Hills, and north of the Indo-Gangetic Plain.
Thakbast	:	Demarcation survey.
Tilaka	:	A mark worn on the forehead. The mark can be as simple as a *bindi* (dot) or cover the entire forehead or even other parts of the body.
Tols	:	Typically 'open air' schools dedicated to traditional (Vedic) education by a single master.
Udgātr	:	The Brahmin chanters of hymns.
WDRs	:	World Development Reports, published by the World Bank.
Zamin	:	Land.
Zamindar	:	From the Persian *zamin* or land, and *dar* which is an inflexion of the verb *dashtan*, denoting to have, hold or possess. Zamindars during the Mughal period came to denote all rent receivers above the actual cultivators. They were possessors of proprietary right in the collection of rent but not in land.
Zamindari	:	A zamindar's estate.
Zat	:	A Mughal personal rank that included status and salary.

Acknowledgements

The seed for this book was planted in January 1975, as the author sat talking to a large landowner in a village north-east of Darbhanga town. Our conversation was carried on in a combination of English and Hindi, with a sprinkling of Maithili. He consulted with his friends, who sat scattered around, in Maithili. He mentioned that the village he lived in, and where we were chatting, and several others were part of his zamindari. Although the idea of zamindari was far from my core study, I catalogued the word in my head, where it remained untouched for more than thirty years.

Then, in 2008, as a result of work I was doing on flooding in Bihar, I remembered the encounter with this gentleman. I remembered the pride that he seemed to attach to being a zamindar, which, as far as I understood it, was a term no longer used because it was either deemed politically incorrect or the zamindars had been eliminated through land reform legislation decades earlier. I was wrong.

I began my researches for this book as a part of the research I was doing for a book dealing with the causes of hunger and poverty in South Asia. Once that book was completed, I threw myself headlong into my 'zamindar book'. Six years later, 'the book' was completed. It was read by a retired anthropologist who had specialized on Bihar. She politely, but forcefully, informed me that the manuscript was too long (over 600 pages) and contained and represented two connected but separate topics – one dealing with the idea of property in India and the other, development. Nine months later, the first of these two volumes was finished and emerged as *Property, Land, Revenue and Policy: The East India Company c. 1757-1825* (Manohar, 2015). Once that volume was completed, work began on the revision of the current volume.

This volume could not, and would not exist had it not been for the efforts of numerous individuals. Some, because of their steady contributions, need mentioning. First, there is Nona Gardner, a friend and the first soul who sees my ideas on paper. She is the one who wrestles with my prose, deciphering my arcane references and inferences, making them readable for others. Thank you.

Barbara Romeo of the Barrie Public Library, Interlibrary Loan Office, has, with few exceptions, found impossible to find volumes for me to consult. I am indebted to her for her tenacity and pure detective work. This book would never have become a reality without her assistance.

Carolyn Brown Heinz, now a retired professor of anthropology, who is putting her time to good literary use, was responsible for the observation that my monster manuscript was in actuality, two books in one. As the author, I was too close to the subject to be able to separate the trees from the forest. With a not-so-gentle nudge, I acquiesced. For her willingness to take time from her busy schedule to review a very sloppy initial draft, I thank her.

Stephen Henningham, formerly the High Commissioner to Samoa for Australia, I thank you, first, for your scholarship on the Darbhanga Raj, and second, for the many e-mail conversations we conducted over topics that few others would probably find interesting or endurable. You provided insights, generally, when I was in need of that little bit of encouragement to get me on to the next paragraph. Your friendship and advice will endure.

Tejakar Jha, the son of the noted sociologist Hetukar Jha, and nephew of the Maharaniadhirani Kam Sundari, the widow and third wife of the last Maharajadhiraja Kameshwar Singh of the erstwhile Darbhanga Raj. Tejakar has been an indispensable source of inspiration and a well-spring of information, especially with regard to the Darbhanga Raj. He has taken time away from his own personal literary and photojournalism projects to assist the author in the completion of this and two previous books. In all likelihood, no other person has been as closely associated with this volume as Tejakar. I cannot adequately express my gratitude.

I cannot thank Ramesh Chandra Jain, my publisher, and Siddharth Chowdhury, my editor, enough for their attention to detail and their willingness to engage my numerous questions and suggestions. Every contact with these gentlemen has been nothing short of delightful. Thank you so much for everything.

Finally, there is my wife, Hava. Many are the nights she trotted off to bed, alone, peeking in on me as she passed my office, often just shaking her head in amazement. While not personally understanding the allure of my topic, she never wavered in her support for my work. She has been my companion, guardian, and guide for more than twenty years. I cannot personally find the words that are delicate enough and, at the same time, powerful enough to express my appreciation for all she has done to make all my books possible. No one could possibly have been given more loving support than I have received over the years it has taken to get this volume completed.

Without each and every one of you, this volume would have remained nestled in some dark recess of my head and would have never seen the light of day. Thank you one and all.

Barrie, Ontario, Canada J. Albert Rorabacher
23 December 2014

Introduction

More than fifty years ago, the anthropologist Kusum Nair trekked the length and breadth of India, stopping and chatting with villagers regarding the impact of development on their lives.[1] Her treatment was narrative and descriptive rather than rigorously analytical. Why did she choose this methodology over the other equally well suited to her objective? She stated that she believed it better suited the situation, bringing out the attitudes and opinions of the people she was interviewing.[2] In so doing, she drew upon a long tradition of many of the social sciences, one of observation, conceptual analysis, and synthesis; a tradition based more on a form of literature than on a system of painstaking experimentation or report methodologies found in other social sciences or the physical sciences.

She understood that village-level statistics, then, as well as now, are often notoriously unreliable; and yet these very same 'statistics' served, and continue to serve as the foundation of state and international development agencies' programmes and plans. In general, authoritative and accurate village-level statistics still remain elusive and amorphous.

Nair's approach relied on observation and context; drawing conclusions from what she saw and heard. Observations are typically difficult to quantify, except in the case of frequency, but one has to ask, is it any less accurate than any other statistic when talking about development? Statistics for tonnes of steel, quintals of maize, rice, or wheat, or barrels of oil tend to be fairly accurate. They measure numerable, tangible things. Statistics concerning the well-being of humans is an entirely different proposition; one the author finds useful but inherently suspect despite the exactness of their derivation.[3]

While the author accepts the general conceptual utility of comparative indices, like the Human Development Index (HDI) or the Oxford Multidimensional Poverty Index (MPI), one still has to question the statistical basis upon which they are founded. Statistics are the aggregation of collected information beginning at the village level, compiled at the district level then moved vertically through the governmental machinery of the state and then on to the nation and the world. If the foundational data is potentially flawed. . . .

* * *

During the years following Nair's remarkable study, the social sciences have undergone a change. The author would not, however, characterize this change as evolutionary nor revolutionary, as much as he would call it the adoption of a survival strategy. There has always been a rift, a schism between the natural and social sciences. This modest antagonism between the two stems largely from how each interprets the 'scientific method' and how one defines disciplinary legitimacy. The social sciences are typically seen as the 'poor stepchildren' of the hard sciences. This second-class status, while only periodically verbalized by either side, has had the effect of influencing the form and function of the social sciences and creating a certain paranoia amongst its practitioners.

At the heart of the problem between the 'sciences' is the concept of causality. The physical or hard sciences are paradigmatic, that is, there are fundamental principles that define and limit their range of research and the methodologies that are deemed appropriate to that research.[4] Causality is less frequently used within the context of the social sciences. There are several reasons suggested for this. First, they are not as homogenous as the hard sciences. The fields of inquiry range from those of psychology that is somewhat integrated with the natural sciences through medicine, to those that draw more on the humanities such as linguistics, anthropology, and history. This diversity becomes part of the problem because it leads to a diversity of justifications. Geography occupies a unique position, treading the razor's edge, with one foot in the natural sciences and one foot in the social sciences.

Second, the social sciences lack the theoretical robustness of the hard sciences. However, some of the guardians of the hard sciences are increasingly showing chinks in their own theoretical armour, which belies a vulnerability. Many seem riven with the same uncertainties as the social sciences. This is nowhere more evident than within theoretical physics, cosmology, or quantum mechanics.

Third, the social sciences 'come up short' when it comes to their ability to predict consequences, which lies at the heart of science and the scientific method. Human beings, with their cultural diversity, linguistic differences, aspirations, 'psychologies', differing technologies, etc., do not easily nor readily lend themselves to the creation of predictive laws or even generalizations. Social laws derived from regularities in social statistics will never become sufficiently specific to be independent of time and place. Unlike the physical sciences, the social sciences are dynamic and fluid. Social laws derived from correlations of statistical fact can have considerable scientific value but we should not place too much confidence in the inferences we are tempted to draw from them. Equally difficult is differentiating between fact and value. Both are elusive and slippery.

Finally, unlike chemistry, classical physics, or mathematics, the social sciences seem to have problems with replication. Research replication, believed to be an essential feature of good science, because it authenticates the work of others, is generally sorely lacking in the social sciences and when replication is attempted, the results tend to be inconclusive, at best, and often completely different, at worst.[5] This may be a consequence of shoddy or sloppy research, incorrect or inappropriate analysis of field data, sample size, or a function of changing times and conditions.

There is, however, both a down- and up-side to scientific replication. When studies can be reproduced, as in the physical sciences, and have been so on several occasions, there is little incentive for the next generation of scientists to redo the experiments of their predecessors. As a result, old findings, once proven, are seldom revisited. Furthermore, academic journals are more inclined to publish new research with positive outcomes than replication studies.[6] However, just maybe, there is merit in performing social science replication studies. They always seem to produce new results!

This is what truly separates the physical sciences from the social sciences. If experts in each of the social sciences can reach wildly different conclusions using the same field data or observations, it would seem to suggest that there may be something wrong with the way social scientists approach problems; or that they are not locked-in to methodologies that lend themselves to the production of cookie-cutter type results. Further, in general, the social sciences tend to be more comparative than authoritative in their findings; and it is the differences between groups that excite the social scientist. However, comparison and focusing on differences between groups is seldom conducive to the formulation of laws, principles, or axioms.

* * *

It was during the so-called Enlightenment – that sprawling intellectual, philosophical, cultural, and social movement that spread throughout parts of Europe during the 1700s – that a science of man was first deemed a possibility and that it would develop into a 'softer' version of Newtonian physics. Newtonian physics was rigorous, reproducible, and predictable; and it still is.[7] More than two centuries have intervened between the Enlightenment and present day and we appear no closer to the goal espoused by the Enlightenment. In part, this may be because of the dreamers of the time overestimated Man's desire to commit to a common good, believing that Man was, first and foremost, a rational animal. In light of current events, it would seem we have not made much progress since the eighteenth century. Mankind does not seem to be committed to a common good and only infrequently displays glimmers of rationality.

Even before the Enlightenment, science was the domain of philosophers, poets, writers, intellectuals, scholars, or people of erudition – men and women of ideas, reflection, and the pen, and who expressed their ideas through their writings. As alchemy gave way to the 'science' of chemistry, a division between scientists and their scientific method and the humanists, with their rationalism and empiricism began to take shape. As Brodbeck points out:

> Despite the division of labor between the humanist's study of man and the scientist's study of matter, the line soon became a barricade. By its fruits science gained affluence, power, prestige – and resentment. Not surprisingly the resentment deepened when the methods of science were extended to the humanist's ancient preserve, the study of man and society. The extension has always been bitterly resented; the opposition has never been wholly allayed, cropping up from time to time with renewed fervor.

In part the opposition is merely a tedious jurisdictional dispute, backed more by malice and irrelevant snipings at unfulfilled promise than by rational argument.[8]

* * *

The first use of 'social statistics' was to influence social debates. They were used as numeric evidence; numeric statements about social life that brought the authority and precision of mathematics to social problems. Therein lies the foible of modern social science and statistics. Numbers, because of their precision, are readily accepted as being somehow correct and with correctness comes the aura of authority. Statistics are regularly used with no thought given to their veracity, reliability or validity, as long as they appear to support one's arguments. Evidence in support of an argument or problem does not inherently carry with it understanding; and it is more important that we understand a problem than simply define, describe, or quantify it. These processes do not necessarily lead to solutions and often divert us from the real problem. That is the power of statistics.

* * *

The poet W.H. Auden, possibly tongue-in-cheek, once wrote as part of a longer poem:

> . . . Thou shalt not sit
> With statisticians nor commit
> A social science.[9]

This short verse would seem to insinuate that counting and measuring are not, or should not be seen as substitutes for thinking.[10] Yet, statistics and statistical analyses have become the heart of modern social science. Concepts that are not easily quantified appear to lack the rigorousness that has become the hallmark of modern scholarship. The management consultant Peter Drucker once said: 'If you can't measure it, you can't manage it.'[11]

Almost every young researcher is tempted to analyse his data using sophisticated statistical computer programmes, until it says what he believes it should say; believing that he knows the truth. At this stage, he changes his analysis specifications until the statistic he is looking for produces a significant result. One of the author's mentors once observed, while discussing the computer analysis of field data: 'If you massage data long enough, it will say anything you want.' The author must have thought there was something axiomatic about that statement since, now, more than thirty-five years later, it still, maybe more so than ever, haunts him. This statement is analogous to Ronald Harry Coase's dictum: 'If you torture data for long enough, it will confess.'[12]

Coase's statement is very cleverly worded. It is a double-edged sword. On the one hand, the researcher must work the data until it has given up all its informative value. On the other, and especially for novice researchers, there is a tendency to attempt to wring more out of the data than is legitimately there. Torturing data is not necessarily a bad thing but 'making it say more than it is capable of saying' is both imprudent and dangerous; and there is a fine line between torturing data for all it can legitimately say and making it confess.

The maturity of a researcher is measured not by the sophistication of his analysis or algorithms, nor the level of significance or confidence of his statistic but by his willingness to accept unanticipated results and find an explanation for them. Thomas Kuhn would refer to this as paradigm shifting.[13] However viewed, there are times when the researcher's original specifications or hypotheses are, in fact, incorrect. The problem, then, is recognizing the difference.

Instead of fitting the data to the theoretical construct, one must either: (a) find an existing construct that fits the data; or (b) redefine or develop a new construct without torturing the data. Further, much of the mathematics used in scholarly publications today is used to make them appear more complicated and profound than they really are. Others use it as decoration.[14] Decoration, aside from aesthetics, serves no purpose. It would not be decoration if it contributed substantively to our understanding; but what it does is demonstrate that the author is 'up to date' with the most recent and obscure developments in mathematics. In most scholarly publications, pages of formulae are used as window-dressing, adding pages but little in the way of understanding or useful content, since typically, the authors tell the reader in prose what the formulae mean or reveal. When the author finds a journal article or report that seems pertinent, he begins reading in earnest. As he turns the pages and is confronted with formula after formula, appearing like delicate Arabesque designs strewn across the page, he marvels at their beauty and quickly turns the page. The formulae are meaningless by themselves. What they demonstrate or reveal is far more important than their elegance.

According to Marvin Harris, '. . . anthropology . . . in one way or another rejected the scientific mandate' in the belief that it could never discover the origins of institutions or explain their causes.[15] Obviously, this view of anthropology did not go long unchallenged. Nonetheless, cultural anthropology shared with history a tradition of description followed by rigorous analysis but both avoided statements of causality while, at the same time, conveying the impression that an explanation was being offered.[16] The icons of anthropology – Boas, Kroeber, Lowie, Spencer, Mead, Murdock, Lewis, Redfield, Nair, etc. – were describers of culture; analysis followed fieldwork, cultural inventories, and cultural placement.

The social sciences, in general, would all like to be recognized, as the name implies, as sciences. Some may be more amenable than others to this aspiration. However, unlike chemistry and physics, the social sciences lack the precision and predictability of the 'hard sciences'. However, even if one compares anthropology or history with modern physics, is there really such a difference? One need only look to theoretical physics, cosmology, or quantum physics. Much of physics today is little more than speculation, with many claimants to Einstein's *Einheitliche Feldtheorie* (theory of everything) but all unable to grasp the prize, unable to empirically prove the validity of their approach. Classical physics, Newtonian physics, which most closely resembles what we have come to believe to be science is relegated to the mundane tasks of computing rocket and spacecraft trajectories and the movement of celestial bodies through space. The rest, and currently the focus of most mainstream physicists, remains in that murky no man's land somewhere between mathematics, philosophy, and free thinking, where one talks of strings, branes, black holes, cosmological inflation, quantum mechanics, and bosons, quarks having flavours, like up, down, strange, charm, bottom, and top. Is this really the kind of 'science' that the social sciences wish to emulate?

Brodbeck, in her introduction to *Readings in the Philosophy of the Social Sciences*, wrote:

> . . . there are clearly two factions within the social disciplines. One of them exuberantly embraces the scientific ideal; the other exalts its own intuitive understanding as being superior in logic and in principle to scientific explanation of the ways of man. Insofar as the division falls between those who count and measure what is not worth counting or measuring and those who speak shrewdly though imprecisely about more interesting matters, the issue is one of strategy rather than one of logic or principle.[17]

The author will admit he belongs in that constellation of social sciences that exalts intuitive understandings and the literary tradition. However, at the same time, he admires many modern theoretical physicists for their persistence, perseverance, and willingness to throw themselves headlong, during their entire careers, into research that has often proven incapable of empirical (scientific) testing and verification. One has to wonder, if a large number of extremely intelligent people have worked on a number of questions for several decades, and the answer continues to elude them, does this mean that the answer is not easy or obvious? Or, could it be that there is no answer? Why do they do it? Smolin suggests that many young physicists feel that they must pursue topics 'sanctioned' by the mainstream if they are to be respected by their peers and enjoy decent careers.[18]

While this is a sad comment on what the modern academy has become, it is, nonetheless, understandable. Scholarship, after all, is a process, with publication as its product. Therefore, it is important for the successful academic to work within the mainstream of his discipline, where the research grants are most readily available, be as rigorous as possible, and publish. Today, with more and more academics seeking to publish in a limited number of journals and a tightening book market, only those who produce articles or books that are deemed to be in the mainstream and supported by rigorous mathematical constructs will ever see the light of day. This means that other, equally well intentioned studies exploring non-mainstream topics or methods are passed over; even if they are of equal academic merit in the long run.

What, then, are the appropriate methods for studying social or cultural phenomena in a scientific way? If we assume that social phenomena are either sufficiently or significantly different from natural sciences, should they not have their own distinctive methods? Or, is it possible to study social phenomena using the same methods used to study biological phenomena, while at the same time, being distinct from inorganic and organic nature or the hard sciences? It seems to be true that how one should study society depends on what that society is like. Maybe this is why the social sciences appear 'less scientific'. They simply have not progressed to the point where a general theory of society can even be contemplated, let alone formulated. And yet, this is exactly what they are ultimately searching for.

The social sciences seem so separated by focus and method that the creation of a social theory of everything, similar to the physicists' tireless search for Einstein's *Einheitliche Feldtheorie,* is not even within the realm of possibility, at least for now. Essentially, both appear to be on their own quests for their Holy Grail, without any substantial success.

* * *

As we will see in a later chapter, the concept of development has been used in a variety of contexts in the West since the Greeks, but did not take on its current form until the late 1940s and since then it has undergone further refinement and elaboration. From the 1940s and into the 1990s, development was largely focused on economic growth rates, sectoral changes, progress, and issues of underdevelopment, as defined by the developed nations of the world.

In the early 1990s, the term 'human development' was added to the development lexicon. Its addition was the result of efforts by the United Nations (UN), and especially the UN Development Programme (UNDP), and the work done by the economists Mahbub ul Haq and Amartya Sen. Together, Haq and Sen argued that 'human' development should be deemed as important as 'economic' development, if not more so. They emphasized the importance of education, health, gender equality and such demographic indicators as infant mortality, child mortality, maternal mortality, and longevity. Accepting Haq and Sen's premise that human development would usher in or foster raw economic development, the UN and UNDP exerted moral pressure on developing countries to redirect their development efforts toward human development, exclusive of raw economic development.

The UNDP's primary development gauge became the HDI, as reported in its Human Development Reports (HDRs). HDIs provide a summary of human development around the world and at the same time categorize them as developed, still developing, or underdeveloped. Using the HDI, nations can be compared and used to assess progress toward some constantly changing ideal.[19] At the same time, the World Development Reports (WDRs) categorize nations on the basis of systematic global and national economic indicators. Cross-comparisons between the HDIs and the WDRs provide a fairly reasonable framework for the evaluation and successfulness of development programmes. These gauges of progress, however well intended, possess an inherent flaw. They are largely Western conceptions and, therefore, ethno- or Eurocentric-tools used by developed nations to compare themselves with or to developing nations.[20]

In the process of shifting from economic development to human development the language of development among policy makers has also changed insofar as it related to public policy statements. Public policy statements often do not reflect the true nature of policy formulation and implementation, which represents the difference between political economy – real politics – and programme implementation.[21]

In most developing nations, even during the rapid economic global expansion of the mid-1990s, there still remained insufficient economic resources to address all the pressing human development needs recognized by the UNDP. The simultaneous reduction of foreign development funding due to economic reform and contractions in the developed nations of North America and Europe necessitated changes in the development plans of developing nations. Consequently, Jean Drèze and Amartya Sen suggested that developing nations, and especially India with its centralized system of development and resource allocation structures, should pull-back from its heavy economic presence in those areas where it was either uneconomic or unnecessary. Instead, policy and programmatic efforts should be focused on areas of human development that would later result in more profound improvements in India's participation in global markets and globalization.[22] Even so, grassroots development programmes in India remained largely unaffected during this period of transition.

OUR PURPOSE

Originally, the examination of district-level backwardness began as a simple exercise to identify the most backward districts in India and compare their distribution with Banerjee and Iyer's (hereafter, B&I) analysis of British land revenue settlement types and subsequent levels of post-Independence development.[23] Later, Kapur and Kim's examination of British colonial institutions and economic development in India dovetailed with that of B&I.[24] It was not intended to be a replication of B&I's ground-breaking work but rather a simple comparison using a more visual approach – the straight-forward display of frequencies on a Census of India base map. See Map I.1, in the pocket at the end of the book.

Five of the more recent 'backward districts' studies, conducted between 1997 and 2007 were consulted. Each enumerated the backward districts of India using a variety of selection criteria. It was because they used different selection criteria that each was chosen, in the belief that the more often a particular district is enumerated, it is at least superficially and somehow consistently 'more backward' than a less frequently enumerated district.

The distribution of backward districts, in general, did not surprise the author. He had 'assumed (anticipated)' that their distribution would be consistent with B&I's findings; and they were. However, he was astonished with just how concentrated and how few districts were enumerated in all the studies among that group we can collectively call 'the worst of the worst'.

Four states had no backward districts – Mizoram, Tripura, Kerala, and Tamil Nadu. Every other state had at least one enumerated backward district. Considering the range of variables used by the base studies, this was not unanticipated. However, only fourteen districts were enumerated in each of the base studies. This was surprising. The author genuinely believed that there would have been more.

TABLE I.1: DISTRIBUTION OF BACKWARD DISTRICTS BY STATE AS ENUMERATED IN THE FIVE BACKWARD DISTRICTS STUDIES, 1997-2007[25]

State*	No. of Backward Districts	No. of Districts in State	Per cent Classified as Backward	Districts Mentioned in Studies				
				5 Times	4 Times	3 Times	2 Times	Once
Andhara Pradesh	6	23	26.1				1	5
Arunchal Pradesh	8	16	50.0				4	4
Assam	15	27	55.6			1	6	8
Bihar	35	38	92.1	12	10	5	3	5
Chhattisgarh	9	18	50.0				3	6
Gujarat	3	26	11.5				1	2
Haryana	2	21	9.5					2
Himachal Pradesh	4	12	33.3					4
Jharkhand	19	24	79.2	1	3	4	4	7
Karnataka	4	30	13.3				2	2
Madhya Pradesh	30	50	60.0		2	7	5	16
Maharashtra	16	35	45.7				2	14
Manipur	3	9	33.3					3
Meghalaya	3	7	42.9				1	2
Nagaland	2	11	18.2				1	1
Orissa	20	30	66.7		1	3	8	8
Punjab	1	20	5.0					1
Rajasthan	10	33	30.3			2		8
Sikkim	3	4	75.0					3
Uttar Pradesh	43	71	60.6	1	4	5	12	21
Uttarakhand	2	13	15.4				1	1
West Bengal	13	19	68.4			3	5	5
Total	251	537	46.7	14	20	30	59	128
As % of total number of districts mentioned in studies				6%	8%	12%	24%	51%

The fourteen districts deemed 'most backward' were geographically distributed as follows:

1. They were concentrated in India's eastern sector – in the states of Uttar Pradesh, Bihar, and Jharkhand, in areas where the zamindari system of land settlement had been implemented.
2. Twelve districts were located in modern-day Bihar.[26]
3. Eleven districts were located in northern Bihar (north of the Ganga).
4. Twelve districts were concentrated in the proposed modern state of Mithila.[27]
5. One district was located in Uttar Pradesh – Barabanki.
6. One district was located in Jharkhand – Godda.

As soon as the author had completed Map I.1, his eye was instantly drawn to the concentration of backward districts in northern Bihar. Immediately, the focus of this study changed from validating B&I's work to explaining this concentration of district-level backwardness in northern Bihar.

The author immediately sought refuge in all the 'usual suspects' or typical explanations for backwardness – lack of resources, periodic calamities, poor infrastructure, poor markets, poor education, social stratification, rapid population growth, political unrest, etc. – everything that had been mentioned in the World Bank's 2006 study, *Bihar: Towards a Development Strategy*.[28] While each of these causes of backwardness seemed irrefutable and were part of the puzzle, the pieces were simply not fitting together well. There had to be more. There had to be something the author was overlooking. What was missing was the adhesive or mechanism that held all the pieces of the puzzle together or in place.

Unable to adequately cement the pieces of the puzzle together, the author temporarily set this project aside. During the course of subsequent academic meander, the author came across Ian Morris' landmark treatise – *Why the West Rules for Now*. Morris uses the idea of 'social development' as the vehicle to explain how societies get things done by reshaping their physical, economic, social, and intellectual environments to their own ends.[29]

In the West, the idea of social development represents something

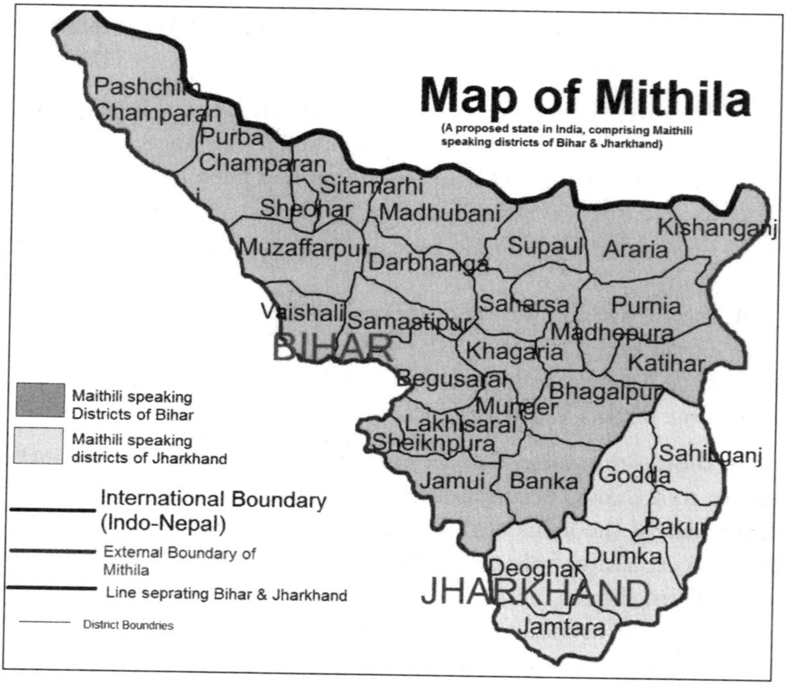

MAP I.2: THE PROPOSED, MODERN STATE OF MITHILA[30]

that seems to be universally considered to be good; because development is deemed to be progress and progress is considered to be either implicitly and explicitly the goal of Man.[31]

Morris observed that 'Greedy, lazy, frightened people seek their own preferred balance between being comfortable, working as little as possible, and being safe'.[32] With change comes new problems and solving them creates even more problems. Change forces people to make hard choices. Forward thinking people generally surmount or at least confront their problems. Others fail to rise to the challenge and development stagnates and sometimes declines.

The last elements of the author's puzzle came in the form of an article written by Jean Drèze and Haris Gazdar.[33] When the author combined the concept of social inertia with Morris' idea of social development and the notion of '*Asabiyya*, he had found the adhesive needed to hold the puzzle pieces in place and an explanation for Mithila's apparent backwardness began to emerge.

As used herein, '*Asabiyya* is a form of socio-economic group cohesiveness; and social inertia is the cessation of social development, which results in the inability of a society to continue to reshape and control its changing social, economic, and political environment. Social inertia, therefore, is a defence mechanism that provides people with an acceptable balance between being comfortable and safe. It is a sociological response to change (history) within a unique geographic environment; and it is the interplay of society and history, within this unique setting that results in the persistence of district-level backwardness in Mithila.

* * *

William H. McNeill and Ian Morris, among others, have sought to reduce the almost randomness of human historical patterns to comprehensible brush-strokes in their seminal writings.[34] Here, within the context and setting of Bihar, northern Bihar, and Mithila, the author has attempted to find some of the more readily identifiable factors and processes that have contributed to Mithila's backwardness. For the sake of convenience, and because they are shadowy, the author will, at least for now, call them Mithila's gossamer threads of history. The remainder of this volume is the author's quest for these historical threads. And because they are shadowy, and not readily amenable to quantification, most developmental economists simply ignore them in favour of more concrete and more easily identifiable 'things' and processes.

NOTES

1. Kusum Nair, *Blossoms in the Dust: The Human Factor in Indian Development*, 7th printing, New York: Frederick A. Praeger, 1961.
2. Ibid., p. xviii.
3. One need only examine the historical and methodological development of the most frequently used development indices, especially the United Nations Human Development Index (HDI) and the more recently developed Oxford Multidimensional Poverty Index (MPI). See, S. Sakiko Fukuda-Parr (2003). 'The Human Development Paradigm: Operationalizing Sen's Ideas on Capabilities' *Feminist Economics*, vol. 9, nos. 2-3, 1 July 2003, pp. 301-17. doi:10.1080/1354570022000077980; and Sabina Alkire and Maria Emma

Santos, *Acute Multidimensional Poverty: A New Index for Developing Countries*, OPHI Working Paper No. 38, Oxford Poverty & Human Development Initiative (OPHI), July 2010, Retrieved 13 June 2013, from http://www.ophi.org.uk/acute-multidimensional-poverty-a-new-index-for-developing-countries/.

4. Here, we are talking about classical physics, Newtonian physics.
5. In 2012, Brian Nosek, a psychologist at the University of Virginia, invited academics from around the world to conduct what has become known as the Reproducibility Project – a project with the express mission of replicating published, high-profile studies. To date, approximately 20 replication attempts have been completed with mixed results. See, for example, Open Science Framework, *About Open Science Framework,* Retrieved 1 July 2013, from: OpenScienceFramework.org: http://openscienceframework.org/about/, 2011-12; Lea Winerman, 'Interesting Results: Can They be Replicated?' *Archives of the American Psychological Association,* vol. 44, no. 2, retrieved 1 July 2013, from American Psychological Association: http://www.apa.org/monitor/2013/02/results.aspx, February 2013; Open Science Collaboration, *The Reproducibility Project: A Model of Large-scale Collaboration for Empirical Research on Reproducibility: Open Science Collaboration,* Open Science Collaboration (OSC), retrieved 1 July 2013 from: http://papers.ssrn.com/sol3/papers.cfm?abstract_id=2195999, 3 January 2013; Kayt Sukel, 'Replicate This', retrieved 6 June 2013, from Mission & State – Pacific Standard: http://www.psmag.com/magazines/march-april-2013/reproducibility-project-science-53141/, 26 February 2013.
6. Kayt Sukel, 'Replicate This', retrieved 6 June 2013, from *Mission & State* – Pacific Standard: http://www.psmag.com/magazines/march-april-2013/reproducibility-project-science-53141/. Comment made by Eric Eich, editor of the journal *Psychological Science.*
7. However, the next stage in physics, the physics of the twentieth century, has pushed it back into the realm of mathematical philosophy, where experimentation and proofs are no longer possible, and mathematical speculation prevails.
8. May Brodbeck (ed.), *Readings in the Philosophy of the Social Sciences,* New York: The Macmillan Co., 1968, p. 2.
9. From W.H. Auden's poem, 'Under Which Lyre', as quoted by MDM [Michael Dennis Mooney], 'Thou shalt not sit with statisticians nor commit a social science', retrieved 5 June 2013, from The Fine-Wrought Figure: http://lightneasy.wordpress.com/2011/04/13/the-hermetic-decalogue-by-w-h-auden/, 13 April 2011.
10. May Brodbeck (ed.), *Readings in the Philosophy of the Social Sciences,* 1968, p. 1.
11. Quoted by Jessica Royer Ocken, 'Enabling Analysis', D. Ganse (ed.), *Synygy Magazine,* vol. 4, 30 September 2008, p. 19.

12. As quoted by Gordon Tullock, 'A Comment on Daniel Klein's "A Plea to Economists Who Favor Liberty",' *Eastern Economic Journal*, vol. 27, no. 2, Spring 2001, pp. 203-7. Tullock's fn. 2 reads: 'I have heard him [Coase] say this several times. So far as I know he has never published it', p. 207.
13. Thomas S. Kuhn, *The Structure of Scientific Revolutions*, 50th Anniversary Edition, 2012, Chicago: University of Chicago Press, 1962.
14. Gordon Tullock, 'A Comment on Daniel Klein's "A Plea to Economists Who Favor Liberty",' 2001, p. 206.
15. Marvin Harris, *The Rise of Anthropological Theory: A History of Theories of Culture*, New York: Thomas Y. Crowell Co., 1968, pp. 1-2.
16. Ibid., p. 2.
17. May Brodbeck (ed.), *Readings in the Philosophy of the Social Sciences*, 1968, p. 2.
18. Lee Smolin, *The Trouble with Physics*, Boston: Houghton Mifflin Co., A Mariner Book, 2006/7, p. xix.
19. In 2010, the Oxford Multidimensional Poverty Index (MPI or OMPI) was added to the UNDP's evaluation apparatus, replacing the Human Poverty Index (HPI) which was a clumsy subset of the HDI. The MPI measures acute multidimensional poverty.
20. M. Adams and P. Hanna, 'Your Past is Not Their Present: Time, the Other, and Ethnocentrism in Cross-cultural Personality Psychology', *Theory and Psychology*, vol. 22, no. 4, 1 August 2012, pp. 436-51, among others, have explored the role of ethnocentrism in cross-cultural research and comparisons, concluding that it is almost impossible to eliminate.
21. Shyam Singh and V. Anil Kumar, *Politics and Public Policies: Politics of Human Development in Uttar Pradesh, India,* Bangalore: The Institute for Social and Economic Change, Working Paper 287, 2012, p. 2.
22. See, Jean Drèze and Amartya Sen, *India: Development and Participation*, New York: Oxford University Press, 1995a; Jean Drèze and Amartya Sen, *India: Economic Development and Social Opportunity*, New Delhi: Oxford University Press, 1995b; and Jean Drèze and Haris Gazdar, 'Uttar Pradesh: The Burden of Inertia', Chapter 2, pp. 33-128, in Jean Drèze and Amartya Sen (eds.), *Studies in Development Economics – Indian Development: Selected Regional Perspectives*, Delhi: Oxford University Press, Studies in Development Economics, 1997.
23. Abhijit Banerjee and Lakshmi Iyer, 'History, Institutions, and Economic Performance: The Legacy of Colonial Land Tenure Systems in India', *The American Economic Review*, vol. 95, no. 4, 2005, pp. 1190-1213.
24. Shilpi Kapur and Sukkoo Kim, *British Colonial Institutions and Economic Development in India*, Cambridge: National Bureau of Economic Research, NBER Working Paper No. 12613, October 2006.
25. The backward district reports used were:
    - Vani Borooah, K. Amaresh and Dubey Amaresh, *Measuring Regional*

Backwardness: Poverty, Gender, and Children in the Districts of India, Munich: Munich Personal RePEc Archive, 2007 (Posted 25 December 2009), retrieved from: http://mpra.ub.uni-muenchen.de/19426/.
- Government of India, *Backward Districts Initiative – Rashtriya Shram Vikas Yojana – The Scheme and Guidelines for Preparation of District Plans,* New Delhi: Government of India, Planning Commission, MLP Division, 2005a.
- Government of India, *Report of the Inter-Ministry Task Group on Redressing Growing Regional Imbalances,* New Delhi: Planning Commission, 2005b.
- Bibek Debroy and Laveesh Bhandari (eds.), *District-Level Deprivation in the New Millennium,* Delhi: Konark Publishers, 2003.
- Planning Commission, *Report of the Committee to Identify 100 Most Backward & Poorest Districts in the Country [aka Sarma Committee Report],* New Delhi: Government of India, Ministry of Rural Areas and Employment, 1997.

26. If one peruses gazetteers or atlases showing the evolution of modern-day Indian districts, especially in Bihar, one is struck by just how often these districts were subdivided and therefore made increasingly smaller, largely for administrative reasons. When Jharkhand was carved out of Bihar in 2000, several of the new districts in Jharkhand underwent subdivision and name changes. These had to be reconciled in the production of the base study map, P.1.
27. Mithila is a proposed state in India, comprising the Maithili-speaking region of North Bihar and Jharkhand. See Map I.1.
28. World Bank, *Bihar: Towards a Development Strategy,* Washington, D.C.: World Bank, 2006.
29. Ian Morris, *Why the West Rules for Now: The Patterns of History and What They Mean About the Future,* London: Profile Books, 2010, p. 24, *passim.*
30. Map attributed to Vikas 11004315, 12 April 2012, http://commons.wikimedia.org/wiki/File:Mithila_Map.jpg
31. See, for example, J. Albert Rorabacher, 'Geo-Historical Approaches to Environment: The Evolution of Environmental Thought in Western Civilization', *Journal of Geography,* vol. 72, no. 4, April 1973, pp. 31-41.
32. Morris, *Why the West Rules for Now,* 2010, p. 28.
33. Jean Drèze and Haris Gazdar, 'Uttar Pradesh: The Burden of Inertia', Chapter 2, pp. 33-128, 1997.
34. Morris, *Why the West Rules for Now,* 2010; and William H. McNeill, *The Rise of the West: A History of the Human Community,* Chicago: University of Chicago Press, 1963/1991.

CHAPTER 1

Development and Backwardness: What are they; How do we Deal with them?

THE MEANING OF DEVELOPMENT

The concepts of 'development' and 'underdeveloped' are contested theoretically, politically, and philosophically and are as complex and ambiguous as they are misunderstood; nevertheless, since the late-1940s, these two simple words have been used to drive and justify the practices of development agencies around the world. They defy definition but not for the want of trying. Economists have been writing about development since the early nineteenth century, or as part of the broader academic discipline of sociology. In both instances development has been perceived as the progressive transformation of society.

If one searches long and hard enough, you can find hundreds of definitions for development, each slightly different from the next. In general, if we focus on the social and economic meanings of development, most contain certain key components. It is a means to carry out a nation's development goals, to promote economic growth, equity and national self-reliance. Or, it can mean providing human beings with the opportunity to develop their fullest potential, enable the poor, women, and peasantry.[1] Depending upon one's audience or constituency, development can mean very different things.

The term 'development', within its current context and most common usage is of comparatively recent origin, possibly dating back to a speech given by President Harry S. Truman.[2] On 20 January 1949, Truman stated: 'We must embark on a bold new program for making the benefits of our scientific advances and industrial progress available for the improvement and growth of underdeveloped areas . . . The old imperialism is dead – exploitation for foreign profit – has no place in our plans. What we envisage is a program of development based on the concepts of democratic fair dealing.'[3]

At the time, no one was quite sure what underdeveloped meant. Nevertheless, thinkers and bureaucrats from the developed countries responded by creating the concept of foreign aid and this promoted industrialization and an increase in the Gross Domestic Product (GDP) *of developing countries*.[4] All efforts at 'developing' areas perceived to be 'underdeveloped' tended to be palliatives that failed to tackle the root problems of backwardness and only served to make the aid-receiving nations dependent upon the aid-providing nations.[5] Some developing nations responded by organizing themselves in an effort to resist the West's newest form of colonial-imperialism – economic dependence – forming such organizations as Organization of Petroleum Exporting Countries (OPEC) to resist resource expropriation. Many other countries simply settled back with willing outstretched hands.

Today, two approaches to development have emerged from the 1950s' indiscriminate aid give-away approach – the basic needs approach that is as much motivated by politics as it is by a genuine concern for the well-being of developing societies; and the capabilities approach as advocated by Amartya Sen which serves to enhance people's potential to be and to do. The basic needs approach focuses primarily on measures of income like GDP. The capabilities approach resulted in the creation of the Human Development Index (HDI) and focuses on providing or awakening human potential.

What, then, are the universal characteristics of developmental success? In reality, there aren't many! Some have to do with growth. Others represent 'well-spent' social expenditures. Success, then, is measured by what is deemed to be the focus of development programming – economic potential and power or human potential and power, which are not always the same and need to be measured differently.

* * *

Part of the confusion surrounding the idea of development stems from the fact that it is difficult to separate immanent development from the intent to develop – one being a natural process, the other a subjective intervention. Immanent development represents the natural evolution of a system, while intentional development presupposes that the action being taken by some outside agency is purposive, the result of conscious, reasoned, decision-making and choice.[6] This latter view of development makes it both a means and a goal. The desire to see change based on the formulation of a goal, defines the means of its achievement, which development agencies then envision as self-fulfilling prophecies. Unfortunately, this development paradigm has not proven itself to be very effective. Recognizing this fact has done little to change the development process as we know it, the agencies responsible for its implementation, or the principles upon which it rests.

Yet, the distinction between immanent and intentional development is the key to understanding the type of development the world envisions for itself – primarily raw, unfettered economic development. In general, the Western conception of development does not consider immanent development to be of much importance. In the eyes of development officials, immanent development is often deemed the root cause of backwardness and economic underdevelopment. It is intentional, goal-specific development that pushes a society to increase its production of goods and services and this is what has motivated the governments of both developed and developing nations to date.

* * *

In the nineteenth century, the solution to issues of development was to invoke the concept of trusteeship. Imperialists and colonialists, believing themselves to be developmentally superior, and possessing superior technological and military might, were in a position to dictate the course of development for those deemed less developed or backward. While the strategy of trusteeship has been justifiably condemned as being Eurocentric, a vestige of European imperialism, it continues to operate. As a strategy, it has been a failure. Nonetheless, every development agency continues to see it as the means by which universal human suffering can be ameliorated or eliminated. The irony is that might continues to make right; and, in large measure, it is the donor nations who define what, when, how, and to whom developmental resources ultimately will be allocated.

* * *

The concepts of development and progress tend to be almost seamlessly bound together until it is almost intellectually impossible to separate one from the other, or determine where one begins and the other ends. For example, Allan Thomas suggests that development is, on one hand, a historical process of social change, transforming societies over a long time; and on the other, it consists of the deliberate efforts of governments, organizations and social movements to promote progress over a much shorter period.[7] Again, natural process versus purposeful involvement. Governments, as the omniscient guardians of the people, see development as a means to ameliorate flaws that occur in the unguided natural process of progress and use their 'development programmes' in an attempt to achieve some preconceived notion of the state and its people.

In this situation, uncertainty exists because governments fail to clearly differentiate between what is intended to be developed and what development means, resulting in the simultaneous process of destruction, renewal, and creation but not sequential revitalization. The intended purpose of development – improving people's lives – seldom builds on what is good in people's lives but rather results in a wholesale transformation of their lives, based on an ideal or image of success in the development agents' minds. This 'visualized' outcome is seldom achieved or achievable without the deconstruction of a sizeable portion of the subject's notion of society, culture, or economy; thus resulting in the loss of much of what was once deemed to be good without a commensurate improvement in the lives of the people.

* * *

When discussing development, underdevelopment, or backwardness, one is quickly caught in a tautology with no clear means of achieving either a definitive or satisfactory conclusion or exit. One is caught in a perpetual, infinite loop, drawing upon the terminology of computer programmers, where there is no terminating condition or one that can be met. And much like a computer caught in an infinite loop, the process of development, as we know it, has become unresponsive to its needs, challenges, and intent.

While we criticize development agencies and programmes for their lack of success, they have been extraordinarily successful in terms of:

- Fostering their own administrative growth, expansion, and proliferation.
- Funding endless and often unproductive and repetitive research.
- The creation of a small, international craft industry dedicated to the design of measurements of poverty and deprivation, often in response to the need to define targets at international conferences and to measure progress against them.[8]
- Squandering monumental amounts of money in the name of progress.
- Avoiding all efforts to make them accountable to their benefactors or the recipients of their services – simple cost-benefit-effect analysis.

* * *

While the terms 'backward' or 'backwardness' are commonly used, they are not typically used by indigenous populations to describe themselves. When used by outsiders – politicians or agents of change – they are used judgementally, whether intended or not. A person may see him- or herself as being poor, with few opportunities, and few inalienable rights, but they do not perceive themselves as backward. Backwardness is only a term used by those who find themselves in a superior position – economically, socially, politically, or technologically. From this perspective, the term backward is, in fact, always pejorative and condescending, and carries with it an implied unilateral need 'to do something', or provides the justification to become involved.

THE ROOTS OF DEVELOPMENT

The first paragraphs of Gilbert Rist's Introduction to *The History of Development: From Western Origins to Global Faith* are, possibly, some of the most poignant statements ever written regarding the concept of development:

> The strength of 'development' discourse comes of its power to seduce, in every sense of the term: to charm, to please, to fascinate, to set dreaming, but also to turn away from the truth, to deceive. How could one possibly resist the idea that there is a way of eliminating the poverty by which one is so troubled? How dare one think, at the same time, that the cure might worsen the ill which one wishes to combat. . . .
>
> How could it have been thought necessary and urgent to do everything to speed up the process of 'development', ostensibly favouring the prosperity of countries in both North and South?
>
> After all, for centuries no one – or virtually no one – took it into their head to relieve the misery of others, . . . especially when they lived in different continents. What is the origin of this collective task which, though constantly criticized for its lack of success, appears to be justified beyond all dispute? . . . How are we to explain this whole phenomenon, which mobilizes not only the hopes of millions but also sizeable financial resources, while appearing to recede like the horizon just as you think you are approaching it?[9]

Development is truly a double-edged sword. It promises great things but seldom rewards either the benefactor or the recipient in equal measure. Large quantities of talent, time and money are invested by the benefactor, with little or no lasting consequential benefit for the recipient; and the perceived misery of the recipient goes largely unresolved.

It has been suggested that misery is created mainly by wars or dictatorial regimes, by insane economic policies, by financial speculation, by the absence of agrarian reform, and ineffectual fiscal policies. Aid and development programmes attend to the misery that frequently results from ineffective or unjust policies. However, if those providing the aid and development programmes do not get their priorities right, any action will be, in all likelihood, in vain. This is the pattern we have seen repeated year after year in country after country, whenever and wherever foreign or domestic development programmes have been initiated. At the heart of every development programme is the rabid belief that the target population will benefit from the beneficence of the foreign aid advisors or domestic change agents.

In large measure the history of development, as Rist has pointed out, is fundamentally of Western origin and has evolved into a global obsession.[10] The dominance of Western thought now stands as the standard by which all development is measured, fusing liberal democracy and industrial capitalism into an inseparable amalgam and appears to have become the only generally accepted basis for modern society.[11] On the one hand, this is ethnocentric; on the other, egocentric. Consequently, and by extension, the idea of development, practically and philosophically, is inherently a flawed concept.

Rist contends that the concept of 'development' is part of the core beliefs of Western civilization, as potent as Christianity or as powerful as Islam in the Middle East. He argues, with some success, that the ideas of growth and progress are among some of the most deeply seated beliefs in Western society; and it is these beliefs that distinguish Western civilization from that of the rest of the world and contribute to the West's felt sense of superiority.[12] It is the West's belief in growth and progress that has infected the thinking of the rest of the world. As a consequence, the idea of development is, now, as much a motive force as it is a process. The believers contend that with sufficient time, diligence, and resources, everyone can prosper. Unfortunately, not every culture or society subscribes to these fundamental precepts. If the Western evangelists of development are to be believed, it is only a matter of awakening the entrepreneurial spirit in other cultures.

Whether entrepreneurial spirit, democracy, or industrial capitalism are ultimately proven right or wrong within the context of developing societies, is a matter of time. To date, however, the process of awakening traditional peasant societies has been excruciatingly slow, with little observable or enduring success. Further, it seems that democracy and capitalism, when applied outside predominately Western centres of influence often seem unworkable and impractical.

* * *

In the process of wanting to improve the backwardness of people, no one seems to be asking whether what *we* want 'backward people' to have are the things *they* genuinely need or want. No one is asking the basic philosophical questions: Is there something intrinsically wrong with being poor? Are the poor really unhappy? Is it possible to live in 'happy poverty?' Admittedly, there are minimum human requirements – food, housing, clothing, and healthcare – but after that, what is necessary to make someone happy? Once basic needs are fulfilled, is not everything thereafter a want?

For economists and agents of change, fundamental needs are key to the ongoing functioning of a society but it is wants that drive the demand for more and more goods and services which, in turn, are deemed economic development. Part of this demand for additional goods and services is based on knowledge – the knowing that there are other goods and services 'out there' that could potentially make one's life more pleasant. Once the existence of other goods and services is realized, the process of choice is initiated which determines what goods and services can be obtained based on one's purchasing power or, stated another way, the importance or value one places on a good or service based on one's the ability to 'pay' in the form of service, benefit, other goods, kind, or some recognized form of monetary exchange. Demand combined with the scarcity of a good determines its 'price'. And price determines who will be able to consume or obtain those available goods.

At the heart of this demand-production-exchange sequence is the intangible notion of desire. Without the desire to possess or consume a 'good', there is no demand and, therefore, no need to produce or exchange, even if knowledge of the 'good' exists. It is this intangible notion of desire that economists generally ignore in their theories of demand, production, and allocation. They 'assume' that everyone is rational, well informed, and possesses a certain level of purchasing power. However, this is entirely, again, a Western conception of the economic process. In many non-Western societies, economic growth, or making money for its own sake, is not a *raison d'être.* Further, the West's insatiable desire to consume does not necessarily have an equivalent in many non-Western cultures. As a consequence, Western economic models may have limited validity in such societies.

The so-called 'developed societies' have transformed wants into needs; and as a result, Westerners automatically feel they should have more and, at the same time, they feel compelled to help the less fortunate and less informed, which means, they want to change them.

Is the West not simply projecting its needs, desires, values, and emotions onto the world's 'less developed people'?

Is living a simple life to be applauded or even appreciated? [For some, the words 'simple', 'poor', and 'poverty stricken' are interchangeable.] Are the Haves of the world even capable of appreciating or understanding the world of the Have-nots? The answers to these and all the questions relating to poverty and backwardness are truly dependent upon the answer to the greater question of: What does it mean to be poor or backward? Can we justifiably define poverty and backwardness in only economic terms or using such indices as the HDI or MPI, which are fundamentally economic constructs?

DEFINING POVERTY AND BACKWARDNESS

Poverty

A survey of the existing development literature reveals that almost invariably it ignores the role of history in development – including the importance of foreign ideologies and personalities. The emphasis has been quite observably focused on quantifiable material outcomes. The primary focus, or the key variable in development studies is deemed to be an economic one; and the term poverty is commonly used as a substitute for backwardness. Monetary or income-based measures and definitions are most frequently utilized because they are generally regarded as sufficient on their own or seen as adequate proxies for poverty. That said, what then is poverty or backwardness?

Over the last decade, since the creation of the Millennium Development Goals by the United Nations, an on-going debate has ensued regarding the meaning of poverty, as well as the many different indicators used and proposed to monitor it. At the forefront of both arguments has been the importance of monetary variables, on objective or subjective measures, and on the link between material income and one's ability to participate in society. Most observers agree that income is an imperfect measure, yet in almost all measures of poverty, it generally becomes the cornerstone for such measures. Another component of poverty is the idea of relative deprivation – an idea that is widely accepted but often times only in theory.

Does poverty mean:

- A predetermined income level?
- Being too poor to afford the basic necessities like food, clothing, shelter?
- Access to clean, potable water?
- Access to health care?
- Being able to send one's children to school?
- Being 'part of the system'?
- Discrimination or disenfranchisement, or marginalization?
- Being sufficiently free to be able to make choices?

With such a range of themes used to describe or define poverty, can there possibly be a single, comprehensive definition? The answer is, categorically, 'No'. It would be virtually impossible to include every individual facet of what constitutes poverty in any concise and meaningful way. It may be possible, however, to simplify the components, thus producing a working definition.

First, poverty is an individual problem, regardless of the individual's position within myriad socio-economic networks like the family, the household, the community, or the nation in which he or she resides. Second, poverty is situational, seasonal, or cyclical, and may result from internal or external social, economic, or environmental changes. Third, poverty is reflected in monetary or personal deprivation, whether in the form of employment, food, shelter, health, clean water, or education, which might be defined as one's basic needs.

Further, the utility of defining individuals and then making the intellectual or methodological leap to larger aggregated populations like regional, national, or international populations, may or may not be defensible and may or may not provide planners with reliable and useful data or information. Herein lies the problem for developmental statisticians. Each model of poverty requires a different indicator. Money metric models require information on income; vulnerability models use indicators of wealth and exposure to risk, as well as income; models concerned with capability and functioning require indicators that measure life expectancy or educational achievement; models of well-being or social exclusion demand measures of social support. Each model requires its own type of data and correlates of poverty and in most developing countries, these data are either incomplete or missing at the level required by the planners and development aid agencies.

The proliferation of concepts, indicators, and definitions used to describe poverty would not matter if the same populations were being identified by all the measures and covered by all the definitions. However, each indicator defines and measures its own population. Admittedly, the different populations being identified reflect some subset of the impoverished community but to what extent? Unless a universal definition and indicator(s) are used, the true magnitude of poverty and deprivation remains conjectural.

Despite these intellectual and methodological inconsistencies and drawbacks, indicators are routinely used to assess poverty or backwardness, deprivation, vulnerability, well-being, human development, and inclusion, and are the basis for the creation of plans and programmes to ameliorate or eliminate the socio-economic woes of 'backward people'. Is it any wonder that little has been achieved? Neither the target populations, the data collectors, nor the planners and development officers perceive the same problems in the same way. Essentially, everyone is 'talking mutually unintelligible languages' to describe the same problems and devise solutions, and the 'solutions', almost invariably, are designed and implemented from the top down, without input from the target population. Generally, the target population's vision of poverty is very different from that of the development bureaucrat sitting in his air conditioned office in the capital.

* * *

The planners, administrators, politicians, and governments throughout South Asia have been struggling with the issue of backwardness and regional imbalances since independence. In India, alone, nearly two dozen official government-sponsored committees and task forces have studied, identified, and recommended action plans and programmes for regional and district-level development since 1960. In addition, several individual states have sought to devise plans for the elimination of district-level backwardness.[13] To this already long list of committees must be added individual non-government organizations (NGOs) who have investigated various elements of backwardness.[14]

If every government is studying the problem of backwardness, why has so little progress been made toward its elimination? Little progress has been made because: (a) there is no consensus on what constitutes backwardness, or equally important, (b) there is no politico-economic benefit to be derived from its elimination.

BACKWARDNESS

With each new study has come a different set of evaluation criteria, used to identify exactly what constitutes 'backwardness'. As a consequence of changing evaluation criteria, it is difficult to make meaningful comparisons among or between the various studies. Therefore, any attempt at comparing levels of development within and between countries is fraught with methodological problems.[15]

Generally, there are four underlying conditions that must be met before any government will authorize the disbursement of scare resources for development programmes and grants. These are:

1. There must be a potential for further development.
2. Some identifiable inhibiting factor must exist that prevents development.
3. There must be a demonstrated need for the implementation of a programme designed to either remove or mitigate the inhibiting factor(s), thus permitting further development.
4. Some defensible measure of backwardness must indicate intervention is necessary.

While these conditions are not always specified, they are the bedrock upon which every development plan is based. Every area has the potential for further development and there is always some inhibiting factor that prevents further development, whether it is technical, economic, or cultural. Therefore, the first two conditions are without a doubt, givens. The more difficult problems are those associated with the need to remove or mitigate the inhibiting factor(s), and the development of a technically defensible index to justify the removal or mitigation of the inhibiting factor(s).

Indices

In the end, it is the index that identifies the need and becomes the justification for action. This index, then, defines the problem, as well as the solution. The index is, therefore, a very important component of any development scheme. It must include:

- A set of indicators;
- A procedure for weighting or aggregating the indicators;
- A procedure for reducing the individual weighted indicators to a single measure; and
- A threshold value that justifies intervention.

In principle, the statistical components of the index are the simple part. They are objective measures. It is the definition of the threshold value that becomes subjective. In most instances, the final decision on the threshold value is based on debate and consensus, not irrefutable and technically defensible criteria. It is much like asking ten people about whether a particular temperature is comfortable. Comfortable is a subjective evaluation, and there may be other influencing factors, like, is there a breeze, humidity level, is one in the shade or direct sunlight, the clothing one is wearing, etc., and so it is with the threshold index value.

Almost every study of backwardness includes certain salient criteria. Among these are:

- A measure of poverty,
- A measure of hunger,
- A measure of literacy or education,
- A measure of healthcare,
- A measure of communication,
- A measure of gender equality.

However, within each of these criteria categories, there are numerous subsets of questions and measures. Each study ascribes its own conceptions of what constitutes backwardness and this is been done through assigning weights to each general category and to each subset within each category. The net result, then, is that the studies are tailored to the needs of each individual fact-finding work group, making cross-study comparisons virtually impossible.

Furthermore, poverty, hunger, illiteracy, poor healthcare, inadequate communication and gender inequality, while certainly manifestations of backwardness, are not causes. They are symptoms.

The difficulty present in both the data and the methodologies associated with index-based approaches to the identification and formulation of development plans for backward areas was recognized by the Indian government as far back as the early 1960s, and yet, each successive report and programme is based on its own set of indicators, weightings, aggregations, and indices.[16]

THE POLITICAL ECONOMY OF BACKWARDNESS

In theory, the eradication of poverty goes hand-in-hand with development. The struggle by developing nations to allocate scarce resources becomes a dangerous balancing act for many politicians, whose fates depend on their popularity. It is far more important to 'look good' than it is to 'do good'. In a proverbial nutshell, politics is all about popularity and vote banks. When electioneering, it does not matter what you say or do, as long as, when you step away from the podium, or take your seat on the bench, you have left a good impression.

It is often said that the lack of political will is the root cause of government's failures. Or that self-serving politicians prevent real social and economic change. From the outside, both of these criticisms appear to be axiomatic. In reality, such thinking demonstrates a lack of understanding or conceptualization of what the political process is really all about. It does not take into consideration the comparative efficiencies of policy alternatives nor the politician's ability to set priorities. Every politician must make his or her own choices by weighing the benefits to be realized from any decision versus the economic and political resources available. What appears to be a lack of political will may simply be a trade-off that the politician must make to achieve an even more important goal, which usually means for the acquisition of more power or re-election. The problem is that most politicians are unwilling or unable to share the true motivations driving their decision-making with their constituencies. Thus, they often appear haute and disconnected from the public they serve. For every politician, power increases with his ability to generate political capital and then utilize it; and often times personal beliefs, personal gain, and public policy must be weighed against public demands.

For politicians, economic development is, at best, a slippery slope. It is difficult and usually a slow process. There are seldom any quick fixes. Some choices may accelerate the process without easing immediate concerns or needs. In these situations, the politician must decide between long-term gains for his constituency which may alienate some or all of that same constituency in the short-term. Thus, with every decision, the politician must calculate the political and social costs associated with every plan and proposal. What may appear as a lack of political will may be just a short-term strategy to achieve a more important, larger, long-term goal.

* * *

Alexander Gerschenkron, the noted economic historian, addressed the question of using a historical approach to analyse current problems.[17] He wrote: 'No past experience, however rich, and no historical research, however thorough, can save the living generation the creative task of finding their own answers and shaping their own future.'[18]

This is analogous to George Santayana's now axiomatic statement: 'Those who cannot remember the past are condemned to repeat it.'[19]

While we are the product of our pasts, as individuals, societies, and nations, we almost always refuse to look back at our mistakes and learn from them. Such is the case with development. Time and again, government committees and aid and development organizations and agencies study and formulate programmes designed to foster progress among 'backward' segments of societies around the world. In the end, large sums of money are spent with little progress being made. If we assume that government policies and institutions are designed to provide incentives and rewards that foster economic growth and development, why do so many of the intended recipients respond in a manner that is counter-productive or result in socio-economic backwardness?

In the case of India, and much of South Asia, it could be what political economists might call socio-economic replacement effect.[20] Social and political elites will tend to block changes when and if they deem such change will either destabilize the existing social, economic, or political system or increase the likelihood they will lose either influence or power. In essence, there is no effective way to combat or prevent the socio-economic replacement effect since there is no realistic way to compensate social, political, and economic elites who lose power, *ex post facto.*

Change is always difficult and elites that perceive change as a threat to their elite status will attempt to block it. The recalcitrance of the elites, therefore, is proportional to their sense of insecurity. The more secure elites feel, the greater the likelihood they will oppose change. Insecurity, on the other hand, will tend to foster a greater likelihood of cooperation. Technical, social, economic, or political innovations, and or change, tend to erode the so-called incumbency advantage that comes with elitism.

DEVELOPMENT AS CASH COW

At least at the national level, there may be another explanation. Development is a cash cow for most developing nations. The developed nations of the world pour billions upon billions of dollars into developing countries year after year, after year, with no demonstrable effect. In India, after more than sixty-five years of almost continuous aid, grants and programmes, nearly half of India's population is still undernourished. The government has promised food security programmes that would provide cheap food for the poor. Such programmes are debated, approved, but insufficiently funded or implemented.

Action Aid, an international development organization founded in 1972 to free the world of poverty and injustice, published several reports in September 2010. One report – *Who's Really Fighting Hunger?* – suggests that the world is going backwards with regard to the UN's Millennium Development Goal (MDG) on hunger. The world has never been on track to achieve the goal of halving poverty and hunger from its 1990 levels by 2015, but since 2007, there has been a dramatic reversal. The number and proportion of hungry in the world has been increasing, rather than decreasing.

South Asia and Sub-Saharan Africa have lost the most ground in the race to meet the MDG on hunger. In 2009, the prevalence of hunger in India surpassed its 1990 level. Worldwide, one person in seven goes to bed hungry. In India, that ratio is one in five. Forty-six per cent of South Asia's children are still underweight, despite the fact that per capita income has more than tripled over the last two decades.[21] Obviously, something needs to be done, and yet, one continues to encounter news briefs about government actions that are almost too ridiculous and too far-fetched to be believed.

The sad thing is that these news reports are not new. Such stories have been circulating since India became a net food exporter in the late 1970s and early 1980s.[22] In 2002, Amy Waldman, writing for the *New York Times*, reported that surplus wheat was mouldering in the fields of Punjab. At the same time, previous years surpluses were being stored in godowns, and yet people starved.[23] Every year, similar stories appear in newspapers and magazines and, with the advent of the Internet, the number of such stories has only proliferated.[24]

More recently, in August 2010, in an unprecedented move, the Indian Supreme Court castigated the Central Government for allowing 67,000 tonnes of improperly stored food grains to rot, and ordered the government to distribute another 17.8 million tonnes of grain in imminent danger of rotting.[25] The prime minister protested, saying the court had overstepped its bounds and that distributing free food to the hungry only destroyed all incentives for farmers to produce. Despite the prime minister's admonitions, the Court stood firm. It was an order, not a suggestion, the judges said.[26] Further, the prime minister's objection on the grounds that to distribute free food would undermine incentives, is simply callous, insensitive, and uninformed. Farmer incentives are one thing, a population of hungry and starving people is quite another. Typically, hungry people do not need incentives. Their hunger is a constant incentive. Starving people are at an even greater disadvantage, for starvation robs them of their health and ability to work.

For the government, the storage of strategic reserves of resources is quite understandable when trying to prevent market fluctuations but permitting those stores to moulder, rot, or be eaten by vermin, losing any value it might have, is almost criminally tragic, especially when hunger exists. With surpluses rotting in government-supervised storage facilities, is there any reason for people to go hungry? There are presently more than 430 million chronically hungry people living in India and that number is increasing, not decreasing.[27] How does one reconcile food surpluses with hunger, starvation, and backwardness?

An even more insidious thought to consider is the almost unthinkable possibility that inaction on the part of government with regard to the disbursement of food stockpiles is simply a tacit form of population control. To even contemplate such a strategy is gruesome and macabre; but not totally implausible, unfortunately.

A New Food Programme for India – An Aside

On 27 August 2013, in an unprecedented move, the Government of India passed a flagship 18 billion US$ programme to provide subsidized food to the poor, with the intention of 'wiping out' endemic hunger and malnutrition in India. At the time of its passage, it was anticipated that up to 830 million hungry people would benefit from this programme. Under the new programme, the Indian government would buy staple foods from small farmers at administered prices, generally above market levels, thereby supporting the incomes of some of the country's most impoverished people. From those stocks, the government will provide food to the poor, generally at below-market prices.

While the programme, known as the National Food Security Act (NFSA) is philosophically and ethically admirable, it is practically flawed. For people with little or no money, even subsidized food may be beyond their financial means.

On the heels of the legislation's passage, the US Government immediately objected to the programme! But why would America object to a programme that fulfils the UN Human Rights Declaration's intent and stated goals to eradicate hunger? The Obama administration's objection was that such a programme violates the trade rules agreed to when the World Trade Organization (WTO) was set up in 1994. At issue are those arcane and biased rules that treat government-supported prices to farmers as a form of 'trade-distorting support', even if that support is for food security and supports only domestic production for the domestic market. The WTO marginalizes the issue, treating food security as a deviation from the primary objective of agricultural trade liberalization. In large measure, many of the WTO's rules and regulations were and are designed to protect the economies of developed countries and not those of developing countries. The rules are designed to reduce developing nations' tariff and protection policies and open their markets to the multinational corporations of the developed countries.

Attempts by WTO's Director General, Roberto Azevedo to mediate India's new food programme with WTO rules went nowhere in late 2013, but at subsequent meetings a few months later, on a temporary basis, the WTO agreed that India would be allowed to protect its food security programming in its efforts to provide subsidized grains to the poor.[28] Until final rules are adopted by the WTO, individual countries of the organization will undoubtedly continue to challenge India's subsidization of domestic agriculture, even if it means cheaper food for the hungry.

Since its passage, the implementation of the NFSA programme has been hampered by fiscal policy problems and pending elections. BJP leader and two-time Finance Minister, Yashwant Sinha noted that managing inflation has to be a priority which has an impact on the growing fiscal deficit facing the Centre and the new food programme, and the NFSA will be a deficit-increasing venture. The cost of the food programme has been estimated to be approximately Rs 88,500 crore, according to a *Times of India* article.[29] Likewise, electioneering on all sides, leading up to the second quarter 2014 elections, has taken up much of the MPs' valuable time and attention.

Accordingly, it is unlikely that any part of the new food act will begin to be phased in before 2015. This will provide all potential beneficiaries with the time to establish bank accounts, familiarize themselves with money transfer services and procedures, and receive their digital ration cards! Is the author missing something here? People with little to no money will need bank accounts, money transfer services, and have to use digital ration cards before they can participate in the new food security programme? This seems like a perfectly designed programme that has built-in procedural hurdles destined to disenfranchise many if not most potential beneficiaries.

* * *

One has to remember that even the idea of the human right to food is a comparatively recent concept. It has its contemporary origin in the UN Universal Declaration of Human Rights (UDHR) of 1948. The main reference point is Article 25, which states, 'Everyone has the right to a standard of living adequate for the health and well-being of himself and his family, including food . . . .'[30] It provides a reference point for human rights legislation that follows but is not itself a binding international legal instrument. It is the implementation of this human right that has proven to be so difficult. Further, while a human right within the UDHR, there is no international mechanism for its enforcement, there are no international food rights tribunals to adjudicate the individual's right.

There is No Incentive to Eliminate Poverty and Hunger

At the national level, and at every other level of the political hierarchy in developing countries, there is no incentive to resolve the issues of hunger, starvation, poverty, and backwardness; because to do so would mean a reduction in foreign aid. Foreign aid has become a dependable source of foreign investment and a source of foreign hard currency exchange. Foreign aid, for many developing nations, has become an institutionalized income line item, helping balance the foreign trade balance sheet. The national leaders in the developing nations recognize this function of foreign aid. The giving nations, however, ignore this reality because as long as hunger, poverty, and backwardness exist, the bureaucracy involved in international development are able to justify their continued existence.

If all the developing countries of the world were to 'solve' their problems of hunger, poverty, and backwardness, what would the developed nations of the world do with all their new-found cash reserves? This is a very frightening scenario to contemplate – governments with surpluses!

THE ROLE OF FOREIGN AID

We hear world organizations, like the United Nations, aid organizations, and national governments, profess that they are actively working on the issues of poverty and hunger but things are only getting worse for the poorest and hungriest segments of the world's population. How is it possible that some of the brightest and most talented people in the world – people like Jeffrey Sachs and William Easterly – cannot devise a programme that can and will address these problems?

To simply say that the problems of hunger and poverty cannot be solved may sound glib but, for decades, massive amounts of foreign aid have been poured into developing countries with no appreciable benefit. Easterly, probably more tongue-in-cheek than academically, is reported to have said: 'If foreign aid was the answer, and the intended recipients of this aid (the poor) are caught in a poverty trap, as suggested by Sachs, with all the foreign aid monies developing countries have received over the years, they could have bought their way out of poverty.'

Over the last fifty years, $2.3 trillion has been spent by the world's wealthiest nations on poverty reduction worldwide; and yet, roughly half of the world's 6+ billion people still claim to be poverty stricken.[31] Are the poor lying to us?

It would seem obvious that aid only works sometimes. It is now time to stop the endless debates that get us nowhere and begin to design and test poverty alleviation programmes to see which ones work, not just some of the time but consistently. Then, apply these tried and true strategies.

Unfortunately, that is not what is happening. To design and test a variety of strategies and implement the consistently successful ones is rational and logical. However, the *status quo* remains. Given this reality, what are the problems with current foreign aid programmes? The real problems are:

- They are wasteful.
- There is no accountability.
- There is no feedback.

Wasteful

The waste inherent in foreign aid programmes stems from ill-conceived projects. Donor agencies and organizations focus on aid distribution as the preferred measure of success. If the donors exhaust their budgets, they have done their job and can ask for more. Their budgets are their reason for and source of existence. Since it is their budgets that define these organizations, they have no incentive to be efficient, either within their individual organizations or the projects they promote.

As a consequence, the aid organizations and agencies have little or no need for external accountability. The public doesn't care where the money goes once it has been given. The only accountability within the organizations and agencies is entirely internal – where does the money go within the organization or agency? How much of the allocated funds reach the intended target populations is usually immaterial.

Accountability

In 2000, a World Bank study of evaluation began with a startling confession: 'Despite the billions of dollars spent on development assistance each year, there is still very little known about the actual impact of projects on the poor.'[32] Most developing countries are, to use an astrophysical metaphor, fiscal 'black holes'. They take in foreign aid, it simply disappears, and no measureable good is ever seen; because, as Easterly points out, there is no accountability.[33] Neither the aid agencies nor the recipient governments are held accountable; and without accountability there is no incentive to find out what does and what does not work. Most aid agencies have no independent project evaluations. Most project evaluations are performed by the same people who implement the projects. Independent or objective project evaluation would mean having the aid agencies take responsibility for specific tasks and determining if the anticipated outcome was achieved. Such evaluations would create more incentive for performance. As it stands now, largely positive project evaluations camouflage generally poor development outcomes. No one is held accountable for the millions of dollars pumped into developing countries. Is it any wonder that little or nothing is accomplished?

Easterly suggests that poverty has never been eliminated by foreign experts or foreign aid. Poverty will end as it has everywhere else, through what he terms 'homegrown' political, economic and social reformers and entrepreneurs. It is they who will unleash the power of democracy and free markets.[34] Yet, the money continues to flow.

The donors, because they are budget-driven, prefer to set broad, sweeping goals like 'ending extreme poverty', instead of more manageable and definable objectives. For reasons of political economy, politicians and bureaucrats prefer large-scale projects that will have the greatest impact and likelihood of satisfying the greatest number of potential recipients, even if there are no long-term, concrete, positive outcomes.

It has already been demonstrated that much of donor aid is based on political motivation, not necessarily given to those who need it most.[35] Need is secondary to donors' political strategies and agendas. Much of foreign and development aid can be seen as incentive driven and not driven to achieve measureable and realistic goals. Aid money is, within this context, reward money.

Feedback

Bureaucracies work best when there is a robust desire for feedback from targeted beneficiaries, strong incentives for the bureaucracy to respond to that feedback, easily observable or measurable outcomes, a willingness to change programmes to fit real world needs, and competition between other bureaucracies and agencies. As currently constituted, very few of these conditions exist within foreign aid.

By their very nature, bureaucracies are insulated. Their complexity and organization militates against outside influence. Added to their complexity is the generally unspoken axiom that any admission of present or past failure is a threat to future funding. Directly related to their insulated nature and their need for positive outcomes is the fact that when aid agencies report on their projects:

- There is little or no attempt to obtain input from those most affected.
- The reports focus on the successes and claim credit for what worked but seldom objectively analyse their shortfalls or mistakes.

The absence of feedback from targeted populations stems from the fact that the aid agencies are not subject to the same 'standards' of what some have called market feedback. If a product fails, the manufacturer wants to know why, so they can either reformat or re-engineer the product to meet the customers' needs and wants; they must compete with other similar products 'out there' that can be used for the same purposes – substitution. This is not the situation with government or private aid agencies. In general, there is no competition and, therefore, there is little or no need to actually seek 'customer' input. Success or failure is solely gauged on the disbursement of the agency's funding, not tangible results or customer satisfaction. There are virtually no mechanisms for obtaining programme-adjusting feedback, since there are no adverse consequences if the target population is dissatisfied. When a programme or project does not meet expectations, the development agents simply throw their hands in the air, shake their heads in derisive disbelief, turn their backs on the recipient population, and walk away to start another new programme somewhere else. They did their part.

When projects fail, there are discussions but no one is held responsible. Project managers move on to manage new projects. Field personnel 'go back to school', become academic researchers, teachers, or write books and articles, or simply move on to something new. No one is fired for incompetence or non-performance. Again, they did their part. The blame for programme failure is almost always placed on the recipient population. 'If the recipient population had only . . . '.

Furthermore, whether aid or development programmes are initiated from inside or outside the recipient nation, they are provided by monopolistic providers. No two agencies will simultaneously serve the same constituency. Therefore, there is no need for feedback, since there is no competition and there are no options for the programme's 'customers.'

* * *

The current system of foreign aid disbursement, almost invariably, requires that projects be implemented through the receiving nation's bureaucracy. These bureaucracies, and especially those in former British colonies, have had centuries to refine their obstructive abilities.

Neither the politicians nor the bureaucrats have any incentive to see poverty or hunger alleviation programmes succeed, as the aid agencies are little more than cash cows. This is not to say that indigenous politicians do not want their constituencies' lives to improve and benefit. They are not that heartless but, if the problems are solved once and for all, aid would no longer be necessary, and the flood of easy money would cease. That is not in the best interests of the politicians or the bureaucracies. It is much preferable to have the ineffectual programmes continue. As long as aid funding is available, the politicians, the bureaucrats and their bureaucracies, and the poor and hungry benefit, even if it is only marginally. The recipients, who receive the least benefit, can see that their political leaders are 'working' for them. Within the context of political economy, even ineffectual programmes have fiscal and political benefits for everyone, even if the problems they were designed to resolve persist.

THE LIMITS OF GROWTH

According to modernization theories, internal factors in the countries, such as illiteracy, traditional agrarian structure, the traditional population attitude, the division of labour, the lack of communication and infrastructure, etc., are all deemed to be factors contributing to underdevelopment. Differences in structure and historical origin are considered of little importance; internal dependencies are not taken into account.

Consequently, a change in endogenous factors is viewed as the primary target for most development programmes. The industrialized nations become the blueprint for everyone's future; and it is believed every nation will inevitably succumb to the Western socio-economic model, sooner or later. There is a continuum between the least and the most developed countries, and each country has its position along this line. The difference between industrialized countries and 'underdeveloped' countries is the degree of backwardness which needs to be addressed. Progress is measured in terms of the modernization of the production apparatus, capital aid, transfer of know-how, so that the developing countries can reach the stage of industrialized countries as quickly as possible. Development, then, is seen as an increase of production and efficiency and measured primarily by changing per capita income.

Professor Frithjof Kuhnen suggests that there are certain 'basic needs' that must be addressed with regard to development. These are:

- Economic growth to secure food and other requirements for the population.
- Social justice to reduce inequality.
- Employment as a means of earning an income but, as well, because of its ethical and social values.
- Participation, politically and socially.
- Independence as freedom from external domination.[36]

While individual societies may have different opinions on the priorities of these goals, in the absence of a general theory of development one can use the criterion of fulfilment of these goals as a yardstick in development. Development is then understood as progress towards these five goals.

There is, as demonstrated by Rist, a cultural imperative within Western cultures – individually and collectively – to pursue growth and progress. This 'need' has pushed the developed nations of the world to their current levels of social, economic, and political development, and these countries, in turn, have become the self-proclaimed standard by which all development is gauged and measured.

This, in turn, begs the question: Could everyone attain the same middle class standard of living we see throughout Europe and North America? As disturbing as it may be, the answer is a categorical no, at least not at our current levels of technology and known reserves of natural resources.

Eventually, every human population reaches a point where there are insufficient resources to support it. This is referred to as the 'overshoot and collapse' principle – Rise and Fall. How many historical volumes have been written with titles that begin: *The Rise and Fall of the . . .* ? Ultimately, it is a question of limits of growth, an idea popularized in the early 1970s with the publication of *Limits to Growth*.[37] If 1.44 to 1.71 billion people of the world's population of 6+ billion are already poor, it is inconceivable that our planet could support 10 billion without a greater percentage of the population falling below the poverty threshold or starving outright.[38] And, if the current trends are real, the world's population should reach 10 billion early in the next century.[39] Are we fighting a losing battle?

One must then ask, is our preoccupation with backwardness misplaced or misguided? Can development advocates justifiably and ethically promote development among all backward people, when there is little or no real likelihood that any substantive gains can be made without jeopardizing the livelihoods and cultures of those who are the target population? Within this context, one must determine growth of what and for whom.

For some groups, as Vandana Shiva suggests, development is a trick played on the people of the Third World to rob them of their resources and wealth, leaving them dispossessed and in debt.[40] This scenario is frequently played out in resource-rich Third World countries, where their resources are snatched from them, converting the residents into development refugees. The resources sought are often, mineral, but the same strategy applies to the expropriation of land for the development of hydroelectric-producing dam projects, highways, industrial parks, etc. In these cases, it is the First World nations, their global corporations or the national governments of these Third World nations that benefit the most.

Within the context of South Asia, the concentration of developmental backwardness, especially in the eastern Gangetic plain, is not situated in a mineral-rich area but, rather, in a primarily agricultural area in alluvial basins and floodplains. Therefore, development in such areas is directed at agricultural and technological development, not extractive resource development by First world multinationals. Within these areas, the peasants are the focus of development, not their displacement for the sake of economically valuable resources. These peasants are small producers with multiple identities, multiple roles, multiple rights and duties, and are not currently envisioned as the target of the agro-chemical giants like Monsanto, Cargill, or DuPont, unlike the situation in Sub-Saharan Africa.[41]

Bill Emmott, formerly the Editor of the *Economist*, counters much of Shiva's anti-development rhetoric when he states:

> . . . the 1.2 billion who live in extreme poverty; the billions more who have stunted lives, with poor diets, a lack of access to health and education, a lack of opportunity to make a difference for themselves and for their children. The point of development is, or should be, those people: to give them opportunities and freedoms to change and improve their lives, if that is what they want.[42]

The most important words within Emmott's statement of what he believes development should be, and the entire debate over the merits of development, rest in the words, 'if that is what they want'. None of the aid agencies, the development agencies, the national development committees or programmes seem to address 'what the backward people want'. Development is almost always defined from the top down and by the values, desires, aspirations, and philosophies of outsiders, not those being 'developed'. From this perspective, the term backwardness is, in fact, pejorative and condescending. Again, we are left with the question: What are development and backwardness? It all depends on who you ask.

OUR MAP OF BACKWARDNESS

Each of the studies consulted for this current work identified between 69 and 170 backward districts, scattered throughout India. There is no doubt that backwardness can be identified in almost any state in India, if one chooses the right set of indicators. However, if using a variety of different measures one finds the same districts appearing time and again in the lists of backward districts, then it might be safe to assume they represent the core group of backward districts. Map I.1, located in the pocket at the end of the book, is a graphic representation of the cumulative findings of five studies.

Even when viewing Map I.1 in a cursory manner, a pattern is readily observable. The majority of developmentally backward districts in India are concentrated in the eastern and central Indian states of Bihar, Jharkhand, Orissa (Odisha), Uttar Pradesh, and Madhya Pradesh. Further, the most backward districts, while scattered throughout these states, also tend to cluster together, contiguously, within each state. They are not scattered randomly.

Combining the information displayed in Map I.1 and Table I.1, reveals:

- Only seven districts – Sirsa and Kaithal districts; Tehri Garhwal, Chamoli, and Champawat districts; Chittoor district; and Chittaurgarh district – were isolated backward districts not contiguous with other backward districts.
- All the other remaining backward districts were contiguous with one or more other backward districts.
- The greatest concentration of backward districts (those mentioned more than three times in the five studies) are located in the states of Bihar, Uttar Pradesh, Jharkhand, Madhya Pradesh, and Orissa.
- Twelve of the fourteen districts mentioned in every study are located in Bihar. Of these:
  - Eleven are in northern Bihar.
  - Eleven are located in Mithila (including Godda, which is within the Jharkhand portion of modern Mithila).
- Bihar also has the largest number of backward districts mentioned in four of the five studies (10).
- The two districts that appeared in every study but were outside Bihar were located in Uttar Pradesh and Jharkhand, Barabanki and Godda, respectively.
- Uttar Pradesh had the largest total number of enumerated backward districts with 43 of 71, followed by Bihar with 35 of 38, Madhya Pradesh with 30 of 50, Orissa with 20 of 30, and Jharkhand with 19 of 24.
- All fourteen of the common backward districts – those that appear in each of the lists of backward districts – fall within what was once Imperial Bengal. Eleven backward districts fall in a historically recognized, culturally important, compact area commonly known as Mithila, an area that, since independence, has sought its own independent state status.

Is this pattern of backwardness coincidental or simply anecdotal? How did these districts and states become backward when history suggests that they were among the most politically and socially vital and agriculturally and economically productive states in all of South Asia? How do we explain this concentration of backwardness, especially

MAP 1.1: BACKWARD DISTRICTS OF MODERN BIHAR AND JHARKHAND

after more than sixty-five years of continuous governmental and international aid agency study and intervention?

OBSERVATIONS

The debate over what development is often fails to recognize the fact that whether immanent or intentional, development is fundamentally a historical process. As a consequence of our preoccupation with its sociological, political, and economic aspects the processes of development and underdevelopment have blinded us to the fact that it has become a global obsession or aspiration.[43] This is 'what' development is. It does not, however, answer the question of 'how' development occurs. And it is this 'how' that results in more failures than successes.

Development can be seen in two quite different ways: First, as a historical process of social change. Here societies are transformed over time, in response to internal and external forces. Second, as a deliberate attempt by development agencies, including governments and non-government organizations, or social movements. In either instance, development is not always positive. Often, whether immanent or intentional, development does not succeed due to social, political, economic, or cultural resistance.

NOTES

1. Michael P. Cowen and Robert W. Shenton, *Doctrines of Development*, New York: Routledge, 1996, p. 3.
2. Gilbert Rist, *The History of Development: From Western Origins to Global Faith*, 3rd edn., 2nd impression, P. Camiller, Trans., London: Zed Books, 2010, p. 485. Although Rist attributes the 'invention' of the concept of underdevelopment to Truman's speech writer in 1949, Michael P. Cowen and Robert W. Shenton, *Doctrines of Development*, 1996, p. 7, suggest that the concept of development and underdevelopment can be traced to a speech by Sir Bernard Henry Bourdillon,the then Governor of Nigeria in 1937, or to Joseph Chamberlain's suggestion that Britain should develop our 'undeveloped' estates in Africa in 1905. See, also, Michael P. Cowen and Robert W. Shenton, 'Bankers, Peasants, and Land in British West Africa, 1905-1937', *Journal of Peasant Studies*, vol. 19, no. 1, 1991, pp. 26-58.
3. Harry S. Truman, 'Harry S. Truman, Inaugural Address, Thursday, January 20,1949', retrieved 8 December 2012, from Bartleby.com - Inaugural Addresses of the Presidents: http://www.bartleby.com/124/pres53.html, 2012, ¶ 44 & 53, 4. Tori Roeck, 'Oxford Professor Emeritus Charts Human Development', retrieved 26 February 2014 from *The Observer*: http:// ndsmcobserver.com/2014/02/ oxford-professor-emeritus-charts-human-development/, 19 February 2014.
5. Planning Commission, *Report on General Issues Relating to Backward Area Development*, New Delhi: Government of India, National Committee on the Development of Backward Areas, November 1981, p. 4.
6. See, Michael P. Cowen and Robert W. Shenton, *Doctrines of Development*, 1996, Chapter 4, pp. 173-253, especially p. 173.

7. Tim Allen and Alan Thomas, eds., *Poverty and Development in the 1990s*, Oxford: Oxford University Press in association with the Open University, 1992, p. 7.
8. Simon Maxwell, *The Meaning and Measurement of Poverty - ODI Poverty Briefings Issue 3*, retrieved 3 January 2011, from ODI - Shaping Policy for Development: The Meaning and Measurement of Poverty - ODI Poverty Briefings Issue 3, February 1999.
9. Rist, *The History of Development: From Western Origins to Global Faith*, 2010, p. 1.
10. Ibid.
11. Francis Fukuyama, *The "End of History?"* Washington, DC: US Institute of Peace, no. 11, 1989.
12. See, for example, William L. Thomas, ed., *Man's Role in Changing the Face of the Earth,* Chicago: University of Chicago Press, 1956/1971; Clarence Glacken, *Traces on the Rhodian Shore: Nature and Culture in Western Thought from Ancient Times to the End of the Eighteenth Century*, Berkeley: University of California Press, 1967; and J. Albert Rorabacher, 'Geo-Historical Approaches to Environment: The Evolution of Environmental Thought in Western Civilization', *Journal of Geography,* vol. 72, no. 4, 1973, 31-41.
13. The primary efforts to define and address district-level backwardness include:

    1. Committee on Dispersal of Industries (1960)
    2. Patel Committee Report (1964)
    3. Planning Commission Study Group (1966-71)
    4. Pande Committee Report 1968)
    5. Wanchoo Committee Report (1968)
    6. Sukhamoy Chakravarty Committee Report on Backward Areas (1972)
    7. National Committee on Development of Backward Areas (1978)
    8. Development of Backward Hill Areas (1981)
    9. Hyderabad Karnataka Development Committee (1981)
    10. Fact Finding Committee on Regional Imbalances (1983)
    11. Committee for the Development of Backward Areas (1983)
    12. 100 Backward Districts (Sarma Committee) (1997)
    13. District Industries Centre Action Plan (1979-80)
    14. Kurian's Note (2001)
    15. Task Force on the Identification of Districts for Wage and Self-employment Programmes (2003)
    16. District-level Deprivation in the New Millennium (2003)
    17. Inter-Ministry Task Group Redressing Regional Imbalances (2005)
    18. Report of Fact Finding Team on Vidharbha (2006)
    19. Borooah and Dubey; and Borooah, Amaresh and Amaresh (2007 & 2008).

14. See, for example, B.M. Bhatia, 'Back to Mandal', *The Hindustan Times*, 3 December 1992; N.J. Kurian, *Widening Regional Disparities in India,* retrieved 21 December 2012, from http://planningcommission.nic.in/reports/articles/ncsxna/art_wide.pdf, n.d.; N.J. Kurian, 'Review Article: Widening Economic & Social Disparities: Implications for India', *Indian Journal of Medical Research,* vol. 126, no. 4, October 2007, pp. 374-80; N.J. Kurian, *Regional Disparities in India,* New Delhi: Planning Commission of India, 2001; Vani Borooah, K. Amaresh, and Amaresh Dubey, 'Measuring Regional Backwardness: Poverty, Gender and Children in the Districts of India', *Journal of Applied Economic Research,* vol. 1, no. 4, 2007, pp. 403-40; Planning Commission, *Task Force on Identification of Districts for Wage and Self Employment Programmes*, New Delhi: Planning Commission, Government of India, 2003; and Rohini Nayyar, *Planning for the Development of Backward Districts,* New Delhi: Planning Commission, Government of India, 2004.
15. Even within India, the Government of India frequently uses still other systems to evaluate levels of socio-economic development for internal purposes. India's National Informatics Centre (NIC) was created 1976 with the financial assistance of the United Nations Development Program (UNDP) and provides support for e-Governance to the Central Government. Among the services NIC provides is a nationwide data base with links to almost every district. Each district website typically provides, among other categories of information, listings called *District at a Glance* and *Profile*. The profiles, in particular, often provide a wealth of information, often including the district's Relative Index of Development, based on a 100 point system. See, for example, Darbhanga District in northern Bihar: http://darbhanga.bih.nic.in/. See, also, Wikipedia's *List of Districts of India,* which provides state-wise listings for India's states and individual district website links. http://en.wikipedia.org/wiki/List_of_districts_of_India.
16. See, Planning Commission, *Report on General Issues Relating to Backward Area Development,* New Delhi: Government of India, National Committee on the Development of Backward Areas, November 1981, p. 7, § IV, para 4.24.
17. Alexander Gerschenkron, *Economic Backwardness in Historical Perspective: A Book of Essays,* Cambridge: Belknap Press of Harvard University Press, 1966.
18. Ibid., Essay I: 'Economic Backwardness in Historical Perspective', p. 6.
19. George Santayana, *Reason in Common Sense,* New York: Dover Publications, 1980, vol. I, chapter XII, p. 284. The greater quotation is:

    'Progress, far from consisting in change, depends on retentiveness. When change is absolute there remains no being to improve and no direction is set for possible improvement: and when experience is not retained, as among savages, infancy is perpetual. Those who cannot remember the past are condemned to repeat it.'

20. Daron Acemoglu and James Robinson, *Economic Backwardness in Political Perspective,* Cambridge: National Bureau of Economic Research, NBER Working Paper No. 8831, March 2002, p. 2. Acemoglu and Robinson used the phrase – political replacement effect within a purely economic and political setting. For our purposes, it may be more useful to expand the idea to include social and economic spheres of influence as well.
21. Data on per capita income in South Asia, 1990-2010, from International Monetary Fund Data Mapper. In Purchasing Power Parity terms, per capita income more than tripled, from under US $850 per year in 1990 to almost US $3,000 per year in 2010.
22. See, for example, Jason Overdorf, *India: Food Rots as People Starve*, retrieved 4 November 2012, from Global-Post: http://www.globalpost.com/dispatch/news/regions/asia-pacific/india/120712/food-security-hunger-starvation-wheat-prices, 16 July 2012, RT Question More, *Indian Poor Starve While Grain Rots in Depots*, retrieved 12 August 2012, from RT Question More: http://rt.com/news/india-hunger-grain-depot/, 11 August 2010, *The Irish Times*, *India's Children Starving to Death While Grain Rots in Fields*, retrieved 3 November 2012, from IrishTimes.Com - On-line: http://www.irishtimes.com/newspaper/world/2012/0703/1224319264513.html, 3 July 2012; Ram Kishen, 'India's Poor Starve as Politicians Steal Their Food', retrieved on 19 December 2012 from BloombergBusinessweek - Global Economics: http://www.businessweek.com/articles/2012-09-06/indias-poor-starve-as-politicians-steal-their-food, 12 September 2012; and Amy Waldman, 'India's Poor Starve as Wheat Rots', retrieved 3 January 2011, from *The New York Times* – Asia Pacific – On-line: http://www.nytimes.com/2002/12/02/international/asia/02FARM.html?pagewanted=all, 2 December 2002.
23. Amy Waldman, '*India's Poor Starve as Wheat Rots*', 2 December 2002.
24. See, for example, *The Irish Times*, 'India's Children Starving to Death While Grain Rots in Fields, 3 July 2012; Jim Yardley, India Asks, Should Food Be a Right for the Poor?' retrieved 14 December 2012, from *The New York Times* – Asia Pacific: http://www.nytimes.com/2010/08/09/world/asia/09food.html?pagewanted=all&_r=0, 8 August 2010; RT Question More, 'Indian Poor Starve While Grain Rots in Depots', 11 August 2010; Jason Overdorf, 'India: Food Rots as People Starve, 16 July 2012; and Mehul Srivastava and Andrew MacAskill, Poor in India Starve as Politicians Steal $14.5 Billion of Food, retrieved 5 November 2012, from Bloomberg.Com: http://www.bloomberg.com/news/2012-08-28/poor-in-india-starve-as-politicians-steal-14-5-billion-of-food.html, 29 August 2012.
25. Gethin Chamberlain, 'Hunger in India: The Real Cause is Lack of Political Will', retrieved 15 October 2012, from *The Guardian* – Global Development:

http://www.guardian.co.uk/environment/2010/se/14/hunger-india-actionaid, 14 September 2010.
26. Ibid.
27. Joachim von Braun, M.S. Swaminathan, and Mark W. Rosegrant, *Agriculture, Food Security, Nutrition and the Millennium Development Goals,* Washington, DC: International Food Policy Research Institute, 2004, p. 5.
28. Zeebiz.com, 'Pushing Food Security at WTO is a Challenge: India', 1 March 2014, retrieved from, http://zeenews.india.com/business/news/economy/pushing-food-security-at-wto-is-a-challenge-india_96013.html.
29. ET Bureau, 'Implementing Food Security Law to Cost Government Rs 88,500 Crore', 17 February 2014, retrieved from *Times of India* – On-line from http://timesofindia.indiatimes.com/business/india-business/implementing-food-security-law-to-cost-government-rs-88500-crore/articleshow/30665108.cms.
30. UN (United Nations), 'The Universal Declaration of Human Rights', Article 25, retrieved from, http://www.un.org/en/documents/udhr/index.shtml#a11, 2014.
31. von Braun, Swaminathan, and Rosegrant, *Agriculture, Food Security, Nutrition and the Millennium Development Goals,* 2004, p. 3.
32. Judy L. Baker, *Evaluating the Impact of Development Projects on Poverty: A Handbook for Practitioners*, Washington, DC: World Bank, 2000, p. vi.
33. William Easterly, 'Why Doesn't Aid Work?' retrieved 4 November 2012, from Cato Unbound: http://www.cato-unbound.org/2006/04/03/william-easterly/why-doesnt-aid-work/, 13 April 2006.
34. See, William Easterly and Steven Radelet, *The Effectiveness of Foreign Aid,* retrieved 23 December 2011, from Council on Foreign Relations: http://www.cfr.org/foreign-aid/effectiveness-foreign-aid/p12077, 1 December 2006.
35. P. Mosley, 'The Political Economy of Foreign Aid: A Model of the Market for a Public Good', *Economic Development and Cultural Change*, vol. 33, no. 2, 1985, pp. 373-93; Bruno S. Frey and Friedrich Schneider, 'Competing Models of International Lending Activity', *Journal of Development Economics,* vol. 20, no. 2, 1986, pp. 225-45; and William N. Trumbull and H.J. Wall, 'Estimating Aid-allocation Criteria with Panel Data', *The Economic Journal,* vol. 104, no. 425, 1994, pp. 876-82.
36. Frithjof Kuhnen, 'Causes of Underdevelopment and Concepts for Development: An Introduction to Development Theories', *The Journal of Development Studies*, vol. 8, 1986-7, pp. 11-25, especially p. 23.
37. Donella H. Meadows, *The Limits to Growth: A Report for the Club of Rome's Project on the Predicament of Mankind,* New York: Universe Books, Potomac Association Books Series, 1972. This book was updated and republished in 2004.
38. See, D. Morrell, 'Who is Poor?' retrieved 3 November 2011, from *Harvard*

Magazine – On-line: http://harvardmagazine.com/2011/01/who-is-poor, January-February 2011. Morrell references the World Bank's estimate of 1.44 billion poor and Amartya Sen's estimate of 1.71 billion. See, also, Jean-Louis Warnholz, *Poverty Reduction for Profit? A Critical Examination of Business Opportunities at the Bottom of the Pyramid*, AEH Working Paper Series QEHWPS 160. Oxford: Queen Elizabeth House Working Papers Series, October 2007.

39. United Nations Press Release, *World Population to Reach 10 Billion by 2100 if Fertility in All Countries Converges to Replacement Level*, New York: United Nations, 3 May 2011.
40. Vandana Shiva is a philosopher and environmental activist, and one of the leaders and board members of the International Forum on Globalization. In Bill Emmott and Vandana Shiva, *Is Development Good for the Third World?* retrieved from Word Document on-line: http://www.amerika.org/texts/is-development-good-for-the-third-world-vandana-shiva/, 2000. Vandana 'debates' with Bill Emmott, the editor of the *Economist*, whether development is good for the Third World.
41. The current literature is rife with debates over the exploitation of emerging nations in Sub-Saharan Africa, especially as regards the agro-chemical, multinationals' attempts to penetrate this largely untapped market for genetically modified, transgenic plants, including 'terminator' technologies. See the discussion in J. Albert Rorabacher, *Hunger and Poverty in South Asia,* Delhi: Gyan Publishing, 2010.
42. Bill Emmott and Vandana Shiva, 'Is Development Good for the Third World?', *The Ecologist*, vol. 30, no. 2, April 2000, p. 25. See also, E. Miller, 'Is "Development" Good For The Third World?' (Vandana Shiva), retrieved 5 December 2012, from America.org: http://www.amerika.org/texts/is-development-good-for-the-third-world-vandana-shiva/, 29 April 1970. See, also, Vandana Shiva, *The Enclosure and Recovery of the Commons,* Delhi: The Research Foundation for Science, Technology and Ecology, India, 1997.
43. Henry Bernstein, ed., *Underdevelopment and Development: The Third World Today: Selected Readings,* Harmondsworth: Penguin Books, 1973, p. 13.

CHAPTER 2

Bihar and Mithila: What Went Wrong?

INTRODUCTION

Modern Bihar is a very different place from that which existed in early historic times or, for that matter, until shortly after Independence. The course of Bihar's long illustrious history began to change and within little more than a decade, by the time of the 1961 Census of India, Bihar was rapidly becoming the economic backwater that everyone has come to know.[1] Biharis, by the thousands, were seeking employment and educational opportunities outside their home state, from landless agricultural labourers to those of the professional classes. In 2005, Rakesh Ankit wrote: 'The professional class in Patna is skeletal, with the best and the brightest having evacuated.'[2] Only the landlords, politicians, aged, ill, and feeble seemed to remain behind. Then, in the same year, Nitish Kumar became the chief minister and the history of Bihar began to change. It was not a dramatic change in the observable living conditions of the people, as much as it was a change in the people – a glimmer of hope.

In 2007, the author contacted the Centre for Monitoring Indian Economy (CMIE), an independent economic think-tank headquartered in Mumbai that produces economic and business databases, including monthly state activity and analysis reports for decision-makers. He questioned why Bihar, Jharkhand, Chhattisgarh, and Orissa, among other mainland states of India, were conspicuously missing from its Monthly State Analysis Service Map. The company's response, while shocking was, at the time understandable (paraphrasing): 'There is not sufficient economic activity in these states to justify their inclusion in our monthly reporting system and it is difficult to obtain reliable data.[3]'

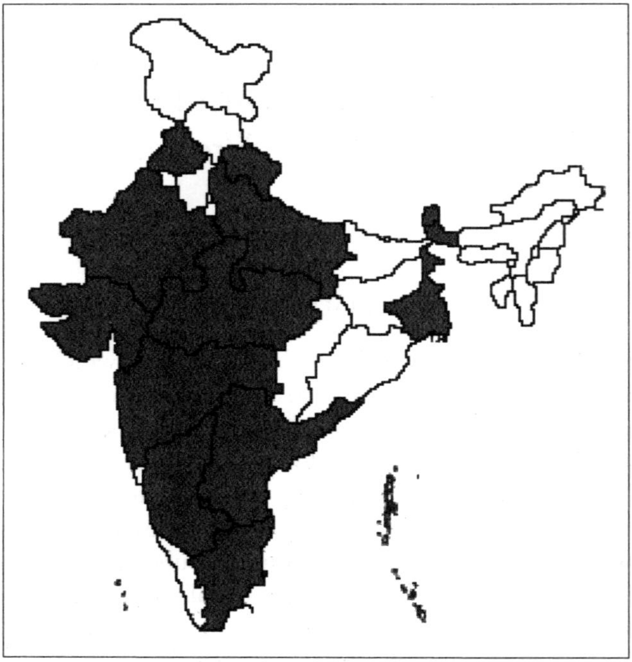

MAP 2.1: CMIE MONTHLY STATE ANALYSIS SERVICE MAP

Even after nearly a decade of unprecedented economic success, almost every indicator or statistic used to describe Bihar places it at or near the top or bottom of each category. For Bihar, there seems to be no middle ground. When compared with India's other major states, it continues to post some of the most amazing and depressing statistics:

- Population density – 1,106 people per sq km – the highest.[4]
- Population decadal growth rate – 25.07 per cent – the highest among the major states of India.[5]
- Rural population – 88.7 per cent – second highest. Indian average, 68.84 per cent.[6]
- Urban population – 11.3 per cent – second lowest. Indian average 31.16 per cent.[7]
- Literacy – 63.82 per cent – lowest.[8]

- Economic growth rate – 11.03 per cent from 2005-10 – highest in India.
- Per capita income – Rs 22,691 – lowest. The national average – Rs 35,993.[9]
- Poverty ratio – 33.5 per cent – highest.[10]
- Percentage of population living below the poverty line (BPL) – 55 per cent – second worst. All India average is 37 per cent.[11]
- Human Development Index – 0.367 – Lowest. India average is 0.467.[12]
- Oxford Multidemensional Poverty Index (MPI) – 0.499 – lowest of all Indian states. India average is 0.296.[13]
- Life expectancy at birth – Bihar – 61.6 years. India – 63.5 years.[14]
- Cellphone ownership in 2005-6 – 4.2 million mobile phones registered; today, more than 46 million mobile phone connections![15]
- Km. of road per person: Bihar – 0.0108; India – 0.262.[16]

* * *

Why did Bihar fall from social, political, and economic grace? At one time, it was one of the beacons for all that was good in India. At one time, as the historian Romila Thapar stated: 'the early history of India *was* the history of Bihar'.[17] The fall of Bihar took little more than a decade, beginning in the mid-1950s. Each successive decade only added another layer of misery.

Bihar's downfall was not just a matter of economics, politics, sociology, psychology, education, health-care, communication, or that elusive component we call infrastructure. One cannot simply disaggregate Bihar, investigate its component parts, and hope to understand what 'makes it tick'.

Everyone has an explanation but every programme, thus far designed to ameliorate or eradicate the causes of Bihar's failure to thrive, has been, at best, disappointing to disastrous; and it has been so for decades. Some have suggested that the machinery of government is unresponsive and corrupt. Some blame the people and the state's system of education; however, with many young Biharis frequently passing the prestigious entry-level civil service exam with honours, year after year, it is obviously not a problem with the people.[18] Faced with institutional and infrastructural inadequacies at every turn, one is left with the impression that the people have simply given up. Alternatively, they may not have surrendered to their situation so much as they have simply resigned themselves to the fact that the state is either unwilling or incapable of helping them. Consequently, they are attempting to live their lives the best they can, much like their ancestors. Over time, this resignation has chipped away at the people's ability to visualize or conceive of a life without poverty. Unable to visualize prosperity, they are unable to achieve it.

There are those who blame modern Bihar's problems on the bifurcation of the state in 2000 – forming the reduced modern state of Bihar and the state of Jharkhand. Jharkhand was the fiscal beneficiary of the bifurcation. It received most of the tax and revenue generated by the industrial and mineral resources of old Bihar. Residual Bihar, on the other hand, retained most of the state's liabilities, especially those associated with flood relief and land reform compensation payments, since residual Bihar is the area hardest hit by annual flooding and historically the home to numerous large zamindari estates.

At the time of bifurcation, a major portion of the Rs 30,000 crore liability of undivided Bihar fell on residual Bihar. As a consequence of its loss of revenue, the state was unable to provide for the much-needed capital spending.

While it was able to maintain most of its basic social programmes at a minimalist level, education and healthcare suffered profoundly. Bihar has been unable to sustain its basic economic services and infrastructure. As a consequence, roads and bridges deteriorated, schools remained in disrepair, teachers abandoned their posts because they went unpaid, clinics were left to operate without supplies and medical staff, rural electrification and sanitation programmes stagnated, and flood protection became little more than a memory. Bereft of virtually all industrial capacity and industry-related revenue, Bihar quickly faced fiscal insolvency.

While bifurcation may have exacerbated the economic woes of

modern Bihar, it was not the cause of the state's economic collapse. Its downward spiral had begun long before the idea of Jharkhand had entered the heads of sitting politicians in Patna, Ranchi, or New Delhi.

One observer, Saibal Gupta went even further, suggesting that: 'The only reason the state [residual Bihar] has managed to keep its deficit down is that it has refused to spend. All the government departments are flush with funds being surrendered year after year.'[19]

Gupta's assertion is difficult to even comprehend. A state in financial ruin, begging for investment capital, and it refuses to spend its budgeted funds? This is little short of insanity but it happened; an example of the government's failure to fulfill its fiduciary responsibility to its citizens, a violation of the public trust, and blatant bureaucratic malfeasance, all of which are but the outward symptoms of government corruption within a failed state.

* * *

It was not until Nitish Kumar began to trumpet 'good governance and development' in 2005 that things began to change and Bihar's economy seemed to magically spring to life. Whether that economic upsurge will continue remains to be seen. Nevertheless, Bihar's apparent war on criminality did much to repair its severely tarnished image, inspiring a newfound optimism that has become almost palpable. Despite an astonishing growth rate of 11 per cent, Bihar has failed to bring about similar changes in poverty reduction, *per capita* incomes, and literacy.

The most important question, now, is whether Bihar has entered a new era of prosperity or is the state's recent economic success simply a deft politician's use of smoke and mirrors. If it was all political and economic chicanery, ultimately the truth will be unearthed. It cannot go on forever. However, even if it was not real and lasting, at least for a brief shining moment Bihar, again, had a fleeting wisp of glory; and for a state that has experienced decades of neglect and pessimism, any glimmer of hope is something to be genuinely appreciated.

The suggested causes of Bihar's abysmal state of affairs, or condition, are but broad strokes on a very large socio-economic and physical canvas. They can all be viewed, in one form or another, as environmental problems – the economy, politics, finance, crime, illiteracy, poor health-care, and, of course the fall-back, catchall problem, infrastructure.

* * *

After more than nine years of economic success, unfortunately, the landscape of Bihar seems only slightly altered from that described by Ankit in 2005, when he wrote:

> Most of the rampant stereotypes about Bihar's underdevelopment are actually true. The state is marked by deep-rooted poverty, little opportunity for upward mobility, a dismal education system, and a sky-high crime rate; extortion in particular has emerged as a major industry. All this is coupled with an unresponsive and corrupt civil administration. For nearly a half-century, Bihar has been consistent in one respect: poor ranking on almost all major social and economic indices. Education remains, simply put, a dead loss. With the great schools and colleges of the past having lost all strength and credibility, anyone who can afford it sends their charges to Delhi, Calcutta, or elsewhere, as long as it is outside Bihar. With young Bihari men and women clearing the country's most prestigious entry-level civil service exams year after year, it is obvious that the problems of Bihar lie not with its people.
>
> The rotten state of Bihar's roads provides a window into the state's abysmal physical infrastructure. The lack of productive employment pushes un-organized labour to the metropolises in western India, Delhi and Calcutta, while organized labour within the state is used as cannon-fodder by the various political parties. The professional class in Patna is skeletal, with the best and the brightest having evacuated. A heavily compromised bureaucracy and judiciary are used to uphold the status quo. Faced with such a wall of inadequacy in governmental institutions, the people have decided to tune out and live their lives as best they can – in the manner of their ancestors, who similarly did not expect help from the state.[20]

In early 2010, shortly after it was announced that Bihar had experienced what was believed to be an unanticipated and unprecedented 11-plus per cent economic growth rate over the previous five years, Lydia Polgreen of *The New York Times* was still able to describe Bihar using many of the same terms and phrases as her predecessors had. She wrote:

> For decades the sprawling state of Bihar, flat and scorching as a griddle, was something between a punch line and a cautionary tale, the exact opposite of the high-tech, rapidly growing, rising global power India has sought to become.
>
> Criminals could count on the police for protection, not prosecution. Highwaymen ruled the shredded roads and kidnapping was one of the state's most profitable businesses. . . . Its economy, peopled by impoverished subsistence farmers struggling through alternating floods and droughts, shrivelled. Its government, led by politicians who used divisive identity politics to entrench their rule, was so corrupt that it required a newly coined phrase: the Jungle Raj.
>
> The name captured everything that was wrong with old India – a combustible mix of crime, corruption and caste politics in a state crucible that stifled economic growth.[21]

Some would argue that Ankit's and Polgreen's descriptions of Bihar are no longer accurate, citing the state's economic turnaround. It is readily admitted that Bihar's economic indicators suggest things have changed. Yet, despite reports of spectacular economic growth in recent years, Bihar remains largely and visibly unchanged. Sadly, it continues to be characterized by a pall of poverty which is visible and palpable almost everywhere – poor infrastructure, the appearance and disrepair of government, historic, and private buildings, and even worse, on the people's faces, something Usha Alexander commented on more than a decade earlier.[22]

Blair Glencorse, writing in *Himal* recently, suggested that, while driving around Bihar in late 2011, it was apparent that the state had not been transformed into the orderly, prosperous society that the media and the government would like us to believe now exists.[23] The economic revival of Bihar's economy has not been felt everywhere and by everyone. The benefits of the remarkable rise in Bihar's economic expansion was unevenly distributed. It was most readily felt by Bihar's urban dwellers, not the 88.7 per cent of the state's population living in rural areas.

While numbers and statistics do not lie, how they are derived, used, and the inferences we draw from them often make them

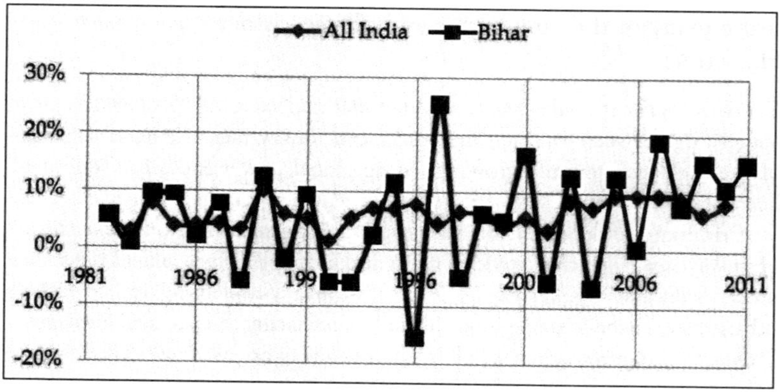

FIGURE 2.1: ANNUAL ECONOMIC GROWTH RATES, ALL-INDIA AND BIHAR, 1981-2011[24]

misleading. Equally important is the fact that statistics are often more descriptive than analytical, often providing simplistic, linear conceptions of transformations. In general, developmental statistics reflect points in time. They are constantly changing. For a pattern to emerge takes time. A single number, or even a short series of numbers over months or even several years, do not a pattern make, witness Figure 2.1.

From the author's perspective, there are possibly three patterns depicted in Figure 2.1:

- Bihar's annual economic growth rates are highly variable year to year.
- In general, every year of increase is followed by a year of nearly equal or greater decline.
- There is no consistent trend one way or the other, even during the years now considered to represent Nitish's 'economic turnaround'.

At the same time, the all-India growth rate has trended, albeit slowly, consistently upward.

* * *

Immediately following the government's announcement that Bihar had experienced an 11.03 per cent economic growth rate, Professor

N.K. Chaudhary, Department of Economics, Patna University, questioned the figure; at first from the point of view of simple academic curiosity. He wanted it to be true. He hoped it was true. However, at the same time, he doubted its veracity. He knew that for at least three of the five years between 2004 and 2009, agricultural production had shrunk. He referred to Bihar's state economic survey for 2008-9, which contained the economic statistics for the preceding five years. Using a harmonic mean he calculated the gross domestic product for Bihar, finding it to be somewhere between 6 and 7 per cent.[25] Further investigation showed that the data for 2009-10 had been omitted from the Legislative Assembly's economic report and the data from previous years had been:

> tinkered with to reach the magical figure of 11.03 per cent: most of the lagging figures had been quietly jacked up. . . . the agriculture growth data for 2008-09 was changed from -6.7 to +13.33 per cent, a mysterious jump of 20 per cent. That year, severe floods in Bihar's Kosi River and the subsequent drought adversely impacted Bihar's agricultural output.[26]

If the figures were changed covertly, does that mean the economic surveys tabled in the state legislature in previous years were also wrong? Or are the numbers in the 2009-10 report wrong? '. . . [a] 20 per cent [jump] in agriculture, a sector that is bleeding in Bihar, raises serious doubts about the veracity of the magical 11 per cent. . . .' The credibility of that data was further weakened by a caveat appended to that report by Pronab Sen, the Chief Statistician of India: "This data is not authenticated by the Central Statistics Organization".'[27]

It has been suggested that much of the economic activity in Bihar over the last five to seven years is largely a function of heavy spending on road construction projects. It really does not matter if this 'observation' or 'criticism' is correct or not. Today, Bihar has potholes where formerly it didn't even have roads. Although one writer suggests, based on his review of government documents, '. . . public works programme[s] did the job, as there is evidence of a substantial reconstruction of roads and bridges (though perhaps not of new roads) funded by the Asian Development Bank (ADB) and national programmes that seem to have boosted overall output growth'.[28]

Despite Bihar's impressive economic gains, it continues to be among the poorest states in India; and its social indicators continue to be weak in contrast to the positive economic image the state has begun to enjoy. Nevertheless, there is a sense of change and anticipation in the air, and should Nitish falter, all his successes could be easily undermined by unfulfilled expectations. What the Nitish's government has been able to accomplish, where all the other governments before have failed, is the recognition that change was not only feasible but possible. However, to make that possibility a reality required that the dysfunctional and corrupt system of public finance in the state submit to strict supervision and external oversight or audit, forcing bureaucrats throughout Bihar to become accountable to the state's bureaucracy, the state ministers, and the people. After all, this is what good governance is all about. Furthermore, Bihar has begun to comply with national compliance requirements in return for state grants-in-aid and low-interest loans.

* * *

Nevertheless, economic analysts, political writers, and everyday citizens are already beginning to complain that Nitish's government has fallen short of its ambitious development plans. But at least it appears that Nitish continues to have ambitions, both for himself and his state. Nitish's predecessor, Lalu Prasad Yadav, did not offer development. At best, he promised *izzat*, or self-respect, to the downtrodden castes – the Backward Classes (BC) and Other Backward Classes (OBC) – who once voted as their landlords demanded, and who later began to elect caste and communal candidates with whom their 'superiors' could or would not cooperate. The irony of Nitish's successes is all the more surprising since he was a staunch ally of Lalu and preceded him as union railway minister and followed him as chief minister.[29]

Nitish did not become chief minister without bringing along 'Lalu-like baggage', however. In 2010, P.K. Sinha, president of Loktantrik Samata Dal, accused Nitish of participating in a Rs 4,000-crore concrete sleeper scam during the time he was the union railway minister.[30] The case was only recently dismissed by the Delhi High Court. As with many claims of corruption, whether true or not, such claims are often used to manoeuvre or compromise political opponents or future allies.

While the veracity of the claims against Nitish will undoubtedly never be substantiated nor completely forgotten, Nitish finds himself in the midst of a growing political maelstrom. In June 2013, Nitish and his JD(U) party broke away from their alliance with the Bharatiya Janata Party (BJP) creating an opportunity for the re-emergence of the likes of Lalu Prasad Yadav in the next parliamentary elections and simultaneously prompting the rancour of the BJP's national leader, Narendra Modi of Gujarat.[31]

The rumour of this split began to fuel political controversies and speculation in Bihar's complex system of caste and communal politics, even before it was announced. In Bihar, political alliances are everything and at best tenuous. Without clear political dominance, alliances are the only way to form a working government under the parliamentary system. With each new election, every party leader jockeys for support and position, often changing party affiliations and alliances to achieve their political goals. Therefore, the fluidity of Bihar politics, at least in part, explains much of the state's lack of social, political, and economic direction, leadership, and continuity. Political careers in Bihar are often measured in days rather than years or decades. They are often chaotic, fast and furious, and frequently fleeting.

Bihar has a very long way to go before it has fully recovered from the decades lost to social, political, fiscal, and economic mismanagement. Poverty reduction still seems to be an almost impossible dream, an unreachable star, to draw on *Don Quixote*. However, it is imperative that the leaders of Bihar continue to nurture and support the state's current economic surge, real or not, and with or without Nitish. Already, there are those who are sounding the final drum roll for Nitish. Among these is Narendra Modi, Nitish's former colleague within the NDA. Following Nitish's split with the BJP, Modi warned that those who betray the people's mandate in Bihar 'will be taught a lesson', a statement that sounds ominously similar to Shakespeare's famous line from *Julius Caesar*. 'Beware the Ides of March', the soothsayer's message to Julius Caesar, warning of his impending doom.[32]

* * *

Bihar did not 'come apart at the seams' overnight, in a year, or even a decade. However, with each succeeding decade, it declined, and then began to spiral out of control. Even before the eventful 1980s, per capita income in Bihar was well below the national average. The already low *per capita* income began to fall relative to the rest of India as the Indian economy began to expand, and per capita income in Bihar continued to decline. While growth accelerated in India, it slowed in Bihar, transforming an already poor population into an even poorer one. The gap between India and Bihar expanded rapidly, and by 2000, per capita output for Bihar was a third of the national average.[33]

While the economic bottom was falling out, at the same time, monumental changes were occurring within the state's sectoral make-up. The sectoral pattern was moving inexorably toward one more consistent with a modern economy. Agriculture, once the backbone of the Bihar economy and the dominant economic activity, was giving way to the service sector, a pattern that was evolving everywhere in India (see Figure 2.2).

While the sectoral share of the state's economic productivity was becoming increasingly service oriented, the percentage of people employed in the agricultural sector showed little change which suggests

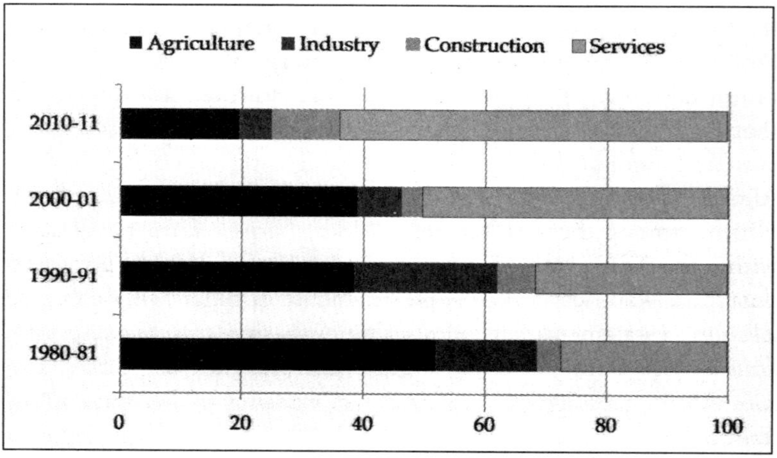

FIGURE 2.2: SECTORAL CONTRIBUTIONAL CHANGES IN BIHAR'S ECONOMY, 1980-2011[34]

a decrease in agricultural productivity. Employment statistics also suggest that the non-agricultural sector was not siphoning off surplus agricultural labour. At the same time, non-agricultural labour was becoming increasingly more productive – doing more work with no appreciable increase in the ratio of non-agricultural to agricultural workers. This meant that for the vast majority of Bihar's population – those living in rural areas – the standard of living or quality of life was declining as measured by *per capita* income levels.[35] This pattern can be readily seen in Figure 2.3.

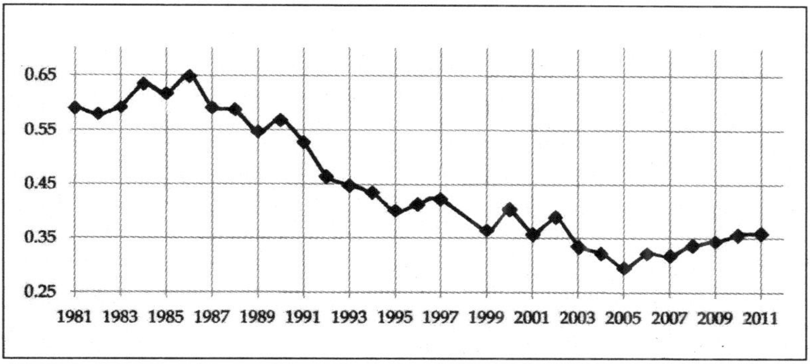

FIGURE 2.3: THE RATIO BETWEEN PER CAPITA INCOMES IN BIHAR AND ALL-INDIA, 1981-2011[36]

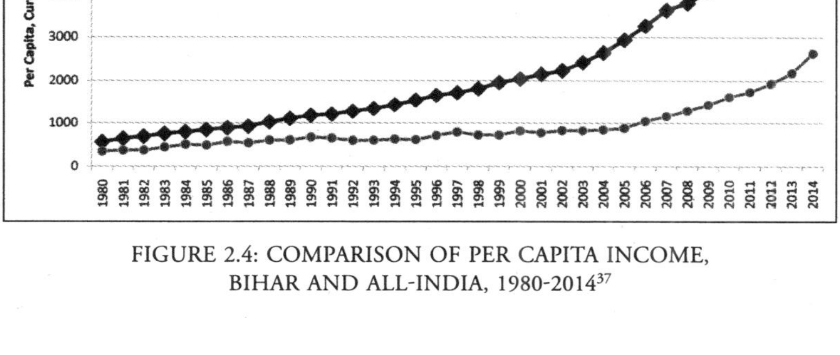

FIGURE 2.4: COMPARISON OF PER CAPITA INCOME, BIHAR AND ALL-INDIA, 1980-2014[37]

Until *c.* 2005, the ratio between all-India and Bihar per capita incomes fell steadily. This decline was the consequence of two simultaneous processes. First, all-India incomes were advancing steadily as the economy experienced unprecedented growth, expansion, and diversification. Second, Bihari incomes and productivity declined independently of what was happening in terms of national economic growth and incomes. Finally, in 2005-6, this steady decline was reversed and it continues to improve – a response to Nitish's economic programming? Further, changes in the numbers of the urban population are generally associated with a shift from a largely rural, agricultural population and labour force to an urban non-agricultural labour force. While urbanization in India is amongst the lowest in the world, Bihar continues to have the lowest level of urbanization in India, which would indicate, again, that the agricultural labour force is not making the transition to urban, non-agricultural occupations.[38]

* * *

In a state that for decades has been the but of pejorative comments and jokes, a sub-national identity has been all but absent for decades. Over the last fifty years, Biharis generally identified themselves by caste or nationality and not as a Bihari. For a population so ostracized and depressed, impressive economic development figures are important. With the announcement of Bihar's rapid economic growth, everyone is finally talking about Bihar, not of its bandits, lack of electricity, poor roads, or squalor but because of its development. It is no longer an insult to be referred to as a Bihari. Even if, in the end, the current development bubble is illusory or transitory, it is serving as a powerful symbol. It is changing how outsiders view Bihar, and even more important, how Biharis view themselves. And, that after all, may be what is really important.

In 2006, the World Bank in its landmark study – *Bihar: Towards a Development Strategy* – emphasized the fact that many of Bihar's socioeconomic problems result from misperceptions and self-perception and it is imperative that these be changed if Bihar is to progress.[39] The 'big turnaround' could be the 'thin edge of the wedge' in achieving a new mind-set for both outsiders and the people of Bihar. Anuj Chopra understood the importance of this change when he observed:

> The state now has mediocre roads, many of which are dirt tracks with bone-jarring depressions. Its villages have four hours of electricity, compared to no electricity at all. Its hospitals have doctors and schools have teachers, albeit poorly qualified, but still a radical departure from the days of rampant truancy. If you build a state from scratch, every little thing you add is a plus. Every small achievement is perceived as a big one.[40]

INFRASTRUCTURE, POLITICS, AND GOVERNANCE

Typically, when the term infrastructure is used, it refers to public services or systems – that constellation of physical systems that are considered essential to productivity and the facilitation of economic activity. These include transportation, roads, power, large-scale flood control and irrigation, markets, telecommunications, development programmes, the legal system and law enforcement, schools or education, and healthcare. All these services or systems play a part in human economic activity.

Infrastructure, while composed of a broad range of services or systems, cannot be viewed as isolated, independent components. They are too vitally interconnected, each serving or assisting the others accomplish their specific function. No one component of infrastructure can stand or exist in isolation. However, if any component of infrastructure fails, it affects all the others, often in a dramatic domino fashion.

Infrastructure is metaphorically the lubricant used in a machine or engine. It facilitates, impedes, or reduces the efficiency of the machine and thus affects the machine's output. Continuing our machine metaphor, infrastructure requires constant attention. It needs to be 'checked', just as one 'checks' the oil level in an automobile engine. Adding too much oil causes overflow and loss. Too little oil and wear and tear increases and can even lead to the catastrophic breakdown of the engine, requiring even more costly repairs or replacement. In other words, infrastructure requires oversight and maintenance to serve its purpose, which is ultimately to facilitate economic activity, growth, and progress.

In an automobile engine, oil serves a number of functions. First, it helps keep engine components working smoothly together. Second, it helps dissipate heat. Finally, it helps prevent the accumulation of abrasive, wear-causing metal shavings and compounds. With infrastructure, people and government are both the lubricant and the abrasive. People construct it and they also cause its failure. In Bihar, nothing escapes or is immune to politicization, exploitation, and corruption, even in the best of circumstances and with the best of intentions. It is these human activities that have traditionally caused the infrastructure of Bihar to fail to support the state's economic progress.

Developing infrastructure, however, often requires making large capital investments, but generally there are simultaneous economies of scale to be realized since an investment in one area of infrastructure typically has an effect on another. In most cases, the lack of capital is the reason for infrastructural deficiencies. Surprisingly, however, in the case of Bihar, it has not always been the absence of infrastructural capital but its misuse and *non-use* by lackadaisical and corrupt administrators and ministers that has constrained Bihar's development. This was, indeed, the case until Nitish's arrival on the political scene in Bihar as its chief minister in 2005.[41]

* * *

Almost immediately after taking office in 2005, Nitish's government focused its efforts on good governance – first addressing inter-caste enmity, crime, communalism, and corruption; and amazingly, it worked. Nitish's commitment to good governance and the suppression of crime bore both political and economic fruit. Crime rates plunged by 50 per cent, and the number of kidnappings for ransom, at one time deemed Bihar's only growth industry, plummeted dramatically from 1,390 cases during the previous government's term to 315 in Nitish's first full term.[42] Improved law and order fostered a sense of security, which served to convince outside investors that it may be time to begin investing in Bihar again.

In the wake of these institutional changes in government, Bihar's economic growth began to sputter to life and by 2011, it posted an unprecedented 11 per cent growth rate over the previous five years, one of the highest economic growth rates in all of India. Much of this economic growth has been attributed not to private sector investment but to the Nitish government's preoccupation with much-needed capital-intensive construction projects funded through large grants-in-aid and low-interest government and ADB loans. The Nitish government focused on power grids, bridges, dams, roads and urban infrastructure development, all of which were sorely in need of rehabilitation or replacement.

Nitish's government, following a stern nudge from the Supreme Court, provided 232,000 teachers with contracts and guaranteed salaries in 2006. At the time, an estimated 12 per cent of the school-age population was not enrolled in schools. The truancy rate dropped to 3 per cent by 2010.[43] While healthcare in Bihar is demonstrably behind healthcare in the rest of India, the Bihar government expects it to be 'better than the national level within the next five years'.[44]

Nitish's government recently received a commendation from Amartya Sen, the economics Nobel laureate. Sen, in a TV interview, stated:

> If there is dynamism, is it in India's interest that Bihar makes good use of that dynamism and proceeds forward fast? Yes. The fact that things are moving is not an inequity argument, it is an efficiency argument. Is there a case for putting your money more on places where things are happening, radically changing? Yes. So, as a citizen of India and the world, I would say there is a strong political and economic case for having that kind of a priority.
>
> In terms of maintaining the quality of human life while not neglecting economic growth but trying to increase it through enhancing social infrastructure, improving education, healthcare and so on – that is the way I would like to see India go and Nitish fits into that pattern much more easily than a focus which is primarily business and profit oriented.[45]

* * *

Years, decades of misrule allowed the infrastructure of Bihar to succumb to the ravages of time, largely due to the lack of preventive and regular maintenance, increased use, and flooding.[46] Every year

Bihar's roads, bridges, and utilities needed to provide access and power and communication to an ever-growing human population.[47]

Of the various types of infrastructure, roads (and bridges) may represent one of the most important; because roads are the chief means of communication, short distance travel, and farm-to-market-to-farm commerce. Therefore, rural road connectivity is essential to support agricultural growth, especially in a state already showing signs of growing food insecurity.[48]

The World Food Programme and Institute for Human Development, *Food Security Atlas of Rural Bihar,* in a series of maps, depicts the status of district-level food security as a function of connectivity.[49] Only 6 of the state's 38 districts are classified as secure. Two of these are north of the Ganga – Siwan and Khagaria. Khagaria is the only food secure district in the Bihar portion of modern Mithila. All the rest are moderately to extremely food insecure. The districts of Mithila lying in Jharkhand are all moderately to severely food insecure.[50]

Further, Hanan Jacoby has shown that roads, in general, and rural roads in particular, tend to raise agricultural productivity and the value of land for poor farmers.[51] Government expenditures on roads have been found to have the single most positive impact on productivity and growth; because, transportation, transport, and connectivity are intimately linked with marketing and access to markets in rural areas. The inability to get produce to market or obtain inputs causes a combination of problems:

- Making it impossible for producers to sell their surplus produce, thereby eliminating or curtailing disposable or discretionary income.
- Resulting in waste and spoilage, thereby reducing both the quantity and quality of their saleable product, reducing income.
- Eliminating both the exchange of goods, supplies, services, ideas, and information.

The use of fertilizers, high-yielding seed varieties and labour inputs are positive determinants of aggregate agricultural productivity. Market access (the time taken to get to market) has a negative effect on productivity, which suggests that aggregate productivity increases with 'decreasing time to markets' (or improving market access).[52] Stated in more geo-sociological terms, proximity, as gauged by either the variable of distance or travel time, or ease of access, plays a crucial role in the diffusion of information, ideas, and the procurement of goods and services.[53]

In general, if one is able to mentally overlay and compare Map I.1: Distribution of District-level Backwardness in India, (in the book pocket); with Map 2.2: Food Security Map of Rural Bihar; Map 2.3: Status of Agricultural Production in Rural Bihar; Map 2.4: Status of Connectivity in Rural Bihar, and Map 2.5: Bihar Road Map, from the *Food Security Atlas of Rural Bihar,* one finds that there is a clear pattern. Backwardness, food insecurity, and road infrastructure patterns show a very similar pattern.[54] Where road connectivity is limited, especially with regard to paved, year-round, all-weather (*pucca*) roads, district-level backwardness and food insecurity tend to be highest.

According to Government of Bihar statistics, Bihar has 2,318 km of national highways, 4,192 km of state highways, 12,579 km of district roads and over 69,000 km of village roads.[55] The length of *kutcha*, village roads dwarfs the kilometres of paved, all-weather roads.

It is difficult to conceive that, according to government reports, over 1,400 km of fully completed and operational *pucca,* national-grade roads have been added to the state's highway inventory, especially in light of recent civilian comments and commentaries.[56]

Table 2.1 indicates that there are no *kutcha* roads outside the villages. One would then expect all the roads, at least in the cities, to

TABLE 2.1: ROAD LENGTHS IN BIHAR BY CATEGORY AND TYPE ACCORDING TO THE NIC[57]

Category	*Pucca**	*Kutcha**	Total*
National Highways	3,734	0.00	3,734
State Highways	4,857	0.00	4,857
Major District Roads	9,030	0.00	9,030
Other District Roads	20,190	0.00	20,190
Village Roads	21,348	46,461	67,809
Total	59,159	46,461	105,620

Note: *Rounded to the nearest km.

be *pucca*. M. Shamsur Rabb Khan, writing for *The Bihar Times*, would disagree. He wrote:

The most difficult question for pedestrians is how to walk properly on slippery roads and encroached pavements where any wrong step could lead you in a shallow shit, if not deep. The glaring truth about road infrastructure is mindboggling, as most of the roads that I found to be in utter dilapidated conditions asking for immediate repairs, and those near the market places are covered with piles of rotten spinaches and peels of various fruits and vegetables.[58]

Another traveller, Welkin Siskin, an émigré from Bhutan, now living in the US, during a road trip to Bhutan, elected to drive through Bihar in mid-2010, taking National Highway 57. He estimated the distance to be approximately 310 km, representing an estimated driving time of 10 hours. Due to road construction and other conditions, Siskin was able to travel approximately half that distance in *15 hours* before finally abandoning Bihar's highways altogether. He wrote:

. . . we drove into Nepal because crossing Bihar was IMPOSSIBLE. The roads . . . unimaginably bad. I am [a] good writer, know the English language reasonably well, but I just don't have [the] words [to] describe [the] road conditions, the people, the environment, . . . everything of that place. In fact, while I was there I thought I was in Afghanistan. The situation is really that bad.

Well, here [are] some pictures of the NH 57. The last picture is very important. It depicts the final problem that we faced in Bihar.

[T]hat made me LOSE courage.[59]

There is absolutely no denying that over the last five to seven years, there have been major improvements in Bihar's system of roadways, at least as evidenced by the growth in the construction sector of the state's economy and the influx of highway construction grants from the Centre. According to news releases, 6,800 km of roads and more than 1,500 bridges were constructed during Nitish's first full term as chief minister.[60] However, the inconvenience associated with highway construction; combined with road entropy – the result of natural decay stemming from the perennial lack of routine maintenance and damage caused by flooding – causes persistent dislocations in both

PLATES 2.1A & B: SISKIN'S NATIONAL HIGHWAY 57, BIHAR, PHOTOS, *c.* 2010

routine communication, travel, and the transport of goods to and from markets.

During previous tenures, major portions of the allocated infrastructure funding remained unused as a result of the lackadaisical attitude of the authorities and ministers concerned, as well as graft.[61] Government spending on infrastructural construction projects, single-handedly, has spawned the resurrection of what was heretofore perceived to be a failed state.

SPECIAL CATEGORY STATE STATUS FOR BIHAR?

Even before Nitish's administration, beginning in 2002-3, Bihar began receiving special attention from the Centre as part of the Backward Regions Grant Fund (BRGF) programme, which was designed to address regional imbalances in development. Bihar has received Rs 1,000-1,500 crore annually.[62] Much of this funding was either unused or simply vanished from the government's coffers.

The BRGF fund provided financial resources for supplementing existing developmental cash flows, allowing states to:

- Bridge critical gaps in local infrastructure and other development requirements that are not being adequately met through existing state funds.
- Strengthen local-level governance through the provision of facilities and oversight.
- Provide professional support to local bodies for planning, implementation and monitoring their plans.
- Improve the performance and delivery of critical functions assigned to Panchayats.[63]

Beginning with 'behind closed doors' discussions with the Centre as early as 2011, Nitish began negotiations for the recognition of Bihar as a state requiring special attention. Then, in 2012, he began 'demanding' that Bihar be recognized as a 'special category state', which would make it eligible for even more low-interest (cheap) money from the Centre and would also carry with it tax breaks. Nitish took his campaign for special category status to the streets in September, initiating a march from Bettiah in West Champaran. Later, as part of his strategy to woo voters to the JD(U) for the upcoming parliamentary elections in early 2014, he broadened his campaign to include other states.

In 1969, Dhananjay Ramchandra Gadgil, the head of the Planning Commission, had developed a formula by which New Delhi would share its finances with state governments. Part of this formulation involved the recognition of what were referred to as Special Category States (SCS) – states with international borders, conflicts, sparse population, and difficult (hilly) terrain. Most of the targeted states also displayed a general lack of infrastructure. The underlying principle of SCS status, it seems, was to provide a mechanism for levelling the playing field between the states and push or encourage development.

The formulation for SCS status was originally intended to be applied to states like Assam, Nagaland, Jammu & Kashmir (J&K) but soon, it was expanded to all the states of India's north-east, J&K, Himachal Pradesh, and Uttarakhand. The status provided central development resources and lots of nearly free money. The 'nearly free money' provision was instituted to counter the growing indebtedness of the SCS. Each of these north-eastern states had state and institutional indebtedness in excess of 50 per cent of their economy's worth.[64] Tax breaks were provided to encourage investors, industrial development, and the generation of jobs.

Bihar's indebtedness was among the nation's highest at 28 per cent of its state economy but substantially lower than for most of the states in the north-east.[65] Nitish lobbied to have Bihar recognized as a SCS based on the state's appalling human development indicators. It was at the bottom of all the states in terms of literacy, nutrition, child mortality rates, and percentage of the population below the poverty line (BPL).[66] Further, the Centre recognized the unique circumstances resulting from the 2000 bifurcation of Bihar and its subsequent economic dislocations. Once recognized as on SCS, Nitish will be able to 'demand' cheap infrastructural loan monies from the Centre; and it is from these low-interest loans that Bihar hopes to manufacture and continue its amazing economic turnaround.

Inasmuch as the SCS selection criteria and those used by the BRGF are almost identical, it would seem that Nitish need not sound quite so adversarial with the Centre in his efforts to obtain the additional funding he wants and needs so desperately. Recognizing the similarities between the BRGF and SCS programmes and due to the active campaigning of Nitish, the finance minister, P. Chidambaram, in his 2013-14 budget speech, suggested that new or amended selection criteria be established to separate and refocus the two development programmes. The reason for Chidambaram's comments stem from the fact that other states are already beginning to demand SCS status in the off-chance that Bihar will be recognized as a legitimate SCS candidate. Among these are West Bengal and Orissa, and more are likely to join the contest. With limited resources, it is unlikely that either or both programmes could address all the potential claimants to these preferential development funds.

If Bihar is, in fact, accorded SCS status, it would mean that the Centre, in addition to altering its selection criteria, would have to alter its current loan formula. The current formula of 30 per cent loan and 70 per cent grant would need to be revised to 10 per cent loan and 90 per cent grant for centrally-sponsored programmes and external aid. The benefit of SCS status over BRGF funding lies primarily in potentially much larger grants being available under identical terms.

Like any 'free money' programme, both the SCS and BRGF programmes are political tools. While they come with the appearance of cheap money, there are always political strings attached, and it may be these strings that are being pulled by the Centre's leadership to manipulate Nitish, as witnessed by his split from the BJP in the June of 2013.

It may well be that because the two programmes are so similar, the funding formula would need to be revised, and there would be so many claimants that the government initially rejected Bihar's plea to be recognized as an SCS. Already 11 states have been accorded this status – mostly the smaller states of India's north-east. Changes in the SCS would almost surely attract the larger states of mainland India. These could easily include the Bundelkhand region, West Bengal, the Kalahandi-Bolangir-Koraput region of Orissa and the 82 districts under the Integration Action Plan, aimed at tribal and backward districts.

* * *

While the recent progress seen in Bihar has been driven mostly by large-scale public outlays, these outlays come with a downside. Eventually, the supply of nearly free money will dry up. The return to self-funded, infrastructural development projects will prove difficult;

because 'free money' generally has an addictive effect, especially among state contractors, administrators, and ministers. They become habituated to almost limitless quantities of public funds with few or no strings attached which, in turn, promotes a rise in white-collar graft, possibly Bihar's newest growth industry, replacing kidnappings for ransom.[67]

If it was good governance, indeed, that has prompted much of Bihar's recent economic success, and has permitted the state to obtain loans for the purposes of rehabilitating existing infrastructure and the construction of new infrastructure, it would seem essential that the current state of good governance be maintained and perpetuated. However, Nitish's landslide election in 2010, according to some observers, has changed the chief minister's focus. He now has his eye on the 2014 Parliamentary election. According to Kumar and Bhattacharya, '. . . governance has taken a backseat'.[68] If Nitish has, indeed, refocused his energies, the darker elements of Bihar's society have quickly begun to capitalize on it and are profiting. In 2005, 104,778 felony crimes were reported. In 2011, that number had risen to 147,633.[69] The increase in offenses was attributed primarily to an increased number of kidnappings, thefts, and rioting.

Nitish brought the rule of law to Bihar, and thousands of criminals were jailed, both blue- and white-collar criminals. Nitish became a national hero for secular, political and economic salvation. Now, both the political climate and Nitish's good governance policies are beginning to show signs of vulnerability. The state has failed to attract private investors; although many Bihar expatriates, at one time, began to reinvest in Bihar based on the apparent elimination of street crimes and the rapid increase in infrastructure-development projects. This temporary euphoria quickly faded as private investors were faced with the non-availability of land for industries, power shortages, and a lackadaisical and uncooperative bureaucracy.[70]

At the end of 2008, while the State Investment Promotion Board announced it had 164 proposed new investments worth Rs 133,841 crore 'on the books', only 15 projects worth Rs 628.49 crore have taken off.[71] While infrastructural development has been the basis of Bihar's recent growth rates, infrastructure alone is not enough to promote overall development, especially in rural areas where there is little direct, long-term financial impact. The immediate financial benefits of these large-scale projects accrue principally and directly to urban-based contractors, engineers, architects, and suppliers and indirectly to bureaucrats and ministers.

Government spending increased from Rs 4,000 crore a year to Rs 34,000 crore. With this 850 per cent increase in spending came more opportunities for graft and corruption among government officials. Nitish began confiscating the properties of corrupt officials, only to have the courts subvert and thwart his attempts at rooting out corruption within his bureaucracy. Graft and fraud have since continued unabated.

Mahatma Gandhi National Rural Employment Guarantee Act (MGNREGA) programmes, when audited, found that 73 per cent of their budgets were siphoned off by local authorities between 2006 and 2010.[72] Programmes designed to stem the high rate of girl drop-outs from schools were pilfered from as well. It is estimated that of nearly half-a-million children enrolled in only 11 of the state's 38 district schools, half were fraudulent admissions.[73] Not only did the programme's funds disappear but it also had a significant impact on the veracity of human development statistics.

While Nitish has advocated strong sanctions against criminals, at least publically, recent revelations suggest that he personally has had long-term liaisons with certain criminal elements. Ajay Kumar, involved in over two dozen cases of murder, kidnapping and extortion in Siwan, is married to Kavita Singh who became an MLA. The JD(U), Nitish's party, plays host to MLAs like Bima Bharati, wife of alleged gangster Awadhesh Mandal; Annu Shukla, wife of the jailed former legislator Munna Shukla; and Lesi Singh, wife of the late Butan Singh, a known mobster.[74] Ranvir Yadav, the husband of MLA Poonam Devi, participated in the September 2012 shootings in Khagaria in front of the chief minister, against protesting teachers. Nitish defended Ranvir's actions.[75]

Currently (mid-2013), eight JD(U) ministers have criminal charges pending against them – charges including murder, attempted murder, and gangsterism. This would seem to be incongruous for a ruling party that was catapulted to power under a banner of good governance and a promise to crackdown on criminality. Lalu Prasad Yadav, it is suggested, promoted what one journalist called 'criminals-turned-politicians'.[76] Lalu was almost unapologetic about his backers and cronies. Nitish, it would seem, shares similar tendencies but does so with more finesse, deftness, or discretion. The support of powerbrokers, gangsters, and thugs, in the past, allowed Nitish to get to where he is today; and had he not become the chief minister of Bihar when he did, Bihar might not be basking in the limelight of economic super-stardom.

On 2 August 2013, however, in the Bihar Assembly, the BJP alleged that after seven years of apparent law and order, Bihar '. . . [is] returning to "jungle raj"'.[77] The BJP called to the Assembly's attention the Bodh Gaya serial bombings, the use of deadly force in Bagha, the Maoist attack in Aurangabad, and a rise in the number of cases of kidnapping for ransom, rape, murder, and *dacoity*. The BJP suggested that Nitish's government and coalition were losing control in the area of law and order due to the chief minister's 'over engagement' in saving his chair in a period when political alliances seem to be becoming increasingly volatile and fragile, at best. The rhetoric, inevitably, suggests that the chief minister is betraying the people's mandate and the faith of the those who had voted him into office, and that Nitish's government is on the path for a return to a Lalu-form of 'jungle raj'.

Nitish has, for nearly eight years, propelled himself and his state to new heights. He is seen as the great hope, the man who brought Bihar out of a long economic coma – a condition that many thought was terminal. Part of Bihar's problem was the almost complete absence of law and order. Corruption was rampant. Casteism fed violence and perpetuated abject poverty. Nitish superficially eliminated the pall of crime and lawlessness, replacing them with an idea – the idea that Bihar could be economically successful, in spite of itself. He fulfilled his electioneering promises but at what costs?

How much farther can Nitish take Bihar? The big-money infrastructure projects will soon have run their course. Infrastructure alone will not guarantee future economic success nor growth. Infrastructure only provides an environment within which development can take place. The unrest that seems to be building throughout Bihar is certainly the result of several years of economic success. The people of Bihar are becoming impatient. They want more and they want it now. The hungry want more food. The unemployed and under-employed want gainful employment. Villages want *pucca* roads. Villagers want the luxury of guaranteed 'on demand' electricity. They want telephone and internet services. They want to be healthy and educated.

Nitish's own success and popularity are possibly the most serious source of the problems he faces. It would seem that he has convinced himself that his successes have been entirely because of him and that he no longer needs the vote bank of the Bharatiya Janata Party (BJP). How can success and popularity undermine a sitting chief minister one might ask?

BIHAR AND THE REACH OF NATIONAL POLITICS

In India, national politics cannot be separated from state politics. Nitish's success and popularity are having an effect on the national power struggle which is currently focused on Narendra Modi of Gujarat, the leader of the BJP – the largest and strongest party within the National Democratic Alliance (NDA) – and the Indian National Congress party (Congress). The NDA, in effect, has become the main player as the opposition to Congress. From the perspective of Congress's national leadership, the only way to derail the rise of Narendra Modi and his BJP is to force or seduce Nitish and the JD(U) to abandon the NDA. On 16 June 2013, Nitish did exactly that. He announced that he and the JD(U) were leaving the NDA after a 17-year long alliance. Their departure from the NDA infuriated Modi. At the same time, it effectively derailed any of hope of Nitish becoming the next prime minister, for now he had no national alliance support.

For his part, Nitish fulfilled his role. Now, it is time for Congress to come to Nitish's rescue if he is to remain in power in Bihar. Without the support of the BJP, the JD(U) has no hope of winning a sufficient number of seats in the Bihar Assembly to give Nitish a third full term as chief minister, assuming that is what Nitish actually aspires to. Nitish has already served as a union minister and this may be where his manoeuvrings will take him, back to New Delhi.

The politics of Bihar are so severely fragmented that to remain chief minister after the next election in 2015, Nitish's party will need to obtain at least a 30 per cent vote share which requires that each seat be contested by three or more candidates. Nitish can run on the past glories of his JD(U) party's record and his developmental successes, and this would normally ensure sufficient seats in the Bihar Assembly to permit a majority alliance. However, his split with the BJP almost assures that the JD(U) cannot earn enough seats to return Nitish to the position of chief minister for a third term. The outcome of recent by-elections have gone against Nitish's party. This has had to be sobering for Nitish. However, if he successfully realigns himself with the Congress, he and the JD(U) may, in fact, obtain the required number of seats to keep him in power.

Having cast his die, Nitish finds himself in an unenviable position, a kind of political non-man's land. He has alienated his ally Modi and the BJP, the real vote-getters. He will need to cultivate the backward caste factions and win over the forward castes – no mean feat in Bihar. If he ignores the forward castes while attempting to knit together a block of backward castes and minorities, there may be no hope. Likewise, he cannot take the backward castes alone for granted, nor the forward castes. Congress support is his only hope. Having 'tinkered' with a winning formula, Nitish's political future, at least in the short term, does not look good. In fact, the people of Bihar fell victim to inter-party intrigue.

Nitish's efforts to secure SCS status came to an abrupt end in February 2014, when Congress stopped Bihar's application. The denial announcement was strategically timed. It was generally believed that Congress had delayed Bihar's application as it weighed the possibilities of a political alliance with Nitish's JD(U) for the upcoming parliamentary elections. Failing to forge an alliance, Congress derailed Bihar's SCS application. As a consequence, Nitish ultimately resigned from office following the Lok Sabha elections in mid 2014 and Bihar lost its opportunity for much needed development funding. The application and denial were a classic party-politics 'carrot on a stick' strategy played at the highest levels of government, with the people of Bihar, again, becoming the ultimate losers.

* * *

Mithlesh Kumar Singh, who has sought to reopen the Central Bureau of Investigation's case file in the sleeper scam in which Nitish has been implicated has suggested '. . . that the repeated dismissal of his motions in Delhi High Court are due to Congress party trying to woo Nitish Kumar and JD(U) away from BJP'.[78] This observation, in light of recent political realignments, may have some merit. Only time will tell.

Furthermore, the breakup of the NDA also opens the door for Lalu Prasad Yadav, who has been relegated to the political sidelines in recent years due to legal problems. No one can deny that Lalu has lived a charmed political life and his successes have been forged by design, not luck. He foresees Bihar headed for a fight between Narendra Modi's BJP and himself. Modi recently commented: 'Nitish Kumar has been relegated to irrelevance after his stage-managed break-up with BJP for minority votes. BJP controls 80 per cent of the votes NDA had prior to the break-up.'[79]

Modi's words as it turns out were prophetic. Nitish Kumar's party, the JD(U) is expected to finish a poor third, and Lalu Prasad Yadav's Rashtriya Janata Dal (RJD) has positioned itself as the main challenger to Narendra Modi's BJP in the 2015 Legislative elections in Bihar. What does this portend Nitish's political future in Bihar?[80]

With his enemies divided and the vote bank of the BJP significantly more important than that of the JD(U), it would appear that Lalu's assessment may be correct. The contest in Bihar could well be between the followers of Modi and BJP and Lalu's home-grown RJD party, BC, and OBC supporters. The only flaw in Lalu's comeback plans lie in the outcome of the last of more than 52 cases prompted by the so-called 'fodder scam' which Lalu has deftly managed, through endless legal filings.

Both Lalu and Nitish can survive politically only by destroying one another. For his part, Lalu is attempting to organize support among the Yadavs, Rajputs and Muslims – an alliance that has worked for him in previous elections. For his part, Nitish, as a 'secular' leader, may find support in the form of an alliance with the Congress. After Nitish's break with the BJP, prime minister Manmohan Singh reached out to him, saying that Nitish was secular and that the Congress has always sought out 'right-minded' people. He went on to say, 'In politics there are no permanent friends or enemies. We will decide as [the] situation evolves'.[81] From all indications, Nitish has not reached out and grasped the olive branch offered by Manmohan Singh. He appears ready to forge ahead alone.

A short prison term for Lalu could have the effect of generating sympathy support and buttress his political prospects. If he is sentenced to a longer prison term, as the head of the RJD, his position of party leader will fall to either his wife or one of his adult children, through whom he would run the party, even from his prison cell – a practice very similar to that seen among mafia dons in the United States. They run their criminal empires from behind bars.

[In October 2013, Lalu was found guilty in one of the fodder scam cases and was sentenced to five years' rigorous imprisonment. This automatically disqualified him from the Lok Sabha and his party lost its leader when he was escorted to prison. Surprisingly, six months later, the RJD appears to have rebounded during the 2014 elections. Nevertheless, Lalu will be barred from contesting in the polls for ten years following his confinement. This indefatigable campaigner and partly leader may well lead his party from his prison cell, as he has in the past when he has run afoul of the law or has been banned from holding office. No one should count Lalu Prasad Yadav out for a long time to come.][82]

BIHAR'S MODERN POLITICAL IMPLOSION

Set against such a glorious beginning, it is difficult to conceive of modern Bihar as being in its current state. Of all its historical attributes or accomplishments, one seems to have endured through the centuries – its political vibrancy; but that too has run amok. Now, rather than unifying Bihar, politics is tearing it apart. Bihar society has become politicized down to its lowest levels and its politics are used, often in a Machiavellian fashion, to exploit and control its poor, illiterate masses and as a tool of economic exploitation. Politics has become an instrument of abuse and control and just another 'profit centre' for the criminal element.

Nitish's government sought to reinforce the rule of law by adopting a three-pronged strategy – making full use of the existing laws, protecting the police from political interference, and speeding up the judicial process. Almost immediately, street crime rates for murders, kidnappings, robberies, and theft began to decline. The streets soon became safer at night for pedestrians and drivers alike.

While street crime – the most visible form of crime in Bihar – quickly saw major reductions; for less visible 'white collar' crimes, it was business as usual. Early in Nitish's tenure as chief minister, there were a few 'high profile' quick fixes to the bureaucratic looting that was going on in government. In fact, during the first year after his election, there seemed to be little or no change. Then, came the first indictments of public officials, followed by swift trials and sentences that, at least for one of the accused, included capital punishment.[83]

To emphasize his determination to root out bureaucratic criminals, Nitish sought to confiscate the property of politicians accused of malfeasance, corruption, or graft, only to have the courts reject this strategy after homes of some accused officers were converted into schools or other public places. While the enforcement of laws against corruption and graft continue to be enforced, some of the bite of law enforcement has been dulled.

Any attempt to decriminalize Bihar's politics has been much less successful than the enforcement and prosecution of street crimes. As late as 2010, according to the Association of Democratic Reforms and the National Election Watch, 43.8 per cent of the candidates for recent Assembly elections had criminal backgrounds or records.[84] Among the crimes these candidates were accused of, or had been sentenced for, were murder, criminal intimidation, extortion, assault, looting, and wrongful restraint (kidnapping).

The war on crime is far from over in Bihar. Certain kinds of criminality have simply become more covert. Under Lalu, criminality was deemed a part of the process, the political system at work. Nitish has, at least superficially, attempted to right this wrong but, at the same time, he cannot press too hard. He cannot step on the neck of the snake that got him to where he is today. Like the *Ouroboros*, the snake biting its own tail, one misstep and Nitish could miss the neck of his snake, step on its tail, and be bitten. For, like most politicians in Bihar, no one, not even Nitish can claim to have completely clean hands.

THE SEARCH FOR AN EXPLANATION

If we are searching for a defensible explanation for Bihar's apparent backwardness, we have to ask ourselves what is holding it back? First, over 88 per cent of Bihar's population is rural, practicing a form of subsistence agriculture that has changed very little in the last sixty years despite the 'Green Revolution' and government efforts to stimulate rural development.

Second, the political economy of Bihar is fundamentally semi-feudal. It is held together by long-standing patterns of social and political patronage, support, and exploitation. The primary responsibility of the elites within this arrangement is to maintain the *status quo* and keep themselves in power. This is accomplished by stressing traditional obligations at the lowest levels of organization, between the villagers and their landlords, the maintenance of peace, and the collection of rents or revenues. This is accomplished through the use of customary patron-client relationships, moneylending, sharecropping, wage controls, control over the systems of local self-government through strong-arm tactics that are ignored by the machinery of state, and political patronage.

The landlords and landowners maintain liaisons or alliances with state office holders, who assure landowners' property rights by refusing to implement and enforce land reforms. In return for their support, the landowners receive patronage in the form of rural development spending and the opportunity to siphon off funds from these programmes. Through these traditional systems, a form of rural homeostasis is maintained between the rural elites, the powerbrokers, cultivators, landless labourers, and state political leaders.

When viewed as a group of rural elites endeavouring to maintain themselves, their customs, and position, their frequent disregard for income maximization becomes more understandable. Likewise, if survival in a labour-rich environment is the determining factor for cultivators and labourers, the acceptance of a system of elite rule is frequently the price that must be paid to insure one's survival. If compliance insures survival, the bargain becomes less onerous, when compared to the alternative.

Third, Saibal Gupta, an outspoken member secretary to the Asian

Development Research Institute in Patna, suggests that the zamindari system institutionalized under the British in the form of the Permanent Settlement of 1793 is one of the leading factors in Bihar's devolution. The zamindars, have no incentive to invest in their land or increase productivity, unlike in *ryotwari* tenure areas. This has resulted in the stagnation of Bihar's agriculture and rural economy for generations.

Further, land reforms, which could have addressed both the dominance of the zamindars and the political fragmentation at the local level, failed on both accounts, and only resulted in the re-inforcement of colonial, social, political, and economic institutions. Nowhere is the gulf between the articulation of ideals and accomplishment more conspicuous than in the case of Bihar and its land reforms legislation.[85]

F. Thomasson Januzzi's contention is that the failure of land reforms in Bihar is partially responsible for the state's lack of development. While land consolidation and fragmentation have had some success they were not sufficient to significantly alter the general agricultural landscape of Bihar. Recent studies support this assertion.[86]

Banerjee and Iyer (B&I) sought to explain the performance of the agricultural sector as a function of British colonial institutions and land revenue and tenure systems.[87] While B&I and Kapur and Kim, at least superficially, appear to make a strong case for the influence of British colonial institutions and policies on post-Independence agricultural development, recent research has tended to undermine the very premise of that argument.[88]

Recently, the role of institutional differences has become a 'hot topic' among development pundits. The emerging consensus is that long-term productivity differences are the result of 'institutional quality'.[89] Property rights or the institution of property among these, it seems, is a central concept in explaining aggregate agricultural and non-agricultural productivity in developing nations. The institutional structures associated with the social, legal, and political recognition of personal or individual property rights provide incentives for productive effort, rather than the less productive rent-seeking or economic predation of more feudal socio-economic structures.

Third, after the First Indian War of Independence in 1857, the more conservative elements of those living within the so-called

'Gangetic Belt' began to denounce Western culture. Hindi rapidly supplanted English as the *lingua franca* at all levels in government. In even more conservative areas, like Mithila, people retreated even further, emphasizing Sanskrit and its more modern off-shoot Maithili. The repudiation of Western culture permitted and even reinforced the perpetuation of traditional thought, organization, and action. As a consequence, these more isolated areas failed to modernize and accept the new Western ideas that were sweeping across the country. People preferred to embrace the past and traditionalism. This preference has contributed to Bihar's backwardness and is consistent with Thapar's suggestion that during ancient times, the more independent-minded settlers of the Gangetic Plains, rebelling against the strength of the monarchies, moved toward the foothills of the Himalayas and established communities which were more in keeping with their tribal traditions, taking on an orthodoxy of their own. The nature of the republican reaction to Vedic orthodoxy indicates that the people of the republics were maintaining an older and continuous tradition.[90]

Recently, the author heard a comment, and while it was in response to a question regarding Hinduism, it could just as easily have been a response to a question regarding 'development' in general: The Indian outlook is historical not merely ideological.

Fourth, Bihar's sub-nationalism is a symptom of a much larger and deeper problem. When a Punjabi travels he or she proudly announces, without hesitation: 'I am a Punjabi'. The same is true for Bengalis, Marathis, Gujaratis and the rest of the Indian states. Until very recently, the people of Bihar have tried to disassociate themselves from their home state, avoiding identification with Bihar. Traditionally, in Bihar there have been two forms of nationalism. The first is Indian and the second is one's caste. A Bihari is always an Indian first and then the member of a specific caste. Without some sense of state pride, there is no one to speak for Bihar at the national level. This may or may not be changing.

On the one hand, for a while, Nitish appeared to be one of the rising stars of Indian politics. He led his impoverished state to new heights in economic growth. That growth, in turn, brought him to national attention. For a while, some envisioned him to be a possible candidate for prime minister. Then came his split with the BJP. Nitish's political and economic stock has since plummeted. He appears to have little, if any, popular support in his home state, and even less nationally. That leadership role has fallen squarely to Narendra Modi and the BJP. As such, Nitish could well become little more than a historical footnote in the history of Bihar. However, one should never count a career politician out; Nitish is a survivor. He will surely regain his political footing and find or create a new political alliance that again could establish him as worthy of front page political coverage.

Fifth, when Bihar was bifurcated in 2000, there were few protests over the decision, and the protests that did occur were, in general, modest. The lack of vociferous, belligerent protests and marches only suggests that the average Bihari simply did not care. If the States Reorganisation Commission was to suggest that Punjab be bifurcated, no matter what the reason or logic, rebellion would ensue; but not in Bihar.

It is entirely conceivable that a modern state of Mithila could, one day, be carved out of the current residual state of Bihar and north-eastern Jharkhand – twenty-five districts taken from Bihar and six from Jharkhand. Suggestions for a free state of Mithila have been circulating, at least since Independence (see Map 2.2). What would be left of Bihar then? Thirteen districts south of the Ganga? Could they legitimately be considered a state? What would happen to them? Would they be integrated into Uttar Pradesh or Jharkhand, or divided between the two larger states? Would the Biharis protest? What about the people of Jharkhand or Uttar Pradesh?

The history of Bihar has been one of diminution. Areally, Bihar's influence once extended well beyond its borders. Over time, the state has shrunk, as have the districts within it. In general, the earlier downsizing of the state and its districts was done for political/administrative reasons, as population grew. Now, the state is being carved into smaller and smaller states in response to ethnic and linguistic agitation. If Mithila should eventually achieve state status, there will be little left of the 'Hindu Heartland'; and the name, Bihar, will only exist in the history books, a sad epitaph for a state that has traditionally played such an important role in Indian history and culture, despite its recent economic and political problems. Does

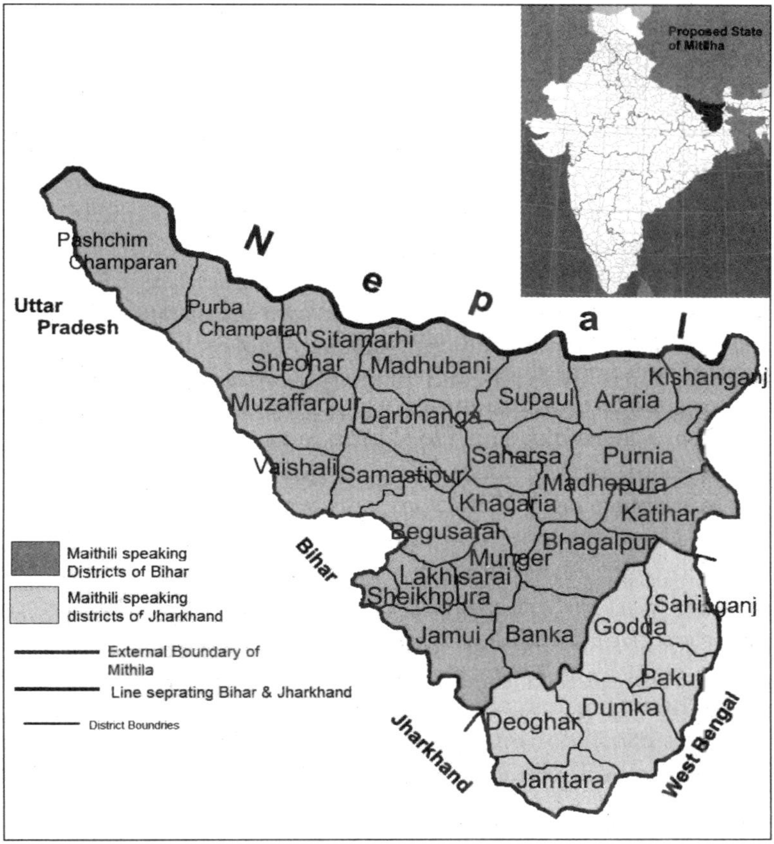

MAP 2.2: THE PROPOSED MODERN STATE OF MITHILA[91]

anyone genuinely believe the downsizing of Bihar will solve its social, political, and economic problems?

Finally, there is Bihar's image. Politicians in Bihar are synonymous with criminals, and consequently, the people justifiably fear them. Why, because to win elections candidates coerce people to vote for them. Surprisingly, the connection between crime and politics is traceable to the Jayaprakash Narayan (JP) Movement that began in the early 1970s as a reform movement and a challenge to then prime minister Indira Gandhi and her autocratic style.

Narayan urged people to simply become involved and there was no need for party membership. People began participating in 'politics' without party affiliation or political ideology. The goal was to simply mobilize the people for a common goal. But, in so doing, ideology and party no longer held the same importance for the people as it had during the Independence movement under Gandhi and the Indian National Congress party. It was every man for himself.

At the end of the JP Movement, the parties found it increasingly difficult to mobilize people to support them. The criminal element saw this as an opportunity. Using their own organizations, money, and muscle to mobilize support, they were able to make their way into the Bihar Assembly and ministry positions. From then on, criminals were either the politicians or they owned those who were; thus controlling office appointments through patronage – a practice not unlike the *jajmani* system. Politicians ostensibly became the rulers over petty fiefdoms wherein they were largely immune to the rule of law.

It is this image that has come to haunt the people of Bihar and from which they have not fully escaped. Despite his efforts to reform Bihar and institute the rule of law, Nitish has not been able to fully root out corruption and graft, or malfeasance; and it is this almost impossible task that perpetuates the image of Bihar as a Jungle Raj. The task of changing Bihar's image is made all the more difficult by the very character of Bihar politics itself.

Bihar society is complex and highly stratified, fragmented by caste, socio-economic class, religion, and ideology. There are more powers at work generating disintegration than cohesion. All these repulsive forces are mirrored in Bihar's political structure and party make-up. There are dozens of political parties and subsets of parties that form, at best, tenuous and short-lived alliances, used to assert caste or communal claims, avenge real and perceived slights, and extend personal agendas. Under the circumstances, it is absolutely amazing that a government, let alone a functioning government, is ever formed, and this political chaos is counter-productive to the needs of social, political, or economic development, whatever form it takes.

A Canadian writer once commented on Canada's policy of multiculturalism and its influence on the Canadian character and its national identity. The writer, Frank R. Scott wrote: 'There are two miracles in Canadian history. The first is the survival of French Canada, and the second is the survival of Canada.'[92]

Similar problems exist within India. Canada's multiculturalism is a microcosm of India. The Hindu-Muslim schism remains unsolved and unresolved, and tears at the fabric of India's identity. Further, the penchant to recognize and respond to every ethnic or linguistic group's demand for recognition only serves to undermine India's identity and unity at the subnational level. If this process is permitted to continue, it is conceivable that national India, as we know it, could well partition itself out of existence. An argument could easily be made for the partitioning of India into three or four sizeable national states, or a dozen or more smaller states based purely along ethnic or linguistic lines.

Canada is bound together by secular, cosmopolitan, democratic values. Canadians tend to recognize civic values such as democracy, the rule of law and the protection of human rights as far more important than national or ethnic origin, or language or faith. India, on the other hand, while espousing secular, cosmopolitan, democratic values, is rife with divisive forces based on ethnicity, language, and faith; and it is these latter forces that India must guard against if it is to remain strong and united. The very same forces are at work tearing away at Bihar.

NOTES

1. Ashok Mitra, *Census of India, 1961: Levels of Regional Development in India*, vol. I, part 1-A (I & II), New Delhi: Registrar General of India, 1965-6, placed Bihar among the least developed states in India, and several of its districts among the most backward.
2. Rakesh Ankit, 'Analysis: Modern Zamindari', *Himal Southasian,* vol. 18, no. 2, November-December 2005, p. 91.
3. Now, six years later, I can report that CMIE provides reports for most of India's major and minor states. Furthermore, the Monthly State Analysis Service Map, as depicted, no longer appears anywhere on the company's website.
4. Government of India, *Census of India 2011, Provisional Population Totals.* Patna: Office of the Director of Census Operations, Bihar, 2011a, p. iii.

5. Ibid. Only Himachal Pradesh at 89.96 per cent is higher.
6. Indiafacts, *Urban and Rural Population of India,* retrieved from Indiafacts, http://indiafacts.in/india-census-2011/urban-rural-population-oindia/ *2011,* 20 July 2011.
7. Ibid. Only Himachal Pradesh at 10.04 per cent is lower.
8. Government of India, *Census of India 2011, Final Provisional Population Totals*, New Delhi, 2011b, Statement 23(1), p. 110.
9. Minhaz Merchant, 'Gujarat vs Bihar: Which Development Model Works Best?', retrieved from *The Economic Times*: http://blogs.economictimes.indiatimes.com/headon/entry/gujarat-vs-bihar-which-model-works-best, 1 August 2013. This figure represents an 85 per cent increase over the 2011-12 figure of Rs 13,362. *TNN, 13362 Per Capita Income in Bihar*, 29 March 2012.
10. Merchant, 'Gujarat vs. Bihar: Which Development Model Works Best?', 2013.
11. Dipak Mishra, 'BPL Population of Bihar 55%, says Report', retrieved from the *Times of India*, Patna: http://articles.timesofindia.indiatimes.com/2009-12-12/patna/28109823_1_bpl-families-bpl-population-bpl-list. 12 December 2009; and Rupashree Nanda, 'It's Official: 37 pc Live Below Poverty Line', retrieved from IBN Live - India: http://ibnlive.in.com/news/its-official-37-live-below-povertyline/113522-3.html. 10 April 2010. Only Orissa at 60 per cent is higher.
12. Merchant, 'Gujarat vs Bihar: Which Development Model Works Best?' 1 August 2001. The highest possible score is 1.
13. Sabina Alkire and Maria E. Santos, *Multidimensional Poverty Index Research Brief,* Oxford: Oxford Poverty & Human Development Initiative, July 2010, p. 6. There are more MPI poor people in eight Indian states than in the 26 poorest African countries combined – 421 million. Sabina Alkire and Maria E. Santos, *Multidimensional Poverty Index Research Brief,* July 2010, p. 4. The lowest score is 1.
14. Government of India, *Census of India 2011, Final Provisional Population Totals*, 2011b, Table – A.13.1.
15. Press Trust of India, 'Telephone Boom in Bihar Most Visible Sign of Economic Growth', retrieved from *Business Standard:* http://www.businessstandard.com/article/economy-policy/telephone-boom-in-bihar-most-visiblesign-of-economic-growth-113022400147_1.html, 10 August 2013; and Faizan Ahmad, 'Bihar Ranks Poorest Despite Giant Strides', retrieved from *The Times of India,* Patna: http://articles.timesofindia.indiatimes.com/2011-02-23/patna/28626349_1_lakh-tonnes-economic-survey-capitaincome 23 February 2011. One of the most visible signs of economic growth in Bihar is in the mobile phone sector. Now, on average, every household has two mobile phones (Press Trust of India, 'Telephone Boom in Bihar Most Visible Sign of Economic Growth', 10 August 2013).

16. Saibal Gupta, 'Bihar on the Wings of Progress', retrieved from *The Times of India,* Patna: http://articles.timesofindia.indiatimes.com/2012-05-15/patna/31711061_1_bad-roads-pratyaya-amrit-governance, 15 May 2012; Indiaonlinepages.com, 'India's Population 2013', 8 August 2013; and National Highways Authority of India, 'Indian Road Network', retrieved from Indiaonlinepages.com: http://www.indiaonlinepages.com/population/india-currentpopulation.html. August 2013.
17. Romila Thapar, *A History of India,* vol. I, Baltimore: Penguin Books, 1966, chapter 3 – 'Republics and Kingdoms'.
18. See, Ankit, 2005, op. cit.
19. D. Mishra, 'Bihar Feels the Pinch of Bifurcation', 15 November 2001, retrieved from *The Times of India,* Patna: http://articles.timesofindia.indiatimes.com/2001-11-15/patna/27259995_1_bihar-bifurcation-economist-saibal-gupta.
20. R. Ankit, 'Analysis: Modern Zamindari', November-December 2005, p. 91.
21. Lydia Polgreen, 'Turnaround in India's State Could Serve as a Model', retrieved 16 July 2013, from *The New York Times,* On-line: http://www.nytimes.com/2010/04/11/world/asia/11bihar.html?_r=0, 10 April 2010.
22. Usha Alexander, 'Bihar', retrieved 22 September 2012, from *Shunya's Notes*: http://blog.shunya.net/shunyas_blog/2007/11/bihar.html, 28 November 2002.
23. Blair Glencorse, 'Analysis: Building on Bihar', retrieved from *Himal:* http://www.himalmag.com/component/content/article/4836-building-onbihar.html, December 2011.
24. Arnab Mukherji and Anjan Mukherji, 'Bihar: What Went Wrong? And What Changed?' New Delhi: National Institute of Public Finance and Policy, Working Paper No. 2012-107, 2012, with permission, p. 71.
25. Anuj Chopra, 'The Great Leap Forward?' *Caravan Magazine*, retrieved 16 July 2013, from http://caravanmagazine.in/reportage/great-leapforward, 1 July 2010.
26. Ibid.
27. Ibid.
28. R. Nagaraj, 'How Real is Bihar's Growth Story', retrieved from *RediffBusiness*: http://www.rediff.com/money/column/guest-how-real-is-biharsgrowth-story/20100304.htm, 4 March 2010.
29. *The Economist*, 'The Bihari Enlightenment', retrieved from *The Economist - Development*: http://www.economist.com/node/15393980, 28 January 2010. Nitish was closely aligned with Lalu for years before they parted ways and the Samata Party came into existence in 1994.
30. 'Bihar at a Glance – Scam', retrieved from *The Telegraph*, http://www.telegraphindia.com/1130711/jsp/bihar/story_17102824.jsp 11 July 2013; and Delhi High Court PR Wire, 'Delhi High Court Dismisses Reopening CBI Report in Nitish Sleeper Scam', retrieved from India News Co.: http://

politicsindianews.rhcloud.com/news/delhi-high-court-dismisses-reopening-cbi-reportnitish-sleeper-scam-6917042, 19 July 2013.

31. See, Staff Reporter, 'Fodder Scam: Jharkhand HC to Decide on Lalu's Transfer Plea', retrieved from *The Hindu*, Online: http://www.thehindu.com/news/national/other-states/fodder-scam-jharkhand-hc-to-decide-on-lalustransfer-plea/article4860469.ece, 28 June 2013; Faizan Ahmad, 'Fearing Jail, Lalu Prasad the Father in Hurry', retrieved from *The Times of India,* Patna: http://articles.timesofindia.indiatimes.com/2012-05-06/india/31596780_1_lalu-and-rabri-lalu-prasad-lalu-confidant, 6 March 2013; Saryu Roy, 'Mr Lalu Prasad at his Wily Worst in Fodder Scam, retrieved from *Governance Now*: http://www.governancenow.com/news/regular-story/mr-lalu-prasad-his-wily-worst-fodder-scam, 2 August 2013; PTI, 'Fodder Scam: Supreme Court Reserve Order on Lalu's Plea to Change Judge', retrieved from *The Economic Times*: http://articles.economictimes.indiatimes.com/2013-08-06/news/41131972_1_fodder-scam-shantibhushan-plea-seeking-transfer, 9 August 2013d; and Live Mint, 'Fodder Scam Trial: SC Reserves Verdict on Lalu Prasad's Plea', retrieved from *Live Mint and The Wall Street Journal:* http://www.livemint.com/Politics/Hdt5TvicWCOoNO4IDfzEAK/SC-reserves-verdict-on-Lalus-pleato-transfer-fodder-scam-t.html, 11 August 2013. Lalu's political future will be determined by whether or not he is successfully prosecuted over what has become known as 'the fodder scam' which could involve a prison sentence of up to ten years.
32. Zee Media Bureau, 'Nitish Kumar Will be Taught Lesson for Betraying BJP: Narendra Modi', retrieved from Zeenews.com: http://zeenews.india.com/news/nation/nitish-kumar-will-be-taught-lesson-for-betraying-bjp-narendramodi_860316.html, 6 July 2013a.
33. Mukherji and Mukherji, 'Bihar: What Went Wrong? And What Changed?' op. cit., 2012, p. 8.
34. Ibid., 2012, with permission, p. 69.
35. TNN, '13,362 Per Capita Income in Bihar', retrieved from *The Times of India,* Patna, Online: http://articles.timesofindia.indiatimes.com/2012-03-29/patna/31253879_1_capita-income-gender-budget-special-status, 29 March 2012. 'Deputy CM said the 2011-12 per capita income in Bihar was Rs 13,362, which was one third of the national average of Rs 35,993 . . . ', Bihar, consistently, has had the lowest per capita income levels among the Indian states.
36. Ibid., with permission, p. 68.
37. This figure is based on Mukherji and Mukherji's work, op. cit., only converted to PPP$ (Current Purchasing Power Parity, international Dollars for India). Source for PPP$ for India: 'GDP per Capita by Country 1980-2014', Retrieved from *Knoema*, from: http://knoema.com/pjeqzh/gdp-per-capita-by-country-1980-2014#India, 5 May 2015.

38. Based on the *2011 Census of India*, India's level of urbanization was 31.2 per cent, while that of Bihar was 10.5 per cent. National Informatics Centre, *The Changing Face of Urban Bihar*, New Delhi: National Informatics Centre, 2011.
39. World Bank, *Bihar, Towards a Development Strategy*, Washington, D.C.: The World Bank, 2006.
40. Anuj Chopra, 'The Great Leap Forward?' *Caravan Magazine, On-line*, 1 July 2010.
41. Nitish was appointed as chief minister briefly in March 2000. His first elected, full term was 24 November 2005 – 24 November 2010. His third and current term began 26 November 2010.
42. Abhirup Bhunia, 'Nitish Shows the Way: Bihar's Enviable Story', retrieved from *The Herald of India*: http://www.heraldofindia.com/article.php?id=457 6 August 2013. There are, however, indications that criminality, especially murder and gangsterism, is again on the rise; and it is suggested that this is due to political changes, or the return to earlier political policies and alliances.
43. Satyavrat Mishra, 'A Tricky Lesson for Bihar', retrieved from *Business Standard:* http://www.business-standard.com/article/beyond-business/a-trickylesson-for-bihar-113032200484_1.html, 22 March 2013. Later it was discovered that many of the new hirees were unqualified and even more recently, these same teachers began rioting over salary parity with other teachers. See, A. Archana Masih, 'Has Change Really Come to Bihar?', retrieved from *RediffNews*: http://www.rediff.com/news/report/what-change-is-really-like-in-nitishkumars-bihar/20130523.htm, 24 May 2013. In his second term, Nitish government proposed that 1,000 secondary schools will be built annually and two or more schools in each panchayat. Today, one sees 'girls cycling to school . . .' wearing school uniforms, having textbooks, and receiving midday meals; although recently, even the midday meal programme has caused a political uproar with the death of 23 students and 150 falling ill PTI, '150 Students Fall Ill after Midday Meal in Bihar', retrieved from *DNA*: http://www.dnaindia.com/india/1868262/report-150-students-fall-illafter-midday-meal-in-bihar 31 July 2013b.
44. See, IBNS, 'Bihar Lagging Behind in Healthcare: Govt', retrieved from Sify News: http://www.sify.com/news/bihar-lagging-behind-in-healthcare-govtnews-health-mjdlHfgdbjc.html, 3 September 2012; and Pratyaya, 'Bihar Tragedy: The State of Education and Healthcare Infrastructure', retrieved from *Pratyaya – Indian Education Policy:* http://pratyaya.nationalinterest.in/2013/07/18/bihar-tragedy-a-reflection-on-the-state-of-education-and-healthcare-infrastructure/, 18 July 2013.
45. Amartya Sen, 'Credit Nitish for Focus on Growth, Quality of Life', *CNBC-TV 18*, 29 July 2013.
46. While our focus, regarding infrastructure will appear to focus on traditional infrastructural components, similar attention has been paid to other less physical components like education, by the current government of Bihar.

47. During the census decade of 2001-11, Bihar's population grew 25.07 per cent. During the previous decade (1991-2001) the state had grown by 28.62 per cent. According to recent estimates, Bihar's population will double by 2051. PTI, 'Bihar CM Worried over Population Growth Rate', 2 March 2013a; and *The Economic Times*, 'Bihar's Decadal Population Growth Rate Dips', 22 April 2011.
48. See, Shoumojit Banerjee, '12 Districts in Bihar Identified as "Highly Food Insecure"', 21 May 2010.
49. World Food Programme and Institute for Human Development, *Food Security Atlas of Rural Bihar*, New Delhi: Institute for Human Development, 2009, p. 79.
50. See, United Nations World Food Programme, Institute for Human Development, *Food Security Atlas for Rural Jharkhand*, New Delhi: Institute for Human Development, 2008, Map 7.1: Food Security Map of Rural Jharkhand, between pp. 62-3.
51. See, Hanan G. Jacoby, 'Access to Rural Markets and the Benefits of Rural Roads', *The Economic Journal*, vol. 110, no. 465, 1 July 2000, pp. 713-37; and Shenggen Fan, P. B. Hazell and Sukhadeo S. Thorat, *Linkages Between Government Spending, Growth and Poverty in Rural India*, Washington, DC: International Food Policy Research Institute, 1999.
52. A.B. Kamara, 'The Impact of Market Access on Input Use and Agricultural Productivity: Evidence from Machakos District, Kenya', *Agrekon*, vol. 43, no. 2, June 2004, p. 210. Although Kamara's work was undertaken in Kenya, similar patterns and results are applicable within most developing nations that are largely rural in character. See also, Mia Mikic, *Preferential Market Access Issues*. In *Studies in Trade and Investment* (pp. 25-37), New York: United Nations Economic and Social Commission for Asia and the Pacific (ESCAP), 2011; S. Chaturvedi and S.K. Mohanty, *Assessing the Market Openness Effects of Regulation in India: An Overview of Emerging Trends and Policy Issues*, Macao Regional Knowledge Hub (Markhub) - Working Papers, no. 7, United Nations Economic and Social Commission for Asia and the Pacific (ESCAP), October 2008; TNN, 'India Won't Link Subsidy, Market Access', 26 November 2005; Renuka Mahadevan, 'Productivity Growth in Indian Agriculture: The Role of Globalization and Economic Reform', *Asia-Pacific Development Journal*, vol. 10, no. 2, December 2003, pp. 57-72; M. von Oppen, B.K. Njehia and A. Ijaimi, 'The Effect of Interregional Trade and Market Infrastructure on Aggregate Productivity', *Journal of International Development*, vol. 9, no. 1, 1997, pp. 117-31; M. von Oppen, *The Effect of Interregional Trade and Market Infrastructure on Aggregate Productivity*, Pantacheru, India: International Crop Research Institute for Semi-Arid Tropics, Economic Programme, 1978.
53. There is an entire literature devoted to the patterns of diffusion, beginning

with the work of Walter Cristaller and Everett Rogers. See, Walter Cristaller, *Die zentralen Orte in Suddeutschland*, Jena: Gustav Fischer, 1933; Everett M. Rogers, *Diffusion of Innovations,* Glencoe: Free Press, 1962; Everett M. Rogers, *Diffusion of Innovations,* New York: Free Press, 1983; and B. Wejnert, 'Interacting Models of Diffusion of Innovations: A Conceptual Framework', *Annual Review of Sociology,* vol. 28 (Annual Reviews), 2002, pp. 297-306.

54. World Food Programme and Institute for Human Development, *Food Security Atlas of Rural Bihar,* New Delhi: Institute for Human Development, 2009, p. 80.
55. M. Shamsur Rabb Khan, 'Building Infrastructure in Bihar: Roads Need Urgent Attention', *The Bihar Times*, retrieved from: http://www.bihartimes.in/articles/msrabbkhan/roads.html, 9 March 2007. Government of Bihar statistics as reported by Khan.
56. Unless it can be verified, the author believes that some of the figures in Table 2.1 represent the 'simple, convenient reclassification' of some existing roadways. From the author's own experience, what the state might categorize as *pucca* is often little more than a dusty, un-rutted dirt or gravel roadway, unlevelled and pitted with potholes, screaming for maintenance.
57. http://rcd.bih.nic.in/Network.htm.
58. M. Shamsur Rabb Khan, 'Building Infrastructure in Bihar: Roads Need Urgent Attention', 9 March 2007.
59. Welkinzer, *Trip to Bhutan: Road Conditions in Bihar*, 11 April 2010.
60. Abhirup Bhunia, 'Nitish Shows the Way: Bihar's Enviable Story', 6 August 2013. See, also, PolyEyes Staff, 'Bihar Economy Statistics: Infrastructure and Communications', retrieved 4 August 2013, from *PolyEyes*: http://www.polyeyes.com/Article/Bihar-Economy-Statistics-Infrastructure-and-Communications, 2 May 2013.
61. Ibid. A recent report by Ernst & Young's Fraud Investigation & Dispute Services (FIDS), *Bribery and Corruption: Ground Reality in India: A Survey by Fraud Investigation and Dispute Services*, Kolkata: Ernst & Young LLP/FICCI, 2013, suggests that corruption continues to loom large and tears into the fabric of good governance, and is '. . . growing by leaps and bounds in India. As the nation grow, the corrupt also grows to invent new methods of cheating the government and public' (p. 8). Infrastructure and real estate are among the most vulnerable sectors to corruption (p. 20), due to weak law enforcement.
62. Sanjeeb Mukherjee, 'For Now, Bihar Likely to get just a "Backward" Boost', retrieved from *Business Standard*: http://www.business-standard.com/article/economy-policy/for-now-bihar-likely-to-get-just-a-backwardboost-113032600438_1.html, 4 August 2013.
63. Panchayati Raj: http://epanchayat.gov.in/mopr/viewPortalPage.do?cToken=null, 4 November 2009. Recent announcements suggest that

the BRGF may increase Bihar's annual grant to Rs 11,500 crore for the financial year 2013-14.

64. Abheek Barman, 'A Special Curse for Nitish', retrieved from *The Economic Times*: http://blogs.economictimes.indiatimes.com/folk-theorem/entry/a-special-curse-for-nitish, 27 March 2013.
65. Compare state indebted rates: Bengal: 36 per cent, Uttar Pradesh: 37 per cent, Punjab: 32 per cent, Kerala: 27 per cent.
66. Bihar currently rates at the bottom with 53.3 per cent of its population living below the poverty line.
67. Sanjeeb Mukherjee, 'For Now, Bihar Likely to get just a "Backward" Boost', 4 August 2013.
68. See, Ernst & Young's Fraud Investigation & Dispute Services (FIDS), *Bribery and Corruption: Ground Reality in India - A Survey by Fraud Investigation and Dispute Services,* 2013, for a eye-opening exposé on the state of bribery, corruption, graft, and fraud in modern India. The boom within India's economy is ripe with new opportunities for the exploitation of public, infrastructure scams, graft, and fraud.
69. Ajay Kumar and Santwana Bhattacharya, 'The Fall of an Icon', retrieved from *The New Indian Express*: http://newindianexpress.com/magazine/The-fall-ofan-icon/2013/08/04/article1712213.ece, 4 August 2013.
70. Ibid.
71. Energypedia, *Bihar Energy Situation*, retrieved from Energypedia: https://energypedia.info/wiki/Bihar_Energy_Situation, 25 June 2013. In 2009, Bihar's per capita electrical consumption was 95 units, against a national average of 717. 'Only 52.8 % of villages and 6 % of households of the state are electrified, leaving about 85 % of the population with no access to electricity', and those villages that were 'electrified' only received intermittent service. One village received power 17 years ago, had it for 3 months, and then lost it for the next 17 years. Sabyasachi Dasgupta, 'In Nitish's Bihar, A Village's Power Cut has Lasted 17 Years', retrieved from NDTV: http://www.ndtv.com/article/india/in-nitishs-bihar-a-village-s-power-cut-has-lasted-17-years-298262, 28 November 2012. India TV, 'Electricity to all Villages in Bihar by 2015, Promises Nitish', retrieved from *India TV*: http://www.indiatvnews.com/politics/national/electricity-to-all-villages-in-bihar-by-2015-promises-nitish-5449.html, 23 September 2012. This would be quite an accomplishment assuming that only slightly over half of Bihar's villages do not yet have electrical power.
72. Ajay Kumar and Santwana Bhattacharya, 'The Fall of an Icon', 4 August 2013. See, for example, Rediff News, 'Bihar Govt to Probe in Misuse of Rs 5,900-Cr NREGA Funds', retrieved from Rediff.com News: http://www.rediff.com/news/report/bihar-govt-orders-probe-in-misuse-of-rs-5/20121126.htm, 26 November 2012c; and Parshuram Rai, 'The Great

MNREGA Robbery: Wretched of Bihar Robbed of Nearly Rs. 6000 Crore', New Delhi: HIVOS and Centre for Environment and Food Security, 2012.

73. See, for example, Rediff News, 'Bihar: Govt-run Schools have More than 3,000 Fake Students', retrieved from Rediff.com News: http://www.rediff.com/news/report/bihar-govt-run-schools-have-more-than-3000-fake-students/20120112.htm, 12 January 2012a; Rediff News, '15 Lakh "Fake" Students Enrolled in Bihar Schools', retrieved from Rediff.com News: http://www.rediff.com/news/report/lakh-15-fake-students-enrolled-in-bihar-schools/20120510.htm, 10 May 2012b; and S. Ahmed, Loss of Innocence: School-children Used as Tool to Loot Money in Bihar', retrieved from *Zakat Foundation of India/TwoCircles.net*:http://twocircles.net/2012jan25/loss_innocence_schoolchildren_used_tool_loot_money_bihar.html, 25 January 2012.

74. See, *India Today* 'A Wedding Gift for Bihar Strongman's Wife', retrieved from *India Today.in*:http://indiatoday.intoday.in/story/assembly-pollswife-of-bihar-strongman-bags-jdu-ticket/1/152604.html, 25 September 2011; Communist Party of India, 'Rising Injustice, Crime and Repression in Nitish's Bihar - Cover Feature', retrieved from *Communist Party of India - Online:* http://www.cpiml.org/liberation/year_2012/june_2012/cover_feature.html, June 2012; TNN, 'MLA's Husband Awadhesh Mandal Arrested', retrieved from *The Times of India, Patna*: http://articles.timesofindia.indiatimes.com/2012-06-01/patna/31958239_1_habitual-offender-nazir-manhandling, June 1, 2012b; *India Today*, 'Two Woman Legislators of JD-U at Loggerheads over Murder in Bihar', retrieved from *India Today*, in http://m.newshunt.com/India+Today/East/21359123/993. 9 May 201; Giridhar Jha, 'Lawless in Bihar: Ex-JD(U) MLA Makes Extortion Calls in the Name of Nitish's Rally While Still in Jail', retrieved from *India Today*, in http://indiatoday.intoday.in/story/bihar-munna-shukla-extortion-nitishs-rally/1/226612.html, 28 October 2012; *The Times of India* (29 October 2012). Popular articles about Munna Shukla, retrieved from *The Times of India - Online*: http://articles.timesofindia.indiatimes.com/keyword/munna-shukla, 29 October 2012; and IANS, 'Jailed Criminal from Nitish's Camp Wins', retrieved from *HindustanTimes - Online*: http://www.hindustantimes.com/India-news/Bihar/Jailed-criminal-from-Nitish-s-camp-wins/Article1-630552.aspx. 24 November 2010.

75. See, Press Trust of India, 'Sharad Yadav Gives Clear Chit to Gun-totting JD(U) Leader Ranveer Yadav', retrieved from NDTV: http://www.ndtv.com/article/india/sharad-yadav-gives-clean-chit-to-gun-totting-jd-u-leader-ranveeryadav-273945, 20 September 2012a; Press Trust of India, 'No Case Against Ranvir Yadav: Police', retrieved from ZeeNews.com: http://zeenews.india.com/news/bihar/no-caseagainst-ranvir-yadav-police_802760.html, 29 September 2012b; and 'Madan Kumar, JD(U) MLA's Husband Snatched

Police Carbine at Khagaria', retrieved from *The Times of India* - Patna: http://articles.timesofindia.indiatimes.com/2012-09-29/patna/34162804_1_khagaria-elections-ljpcandidate, 29 September 2012.

76. Amitabh Srivastava, 'Nitish's Most Favoured Dons', retrieved from *India Today,* in http://indiatoday.intoday.in/story/nitish-kumar-bihar-chief-ministertainted-cabinet-ministers-criminal-records/1/284623.html, 1 July 2013a.
77. PTI, 'BJP Alleges Return of "Jungle Raj" in Bihar', retrieved from *The Hindu - Business Line*: http://www.thehindubusinessline.com/news/states/bjp-alleges-return-of-jungle-raj-in-bihar/article4981845.ece, 2 August 2013c.
78. Delhi High Court PR Wire, 'Delhi High Court Dismisses Reopening CBI Report in Nitish Sleeper Scam', 19 July 2013.
79. Amitabh Srivastava, 'Why Lalu is Laughing', 15 July 2013b.
80. Devesh Kumar and Manish Kumar, 'Nitish Kumar Admits Outcome of General Election will Impact his Government's Survival', retrieved from *NDTV – India Votes 2014* from: http://www.ndtv.com/elections/article/election-2014/nitish-kumar-admits-outcome-of-general-election-will-impact-his-government-s-survival-512208, 22 April 2014.
81. Zee Media Bureau, 'Nitish Kumar is Secular, Have Always Sought Support from Right-minded People: PM', retrieved from ZNews: http://zeenews.india.com/news/nation/nitish-kumar-is-secular-have-always-sought-supportfrom-right-minded-people-pm_855637.html, 13 August 2013b.
82. Devesh Kumar, 'RJD Bouncing Back in Bihar, but Lalu Prasad Remains Grounded', 24 April 2014, retrieved from NDTV – *India Votes 2014,* from http://www.ndtv.com/elections/article/election-news/rjd-bouncing-back-in-bihar-but-lalu-prasad-remains-grounded-513494?curl=1399095082.
83. 'No Bribe, Changing Bihar, Slowly', retrieved from *No Bribe - Corruption Free India*: http://www.nobribe.org/changing-bihar-slowly, 9 November 2009.
84. Rediff News, 'Crime and Politics go Hand-in-hand in Bihar Polls', retrieved from *Rediff News*: http://www.rediff.com/news/slide-show/slide-show-1-criminals-politics-go-hand-in-hand-in-bihar/20101007.htm, 7 October 2010.
85. F. Tomasson Jannuzi, 'An Account of the Failure of Agrarian Reforms and the Growth of Agrarian Tensions in Bihar: 1949-1970' , in R.E. Frykenberg (ed.), *Land Tenure and Peasant in South Asia*, New Delhi: Orient Longman, 1977, pp. 211-12.
86. Daniel Monchuk, Klaus Deninger and Hari Nagarajan, *Does Land Fragmentation Reduce Efficiency? Micro Evidence from India,* Denver: Agricultural and Applied Economics Association 2010 AAEA, CAES, and WAEA Joint Annual Meeting, 25-6 July 2010.
87. Abhijit Banerjee and Lakshmi Iyer, 'History, Institutions, and Economic

Performance: The Legacy of Colonial Land Tenure Systems in India', *The American Economic Review*, vol. 95, no. 4, 2005, pp. 1190-1213.

88. Shilpi Kapur and Sukkoo Kim, *British Colonial Institutions and Economic Development in India*, Cambridge: National Bureau of Economic Research, NBER Working Paper, no. 12613, October 2006. See also, Vegard Iversen, Robert Palmer-Jones and Kunal Sen, *On the Colonial Origins of Agricultural Development in India: A Re-examination of Banerjee and Iyer, 'History, Institutions and Economic Performance'*, Manchester: Brooks World Poverty Institute, BWPI Working Paper 174, 2012.
89. See, for example, Douglass C. North, *Institutions, Institutional Change and Economic Performance*, Cambridge: Cambridge University Press, 1990; Stanley L. Engerman and Kenneth Lee Solokoff, 'Factor Endowments, Institutions, and Differential Paths of Growth Among New World Economies: A View from the Economic History of the United States', in S. Faber (ed.), *How Latin America Fell Behind: Essays on the Economic Histories of Brazil and Mexico, 1800-1915*, Stanford: Stanford University Press, 1997, pp. 260-304; Robert E. Hall and Charles I. Jones, 'Why do Some Countries Produce so Much More Output Per Worker?', *Quarterly Journal of Economics*, vol. 114, no. 1, 1999, pp. 83-116; Kenneth L. Sokoloff and Stanley L. Engerman, 'History Lessons: Institutions, Factor Endowments, and Paths of Development in the New World', *Journal of Economic Perspectives*, vol. 14, no. 3, Summer 2000, pp. 217-32; Daron Acemoglu, Simon Johnson and J. James Robinson. 'The Colonial Origins of Comparative Development: An Empirical Investigation', *American Economic Review*, vol. 91, no. 5, 2001, pp. 1369-401; Daron Acemoglu, Simon Johnson and James A. Robinson, 'Reversal of Fortune: Geography and Institutions in the Making of the Modern World Income Distribution', *Quarterly Journal of Economics*, vol. 117, no. 4, 2002, pp. 1231-94; and William Easterly and Ross Levine, 'Tropics, Germs, and Crops: The Role of Endowments in Economic Development', *Journal of Monetary Economics*, vol. 50, no. 1, January 2003, pp. 3-39.
90. Romila Thapar, *A History of India*, vol. I, 1966, p. 50.
91. Adapted and modified from original map of Mithila attributed to Vikas 11004315, *Map of Mithila*, 12 April 2012.
92. Frank R. Scott, 'Canada et Canada français', *Esprit* (Paris), August-September 1952, nos. 193-4, p. 178.

CHAPTER 3

The Environmental Roots of Backwardness in Bihar and Mithila

Part I: Floods

Despite the historic image of Bihar as one of several 'bread baskets' of India, that appellation no longer seems to ring true. More recently, Yadav, Gupta, and Kumar have demonstrated that agricultural yields in Bihar are among the lowest in all-India; not only on a *per capita* production basis but also in terms of basic real yields per acre.[1] It is this decline in real yield per acre that has contributed to the rapid shift in Bihar's overall economy, away from agriculture. Since 'backwardness' is generally associated with a lack of productivity, and in a state that is predominantly agricultural, at least in terms of the numbers of people occupied by it, agriculture's failure to perform could explain why Bihar has appeared to be so economically backward for so long. Bihar's agricultural sector is the primary component of the rural economy and society, and it continues to operate on the margins of human enterprise. Without increasing returns, not much can be done realistically to develop the state's overall economy in the long run. Thus, agriculture continues to define both the long-term potentialities and constraints to development.

The question, then, is why has Bihar's agricultural productivity declined so appreciably? In general, the decline in *per capita* productivity can easily be explained as a simple function of increased population set against agricultural productivity rates. Assuming no net increase in agricultural productivity, as population grows, *per capita* productivity will naturally show a decline. When population increases and real agricultural productivity decreases, the magnitude of the problem is multiplied.

While there is a plethora of potential socio-economic causes for declining agricultural productivity, here we will go back to the basics of agricultural production – the environment. Since agricultural productivity is, at its most basic level, the direct interaction of human energy with the earth, changes in productivity could be attributed to changes in the environment, especially if those changes prevent cultivation, the loss of crops, or results in the loss of productive means.

* * *

The physical environment of Bihar can be summed up as: alluvial in nature, with riverine systems that annually flood, depositing mineral-rich silt, much like the Nile; climatically sub-tropical monsoon; abundant rainfall, although variable from season to season, year to year, and place to place; and capable of being cultivated year-round.

For centuries, this description of Bihar and Mithila stood the test of time. One author suggests that the climate is generally warm but not oppressive, there is abundant rainfall, most of which falls during the June-August monsoons, the soil was so fertile that the people had to work little to sustain themselves, and two to three crops could be harvested from the same field each year and, as a consequence, 'the area has rightly been described as the granary of north India'.[2]

On the surface, these idyllic-sounding environmental descriptions suggest a soil-rich area blessed with all the environmental attributes of a highly productive agricultural region. Ironically, this generalization belies a variability and a reality that alters the Garden of Eden-like description, turning it into a region where the people have, for more than half a century, simply fought to survive.

In 2001 and again in 2007, the United Nations Environment Programme published a series of state studies under the omnibus title of *State of the Environment*.[3] These studies were designed to define and assess the importance of environmental factors, especially environmental degradation and the incidence of natural disasters in South Asia, and to gauge people's vulnerability to them. The list of natural disasters included: floods, droughts, landslides, mudslides, earthquakes, forest fires, cyclones, thunderstorms (including hail-storms), heat waves, and lightning.

In late 2010, a number of development agencies met to further explore the risk of natural disasters occurring in or affecting Bihar.[4]

One of the forum's observations was that 'the state of Bihar is a classic example of the incidental loss to development due to recurring disasters such as flood, earthquake, drought and fire'.[5] Of the various types of disasters, two are possibly the most frequent and devastating – floods and droughts. In essence, in Bihar, where the land has been traditionally and naturally fertile, it is water – either too much or too little – that most often plagues the state's agricultural economy.

The other disaster-types, while representing genuine threats to the people and economy of the state, are neither as frequent nor as devastating as floods and droughts. However, the incidence of all types of natural disasters, especially those relating to climate and weather – particularly storms and floods, and more recently, heat waves – is increasing in both frequency and magnitude, worldwide. Figure 3.1 depicts the incidence of natural disasters occurring worldwide from 1900 to 2010. There has been a clear, almost exponential increase in the occurrence of natural disasters since the mid-1970s. Much of this increase has been attributed to that catch-all phrase Global Warming, whether it is part of a natural process or cycle or whether it is being hastened by anthropogenic activity, especially the use and consumption of fossil fuels. Some of the more

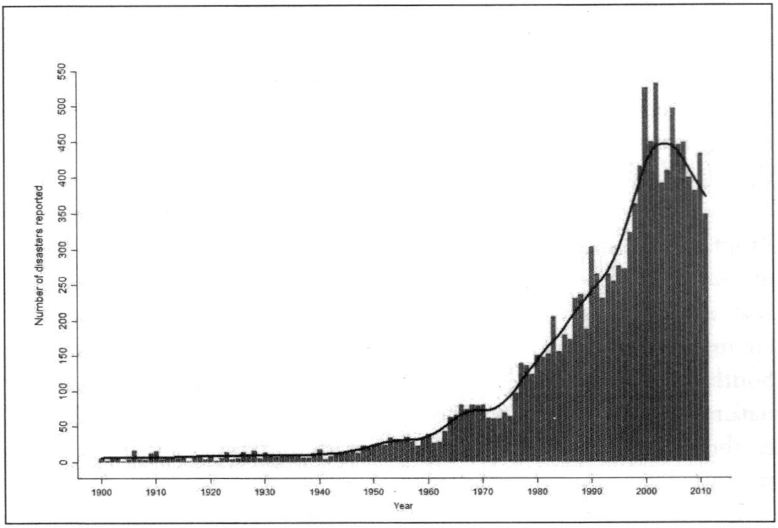

FIGURE 3.1: INCIDENCE OF NATURAL DISASTERS, WORLDWIDE, 1900-2010

readily recognized consequences of global warming are more intense summer and winter storms, both of which can have an impact on agricultural productivity.

* * *

The monsoons, which last from June and often into September, are marked by large regional and temporal variability. The rainfall is generally sharp and intense from the date of onset but its magnitude, duration, and intensity can be highly variable. Sudden cloudbursts, which can generate almost 500 mm of rainfall in a single day are not uncommon in the mountains of Nepal and can increase the water levels in the rivers by 6.1 to 9.1 m within 24 hours. At the end of the monsoons, when the land is saturated, the contribution of cloudbursts to riverine and overland flows frequently leads to devastating effects.[6] While rainfall has increased in the Himalayas, largely as a function of Global Warming, as well as causing temporal and quantitative changes in ice and snow melt, the average rainfall within Bihar has decreased appreciably since 1970.[7]

While agriculture, anywhere in peninsular India, is dependent upon the monsoons, in Bihar the bulk of the water used for agriculture now comes from surface water in the form of annual riverine floods and not directly from monsoon rainfall. Monsoon rainfall in Bihar has become increasingly unpredictable and, therefore, undependable. As a consequence, the threat of drought has increased proportionally with the decline in Bihar's annual rainfall; and stored water, following the annual floods, or groundwater accessed through tubewells, provides the bulk of the water for post-monsoon agriculture, October through May.

As a consequence, rivers have, and continue to play a critical role in the lives of the people of Bihar as they are an invaluable resource. However, the relationship between the people of Bihar and their rivers is fraught with difficulties due to changes in the rivers' discharge, which is manifested in the form of floods. Floods destroy human settlements, communications, transportation and power networks, and are capable of destroying his land; and many of these problems have been exacerbated by the actions of government through ill-conceived and poorly executed and maintained intervention schemes.

FLOODING IN BIHAR: THE PHYSICAL CONTEXT

Bihar has been recognized as the most flood-prone state in India. Nearly every district in the state has experienced life-altering floods at one time or another, and for many, flooding is literally an annual event. Approximately 73 per cent of the geographical area of Bihar is subject to flooding.[8] Seventy-six per cent of the population of northern Bihar lives under the recurring threat of flood devastation. There is not a single river in northern Bihar that does not flood, or that does not flood regularly, due to the basic morphology of the rivers themselves and the general lack of topographic relief throughout the north Bihar and Gangetic plains. Despite repeated attempts to resolve Bihar's flooding, the frequency and severity of it has only increased.

The Bihar plains are broken into an intricate mosaic or lacework of swamps, marshes (*bils*), rivulets, small streams, small and large rivers, punctuated by alluvial mounds, not quite reaching the status of hills. Historically, this riverine landscape has made travel difficult and has traditionally impeded communication with the outside world. It has also served as a formidable barrier against military invasion, acculturation, and change.

PLATE 3.1: FLOOD VICTIMS IN BIHAR

For those not living in monsoonal areas, and especially those living in North America or most of Western Europe, the image of flooding is one of the local creek or river overflowing its banks, often during the spring thaw, a shallow sheet of water spreading across the low-lying floodplain, filling the basements of unprepared homes. Or, in mountainous areas, as flash floods cascading down valleys hemmed in by foothills or mountains, destroying everything in its path, often triggering massive mudslides. The scope of flooding in monsoonal areas, and particularly in Bihar, is almost unfathomable.

Southern Bihar

The rivers of southern Bihar, the area lying south of the Ganga, flood regularly but the nature of that flooding differs significantly from that of northern Bihar. The rivers here are morphologically and qualitatively different from those of northern Bihar. Their channels are wide, but not as wide as those in the north (4-5 km wide versus up to 10-16 km), equally shallow but with narrower floodplains. With the exception of the Son, which is the largest and longest of Bihar's southern rivers, the remaining rivers are comparatively short, draining significantly smaller catchment basins. Unlike the rivers of the north, the rivers of southern Bihar have markedly steeper gradients which results in rapid run-off. These rivers flood in response to the monsoons but their capture basins are neither as high, nor as large as those of the rivers of northern Bihar.

Unlike the Himalayas, the hills of southern Bihar, where these rivers originate, seldom rise above 500 m and beyond lies the Chota Nagpur and Vindhyan plateaus. Therefore, the floods do not have the same devastating qualities, intensity, or debris-carrying capacity as the mountain-fed rivers emanating from Nepal and Tibet. Their floods are neither as extensive nor as long-lasting, although, when these flood waters are caught behind the rivers' natural levees, waterlogging frequently occurs. Often, the rising Ganga will push back the flood waters of many of these southern rivers and this then, becomes the active agent in their flooding, delaying the flood waters from returning to the river's main course.

Northern Bihar/Mithila

Northern Bihar can be described as a series of alluvial floodplains, the product of the megafans of the major rivers.[9] More than a dozen primary and secondary rivers, plus their tributaries, pour onto the north Bihar plain from Nepal, each building up its own uniquely shaped megafan which overlaps or merges with that of its neighbours. Map 3.1, depicts the major river basins of Bihar.[10]

The plains are broken into an intricate mosaic or lacework of swamps, marshes, rivulets, small streams, small and large rivers, punctuated by alluvial mounds, not quite reaching the status of hills. Historically, the riverine landscape of northern Bihar has made travel difficult and has traditionally impeded communication with the outside world. It has also served as a formidable defence against invasion, acculturation, and change.

* * *

Flooding is a natural feature of most monsoon-fed mountain-originating rivers and streams. Nearly all the rivers of the northern India have long histories of flooding, triggered by heavy monsoonal rainfall combined with ice- and snow-melt in the rivers' mountainous catchment basins in Nepal and Tibet.

Unless there is an unusually high amount of precipitation or ice and snow melt in a river's catchment, its main channel is generally able to accommodate the surplus volume without spilling over its banks or levees onto the floodplain beyond; and, therefore, flooding does not become an annual or perennial problem. In the case of the Kosi, Gandak, Burhi Gandak, Bagmati, Adhwara, Kamal-Balan, and Bhutani rivers, however, flooding is a recurring, almost annual event. There is no single cause for this annual pattern but rather a combination of factors or conditions, with each river having its own unique combination of factors. Among these are:

In the mountains:

- Large accumulations of mountain ice and snow in Nepal and Tibet.
- Rapid and heavy monsoonal rainfalls.
- Large mountainous, high-elevation catchment basins.

- Narrow, steep, and deep valley profiles within the catchment basins.
- Steep channel gradients.
- Increased ice- and snow-melt, and glacial lake outburst floods (GLOF) attributed to Global Warming.

On the plains:

- Shallow, wide, low-gradient primary river channels with low natural levees in the plains.

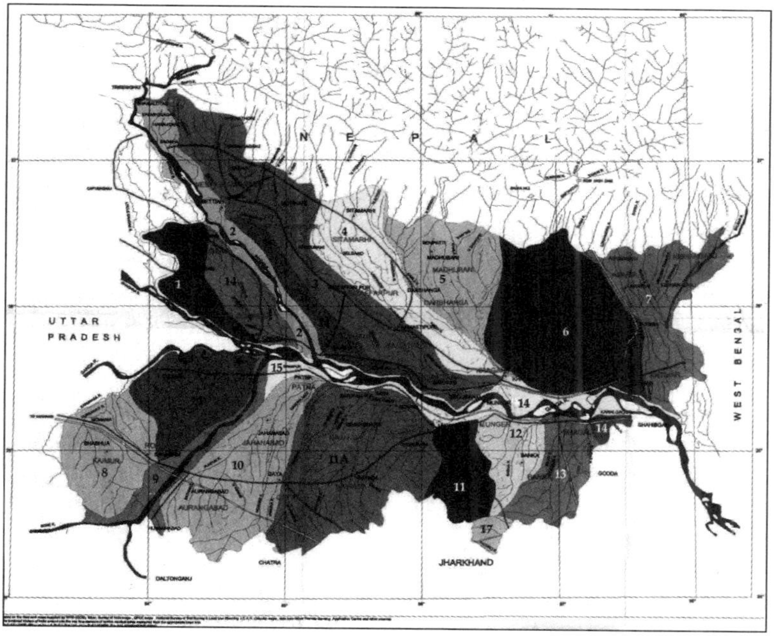

MAP 3.1: THE MAJOR RIVER BASINS OF BIHAR[11]

The major river basins and sub-basins in Bihar include:

1. Ghaghra, 2. Gandak, 3. Burhi Gandak, 4. Bagmati-Adhwara, 5. Kamla-Balan, 6. Kosi, 7. Mahananda, 8. Karmnasa, 9. Sone (Stem), 10. Punpun, 11. Kiul, 12. Harahar, 13. Badua-Belhama, 14. Ghandan-Belhama, 15. Ganga-Stem, 16. Kao-Gangi, 17. Baya, 18. Koa-Bhena, 19. Mahi. With exceptions of the Bagmati-Adhwara and Kamla-Balan, which empty into the Kosi, and the Harahar, which empties into the Kiul, all the rivers empty into the Ganga, which ultimately empties into the Bay of Bengal. [The numerical figures on the map represent the Bihar Flood Management Information System (FMIS) assigned basin designation for each of the rivers/basins.]

- Unusually high quantities of geologic debris – boulders and rocks – as well as sediment composed of gravel, sand, silt, and organic matter that are deposited in the river channels.
- A highly braided network of secondary channels spreads the in-coming water flow and slows the rate of flow-through to the Ganga.
- The rivers carry between ten and twenty times more water during the monsoon than during the rest of the year but, during periods of intense rainfall in the catchment areas, their volume can increase 100-fold.[12]

THE KOSI

Among the rivers of northern Bihar, the Kosi is the largest tributary of the Ganga and exemplifies many of these factors. We will focus on the Kosi not because it is a 'typical river of northern Bihar' but because it exemplifies all the worst and most extreme characteristics of all the rivers in northern Bihar. Equally important is the fact that the effects of human intervention, in the name of flood prevention, have made the Kosi a perfect example of what not to do. Dilip Kumar, a professor of flood management, stated:

> The Kosi River Basin is the most complicated and difficult river to be harnessed. Floods happen frequently and bring huge disasters to the residents along the river. After fifty years of harnessing of the Kosi River, great achievement has been obtained. However, the problems of the Kosi River are still serious, and many natural foundational rules have not been known and mastered. The flood threat is still the serious potential and hidden danger. Water and soil losses as well as ecological environment deterioration have not been controlled effectively, which threaten the life and property of the people along the river and restrict the development of economy and society in the basin and its relative areas.[13]

The Kosi has one of the largest catchment basins in South Asia, 74,030 sq km, 84 per cent of which falls within the Himalayas. The upland-to-plains ratio is extraordinarily high – 5.49, the highest for any river in South Asia.[14] More than 50 per cent of the Kosi's catchment basin is 4,000 m above sea level, and the area below 120 m constitutes only 16 per cent of the total area. The catchment area has very high basin relief (highest in the world), combined with an unusually steep channel gradient. In Nepal, the rivers that combine to create the Kosi cascade through steep, narrow and deep gorges. The Sun Kosi, Arun and Tamur rivers, whose tributaries and catchment basins include much of the eastern one-third of Nepal and parts of Tibet, come together near Tribeni Gatt in Nepal to form the Sapta Kosi which becomes the Kosi as it enters Bihar. Figure 3.1, provides a graphic representation of the relative physiographic differentials between the Kosi's headwaters and the alluvial floodplain of northern Bihar.

When the Kosi exits the mountains and emerges onto the Bihar plain, the main channel is neither deep nor wide enough to handle the river's accumulated discharge, estimated to be approximately 52×10^9 m^3 on average.[15] In the mountains, the waters are confined to deep, steep-walled mountain valleys where they 'pile up', nearly filling the smaller canyons and gorges. These valleys and gorges typically vary in width at the bottom from only 2-3 km with steep channel gradients.

After reaching the plains, the bed of the Kosi flattens abruptly, spreading to a distance of 6-10 km. After traversing a distance of about 50 km in Nepal, the river enters Indian territory near Bhim Nagar. The high width-to-depth ratio and low channel gradient together mean that the river is no longer able to sustain its colloidal suspension of geologic debris. This causes the river to jettison a large portion of its massive rock, stone, gravel, sand, and silt burden, filling the river's channel and forcing the river's volume, along with the lighter gravel, sand and silt, over the river's natural levees and onto the adjacent floodplain – in the form of historically gentle sheet-flooding. See Diagram 3.1.

Although the overall velocity of the river is altered as it enters the plain, the velocity in the main channel continues to remain sufficiently high enough to allow it to transport organic laden silt, sand, gravel, and rocks downstream – boulders and large rocks having been deposited in the river's channel soon after entering the Terai plains at Chatara. Ninety-five per cent of the annual sediment load of the Kosi is carried during the monsoon months – June through August. As the river's velocity continues to decline downstream, its carrying

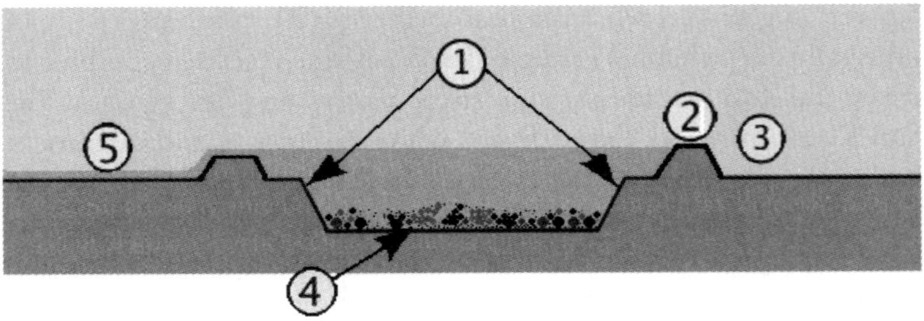

DIAGRAM 3.1: CROSS-SECTION OF TYPICAL UNALTERED NORTH BIHAR RIVER[16]

Notes: Vertical relief exaggerated. NTS.

1. Low water channel – In the case of the Kosi, while variable, the low water channel is often miles across and has depths of only a few feet.
2. Natural levees – originally these were only a few feet high.
3. Active Flood Plain, outside the natural levees on either side of the river.
4. Geologic Debris/Sediment – fills the low water channel, raising the mean water level annually. In the case of the Kosi, sediment (fine silt) accumulates at a rate of approximately 10 cm per annum.
5. Sheet flooding. High water levels, often more than once during the flood season, crest the natural levees and the water flows unimpeded across the floodplain.

capacity declines, depositing the heaviest debris first.[17] Silt, sand, and organic material continue in suspension until a portion is deposited on the Bengal Submarine Fan in the Bay of Bengal[18] (see Figures 3.2 and 3.3).

The process of floodplain, delta, and fan building is typically calculated in terms of centuries or millennia. Recent research, however, suggests that this process is quickening due to global warming, which is causing glaciers and snow in the Himalayas to melt more quickly and earlier each season. In addition, warmer air over the Bay of Bengal increases evaporation rates, providing more moisture that is deposited by the monsoons in the Himalayas as heavier and more intense rainfall. Together, increased ice and snow melt, as well as heavier rainfall discharges changes the peak water flows in the rivers, and their timings. The rivers run faster and deeper and are capable of carrying more sediment which contributes to an accelerated rate of floodplain, delta, and submarine fan building, which may also have an effect on overall global climatic change by sequestering large quantities of organic carbon.[19]

As the individual river channels are aggraded and degraded they frequently abandon their channels and begin to shift their course through a process known as avulsion. Avulsion represents the sudden movement of a river around a nodal point, a divergence point, and occurs when the flood level of the river reaches its avulsion threshold.[20] This threshold, however, can be reached even when a flood is not at its greatest. The true triggering event is a function of the instability or weakness of the channel walls and natural levees, and not the magnitude of the volume of water. The most common mechanism of avulsion is the re-occupation of a former, pre-existing channel, often referred to as a paleochannel. Another form of avulsion is called crevasse splaying, which involves the gradual breaching of the river's banks and the development of a new channel. The former is often a rapid and convulsive action, while crevasse splaying is a much longer process.

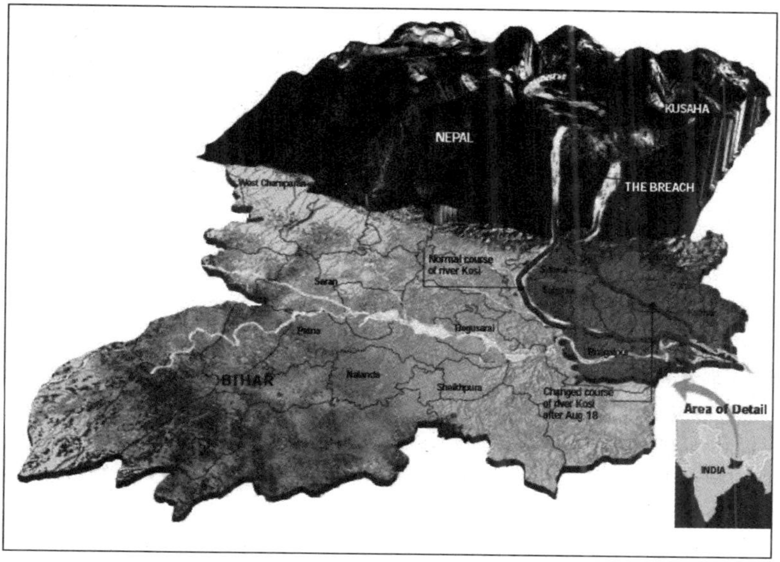

FIGURE 3.2: A GRAPHIC REPRESENTATION OF PHYSIOGRAPHIC DIFFERENTIALS BETWEEN THE HIMALAYAN MOUNTAINS AND TERAI OF NEPAL AND NORTH BIHAR PLAIN

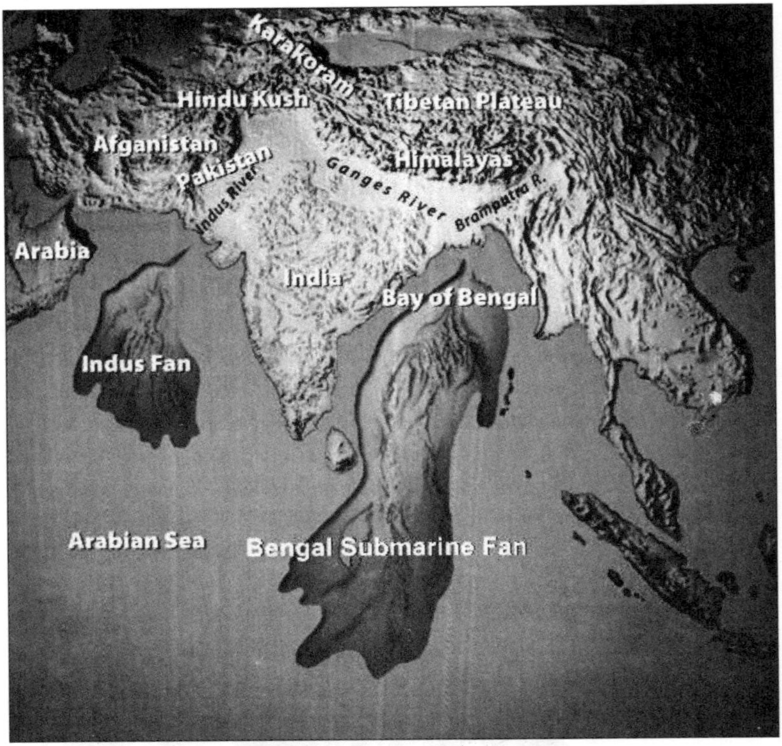

FIGURE 3.3: THE BENGAL AND INDUS SUBMARINE FANS[21]

Contributing to the instability of the channel is the enormous quantity of sediment and its composition. Each constituent part of the sediment load and the timing of its deposition affects the channel's structural integrity. The mean annual suspended-load transported by the Kosi is estimated to be 130 million cu m of debris, possibly the highest of any river of its size in the world.

Of all the rivers of north Bihar, the Kosi has changed its course possibly more often than any other. Until 2008, when it reversed its general movement, the Kosi had tended to move westward (see Figure, 3.4). Gole and Chitale explained the continuous movement of the Kosi in one direction as a function of the Kosi's cone-shaped megafan, which is unique among the rivers of northern Bihar.[22] The other rivers

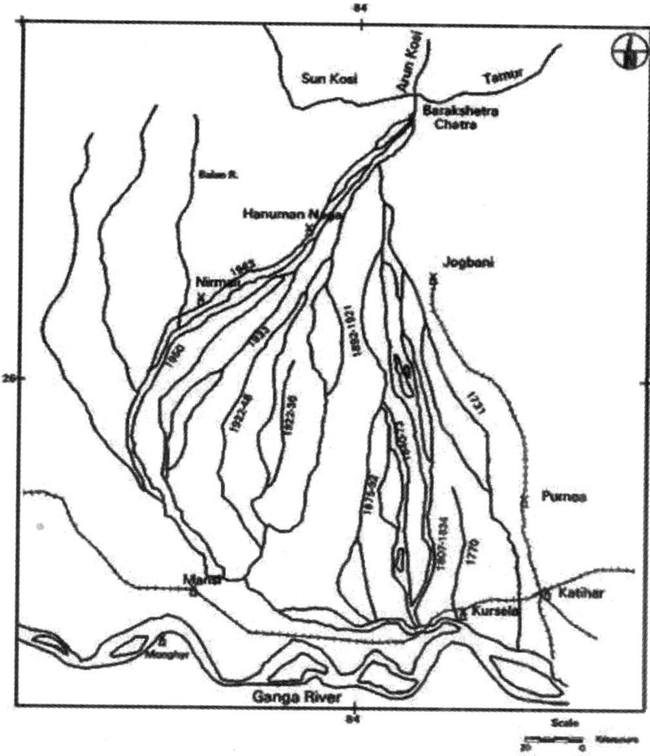

FIGURE 3.4: THE WESTWARD MIGRATION OF THE KOSI RIVER, PRE-1736 TO 2008[23]

are largely longitudinal in shape, making them comparatively long and narrow.

Writing in 1966, Gole and Chitale suggested that after reaching its westernmost limits, the Kosi would eventually begin to move in the opposite direction, eastward, due to the on-going process of deposition.[24] This prediction was realized in August 2008, when the Kosi breached the Afflux Embankment at Kusaha in Nepal and returned to one of its more eastern paleochannels with disastrous consequences – a channel it had not occupied in over two-hundred years, through the districts of Supaul, Madhepura, Araria, Saharsa, Katihar and Purnea districts.

Changing Perceptions of the Kosi

Until the mid-1950s, the Kosi was permitted to sheet flood over the floodplain on either side of the river, spreading across the landscape for many miles in either direction. James Inglis, an English adventurer and planter in 'Purneah and North Bhaugulpore', in the late nineteenth century, commented:

> The Koosee comes directly down with a turbulent impetuous rush from the towering Himalayas, . . . The main stream flows with swift milky flood, dividing the two great indigo and rice districts of Bhaugulpore and Purneah. When swollen by the melting of the snows or the annual rains, the river overflows its banks, and at such times presents the appearance of a broad swiftly-flowing sea, for its breadth from bank to bank is often ten, and in some places nearly twenty miles across. In the dry season, the waters – always of the same milky hue – are confined to innumerable channels; so shallow that the silted plover can wade across; and others running deep and strong, with a ceaseless gurgling swish that would sweep the stateliest elephant off its feet, and carry its ponderous bulk far down the stream. These streams seem to run at random over this deltaic plain. Diverging here, reuniting there; forming a wide bend in one place, and cutting direct through the sandy soil in another; the face of the country is split up into an infinitude of islands, and reticulated everywhere by a network of dry channels and shifting sand banks; . . . where the silent river pursues its impetuous course, to join the dark mysterious waters of the mighty Gunga.
>
> Every year the river spreads here a layer of fertilizing mud, there a covering of destructive sand over the valley, or rather plain – for it seems as flat as a board. . . .[25]

Flooding, in the absence of human involvement, was just a flood, part of a millennia-old natural hydrologic cycle and process. Floods were appreciated, revered, putting people in awe – the raw power of water spreading across the landscape was an unstoppable natural force, neither all good nor bad. However, whenever humans see themselves as separate from or above Nature, floods generally take on a malevolent character. They are no longer natural phenomena but become disasters, catastrophes, calamities, or tragedies, and often people lose their lives, their possessions, and their means of livelihood.

In his article, 'Life with Floods', Naren Karunakaran, with a certain sense of melancholy, suggests: there was a time when the people of Bihar celebrated the monsoons and lived in harmony with the water. The coming of the monsoons and the floods was a good omen. They brought prosperity. It was a festive time. Women would pole out onto the water in their boats on starlit nights, singing and celebrating. There was a kinship and close relationship between the people, the river and its floods. Flooding was such a part of the people's culture that they had words for every permutation and nuance of the river's annual cycle – from the time the rivers began to swell with the abundance of the first mountain rains until the floods peaked and then receded.

Occasionally, the waters would overwhelm the people but they understood the river and its floodwaters, and were generally aware of their every aspect – depth, duration, and retreat – and they took reasonable precautions. The floods came, washed over the landscape, known as *boh*, and then retreated, leaving behind a rich layer of nearly white silt, Nature's natural fertilizer.[26] The silt is so fine that it often becomes airborne when disturbed and coats the people and their animals, giving them an almost ghostly appearance. Yet, it is was the silt that sustained the fertility of the soil. In much of Mithila there was a saying: 'Let the *Balan* [river] spill this year, we will build a new extension on our house: if it doesn't, then we lose whatever we have in the house.'[27] Life with floods, in general, was good.

This same silt, when combined with Himalayan sand and gravel often makes agriculture impossible when it settles as a thick layer over broad swathes of the floodplain, smothering the land. If the people are lucky, these lands are only rendered temporarily fallow. In some cases, depending on the thickness of the sand-gravel deposits, the land is made permanently uncultivable, as there is no means of reclamation. Then it is referred to as sand- or gravel-casting, or locally, as *patpar*.

From time immemorial, the people of northern Bihar have been the victims of floods and the shifts in the courses of the rivers. However, at the same time, the silt-laden spillover from the rivers often became the basis for the development of the earliest civilizations along such rivers. Annual silt deposits permitted population densities to increase as opposed to drought-affected areas. Communities opted to stay in the fertile flood plains; and they adapted to the rivers' annual cycles and learned to live with the floods. They had neither the means nor the inclination to control the rivers.

As population grew and human densities increased, however, especially in the twentieth century, the demand for land and the need to make it more productive conflicted with the natural cycles of the river. Over time, people extended their cultivation into ever lower, low-lying, flood-prone areas, knowing they were susceptible to long-term flooding. These low-lying areas, often referred to as *bils* or marshlands, had previously served as buffers, absorbing significant quantities of floodwater and providing mitigation against catastrophic flooding. The people knew these lands were vulnerable and yet, out of necessity, they cleared and reclaimed them, putting themselves in harm's way, directly in the path of the annual floods. These were the first people to cry for flood relief. At first, they were pioneers, clearing the *bils* of tangles of *jhaua* (tamarix), *kas* (patch grass), and *pater* (typha), converting them into productive agricultural fields; then they became the first victims of the floods, due in large measure to their own actions.

With each successive generation and no new land to clear and cultivate, the farmers needed to work their existing plots more intensely, which required more time in the fields to grow more to feed those dependent upon them. The floods prevented the farmers from returning to their fields, precious time was being lost. They lamented their plight. It was simply a human expression over an insoluble and exasperating problem. There was no inherent suggestion of a solution. At the same time, the benefits accruing from the floods – the silt-fertilization – were forgotten. The peasants felt it was more important to be on their land, working it. Their laments were ultimately heard by the politicians, who quickly turned the peasants into the victims of the floods they had once worshipped.

The farmers sought 'protection' from the floods. In general, this simply meant diverting the flood waters temporarily away from productive lands and onto less or non-productive lands. For generations, the peasants had constructed temporary embankments to protect their fields, often abandoning them after only one season, as the river and its course changed season to season. However, in their quest for more and more cultivable land, they had settled on the very lands that had once protected them. There was now little or no unproductive land. It was being occupied by fields and dwellings. And there was nowhere else for the floodwaters to go.

The politicians, instead of hearing a plea for 'protection', heard 'prevent the floods'. As early as 1937, seminars were held to examine the nature of flooding in Bihar. Then Governor Maurice Hallett observed that, of the floods that had occurred since circa 1877, '22 per cent are sub-normal, 55 per cent are normal, 22 per cent are abnormal and only two per cent are extremely abnormal. In other words, the dwellers in India [Bihar] can expect to be flooded rather badly once every five years, on the average, and to have a really dreadful flood once every fifty years or so.'[28] This was Nature at work. When Man became involved in the 'management' of the river, the frequency, severity, and destructiveness of the floods increased.

THE BIHAR FLOOD SOLUTION

Following a particularly severe flood in 1953-4, the Bihar government initiated an ambitious programme of dam and levee construction designed to tame the Kosi and 'train' it into a well-defined course. This strategy was simply known as the 'Kosi Project'. The project consisted of: (a) a barrage at Bhim Nagar and an afflux levee or embankment to redirect the river's flow; (b) embankments downstream from the barrage on both sides of the river; (c) an eastern and western weeping, drainage canal system; (d) a hydroelectric station in the eastern canal; and (e) a high dam at Barahkshetra. The project's purpose was to control flooding and simultaneously provide irrigation and electricity for agricultural purposes.

The programme ignored: (1) the sediment load carried by the Kosi, which piled up between the rivers' banks and natural levees, making avulsion more and more likely; (2) prior British efforts to 'channelize' the rivers of Bengal; (3) the deleterious environmental effects of the embankments, such as rising river levels, drainage congestion, water-logging, a reduction in crop productivity, and the loss of productive land; and (4) the needs and desires of the local populations, who were effectively abandoned to their fates once the levee systems were completed.

In 1954, the embankments in Bihar began as 100 km of intermittent, poorly constructed *maharaji* and *zamindari* embankments. When completed in 1998, the Bihar embankment system consisted of 3,430± km of embankments, constructed at a cost in excess of Rs 746 crore.[29] By 'channelizing' the silt-laden rivers of northern Bihar, the flood-prone areas have actually increased, rather than decreasing.[30] Before its inception, it was estimated that 2.5 million hectares were flood prone. When the embankments were completed, the flood prone area had *increased* to 6.88 million hectares – an increase of 175 per cent.[31]

The irony of Bihar's flood protection programme is that, for whatever reason, the government of Bihar either refused to acknowledge the efforts of the British to control the Damodar and other smaller rivers in Bengal – it did not equate the similarity of the Damodar River to the rivers of northern Bihar – or it simply chose to ignore history. The euphoria that accompanied Independence and the desire to demonstrate that the newly elected independent government of Bihar was capable of solving its own environmental problems, served to feed the idea that the people of Bihar could succeed where the British had not. Equally important was the fact that more was known about riverine hydrology than when the British had attempted to 'tame the Damodar' nearly a century earlier. However, this additional hydrologic knowledge and the experience of the British were ignored largely because of politics more than an unwillingness or inability to apply good engineering principles and practices to the problems of flooding in the state.

Further, the 'taming' of the rivers of northern Bihar gained both political and technical legitimacy following a visit of Dr. K.L. Rao and Kanwar Sain, who had seen the positive effects of constructing embankments in China, along the Hwang Ho.[32] On the heels of Rao and Sain's reports, the Kosi Project was begun in earnest in 1954.

The British and the Damodar Experiment

The British had recognized the nature of the rivers of Bihar and Bengal very early on. They found the rivers to be, as G.W. Lamplugh stated:

'wayward and restless, ever shifting from place to place within the bounds of the valleys that are theirs to sprawl across at will . . . '.[33] They also observed the positive effects of the more-or-less gentle process of sheet-flooding that took place each year. William Willcocks suggests that prior to British intervention seasonal flooding replenished fertility and were part of an elaborate system of irrigation.[34] He maintained that the 'overflow irrigation of the ancient kings' of Bengal had ensured the country's prosperity and freedom from malaria. Overflow irrigation was a system by which the nutrient-rich, silt-laden monsoon floodwaters from the upper regions of the various rivers flowing into Bengal were distributed evenly over the floodplains of Bihar and the delta of Bengal, watering and more importantly fertilizing fields, spreading fish over the countryside and sweeping away the mosquito populations that spread malaria. Floodwater was not simply allowed to go where it would; rather, it was directed through a system of wide, shallow canals with minimal embankments, in which, at an appropriate time during the yearly monsoon, breaches were made to allow more even flooding. The proper distribution of this water was put in the charge of local water boards which worked with cultivators. The canals also drained the land, preventing water-logging. This system worked marvelously as long as it was maintained in good working order, with the canals being kept clear of silt or sand and vegetation.

As a counterpoint to Willcocks, George Lamplugh suggested that 'For many reasons, human interests demand that a stream shall have a fixed course'.[35] This principle was adopted and it was applied to the Damodar, in the belief that agricultural productivity and prosperity were dependent upon the control of the rivers. Possibly to a lesser degree, this same logic was later applied to Bihar's flood problems by its indigenous government leaders.

Before the British, cultivators had constructed crudely-built, earthen embankments that were typically washed away during the next flood cycle. The British had noted these embankments along the rivers within some of the major zamindaris, and they were informed that such embankments had been in existence for a long time.[36] However, these embankments were sporadic, exhibiting no uniformity in height or length, design, layout or pattern. It was commonly understood that under the *pulbandi* system, the zamindars were responsible for the protection of their lands from inundation by renovating or repairing the embankments. However, in the absence of any enforceable legal imperative, the zamindars generally left the maintenance and repair of the embankments to their tenants, avoiding as much involvement, responsibility or liability, as possible.[37] Lacking any continuity, these earthen embankments afforded only localized flood protection, with the floodwaters flowing through the gaps between them.

The British failed to recognize that the intermittent placement of the embankments was intentional and the key to their success. The peasants understood that, at any one time, only a portion of the productive land could be 'protected' from flooding – essentially an experiential form of modern game theory. The British extrapolated that if intermittent embankments were able to protect only a portion of the land, continuous embankments could protect *all the land*. This simple extension of an idea would, eventually, came to haunt the British administration and would be their downfall.

Until 1846, the issues surrounding embankments were left in the hands of the peasantry and the zamindars, who, technically, owned them. The British 'hands off' policy stemmed from the fear that any involvement with the issue of embankments would result in some kind of fiscal liability. Even so, as early as 1798, the Board of Revenue was forced to take action to repair neglected embankments. The Collectors in the affected districts were then ordered to seize and sell the lands of the 'defaulting' zamindars to recover the costs of the repairs under the provisions of the Permanent Settlement Act of 1793.[38] While the legitimacy of the government's actions, in retrospect, might appear questionable, it had sufficient authority to authorize the taking and sale of zamindari lands to effect the embankment repairs.

By taking responsibility for the repair and maintenance of the embankments, the East India Company, as the government, had inadvertently also assumed the responsibility for embankment oversight and monitoring. The Company, by extension, had placed itself in a position of defining what lands should be protected from floods. Soon, the Company felt compelled to extend the existing system of embankments to protect and ensure the production of the land. In time, the colonial mind of the British gradually extended its responsibilities and authority. The Company came to see itself as having the administrative responsibility of protecting all cultivable land from any threat from the rivers. It was deemed the only way to ensure the prompt and full payment of the revenue by the landowners. The Company saw its actions as simply 'protecting its investment', thus becoming a self-fulfilling prophecy.

The embankments, or *bunds,* while protecting the land also created other environmental problems for the Company. While intended to protect, when they were breached or there was overflow, the water on the outside of the levees often became trapped, with no way back to the river's channel. In these circumstances, the cultivators would often make 'cuts' in the embankments to allow or quicken the return of the water to the river, thereby avoiding standing water and what was called waterlogging if the standing water persisted.

In time, the government came to recognize that native embankments served a variety of purposes depending on the season or situation. During the monsoons, they protected the fields. Later, they helped retain water for later use for irrigational purposes. Consequently, many of the embankments constructed by the peasantry were not meant to be permanent, and they were not averse to abandoning them even if used for only a single season.[39] The monolithic view of government – embankments were meant to separate and protect cultivated lands from water – was oftentimes at odds with the less rigid view of the cultivators. For the cultivators, water and land, flood and irrigation were not necessarily discrete and mutually separable and exclusive resources. Each played its part in turn, a conception not necessarily shared by the imperial administrators. For a government, however, long-term adaptive thinking is often seldom possible.

In 1846, a British inquiry was made into the possibilities of embanking all those rivers subject to flooding. When the expert committee's report was released, there were two startling recommendations: (1) all the rivers of Bengal should remain unconfined; and (2) all existing embankments should be removed.[40] The basis of the committee's recommendations hinged on the fact that the embankments resulted in the gradual shallowing of river channels through the process of sedimentation, and there were also the overriding fiscal demands of embankment construction and maintenance. In a narrower context, there was the genuine concern for the consequences of preventing the fertile silt from being deposited on the levee-protected agricultural lands outside the levees.[41] Silt deprivation could only result in the deterioration and subsequent devaluation of the land. Both would have a fiscal impact on the peasants as well as the zamindars and, ultimately, the government.

In 1852, Captain J.P. Beadle, the Superintendent of Embankments, was possibly the first to propose that a portion of the right bank embankment of the Damodar be removed to facilitate the river's discharge during the monsoons and the elimination of standing water outside the embankments, which was causing waterlogging and creating breeding grounds for malaria-carrying mosquitoes. His opinion, however, was not unanimously held by many observers.[42] It was not until May 1855 that orders were handed down by the Bengal Government to demolish 32 km of embankments along the right bank of the Damodar, from Sungutgolah to Begua.

After weighing the advantages and disadvantages of 'taming' the rivers of eastern India and after nearly fifteen years of experimentation with the Damodar, the British abandoned the idea of state-sponsored embankment programmes alltogether. By 1869, the British refused all demands to control the waters of any river where embankments were involved. If flood control resulted from the construction of dams and barrages, all well and good, but embankments had proven to be a worthless alternative. Even so, it was not until 1918, almost fifty years after the initial decision had been made to discontinue the use of embankments, that the final order for the complete removal of the government's network of embankments was finally promulgated.

A number of factors contributed to the delay in implementing the government's plan to remove all government-constructed embankments. First, and foremost, the decision makers were concerned with questions of cost. They feared that the removal of the embankments would require the payment of compensation for lands likely to be inundated. They were also concerned with the possibilities of adverse effects that might accrue to the rivers' courses. The fate of embankments on the Damodar reflected the British concerns over what might happen to the Hoogly River and eventually the impacts on the port of Calcutta (now Kolkata). In the end, the use of embankments as a safeguard against flooding had never proven a workable solution.

Yet, in many developing countries, embankments continue to be the preferred strategy for the mitigation of floods. In the case of the Kosi's system of embankments, the initial, primary design considerations were:

- The area(s) to be protected.
- The anticipated magnitude of the peak flood discharge.
- The local availability of materials for the construction of the embankment – typically sand, soil, and clay.
- Finances.
- Human resources, i.e. labour.
- Local and state politics.

Independent Bihar's initial embankments were constructed to a height of 15 to 18 ft (4.5 to 5.5 m), depending on their location. After the flood of 1987, they were raised an additional 6 ft (nearly 2 m) in certain areas. After the Kusaha breach in 2008, according to Dinesh Mishra, 'the entire stretch of embankments on either side [of the Kosi] was raised by 5 to 6 ft [1.5-2 m] with a black top road on them. I have a feeling that the embankment will have to be raised by another 12 to 15 ft [3.6 to 4.5 m] . . . if the pace of sedimentation continues the way it had been doing in the past.'[43] Currently, at their highest, the Kosi embankments average 30 feet (9.14 m), and if Mishra is correct, and the height will need to be raised to accommodate or compensate for increased mean low water levels, due to the sedimentation of the main river channel(s), and the embankments could easily reach an average height of 45 ft (13.7 m)!

Assuming Mishra's assessment to be correct and we accept the basic principle of civil engineering – that embankments taller than about 12 m (39.3 feet) are generally deemed uneconomical – the Kosi embankments are already approaching the limits of economic tenability.[44] Using land-side slopes of 1:3 and river-side slopes of 1:2, as advocated by the FAO for the construction of unfaced, homogeneous embankments, the embankments along the Kosi are massive earthworks. However, they are also highly susceptible to scouring, erosion, seepage, tree growth, subsidence, and animal and insect damage; thus, requiring continual maintenance to insure structural integrity. The Government of Bihar has habitually ignored routine maintenance with disastrous consequences. Unfortunately, regular maintenance of embankments, or of most government structures for that matter, is not part of the normal social or political ethos.

The Problems with Embankments

Embankments suffer from a number of inherent problems. Among these are:

- The rapid build-up of silt, sand, gravel, and stones in the riverbeds/channels, which results in an increase in the mean height of the river's water level.
- Embankments are typically constructed with earth locally available from river beds and banks, and are generally unfaced.
- The scouring of the unfaced embankments results in catastrophic breaches.
- The increased height of the river's mean water level plays a role in exacerbating the damage caused from inevitable levee breaches, as higher mean water levels requires that embankments be built higher increasing the 'cascade effect' of the breaching waters. The Kosi's riverbed has risen by as much as 3.7-4.6 m above its original floodplain.[45] Trapping water outside the embankments delays the 'drying-out' of agricultural lands and often leads to waterlogging.
- Waterlogging is largely the result of the levees themselves, which do not allow the water to return to the river.

The Kosi embankments initially demonstrated their utility. For a period, they held back the waters of the Kosi, then the river channel filled with debris and rose, cresting the embankments and, in places, the embankments were breached. Water poured onto the floodplain, where it became trapped. Just as the embankments had prevented floodwaters from washing over the floodplain, they also prevented the spill-over waters from returning to the river's course, frequently

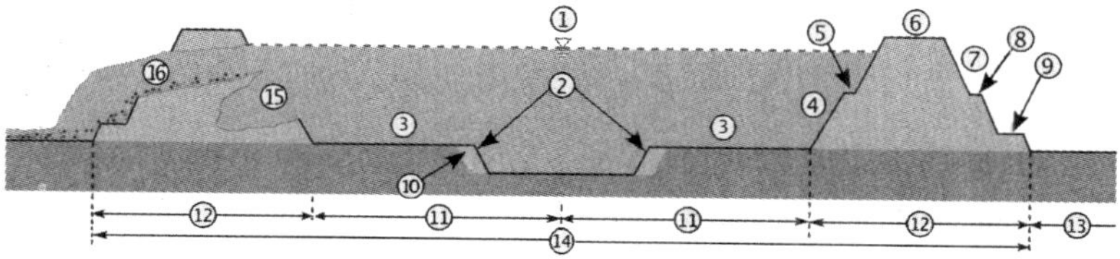

DIAGRAM 3.2: RIVER AND LEVEE CROSS-SECTIONS, SCOURS AND BREACHES

Not to Scale

1. High Water Level
2. Low Water Level/Channel
3. Flood Channel
4. Riverside Slope of Levee
5. Riverside Banquette
6. Levee Crown, may be up to 12-13 m high.
7. Landside Slope of Levee
8. Landside Banquette
9. Berm
10. Low Water Revetment
11. Riverside Land. Distance between the Kosi's Levees varies but may get up to 16 km.
12. Levee
13. Protected Lowland
14. River Zone
15. Scour, or undermining of levee
16. Breach, laden with debris – rocks, gravel, and, and silt. Water trapped outside levee causes waterlogging of the soil.

waterlogging the land. Unable to drain itself, the water stood until it evaporated, sometimes taking up to a year, and frequently, the lands never fully dried. Then the water hyacinths took over and the land was permanently lost to cultivation. Sometimes, these waterlogged soils can be reclaimed, at considerable expense. Generally, they go un-reclaimed.

Throughout Bihar, West Bengal, and Bangladesh, which share similar types of water-related problems, especially flooding and waterlogging, government and private embankment systems have been constructed. The smaller, private embankments pose much less of a problem than the government-sponsored and maintained embankments. Inevitably, the floods that breach the government levees are more destructive and longer lived than for the lower private levees. After years of floods, villagers insist that they are prepared to deal with natural floods. 'It is man-made floods that have wreaked havoc on them [cultivators] all these years.'[46]

There is a growing movement among a number of flood-watch groups to 'go back to the old ways' of dealing with the floods. This would mean either the elimination of the embankments or permitting breaches to remain un-repaired, which would allow the flood waters to 'sneak in like cats', as Dinesh Kumar Mishra, the convener of the *Barh Mukti Abhiyan*, so eloquently stated it, rather than 'roaring like lions'.[47] Mishra's comment reflects the difference between the sheet flooding that preceded the construction of the embankments. During the post-embankment construction phase, floods occurred as catastrophic breaches, permitting water, sometimes four or more metres above the mean water level of the river to cascade down through narrow breaches onto the agricultural lands below, with the force of a fast-flowing waterfall, destroying everything in its path.

These breach floods, in addition to their ferocity, are also accompanied by river sediments other than silt. These other sediments – sand, gravel, and stones – that normally would have been deposited in the river channels are now cast onto the farmlands. In the past, it was not uncommon for sand and silt to be deposited during the initial phases of sheet flooding but breach flooding, in addition to silt and sand, often brings with it gravel and stones. In some areas, the casting of sand and gravel has made otherwise productive land unworkable.

More land has been lost to embankments and problems associated with them than has ever been lost due to over-cultivation. Consequently, Bihar's agricultural productivity has declined. According to Pratyaya Amrit, an Additional Commissioner in Bihar's disaster management department: 'There is a saying in [these] parts – Wherever the Kosi goes, not even a blade of grass grows there for 20 years.'[48] Amrit was referring to the fact that the Kosi, more so than any other river in northern Bihar, brings in addition to fertile silt, course sand and gravel from the upper reaches of the river's catchment. It is this sand and gravel that makes the land barren and this, in turn, affects the food security of the state and if it can be repaired, it will take a very long time and an extraordinary amount of money.

The population in Bihar is perennially affected by floods – 30 of its 38 districts are flood-prone and afflicted by floods almost annually. The five districts within, or west of the Kosi megafan, are most affected by the flooding and are among the least developed districts in the state, lagging behind the state as a whole.

Part of Bihar's flooding problems is the direct result of outdated notions regarding river management dating back to the British. The British, however, were at least astute enough to realize that because of the character of the rivers of eastern India, embankments typically caused more problems than they solved. It is for this reason that they abandoned every effort to channelize the rivers of Bengal and Bihar using embankment techniques. The follow-on, Indian politicians, engineers, and contractors, however, ignored the experience of the British and saw an opportunity to cash in. As a result, the people of Bihar have been made to suffer the effects of uncontrolled flooding for sixty years.

Since the inception of the Kosi embankment programme in the 1950s, our technical understanding of the river's physical behaviour has improved, with the 2008 breach serving as a major, albeit costly, instructional opportunity. Increasingly, different points of view are being heard by both politicians and government. Together a kind of convergence is emerging. New innovative strategies of breaching the levees and allowing controlled flooding and sediment transport through the network of abandoned river channels during high flows is gaining support. But more importantly, there is the recognition that no one at any stage in this shameful saga actually bothered to ask the residents of the Kosi region, or any of the other rivers that have been channelized, what they wanted from flood control, or indeed whether they wanted it at all. The Bihari culture had long ago adapted to yearly floods, and this was incorporated into crop rotation, patterns of migration and ways of sharing resources between villages during bad years. Now, the residents of the region have no voice in the decisions that are being made about their lives, their livelihoods, their property, or their possessions.

UNCONTROLLED FLOODING

In the final analysis, floods have been a part of the normal life cycle of the people of northern Bihar for millennia. The people knew when they would come and typically how long they would last. There were no surprises. With the advent of the embankments, beginning in the mid-1950s, the character of the floods began to change. They became more widespread and devastating. This too, the cultivators came to know. What the cultivators had not anticipated, however, were the consequences of the embankments. They had thought that the embankments would protect them from the floods. Soon, they realized that this assumption, too, was incorrect. It was the inability of the flood waters to make their way back to the river channel that they had not anticipated. As a consequence, many thousands of hectares of valuable, formerly productive farmland have become waterlogged or sand-casted, and there was little anyone could do to change this, neither the planners, the contractors, the politicians, nor the cultivators.

Knowledge about what can and will, in all likelihood, occur does not necessarily prepare a person for the actual event. What does happen, however, is the person steels himself to the probability of the event. If it occurs, he knows what to do. If it does not occur, he has been spared. In the case of the cultivators who experience flooding, oftentimes on an annual basis, relief, relief payments, and compensation have become the new way of life. The word relief was not even part of the average villager's vocabulary until 1936. However, when relief became available for the first time in 1938, things began to change. Initially, many villagers felt that these government handouts were degrading and made them feel like beggars. These were proud people. Many, initially, even refused the assistance. At one time, *khichri* – a traditional rice, dal, and spice dish – was simply an inexpensive and easy-to-make menu item. But, because it was easy to prepare, the government used it as part of its food relief programmes during floods; feeding those who occupied the embankments to escape the flood waters. In the past, old women would have normally distributed *khichri* to the needy and suffering. That was then, now, the floods have become almost an annual event, and those that once distributed *khichri* are now recipients. In more recent times, the term, *khichri* has taken on a new colloquial meaning. It has become synonymous with welfare, charity, or help; and a new generation with a different set of values and a different work ethic now occupies the embankments. With the onset of the rainy season, 'everyone is busy harvesting the fourth crop of the year: flood relief funds'.[49]

The cultivators who inhabit the lands just beyond the embankments pine for the 'good old days' – a time before embankments and ferocious flooding. They recognize that man-made floods are much worse than those before the embankments. The water once overwhelmed the people and the land but it was nowhere as destructive as modern-day flooding. The people understood the floods. They did not wait in dread, wondering if, or when, the levees would fail, sending a deluge down onto their homes and across their fields. Over time, the people have undergone what might be referred to as 'a nomenclature change – from "worshippers of floods" to "victims of floods"'.[50]

Have the people of northern Bihar been defeated by the floods? No. Flooding is simply part of northern Bihar's new 'normal' pattern of life. The people have adapted, just as any cultivator does to changing conditions, whether it is climate, flooding, economic, or social. These people are hardy and proud. They are survivors. They and their ancestors have lived with the same, but slightly different environmental problems for millennia. There is little they have not seen. Some years are worse than others but some are also much better than others. These are practical, industrious people.

Can the backwardness seen in the 'backward district studies' be attributed to flood? In all likelihood, no. Floods, while often attended by destruction and the loss of life, have been part of Bihar's cycle of life for millennia. At least to the limit of the society's social, economic, and technological ability to cope with these calamities, floods have always been a regular part of rural agrarian life in northern Bihar.

However, whether cause or effect, or coincidence, the economic fate of Bihar began to decline almost simultaneously with the Bihar government's obsession and preoccupation with its embankment and flood control programmes. Billions of rupees were diverted from other development programmes to dam, barrage, and embankment projects. One has to wonder, or at least question whether embankments were the cause or mechanism of Bihar's economic undoing. Is it only coincidence that Bihar's storied place in Indian agrarian history should begin to wane and crumble at about the same time as the state began making unprecedented investments in ill-fated flood protection schemes?

The construction and maintenance of the infrastructure of flood control was inordinately expensive. To these costs must be added the costs associated with waterlogging and casting which, ultimately, resulted in the wholesale loss of productive agricultural land. And the catastrophic flooding, resulting from the embankments and periodic breaches, have resulted in massive and increasingly expensive relief and rehabilitation costs, as well as the costs associated with the loss of human lives, livestock, crops, and dwellings and other infrastructural items like roads, bridges, railway lines, electricity and communications.

In an attempt to 'protect' the cultivators, the Government of Bihar substituted the inconvenience of periodic sheet flooding with catastrophic large-scale flooding. Worship of the floods became fear and the government's solution loathsome. As Hanuman Prasad, an old farmer in Bihar stated with regard to the Kosi embankments: 'You have ruined the relationship we had with the river. It was a relationship of equals. By building embankments you have given the river a bow. The stronger you make the bow the stronger will be the force of the arrow [water].'[51]

Another villager, Akhilesh Mishra pointing to his waterlogged land from atop the embankment he occupied during a recent flood, commented: 'Now I can fish here instead of growing crops.'[52] While amusing, his statement brings into focus the dimensions and consequences of one of the real threats of the Kosi and its embankments.

* * *

According to the *Rashtriya Barh Ayog* (the National Commission on Floods) today, 16.5 per cent of the entire flood-prone area of India is located in Bihar and 22.1 per cent of the total flood-affected population within the country resides in the flood plains of Bihar. The flood-prone area of Bihar was only 25 lakh hectares in 1954, when the First National Policy on Floods was announced. It rose to 43.2 lakh hectares in 1971 and further to 64.51 lakh hectares by

1982.[53] A Planning Commission special task force concluded that almost 41 per cent of the total cropped area in Bihar is now flood prone, and noted that there is not much scope for improvement in yield due to waterlogging, poor drainage, and water management, recommending urgent government investment in measures like drainage and the desilting of rivers.[54]

The 2008 Kosi Afflux breach, for the first time since the mid-1950s, shocked planners and politicians alike. They had become inured to the nearly annual floods, and the relief efforts provided an opportunity for both the national and foreign relief agencies, as well as local politicians, to obtain recognition for their work. Although most observers of flooding in Bihar are familiar with the eight main breaches, floods and devastation, the government acknowledges the existence of as many as 371 breaches over the past twenty-four years on almost all of the rivers under its jurisdiction, including the Kosi, Kamala, Gandak, Bagmati, Burhi Gandak and Mahananda.[55] While officially refusing to acknowledge that these breaches ever happened, the government has accepted claims based on them. The policy seems to be – yes, the breaches occurred, we're responsible but we don't want to talk about them.

FLOODING IN BIHAR: THE SOCIO-ECONOMIC CONTEXT

Following the 2008 breach, for the first time, the debate surrounding flood protection moved away from engineering solutions. The debate broadened with all sides showing a never-before-seen openness and willingness to debate rather than subscribing to outdated doctrinaire positions. It may be that, also for the first time, efforts will be made and solutions found that will permit the mitigation of the threat of floods; this may improve the security of those living along the rivers. In the past the views and concerns of those most directly affected by the floods were ignored. Now, villagers and cultivators are becoming part of the debate.

The debate has shifted from flood-proofing to flood-management. One of the most enlightened studies to come out of the 2008 Kosi breach is the United Nations Development Programme's study, titled *Kosi Floods 2008: How We Coped! What We Need – Perception Survey on Impact and Recovery Strategies.*[56] Instead of being a typical post-disaster event that 'needs assessment', the study looked at how people experienced the floods, their perception of how the floods affected their lives and livelihoods, and how they coped economically and socially. This alone can be seen as a radical departure from previous flood relief programmes and strategies. It actually examined the suffering of the victims as well as the effectiveness of public action on mitigating the impacts of the disaster. This report clearly demonstrated a new approach to old problems of dealing with natural disasters.

Both national and international debate over what needs to be done is finally going beyond simple flood relief – polyethylene sheets, food packets, *khichri*, salt, candles, and portable sanitation facilities. For the first time in generations, welfare is taking precedence over political expediency when it comes to the problems associated with flooding in Bihar. With over three-quarters of the total area of north Bihar affected by floods and 87 per cent of the population of north Bihar dependent upon agriculture for its livelihood, flooding and waterlogging are life-threatening events. It may be that statistics, combined with events, are finally pointing in new directions for solutions. Clearly, the situation demands serious and urgent action and not platitudes, pandering, and posturing.

Likewise, ground-level participation in the planning process has been institutionalized through the creation of an unprecedented set of operational guidelines which emphasize community participation in quality planning, implementation, social audit and transparency through the MGNREGA. Working through the implementing agency of the Gram Panchayat, these guidelines place a complete ban on the use of contractors and lay an emphasis on labour-intensive work for water conservation, drought and flood-proofing, underscoring water security as the prerequisite and foundation for rural transformation in India.

* * *

By early 2009, the breach at Kusaha had been repaired. Shortly after the Kusaha embankment was restored, at least a portion of the Kosi returned to its pre-breach channel, while the remaining volume continues to flow into and through several of its paleochannels. However, a question continues to linger. What is to be done with the Kosi?

Currently, there are several strategies being considered but none have gained consensus among the authorities or the government. The primary alternatives include:

- Embank the Kosi in a straight line, shortest route, from Chatra to Kursela where it joins the Ganga.
- Disperse the water of the Kosi into several of its former channels, which would have the effect of disbursing the river's volume and burden over a broad area.
- Try to return the full volume of Kosi to its pre-2008 embanked course.[57]

Of the alternatives currently under review, the author can only subscribe to the second proposal – shunting the water of the Kosi into former channels and, thereby, distributing the river's volume of water and sediment over a much larger area. Since 2008, the Kosi has been sending its volume, alternately, through a number of its old channels. The effect has been that there have been no catastrophic breaches or floods. Compare this with the annual flood patterns prior to 2008. Each August and September, one would typically read of a minor breach and flood here and a minor breach and flood there, with thousands of villagers scrambling for high ground as the river flooded one area after another. Even though there were 'minor breaches' between the highly reported massive breaches, these minor breaches still flooded thousands of hectares of land, drowning people and livestock, and destroying crops and croplands.

Those who have advocated the dismantlement of the embankments may well have realized an opportunity. Since the Kosi has not been straight-jacketed by embankments, over the last six years, there have been no disastrous, catastrophic flooding. To be sure, there have been floods, but there has been a type of normalcy to them. They come.

They go. The only appreciable change in the floods is the increased amount of discharge coming out of the mountains. Each year, the absolute volume of water seems to be increasing and with it, ever larger areas are enveloped and it takes longer for the floods to recede, returning the farmland to the cultivators.

Allowing the river to wallow through the labyrinth of the river's much braided courses has served to 'tame' the turbulent and destructive nature of the Kosi, at least in terms of catastrophic, breach flooding. Isn't this, after all, what the cultivators were asking for back in the 1950s, before the government decided what was best for its constituents? For sixty years those living outside the embankments have waited patiently for flood protection. Now, that protection has come in the form of flood management by allowing the river to idle its way to the Ganga via numerous river channels, and this has had the effect of turning a tiger into a comparative pussy cat, with all the benefits of a silt-laden river that gently floods the farmland and then gently recedes to continue on its way to the Bay of Bengal.

The rivers will never stop flooding. That is a function of their morphology and the monsoons. But, now, the people seem more able to return to living with the rivers instead of living in fear of them. Maybe one day soon the cultivators will return to being worshippers of the rivers, no longer victims of them. In large measure, that transformation now lies in the hands of the politicians and the bureaucracy's planners.

The Nowhere People

There is, however, one other feature of river flooding that bears mentioning. When the state of Bihar initiated its embankment programme, more than 250,000 villagers were asked to leave their villages and homes because they lived *between* the proposed embankments of the rivers. Along the Kosi alone, more than 192,000 people, living in more than 300 villages, were asked to leave their homes, villages, and fields in the districts of Darbhanga and Saharsa. Today, the number of people living between the embankments has grown to nearly 1.2 million.[58]

When one thinks of embankments, one envisions large levees being built that will channel and direct the river, with the distance between these levees being comparatively short. In the case of the Kosi, however, the distance between the embankments is frequently 10 to 16 km in places.

Promises were made to these displaced villagers that they would be 'rehabilitated'. However, the government did not have the financial resources to relocate all the villagers and simultaneously provide them with cultivable land. In part, this was due to the non-availability of land beyond the embankments. The government could, however, relocate the villagers' residences at a substantially lower cost. These new homesites were, however, scattered outside the embankments and, on average, 10 km from the embankments, thus dispersing the villagers. Old social units and networks ceased to exist. Their farm lands, however, remained accessible between the embankments and could be worked once the floodwaters receded and the rivers returned to their minimum channels.

By 2009, all the villagers were not yet rehabilitated.[59] Most abandoned their 'new homesites' in favour of moving back to their ancestral villages between the embankments. A number of factors contributed to their decision to move back in harm's way. Most simply missed being together as a village. Many of their new homesites were located in areas prone to waterlogging. And the government repeatedly failed to live up to its financial and support commitments. The government promised the people whose lands were between the embankments rehabilitation, employment, and a place to live. These promises were largely 'paper promises'. Ironically, those who moved back to their old villages in-between the embankments did so knowing, when the river rose, they would be flooded out. One villager, Ram Vilas Sharma, put it this way: 'I'd rather brave the floods than live under impossible conditions.'[60] Is not living in an area that has a 100 per cent likelihood of being inundated each year an equally impossible condition?

From the government's perspective, however, the Nowhere People are not supposed to be living near or within the embankments. Therefore, they are not the government's responsibility. Nevertheless,

PLATE 3.2 A, B & C: FLOODS AND ELEVATED LIFE

with each inundation, it is the government that provides flood relief supplies and makes relief payments to these same Nowhere People.

As a consequence, every year these villages are inundated as the rivers spread out from their central channels, filling the area between the embankments. When the waters begin to rise, the villagers collect their meagre possessions and move to higher ground inside and outside the embankments, usually elevated roadways. Some of the lucky ones find refuge in refugee camps with proper emergency facilities. Others, along with their animals occupy plastic shelters with no proper sanitation. And life goes on.

* * *

So, why have the Bihar Project's embankments not been either allowed to decay and crumble, or been demolished like those along the Damodar? The answer is quite simple. It is due to political economy. Contractors and their political patrons make huge sums of money through such civil works. The flood business, funded by government relief, is worth thousands of crores of rupees; and as long as there is money to be made, legitimately or not, and there is corruption within the government, embankments will continue to stand, be rebuilt, built up, improved, and perfunctorily repaired.

Dinesh Kumar Mishra, possibly, said it as succinctly as anyone, when he commented: 'When you have politicians behaving like engineers and vice-versa you will obviously land everyone in trouble. Unless these roles are kept in order, nothing will happen.'[61]

NOTES

1. C.P. Yadav, B.S. Gupta and S. Kumar, 'Export Potential of Agriculture', in Jagdish Prasad (ed.), *Export Potential of Indian Agriculture: Bihar – Perspective and Issues*, Delhi: Mittal Publications, 2000, pp. 113-22.
2. P.C. Roy Chaudhury, *Bihar District Gazetteers – Darbhanga*, Patna: Superintendent, Secretariat Press, 1964, p. 24.
3. UNEP, *South Asia: State of the Environment 2001,* Pathumthani: United Nations Environment Programme/Regional Resource Centre for Asia and the Pacific, 2001; and Bihar State Pollution Control Board; Department of Environment and Forest, GoI, *State of Environment Report, Bihar,* Patna:

Bihar State Pollution Control Board; Department of Environment and Forest, GoI, 2007.

4. Bihar Inter Agency Group; US Aid; Project Concern International; Global Forum for Disaster Reduction, *Bihar State Forum for Disaster Risk Reduction (BSFDRR),* Background Paper, Patna: BIAG; US Aid; PCI/India; GFDR, 2010.
5. Ibid., p. 1.
6. Ajaya Dixit, 'Kosi Embankment Breach in Nepal: Need for a Paradigm Shift in Responding to Floods', *Economic and Political Weekly,* vol. 44, no. 6, February 2009, p. 71.
7. C.P. Sinha, 'Climate Change and its Impact on the Wetlands of North Bihar', *Lakes & Reservoirs: Research & Management*, vol. 16, no. 2, June 2011, p. 110.
8. Special Task Force on Bihar, *Bihar's Agriculture Development: Opportunities & Challenges,* New Delhi: Government of India, 2008, p. 16. Of Bihar's total area of 94,163 sq km, 68,795 sq km are deemed to be flood prone.
9. Megafan – an alluvial fan formed where fast-flowing streams flatten, slow, and spread, typically at the exit of a canyon onto a flatter plain. All the great rivers of Northern Bihar have formed megafans, each with its own unique physical characteristics, due to the nature of its exit from the canyons of Nepal and the greater floodplain of northern Bihar.
10. A much larger and more detailed river basin map of Bihar can be found at: http://fmis.bih.nic.in/RiverBasinMap.jpg.
11. Adapted from Flood Management Information System, Bihar, map series.
12. Praveen Singh, Nilanjan Ghose, Nitin Chaudhary, and Regina Hansda, *Live in the Shadow of Embankments: Turning Lost Lands into Assets in the Kosi Basin of Bihar, India,* Kathmandu: International Centre for Integrated Mountain Development (ICIMOD), 2009, p. 6.
13. Dilip Kumar, 'Millennium Strategy for the Kosi', Patna, n.d.
14. Rajiv Sinha and Peter F. Friend, 'River Systems and their Sediment Flux, Indo-Gangetic Plains, Northern Bihar, India', *Sedimentology* (Oxford, Boston: Blackwell Scientific Publishers), vol. 41, no. 4, 1994, p. 830. Sinha calculates the Kosi's uplands-to-plains area ratio at 5.31. However, he used a slightly lower figure for the mountain catchment basis – 59,503 sq km. Whereas we have used the figure 62,620 sq km, thus slightly increasing the ratio to 5.49.
15. Vishwas S. Kale, 'Catastrophe that Engulfed North Bihar', *Journal of the Geological Society of India,* vol. 72, December 2008, p. 715.

    Original graphic decolorized and edited, from 'How Kosi River Changed its Course', *Zakaria Siddiqui's Blog: Blog on Issues of Development,* retrieved on 10 April 2013, from http://zakku78.wordpress.com/, 28 September 2008.

16. Modified based on Wiki Commons. *River Levee Cross Section Figure.pn,* 13 November 2005, http://commons.wikimedia.org/wiki/File:River_Levee_Cross_Section_Figure.png, accessed 3 March 2014, River Levee Cross Section Figure.png.
17. As the velocity declines, the boulders, then the, rocks, gravel, and sand are deposited. The silt is deposited proportionally all along the river's course during the floods in both the channel and across the floodplain.
18. Although clearly recognized as the world's largest delta, the Ganga-Bhagirathi Delta, is, as Kalyan Rudra suggests, disappearing into the Bay of Bengal. See, Kalyan Rudra, *Atlas of Changing River Courses in West Bengal, 1767-2010,* Kolkata: Sea Explorers' Institute, 2012. While the delta 'appears' to be disappearing, the submerged delta continues to expand in all directions into the Bay of Bengal, gradually filling it.
19. See, Jacob A. Covault, 'Submarine Fans and Canyon-Channel Systems: A Review of Processes, Products, and Models', *Nature Education Knowledge,* vol. 3, no. 10, 2011. Covault suggests that the burial of organic carbon sediment is capable of influencing the global inventory of carbon and is potentially a key to the control of carbon dioxide concentrations over millions of years. The Bengal Submarine Fan is responsible for 10-20 per cent of the global burial of organic carbon derived from terrestrial plant detritus from the Himalayas. See, also, Peter J. Telling, James Hunt and Ian Harding, *How Efficient is Organic Carbon Burial and Sequestration by Large-Scale Sediment Flows in the Deep Ocean, and What are the Implications for Global Carbon Cycle?* 2014, http://noc.ac.uk/gsnocs/project/how-efficient-organic-carbon-burial-sequestration-large-scale-sediment-flows-deep-oce; and Victor J. Galy, C. France-Lanord, O. Beyssac, P. Faure, H. Kudrass and F. Palhol, 'Efficient Organic Carbon Burial in the Bengal Fan Sustained by the Himalayan Erosional System', *Nature,* vol. 450, November 2007.
20. Rajiv Sinha, 'Dynamics of a River System – The Case of the Kosi River in North Bihar', *e-Journal Earth Science India,* vol. 2, no. 1, January 2009, p. 35.
21. Woods Hole Oceanographic Institution, *Images: Moving Heaven and Earth,* http://www.whoi.edu/oceanus/v2/article/images.do?id=2510. The Bengal Fan extends 2,500 km south into the Bay of Bengal and is 22 km thick.
22. C.V. Gole and S.V. Chitale, 'Inland Delta Building Activity of Kosi River', *Journal of Hydraulics Division, American Society of Civil Engineers,* vol. 92, no. 2, 1966. Others, like Mohd. Danish, Priyank Gupta, Javed Alam and Mohd. Muzammil, *River Kosi, Sorrow of India: An Overview, Paper-CV-111,* 2nd International Conference on Emerging Trends in Engineering and Technology, 12-13 April 2013, suggest other possible causes for the waywardness of the Kosi.
23. Amurt Deutschland, e. V. *Bihar - Kosi River,* 1998-2012, http://www.amurt.

eu/node/21. See also, original diagram obtained from Dinesh Kumar Mishra, 'Kosi Changes its Course', *Abc - An Opinionated & Politically Incorect[sic] Blog*, retrieved 2 December 2014, from http://drdivas.wordpress.com/2008/09/09/kosi-floods-establishment-refuses-to-learn-any-lesson/, n.d.

24. Gole, and Chitale, 1966, op. cit.
25. James Inglis, *Tent Life in Tiger Land; and Sport and Work on the Nepaul Frontier*, London: Sampson Low, Marston & Co., 1892, pp. 6-7. The author has seen all or portions of this lengthy passage quoted elsewhere but using 'modern' punctuation and spelling. The author prefers to rely on the original version here.
26. An old word, 'humma', meaning a major, destructive flood is now used far more frequently than *boh* . As Kameshwar Kamati stated: 'There is no boh now, only humma.' See, Meena Menon, 'The Nowhere People', 19 March 2010, http://www.thehindu.com/todays-paper/tp-opinion/the-nowhere-people/article731085.ece.
27. Naren Karunakaran, 'Living With Floods', 10 September 2004, http://www.countercurrents.org/en-naren100904.htm, accessed 1 September 2012.The original saying goes: 'Ael Balan ta banhaloun dalaan; gel Balan ta tutale dalaan.'
28. As quoted by Dinesh Kumar Mishra, 'The People vs. the Environment', March 2011, http://www.himalmag.com/component/content/article/4288-the-people-vs-the-environment.html, accessed 2 September 2012.
29. R. Krishnakumar, 'Flood Management: The Kosi Untamed', September-October 1999, http://www.frontlineonnet.com/fl1620/16200650.htm, accessed 1 September 2012.
30. Sudhirendar Sharma, 'Missing the River for the Dam', August 2008, http://infochangeindia.org/environment/analysis/missing-the-river-for-the-dam.html, accessed 11 September 2012, 'Strait-jacketing the silt-laden Kosi has actually caused flood-prone areas in the state to increase threefold since independence, from a low of 25,00,000 hectares to a high of 68,00,000 hectares today. No less than 73% of the entire land mass of Bihar remains flood-prone.' Sharma was part of an Ashoka Fellowship Initiative fact-finding mission to assess the perpetual flood cycle in North Bihar.
31. Eklavya Prasad, 'Bihar's Flood Survival Mechanism', 2003, http://www.indiawaterportal.org/sites/indiawaterportal.org/files/floodissuecore11-30.pdf, accessed 2 September 2012.
32. See, Dinesh Kumar Mishra, 'The Bihar Flood Story', *Economic and Political Weekly*, vol. 32, no. 35, January 1997; and Praveen Singh, 'Colonial State, Zamindars and the Politics of Flood Control in North Bihar (1850-1954)', *Indian Economic and Social History Review* (Elsevier B.V), vol. 45, no. 2,

June 2008, for a discussion of the debate over embankments in Bihar.

33. G.W. Lamplugh, 'Physiographical Notes II: On the Taming of Streams (Continued)', *Geographical Journal,* vol. 43, no. 6, 1914, p. 651.
34. William Willcocks, *Ancient System of Irrigation in Bengal and its Application to Modern Problems,* Delhi: B.R. Publishing, 1928 [1984].
35. G.W. Lamplugh, 'Physiographical Notes II: On the Taming of Streams (Continued)', p. 651.
36. See, Lewis Sydney Steward O'Malley and Monmohan Chakravarti, *Bengal District Gazetteers, Howrah,* vol. 18, Calcutta: Bengal Secretariat Book Department, 1909, p. 82; Kumkum Bhattacharyya, 'Applied Geomorphological Study in a Controlled Tropical River: The Case of the Damodar Between Panchet Reservoir and Falta', unpublished Ph.D. dissertation, Burdwan: The University of Burdwan, 1998; and Kumkum Bhattacharyya, *The Lower Damodar River, India: Understanding the Human Role in Changing Fluvial Environment,* Dordrecht: Springer, 2011, p. 74.
37. It must be noted that the *pulbani* system applied as a function of custom, not a legal requirement. As long as the zamindars were traditional, customary officials, *pulbani* prevailed but once the British system of law became the law of the land, tradition and custom could be subverted. If the settlements did not include *pulbani,* the government or those who benefited from the embankments must be responsible for their construction, repair, and maintenance.
38. Embankments in Murshidabad, Selection from the Records of the Government of Bengal Relating to the Nadia Rivers, 1848 to 1926 (Calcutta, 1931), p. 53.
39. *Embankments in Bengal: Note on their Origin, Development and Utility (1772-1850),* pp. 33-8, Land Revenue Records (28 March 1851), pp. 20-1, in *Index to Land Revenue Records (1838-59),* vol. II, National Archives of India.
40. As referenced by Kumkum Bhattacharyya, *The Lower Damodar River, India: Understanding the Human Role in Changing Fluvial Environment,* 2011, p. 75.
41. Ibid.
42. Henry Leland Harrison, *The Bengal Embankment Manual: . . . ,* Calcutta: The Bengal Secretariat Press, 1875. This volume is an invaluable resource for understanding the general change of policy within the Company with regard to its responsibilities and obligations vis-à-vis embankment building, maintenance and repair. See, especially the section titled: Historical Outline and Discussion of the Main Principles of the Act. It also provides references to Beadle's suggestion that the right embankment of the Damodar be razed. See, for example, the communications in Appendix B.

43. Dinesh Kumar Mishra, personal e-mail communication, 6 March 2014.
44. R.J. Garde and K.G. Ranga Raju, *Mechanics of Sediment Transportation and Alluvial Stream Problem,* New York: John Wiley, 1985, p. 576.
45. Sudhirendar Sharma, *Missing the River for the Dam,* retrieved 11 September 2012, from Infochange-Environment: http://infochangeindia.org/environment/analysis/missing-the-river-for-the-dam.html, August 2008.
46. Naren Karunakaran, 'Living With Floods', 10 September 2004.
47. Personal communication with Dinesh Kumar Mishra, as well as cited by Naren Karunakaran, 'Living With Floods', 10 September 2004.
48. Writer at Large, 'Killer Kosi Could Leave Bihar Barren', 9 September 2008, http://rovingwriter.blogspot.ca/2008/09/killer-kosi-could-leave-bihar-barren.html, accessed 7 September 2012.
49. Dinesh Kumar Mishra, 'Harvesting Flood Relief', August 2004, http://www.indiatogether.org/2004/aug/opi-floods.htm, accessed 11 August 2012.
50. Karunakaran, 'Living With Floods', 10 September 2004.
51. Down To Earth, 'Engineered Chaos', 30 September 1999, http://www.downtoearth.org.innode/20456.
52. Meena Menon, 'The Nowhere People', Retrieved from *The Hindu On-line*: http://www.thehindu.com/todays-paper/tp-opinion/the-nowhere-people/article731085.ece, 19 March 2010.
53. Dinesh Kumar Mishra, 'Special Articles: The Bihar Flood Story', *Economic and Political Weekly*, vol. 32, no. 35, August 1997.
54. Planning Commission, *Bihar's Agriculture Development: Opportunities & Challenges, Report of the Planning Commission Special Task Force on Bihar*, New Delhi: Government of India, April 2008, pp. 5 and 17.
55. Dinesh Kumar Mishra, 'The People vs. the Environment', retrieved 2 September 2012, from Himal Southasian: http://www.himalmag.com/component/content/article/4288-the-people-vs-the-environment.html, March 2011.
56. UNDP, *Kosi Floods 2008: How We Coped! What We Need – Perception Survey on Impact and Recovery Strategies*, New Delhi: United Nations Development Programme, 2009.
57. Personal communication with Dinesh Kumar Mishra, convener of the *Barh Mukti Abhiyan*, 13 September 2012.
58. Today, there are 414 villages (380 in India and 34 in Nepal) that are located within the embankments of the Kosi with an estimated population of nearly 1.2 million. Within the embankments of the Mahananda there are 66 villages, the Kamla: 104 villages, the Bagmati: 95 villages (Dinesh Kumar Mishra, 'Managing Embankments to Manage Disasters', South Asia Network on Dams, Rivers and People, retrieved from http://sandrp.in/floods/Managing_Embankments_to_Manage_Disasters.pdf, April 2012, p. 2).

59. Dinesh Kumar Mishra, 'The Kosi is Back to Its Permanent Clientele', 7 August 2009, d-sector, http://www.d-sector.org/article-detailCon.asp?id=12, accessed 20 September 2012.
60. Down To Earth, 'Engineered Chaos', retrieved from *Down To Earth*: http://www.downtoearth.org.in/node/20456, 30 September 1999.
61. Ibid.

CHAPTER 4

The Environmental Roots of Backwardness in Bihar and Mithila

Part II: Drought

Unlike floods which are often sudden and traumatic events, droughts, at least in the beginning, are much more subtle and for this reason, more insidious. They do not destroy man's physical inventory of things but often result in starvation. The irony of the situation in Bihar is that these two destructive forces – floods and droughts – can be visualized as adjacent links in the Bihari chain of life. Floods can and often are immediately followed by droughts, and the cycle has been repeated again and again.[1] Within the climatic context of Bihar, it is difficult to even contemplate the possibility of drought following on the heels of a flood.

If we accept Amaryta Sen's contention that: (a) starvation is the characteristic of some people not having enough to eat; and (b) it is not the result of there not being enough food to eat, but is more the result of social policies and poverty than actual agricultural production, then the people of Bihar are among some of the most vulnerable people in India.[2] This is because low agricultural productivity, often caused by flooding or drought, or both, results in or causes poverty and serves to reinforce backwardness. And the government of Bihar seems incapable or unwilling to help in any meaningful way, except to provide relief during such calamities.

DROUGHTS

Droughts occur in nearly all climatic zones at one time or another but are found predominately in the tropics and adjoining areas. Due to the fine line between normal conditions and drought conditions, the onset of a drought is often difficult to identify and more difficult to predict. The distinction between a 'dry spell' and a drought is only the dry spell's persistence. As a disaster, it is recognized only well after it has begun. The end of a drought is easily recognizable. While most people intuitively know what a drought is, attempts at defining it are rife with controversy. What makes it controversial is that there is no standard by which one can say with certainty that a drought does or does not exist. Droughts are difficult to quantify, and different disciplines use different criteria or thresholds to define them, and even these vary from region to region. Thus, drought is a situational or perceptual phenomenon.

In developing societies like Bihar, where nearly 90 per cent of the labour force is involved in cultivation, dependent upon agriculture for employment, and the steady production of staples and industrial raw materials, drought is often used synonymously with famine, although the two are distinctly different phenomena.[3] One results in the absence of food being produced and the other the non-availability of food. One is environmental; the other is socio-economic. Absolute scarcity – insufficient food to feed everyone – is extraordinarily rare.[4]

In areas where rainfall is seasonal, agriculturalists generally adapt themselves to this cycle or the rhythm of the rains. The monsoons, through their intensity, duration, and areal extent define whether there will be normal, above normal, or below normal conditions. Too much rain, as we have seen, can cause hardship in many forms. Likewise, too little rainfall can become an inconvenience or become the ruin of areas, regions, nations, and even civilizations.[5] Conceptually, drought is a lack of rainfall so great and for so long as to adversely affect all established human activities of a given region.[6] The Indian Meteorological Department (IMD) uses a simple formula to define drought – a deficiency in the amount of rainfall in any area that is ≥ 26 per cent of its long-term norm.[7]

Within an environment that is deemed semi-tropical, continental monsoon, it is difficult to contemplate the likelihood of drought occurring anywhere in Bihar. Further, with an annual threat of flooding, drought, using the typical interpretation of the term – a lack of water – would seem almost oxymoronic. Yet, drought is a very real problem in Bihar, and particularly so in Bihar's flood-prone districts of the north.[8] History has shown that drought conditions exist almost every other year in some part of the state. However, this observation seems to contradict the findings of the IMD which suggests that between 1875 and 2004, Bihar had experienced eleven moderate droughts, no severe droughts, and has never experienced two, or more than two consecutive years of drought.[9]

In 1975, when the author was in Darbhanga, he spoke at length with the then District Magistrate (DM) about the occurrence of drought conditions in the district. The DM commented: 'At least 25-30 years of near-famine could be added to the 24 years of official famine in the district between 1869 and 1967.' And since 1975, there has been a statistical decline in the quantity of rainfall, attributed to the effects of Global Warming.

UNICEF reports that in the summer of 1966, Bihar and Eastern Uttar Pradesh experienced one of the worst droughts in the history of the region during the twentieth century, with approximately 60 million people suffering acute food and water shortages.[10] The IMD's, the DM's and UNICEF's drought assessments are not unanimous. Are their differences simply a question of definition or is it a question of governmental face saving?

Part of the problem with droughts is that there are different kinds of drought which are progressive and sequential. Typically the type and sequence of drought are:

- *Meteorological drought* – The simple absence/deficit of rainfall from the norm. It is the least severe form of drought.
- *Hydrological drought* – Meteorological drought often leads to reduction of natural stream flows or groundwater levels, plus stored water supplies. In this situation, the main impact is on water resource systems.
- *Agricultural drought* – This occurs when the moisture in the soil is insufficient to maintain average crop yields which, in the case of Bihar, are already low. Initial consequences are in the reduced seasonal output of crops and other related production. An extreme agricultural drought can lead to a famine, causing widespread disease and death from starvation.
- *Socio-economic drought* – Socio-economic drought relates to the supply and demand of goods and services associated with the three above-mentioned types of drought. When the supply of certain goods and services are curtailed by the other drought types, it often results in the shortage of still other economic goods and services.

Due to the diversity of drought types, which are based on sound physical and social scientific principles, and acknowledging the tendency of both bureaucracies and governments to play word or definitional games for the sake of appearance, is there any wonder there is no definitive answer when someone asks the simple question: How often do droughts occur? To muddle the question even further, where does one place the classification 'near drought' which can have an impact on people's lives as well?

One need only peruse the headlines of the major Indian and international newspapers and periodicals over the last decade for stories regarding Bihar's battles with catastrophic flooding and drought. Each of these stories is typically accompanied by a series of photos much like those in Plate 4.1A and B, taken from similar locations

PLATE 4.1 A & B: IMAGES OF FLOOD AND DROUGHT IN BIHAR

looking across the Kosi – one during the height of the annual flood and the second during a following 'semi-drought' period.

* * *

The monsoons arrive almost simultaneously in Bihar and Nepal, generally beginning in mid-June and last well into August and sometimes September. By the time the showers on the plains are beginning to wane, the rain that has fallen in Nepal swells the river channels as they course their way toward the Nepal-Bihar border. The river channels that have been filling with water since June can no longer contain the unrelenting volume of water and by August floods begin to take over the landscape, turning much of the floodplains into vast stretches of water as far as the eye can see, here and there dotted with tree lines, villages and huts rising above the surface of the water (see Plate 4.1A and B).

Meteorologists around the world, using sophisticated statistical models, attempt to predict the Indian Summer Monsoon Rainfall (ISMR) since it plays a vital role in the future of millions of people and India's economy, in general. Higher than anticipated rainfall portends above-average flooding. Lower than normal rainfall means the possibility of drought, crop failures, and hunger. Likewise, if the monsoons arrive late (usually arriving between 12 and 14 June) or

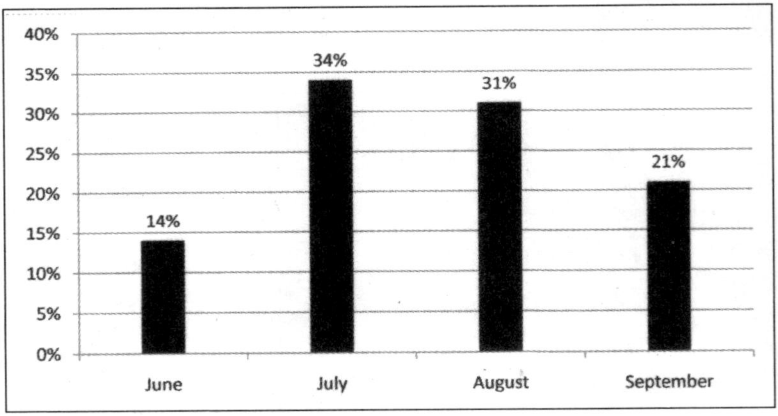

GRAPH 4.1: AVERAGE MONTHLY RAINFALL DISTRIBUTION AS PER CENT OF ANNUAL RAINFALL[11]

are scanty, the planting of certain crops must be delayed, often with serious consequences.[12] The average June rainfall in Patna is approximately 160 mm.[13]

- In 2009, the monsoons arrived in June but with rainfall deficits ranging from 31 to 60 per cent for the state.[14]
- In 2010, the monsoons deposited 172 mm of rainfall.
- In June 2011, they arrived depositing 152 mm of rainfall and there was a bumper paddy harvest.[15]
- In 2012, the monsoons arrived more than two or three weeks late, delivering only 89 mm of rainfall.
- In 2013, the monsoons arrived on 10 June, but there was a 30 per cent annual shortfall; even so, Bihar faced some of its worst floods in fifty years.[16]

Annually, rainfall totals vary throughout the state. On average, the state receives 1,140 mm, most of which falls between June and August, rapidly declining in September, with almost no rainfall from November through April. Any significant deviation from this normal pattern of rainfall, whether more or less, or early or late, typically has an impact on the subsequent harvest. This is especially true for paddy, which is less tolerant of deviations in temperature, sunlight, or rainfall amounts than many of the other staple crops, like wheat, maize, and barley. As a consequence there is an irrigation imperative.

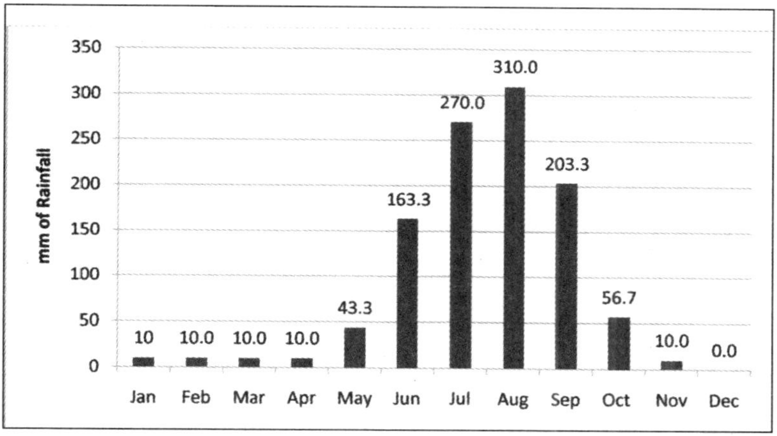

GRAPH 4.2: AVERAGE RAINFALL PATTERN FOR THREE CITIES IN BIHAR[17]

THE NEED FOR IRRIGATION

Due to the scanty rainfall from the end of the monsoons to their return the next year, many of the main rivers become little more than streams within a broad and nearly flat river channel/floodplain. For some of the embanked rivers in northern Bihar, cultivators venture out onto the floodplain between the natural levees and the man-made embankments in search of cultivable land. Those who claim the land closest to the river's diminished channel use its waters for irrigation. Those farther away or those outside the embankments have little or no chance of using gravity-fed irrigation. Thus, the cultivators must, if possible, obtain irrigation water from other, non-riverine sources.

Approximately 54 per cent of Bihar's area is currently irrigated, which is higher than the national average of 42 per cent, but its irrigation efficiency is the nation's lowest, according to R.K.P. Singh, former advisor to the Bihar State Farmers Commission.[18] It was not until comparatively inexpensive tubewells and pump-sets became available that irrigation became commonplace, especially in northern Bihar. Currently, tubewell irrigation represents 62 per cent of the total irrigated area and this is achieved using private tubewells, since 90 per cent of the government's tube wells have been abandoned or are inoperable due to lack of maintenance. Government tube wells irrigate less than 124,000 acres out of an estimated 11.86 million acres.[19]

In many other areas, canal irrigation is generally considered to be the least reliable and least expensive source of irrigation. Canal irrigation is deemed the least reliable of all sources of irrigation due to the highly seasonal nature of the water supply. During 2009-10, the state's canal irrigation system provided reliable water to less than 50 per cent of its command area. Despite increasing state expenditures on the development and maintenance of its irrigation canal systems, there has been no corresponding increase in irrigated area or improvement in the state's irrigation infrastructure. Since less than 55 per cent of the state's ground water remains unexploited for irrigation purposes, there still remains a large potential for increased irrigated area in Bihar.

While it cannot be denied that the state's system of canal irrigation is in need of much routine maintenance and repair, this is not its only problem. The reliability of canal irrigation is dependent on the monsoons. When the state's canals is most needed, the monsoons cease their delivery of water and the rivers begin to dry up. There is no source water and no water reserves to tap. Historically, in northern Bihar, the cultivators would dam small rivers and streams creating their own post-monsoon water reservoirs. This only deprived people downstream of a supply of water. Due to the uniformity and gradual gradient of the landscape, the water from these reservoirs was diverted to the adjoining fields, flowing freely from one field to the other until it was gone. No further canals or artificial water courses have been constructed. This system, however, has limited utility, as it does not serve a large area and is, therefore, very localized. Further, the earthen dams constructed by the cultivators are intended to be temporary and are washed away or cut when the last of the water has been used.

Elsewhere, well irrigation was used when the surface water supplies dried up, using simple lifting devices like the *ektha*, or using a counter-weighted bucket (*dole*) suspended from a bamboo pole, or the two-man swing basket. Some well-to-do farmers used Persian wheels, locally known as *rahats*.

Observations on Canal Irrigation

Since time immemorial gravity flow irrigation has been a central component of Indian agriculture and social history. Large-scale irrigation projects by the British began in the early years of the nineteenth century but it was not until the latter years of that century that canal irrigation systems of British India experienced their greatest expansion, with the advent of the 'Canal Colonies' of Western Punjab, in what is now Pakistan. While the construction of canal systems in the Indus Basin was new construction, the British rightly observed the utility and low cost associated with the rehabilitation of derelict and abandoned systems from earlier times.[20] Each new canal project and each canal rehabilitation project produced for the government a handsome return on its investment.

Early rehabilitation projects in the Indus and Ganga basins consistently resulted in returns of 8-10 per cent on monies invested.[21]

Robert Burton Buckley considered canal irrigation to be an excellent investment and business enterprise for the government. He wrote:

The capital cost of the works in operation of which capital accounts are kept was about 45 crores of rupees, or £30,000,000 sterling, at the end of the years 1902-1903. In that year the value of the crops irrigated by these works was about 40 crores of rupees, say, £26,000,000. Taking all the circumstances into consideration, it may be safely said that one-third of this sum – say, £9,000,000 sterling – represents the increased value of the crops due to the irrigation; for this increase in the value of the out-turn the people paid about £3,000,000 in water rates.[22]

The return the British realized was due largely to improved production on previously marginal and unproductive land; land that simply had lacked water. In areas like Bengal and Bihar, the land was already at its peak of production and investments in large-scale irrigation projects were deemed comparatively uneconomic.

The profitability of these large-scale irrigation projects continued well into the twentieth century. Then in the 1980s, researchers began to notice that these systems were increasingly underutilized and not fulfilling their intended purposes. Only a portion of the entire command area was being serviced.[23] The reason for this was poor maintenance and system management. The water was simply unavailable to those in need of it. 'The Colonial irrigation's ethos of "build-manage-generate surpluses-maintain" gave way to the "build-neglect-rebuild" syndrome of the modern Indian government.'[24]

* * *

Drawing upon the writings of Karl Wittfogel and others, it would seem that there is a direct relationship in ancient civilizations between successful, irrigated agriculture and the presence of a strong, organized and stable central government.[25] Only when government controls weaken, due to overextension or growing inefficiency, do the irrigation systems and the whole agricultural regime collapse. India's irrigation systems are falling into a state of disrepair, with per capita and overall agricultural productivity declining. Is it only a matter of time before the Government of India joins its irrigation systems and agriculture, and collapses under its ponderous inefficiencies and its inability to maintain that which it has built.

Further, in the last few decades, there has been a rapid exploitation of India's groundwater resources through the increased use of tubewells and pumpsets, thus raising questions about the relevance and efficacy of traditional canal irrigation altogether. Now, when cultivators ask for and expect on-demand irrigation capabilities year round, they are referring to tubewell irrigation.

In the Wake of Tube Wells

While canal irrigation systems have largely fallen into disrepair, cultivators have had no choice but to invest in tube wells and pumpsets to either complement canal irrigation or replace it entirely. These provide reliable and flexible sources of irrigation water from groundwater sources, as the old irrigation canal systems and the major rivers dry up due to natural water losses and over-use by upstream cultivators.

However, as the use of tubewells and pumpsets has proliferated, irreparable damage is being done to the groundwater resources inventory and the environment. Groundwater is rapidly being depleted and simultaneously contaminated and polluted. Natural replenishment/recharge has not been able to restore nor keep pace with the water being withdrawn and the water supplies and water levels have declined precipitously. This pattern was first observed and has been most profound in Punjab but the same problems and processes are at work wherever tube wells are used in lieu of surface water sources.[26]

The falling water table was first observed in Punjab in the late 1970s and early 1980s. Initially, an 18 cm fall was recorded. This increased to 42 cm during 1997-2002, and further to 75 cm during 2002-6.[27] The falling water table has forced many cultivators, who had already invested in tubewells and portable centrifugal pumpsets (either diesel or electric-powered) to deepen their wells and switch to submersible pumps since centrifugal pumps are generally incapable of lifting from depths in excess of 6.6 m.[28]

Although deemed as little more than a by-product of tubewell use, when tubewells are located just beyond the embankments, they have the effect of draining trapped, standing water, thus reducing water-logging and salinity.[29] Within this context, tube wells operate as instruments of reclamation.

Nonetheless, canals provide a number of advantages over more mechanized forms of irrigation. These include:

- They are effective, despite their dependence on gravity as the mechanism for the distribution of water.
- They generate income for the government in the form of irrigation revenues.
- Canal water is less expensive for the end user.
- They are an effective hedge against droughts.
- They help control floods.

Simultaneously, they embody certain disadvantages. These include:

- They often are responsible for problems of water-logging, increased alkalinity, and salinization of croplands, when not coordinated with adequate drainage systems.
- They lose large quantities of water to seepage and evaporation. On average, only 50 per cent of canal water reaches the fields.[30] Thus, they are inefficient transporters of a valuable resource, at best.
- The release of water into the canals is controlled by often disengaged and disinterested government officials and not by the cultivators in the fields.
- Downstream cultivators are often deprived of their 'fair share' of the canal's water supply.
- They are increasingly affected by global warming and rising temperatures and changing rainfall patterns.

As the rivers and canals prematurely dry-up and severe water shortages set in downstream, cultivators are forced to secure alternate sources of water, pushing them increasingly to invest in tube wells and pumpsets. In the end, both the surface water and groundwater supplies of irrigation water are exhausted, resulting in or leading to the desertification of the environment, and the need to drill deeper and deeper to find water.

In 2010, irrigation and livestock accounted for 91 per cent of all the water withdrawals in India and of this, canals withdrew 29 per cent, surface water tanks utilized 4 per cent, and groundwater wells withdrew 63 per cent, and of the techniques used for the control of irrigation, 97 per cent of the water extracted was used for surface irrigation.[31] Since only 10 to 20 per cent of precipitation enters the water-bearing strata or aquifers, when groundwater is withdrawn, especially during periods of drought or near-drought, the aquifers are unable to recharge.[32] In the end, the water table recedes, requiring deeper wells and more powerful pump-sets to extract it.

In a 2011 report, Shiv Kumar Tiwari, Regional Director, Minor Water Resources Department, Ground Water Directorate of the Government of Bihar announced:

> If the state receives poor rainfall this year like the past two years, the situation will be very challenging. The plunge in the water table is a result of the decline in rainfall in the past two-three years, complemented by excess extraction of shallow water for irrigation and drinking purposes. Our concern is depletion of shallow water level across the state that goes as deep as 70 ft below ground level. While we advise all individuals and agencies extracting shallow water to tap deeper levels, we have made a special request to the state government to drill deep-water tubewells in every block or district centre and distribute water through water tanks and tankers. Drinking water problems should be addressed first through these tubewells and then irrigation purposes should be served.[33]

Further, groundwater levels had already dropped in most areas, varying between one to four metres. This decline is, at least in part, explained by the combination of deficits in rainfall coupled with the rapid increase in the number of tubewells being used for agricultural irrigation purposes. Rapid groundwater development took place in Bihar powered by both policy push and private initiative. The density of tubewell and pumpsets has experienced exponential growth rates over the last two decades. Between the two minor irrigation censuses in 1986-7 and 1992-3, the pump density increased fourfold in Bihar, and has continued to increase ever since.[34] As a consequence of the rise in the number of tubewells and pumpsets, both in Bihar and all-India, some experts, including the World Bank, suggest that 60 per cent of the aquifers in India will dry up within the next 15 years.[35] Equally disturbing is the fact that 15 per cent of India's food production is dependent upon unsustainable groundwater exploitation in rain-fed or drought-prone areas. A spiralling cycle of well deepening and new, more efficient pumpset purchases has been triggered by the lowering of aquifers and water tables. This scenario is all the more disturbing when one considers that between 60 and 69 per cent of India's irrigated agriculture is dependent, almost exclusively, on groundwater.[36]

Surprisingly, the main driving force behind the increased exploitation of groundwater for irrigational purposes is not necessarily improvements in agricultural productivity or expansion into previously uncultivable or uncultivated lands but rather, the availability of electricity. The first mobile pumpsets were diesel-powered but the availability of comparatively cheap electrical power made tubewells and pumpsets the way of the future. Of the 18.50 million groundwater wells 16.43 million are in use (7.85 million dug wells, 8.10 million shallow tube wells and the rest deep tube wells). While the development of groundwater resources varies from state to state, groundwater is still available for exploitation in the eastern parts of the country – in Madhya Pradesh, Chhattisgarh, specific pockets of Andhra Pradesh, Karnataka, Maharashtra, and Jammu & Kashmir. In Punjab, Haryana, Rajasthan, Gujarat and Tamil Nadu, the exploitation exceeds the recharge rate to groundwater.

There are severe uncertainties attached to the continued exploitation of India's water resources. There is a need to produce as much as 325-350 million tonnes of food grains by 2025 to meet the food, feed, fodder and fibre requirements of the nation. To meet this demand it is assumed that the overall irrigation efficiencies will need to be in the order of 50 per cent for surface water systems and 72 per cent for groundwater systems, compared to the present levels of 35-40 per cent, and that the national average food grain production will need to increase accordingly.

In the wake of the development of large-scale irrigation facilities, several serious problems of degradation of soil, water, and environment have emerged, threatening the sustainability of India's agricultural production altogether. These include:

- Further land availability for agriculture is extremely limited.
- A total of 8.53 million hectares is subject to or already waterlogged.
- Over 22.5 million hectares have been degraded by floods, water and wind erosion.
- The per capita availability of water as a resource is expected to decline to 1,335 cu m/year by 2025.

- Indian agriculture will face stiff competition for water from other sectors. By 2025, the government plans to reduce agricultural water withdrawal to 70 per cent of total withdrawal, against 90 per cent at present.
- The nation's system of irrigation tanks has been neglected and most of them have become non-operational.
- Continued extensive pollution of water bodies both from point and non-point sources continues to affect the quality and availability of water resources, further depleting the utilizable water.

OBSERVATIONS

Due to the unique pattern of the monsoons – where more than 90 per cent of the annual rainfall occurs during the months of June through September – a period of overabundance, often resulting in flooding, is followed by a period of almost genuine aridity in Bihar. Although around 57 per cent of Bihar's gross cultivated area is irrigated, irrigation itself is crucially dependent on the monsoons, as it is largely dependant on the use of surface water.[37]

In addition, the nearly relief-less alluvial topography of northern Bihar militates against the existence of natural reservoirs for the retention and long-term storage of water for use during the 'dry season'. At one time, northern Bihar was renowned for its system of tanks, generally small earthen-walled reservoirs used to impound and store water for irrigation purposes, using channels for distribution. In addition, the term 'tank' was commonly used to describe small irrigation reservoirs along with man-made lakes. Some zamindars constructed elaborate stone tanks. Of these, few of the earthen tanks have survived. Many of the stone tanks have survived, albeit showing their age due to lack of maintenance and repair.

In the *Arthashastra,* Kautilya describes kings digging tanks, even where water for irrigation was plentiful.[38] Tanks as a source of irrigation have been commonly used for centuries. Pant and Verma find reference to the use of tanks dating back to the first and fourth centuries AD, with many still being used today.[39] In the absence of natural reservoirs for the long-term storage of water for irrigational purposes, tanks served as a reasonable man-made alternative. However, tanks for

PLATE 4.2 A, B & C: EXAMPLES OF STONE AND EARTHEN TANKS IN MITHILA

irrigation served only a very small command area. As population rose and with it, the search for additional cultivable land, tanks were unable to provide irrigation to these newly incorporated areas in terms of extent and water capacity.

The use of tanks for irrigation has declined, especially in the last seventy-five years. The primary reason for the decline in their use is that the large zamindars who constructed and maintained them, for both practical and reasons of status, are gone now. After the abolition of the zamindars, there was no government provision made for the maintenance and repair of such *ad hoc* irrigation systems. Also, a number of alternative, more efficient forms of irrigation have become available to cultivators. The increase in tubewell use, especially during the Green Revolution and thereafter, was phenomenal but not without environmental consequences. Finally, tanks have not been integrated into Bihar's overall flood and irrigation schemes. As a consequence, many tanks have fallen into disrepair, often covered with algae, clogged with water weeds, water hyacinth, and serve as little more than mosquito breeding-grounds and relics of times gone by.

* * *

Of the several sources of irrigation, it is apparent that tubewells (63 per cent), followed by canal (30 per cent) dominate the irrigation networks of Bihar, with canal irrigation showing a declining use-rate and the use of wells and ponds is negligible.[40] Throughout much of Bihar, irrigation is dependent upon tubewells, using diesel-powered pumpsets due to lack and intermittent nature of the power infrastructure in many the rural areas; this means high cost and inefficient irrigation.

Despite previous efforts, groundwater resources still remain largely under-utilized in the state. To tap the huge potential of groundwater irrigation, the Million Shallow Tube Well Programme was initiated with the intent of irrigating an additional 20 lakh hectares. About 6.97 lakh diesel tubewells and pumpsets were to be distributed by March 2007 under this programme. Farmers were given a grant of 30 per cent and a loan of 50 per cent of the total costs under the programme. To date, only 3.72 lakh private shallow tubewells have been sunk. The distribution of tubewells has been delayed by the terms of the programme itself. The programme provided for wells to be sunk to a depth of 4.5 m; however, to permit deeper wells, as needed in many areas, would require Planning Commission permission and this has not been forthcoming.[41]

In general, even though tube well irrigation has expanded in much of Bihar, in northern Bihar there was an aggregate decline in tube well irrigated area. The decline has been attributed to non-functioning state-owned deep wells.[42] P.C. Bansil reports that the majority of the state's tube wells are simply no longer operable.[43]

Further, the areas where irrigation lagged most perceptibly was in Bihar's north-west and eastern plains, while the south-west registered the greatest growth increases, with 81.14 per cent of its area irrigated, as opposed to only 45.05 per cent across northern Bihar. While the number of tube wells increased across northern Bihar, the area irrigated either stagnated or declined, which seems inconceivable.

Those areas most frequently irrigated are typically planted with food grains, representing 93.07 per cent of the total area irrigated. These included paddy, wheat, and maize, and of these grains, wheat had the highest irrigation coverage at 85.52 per cent.[44]

As in the country as a whole, the expansion of irrigation in Bihar is limited, not so much by the lack of will on the part of planners and politicians but, rather, due to the enormous backlog of deferred maintenance of the infrastructure needed to accomplish the intended ends. The backlog has in general resulted from a disproportionately large portion of the state's budget being spent on staff, personnel, flood reconstruction and relief and the government's inability to collect the agricultural and irrigation revenue year after year (see Graph 4.3).

The graph compares the irrigation revenue demand made by the Department of Water Resources, the amount of irrigation revenue collected, and the cost associated with the collection of that revenue. During each time period, the demand has risen but at the same time the gap between demand and collection has also increased, and the cost of collection has continued to rise. Irrigation revenue collections are hardly 6-7 per cent of the amount due and the cost of collection has doubled at the same time. Invariably, the Water Users Associations have not been able to collect the revenue required to maintain the

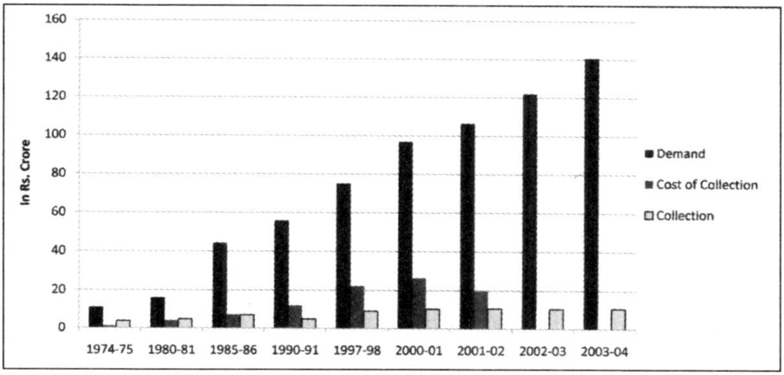

GRAPH 4.3: IRRIGATION REVENUE IN BIHAR[45]

networks and systems over which it has authority.[46] Is it any wonder that they have never been able to maintain the embankments or provide the equipment for the services demanded of it?

This lack of revenue results in a constellation of problems for the state and end-users of the state's irrigation and flood-protection systems. Among these:

- The majority of villages are electrified but the supply of electricity is erratic.
- Diesel suppliers exist but fuel availability in rural areas is often inadequate and costly.
- Most of the private tubewell drilling rigs are not registered with the State Ground Water Investigation Organization or SGWIO, especially when bank financing is involved, which requires licensed drillers.

OBSERVATIONS OF THE ENVIRONMENTAL ROOTS OF BACKWARDNESS

There are many lessons to be learned from our examination of the dominant environmental factors that have been linked to district-level backwardness:

1. Floods and droughts have been an almost perennial part of the Bihar way of life for centuries.

2. While there are always costs associated with floods or droughts, in general, the people of Bihar had lived in harmony with Nature and they understood it; and, at least the rhythm of the floods, were looked upon as a good omen, something to be celebrated.
3. It was not until population pressure on the land rose that people's views began to change with regard to their relationship with the rivers and floods. Their relationship became adversarial, not complementary.
4. Politicians exploited the frustration of the cultivators, turning them into 'victims of floods' rather than the beneficiaries of the floods; and sought to resolve the plight of the cultivators through the construction of monolithic embankments that were neither suited to the character of the rivers nor the needs of the people. As a consequence, in the case of the Kosi, it became the uncontrollable 'Sorrow of Bihar', destroying everything in its path – life and property.
5. To combat the rising frequency of drought or drought-like conditions, the people of Bihar have resorted to the use of tube well and pumpset systems of irrigation and, in so doing, they have caused what may be, in the long run, catastrophic damage to the environment by overexploiting what had been deemed an abundant groundwater resource.

The people of Bihar had developed social and economic coping mechanisms to deal with the vagaries of nature. They had adapted to their environment. It was only when they placed themselves above Nature that things began to go wrong. Combating the floods only resulted in greater losses of time, energy, life, and land; just when Man's demand on the land was growing increasingly acute due to increased population pressure. By exploiting and eliminating the *bils,* which had served as buffers against catastrophic flooding, subsequent flooding became worse.

The embankments compounded the destructiveness of the floods by raising the mean water level in the rivers and concentrating the fury of the floodwaters as they crested or breached the embankments. The flooded lands, in the absence of any mechanism for the removal of the water, either had to wait for the water to evaporate or, in the event it did not evaporate, it became waterlogged.

The people who live between the levees annually seek refuge on the embankments, elevated roadways or railroads, refugee camps, or any high ground, and receive relief assistance, returning to their inundated villages and fields after the flood waters have receded. For these people, there is no protection from floods.

When the rivers crest or breach the embankments, those who live outside the levees are flooded; their homes destroyed, their cattle die, and they too must seek relief assistance from the government.

Before the embankments, there was a type of equilibrium between the people and the rivers and the floods. The people understood them. Today, both the rivers and the floods have become unpredictable and, therefore, more dangerous.

The likelihood that the embankments will be left to decay and crumble and disappear or will be demolished, within the context of modern Bihar politics, is genuinely unlikely. The very existence and continued existence of the embankments represents a vast amount of money for the politicians, the contractors, the suppliers, and the engineers.

The embankments were ill-conceived when they were originally constructed, as was each subsequent rehabilitation. This scenario has been made all the more tenuous through the systematic lack of inspection and maintenance. Vast sums of money have been wasted on the construction of the embankments; while only worsening the effects of subsequent flooding.

In general, the Government of Bihar has failed to provide protection against floods and has failed to provide reliable and cost-effective methods of providing irrigation during the increasingly frequent incidence of post-flood drought. Precious state funds are squandered or simply disappear. When funds are dispensed, they are often used to support ineffective, ill-conceived, and poorly implemented schemes that, in the long-term, produce as many or more administrative and real problems than they solve.

While environmental problems cannot be overlooked as a contributing influence on Mithila's development, they have been in existence of centuries and the people have, in general, adapted to the natural cycle of flood and drought. Therefore, if we are looking for the roots of Mithila's backwardness, we need to look in other, uncharted directions. There is, however, another side to the contribution of the environment to Mithila's backwardness. In general, the environmental problems that the people of Bihar face have been compounded by the actions of government and the role of disruptive and divisive politics.

One, however, cannot ignore the influence or importance of the Kosi Project. The Kosi Project was begun in the mid-1950s. At about the same time Bihar began its economic downward spiral. Is this mere coincidence or is there a causal relationship at work? Tremendous amounts of money, resources, and man-hours were consumed in the construction of the embankments in Bihar. Considering the long-term effects of these embankments, could the state's monies not have been spent more productively? Did the siphoning off of these funds from the state treasury for the construction of the embankments precipitate or at least contribute to the economic downfall of Bihar? Further, the direct consequences of the construction of the embankments resulted in on-going and ever-increasing expenditures for rehabilitation, compensation payments, relief operations, and welfare payments. Each year these expenditures only increase, taking monies away from programmes that might actually improve the people's day-to-day lives, rather than simply getting them through to the beginning of the next cycle without much improvement.

NOTES

1. The distinction between food shortages, famine, and starvation is largely a function of bureaucratic interpretation and is separate from drought. Democratic governments are loathe to admit to the existence of famine conditions or starvation but are willing to acknowledge food shortages, even if those suffering perceive no substantive difference. Likewise, the line between famine and near-famine is very imprecise.
2. Amartya Sen, *Poverty and Famines: An Essay on Entitlement and Deprivation,* 16th Impression, Delhi: Oxford University Press, 1981/2011, p. 1.
3. Department of Agriculture, *Online Reporting*, 20 September 2012, http://krishi.bih.nic.in/, accessed 20 September 2012.
4. Sen, *Poverty and Famines,* p. 7, *passim.*
5. Recent archaeological and paleoclimatological research suggests that due to historical climate change, desertification spread across Egypt, the Middle East, and may have brought the downfall of the Indus Civilization. See, only as a

sampling, Chris J.D. Kostman, 'The Demise of Utopia: Contexts of Civilizational Collapse in the Bronze Age Indus Valley', *Journal of the Association of Graduates in Near Eastern Studies,* vol. 6, no. 1, Fall-Winter 1995; Fekri A. Hassan, 'Climate Change, Nile Floods and Riparia - English Translation', *Bar International Series,* vol. 2066, January 2010; Charles Choi, 'Huge Ancient Civilization's Collapse Explained', 28 May 2012, http://www.livescience.com/20614-collapse-mythical-river-civilization.html, accessed 13 September 2012; and Eddie Wrenn, *Climate Change Wiped Out One of the World's First, Great Civilizations More than 4,000 Years Ago,* 28 May 2012, http://www.dailymail.co.uk/sciencetech/article-2151143/Climate-change-wiped-worlds-great-civilisations-4-000-years-ago.html, accessed 12 September 2012.

6. Richard A. Warrick, *Drought Hazards in the United States: A Research Assessment, Monograph # 4,* Boulder: Institute of Behavioral Science, University of Colorado, 1975.
7. M.P. Shewale and Shravan Kumar, *Climatological Features of Drought Incidences in India,* Pune: India Meteorological Department, 2005, p. 4.
8. Praveen Singh, Nilanjan Ghose, Nitin Chaudhary and Regina Hansda, *Life in the Shadow of Embankments – Turning Lost Lands into Assets in the Kosi Basin of Bihar, India,* Kathmandu: International Centre for Integrated Mountain Development (ICIMOD), 2009, pp. 13 and 14 – Table 2 – Frequency of droughts between 1966/7 and 1986/7. Likewise, K.G. Parameshwarappa, *Climate Change and Perspectives for Indian Agriculture,* n.p.: IOP Conference Series: Earth and Environmental Science 6: Climate Change: Global Risks, Challenges and Decisions, 2009, suggests that northern Bihar has the second highest probability of experiencing drought conditions – a 30-40 per cent probability every year (p. 2, Figure 2). The remainder of the state has an even higher probability – 40-50 per cent.
9. M.P. Shewale and Shravan Kumar, *Climatological Features of Drought Incidences in India,* 2005, p. 15, Table 2 and pp. 18-19, Table 5.
10. UNICEF, Bihar *Drought,* n.d., http://www.unicef.org/india/media_2645.htm, accessed 13 September 2012.
11. 'After Angel Commodities', *Monsoon Report,* June 2013.
12. The monsoon is considered normal if the rainfall is between 96 per cent and 104 per cent of the long-period average (50-year average) of 98 cm in the four months monsoon period beginning 1 June, Angel Commodities, *Monsoon Report.*, Mumbai: Angel Commodities Brokering, June 2013, p. 3.
13. IMD & WMO, *Average Rainfall for India in June,* India Meteorological Department and World Meteorological Organization, http://www.currentresults.com/Weather/India/precipitation-june.php, Average Rainfall for India in June.

14. 'Bihar: Fear of Drought Looms Large', *India Today*, 3 July 2012, http://indiatoday.intoday.in/story/bihar-drought-monsoon/1/203520.html, accessed 12 September 2012. See, also, *Krishibhoomi*, 'Drought Situation to Emerge in Bihar with Delayed Monsoons', 4 July 2012, http://www.krishibhoomi.in/detailnews.aspx?Dept=weatherwatch&SID=41, accessed 8 September 2012.
15. 'Bihar: Fear of Drought Looms Large', *India Today*, 3 July 2012.
16. Cordaid, *Bihar Floods 2013,* December 2013, http://www.cordaid.org/.en/projects/bihar-floods-2013/110243/; and The Extinction Protocol, *Northern India Hit by Worst Flooding in 50 years: 100 Villages Swamped in Bihar,* 12 July 2013, http://theextinctionprotocol.wordpress.com/2013/07/12/northern-india-hit-by-worst-flooding-in-50-years-100-villages-swamped-in-bihar/.
17. Data based on average precipitation for Patna, Arrah, and Darbhanga, Bihar, Wikipedia, *Climate of Bihar,* 20 June 2012.
18. R.K.P. Singh, *Changing Face of Agriculture in Bihar,* 11 August 2011, http://www.bihartimes.in/articles/RKP/Agriculture.html, accessed 14 September 2012.
19. Ibid.
20. Tushaar Shah, *Past, Present and the Future of Canal Irrigation in India,* Colombo: International Water Management Institute, 2011, pp. 2-3.
21. Elizabeth Whitcombe, 'Irrigation', vol. 2, in *The Cambridge Economic History of India, c. 1757-1970,* ed. K. Kumar and M. Desai, pp. 677-737, Hyderabad: Orient Longman, 2005.
22. Robert Burton Buckley, *The Irrigation Works of India*, London: E. & F.N. Spon, 1905, p. 318.
23. S.R. Daines and J.R. Pawar, *Economic Returns to Irrigation in India: A Report Prepared for the U.S. Agency for International Development Mission to India,* New Delhi: SDR Research Groups Inc. & Development Group Inc., 1987.
24. Shah, *Past, Present and the Future of Canal Irrigation in India,* p. 8.
25. Karl Wittfogel, *Oriental Despotism: A Comparative Study of Total Power,* New York: Vintage Books, 1981; Robert McCormick Adams, *The Evolution of Urban Society: Early Mesopotamia and Prehispanic Mexico,* New Brunswick: Aldine Transactions, 2005; and Thorkild Jacobsen, *The Treasures of Darkness: A History of Mesopotamian Religion,* New Haven: Yale University Press, 1978. See also, William Hardy McNeill, *The Rise of the West: A History of the Human Community,* Chicago: University of Chicago Press, 1963/1991.
26. For example, Priya Yadav, 'Ground Water Level Declining, Contamination Rising in Punjab', 29 June 2012, http://articles.timesofindia.indiatimes.com/2012-06-29/india/32472235_1_ground-water-nitrate-water-table, accessed 17 September 2012; R.S. Sidhu and Kamal Vatta, *Degradation and Management of Groundwater Resources in Indian Punjab,* Ludhiana:

Department of Economics and Sociology, Punjab Agricultural University, 2010; Gagan Ramoo, 'Punjab: Declining Water Table Reduce Area Under Paddy, Water Board Tells Govt', 25 February 2012, http://agrariancrisis.in/2012/02/25/punjab-declining-water-table-reduce-area-under-paddy-water-board-tells-govt/, accessed 17 September 2012; K. Singh, 'Water Table Behaviour in Punjab: Issues and Policy Options'. Conference Paper, no. h042912 International Water Management Institute, 2008, http://ideas.repec.org/p/iwt/conppr/h042912.html; http://publications.iwmi.org/pdf/H042912.pdf, accessed 12 September 2012; A.K. Jain and Raj Kumar, *Water Management Issues: Punjab,* Ludhiana: Punjab Agricultural University, 2009; GoI Monitor Desk, 'Watering the Future Disaster', 25 August 2012, http://www.goimonitor.com/story/watering-future-disaster, accessed 17 September 2012; Sheetal Sekhri, *Sustaining Groundwater: Role of Policy Reforms in Promoting Conservation in India,* Washington, DC: National Council of Applied Economic Research, Indian Policy Forum 2012 - Brookings Institution, 2012; and Sudhir-Yadav et al., 'Water Balance in Dry Seeded and Puddle Transplanted Rice in Punjab, India', *Soil Solutions for a Changing World.* Brisbane: 19th World Congress of Social Science, 2010, pp. 43-6. See also, Ministry of Water Resources, *Ground Water Resources Estimation Methodology,* New Delhi: Government of India, Ground Water Resource Estimation Committee, 2009.

27. G.S. Hira, S.K. Jalota and V.K. Arora, *Efficient Management of Water Resources for Sustainable Cropping in Punjab,* Ludhiana: Department of Soils, Punjab Agricultural University, 2004; and Karan Singh, *Fall in Water Table in Central Punjab: How Serious,* Chandigarh: The Punjab State Farmers Commission, Government of Punjab, 2006.
28. See, H.S. Sidhu, 'Production Conditions in Contemporary Punjab Agriculture', *Journal of Punjab Studies,* vol. 112, no. 2, Fall 2005, pp. 206-7. See, also, Shri Suryawanshi, Raj Bhasha and Sanjay Swarup, *Principles of Pumps and Pumping Installation,* Nasik: Institution of Railway Electrical Engineers, 2010, p. 23.
29. Syed Mohammad Bilal and Tahir Sarwar, 'Effect of Tube Well Drainage on Water Logging and Salinity in Kafur Dheri Unit Pesawar', *Sarhad Journal of Agriculture,* vol. 24, no. 1, 2008, p. 48; M.A. Kahlown, M. Iqbal, G.V. Skogerboe and S. Rehman, *Waterlogging, Salinity and Crop Yield Relationships,* Mona Reclamation Experimental Project; International Irrigation Management Institute, 1998; V.S. Kale, 'Flood Studies in India: A Brief Review', *Journal of the Geological Society of India,* vol. 49, no. 4, 1997; and Bakhshal Khan Lashari and Shafi Mohammad Kori, 'Drainage Scavenger Tube Wells Can Sustain Rural Livelihoods: Evidence from Sindh Pakistan', *Proceedings of IWRM2010,* Nanjing: IAHS, 2010.
30. Geosynthetic Materials Association. *Geosynthetics,* 2012, http://

geosyntheticsmagazine.com/articles/wp5_canal.html, accessed 18 September 2012; and C. Brouwer and K. Prins, *Training Manual No. 4: Irrigation Water Management: Irrigation Scheduling,* Rome: Food and Agricultural Organization of the United Nations, 1989, Annex 1: Irrigation Efficiencies. In some areas, evaporation rates can exceed local rainfall, resulting in what is termed 'water deficiency' – a deficiency which can be temporary, lasting only a month or two, a year, or permanent. In addition to surface evaporation and seepage, canal water is lost to percolation, overtopping of bunds, bund breaches, run-off and rat holes in the canal bunds. As Brouwer and Prins state: '. . . bad maintenance may lower the [conveyance efficiency] values by as much as 50%.' Thus, depending on the soil type of the earthen canals, conveyance efficiencies could decline to as little as 30 or 40 per cent based solely on the level of maintenance.

31. Avanish K. Panikkar (Content Source: FAO), *Water Profile of India,* 19 March 2012, http://www.eoearth.org/article/Water_profile_of_India, accessed 18 September 2012.
32. Ministry of Environment & Forests, Government of India, 'Status of Surface and Groundwater in Bihar', 2014. http://bhenvis.nic.in/intro_water.html, Groundwater.
33. Piyush Kumar Tripathi and Khwaja Jamal, 'Groundwater Crisis Runs Deep', 26 March 2011, http://www.telegraphindia.com/1110326/jsp/bihar/story_13743985.jsp.
34. See, Avinash Kishore, 'Understanding Agrarian Impasse in Bihar', *Economic and Political Weekly*, vol. 39, no. 31, July 2004, p. 3485. In 1975, when the author did his dissertation research in Darbhanga district, he never saw a pumpset being used in any of the villages he worked in. At the time, many villages had no electricity and no in-coming electric lines or phones, and some were approachable only via well-worn trails, not even approaching the status of a road. To get to one isolated village, due to the lack of roads and bridges over the labyrinth of streams and rivulets, the author hired an elephant for transport.
35. Ajith Athrady, 'India's Ground Water Table to Dry up in 15 Years', 10 March 2014, http://www.deccanherald.com/content/56673/indias-ground-water-table-dry.html; and World Bank, *Deep Wells and Prudence: Towards Pragmatic Action for Addressing Groundwater Overexploitation in India,* Washington, D.C.: The International Bank for Reconstruction and Development/The World Bank, 2010.
36. World Bank, *Deep Wells and Prudence: Towards Pragmatic Action for Addressing Groundwater Overexploitation in India*, 2010, pp. 1 and 5; and World Bank, *India's Water Economy: Bracing for a Turbulent Future,* Washington, DC: The International Bank for Reconstruction and Development/The World Bank, 2005.

37. Bihar Agricultural Management and Extension Training Institute, 'Status of Agriculture in Bihar', in *Bihar State Profile*, by Bemati.Org, Government of Bihar, 2008, p. 13.
38. See, R.P. Kangle, *The Kautiliya Arthasastra,* vol. II, 3 vols., Delhi: Motilal Banarsidass, 2010 (7th rpt.), 2. 1. 20-25, p. 57, and associated footnotes.
39. Niranjan Pant and R.K. Verma, *Tanks in Eastern India: A Study in Exploration,* Hyderabad and Lucknow: IWMI-Tata Policy Research Program and Centre for Development Studies, 2010, p. 3. See, also, Ruth Suseela Meinzen-Dick, *Local Management of Tank Irrigation in South India: Organization and Operation,* Ithaca: Cornell University - Cornell Studies in Irrigation, no. 3, 1984.
40. Bihar Agricultural Management and Extension Training Institute, 'Status of Agriculture in Bihar', in *Bihar State Profile*, 2008, p. 23.
41. P.C. Bansil, *Bihar Agriculture: A Perspective,* Delhi: Concept Publishing, 2011, p. 108.
42. T.N. Jha and K.U. Viswanathan, *Problems and Prospects of Agricultural Development in Bihar: Occasional Paper – 10,* Mumbai: National Bank for Agriculture and Rural Development, 1999, p. 149.
43. Bansil, *Bihar Agriculture: A Perspective,* 2011, p. 110.
44. Ibid., p. 156.
45. Data from P.C. Bansil, ibid., 2011, p. 112, Table 14.3, constructed using data from the director of Revenue, Department of Water Resources, Government of Bihar.
46. Of the 12 states with WUAs, listed by K. Palanisami and P. Paramasivam, *Irrigation Sector in India: Trends, Issues, and Prospects,* Coimbatore: Tamil Nadu Agricultural University, 2007, computer script, Bihar is the only state with but one WUA. After Bihar, the number of WUAs range from 30 (Assam) to 10,000 (West Bengal). See, also, M. Venkata Reddy, 'User Organizations as a Demand Management Option: Potentials, Problems, and Prospects', chapter 7, in *Strategic Analyses of the National River Linking Project (NRLP) of India, Series 3 – Promoting Irrigation Demand Management in India; Potentials, Problems and Prospects,* ed. Rathinasamy Maria Saleth, pp. 147-70. Colombo: International Water Management Institute, 2009, p. 153.

CHAPTER 5

Orientalism and India's Gordian Knot: Religion, Secularism and Caste

In an age where change, innovation, and technological advances are measured not in decades or years, but in months and, sometimes, in weeks or days, it seems almost incongruous to be discussing processes and practices that took millennia or centuries to emerge full-formed, or have been handed down, largely intact, for thousands of years. The history of India is far more intimately woven into the fabric of Indian society than its counterparts in Western Europe or the New World. Unlike most Western societies which have thrived on secularism, religion, the philosophy of religion, religious practices, religious influences, and social institutions originating in religion are often inseparable in day-to-day life in India. As 'modern' as India has become over the last two decades, it has not, cannot, and should not ignore its rich historical roots, nor sequester it in the name of secularism or modernity.

Westerners are typically, and at least initially, reduced to a state of total incomprehension when they arrive in India for the first time. There is nothing that can adequately prepare them for the multitude of incongruities that greet them. The sights, sounds, smells, and tastes encountered have few counterparts in the West.[1] One can intellectualize the poverty but it is impossible to prepare oneself for the absolute, abject differences between the Haves and Have-nots of India, or the differences in lifestyles and developmental disparities between urban and rural India. Yet, every sight, sound, smell, and taste is part of the tapestry that makes India so unique and intriguing.

* * *

Measuring levels of development or backwardness is much like measuring poverty. Most people have an inherent sense of what it means to be poor or underdeveloped; however, choosing a definition for either is a very 'tricky' matter. Are they an absolute or relative condition? What represents a acceptable standard of living? These questions have dogged social scientists and development agencies for over half a century.

There is probably no single definition that can adequately convey all the permutations of poverty, underdevelopment, or backwardness. It is different in each country and regionally different within countries. The United Nations has adopted several indices for the measurement of poverty and levels of development, changing from purely economic measures like GDP or an income of '*x* dollars per day' to Human Development Indices and more recently adding the Oxford Multi-dimensional Poverty Index.

While it is agreed that underdevelopment or backwardness is most often seen as an economic condition, i.e. poverty, the causes of poverty may not be economic in origin. This is why measures of under-development and poverty have shifted to definitions and measures based on human development. Poverty and backwardness are social conditions in the spirit of Amartya Sen's concept of entitlement.[2] Therefore, we need to look to social institutions and practices that produce, promote, or result in backwardness.

In this chapter we will explore the veracity of Western scholarship regarding 'the Orient', the role of religion in development, the role of secularism in the development process, the importance of caste, and the role of tradition, or Vedic Overhang (social inertia) in sustaining or perpetuating backwardness in Bihar and Mithila.

ORIENTALISM

Orientalism began with the first on-foot explorer to make his way eastward beyond that imaginary line that separates the East from the West, Asia from Europe. We will never know who he was but many were to follow, all the way through antiquity. Long-distance trade, since time immemorial, has played an important role in cultural, religious, and artistic exchanges.[3] Many of these early trade routes had existed possibly for millennia.

The trade routes served principally to transfer raw materials, foodstuffs, and luxury goods from areas with surpluses to others where they were in short supply. Some areas had a monopoly on certain materials or goods. China, for example, supplied West Asia and the Mediterranean with silk, while spices were obtained principally from South and South-East Asia.[4] These goods were transported over vast distances – either by pack animals overland or by seagoing vessels – along the Silk and Spice Routes. This long-distance trade was generally carried on in segmented and discrete intervals by numerous caravaners and merchants, much like the links of a very long chain. The cost and value of the goods increased as they were handled by successive middlemen and subjected to taxation and tolls while in transit. Only occasionally would one person make the entire trip East-to-West or West-to-East, and even fewer ever returned home. These trade routes served as communications highways, carrying new inventions, religious beliefs, art, languages and social customs, along with exotic goods and raw materials.

While Indian travellers travelled extensively, seeking or teaching the paths of enlightenment or simply satisfying individual wanderlust in Asia and Africa, the first Indian travellers to venture to Europe came in the seventeenth century, with most sailing to Britain aboard English ships. During the first two hundred and fifty years of British Oriental trade, beginning in the early seventeenth century, some 20,000-40,000 Indian men and women of all social classes made this voyage. Some settled, usually marrying into British society; others returned with their personal accounts of the West that they recounted to their relatives, friends, and acquaintances.[5]

Orientalism, as the formal study of the 'Orient', began in earnest with the earliest British traders of the East India Company. For purely practical reasons, the study of indigenous languages, especially Persian, was deemed essential to the fulfilment of the Company's commercial objectives. Many, for personal reasons and simple curiosity, sought to understand the land, the people, the languages, the cultures, the philosophy and religions of India; not as an adjuncts to or a tool of administration but to understand and appreciate that which was so 'foreign' when compared to their own, staid, common English backgrounds. These early 'Orientalists' were frequently simply the collectors of information that also served their commercial interests.

Somewhat later, Orientalism took on a new and more disciplined and academic demeanour. Among this new breed of Orientalists were Charles Wilkens, who translated the *Bhagavad Gita* in 1785; William Jones, who translated the *Gītagovinda* and the *Īśa Upanishad.* Alexander Dow translated several historical works from the Persian. These and others, like Henry Thomas Colebrooke and Samuel Davis, who Warren Hastings referred to as 'bright young men', paved the way for the establishment of the Asiatic Society (of Bengal). The Company, directly or indirectly supported the work of the Society but only as a repository of knowledge. Only later was its support used to subvert the otherwise purely scholarly pursuits of the Society and its members. Will Sweetman correctly points out that, in general, even now, it is still far too early to categorically condemn eighteenth-century Orientalism in India under the aegis of the East India Company.[6]

The work of these 'amateur' scholars, most of whom were indeed servants or officers in service of the Company, paved the way for the great European Orientalists of the nineteenth century – Eugene Burnouf, Max Müller, Paul Deussen – and the dissemination of Eastern philosophy and metaphysics among German and American scholars; and the work of Jones, Wilkens, Colebrooke, and others has continued in an unbroken line into our own time.

The history of Orientalism has always been convoluted, full of ambiguities and contradictions. Without question, Edward Said's celebrated treatise, *Orientalism*, has forced modern Orientalists everywhere to seriously re-evaluate their research, especially as it pertains to cultural bias and the very legitimacy of Orientalism in the West. It has also provided fuel for much of the current geopolitical state of affairs between the West and militant Islamic factions throughout the world.[7]

If the work of the early British Orientalists were as corrupted by Western preconceptions as suggested by Said, why has their work endured? The obvious answer is because it was and continues to represent good scholarship. It was not flawless, to be sure but, then, no original research ever is.

Orientalism, as the recognition of differences between 'the West' and 'the Orient', has always represented, whether intellectually stated or as a simple unconscious thought, the institutionalization of a dichotomy between 'us' and 'them'. Admittedly, that simple distinction is founded to a certain degree on racism. Masoud Kamali boldly pointed out: 'Thinking racially has been an inseparable part of the Enlightenment's philosophy and science.'[8] Currently, this discriminatory and militant view of Orientalism, especially as it relates to Islam, has come to overshadow the early efforts of Orientalists in India although recent scholarship has set about defending Orientalism by exposing the ideological bias in Said's own work.[9]

Said's work is largely an indictment of Orientalism based on the assumption that it represents a racially motivated typology used by Westerners to differentiate themselves from 'those of the Orient'. He suggests that the Orient – essentially Islamic – has been typically described as less developed, less civilized, and less rational than the Occident. Admittedly, many Western writers pitted the Enlightenment's preoccupation with rationality and democracy against the achievements of the Orient.[10] In so doing, the West created an imaginary world it simply called 'the Orient'. This world represented either a conscious or unconscious fantasy filtered by Western fears and desires but not reality. This vision or version of the Orient is justifiably subject to criticism. However, the current preoccupation with European or Western ethnocentrism ignores the efforts of many amateur and professional scholars who remained faithful and objective.

The current militancy and controversy surrounding the form and function of Orientalism has become equally as myopic as that of the imperialists who expropriated it for colonial purposes in the eighteenth and nineteenth centuries. As Rosane Rocher has pointed out, Said and others have conveniently ignored the contributions of German scholars and scholarship during much of the nineteenth and twentieth centuries, when Germany was the centre of Indological studies.[11]

Since the publication of Said's book, no one dares to call himself (or herself) an Orientalist since the word has acquired such negative connotations.[12] Now, more than thirty-five years after its original publication, those interested in Asia or Africa as areas of research continue to look furtively over their shoulder, afraid to offend the academic watchmen, the arbiters of academic correctness. More recently, the pendulum has finally begun to swing back to a more even-handed assessment of Western Oriental scholarship. No longer are Western academics automatically subject to the derisive scrutiny of Oriental scholars as being soulless and spiritually inert creatures, a position Western scholars were relegated to immediately following the publication of *Orientalism*. And yet, some writers like Buruma and Margalit continue to characterize the Western mind-set as follows:

> . . . a kind of higher idiocy. To be equipped with the mind of the West is like being an idiot savant, mentally defective but with a special gift for making arithmetic calculations. It is a mind without a soul, efficient, like a calculator, but hopeless at doing what is humanly important. The mind of the West is capable of great economic success, to be sure, and of developing and promoting advanced technology, but cannot grasp the higher things in life, for it lacks spirituality and understanding of human suffering.[13]

This characterization (possibly more an attack on America than on Europe) is just as racially scandalous and judgmental as that levelled against the British Orientalists of the eighteenth and nineteenth centuries. This new 'Occidentalism', the reverse of Orientalism, portrays the Western mind as sterile, all reason and no soul, self-absorbed, and compassionless, versus the far more spiritual and compassionate mind of the Orient. Both views are cultural fantasies and objectively laughable. In fact, the pendulum may be swinging in the other direction, forcing Asian scholars to take a serious look at their own biases and historical revisionism.

Admittedly, there was both a use and misuse of Oriental research by colonial governments but this, in and of itself, does not negate the contributions such scholarship has made. What is missing in the current condemnation of Orientalism is a fair and even evaluation of (a) what inherent value was there in the original research; and (b) how, if, and why was this research compromised by colonial governments? As with almost any innovation, governments tend to evaluate it first for its military value or potential.[14] The same can be said for all information placed in the hands of government; the first unconscious question is: how can it be used to achieve our goals? Knowledge almost always becomes a tool for the improved and efficient pursuit of government's ends, exploitation, or domination. One need only look to the growing controversy over governments' electronic surveillance of their citizens as the 'logical extension' of this process.[15] There is no reason to believe that the findings of the Orientalists would be treated as somehow sacrosanct and therefore ignored by any colonial or non-colonial government, then or now.

In the beginning, the servants of the East India Company did not see themselves as imperialists. They saw themselves as simply commercial traders. The ideas of imperialism and colonialism were simply not yet formulated nor recognized, despite the fact that the Company was already well on its way to becoming a colonial power. The men of the Company simply were not yet thinking in terms of Kipling's 'White Man's Burden'.[16]

Orientalism developed two very different dimensions, one based on European ethnocentrism and the other as the objective study of Oriental history, culture, and literature. Ethnocentric Orientalism emerged during the Enlightenment and European colonization of Asia and provided a rationalization for colonialism based on a self-serving history in which 'the West' constructed 'the East' as different and inferior, and therefore in need of Western intervention, improvement, or upliftment.[17] In part, it could be suggested that 'the West' came to see itself as much more than a geographical location. It distorted and recreated Asian history and, in so doing, served to modify the Asian cultures it touched, while, at the same time, further altering the European conception of the East. Even legitimate scholarship in the hands of politicians and administrators was misused, as the relationship and influence of 'knowledge' and 'power' served the British colonial interests in India and elsewhere.

The difficulty with objectively examining or evaluating Orientalism stems from the overlapping and interwoven nature of its two variations and the premise upon which each drew its strength. Neither completely absorbed the other but each served to feed, fuel, and influence it. The more that was learned through the serious, objective, intellectual study of the Orient, the more the felt need to change it grew. It was the 'exotic' Orient's 'sinister' and 'threatening' image, its 'splendour', 'sensuality', 'cunning', 'cruelty', 'despotism', and 'mysticism' that spawned the desire to somehow change it for the better.

Coming as explorers and traders, the West's subsequent exploitation and expropriation – the result of the West's perception of the people of the East as being somehow inferior – permitted the West's self-aggrandizement and legitimized its rule. The West came 'armed with gun-and-gospel' and successfully imposed its religions, values, legal and political systems on the East; all the while, either oblivious to or insensitive and indifferent to indigenous social and cultural traditions.[18]

Even in those areas where the East was perceived as far in advance of the West – in the realms of philosophy – there was still an otherness, a strangeness that was attached to it, and to a certain degree, along with this envy and awe, there was fear. In part, the East opened the eyes of the West to an alternate vision of the world, far beyond simple 'rational', national and ideological differences which were immediately evident. This, too, unnerved the West. To 'feel comfortable' with the East, the best strategy, whether consciously or unconsciously conceived, was to change it. The pressure to change and be changed, to a certain degree, has only increased with the globalization of the world culture and economy; and yet, the West continues to go Eastwards as a 'pilgrim in sackcloth and ashes, anxious to prostrate himself at the guru's feet'.[19]

While the West's views of the East may have been clouded by fantasy and misunderstanding, at the same time it astonished generations of scholars and laymen alike, who sought insight and inspiration. In large measure, this phenomenon stems from the very thing that makes the West what it is vis-à-vis the East – self-questioning and self-critical.[20] However, this does not assuage the inherent racism that underlay the consequences of imperialism and colonialism in Asia; a legacy that has not been eliminated by the act of colonial independence. Racism, in its various forms, continues in political interactions and the media today, and can be seen, especially in Africa, in the form of modern, post-colonial national boundaries.[21]

Differentiating between the objectives of Orientalism has only served to muddy the waters, with the result that post-colonial academic Orientalism has incurred intense scrutiny and criticism, and it might be added, not unjustifiably so. Further, everyone who has studied 'the Orient', has done so based on the initial premise that the 'Orient' and the 'West' were somehow mutually exclusive and axiomatically 'different'. In this regard, the author believes Edward Said and other similar critics are undoubtedly correct. In the final analysis, no matter how lofty and 'correct' the philosophical, religious, or spiritual content of the East or the integrity of the Orientalist, the relationship between the Orient and the West has always been one of raw power and domination.

Even today, Said's *Orientalism* continues and only serves to undermine the legitimacy of Western 'Oriental' scholarship and has resulted in a radical shift in our understanding and the meaning of the term. Said took Michel Foucault's concept of power-knowledge and Antonio Gramsci's concept of cultural hegemony to develop a new framework. For Said, knowledge of the Orient, even if intended originally as scholarship, was knowledge meant to serve the colonial power structure.[22] Gramsci's conception of cultural hegemony suggests that every authority ultimately seeks to exchange coercion for intellectual or moral legitimacy, thus giving the oppressor (colonial authority) greater social and political stability.[23] According to Said, Orientalism was used to establish hegemony over the Orient whereby the Europeans appropriated for themselves the authority to make any pronouncements on the Orient and deemed Orientalist knowledge as natural and self-evident truth. Using this formulation or extrapolation of history, Said was able to argue that any comment, statement, or finding by any Western observer, regarding the Orient, was simply a self-serving Western construction, or non-reality, to be used by the colonial state. Even the works of eighteenth century 'Oriental scholars or writers' like Henry Thomas Colbrooke, G.W.F. Hegel, Gustave Flaubert, Charles Wilkens, or William Jones, were thus viewed as simply colonial tracts.

Said's themes, although focused on the West's interactions with the Middle East and Islam, have been extended by other writers to the Oriental literature of India and has been picked up by Indian writers. For example, Gyan Prakash argues that Orientalism was, from the beginning, an English enterprise dedicated to the objectification of the Indian people making them simply objects of knowledge.[24] In so doing, such 'scholarship' provided a justification for colonial domination. This aspect of Indian Orientalism, however, seems more driven by ideology. Thus, both the critic and the criticism are hoist with their own petard.

There are no (or at least very few) academic saints. If they are human, they are inherently flawed. However, good academics are generally responsible and frequently examine their own work for bias.

Or, they clearly acknowledge their ideological bias. To this is added the peer-review process. Together, self-assessment and peer-review winnow out much of the unintentional or unacceptable bias in books and journal articles, or at least that is what it is supposed to happen; and, in general, Western scholarship has been reasonably objective. But, if cultural bias resides at a subconscious level, even self-assessment and peer-review might not be enough to eliminate it. From this standpoint, one has to at least entertain Said's arguments.

If the underlying intent of *Orientalism* was to serve as a tool of propaganda or to distract Western academic research away from the further exploration of Arab-Western or Islamic-Western conflicts, whether ideological, religious, or political, it has been successful. By politicizing Orientalism, by making any discussion of differences of culture, philosophy, or religion politically incorrect, especially between the West and the Islamic world community, any comments made by Western observers or scholars can be immediately labelled as axiomatically racist and are therefore automatically discreditable. Such positioning or posturing, especially within the realm of international statesmanship and diplomacy gives the East and Islam a commanding advantage.

It has also tended to cause many Western scholars to second-guess every conclusion and statement, for fear of falling prey to Said's well-laid racial trap. There is no doubt that Said's arguments are both suggestive and, more often than not, superficially correct; but to condemn all Oriental research by Western scholars is unfair and equally racist.

As Anirudh Raghavan states: 'Said and others who have followed a similar argument seem to have fallen prey to the same essentialism that they accuse Orientalists of. They could in some ways be called "Orientalists-in-reverse" as they present the West as unified, constant throughout history and incapable of producing any true knowledge about the Orient.'[25]

Said's denunciation of Orientalism ignores the scholarly work undertaken by the non-colonial nations of Western Europe and, in particular Germany, Austria-Hungary, and the countries of Eastern Europe, e.g. Czechoslovakia, Russia, etc. German scholars showed particular interest in Indian linguistics; for example, one need only examine the work of Max Müller. Likewise, Wilhelm von Humboldt, Max Weber, and Jürgen Habermas wrote extensively on India. However, at no time did the Germans have imperial designs on India and only later did they even take part in the colonial process in Africa, which was late coming and from which they exited early.[26]

Western, European depictions of 'the Orient' prior to the establishment of British colonial rule simply do not contain the causal connections between colonial power and Oriental scholarship that are required to satisfy Said's premise. Said's generalizations are simply invalid when extended backward into much of the seventeenth and eighteenth centuries and possibly the early nineteenth century, especially when applied to India. Awe and appreciation of non-Western systems of culture, language, philosophy, literature and religion cannot and should not be confused with colonial intent or administration. Where one ends and the other begins is the role of further historiographical research.

RELIGION

Richard King suggests that religion and the history of religion are bound together with the cultural and intellectual history of every culture and ultimately is simply the study of history. Even the term 'religion' bows to this assertion, being derived from the Latin *religio* which is a derivative of the word *relegere* – to re-trace or re-read. Thus, religion involves retracing the ritual lore or practices of one's ancestors or the ancestors of others.[27] As understood and conceived by the Romans, religion represented the study of traditions, the performance of rituals, and paying homage to the gods; and the recognition that people have different cultural and ethnic origins, therefore, religion was pluralistic – it encompassed a broad range of religious practices. As thus conceived, there could never be only one religion. S.N. Balagangadhara states:

> When you look at religion as tradition, that is, as a set of practices transmitted over generations, then the term appears as a minor variation of our intuitive notion of culture: to have religion is to have culture. . . . Tolerance of different traditions, 'respect' for tradition demonstrated actually by practising the tradition of the other where and when necessary, appear to characterize the Roman religion.[28]

This early interpretation of religion was later challenged and gave way to the political, exclusionary needs of Roman leadership. Lactantius, an early Christian writer and rhetorician, successfully argued that *religio* was derived from *re-ligare*, meaning to bind together or link. This allowed Romans to reject the all-inclusive nature of *religio* and substituted a system of worship that permitted, even mandated, the rejection of all but the one and true religion of the Romans.[29] Thus, early religious tolerance among the Romans was replaced by intolerance and sectarianism. Thereafter, each 'religion' was empowered to reject the rituals and practices of those who did not conform to the accepted and institutionalized beliefs and practices of the predominant religion, creating rivalries and domains of influence for the dominant and more successful religions.

This conceptualization of religion reinforced the idea, among the major, universal, proselytizing religions of the world, especially Christianity and Islam, that there is 'only one way' to achieve salvation. Not only does this principle operate between religious faiths but also between sects within these faiths. The irony of active, often coercive proselytism in today's world is that it violates the United Nations Declaration of Human Rights, Article 18: 'Everyone has the right to freedom of thought, conscience and religion; this right includes freedom to change his religion or belief, and freedom, either alone or in community with others and in public or private, to manifest his religion or belief in teaching, practice, worship and observance.'

In the West, the rise of Christianity as the true religion, even with its various sects, permitted and reinforced the monotheistic and exclusionary nature of religion; and Christianity became the normative paradigm for the understanding of what a religion was, and more importantly, what it should be. Western pagan traditions gave way to religions that possessed sacred texts and the importance of their proper interpretation by a trained clergy. Religion became increasingly concerned with doctrine based on accepted beliefs (orthodoxy) and exclusionary, which then became the new tradition.

What differentiated Western religion from paganism or other religions of the world was the Western preoccupation with historical authenticity based on a system of reinforcing belief(s). For Christianity, the message must be believable but need not necessarily be true -- the truth of the message is more important than reality. It is this system of beliefs that permits the existence of 'miracles' within the sacred texts. They reinforce and illustrate the message but are dependent upon faith for their believability.

As a consequence of the economic and industrial success of the West, Christianity, in its various forms, became the prototypical form by which all other religions were judged. Further, at least in the eyes of Westerners, Christianity bore the mark of a 'rational', common-sense approach to the divine. It was this system of thought the British brought with them to India and served as the intellectual basis for subsequent scholarly research into Eastern religions and practices.

Due to historical circumstances, a 'text-oriented' approach to both education, knowledge, and religion developed in the West. The first mass-produced book in the West was the Bible, thus making the Scriptures available to all who could read. In turn, this stimulated the demand for rudimentary education to give the ordinary citizen access to the Scriptures, which further stimulated the production of still more books to fulfil the demand for 'reading material'. As a consequence, a comparatively highly literate culture developed in the West, and has become an identifiable component of nearly all 'developed' nations.

The reliance on the Scriptures in the West is all the more prophetic when one considers that of the thousands of human languages spoken throughout the world and throughout history, only 106 have ever developed what might be termed a literary tradition.[30] This has resulted in what could be called a literary bias when it comes to notions regarding religion and it is, at least initially, through 'texts' that the West has come to know its own religions and those religions and philosophies of the East, rather than firsthand, direct, personal exposure.[31] Illustrative of this phenomenon is the cyclic, generation-by-generation 'rediscovery' of the *Bhagavad Gita* and its message.

At least in part, the reliance on the ability to read the Holy Scriptures for one's self diminished the role of the clergy. One can worship, have personal communication with a transcendent God, through personal prayer. No intermediary priesthood is necessary; because communication with one's God is personal and not predicated on the performance of elaborate, highly scripted rites, rituals, and sacrifices. Individual prayers need not conform to a rigid format to be effective, further depreciating the need for priestly intervention or involvement. However, at the same time, the tradition of liturgy – customary public gatherings for the purposes of worship, convened and officiated by a clergy – dominates in most Western religions, binding adherents together.

The liturgies of the West are differentiated from the religious practices of most Eastern religions by being a communal response to the sacred by giving praise, thanksgiving, supplication, or repentance to a diety that can confer salvation. In Hinduism or Buddhism, salvation is self-obtained and is not granted by the deity in the form of a 'judgement'. Thus, Hindu practices seek guidance in achieving self-realization, with the goal of becoming 'one with god' and this is achieved through *darshan*, the act of seeing and being seen by a deity. No liturgy is necessary. The individual charts his own path to achieving enlightenment and the purification of the soul, which may require numerous lifetimes. In Western religions, one's deeds, during a single lifetime, determine the ultimate and final fate of the soul.

Hinduism's orthodoxy is defined largely by its tolerance of different points of view which has allowed it to encompass a great many doctrinal stresses without causing convulsive harm. In part, this is due to the lack of a central authority that determines 'right thought, right content, or right practice'; therefore, there have been few debates that could not be integrated, in lieu of irreparable internal philosophic schisms within Hinduism. The Hindu attitude has largely been one where various beliefs and paths are appropriate to different people at different times. Likewise, Hinduism has been equally tolerant with regard to orthopraxy, or proper religious practice. The result, unlike with most Western religions, is that Hinduism can be viewed (or possibly should be viewed) as consisting of small groups, castes, subcastes, and regional traditions setting down no clear or immutable guidelines for either orthodoxy or orthopraxy. All are tied to the Vedas, but most are only loosely tied to these ancient texts. There are, however, often large groups of orthodox and orthopraxic Hindus who remain steadfastly tied to the Vedas in form and function, for example the Maithil Brahmanas of Mithila.

At the same time, as David Kinsley has pointed out, the vast majority of Hindus have never practiced, nor been allowed to practice the rituals prescribed in the Vedas since many of these rituals, for the most part, are for upper caste Hindus only.[32] For the vast majority of Hindus, Hinduism represents non-Vedic rituals, pilgrimages, festivals and devotion to local deities. Some of these non-Vedic traditions, undoubtedly, stem from anti-Brahmin movements resulting in an indifference to Vedic Hindu tradition, or a tacit protest against it.

* * *

Mark Muesse suggests, much like Richard King, that the English concept of religion was based largely on European experiences with Catholicism, Protestantism, and Judaism; and for most Westerners, a religion was, first and foremost, a fundamentally unified set of doctrines pertaining to one's belief in a god and a code of behaviour based on those doctrines and beliefs.[33] They also had sacred books upon which the religion's doctrines were based, a clergy that was responsible for the interpretation of those texts, and temples or churches where the believers assembled to express and declare their faith.[34]

The British studied the religions of others seeking parallels between their own religions and worship practices. In India, they attempted to fit what they knew with what they saw. They tried to reconcile Indian religion and practices with their conception of what a religion 'should be'. This Western 'checklist' of what a genuine religion should contain included:

- A written scripture. In India, the British identified the Vedas as the scriptural and philosophical source or basis of India's religion.
- Rituals, ceremonies, and practices. Here, the British discovered a bewildering diversity of beliefs and practices routinely being carried out, often on a daily basis and accentuated by frequent religious holidays.
- A clergy. The Brahmins were quickly identified as the priestly class and who were responsible for the religion's rites and ceremonies but they were not the interpreters of the religion.
- Houses of worship. In India, the British found no shortage of temples and holy sites.

All the components of a religion were present, and while it was comparatively easy to identify Hinduism's scriptures, 'clergy', ceremonies, and temples, there was no indigenous word for the religion. The British needed to be able to identify and describe the amorphous religion they saw and they fashioned a neologism formed by adding the Anglicized Greek suffix *-ism* to the Persian designation for India, *Hindu*. Thus, Hinduism joins Judaism as one of the only world religions named after a place.[35] Once thus conceptualized, it influenced how both the British *and* the Hindus thought about religion; and many Hindus began to rely upon Westerners to tell them what Hinduism was.

Subsequently, increasing numbers of Hindus began to adopt the 'authorized' sacred texts as the true source of their religion, and began to take pride in both their history and religion. At the same time, having a scriptural literature served to unite or unify Hindus and Hinduism, giving the 'ism' in Hinduism much more authority and legitimacy. It was as much the ascription of the 'ism' to that collection of rites, practices, and ceremonies that truly elevated Hinduism to the status of being a 'real and true religion' in the minds of European authorities. At the same time, the British conception of Hinduism as a religion proved to be far too limited to encompass its range of practices, which included monotheism, polytheism, henotheism, animism, pantheism, monism, and even atheism, each of which, for the English, was typically conceived as a separate set of religious practices or as its own religion.[36]

Once the Vedas became the acknowledged source material for Hinduism, there was a reaction in Europe. For many, the elevation of the Vedic, Upanishadic, and epic texts to the status of scripture placed them squarely on the same plane with the Bible or Qur'an Soon, theologians, historians and politicians alike condemned the Sanskrit scriptures. As romantic literature, the Indian classics were possibly something to wile away one's time. Indian literature, with its myths and fables was deemed little more than diversionary by many. These critics argued that if these texts were so important and a fundamental part of Hindu society and religion, why were so very few Indians versed in or even familiar with the Vedas, the Upanishads, or the other epic poems of Hinduism? Among these critics were James Mill and Thomas Babington Macaulay.

In truth, what is now known as 'Hinduism', within the context of the eighteenth and nineteenth centuries' Western conception of religion, was not a religion – a doctrine or set of beliefs and practices shared and celebrated by a definable group of adherents. Hinduism is idiosyncratic. It is different with each practitioner and for the majority of 'Hindus', they are intellectually removed from the very roots of their religion by being unable to directly access the written source material of the religion, because there was no literary tradition, little education or literacy, and many Hindus were barred from many of Hinduism's rituals by caste convention. Thus conceived, it is only with a 'liberal' interpretation of the term that Hinduism becomes a religion with its companion literature.

At the same time, there was a growing lay-interest among Europeans in such translated works as the *Bhagavad Gita* (1785) which brought an alternative view of the universe, duty, and introspection to an increasingly confused and unsure Western audience in rapidly changing, dehumanizing, industrial societies. Today we would call this alienation, and was epitomized best in Charles Dickens' 1854 novel, *Hard Times,* wherein Dickens puts the poverty-ridden factory towns of nineteenth century England on trial, using Coketown's school to recreate the dehumanizing industrial world in microcosm.[37]

Equally reassuring is the fact that the 'sacred texts' of Hinduism have continued to be read by a very small but growing group of people, not all of whom, however, are priests. The Hindu priests, even today, are chiefly concerned with the sacred texts not for inspiration, enlightenment, nor the ability to explain but for the purposes of ceremonial recitation and ritual performance. Yet, many of these sacred texts continue to be read by both academics and a growing lay-audience throughout the East and West.

In his Introduction to Prabhavananda and Isherwood's *Bhagavad Gita: The Song of God,* Aldous Huxley's oft-quoted comment may help to explain, at least in part, the importance of many of the Indian sacred texts as they relate to the Western mind: 'The *Bhagavad Gita* is the most systematic statement of spiritual evolution of endowing value to mankind. It is one of the most clear and comprehensive summaries of perennial philosophy ever revealed; hence its enduring value is subject not only to India but to all of humanity.'[38]

At some indefinable level, the reading of the Indian scriptures simply touches the reader. Even without complete understanding, which requires patience and contemplation, each reading leaves its mark, incrementally simplifying life in an ever more complex world. In these texts lies an alternate view of reality, of truth which the Western mind is unaccustomed to, and it is the possibility of this alternative that is so intriguing and enthrals the uninformed.

THE VEDAS AND EPICS

Despite their inherent limitations as purely historical documents, the Vedas and epics contain the bulk of the philosophical, theological, and ethical ideas covering much of Indian speculation, including Brahmanical instruction in the art of politics and government; speculation on the origin of the universe and religion; in mythology and mysticism; in ritual and the conduct of daily life. They are the roadmaps of Hindu life. They are a tool for instructing past, present, and future generations in the code of right and wrong and moral behaviour. It is for these reasons that these stories, composed millennia ago, have survived, and still play an important role in Indian society today.

John Campbell Oman, writing in 1899, described the Epics, and by extension, the Vedas as follows:

> The . . . precious relics of the springtime of Eastern thought, revealing a new and singularly fascinating world, which differs very remarkably from that depicted in the epic poetry of Western lands. . . .
>
> . . . every Indian History, written within recent years, contains abstracts of the two epics; but these abstracts, I would observe, are skeletons rather than miniatures of the poems; they are the dry bones, on which the historians try to support a fabric of historical inferences or conjectures, and they are necessarily deficient in the mythological, romantic and social elements so important to a proper comprehension of the 'Ramayana' and 'Mahabharata.'
>
> [I have attempted to provide], in a strictly limited space, the main incidents and more striking features of those gigantic and wonderful creations of the ancient bards of India – the 'Ramayana' and 'Mahabharata' – but also to direct attention to the abiding influence of these works upon the habits and conceptions of the modern Hindu.[39]

One need only examine a few 'histories of India' to see that Oman's observation is accurate even to this day. Every Indian history written either begins with or eventually addresses one or more of the Sanskrit epics. Romila Thapar begins her history of India with a discussion of the first king of India, Manu Svayaambhu, borne directly of the god Brahma.[40] Shyam Narayan Singh, in his *History of Tirhut*, quickly invokes the *Śatpatha Brāhmaṇa* and *Bṛhadāraṇyaka Upanishad* to discuss the eastward migrations of the Aryans and the establishment of Videha.[41] Edward J. Rapson's *Ancient India* discusses the *Rigveda*;[42] Peter Robb's discussion of early India[43] and John Keay's Introduction to his *India: A History*;[44] each engages the epics as source material.

That said, numerous other writers have observed that the epics and Vedas are only marginally useful as historical documents. D.D. Kosambi states categorically: 'India has virtually no [ancient] historical records worth the name.'[45] Despite its rich literary heritage, India produced no historical writers comparable to Herodotus, Thucydides, Polybius or Livy. There were kings and there were wars but no one, it seems, thought to compose anything approaching 'a history'.

Ironically, the earliest histories of India are those written by non-Indians, like Nearchus, Alexander the Great's Macedonian admiral and satrap of Lycia and Pamphylia, or the Greek, Megasthenes (*c.* 350-290 BC), who lived in India while serving as an ambassador of Seleucus I at the court of Chandragupta Maurya. If the adage – history tends to be written by the victors and about the powerful – is true, why are there no ancient Indian histories? Where were the native historians and where are their histories?

In 1922, E.J. Rapson pointed out that the materials for the reconstruction of ancient Indian history were supplied from the literature of the Brahmans, Jains, and Buddhists; inscriptions on monuments, coins, and seals; and the accounts of foreign writers – Greek, Roman, Latin, and Chinese.[46] Rapson's list of source material for ancient Indian history, originally enumerated in the early 1920s, remains largely unchanged today. We have more archaeological information, more inceptions on monuments, pillars, steles, coins, and seals but these only mark milestones in time, they are not histories.

There may have been historians or chroniclers but either due to environmental, social, or political reasons, their works were destroyed or lost. Alternatively, it may well be that none were ever composed due to the nature of Vedic Sanskrit itself. In its formal written form, early Sanskrit militated against its use as a vehicle for prosaic topics. It was a language of and about the gods. It was not until the beginning of the Common Era that Sanskrit was reinvented, becoming a complicated code for literary and political expression.[47] Whatever the cause, there are no formal histories written in early or Vedic Sanskrit.

It was not until the Muslim period that we find our first indigenous histories being written. Even the earliest of these historians, Kalhana, a twelfth-century Kashmiri, writing in modern Sanskrit, quickly lapses into legend, myth, or pure romance when attempting to create a history before the seventh century.[48] Abū al-Rayhān Muhammad ibn Ahmad al-Bīrūnī (978-1043), the traveller, historian, and geographer, observed: '. . . the Hindus do not pay much attention to the historical order of things, they are very careless in relating the chronological successions of their kings, and when they are pressed for information and are at a loss, not knowing what to say, they invariably take to tale-telling'.[49]

Robin Donkin suggests that 'there are no native literary works with a developed sense of chronology, or indeed much sense of place, before the thirteenth century'.[50] Donkin's observation, while inherently derisive, does bear further consideration. From the author's personal fieldwork experience across northern India, he was left with the impression that things chronological become difficult for many of India's indigenous people. The author's original research dealt with the diffusion and adoption of agricultural innovations. Most villagers found it difficult to ascertain when they had actually adopted a specific innovation. At least, in part, the author attributed this phenomenon to two operational factors. First, peasant life is geared to the endless cycle of the agricultural seasons and the focus is primarily on one's current attempts to survive. Second, in the absence of widespread literacy, there is no method of long-term recordkeeping that can be used as a referential tool. If, during ancient times, only the priests were literate, and due to the complexity of the language, it is understandable that their writings would be predominately, if not exclusively religious in character, content, and tone.

* * *

Nevertheless, the epics and other philosophical treatises serve as the armature for most of India's political, religious, social history and thinking. As such, they serve, in fact and fiction, as the underlying foundation of much of what India is today. It is inescapable. The people are tied through these texts to the very roots of their culture which predates the composition of the Vedas – the 'Books of Knowledge' – which were being developed long before the Aryan arrival in India.

In the Vedas, we find the primary texts of the Hindus, which have also had a strong influence on Buddhism, Jainism, and Sikhism. Composed as oral chants, they were committed to writing around 300 BCE, using an early form of Sanskrit referred to as Vedic or Classical Sanskrit.

The Vedas contain hymns, incantations, and rituals inspired by the wanderings of the Aryans. Along with the *Book of the Dead*, the *Enuma Elish*, the *I Ching*, and the *Avesta*, they are among the oldest religious texts known. Each of these books also provides a world view of their authors and their audiences, and a glimpse of everyday life as much as four thousand years ago, and provide the most extensive Indo-European language texts known.

By tradition, the Vedas are believed to have been handed down through the generations by word of mouth from time immemorial. The texts are believed to have coevaled with the universe. Generally, the Vedas were either taught by the gods to the sages, or the gods revealed themselves to the sages who were the seers or '*mantradrasta*' of the hymns. As *Śruti,* the Vedas are regarded as the absolute authority for religious knowledge and a test of Hindu orthodoxy.[51] For Hindus, the Vedas are a symbol of unchallenged authority and tradition. Selections from the Vedas are still memorized and recited for religious merit; yet many of the esoteric aspects of the religion presented in the Vedas are unknown today and play little to no role in modern Hinduism, much like the mysticism of Judaism as communicated through the *Zohar* and *Kabbalah*.

The *Rig Veda* is a collection of inspired songs or hymns and is a main source of information on Aryan civilization. Each of the four Vedas has a specific purpose. The *Sama Veda* – The Book of Song – is purely a liturgical collection of melodies (*saman*). The hymns in the *Sama Veda*, used as musical notes, were almost completely drawn from the *Rig Veda* and have no distinctive lessons of their own. The *Yajur Veda* – The Book of Ritual – is also a liturgical collection and was meant to meet the demands of the ceremonial practice of Hinduism. The *Yajur Veda* serves as a guidebook for the priests who execute sacrificial acts muttering simultaneously the prose prayers and the sacrificial formulae (*yajus*). The last Veda, The *Atharva Veda* – The Book of Spells – is completely different from the other three Vedas and is next in importance to the *Rig Veda* with regard to history and sociology. A different spirit pervades this Veda. Its hymns are of a more diverse character than its predecessor and it utilizes a simpler language form. Consequently, some scholars do not consider it an integral part of the Vedas. The *Atharva Veda* consists of spells and charms prevalent at the time of its composition, and portrays a clearer picture of Vedic life and society.

Historical and religious literature is often written from the perspective of the most powerful groups, priests and warrior-kings. Therefore, it unlikely that the Vedas represent or provide a fully panoramic view of Aryan life at the time, or the totality of religious belief and practice in India in the first millennium BCE. This perspective is especially evident in the earlier parts of the Vedas in which the primary concerns are war, rain, and dealing with the 'slaves', or the native inhabitants of India.

It is from the *Rig* and *Atharva Vedas* that much of the 'history' of ancient India is drawn, as it deals with chiefs and kings, with successions, wars, and Aryan tribal life. These Vedas, in general, provide us with a glimpse of the political structure of the tribal groupings of the Aryans that remained little changed until their eastward expansion slowed, then stopped in what is now Mithila.[52] As their tribes settled and more permanent life patterns developed, the nature of Aryan political structure also changed, growing increasingly feudal in nature, a natural extension of a formerly tribal system of political organization. A variant of this feudal socio-economic system of organization continues to exist in modern Bihar, even today.

THE ROLE OF RELIGION IN DEVELOPMENT

In this age of technology and globalization, when one speaks of development, it is generally understood to mean economic development. The emphasis, thus far, has been largely on technological and scientific advances, and only peripherally has religion's role in the development process been addressed or examined.

The idea of progress is firmly rooted in Western culture and religion. Outside Judeo-Christian thought, life and history are largely viewed as cyclic, recurring cycles. Judaism was probably the earliest religion to think in terms of history as being 'linear' or 'progressive' where there was a beginning and there will ultimately be an end, when all human misfortunes will be set right. Later Christian theologians, like St. Augustine in his *The City of God*, extended and refined this notion when he suggested that in God's plan there was no presumption of eternal recurrence, that history has a direction, that it works in a predetermined path.[53] Therefore, according to Christian history and theology, life is not a series of eternal returns; it does not move in circles. This truth was a crucial departure from traditional and Oriental thought.

Alfred Radcliffe-Brown states that:

> In every human society there inevitably exist two different and in a certain sense conflicting conceptions of nature. One of them, the *naturalistic*, is implicitly everywhere in technology, and, in our 20th century European culture, has become explicit and dominant in our thoughts. The other, which might be called mythological, or *spiritualistic* conception, is implicit in myth and in religion, and often becomes explicit in philosophy.[54]

Religion has traditionally been perceived as a personal relationship between people and some unseen god or order but this order influences one's relationship with one's fellow humans and, therefore, it has a material dimension. It is this material dimension that has an impact on development. Assessing the role of religion in the developmental process has been largely ignored by Western-dominated nations and their development agencies, who dole out development funding and foreign aid. This is due to the West's preoccupation with secularism which is presumed to be the source of the West's economic success. As a consequence, religion is deemed socially and economically as irrelevant. This largely secular approach to development has frequently caused tensions when dealing with constituencies that remain religiously devout, with the end result that development fails or is 'less successful' than anticipated by both the developmentalists and the recipients.

Part of the reason that Western secular society has ignored religion as a component of the development process is that secularists suggest that religion should remain a private affair attending to matters of the soul. This position, however, represents a fundamental misunderstanding of the function and nature of religion. It ignores the fact that spiritual growth is a vital part of human well-being and, therefore, an integral part of human development. To marginalize religion, even in the West, limiting it to only the personal domain fundamentally negates one of society's primary sources of values and traditions. Individual freedom and liberty, while powerful concepts in the West, and inherent in most development programmes, are often perceived as antithetical to certain religious beliefs and, therefore, entire programmes are rejected by the intended target population. Development programming must reflect people's ways of life or risk rejection. Development must also acknowledge that a 'cookie cutter' approach to development is both inadvisable and often unproductive. What works within one community, society, or culture will not necessarily work in another without revision. What Muslim, Hindu, or Christian communities need and want are oftentimes very different. This recognition is fundamental to achieving successful development.

The West must recognize that religion, religious values, and religious structures are a reality in many places around the world. It modifies human behaviour as well as providing a framework within which to understand why the world exists, how it works, and provide a normative view of 'how it should be'. In a 2000 survey, when asked why people are rich or poor, many people answered 'Destiny' or 'That's the way God created the earth'.[55] Additionally, the survey indicated that one's well-being was closely aligned with spirituality and religious observance. Equally important was the observation that maintaining social traditions, hospitality, reciprocity, rituals, and festivals was central to the poor's identification of themselves as humans.[56] Excluding, ignoring, or marginalizing the role religion plays in the development process only serves to thwart the genuine efforts of Western development agents and agencies. Religion is an integral part of many communities' culture and its exclusion will, and has affected development programmes and initiatives throughout the world. Engaging and including religious beliefs in development planning is crucial to reducing barriers to programming.

Further, within the last twenty years, religion and the role of religious groups have assumed the role of social and political movements. On the one hand, religion in both the East and West has become increasingly important within civic cultures, providing a focal point for often disenfranchised groups. On the other, it has become a rallying point for militancy, where religion is fused with political agendas.

If development programmes are to be successful, development agents must recognize the extent to which religion influences the individual and the community in which he or she lives. Secularism within the international development process has meant that religion has been largely excluded from consideration. Religion cannot be ignored. It has to be part of the development process. Religious beliefs and values are powerful and they

> . . . harbour within them a latent dynamism which, when properly respected, can serve as the springboard for modes of development which are more humane than those drawn from outside paradigms. When development builds from indigenous values it extracts lower social costs and imposes less human suffering and cultural destruction than when it copies outside models. This is so because indigenously-rooted values are the matrix whence people derive meaning in their lives, a sense of identity, and the experience of continuity with their environment and their past even in the midst of change.[57]

* * *

Historically, religion's role in societies has spanned the spectrum from being fully integrated in political, cultural, and civil affairs to the complete banishment of religion from society; to the point that the United Nations felt it necessary to make religious freedom a part of its mandate.

Faith-based organizations, soon thereafter, became a part of the global web of development agencies, and have contributed significantly in the fields of health and human development, agriculture, environmental preservation, and the media, especially as national governments have cut back on their aid spending. In many foreign-development programmes, today, faith-based development personnel are the only constant presence in many communities and often the last development experts who receive respect from the public.[58]

In India, just as in Africa, the resilience of religion continues to be seen and shows no sign of disappearing from or diminishing in public importance. This reality is quite different from the expectations of development theorists. The role or importance of religion, as part of the development process, has been largely ignored since the work of Max Weber and Emile Durkheim, who together considered the 'disenchantment' of the world – Weber's phrase – as an inevitable consequence stemming from the rise of the modern state and modern economics. This belief has, somehow, become ingrained in the thinking of classic theories of development.[59] Consequently, development theorists, in general, have paid little or no attention to the role of religion as part or cause of development; believing, instead, that it was either irrelevant or possibly even represented an obstacle to the development process.

In his *The Sacred Canopy: Elements of a Sociological Theory of Religion*, Peter Berger seeks to reconcile Durkheim and Weber. He suggests that while religions as social projections once provided communities with an overarching framework and means of cohesion (Durkheim's social function of religion) as societies modernize, this integrative function will shift from religion to science and other disenchanted institutions and discourses (Weber's rationalization and secularization as historical trends).[60] This integration of classical sociology, however, seems to ignore the realities of the late twentieth and early twenty-first centuries. The world seems to be changing and changing rapidly. To use an American idiomatic and colloquial expression: 'We're not in Kansas anymore' – life is no longer quiet and comfortable. Recent events have changed how people perceive and respond to religion. It is no longer some vague set of principles or platitudes with no real-world implications. Religion has taken on a new militancy and, as such, has become a factor in day-to-day life and politics around the world. The platonic discussion of religion, in the classical sense of

Durkheim and Weber, seems almost comical, an intellectual dalliance. Religion has become a new, real, and powerful reality in the world.

* * *

The role of religion in international politics, until possibly 1979, with the overthrow of the Shah of Iran and the Iranian Revolution, was in large measure marginalized. Thereafter, it became clear that religion was not, in fact, a force that was simply going to disappear. Further, with the advent of 9/11, religion has become the subject of almost continuous worldwide debate. Race and religion have combined to foment political and social conflicts throughout the world, especially in Sub-Saharan Africa, the Middle East, and South Asia; and have become fundamental components in defining the West's response in its 'war on terror', which became the basis for overt American military involvement in Iraq, Afghanistan, and Somalia. More recently, as the US began to disengage itself from missions in the Middle East, the Taliban and the Islamic State of Iraq and Syria (ISIS) or variously referred to as IS (Islamic States) or ISIL (Islamic State of Iraq and the Levant) have taken advantage and begun waging jihadist wars in the hopes of establishing a Muslim caliphate in the heart of the Middle East, attended by the use of brutal tactics used against all infidels, everywhere, in the name of Islam.

Whether stemming from religion or race, conflicts are generally regarded as an impediment to development. At the same time, religion as a catalyst for conflict should not and cannot be ignored as one of the factors in the development process.[61] However, one cannot easily ignore religion's role in both world politics and development since, at least for the foreseeable future, it may be the most important single connection between the developed and developing nations of the world. And at long last, the primary international development agencies and financial institutions are discussing the role of religion with regard to the development process.[62]

* * *

Within the context of many developing nations, the shortcomings observed in the wake of development programmes, year after year, have been attributed to the failure of the Western materialist paradigm, leaving what might be thought of as a paradigmatic void. Since the end of World War II, since Truman's first use of the word 'under-developed', the West has invested nearly seventy years and trillions of development dollars on one line of thought with little to show for its time and investment. No one had thought to posit an alternative 'fallback' strategy. There was no alternative to the premise that money (aid) would resolve all the developmental problems of the world, given enough time. Either there was not enough money provided and spent, or there has not been sufficient time. William Easterly, a vocal opponent of 'throwing good money after bad' with regard to foreign development aid, suggests that if development was just a matter of money, the poor of the world could have bought themselves out of poverty with the huge sums already provided by foreign donor countries.[63] If 'development' has taken so much and so long, and the problem of poverty has not been resolved, obviously, money and time were not the palliatives they were deemed to be.

Recently, faith-based developmentalists have suggested that if religion is viewed as a system of knowledge and practices that complement science, it will bring prosperity to all humankind.[64] This approach, it would seem, integrates the Durkheim-Weber duality and finally recognizes the not-so subtle influences of religion in development and politics. These faith-based developmentalists recognize that both religion and science have been misused. Both can and have fallen prey to fanaticism.

Nowhere else is the need for faith-based development more evident than in India. An unparalleled amount of material resources, human effort, experimentation, and methodologies have been implemented in India; and yet, poverty continues to be the prevailing outcome. Modernization in India has focused on industrialization, infrastructural projects, the strengthening of agriculture, poverty elimination, and rural development in an effort to reduce poverty and eliminate income disparities. This was also a period in which the focus turned to appropriate technology, the role of women in development, community and institutional capacity building, environmental preservation, people-centered development, community organization, and project evaluation. Then, an attempt was made to liberalize the Indian economy in the belief that it would somehow push forward the need for better educational institutions, healthcare, the empowerment of women, and would resolve the social and economic problems within the disadvantaged sectors of Indian society.

However optimistic the government's plans and programmes, the global free-market capitalism that was to transform Indian society never materialized. It did raise India's global presence in the world market, becoming an 'emerging economic power', but it did not significantly change the overall conditions for the vast number of rural Indians. This development was largely urban and industrial.

* * *

Today, almost anywhere in India, if one listens closely to virtually any discussion of almost any mundane political, economic, or social matter, you will hear references from one or more of the Indian epics or some other historical or philosophical treatise to buttress an argument, legitimize a position, or emphasize a point. There is no temporal, religious, or philosophical separation between times long gone by and today. At least, in part, this stems from the universality, interpretability, or legitimacy of the well-crafted statements of these historic works.

For many, these ancient texts retain a currency and a durability unparalleled in Western civilization. Rarely are the Bible or Qur'an heard quoted in classrooms, businesses, legislative bodies, or courtrooms. In fact, it is often deemed 'politically incorrect' or outright unlawful to even mention, by inference or otherwise, religious quotes or precepts, as part of the West's concept of the separation of 'Church' and 'State'. Not so in India with regard to the epics and many other ancient discourses. India, although intended to be a secular state, nonetheless, retains religious and cultural ties to the past, ties that stretch back, literally, thousands of years. Would this phenomenon exist today had it not been for the British, assuming Muesse's proposition is correct; that what we know and call Hinduism today is a product of British Orientalism?

* * *

Modernity and religion have been traditionally conceived, somehow, as polar opposites among developmentalists. There is the underlying, often unspoken, assumption that religion has no place or role in the development process. In a country like India, where modernity is largely an urban phenomenon and religion and religious symbols are visible everywhere, influencing society, politics, philosophy, and the economy, one must either accommodate or accept the influence of religion. By either ignoring or rejecting India's religiosity developmentalists underestimate its modern potentialities.[65] Religion among both Muslims and Hindus is more and different than religion in the West. On the one hand, it is more, as much a social system as it is a religion. It is also different in that religion does not have the same additive and derivative impact on every facet of one's life in the West. Both Islam and Hinduism define and sanction the individual's rank, distance, privileges, obligations, rights and duties within the largely rural and traditional socio-economic and political milieu of India. To be sure, the message of each obtains from clearly different philosophical premises but, as applied within village India, they both reinforce similar patterns of human behaviour; and unlike Marx's contention that religion is the opiate of the masses, neither Islam nor Hinduism serves quite that purpose.[66]

Until quite recently, the role of religion as a component of development has remained, at best, marginal, both as a topic of academic interest and within policy circles. Part of the reason that religion has been accorded so little attention in development studies is that the ideas of progress and development, while having deep roots in Western civilization, have largely been thought of as an outgrowth of the Enlightenment, with its emphasis on rationality. Religion, not being inherently rational, therefore, has been given very little attention. This position was reinforced by Western sociologists who predicted that the role of religion would wane as modern society matured; and to a certain degree this has proven to be true. Both Auguste Comte and Max Weber suggested that that religion represented a barrier to rationalism and, therefore, modernity.[67]

In the process of separating Church and State, religious power was transferred to the secular state and its institutions, resulting in a rational legal order. Developed nations, largely Western secular states, as a consequence came to believe that modernization was either dependent upon or emerged from secular socio-economic institutions and if modernization or development was to take place in the developing world, it would necessitate or depend upon the emergence of equally secular states.

Due to development's emphasis on rational choices, the role of religion in that process has been, at worst, largely ignored, and at best, marginalized by development agencies and researchers. It was only due to the expansion of eighteenth-century European historical scholarship that Indian history was subjected to rigorous ideological interpretation, much of which had its origin not in India but in Europe.[68] British influences altered the course of Indian history and historiography. Until this time, Indian history had been largely narratives, lineages, and chronicles of dynasties, and the recital of glorious deeds with little or no analysis or objectivity; where dynastic changes were viewed more as a function of divine intervention than social and political processes.

The Indian connection, verging on a preoccupation with the past, is an everyday fact of life, and was it any other way, Indian society would not be what it is today. The importance of the Vedas and the epics, as the source of Hinduism, lies in the fact that they are accepted as entirely and literally true by millions of Hindus. While some may find in this practice a basis for criticism, it is one of the facets of Indian life that makes India and her problems so unique. Secularization comes at a cost, a cost India has not had to endure and possibly need not.

SECULARISM: A COMPONENT OF DEVELOPMENT?

The West's *apparent* absence of religion in day-to-day affairs can be largely explained as a function of secularism – the separation of religion from most other aspects of one's life – and the introduction, substitution, and integration of ideologies. The author disagrees with this interpretation. He would argue, like Graeme Smith, that while the institutional role of the 'Church' has been restricted by secularism, it has had little or no effect on whether or not the people perceive themselves as being religious or having a belief in God. In the West, people have incorporated the religious tenets of their faith into their daily lives and therefore have or find no need to fall back on or rely upon church doctrine, or state the obvious for their actions. Within this context, non-secular societies seem to misunderstand or are confused by secularism.

The West's response to a history marked by near theocratic domination was secularism – a uniquely Christian response to the role of religion in everyday life.[69] Graeme Smith suggests that secularism is Christian ethics shorn of its doctrine – an approach to life that would be unthinkable for Hindus or Muslims, where the boundary between ethics and doctrine is often, at best, imprecise, non-existent, or blurred.[70]

While the secular state was theoretically 'designed' to prevent organized religion from controlling public institutions, it was not intended to undermine religiosity *per se*, or alienate religious communities. It was, however, conceived as a multi-secular defence against the imposition of the religious values and worldview of one community over another.

In both the United States and Britain, observers are left with the impression that religion plays, at best, a nominal role in the people's day-to-day lives. This is a grievous misunderstanding on the part of outsiders. Two recent polls indicate that despite a decline in people's 'belief in God' or 'church attendance', the vast majority see themselves as religious.[71] In general, religion in the West is a private and personal matter with few overt or outward manifestations. The exception is the practice of church or temple services for Christians and Jews, which is, in fact, on the decline.

Recent survey studies suggest that:

- 78.40 per cent of Americans are Christian. 51.30 per cent are Protestants, while 23.90 per cent are Catholic. 4.7 per cent represent other religions. Only 16 per cent are religiously unaffiliated.[72]
- 59.30 per cent of Britons are Christian. Far back in second place are the Muslims with 4.80 per cent of the British population, and 25 per cent of Britons reported no religious affiliation.[73]

Americans and Britons remain largely Christian, with the Americans showing more religious tenacity than Britons but in both instances, the number of people who believe in God is declining generationally. If we assume that morality is a function of religiosity, will the decline in religious affiliation alter Western behaviour? A recent poll in Britain suggests people are not becoming less moral but increasingly individual; moral values are obtained from one's parents or friends, since a large portion of the next generation appears to be eschewing formal religious affiliations and institutional instruction.[74] Once religiously affiliated parents are gone, society and one's friends will become the primary source of morality. If the concept of altruism is at the heart of religious instruction and morality, is society up to the challenge of inculcating altruistic thinking and behaviour in its future generations? If the current youth generation is any indicator, altrusim may become a lost character trait.

The larger question is why is religion declining in the West? There is, undoubtedly, no one cause but many. Among the most observable, however, are:

- Children in the West have more rights and freedoms, and one of these is the choice to believe in a religion or not.
- Unbiased education reinforces freedom of choice, providing more and more information and, therefore, resulting in more possibilities.
- Bad Press. The foibles of formal religion are increasingly paraded before the public in the media.
- Religion has become burdensome. Many of the practices and canons of the 'church' seem to the next generation to be a waste of time and in opposition to common sense.
- Religion seems to be at the heart of many conflicts – Islam against the world, Christian sects opposed to one another, etc.

In an era of free thought, religion appears to be fundamentally irrational or flawed. Much of it is based on the concept of faith and therefore cannot be substantiated by observation or 'proven'. For example, most religions suggest that God is benevolent and loving and, yet, pain and suffering are visible everywhere. Rationally, how can a benevolent God permit so much pain and suffering? The concept of a benevolent God and reality simply do not seem to equate.

Secularism and Islam

Secularism sets the West apart from much of the rest of the world. Elsewhere, by-and-large, secularism is not as assiduously practiced, especially within the context of Islam, where religious ethics and doctrine are most amalgamated in a unique form of a social-theocratic state; or put another way, there is no separation between mosque and society. This conception only serves to reinforce the notion that Islam does not have a church institution, that it encompasses all domains, and that the state and religious authority are, or should be embodied in the same person. This is the most commonly held view of both Western and Muslim scholars.[75]

Louay Safi suggests:

> For many Muslims, however, the secular state is viewed as an instrument used to undermine religious heritage and deny the relevance of moral teachings to public life. While this perception has an element of truth, it does not necessarily depict the general nature of western secularism. Evidently, Muslim perceptions of secularism are not formed through an understanding of the original purpose and historical circumstances of western secularism, but is influenced by the Muslim experience of secular dogmatism and the intolerance of the secular state in contemporary Muslim societies, most notably that of Turkey and many Arab and Central Asian states.
>
> Reacting to secular dogmatism, populist Islamic groups have advanced a conception of the state that, while different in substance, is similar in purpose and form to the very secular state they oppose. Like Muslim secularists, Islamic populists see the state as an instrument in the hands of ruling powers for imposing a particular conception of the world on the rest of society. They insist, therefore, that the Islamic state should be charged with the duty of imposing Islamic law on the larger society.[76]

Andrew Waskey would refer to such Islamic states as being theonomic theocracies, that is, there is an integration of the social and political state and is therefore seen as an expression of divine will; or, as a religious community with no distinction between faith and civil authority.[77] Hence, '*Islam din wa-dawla*' (Islam is religion *and* state) becomes a rallying cry. Whether it is viewed as a political slogan for those who advocate world domination or those who fear its implications, it is, in essence, dependent upon the context within which it is used.[78] This does not make it any less meaningful for

Muslims or non-Muslims, and for the secular West, it becomes a clarion call, and a call to arms as a means of defending both one's religion and social form.

Secularism in India

In India, the separation of religion and state has never been deemed necessary nor desirable, and all efforts to completely secularize Indian society have been, at best, ineffective and ineffectual. In large measure, the Indian perspective has traditionally been much more historical and individualistic than ideological. In the absence of an organized, identifiable ideological content, Hinduism and the state manifest themselves quite differently than does Islam. With the possible exception of the Hindutva movement, there is no inherent militancy in the conception of a Hindu-based theocracy since there is no underlying proselytizing imperative. It is the urgency of Muslims that all should submit to Islam that truly differentiates it from Hinduism, and surprisingly, more closely aligns Islam with Christianity, both of whom seem locked in a 'winner take all' battle for world domination, with Christianity currently and statistically on the losing side.

THE ROLE OF CASTE IN BIHAR

In the West, possibly more so in America, there is an adage that applies to 'polite society': never talk about religion or politics. Why is this; because everyone seems to have a deep-seated but different opinion regarding each and, as a consequence, such discussions typically result in arguments. So, by not talking about politics or religion, in theory, we avoid argumentation. However, this is not reality. Religion and politics are now about all anyone is talking about since 9/11 and the advent of ISIS.

Just because they are 'hot topics', volatile topics of great importance, it only makes sense that we should be discussing them. If we accept the validity of the dialectic method – a discourse between people holding different points of view on a subject – are we not avoiding the possibility that our differences can be resolved through reasoned argument? This, of course, is based on the assumption that it is within the debators' ability to compromise their positions when confronted with a compelling alternative view.

Within the context of India, a third topic must be appended to this list of things we do not talk about – caste. To ignore caste is like the proverbial 'elephant in the room' or trying to describe an elephant without referring to its size or trunk, two of its most conspicuous features. Yet, public mention of caste has receded to the unfashionable background. The irony of caste is that the Government of India feels it necessary to casually ignore it and legislate against its existence but, at the same time, it selectively specifies privileges and special treatment and programming for 'certain castes'. No matter how justified such legislation might be historically or socio-economically, to right past wrongs, it is nonetheless discrimination; and this is the very situation the government wishes to eliminate. Is 'reverse discrimination' any less noxious and contentious?

* * *

As a separately implemented part of the 2011 Census of India, the Ministry of Rural Development proposed the implementation of a Socio-Economic and Caste Census (SECC), with the intent of collecting caste-specific data on a door-to-door basis throughout the country. Published caste data has not been available since the 1931 census; and a survey by the Anthropological Survey of India found nearly 80,000 caste/community names.[79] By including caste as an enumerable information item, does it not mean that the government is officially recognizing caste as a legitimate institution? Or, is it the institutionalization and acknowledgement of a pre-existing fact?

Ostensibly, the reason for this new schedule was to provide an economic benchmark for castes using a simple headcount. Caste, as defined by the SECC, refers to a social group, members of which marry within the group, follow the same traditional occupation and enjoy the same rank in the hierarchial scale of all castes. The *Instruction Manual for Enumerators* included an introductory dialogue to be used to explain the purpose of the survey to respondents. Included among the stated purposes was the following statement: 'The information you give will be compiled to help the government deliver benefits of schemes more effectively and also formulate policies/schemes for rural development.'[80]

As of early April 2014, according to a spokesman for the Ministry of Rural Development, 'SECC is in the final stages. . . . The data base will be available only after June [2014]'.[81] The SECC has been beset with one technical, political, or legal setback after another beginning soon after the additional census schedule was announced. [Late December 2014, the SECC 2011 had released only the final household information for 97 of India's 640 districts, with no timetable for the release of the remainder of the districts or other data sets.]

* * *

No matter how accurate the SECC data may be, after being collected over a period of more than two-and-a-half years, ultimately it will be used as political grist and fodder for the media and for vote-getting. These data will provide political strategists with tools that will allow them to better target voters and tailor campaign messages to exploit caste concerns and fears, segregating people, making them insiders or outsiders.[82]

Despite India's avowed desire to be a secular state; history and culture continue to play a significant role in every facet of Indian life. Therefore, the influence of religion and caste cannot be summarily legislated away. A political document, like a constitution, while outlining the principles upon which a nation is founded, should not and cannot ignore the existence of customs and traditions that have been in place for, possibly, thousands of years. Caste is a fact of life. This is particularly true when a tradition, however viewed, and legally deemed a non-institution, serves as one of the most volatile and powerful political tools in every politician's arsenal. Whether used for good or bad, caste is often used effectively as a campaign tool; sometimes used to unite but more frequently used divisively. When caste, as a social institution, is politicized it becomes 'casteism' – caste loyalty translated into politics.

Andre Béteille, who Ramachandra Guha, the noted historian called 'The wisest man in India', stated: 'Caste is now the most important political tool for the mobilisation of the electorate.'[83] Politics is the leading contributing factor to the continuation of caste in India. It is no longer sustained by birth, matrimony, occupation, or ritual practices but politics does feed on caste differences and places a special premium on the backward castes as vote banks. Béteille recalls that in his grandfather's day, people carried a map of Hindu society and the caste system around in their heads but now, 'the traditional picture of Hindu society has become fluid, amorphous and has ceased to be legitimate'.[84] Béteille's comment is true in terms of 'modern' urban Indian society but it is much less true in rural India.

In another recent editorial Andre Béteille wrote:

> The leaders of the nationalist movement who successfully fought for India's freedom from colonial rule believed that India may have been a society of castes and communities in the past but would become a nation of citizens with the adoption of a new republican constitution. They were too optimistic. The Constitution did create rights for the citizen, but it did not eradicate caste from the hearts and minds of the citizens it created. For many Indians, and perhaps the majority, the habits of the heart are still the habits of a hierarchical society.[85]

Béteille's comment is all the more perceptive when one considers that the definition used by the SECC's designers harkens back to and sounds very reminiscent of *varna*, with its emphasis on marriage, traditional occupations, and hierarchial rank. Citizenry does not necessarily mean equality.

Caste, in and of itself, is not the problem. It had its origins in the hierarchical nature of most human societies and was crystallized and sanctified religiously and philosophically in Hinduism's earliest writings; then serving sociological and economic purposes. In a much simpler social and economic setting, caste proved itself a useful concept. It was only later that it became a tool of exploitation and discrimination. Today, the four things that make caste a problem are:

- It continues to be used as a tool for social and economic discrimination, resulting in crushing inequality;
- It is exploited by politicians, creating divisions and animus for purely political gain and undermines the principles of democracy;
- It detracts from national efforts to develop a national identity or unity; and

- It reinforces the capacity of the people, and especially the poor to accept poverty.

Because caste is such a fundamental part of the fabric of Indian society, despite attempts to disenfranchise and eradicate it as an institution, both the government and society continue to recognize and manipulate it, institutionally and politically. Therefore, to ignore its role in the development process, especially in Bihar and Mithila, where social stratification and casteism have been refined to an art form, is short-sighted or incomprehensible.

* * *

Despite caste's undeniable and profound impact on Indian society in general, there seems to be a prevailing attitude, especially among cultural anthropologists and sociologists, that any further discussion of caste or religion is irrelevant or derivative. This represents the so-called 'been there – done that' attitude among academics. Today, the roles of caste and religion seem to be more frequently discussed with regard to their contemporary manifestation – casteism – and, consequently, their study has been relegated to political scientists. Here, we will not dwell on the historical development of caste but certain of its aspects must be considered within their historical context since, at least within Mithila, those historical characteristics have changed little, and continue to manifest themselves ceremonially as part of a prevailing worldview.

* * *

Bihar has been the scene of massive peasant movements, violence, popular suppressions, poverty, as well as the epitome of mal-governance. It is often cited as a classic example of a 'failed state'.[86] It is seen as an acute example of why liberal democracy is only partially successful within the context of India. At the centre of each of these matters is the role of caste in governance and politics. Caste, more so than any other factor, prevents the resolution of social conflicts. Instead, it can be seen as a volatile social accelerant of social divisiveness. Castism prevents the modernization and full democratization of India's politics, at least in Bihar.[87] If a solution to Bihar's caste-dominated socio-political governance was available, it could serve as a template for good governance anywhere.

Why is caste, in the twenty-first century, such an issue one might ask? First and foremost, it simply refuses to disappear from either society or the politics of Bihar despite social legislation designed to limit or abolish it, especially within the context of the Nehruvian vision of modern India. Essentially, caste within the system of democracy symbolizes the defeat of Nehru's liberal vision.

Caste resists eradication and change and continues to remain a resilient institution. Since it does not seem amenable to erasure, the politicians of Bihar are forced to deal with it through alliances, networks, and mobilizations, and this forms the basis for interest groups. The difficulty lies in granting the ruling elite legitimacy and, at the same time, drawing upon the support of the majority of the population of a highly complex socially stratified society. As a consequence, caste management becomes a preoccupation for those in power. The cause of this preoccupation lies in the fact that, by in large, until 1990, Bihar politics had been dominated by the three upper castes – Brahmins, including the Maithil and Bhumihars, Rajputs, and Kayastha – which do not constitute a majority of voters.

Traditionally, within the context of the symbiotic *jajmani* system, the Kshatriya landowner/ruler supports the caste-based division of labour, which includes the ritualistic services of the Brahmins, and supports and maintains the hierarchical Hindu social system. In Mithila, however, through a unique variation of the process M.M. Srinivas calls 'sanskritization', the normal socio-economic relationships embodied in the *jajmani* system have been rearranged, which results in a reordering of typical social roles and positions.[88] Through the conservative and self-interested patronage of the Maharaja of Darbhanga, beginning before the rise of British hegemony in Mithila, and its resultant social, political, and cultural changes, the Kshatriyas as the traditional landowning caste were systematically replaced by Brahmins, especially the Maithil Brahmanas. The Maharaja, as the recognized leader of the Maithil Brahmanas, had a vested interest in advancing the position of the Brahmanas, especially as it cemented and bolstered his authority through caste allegiances and his vast land revenue collection personnel. As the 'King', the Maharaja was the final authority when it came to both caste and land disputes and, whenever possible, he replaced quarrelsome and recalcitrant Kshatriya landowners with Brahmanas, thus transferring lands out of the hands of the Kshatriya and into the hands and control of Brahmins. As Carolyn Henning Brown observed, 'The kings, operating as *dues ex machine*, have regularly intervened to reorganize the system when the intrinsic tendency to equalize became a threat to the hierarchical order.'[89]

With each alteration of the socio-economic structure a new equilibrium was eventually achieved and institutionalized by the Brahmins themselves, as the interpreters of dharma for all the castes. Further, the Brahmins may well have been guilty of overstressing the acceptance of the *status quo* among the lower castes and, at the same time, using ambiguities in caste ideology for their own benefit. Since caste hierarchies were never fixed, nor were they unambiguous with regard to the relative positions of local caste groups, the illusion of fixity stemmed from an ideological model that classified castes by *varnas*, which was further institutionalized by British ideological influences and was subsequently accepted by Indian culture itself.

Traditionally in a local and regional caste hierarchy, dominance was based on multiple criteria including land ownership, strength of numbers, political influence, and ritual purity. Competing claims were not unusual in a society that was constantly 'pushing and jostling in an attempt to get ahead'.[90] It were the British who crystallized and fixed caste affiliations through their need to classify and record everyone's status.[91] Subsequently, it was politically economic for caste groups who found themselves in advantageous positions to close the gap between their rising secular status and presumably fixed ritual status by Sanskritizing their ritual practices as a way of legitimizing social rank by claiming a higher ritual position. Traditional Indian society accommodated social mobility while simultaneously resisting structural change. The Maharaja of Darbhanga and the Maithil Brahmanas finessed these inconsistencies in the caste system to their mutual benefits, creating an atypical system of land ownership – a system of Brahmin land ownership rarely found outside Mithila.

Drawing from J.N. Bhattacharya's description of Brahmins in

Hindu society: 'The most remarkable feature in the mechanism of Hindu society is the high position occupied in it by the Brahmans. They not only claim almost divine honours as their birthright, but, generally speaking, the other classes, including the great Kshatriya princes, and the rich Vaishya merchants readily submit to their pretensions as a matter of course.'[92]

The Bhumihars, while classified as Brahmins, gained their power, prestige, and position through grants of land from Brahmin kings, beginning in the sixteenth century largely in north Bihar.[93] Their power and influence grew through meritorious military service, resulting in compensatory land grants for secular services and their recognition as zamindars.[94] The Bhumihars have always constituted a small proportion of Bihari population (around 3 per cent); however, with the partition of Bihar, their percentage has increased to 6 per cent.[95] The Bhumihars now find themselves in a unique position. Their electoral presence has become more visible and this newfound influence has prompted them to form private militias to protect their interests from the demands of Dalits and to fight extremist Naxalite groups who have traditionally represented low-caste Bihar peasants against upper caste exploitation.[96]

The majority of Bihar society, however, is made up of lower castes, many of whom are small landowners, tenants, sharecroppers, and landless agricultural labourers. Many of these people are members of the so-called backward castes – the Yadavs, Kurmis, Koeris, and Dalits and Muslims, although, technically, the Dalits and Muslims should not be grouped with the other backward castes listed.

As with almost any single element or component of India's social order, to talk of any type of cohesion within each caste is a popular form of oversimplification.[97] Nevertheless, within Bihar, probably more so than in any other state, caste plays an increasingly important part in the state's political process as various political groups compete for a share of the political power held by caste members' votes. Unlike elsewhere in India, caste politics seems to be oblivious to prevailing social and economic forces. The empowerment of the marginalized sections of Bihar's population is nothing new. It has been on-going since before Independence. However, its importance waxes and wanes often over extended periods.

The primary castes are also the core groups with whom all the other minor castes function as satellite groups allying themselves to one or more core groups from time to time. The Bhumihars and Brahmins are typically seen as the landed aristocracy who can ill-afford not to be involved in state-wide politics, as they have the most to lose.

During the social struggles of the mid-1980s and 1990s, a sense of empowerment grew within the politically and economically oppressed castes. The Yadavs, Kurmis, and Koeris, aligned themselves with non-Congress groups, thus destroying Congress's domination in the state. The upsurge in the Yadavs, with the election of Lalu Prasad Yadav as the chief minister in 1990, marked the rise to power of the so-called 'backward classes' and a concomitant decline in the power and authority of the upper castes, like the Maithil Brahmanas and Bhumihars. Between 1952 and 2004, the percentage of upper caste MPs returned from Bihar declined from 56.4 to 27.5 per cent, while during the same time period, MPs from the Other Backward Classes (OBCs) increased from 5.5 to 37.5 per cent.[98] No other state appears to be more progressive in its incorporation and integration of the backward classes in modern-day politics than Bihar, which belies the state's reputation as the poorest, most criminalized, most backward, and under-developed state in the Indian Union.

The upper castes, the Brahmins and Bhumihars, began to consolidate, largely in response to their lost political clout, as well as the rise of the so-called Naxalites. The basic demands of the Naxalites revolve around the need for equity, respect for women, payment of minimum wages, an end to the *begari* system, implementation of land ceilings, redistribution of land, and protection of the marginal farmers.[99]

Alarmed by the issues raised by the Naxalites, the landowners began organizing *senas*, privately financed armies. The first *sena* was formed by landlords in early 1994 and was known as The Ranvir Sena. It went unchecked for nearly a decade, and left in its wake a series of murders throughout Bihar. Between 1995 and 2000, the Ranvir Sena was accused of having perpetrated 27 massacres that left a total of 263 dead, mainly in the district of Bhojpur and Jehanabad.[100] Its primary victims were Dalits, Naxalites, and Maoists. Altogether,

13 such militias were formed and supported by both the backward and upper castes. Between 1976 and 2001, there were some 90 recorded incidents of local *sena* massacres resulting in the death of 860 people.[101]

The Naxalites gained a following among the agricultural labourers by organizing their efforts and defending them from landlord violence. The *sena's* aim was to suppress the labourers with a professional militia, with better training, weaponry and leadership. Private armies are a peculiarly Bihari phenomenon.

The *sena*, reportedly, participated in numerous 'massacres' of Dalits and Muslims, many of its victims were women and children. Although the *sena* was officially banned, it continues to operate with impunity throughout central Bihar. None of its organizers have been arrested, or if arrested, they have never been charged or prosecuted. Clearly, the *sena* enjoys, and has enjoyed, the protection of Bihar's elite politicians. And much of this support cuts across party lines. There is no other explanation for the *sena's* 'untouchability' by the law or the courts.

The Ranvir Sena continues to recruit among the unemployed and has gotten used to the power and the benefits that flow from the gun, and has no incentive to allow the confrontation to die out. An end to the cycle of retaliatory attacks, in fact, would erode the power of each of the contenders in these contests, and every time there is any perceived danger of peace breaking out, new atrocities are planned, confrontations intensify, and the platform for further conflict is strengthened. Within the orbit of this unceasing strife, there is no space for political consolidation; and this may be the true purpose for all the *senas* – the prevention of long-lasting political alliances between and among the unorganized political factions in Bihar – landed *versus* landed, tenants *versus* sharecroppers, and cultivators *versus* landless labourers.

* * *

In 2005 Nitish Kumar became the chief minister of Bihar, ousting Lalu Prasad Yadav's wife, Rabri Devi, from that position. He immediately gained popularity by initiating a series of developmental and construction plans, building long-delayed bridges, re-laying roads that had ceased to exist, appointing over 100,000 school teachers, ensuring that doctors worked in primary health centres, and keeping crime in check.[102] His efforts had the effect of propelling Bihar's economy forward.

Only days after the announcement that Bihar had posted a double-digit growth rate, in June 2012, however, another headline announced the outbreak of lawlessness and the murder of Brahmeshwar Singh, the unofficial chief of the outlawed Ranvir Sena. The violence resurrected memories of a Bihar that many had hoped had been put to rest, where lawlessness was a given, and the *sena* plundered and killed as it pleased.[103] In the case of Brahmeshwar Singh's murder, it would appear that those opposed to the *sena* have taken matters into their own hands. It has been said that where social-democracy ends, revolutionary-democracy begins its journey.[104]

Caste allegiances and alliances have dominated the political landscape of Bihar. The current political debate in Bihar is whether development can convince voters to abandon old loyalties in a state that has seen a recent increase in development and stimulated a boom for the growing middle and urban classes, but that has had little or no impact on the rural population. However, the apparent economic boom being acted out in Bihar is, at least in part, illusory, since it is based largely on capital-intensive infrastructural expenditures. In other words, large grants from the Centre account for much of the apparent economic growth, almost entirely a function of a construction boom. Once these funds dry-up, it is quite likely that Bihar's economic boom will go bust.

The apparent economic growth spurt has not been accompanied by equal progress in Bihar's agricultural sector. The agricultural sector's contribution to the state's overall economy is declining. If economic growth is about the creation of durable income-producing employment, Nitish's government, despite all its rhetoric, flag-waving, and hoopla, has not substantially improved the lives of the rural population – the largest block of potential consumers in Bihar.

Nitish is reported to have said: 'Most of the people are talking about development and no longer about caste. Development breaks down all the caste barriers.'[105] This comment would appear to fly in the face of recent events like the murder of Brahmeshwar Singh. Yes, on the one hand, there is visible economic development being achieved, at least within the context of GDP figures but, at the same time, the 'Jungle Raj' that was characterized by kidnappings, Maoist killings, and caste violence under Lalu Prasad Yadav seems to have begun again, in spite of favourable economic figures.

Economic figures aside, the words of a Rashtriya Janata Dal party campaign manager, Ram Bachan Roy, still have a ring of truth: 'Caste is the first election issue. Development is the second issue.'[106] His words bear attention, especially in light of the growing enmity between the landed upper castes and the poor tenants, landless labourers, and their protectors, the Naxalites. In many villages, the main concern still remains work and food. Roads and bridges are fine but it does not put food in the rural population's bellies. As a consequence, caste tensions continue.

* * *

The use of dubious statistics to prop-up any given government always results in problems for politicians. No election can be won on a platform of good governance and economic miracles alone. Caste arithmetic, money and muscle power are the tools used by politicians to influence votes and voters. Lalu's successes as a politician rested on his personal brand of popularism, his communication skills, his charisma, and his aggressive assertion of caste pride. He understood the nature of caste antipathy, social estrangement and constituency arithmetic. He put together alliances between the Muslims and Yadavs. He gave his followers a sense of political consciousness, social respect, security, and involvement. Unfortunately, his own personal foibles resulted in social abuse and despotism; and it was these that brought him down.

On many occasions election to public office changes the incumbent, raising him above the common man because government and state are innately elitist. The incumbent becomes part of the institution of power which carries with it the security of secrecy. It is within this clandestine environment that politics really operates. What goes on 'behind closed doors' is separated from what the electorate sees.

Lalu initially appeared to replace the previous elitist political paradigm, a paradigm that had operated 'successfully' since before Independence. After decades of successfully managing Bihar's political arena, the Congress party's hold on Bihar finally collapsed in 1990. In large measure, Congress's success was based upon social coalitions that included the large landowners, cutting across caste lines but excluded the upper backward castes (the Kurmis, Koeris, and Yadavs); the freedom movement; and its veiled support of Gandhian-Nehruvian socialism. Of these three, it was Congress's commitment to raising up the backward castes, women, Harijans, Muslims, and Adivasis that was, undoubtedly, its undoing. Congress support helped the backward castes to mobilize and organize, with the unanticipated result that they would one day want and demand to participate fully in and occupy their fair share of Bihar's political space, rather than continuing to align themselves with the Congress party.

The 1990 elections in Bihar were a watershed for the Congress. It marked the end of Congress's dominance in Bihar politics, an era that Jeffrey Witsoe has characterized as 'feudal democracy'.[107] From the perspective of the electorate, Congress had failed to deliver on the promises it had made during the independence movement and afterward. There were no tangible consequences from land reforms. Poverty continued unchecked. Prasad, at least initially, offered up individual rights, equity, fair treatment, dignity and, above all, the end to humiliation and discrimination. Congress had attempted to maintain the *status quo* and in so doing, it had lost touch with the largest block of voters in Bihar.

Congress's situation worsened with the appearance of upper caste senas in the late 1980s and early 1990s, designed to counter backward caste demands and Naxalism. The senas, together with blatant nepotism and corruption within government, further alienated Congress from the electorate. Caste empowerment became central to the democratic process and altered the ways in which the state was viewed by both the traditional leaders and the aspiring backward and other backward castes. Many people began to perceive the state and its institutions simply as corrupt sources of political patronage and this served to perpetuate upper-caste dominance and could be used to empower lower-caste groupings. Within this context, corruption was tolerated, sometimes celebrated, but generally simply manipulated to empower lower-caste vote banks.

By manipulating the state's compromised system, Lalu led a successful campaign based on the support of the backward castes and ending Congress's form of elitism. Over the next fifteen years Prasad ruled Bihar, either directly or indirectly the integrity of Bihar governance crumbled and along with it the welfare of the people. The people had simply exchanged one form of caste tyranny for another in the name of political progress. Lalu had effectively immobilized the government of Bihar for his own purposes, bleeding the state dry.[108]

Nitish, on the other hand, seldom mentions caste directly. However, he is not above manipulating castes for political ends. For example, his government recognized the Mallicks – a Muslim caste of central Bihar – as a backward caste, although it is arguably the most developed of all the Muslim castes in the state.[109] The question is why?

The Mallicks form a sizeable block of voters in the chief minister's home district of Nalanda as well as in Jehanabad, Patna, Nawada, Munger, and Gaya. Nitish saw a political opportunity and took it, taking advantage of the recent importance of caste among the Muslim communities in those districts.[110] Also, Nitish recently announced the establishment of an Upper Caste Commission to look into the grievances of the economically weak among the upper castes. If it is the desire of the Bihar government to disregard the role of caste in state politics, there should be no need for an upper caste inquiry. While he may wish caste was a *non sequiter* in Bihar politics, it is and will remain, for the foreseeable future, a potent part of the political process.

Nitish Kumar has brought security to the middle class; thousands have been jailed for crimes and, as a consequence, crime is down. Kidnappings and ransom demands have fallen, dacoit violence has been reduced. Nevertheless, there are three areas that continue to mould Bihar politics, and Nitish cannot simply dismiss them. These are caste, land, and poverty. No matter how successful he is at attracting development funds, he cannot ignore the realities of Bihar politics. Nitish will need to negotiate a new social contract with the people of Bihar if he is to build on his current successes. He will have to deliver on issues of land management (the economics of Bihar), elite power (disenfranchisement and disaffection), and old-fashioned Bihar politics (caste). To succeed, he will need to balance all three of these problem areas. Addressing one will only exacerbate the others.

* * *

When violence is combined with endemic corruption, one is faced with a deadly combination. Under these circumstances, is it any wonder that Bihar's infrastructure is crumbling, public services are nearly non-existent, development languishes, and, as Usha Alexander so aptly put it, an all pervasive 'sense of futility and widespread hopelessness' prevails.

OBSERVATIONS

Politics and politicians often determine the course of events, whether they be emperors, kings, rajas, or chiefs. They consolidate power and claim dominion, whether through the use of the sword or the ballot box.

From their lofty positions as zamindars and landowners, the upper castes dominated the politics of Mithila for centuries and this pattern was not openly challenged until 1990, when the Backward Castes of Bihar were able to seize political, albeit tenuous, dominance of Bihar's political scene. The politicization of the Backward and Other Backward Castes, while having the effect of displacing the upper castes as the dominant political force in Bihar's politics, also has served to destabilize the political process that has been labelled feudal democracy. Unstable alliances determine who rules and these often falter and are dissolved, making caste and caste affiliations the dominant political concern. Within this tenuousness, there is little time or inclination to press forward programmes that address the wants, desires, and needs of the people of Bihar. The maintenance of workable alliances consumes much of the leadership's time, attention, and energy, replacing good works; thus, little is achieved by any sitting chief minister.

Nevertheless, even the political power of the Backward and Other Backward Castes remains dependent upon the cooperation and support of the landed upper castes, which no longer occupy nor dominate the formal roles of leadership within the government of Bihar. Instead, they reap the advantages of power through landownership, the domination of rural society, and serve as unseen economic and political power brokers.

From their sanctuary, away from the public eye, these landowning aristocrats continue to control and prevent all legislation that might infringe upon their station and status. They obstruct, interfere with or blatantly disobey any legislation that poses a threat to them. When legitimate methods are insufficient, they resort to corruption, the manipulation of public services, the police, and judiciary, subterfuge, the redirection of issues, misdirection, and the use of private armies and gangs. While under the guise of opposing the Communist-inspired Naxalites, it would seem the large landowners have come, at least philosophically, full circle, accepting the legitimacy of one of Mao Zedong's favourite quotations, from his 'Little Red Book'. He suggests: Political power grows out of the barrel of a gun.[111]

NOTES

1. The author still remembers his first arrival in India – arriving in New Delhi on Pan Am Flight 002 from Teheran, on a hot and sultry day in mid-August 1974. The flights were still greeted on the tarmac by manually-operated airstairs. There were no jetways connected to the terminal. The instant that the author reached the door from the air-conditioned cabin of the aircraft, he was hit with a blast of hot air and smells he had never encountered before and was almost staggered. It was most overwhelming. Stories from other first-time arrivees are often more humorous due to automatic responses to the heat and smells. Some of these automatic responses were not very dignified. But humans are very adaptable creatures.
2. See, Amartya Sen, *Poverty and Famines: An Essay on Entitlement and Deprivation,* 16th Impression, Delhi: Oxford University Press, 1981/2011.
3. Cf., Michel Louis Séfériadès, 'Spondylus and Long-Distance Trade in Prehistoric Europe', ed. and tr. A.G. Brown, New York University - PDF downloadable article, pp. 178-89, as an example of the work being done to confirm the existence of regular prehistoric trade between and within Asia and Europe. See, also, Anthony Harding, 'World Systems, Cores, and Peripheries in Prehistoric Europe', *European Journal of Archaeology,* vol. 16, no. 3, August 2013, pp. 378-400, fn. 1, referring to Christop Kümmel, 'Frühe Weltsysteme: Zentrumund Peripherie-Modelle in der Archäologie', *Tübinger Texte, Materialien zur Ur- und Frühgeschichtlichen Archäologie* Heidelberg: Heidelberg University, vol. 4, 2001, which provides detailed information on Old World trade systems dating back to the second and third millennia BC.

4. Cf., Susan Whitfield, *Life Along the Silk Road,* Berkeley: University of California Press, 1999; Susan Whitfield and Ursula Sims-Williams, *The Silk Route: Trade, Travel, War and Faith,* London: British Library, 2004.
5. See, Rozina Visram, *Asians in Britain: 400 Years of History,* London: Pluto, 2002; Michael H. Fisher, *Counterflows to Colonialism: Indian Travellers and Settlers in Britain, 1600-1857,* Delhi: Permanent Black, 2004. See, also, Amrita Satapathy, 'The Idea of England in Eighteenth-century Indian Travel Writing', in M.G. Ramanan and T. Mukherjee (eds.), *CLCWeb: Comparative Literature and Culture – Thematic Issue New Work in Comparative Indian Literatures and Cultures,* vol. 14, no. 2, June 2012, Article 3, pp. 1-8.
6. Will Sweetman, 'The Prehistory of Orientalism: Colonialism and the Textual Basis for Bartholomaus Ziegenbalg's Account of Hinduism', *New Zealand Journal of Asian Studies,* vol. 6, no. 2, December 2004, pp. 12-38.
7. Edward W. Said, *Orientalism,* Delhi: Penguin Books, 1978, 2001.
8. Masoud Kamali, 'Conceptualizing the "Other", Institutionalized Discrimination, and Cultural Racism', Miscellaneous E-publication, Department of Sociology, University of Uppsala, Uppsala, n.d.
9. See, Harry Oldmeadow, 'The Debate about "Orientalism"', Bloomington: World Wisdom, 2004, pp. 3-19, especially pp. 10-16.
10. See, Emmanuel Chukwudi Eze, *Race and the Enlightenment: A Reader,* ed. Emmanuel Chukwud Eze, Cambridge, MA: Blackwell, 1997.
11. Rosane Rocher, 'British Orientalism in the Eighteenth Century: The Dialectics of Knowledge and Government', in Carol Appadurai Breckenridge and Peter van der Veer, *Orientalism and the Postcolonial Predicament: Perspectives on South Asia*, Philadelphia: University of Pennsylvania Press, 1993, p. 215.
12. Sigrid Kahle, 'Orientalism Sverige' in the Preface, in Edward Said, *Orientalism,* Stockholm: Ordfront, 1993, pp. 7-62.
13. Ian Buruma and Avishai Margalit, *Occidentalism: The West in the Eyes of Its Enemies,* New York: Penguin, 2004, p. 75. It is ironic that Buruma and Margalit, while suggesting that Occidentalism is the antithesis of Orientalism, have crafted their argument in such a way that their version of Occidentalism seems to get dangerously close to the Orientalism they profess to be arguing against.
14. Gun powder became war rockets. Steel became swords and later tanks. Dynamite became bombs. Nuclear physics brought us atomic and nuclear bombs. Airplanes became fighters and bombers. GPS became guidance systems. Virology and bacteriology became biological weapons. Electronics became guidance systems and communication. The list is endless.
15. While the US appears to be the worst offender in terms of unbridled electronic surveillance, no country can claim to be free of or immune to accusations of the electronic invasion of privacy, the growth of which was spurred on,

exponentially, by the events of 9/11. To some, this is a necessary evil; to others, it is a gross invasion of individual civil liberties. Today, to escape surveillance and reclaim one's privacy is practically impossible. To do so would entail foregoing the use of all electronic devices which, with today's growing dependence on social and economic media – connectivity – would mean withdrawing from society, and most of us are unwilling to disconnect ourselves to ensure our privacy. It is a trade-off many of us are not prepared to make.

16. Holden Furber, 'The History of East India Companies: General Problems', in *Sociétés et Compagnies de Commerce en Orient et dans l'Océan Indien; actes du huitième Colloque international d'histoire maritime (Beyrouth, 5-10 septembre 1966)*, ed. Michel Mollat, Paris: SEVPEN, Bibliothèque générale de l'École pratique des hautes études, Sciences économiques et sociales, pp. 415-18, especially pp. 415-16.
17. Said, *Orientalism,* 1978, 2001.
18. Quote from Arthur Koestler, *The Lotus and the Robot,* New York: Macmillan, 1960, p. 11.
19. Ibid.
20. See, Wihelm Halbfass, *India and Europe: An Essay in Understanding,* Albany: State University of New York Press, 1988, p. 369.
21. Chris Tiffin and Alan Lawson (eds.), *De-scribing Empire: Post-colonialism and Textuality,* Routledge: London, 1994, p. 9. Many modern African national boundaries are simple extensions of late-nineteenth century land-grabs by the European powers that ignored tribal and linguistic differences between native Africans and, even today, contributes to inter-tribal animosities, conflicts, and warfare.
22. See, Michel Foucault, *Discipline and Punish: The Birth of the Prison,* New York: Vintage, 2009.
23. See, Antonio Gramsci, *Prison Notebooks: Selections,* New York, London: Lawrence & Wishart, 1998.
24. Gyan Prakash, 'Writing Post-Orientalist Histories of the Third World: Perspectives from Indian Historiography', *Comparative Studies in Society and History: An International Quarterly,* vol. 32, January 1990, pp. 383-408.
25. Anirudh Raghavan, *British Orientalism in India: Nature and Impact on Indian Society (A Historiographical Survey); Critically Analyze the Nature of Orientalism and its Impact on Indian History with an Emphasis on Edward Said's Arguments,* 2014, http://www.academia.edu/2565126/British_Orientalism_in_India_Nature_and_Impact_on_Indian_Society_A_Historiographical_Survey.
26. See, Suzanne L. Marchand, *German Orientalism in the Age of Empire: Religion, Race, and Scholarship,* Cambridge: German Historical Institute & Cambridge University Press, 2010. See, also, James Hodkinson, John Walker, Shaswati Mazumdar and Johannes Feichtinger, *Deploying Orientalism in Culture and*

History: From Germany to Central and Eastern Europe, Rochester: Camden House, 2013, especially chapter 1, '(Re)translating the West: Humboldt, Habermas, and Intercultural Dialogue', pp. 15-30; Robert Lemon, *Imperial Messages: Orientalism as Self-critique in the Habsburg Fin de Siècle,* Rochester: Camden House, 2011.

27. Richard King, *Orientalism and Religion: Postcolonial Theory, India and 'the Mystic East',* Routledge: London, 1999, p. 35. See, also, Peter Harrison, *'Religion' and the Religions in the British Enlightenment,* Cambridge: Cambridge University Press, 1990, p. 1; Sarah F. Hoyt, 'The Etymology of Religion', *Journal of the American Oriental Society,* vol. 32, no. 2, 1912, pp. 126-9.
28. S.N. Balagangadhara, *'The Heathen in His Blindness': Asia, the West and the Dynamic of Religion,* Leiden: E.J. Brill, Studies in the History of Religions, no. 64, 1994, p. 46.
29. Sarah F. Hoyt, 'The Etymology of Religion', *Journal of the American Oriental Society,* vol. 32, no. 2, 1912, pp. 126-9, DOI: 10.2307/3087765, see, p. 126.
30. Walter Ong, *Orality and Literacy: The Technologizing of the Word,* London: Methuen, 1982, p. 7.
31. Carl A. Keller, 'Mystical Literature', in Steven Katz (ed.), *Mysticism and Philosophical Analysis,* New York: Oxford University Press, 1978, p. 97.
32. David R. Kinsley, *Hinduism: A Cultural Perspective,* 2nd edn., Englewood Cliffs: Prentice-Hall, 1993, pp. 55-7.
33. Mark William Muesse, *The Hindu Traditions: A Concise Introduction,* Minneapolis: Fortress Press, 2011, p. 3.
34. Richard King, *Orientalism and Religion: Postcolonial Theory, India and 'the Mystic East',* 1999, pp. 37-41.
35. Mark William Muesse, *The Hindu Traditions: A Concise Introduction,* 2011, p. 3.
36. Ibid., p. 4.
37. Charles Dickens, *Hard Times,* Champaign: Project Gutenberg, no. 786, 1990.
38. Swami Prabhavananda and Christopher Isherwood, *Bhagavad-Gita: The Song of God, Introduction by Aldous Huxley,* London: Phoenix House, 1947, pp. 6-7.
39. John Campbell Oman, *The Stories of the Ramayana and the Mahabharata,* London: George Bell & Sons, 1899, pp. v-vi.
40. Romila Thapar, *A History of India,* vol. I, Baltimore: Penguin Books, 1966, p. 28. See, also, Radhakrishna Chaudhary, *Mithilā in the Age of Vidyāpati,* Varanasi: Chaukhambha Orientalia, 1973, p. 8; P. C. Roy Chaudhury, *Bihar District Gazetteers: Darbhanga,* Patna: Superintendent, Secretariat Press, 1964, p. 25; and Ranganath Ramachandra Diwakar (ed.), *Bihar Through the Ages,* Bombay: Orient Longman, 1958/9, pp. 94-6.

41. Shyam Narayan Singh, *History of Tirhut: From the Earliest Times to the End of the Nineteenth Century*, 2nd edn., ed. Hetukar Jha, Darbhanga: Maharajadhiraja Kameshwar Singh Kalyani Foundation, Maharajadhiraja Kameshwar Singh Bihar Heritage Series 16, 2012, chapter II, pp. 6-9.
42. E.J. Rapson (ed.), *The Cambridge History of India: Ancient India,* 3rd Indian reprint, vol. I, Delhi: S. Chand & Co., 1968, chapter IV, p. 100. See, also, Maurizio Taddei, *The Ancient Civilization Series: India,* tr. James Hogarth, London: Barrie & Jenkins, 1970, pp. 39-47.
43. Peter Robb, *A History of India*, New York: Palgrave, 2002., p. 28.
44. J. Keay, Introduction, *India: A History,* New York: Grove Press, 2000, p. xxvii.
45. D.D. Kosambi, *Ancient India: A History of Its Culture and Civilization*, New York: Pantheon Books, 1965, p. 9.
46. Edward J. Rapson, *Ancient India: From the Earliest Times to the First Century A.D.*, 3rd edn., New Delhi: Asian Educational Services, 1995, p. 8.
47. Sheldon Pollock, *The Language of the Gods in the World of Men: Sanskrit, Culture, and Power in Premodern India*, Berkeley: University of California Press, 2006, p. 1.
48. Kalhana, the twelfth century Kashmiri author of the *Rajatarangini* (*Chronicle of Kings*), an account of the history of Kashmir.
49. Ainslee T. Embree (ed.), *Alberuni's India*, abridged edition, tr. Edward C. Sachau, New York: W. W. Norton & Co., 1971, chapter XLIX, pp. 10-11.
50. Robin A. Donkin, 'Beyond Price: Pearls and Pearl-Fishing: Origins to the Age of Discoveries', *Memoirs of the American Philosophical Society*, vol. 224, 1998, p. 152.
51. *Śruti* - the body of sacred texts comprising the central canons of Hinduism and is one of the three main sources of dharma. It is considered solely of divine origin.
52. Shyam Narayan Singh, *History of Tirhut: From the Earliest Times to the End of the Nineteenth Century,* 2nd edn., 2012 suggests that in the *Śatpatha Brāhmaṇa*, which is much older than the fifth century BC, Videha was not yet Brahmanized but it also affords clear evidence that the Brahmanical system existed in Videha (Tirhut) by the time of King Janak of Videha, pp. 6-9.
53. Philip Schaff, *NPNF1-02. St. Augustine's City of God and Christian Doctrine.* New York: Christian Literature Publishing, 1890, Box XIII, chapter 19, p. 344.
54. Alfred Reginald Radcliffe-Brown, *Structure and Function in Primitive Society: Essays and Addresses,* Glencoe: The Free Press, 1952, p. 130.
55. Deepa Narayan, Raj Patel, K. Schafft, A. Rademacher and S. Koch-Schulte, *Voices of the Poor: Can Anyone Hear Us?* New York: World Bank & Oxford University Press, 2000, p. 229.
56. Ibid., p. 267

57. D. Goulet, 'Development Experts: The One-eyed Giants', *World Development,* vol. 8, nos. 7-8, August 1980, p. 485.
58. Judith A. Mayotte, 'Religion and Global Affairs: The Role of Religion in Development', *SAIS Review,* vol. 18, no. 2, Summer-Fall 1998, pp. 65-9.
59. Colin Leys, *The Rise and Fall of Development Theory,* Oxford: James Currey, 1996.
60. Peter L. Berger, *Sacred Canopy: Elements of a Sociological Theory of Religion.* Reprint, New York: Anchor Books, 1990.
61. Gerrie Ter Haar, 'Religion: Source of Conflict or Resource for Peace?', in *Bridge or Barrier: Religion, Violence and Visions for Peace*, ed. Gerrie Ter Haar and James J. Busuttil, Leiden & Boston: Brill, 2005, pp. 3-34.
62. For example, The World Bank, the International Monetary Fund, and the Knowledge Centre on Religion and Development. See, also, Katherine Marshall and Lucy Keough, *Mind, Heart, and Soul in the Fight against Poverty,* Washington, DC: World Bank, 2004; Katherine Marshall, 'Development and Religion: A Different Lens on Development Debates', *Peabody Journal of Education,* vol. 76, nos. 3-4, 1998, pp. 339-75; Wendy Tyndale, 'Poverty and Development: Has Religion a Contribution to Make?', *Commentary: International Movement for a Just World,* vol. 1, no. 2, 2001a, pp. 1-5; Wendy Tyndale, 'Towards Sustainable Development: A Shift in Values', *Commentary: International Movement for a Just World,* vol. 1, no. 8, 2001b, pp. 1-4.
63. William Easterly, *The White Man's Burden: Why the West's Efforts to Aid the Rest Have Done so Much Ill and so Little Good,* New York: Penguin Press, 2006.
64. Institute for Studies in Global Prosperity, *Science, Religion, and Development: Promoting a Discourse in India, Brazil, and Uganda - Occasional Papers on Insight and Practice 1,* New York: Institute of Studies in Global Prosperity, 2010, p. 2.
65. Lloyd I. Rudolph and Susanne Hoeber Rudolph, *The Modernity of Tradition: Political Development in India,* Hyderabad: Orient Longman, 1984, p. 5.
66. Marx's full comment reads: 'Religion is the sigh of the oppressed creature, the heart of a heartless world, and the soul of soulless conditions. It is the opium of the people' Karl Marx, 'A Contribution to the Critique of Hegel's Philosophy of Right', Deutsch-Französische Jahrbücher, Proofed and Corrected by Andy Blunden and Corrected by Matthew Carmody, 2005 & 2009, February 7 & 10, 1844.
67. See, Gilles Carbonnier, 'Religion and Development: Reconsidering Secularism as the Norm', April 2013. http://poldev.revues.org/1351.
68. Romila Thapar, 'Ideology and the Interpretation of Early Indian History', *Social Science Information,* vol. 20, no. 2, 1981, p. 239.
69. See, Graeme Smith, *A Short History of Secularism,* London: I.B. Tauris, 2008 for an provocative study of secularism in the West.

70. Ibid., p. 2.
71. Cf., Megan Willett, 'A Fascinating New Poll Shows That Americans are Losing Faith in God', 17 December 2013, http://www.businessinsider.com/new-harris-poll-on-religion-in-america-2013-12; Harris, 'Americans' Belief in God, Miracles and Heaven Declines', 16 December 2013, http://www.harrisinteractive.com/NewsRoom/HarrisPolls/tabid/447/ctl/ReadCustom%20Default/mid/1508/ArticleId/1353/Default.aspx; and Pew Forum on Religion & Public Life. *U. S. Religious Landscape Survey: Religious Affiliations: Diverse and Dynamic,* Washington, DC: The Pew Forum on Religion & Public Life, February 2008.
72. Pew Forum on Religion & Public Life. *U.S. Religious Landscape Survey: Religious Affiliations: Diverse and Dynamic,* February 2008.
73. Office of National Statistics. *Religion in England and Wales 2011.* London: Government of Great Britain, 2012, pp. 1 and 2; and *Scotland's Census 2011*: Table KS209Ca.
74. Andrew Copson, 'Comment: Religion is in Decline – So Why are People so Well Behaved?' 27 June 2013, http://www.politics.co.uk/comment-analysis/ 2013/06/27/comment-religion-is-in-decline-so-why-are-people-so-well-beh. Copson reports that 82 per cent of young adults obtain their moral direction from their parents and 77 per cent from their friends.
75. See, Bernard Lewis, *Islam and the West,* New York: Oxford University Press, 1993, p. 4.
76. Louay M. Safi, 'Islam and the Secular State', 2001, http://www.islamawareness.net/Secularism/secular.html.
77. Andrew J. Waskey, 'The Political Theory of Theocracy', *National Social Science Journal* (National Social Science Association), vol. 28, no. 1, 2007, pp. 116-29.
78. Cf., Charles Tripp, 'All (Muslim) Politics Is Local: How Context Shapes Islam in Power'. Gilles Kepel and Ali A. Allawi explore the troubled relationship between power and Islam and conclude, each in his own way, that Muslims who seek to shape the world according to their religious values are often confronted by the mundane need to bend an often obdurate reality. Retrieved from *Foreign Affairs,* from: http://www.foreignaffairs.com/articles/65229/charles-tripp/all-muslim-politics-is-local, September/October 2009 issue.
79. Purnendu Kishore Banerjee, Registrar General and Census Commissioner, *Management of Statistical Information in Socio Economic and Caste Census – India,* New Delhi: Office of the Registrar General and Census Commissioner, April 2014, p. 3.
80. See, Ministry of Rural Development, *Socio Economic & Caste Census, 2001, in Rural India,* Delhi: Government of India, 25 July 2011. Quotation: Ministry of Rural Development, *Socio-Economic and Caste Census, 2011 –*

Rural Instruction Manual for Enumerators, New Delhi: Government of India, 2011, p. 4.

81. Personal e-mail communication from R. Vineel Krishna, Personal Secretary to M(RD), 3 April 2014.
82. In the same communication from Krishna, above, he indicated that the entire SECC process was in suspension due to the upcoming national elections. Considering the potential volatility of those elections and the inflammatory purposes to which the SECC data could or would be put, it is probably a very sound decision to postpone the release of its findings until after the election, which is to be held between 7 April and 12 May 2014.
83. See, Ramachandra Guha, 'The Wisest Man in India', 4 December 2005, http://www.hindu.com/mag/2005/12/04/stories/2005120400480300.htm; and for Béteille's observation: Express News Service, 'Politics Keeping Caste System Alive', 1 March 2011, http://archive.indianexpress.com/news/-politics-keeping-caste-system-alive-/756166/. Andre Béteille is Professor Emeritus in the Department of Sociology, University of Delhi.
84. Ibid.
85. André Béteille, 'India's Destiny not Caste in Stone', 21 February 2012, http://www.thehindu.com/todays-paper/tp-opinion/indias-destiny-not-caste-in-stone/article2914365.ece.
86. A 'failed state' may be characterized by:
    - The practical loss of control over its territory.
    - The erosion of legitimate authority to make collective decisions.
    - Widespread corruption and criminality.
    - An inability to provide public services.
    - An inability to interact with other states as a full member of the national or international community.
    - A sharp and observable economic decline.
87. Manish K. Jha and Pushpendra, *Governing Caste and Managing Conflicts Bihar, 1990-2011: Policies and Practices, Report no. 48,* Kolkata: Mahanirban Calcutta Research Group, March 2012, p. 4.
88. M.M. Srinivas, *Social Change in Modern India,* rpt., Hyderabad: Orient Longman, 1995/2005, p. 6. 'Sanskritization is the process by which a "low" Hindu caste, or tribal or other group, changes its customs, ritual, ideology and way of life in the direction of a high, and frequently, "twice-born" case.' (p. 6)
89. Carolyn Henning Brown, 'The Gift of a Girl: Hierarchical Exchange in North Bihar', *Ethnology: An International Journal of Cultural and Social Anthropology,* vol. 22, no. 1, 1983, p. 59.
90. M.M. Srinivas, *Social Change in Modern India,* rpt., 1995/2005, p. 4.
91. If, as Metcalf and Metcalf suggest, based on recent scholarship, 'much of the subcontinent was little touched by the four normative hierarchic

categories (varnas) . . .' prior to the British takeover. This would tend to support the argument that it was the British who were largely responsible for the formalization and crystallization of the varnas and the caste system. (Barbara D. Metcalf and Thomas R. Metcalf, *A Concise History of Modern India*, 2nd edn., Cambridge: Cambridge University Press, 2001, 2006, p. 24).

92. Jogendra Nath Battacharya, *Hindu Castes and Sects,* Calcutta: Thacker, Spink & Co., 1896, p. 19.
93. See, Ranajit Guha, Partha Chatterjee, David Arnold and Gautam Bhadra, *Subaltern Studies: Writings on South Asian History and Society,* ed. Ranajit Guha, vol. 9, Delhi: Oxford University Press, 2008; Seema Alavi, *The Eighteenth Century in India,* ed. Seema Alavi, Delhi: Oxford University Press, 2002; Peter G. Robb, *Peasants, Political Economy, and Law: Empire, Identity, and India,* Delhi: Oxford University Press, 2007; Christopher Alan Bayly, *Recovering Liberties: Indian Thought in the Age of Liberalism and Empire: The Wiles Lectures Given at the Queen's University of Belfast, 2007,* Cambridge: Cambridge University Press, Ideas in Context Series, no. 100, 2012.
94. Susan Bayly, *Caste, Society and Politics in India from the Eighteenth Century to the Modern Age,* Cambridge: Cambridge University Press, New Cambridge History of India, IV, 3, 2001, p. 203.
95. Arun Kumar, 'Bhumihars Rooted to the Ground in Caste Politics', 25 January 2005, http://articles.timesofindia.indiatimes.com/2005-01-25/patna/27831627_1_bhumihars-caste-politics.
96. Human Rights Watch, *IV, The Pattern of Abuse: Rural Violence in Bihar and the State's Response,* March 1999, http://www.hrw.org/reports/1999/india/India994-06.htm, Section IV: The Pattern of Abuse: Rural Violence in Bihar and the State's Response.
97. Shree Nagesh Jha, 'Caste in Bihar Politics', *Economic and Political Weekly,* vol. 5, no. 7, February 1970, p. 341.
98. Cyril Robin, 'Bihar: The New Stronghold of OBC Politics', in *Rise of the Plebeians?: The Changing Face of the Indian Legislative Assemblies,* ed. Christophe Jaffrelot and Sanjay Kumar, pp. 65-102, Hoboken: Taylor & Francis, 2012, esp. p. 65.
99. The issue of rape and the denial of minimum wages were initially basic demands. The fight now is for *maan* and *samman,* or self respect, which, in the eyes of the higher castes, translates into a misdemeanour by the lower castes. *Begari,* a term used for work taken from the labourer beyond normal hours or expectations, or work without commensurate pay.
100. N. Jaoul, 'Naxalism in Bihar: From Bullet to Ballot', in *Armed Militias of South Asia: Fundamentalists, Maoists and Separatists,* ed. L. Gayer and C. Jaffrelot, pp. 19-46, Delhi: Foundation Books, 2009, esp. p. 46.

101. Prakash Louis, *People Power: The Naxalite Movement in Central Bihar,* Delhi: Wordsmiths, 2002, pp. 241-6.
102. IANS, 'Nitish Kumar's Development Agenda Makes Waves in Bihar', 1 May 2009, http://indiatoday.intoday.in/story/Nitish+Kumar%27s+development+agenda+makes+waves+in+Bihar/1/39785.html.
103. N. Kesavan, 'Bihar's Caste Curse', 5 June 2012, http://www.thehindu.com/opinion/editorial/article3490670.ece.
104. Vinod Mishra, 'The Heroes have Finally Arrived on the Stage! - Excerpts from the Report from the Flaming Fields of Bihar', 2005, http://www.cpiml.org/liberation/year_2005/january/remembering_vm.htm.
105. Reuters. 'Caste Calculations Still Dictate Bihar Politics', 9 April 2009, http://www.indianexpress.com/news/caste-calculations-still-dictate-bihar-politics/445052/.
106. Ibid.
107. Jeffrey Witsoe, 'Corruption as Power: Caste and Political Imagination of the Postcolonial State', *American Ethnologist,* vol. 38, no. 1, 2011, pp. 73-85.
108. Manish K. Jha and Pushpendra, *Governing Caste and Managing Conflicts Bihar, 1990-2011: Policies and Practices, Report No. 48,* March 2012 provides an excellent analysis of the fall of Congress-led governance and the rise of Lalu Prasad Yadav and the consequences of his 'De-Elitisation of the Government' of Bihar.
109. Soroor Ahmed, 'Beyond Bihar', 10 March 2012. http://www.telegraphindia.com/1110310/jsp/opinion/story_13690337.jsp.
110. The recognition of caste among Muslims, while, in all likelihood having historical roots, is anathema to Islam and its social and political recognition is an interesting social development but even more so for aspiring, vote-hungry politicians.
111. Mao Zedong, *Quotations from Chairman Mao* (The Little Red Book), Peking: Foreign Languages Press, 1964, chapter 5. The longer quotation reads: 'Every Communist must grasp the truth: Political power grows out of the barrel of a gun.'

CHAPTER 6

The Darbhanga Raj: The Heart of Mithila

The Darbhanga Raj was among the last of the large zamindaris in Imperial Bengal at the time of Independence. Unlike the majority of the large zamindaris which had been broken up in response to the Permanent Settlement's oft-referred 'Sunset Law', it had avoided dissolution through personal sale or purchase and had successfully avoided bankruptcy and dismemberment at the hands of the British. In fact, it was one of the few large estates that had grown in extent and revenues from 1860 onward.[1] Its unique ability to survive the vicissitudes of imperial administration was only exceeded by its historical importance and the role it played in Mithila's past and present society, economy, and politics.

Although the Darbhanga Raj ceased to exist as a unified political and economic entity soon after Independence, the title of 'maharaja', or more specifically, maharajadhiraja,[2] was used by the Maharaja of Darbhanga until the death of the last maharaja – Kameshwar Singh Bahadur – in 1962. Despite the fact that Kameshwar Singh died heirless and had not specified a successor, the title of 'maharaja' has continued to be used by court-appointed relatives of the late maharaja until the death of Maharaja Subheshwar Singh Bahadur in 2006. Since then, there has been no maharaja and succession has been the subject of nearly continuous litigation and contention among the maharaja's relatives.

One of the most important and enduring functions of the Maharaja of Darbhanga had been as the secular head of the *Srotriya* division of the Maithil Brahmanas which, in effect, made the maharajas the head of all the Maithil Brahmanas. The *Srotriyas* are Brahmanas who follow the *Shrauta* (*Śrauta*) tradition, having the right to read and teach the Vedas, and who continue to practice what is believed to be one of the most orthodox forms of ritualistic Vedic Hinduism that includes strict and elaborate matrimonial customs.[3]

A BRIEF POLITICAL HISTORY OF THE DARBHANGA RAJ

Tradition suggests that Mithila began with the establishment of the kingdom of Videha, mentioned in the *Ramayana*. Today the terms Videha, Mithila, Tribhukti, and Tirhut, when used geographically, are generally overlapping terms denoting the area from the river Gandak in the west to the Mahananda River (the approximate modern boundary of Bihar and West Bengal) in the east, and from the foothills of the Himalayas – the terai region of south-eastern Nepal – to the Ganga in the south[4] (see Map 6.1).

During the medieval and early modern period, Mithila was never consolidated as a single enduring kingdom. Until the fourteenth century, it was ruled by a series of Bengali kings and local chieftains.[5] As the Muslim rulers swept eastward toward Bengal, Mithila came under successive Muslim dynasties.

Legendary Beginnings of the Darbhanga Raj

There are numerous legends that describe the origin of the Darbhanga Raj. All agree that a land grant was made by the Mughal Emperor Abu'l-Fath Jalal ud-din Muhammad Akbar (aka Akbar) in 1577 to Mahesh Thakur. However, a recent reinterpretation of the historical record tends to push the Raj's origins back by more than two hundred years to 1353. These documents suggest that in *c.* 1326, the armies of Sultan Firoz Shah Tughlaq conquered the rogue territory known as Mithila/Tirhut. The Rajputs who occupied this agriculturally rich territory were little more than warring chieftains, and Firoz Shah was determined to place Tirhut under the umbrella of his growing empire. After defeating the rajas and extracting their promise to acknowledge his authority, suzerainty, and make regular tribute payments to the royal treasury, Firoz Shah's armies withdrew. Peace prevailed and the rajas paid their tribute but this was short-lived. Soon war broke out again between the chieftains.

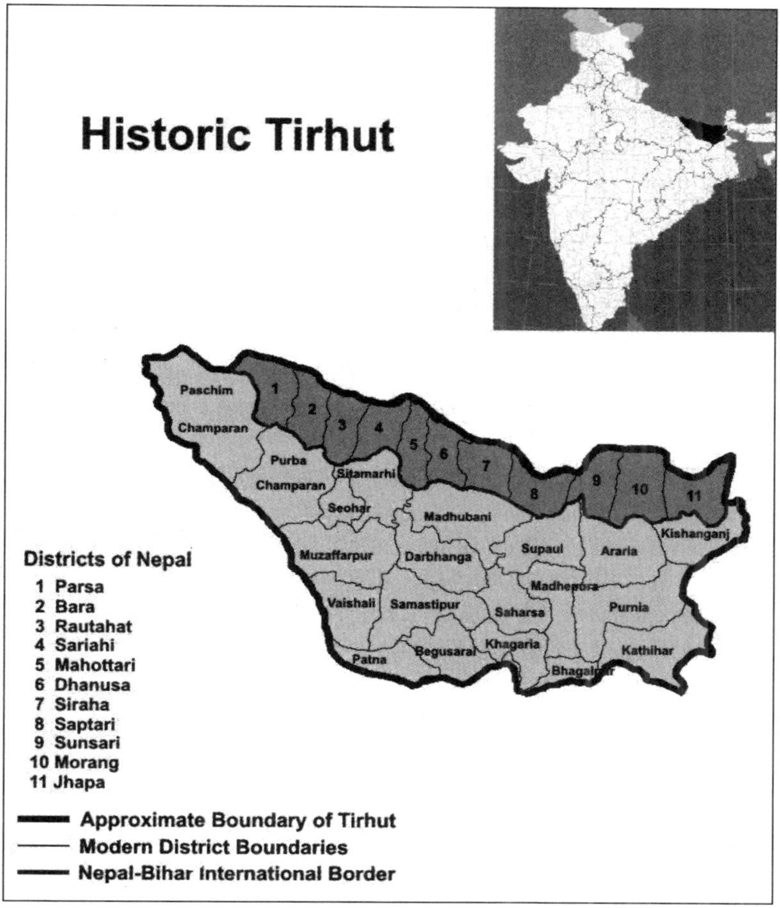

MAP 6.1: APPROXIMATE HISTORIC EXTENT OF HISTORIC VIDEHA/MITHILA/TIRHUT[6]

The Sultan was unable to return to Tirhut to restore peace until 1353 and it was then that he appointed the pundit Kameshwar Thakur as a *karad raja* (a rent-paying king). With his appointment, Kameshwar Thakur became the first raja of the Oinwar Dynasty.[7] This dynasty ruled in Mithila until 1526 when Lakshminath Singh Dev died in battle without an heir.[8]

The Oinwars, much like their predecessors – the Janakas of Videha –

were primarily scholars who patronized religious and philosophical debate, speculation and writing, music and the arts, the development of social regulations and law, all of which became the cultural foundation for Mithila and Maithil society.[9]

For a period of approximately thirty years, following the last of the Oinwar rajas, Mithila fell into a state of lawlessness and, again, small disorganized petty chiefdoms arose. Among these chiefs was Mahesh Thakur, who gradually consolidated his power and became recognized as one of the more powerful petty Brahmin kings in the region. As the recognized King of Madhubani, Akbar chose Mahesh to be the King of Mithila/Tirhut, thus establishing the Khandavala Dynasty.[10] This dynasty flourished, becoming one of the few Brahmin dynasties in India, and henceforth, only Brahmin kings ruled over Mithila.

Mithila had Brahmin kings in the past but foreign invasions prevented the establishment of any long-term dynastic Brahmin rule. The Khandavala Dynasty ruled in an unbroken line of monarchs until 1960, when the last Maharaja of Darbhanga, Kameshwar Singh Bahadur, died without naming a successor.[11]

Over time, the Darbhanga Raj expanded and contracted as territories were won and lost due to intrigue, armed conflict, purchase and sale. While Firoz Shah Tughlaq conferred on Kameshwar Thakur the right to collect taxes within Tirhut, and Akbar, likewise, placed Mithila/Tirhut under the jurisdiction of Mahesh Thakur, the actual estates making up the Darbhanga Raj were territorially much smaller than the *sanad* lands the raja was granted.[12] Map 6.2 depicts the maximum area of the Darbhanga Raj. Ultimately, British intervention in Nepali politics deprived the Darbhanga Raj of its holdings in Nepal.[13] Nonetheless, the Darbhanga Raj was still a very large estate. The Raj was conceptually differentiated from territorial Mithila and Tirhut. Contemporary records suggest that at the time of Independence and just before Maharajadhiraja Kameshwar Singh Bahadur relinquished his claim to the Raj, it comprised approximately 6,200 square kilometres and included nearly 4,500 villages in 14-18 administrative circles.[14] After the loss of its Nepal estates, the Raj still consisted of all or part of 17 districts in northern Bihar.[15] It must be remembered that the process of acquisition and attrition, sale and

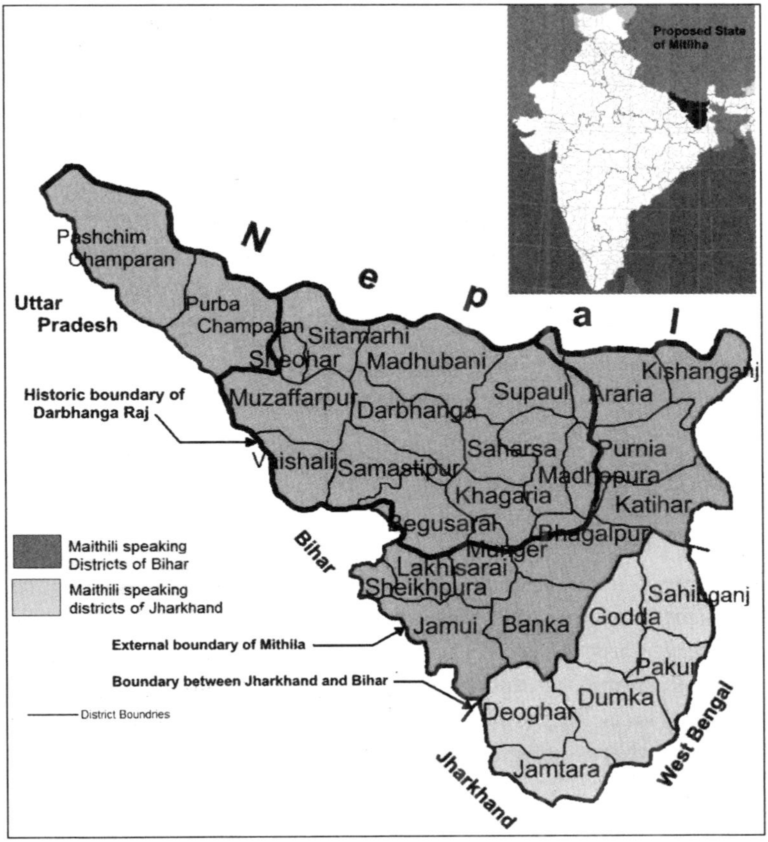

MAP 6.2: HISTORIC EXTENT OF THE DARBHANGA RAJ WITHIN MITHILA[16]

purchase of minor estates by the Raj would have made it appear much like a quilt work of properties. Some would be contiguous, while others might be far flung, scattered, and isolated. Thus, it may be misleading to suggest that the Raj owned entire districts. Here, we suggest only that large portions of these districts were under the ownership or jurisdiction of the Raj's land management corps.

The modern concept of Mithila differs significantly from its historic extent. Mithila has grown in extent due to the expansion of Maithili culture, largely assimilating Bhojpuri populations.[17] Its modern boundaries are depicted in Map I.2, of the Introduction, and includes

31 districts (25 in modern-day Bihar and 6 in Jharkhand). This is an area that is somewhat larger than historical Mithila.

Since the formation of Jharkhand, there has been a growing interest in the creation of the linguistic state of Mithila. The suggestion that a state of Mithila should be created dates back to Independence but to date little has been done by the Centre with regard to recognizing these demands.[18] However, carving yet another state from Bihar, in all likelihood, would have devastating economic consequences for the remainder state, as the diminished number of districts would severely handicap its ability to remain viable or tenable.

The Importance of the Darbhanga Raj

The importance of the Raj stems from: (1) its longevity, existing in one form or another with a largely unbroken chain of rajas from 1353 until 1947 (1962), longer than either the East India Company or the Mughal Empire;[19] (2) it was one of a very few enduring Brahmin kingdoms in northern India; (3) it retained its identity and geographical footprint within northern Bihar, long after other similar kingdoms and zamindaris ceased to exist; and (4) in addition to its profound social, economic, and political impact and influence, it represented a cultural locus for the Maithil Brahmanas, and it may be this aspect of the Raj that is ultimately most important to our purpose.

* * *

Changes for the Khandavalas

The title of king passed down through the generations of the Khandavala Dynasty to Mahinath Thakur. Mahinath's service and exploits on behalf of Emperor Aurangzeb solidified the family's connections with the emperor. Mahinath and his forces supported those of the emperor in the conquest of Palamau in southern Bihar and in the suppression of the zamindars of Morang in the southern terai region of south-eastern Nepal. In *c.* 1684, a letter was sent from Aurangzeb, addressed to the *subedar* (provincial governor) of Bengal Province, Shaesta Khan. This letter forever changed the status of the

Khandavalas, differentiating them from every other zamindar in Bengal and Bihar. The letter included the following passage:

> Since this Hindu Brahmin has displayed such valour, I have by an exalted farman, granted him the Sadr Zamindari and settlement of Sarkar Tirhut, and Zamindari of Pargana Dharampur, Sarkar Monghyr, and conferred upon him a Khilat and the Mhai Maratib [Mughal honors]. The valiant Khan [the addressee Shaesta Khan] too should bestow some consideration upon him which may honour him in the eyes of his neighbours, and send him a letter of approbation *assuring him of the permanent enjoyment of the zamindari* so that other subordinates may be spurred to similar good services.[20] [Emphasis added.]

This letter confirmed that, unlike other zamindars, the lands that had been granted to Mahinath Thakur and his family were to be theirs permanently. Tirhut/Mithila *belonged* to Mahinath. They 'owned' their estate(s) in a form now recognizable as 'fee simple'.[21] This letter would, later, protect the Raj from wholesale British intervention after the Permanent Settlement. The letter also completed the transition of the Thakur family from that of revenue collectors to the rank of hereditary chief. As an indicator of the family's newfound status, the family changed its surname from the Brahmanical Thakur to the Kshatriya surname 'Singh' (Lion), according to Jogendra Nath Bhattacharya.[22]

Aurangzeb's *firman* separated the Darbhanga zamindari from all others. Zamindaris were all technically held under a *sanad* from the emperor until the death of the *sanad*-holder. Custom had tended to make the re-issuance of these *sanads* automatic and, in time, hereditary but, legally, the *sanad* could be revoked at the pleasure of the emperor. The Darbhanga Raj was no longer subject to the terms and conditions of a *sanad*. It had become singularly unique. Its lands had become private property, and may well represent the first indigenous conveyance of absolute property rights in land to an individual in Indian history.

Thereafter, the Rajas of Darbhanga repeatedly refused to pay tribute or remit revenue to either the subedars or nawabs of Bengal or the emperor, and they refused the demands of the British as well. Under the terms of the *firman* issued by Aurangzeb, the lands of the Darbhanga Raj were legally independent of the Mughal emperor, his nawabs in Bengal, and by extension, free and independent of British authority. The Darbhanga Raj was, itself, an independent state. Accordingly, in 1776, Raja Madhu Singh refused to settle with the British when they attempted to settle the revenue in northern Bihar. Madhu Singh genuinely, and rightfully, believed the Darbhanga Raj to be an independent princely state and, therefore, not subject to British authority. His predecessors had successfully refused to pay either revenue or tribute to the Mughals since the reign of Narendra Singh, and the British were deemed no more important than the Mughals by the Maharajas of Darbhanga.

While the British never formally acknowledged the Khandavalas' claim of independent kingship, they were allowed to use the title 'maharaja'.[23] Despite the fact that the British courts would eventually legitimize the Khandavalas' claim of hereditary ownership of their estate, the government refused to officially recognize the Darbhanga Raj as a self-ruling princely state. Nevertheless, the maharajas exhibited all the trappings of a princely state and were outwardly accorded all the privileges of a ruling monarchy by the British. These privileges, at least in part, can be explained by the family's enormous wealth, the size of their estate, and that they were intimate allies of the British Raj once the two rajs had officially recognized the other's rights and authority.

The Hereditary Rule of Kulachar

It is not clear when *kulachar* was first adopted as the means of succession for the Khandavalas but it was not until 1839 that the practice was challenged. Although Brahmins, the Khandavalas practiced a modified form of Muslim-inspired primogeniture in an attempt to keep the family estate intact. Under traditional Hindu inheritance rules, lands of the father were divided equally among all the sons of the deceased, and royal succession was from father to the eldest son. As applied to the Khandavalas, *kulachar* meant that the entire estate was bequeathed to one son, who was not necessarily the eldest, and based on a formal order of succession. As practiced, *kulachar* prevented the subdivision of the estate's lands and the title 'maharaja' and succession was based on a system of tanisty, or the election of a successor by formal appointment by the reigning raja.[24]

In 1839, Chhatra Singh Bahadur, before his death, bequeathed the Raj to his son Rudra Singh and gave villages to his younger son, Rajkumar Bisdeo Singh. Bisdeo, however, sought an equal share of the estate, claiming that traditional Hindu inheritance laws should apply. It was ultimately held by the High Court of Calcutta that ordinary Hindu rules of succession did not apply and the Darbhanga Raj family would have to follow the family custom of *kulachar* – the estate was impartible. Accordingly, Maharaja Rudra Singh Bahadur was declared Maharaja of Darbhanga. This permanently settled the issue of succession and thereafter succession was based solely upon a modified form of primogeniture and each successor needed to be formally specified by the reigning raja.[25] The effect of the court decision was to ensure the future integrity of the family and the estate, eliminating the fragmenting effects of traditional Hindu inheritance law.

* * *

Early in his reign, Raja Raghu Singh (1700-36), often referred to as the King of Madhubani, was one of the first of the Darbhanga rajas to assert his independence from the Mughal nawab. Almost simultaneously, he initiated a war with the Raja of Bettiah, in the hopes of expropriating Bettiah's estates through force of arms.[26] In response, Alivardi Khan, the Nawab of Greater Bengal, in an attempt to mollify Raghu's territorial ambitions, conferred upon him the hereditary title of 'raja' and a *mukarari* lease of the *sarkar* Tirhut.[27]

It was common knowledge that the raja had been exacting high rents from his tenants.[28] If the figures of the *The Golden Book of India* are to be believed, the *mukarari* lease of Tirhut was set at Rs 1 lakh, while the total revenues received from those lands exceeded Rs 7.5 lakh.[29] Under the premise that the raja was abusing the peasantry, the estate was seized and the family imprisoned.[30] The raja and his family were released and the estate was returned with an admonishment that he should '. . . do justice and relieve distress . . . put the country in a flourishing state and keep it so . . . supply the ryots with the necessaries for cultivation . . . and be equally answerable to Government for the revenues collected through his dependents as for those immediately under his own superintendence'.[31]

While the seizure of the estate was ostensibly based on the welfare of the *ryots*, in reality, the nawab had become envious of the wealth the Raj was steadily accumulating as well as the political and social power he commanded. Ultimately, it was concern over the accumulation of wealth that most alarmed the Nawabs and they sought to obtain a larger portion of that wealth for the benefit of the Mughal State.

Although *The Golden Book of India* suggests that the Raja of Darbhanga took heed of the Nawab's admonition to care for the *ryots* under him, subsequent events suggest that the welfare of the tenants was not a high priority – rent collection was. 'Owing to chaotic political conditions prevailing in the country during the reign of the later Mughals the House of Darbhanga, like many others, assumed a somewhat semi-independent chieftainship.'[32]

In 1750, Nawab Alivardi Khan again raised the revenue assessment for Tirhut. This time, Raja Narendra Singh refused to recognize the assessment and defeated the forces sent by the nawab to collect it.[33] Thereafter, until the British won control of Bengal, the Darbhanga Raj was largely an independent state within the Mughal *subah* of Bengal.

The Darbhanga Raj and Permanent Settlement

Raja Madhu Singh refused to settle with the British when they began to assert their land revenue claims in northern Bihar in 1776. Madhu Singh, however, soon discovered that the British were much different than the Mughals. The British attempted to intimidate the rajas by settling the estates with rent farmers. They sold the Raghupur Raunia holdings in Purnia district to recover arrears.[34] The family stood fast, unwilling to yield. The raja intimidated many of the prospective revenue farmers, causing them to refuse the offer of revenue settlement, or interfered with their collection activities. The issue of revenue from the Darbhanga Raj was at a standstill and remained unresolved for nearly twenty years after Permanent Settlement in 1793.

Finally, in 1807, a compromise was reached. It included the waiver of all arrears; the return of all properties previously sold at auction, partial compensation for the losses resulting from the interruption of the maharaja's intermediary rights; and a reduction in the annual revenue demand. In addition, the raja's authority was reduced and redefined, especially in the areas of police and judicial matters. He was no longer considered, nor would he be permitted to be an independent head of state. His status became that of a landed zamindar, a landlord. Although his royal titles were gone, his royal trappings remained intact.

Part of the success of the Raja of Darbhanga lay in the fact that many of his rights and privileges were significantly different from those of most zamindars, large and small. Litigation in the British Courts reaffirmed these rights, which, just like the *firman* given to the British in the form of the *diwani*, bore recognition. The letter from Aurangzeb to the Subedar of Bengal had guaranteed the raja 'permanent enjoyment' of his lands. According to the court, title to these lands had transferred to the rajas. They owned their estates, unlike other zamindars who were only deemed to be hereditary holders of revenue collection rights. The raja's rights had to be recognized and respected, since they preceded even the rights granted to the British by Alam Shah II in 1765.

The inability of the British administration to run rough-shod over the Rajas of Darbhanga was largely due to the limits laid down in the Cornwallis Code. Both the rajas and the administration had to realize and acknowledge each other's powers and rights. The rajas had to accept that they would no longer be permitted to exist apart and separate from the greater political machinery of the State, as Stephen Henningham suggests, 'as a raj within a raj – a kingdom within the kingdom'.[35]

THE COURT OF WARDS AND THE RAJ

When Permanent Settlement was implemented, a relationship of interdependence was created between the landlords of north-eastern India and an imperial ruler. In return for their agreement to pay a fixed land revenue and assistance in controlling the peasantry, the British Government protected the position and privileges of the zamindars. This protection included the assumption of the managerial responsibilities of the zamindari through the agency or a wing of government called the Court of Wards. The Court of Wards protected the landlords' properties from the threat of bankruptcy and dismemberment but only if a minor became the acknowledged owner of the zamindari through succession or inheritance. While the administration was, first and foremost, concerned with the collection of revenue, the Court also provided protection to estates even if it meant protecting these estates from the administration itself, frequently stepping in to preserve the estates from internal mismanagement and providing an opportunity for the improvement of the estate-owner's managerial skills.

In 1860, Maharaja Maheshwar Singh died. The Raj fell to his two-year-old son Lakshmishwar Singh. Almost immediately, the Darbhanga Raj was placed under the administration of the Court of Wards, since both Lakshmishwar and his brother Rameshwar were minors, and there was no regency policy for the management of the estate in the event a minor became the new maharaja. The Court arranged for the education of the boys, first in Darbhanga, then in Muzaffarpur under a Cambridge-trained tutor, Chester McNaughton, and later they were sent to Varanasi for study at the Queen's College.

Lakshmishwar left Queen's College shortly before he came of age. During their schooling, both he and his brother had received a thorough 'English education'. Above all, the young maharaja had learned to manage his own affairs but equally important, he had been instructed in the importance of taking an interest in the well-being of his subjects and *ryots*. On 25 September 1879 the Darbhanga Raj's estates were officially returned to Lakshmishwar Singh.

The estate he received from the Court had grown substantially under the Court's management and many of the problems that had plagued the estate had been resolved, usually in favour of the estate and its owner. One senior revenue official commented specifically on the effects of the Court of Wards on the Darbhanga Raj:

> The truth is that this [income] alone is a most inadequate test of the effects of the management of the Estate by Government officers. The rental, in the time of the late Maharaja and his forefathers, was little more than nominal: it was never realized, and was in fact, not susceptible of realization. The property was assigned away, under fictitious leases to the numerous hangers-on and domestics of the palace, who met all demands for rent with monstrous counter-demands on accounts of supplies and services, which the Maharajas were too ignorant or too indolent to contest, and which were never contested until the Court of Wards appeared on the scene.[36]

The effect the Court of Wards had on some of the largest estates, was to increase the estate's assets, often through acquisitions, but equally important were the changes it wrought in traditional networks and intermediary control of the estates. It was the clearing away of the intermediaries by the Court of Wards, including functionless family parasites, that altered the estates most profoundly and this made them increasingly profitable in the process.

Surprisingly, the agents for the Court of Wards, while improving the position of the proprietors of the estates, did little to benefit the *ryots*. The same kinds of rack-renting that had been practiced under the rajas and their intermediaries continued. Tenancy and occupancy rights were similarly ignored and illegal distraint continued to be practiced.[37] In effect, the Court of Wards continued the same policies and practices of the estate owners, only making them more efficient, without the benefit of improving the conditions of the actual *ryots* who produced the estate's income.

Administration of the Darbhanga Raj[38]

Beginning with the reign of Maharaja Lakshmishwar Singh, the Darbhanga Raj entered a new phase which continued until the Raj was formally abolished in 1950. The Court of Wards had set the tone for the newly enthroned Raja Lakshmishwar Singh when he returned as an adult after nearly twenty years under the guidance of the Court.

By any standard, the Darbhanga Raj was large. By the time of Lakshmishwar Singh, most of the large zamindaris in the province of Bengal had ceased to exist, or were substantially smaller than at the time of the Permanent Settlement. Darbhanga was the last of the large zamindaris. It has been estimated that in area the Raj represented approximately 4,000 sq miles, with holdings in Saran, Muzaffarpur, Darbhanga, Monghyr, Bhagalpur, and Purnia districts. This vast area was administered by a staff of approximately 2,000.[39] In 1876, the estate was organized into 14 circles under the management of circle managers.[40] These circles, however, were changed as deemed necessary, both in size and scope of operation. Below the circle managers were *tahsildars* or assistant managers, each of whom was responsible for sub-divisions within the circles. Below the *tahsildars* were a group collectively known as village servants – these included *jeth ryots*, *patwaris*, peons, and *barahils*.[41]

The *jeth ryots* were responsible for the collection of rents from the tenants in one or more revenue villages known as *mauzas*. For their services, they received a percentage of the rents they collected. The percentage increased as the percentage of the total collection increased. The *patwaris* kept the rent and land records. Peons and *barahils* assisted the *patwaris* and *jeth ryots*.

At the centre there was a law department, with sub-offices in the circles. It was the law department's responsibility to guard the Raj's interests.

Although, from time to time, Englishmen were employed by the Raj, most of the upper and middle management positions were occupied by local high-caste Hindus, particularly those from the Maithil Brahmana community. At the village level, Kshatrias, served as *barahils* and *patwaris*. *Jeth ryots* and peons were also typically high-caste Hindus, with some of the latter group coming from the middling castes. In addition, it had always been the Raj's policy to hire new or replacement personnel from the families of past or present employees.[42] The perpetuation of ties to families cemented the entire organization together, and promotions were almost always from within the organization.

The operation of the bureaucracy was guided by an official set of rules, regulations, and directives for each position within the organization from the *jeth ryots* through the upper-level managers. Periodic meetings and conferences were held, at which time matters of special importance were discussed and upper management advised. Each level of the bureaucracy was responsible for the routine 'touring' (inspection) of the lower-level administrators, with particular attention given to accurate recordkeeping. According to Stephen Henningham: 'Yet, despite rules, directives, records, and inspections, the raj management operated with at best indifferent efficiency.' Reports were oftentimes delayed by months, and in some cases, years, due to the delay in submitting annual reports, beginning with the *patwaris* through every level above them. Many of the causes for the delay in the submission of annual reports stemmed from the difficulty of communication and transportation between villages and circles. Often, the only way to approach many villages was by boat or elephant, since the landscape, especially near the major rivers was typically a labyrinth of small creeks, streams, and rivers that needed to be forded in the absence of formal bridges. Adding to the inconvenience of roads being regularly washed out, employees often waded through mud and rivers and channels full of 'snakes and crocodiles'.

In addition, there was the ever-present issue of corruption. Corruption and collusion were particularly prevalent among and between defendants, pleaders, and circle law clerks, where delays often resulted in lapses in suits and judgements. In part, the imposition of the Raj's legal rights conflicted with the social ties within the Raj bureaucracy, top to bottom, making a mockery of the Raj's enforcement efforts. Surprisingly, however, everyone recognized the collusion that went on between the Raj's staff, from upper management to the lowest *ryot*. It was simply 'a part of doing business'. Personal ties, kin, and caste loyalties were often felt to be stronger and more important than one's responsibilities and obligations to the Raj. It was not uncommon, especially among the *patwaris*, to falsify the land records in favour of powerful village leaders, kin, or fellow caste members, permitting them to hold lands below the standard rent rate.[43] These patterns of subterfuge were common knowledge but nonetheless clandestine. One circle manager stated:

> . . . we are compelled to depend upon patwarys for information, and it is well known that particulars which they supply are not always full and complete . . . [Since the last Survey and Settlement operations] There has been sub-infeudation; tenures have been broken up and some have ceased to exist; holdings have been divided; old tenants have passed away and new ones are filling their places by inheritance, purchase etc. without knowledge of the zamindar . . . changes have occurred . . . of which we have no knowledge at present. . . .[44]

The practice of the *patwaris* of the Raj was little different than that of the *kanungos* of Bengal. The *patwaris* and Bengali *kanungos* were the repositories of information, which they held as a vital trust but, at the same time, could be used for their own benefit or the benefit of others through bribery or clan or caste affiliation. Everyone within the Raj revenue collection organization recognized that the *patwaris* were dishonest and inefficient but, at the same time, they were situated within the bureaucratic hierarchy at a very advantageous level, and one that made them most susceptible to conflicts of interest. Nevertheless, they were responsible for the collection of base level information, which was used by the entire revenue system for decision-making. In reality, the *patwaris* were the foundation upon which the entire revenue system of the Raj depended.

While the *patwaris* falsified the land records, the *jeth ryots*, who did the actual collection of the rents from the peasant cultivators, often demanded *abwabs*. Thus, the information concerning land-holdings and the amounts actually being collected as rent varied from the information the decision-makers possessed. Further, the *jeth ryots* were in a position that allowed many of them to use their collections as a way to fund other moneylending activities, since the rents were generally collected well in advance of their actual due date.

In modern banking parlance, this practice is frequently referred to as 'churning' or 'the holding period;' that is, money is held for a period of time, allowing the bank to make interest on depositors' funds while not having to pay interest on those same funds. For the *jeth ryots*, the holding period could be lengthy, using the excuse that the tenants had delayed their payments – a practice commonly termed simply as UOPM, 'using other people's money'. This practice only works as long as these 'other people' do not demand their money unexpectedly while it is out.

In one extreme example, the villagers of Bhawanipur, in an outlying circle, working with the local *jeth ryot*, avoided paying their rents for twenty-three years![45] While twenty-three years can only be seen as unbelievable, arrears for years was often commonplace. The loss of the revenue, while itself devastating, was often exacerbated by the expenses associated with litigation. Litigation was also no guarantee that the estate would receive its rents. If the defendants were able to stall the proceedings for four years, the claims were deemed time-barred. For the village of Bhawanipur, the first nineteen years of non-payment were barred from consideration and those revenues were lost forever.

For those claims that were heard by the Court, wherein the tenants were found guilty and evicted from their lands, it was not uncommon for such tenants to refuse to leave their lands for years, while simultaneously planting and harvesting the crops and continuing to refuse to pay their rent. Such flagrant disregard for the law and the rights of the Raj was not entirely an isolated event. Anywhere that the villages or circles were at a great distance from the circle offices, or where such offices were understaffed, which was often the case in outlying areas, the avoidance of rent was much more common. When action was taken against the defaulting peasants, they would agitate and incite the locals, further frustrating collection activities. Often rent collection was a battle of wits between the performing *jeth ryots* and the *ryots* themselves.

Errors, omissions, and fraud were often components of managers' reports and the managers throughout the hierarchy did not hesitate to blame those below them for every problem, especially the villagers. Admittedly, the managers' reports were fraught with errors and omissions, but these were compounded by the managers' own dishonesty and inefficiency. Nevertheless, despite the problems inherent in the Raj's system of reporting and accounting, the fraud and collusion, the Raj maintained its authority, although it was tenuous at best. The Raj was able to collect the bulk of the rents that was due and kept most of its land under cultivation. There were always *ryots* who were unwilling to pay, and there would always be attempts at defrauding the Raj, but few zamindaris were generally as well organized or run as that of the Darbhanga Raj, going back to the Court of Wards and, later. The Darbhanga Raj would not have become the last of the large zamindaris, anywhere in India, and could not have lasted until it was officially abolished in 1950, had it not been run with a certain amount of efficiency.

One can select numerous reports, from the thousands that are still extant, reporting incidents of collusion, fraud, corruption, inefficiency, and rebelliousness among the administrative personnel and the villages and individuals but this is because these problems attract our attention, engaging us. They are exciting to read and they are sensational. The vast majority of the Raj's reports, commentaries, and observations, however, are mundane and simply reflect the day-to-day operation of a large corporate structure. If one examines the reports having to do with maladministration, misconduct, and insubordination, most come from circles and villages 'disconnected' and remote from the circle offices, not amendable to easy or efficient administration and oversight.

Henningham provides the following quotation as a counterpoint to the litany of problems the Raj's administrators faced:

> . . . tenants in general of this circle [Jhanjharpur] are very loyal and faithful to the Raj and they are much attached and obedient. They are law abiding and meek. Nowhere I found attached tenants like this to the Raj. The reason of this is that the middle class are learned and have full control over the lower class people and it is an ancient seat of the Raj [*sic*].[46]

In part, the docility and cooperativeness of the villagers in the Jhanjharpur Circle can be attributed to the fact that the 'learned' middle class were largely Maithil Brahmanas, holding their lands not as cultivators but as small landlords at privileged rates. Throughout the Raj where Maithil Brahmanas were the tenure holders, social, cultural, and caste links with the Raj assuaged many of the tensions that typically separated the Raj from its tenants and *ryots*. Rather than criticize the royal family, most tenants chose to show their displeasure by criticizing Raj administrators and personnel. To criticize the royal family, even when it was justified, violated the strict Maithil code of conduct and rankings. One could complain about the 'administrators' but not the recognized head of the caste. This would have been socially unacceptable behaviour. Further, while the Raj may have been economically oppressive at times, and was felt equally by everyone under its jurisdiction, for the Maithil Brahmanas, the burden also came with social, cultural, and religious benefits, and was tolerated because it was simply 'part of the natural order of things'. And it was this attitude that the 'learned' middle class imposed on all those under *their* jurisdiction.

When informal controls, litigation, and the civil and criminal court systems failed and there was unrest, the Raj was not above using force to reassert control. *Lathyals*, or strongmen, often in the form of *barahils*, would be sent to the villages to intimidate and quiet village-level leaders or *ryots*. During the 1920s and 1930s, there was wide-spread peasant agitation within the Raj. With each disturbance, the Raj, using a combination of compromise, coercion and propaganda persevered, retaining its control and authority. Even during the Quit

India campaigns in the early 1940s, there was very little peasant protest within the Raj. Typically, the Raj could call upon the police and the district administrations to quell disturbances but during late 1942, both had collapsed, and as instruments of coercion, they were no longer available to the Raj but, surprisingly, '. . . there was no agitation whatsoever against the Raj . . . [and] though the disturbances were widespread . . . there was no harm to the Raj anywhere'.[47]

Frequently, the *jeth ryots* and *barahils* were unavailable to the administration, often siding with the tenants and *ryots*. One manager reported that the *jeth ryots* belonged more to the tenants than to the administration and were, therefore, at times, of little use. This was the situation during the Quit India campaigns. However, using, alternatively, intimidation and enticement, the filing of suits against important tenants, as well as replacing intractable *jeth ryots* with cooperative rivals generally provided the control the Raj's managers sought. Such 'administrative shake-ups' destroyed or threatened to destroy traditional alliances within the villages, and rather than subject themselves to the possibility of a new and unknown political apparatus, most villages and villagers acquiesced to the demands of the Raj. It was more the fear of the unknown that prompted compliance than the fear of corporal consequences or litigation, real or imagined.

The Raj administrators were clever in the way they exercised their power. If it was within their power and to the advantage of the Raj and its goals, the mid-level managers often terminated hereditary positions, replacing recalcitrant agents with those who would do the Raj's bidding. And when these agents fell out of favour, they too would be replaced. The mere possibility of such a political shake-up was often enough to control entire villages and beyond.

No matter what the means – the threat of violence, legal actions, administrative replacement, cajoling, or the exercise of kin and caste linkages – the Raj maintained its control over both its lands, tenants and *ryots*, a feat most of the large zamindaris in Bihar and Bengal were unable to do. In general, it was able to collect the bulk of the revenue due to it year after year. During the reign of Rameshwar Singh (1898-1929), the rents realized from the *ryots* is estimated to have been approximately Rs 4 million. From this revenue payments to the British provincial government were deducted, approximately 10 per cent (Rs 400,000). In addition, 15 to 20 per cent was spent on administration (Rs 600,000 to 800,000). This left the maharaja with an average net income of roughly Rs 2.8 million to 3 million, just from the operation of his estates. By any standard, this was a massive income. In addition, there was income from the maharaja's other non-agricultural business and industrial investments throughout India.

Not surprisingly, very little of this income was ever reinvested to improve the productiveness of the maharaja's lands. Nearly the entirety of the maharaja's net income was spent in a manner befitting a monarch, a philanthropist, and as a patron of an ancient line of orthodox, Maithil Hindus.

* * *

In 1950, the last maharajadhiraja, Kameshwar Singh, transferred the ownership of his estates to the state of Bihar, an estate that typically had produced a net income of approximately Rs 2.8 million annually. Neither Kameshwar nor any of his ancestors had been intimately involved in the management of the Raj's estates, which were scattered throughout numerous districts. The Raj was simply too large for one man to oversee. The management of the estates was always left to a large, efficient and loyal corporate-like management system. Although the system could not be compared to modern-day asset management firms, with their systems of oversight and accounting checks and balances, it was, by the standards of the day, efficient. The loyalty of the Raj's upper and mid-level managers was not typical of such management organizations within other large zamindaris. Unlike the *amla* attached to these other zamindaris, who were disloyal, corrupt, and self-serving, the Raj's managers, by and large, were efficient and trustworthy. The primary flaw in the Raj's management organization lay with the village- and circle-level *patwaris* and *jeth ryots* – the personnel who had the most direct contact with the individual village elites and *ryots*, and accounted for and collected the land rents. Often, it was difficult to determine to whom they owed their allegiance, the village leaders or the maharaja. The failure or inability of the Raj to monitor the day-to-day activities of the *patwaris* and *jeth ryots* provided opportunities for these petty officials to marginally plunder the revenue destined for the Raj's treasury.

Much like his contemporaries, the maharaja was not concerned with mundane issues of agrarian relations. He was far too removed from any of those involved in the management of his estates, except, possibly, the chief managers at the Raj headquarters. Because of this detachment, no thought was given to reinvesting a portion of the profits in an effort to increase agricultural production and simultaneously to improve the lives of the *ryots*. Likewise, the Raj's bureaucracy, while inherently clumsy and inefficient, was a dependable instrument for the extraction of rents and protecting the interests of the estates. It was not, however, designed nor intended as a mechanism for rural development.

One has to question the source of the loyalty demonstrated by the maharaja's managers and the majority of his petty, village-level officials. The loyalty extended to the maharajas was largely the result of the traditional authority they commanded in what Henningham characterized as 'isolated, backward, and impoverished north Bihar'.[48]

* * *

Kingship, almost anywhere in India, is typically linked to the Kshatriya classes but under the Mughals, at least in northern Bihar, Brahmins became the 'kingly' class, and they separated themselves from their origins sufficiently to effectively wield secular power and authority, while at the same time, not losing touch with the primary source of that power, the Maithil Brahmana community. They cultivated this relationship with the Maithil Brahmanas by fulfilling their religious duties and spending lavishly on ceremonies, festivals, and the maintenance of temples. In addition, they patronized Brahmin pundits and Sanskrit learning and speculation. Further, their steadfast defence of Hindu orthodoxy and the culture of Mithila proved to be an important component in the maharajas' popularity. But being practical men, the importance of gifts and rewards paid to his employees was not lost on the maharajas, thus ingratiating themselves to their rank and file employees. All these acts of charity served to bolster the position of the maharajas and their estates, reinforcing the traditions that legitimized their status and position as the ruling family of Darbhanga.

Likewise, the remission of rents during difficult times of drought or flood generally made a virtue of necessity, and won favour for the family. Ultimately, all the positive gestures made by the maharajas served to promote the image of the maharaja as a good landlord, and although generally perceived as a great and distant ruler, his munificence reflected the prosperity of his realm. This, in turn was translated into a sense of security for everyone under the maharaja's jurisdiction. Spending and display also strengthened the Raj's traditional authority for both insiders and outsiders.

While one can look upon the success of the Raj's revenue administration in monetary terms, possibly even more important was the control that the Raj, in the name of the maharaja, exerted over the people and the reciprocity he received. His money supported and perpetuated a unique form of Hindu orthodoxy, with all its associated trappings, beliefs, attitudes, mores, and values, which can be seen even today in the Mithila region of Bihar. The maharajas left a legacy, one built on the control of vast estates but even more permanent was the cultural legacy they had promoted and left behind.

On the broader stage of India, the maharajas, especially Kameshwar Singh, played an important part in defending the rights of the large landlords, property ownership, promoting nationalism, the endowment of centres of learning, and investing heavily in a broad range of businesses and industries, many of which have contributed to the greater well-being of the Indian people.[49]

The Sources of the Rajas' Power and Influence

For all its efforts, the British administration could not eradicate the rajas' influence and might. At least in part, the rajas' authority and influence was undeniably tied to the size of their estate. In addition to their economic and political power, the rajas' influence, authority, and legitimacy also stemmed from who they were – they were Srotriya Maithil Brahmanas. As the highest order of priestly and landholding Brahmins, the Maithil Brahmanas became 'a royal caste' with its own king and aristocracy, and this resulted in the empowerment of the rajas' family religiously, socially, economically, and politically.

THE MAITHIL BRAHMANAS

The Maithil Brahmanas are distributed across most of northern Bihar from the Gandak to Purnia district, but the cultural heartland is felt to be the districts of Darbhanga and Madhubani. There has been a continuity of Vedic culture in this region from earliest recorded times; and the people have made distinct adaptations to Buddhism, Islam, and the British. Here, Buddhism did not displace Brahmanism. While other areas adapted to the religious and political influences of Buddha and Mahavira, the Maithil Brahmanas resisted, retaining their unique form of Hinduism and social structure. Part of their ability to resist the pressures of reformation can be attributed to the influences of geography.

Mithila is characterized and influenced by its uniquely riverine landscape. Geologically north Bihar constitutes a series of riverine megafans and collectively they form the North Bihar Plain. While this plain exhibits very little relief, it is a labyrinth of rivers, streams, and swamps which historically has made travel into and through the area difficult. As a consequence, it was penetrated only by determined effort. This afforded Mithila a certain amount of physical and cultural isolation.

The Maithil Brahmanas developed their own unique identity which shielded the community from outside influences, allowing them to develop a complex internal social structure through an intricate system of kinship ties, elaborated and formalized through the development of written genealogies known as *panjis*. This elaboration, combined with the social and political support of the rajas of Darbhanga, allowed the Maithil Brahmanas to control much of the social and economic resources of Mithila. This control, to a greater or lesser extent, served to quieten and restrain the violence that later became a trademark in southern Bihar. The rajas of Darbhanga reigned over an all-encompassing, unified system of rank for all Maithil Brahmanas and served as the central authority for these Brahmins, preserving and reinforcing the Maithil Brahmanas' hierarchical system.[50]

One of the most conspicuous aspects of Maithil Brahmanas' ceremony and ritual is the keeping of the *panji* (the genealogical) records which originated before the first Oinwar raja. Tradition suggests that Hari Singh Deva (1296-1324), the last of the Karnataka rulers of Mithila, introduced the four-class structure that now characterizes the social order of the Maithil Brahmanas. He ordered a system of genealogical recordkeeping to insure the purity of Maithil marriages.[51] If, when the first *Panji Prabandha* was undertaken, one's family was not entered into one of the *panjis*, the members of that family were no longer deemed to be Maithil Brahmanas.

The highest classification within the *panjis* is a group known as the Srotriya, a generally poor group befitting their correct code of conduct. They follow a traditional Vedic path, a life of restraint often in poverty. They were expected, due to their high position, to impart their spiritual knowledge to others, surviving on meagre and uncertain rewards in this life. Most are scholars of the *Shastras*, performers of sacrifices, and ideally are supposed to shun profit-making activities.

The holy texts provide for the devout Vedic Brahmins. They suggest that it is the duty of the king to look after the needs of these Vedic Brahmins, the Srotriyas, and to protect those incapable of earning a living.[52] This admonition, therefore, bound the Vedic Brahmins to the king and vice versa.

Modern day Srotriyas are most frequently teachers, professors, writers and government officials. Most, however, are poverty-stricken and, of all the *gotras*, they are generally exempt from the payment of dowry for their brides. One of the most advantageous marriages for these poor Brahmanas is a marriage to a member of the royal family. Such a marriage brought the poor Srotriyas instant wealth.[53]

The raja derived much of his political authority and legitimacy from his superior Srotriya bloodline. He was revered as much for his royal position as he was for being a Srotriya. The irony of this veneration lies in the fact that five generations after the *Panji Prabandha*, a reorganization of the system took place. In the subsequent juggling of *mulagrams*, the lineage of the Oinwar Dynasty, who had been the patrons of the *panji* system, were reclassified becoming a minor lineage and ultimately disappeared from the *panji* records all together shortly thereafter. The winners were those of the newest royal line, that of Mahesh Thakur, the progenitor of the Khandavala Dynasty. He became the founder of a single lineage of Srotriya with only one branch. Brown suggests that Mahesh Thakur initiated the reorganization as part of an effort to erase the Oinwars from the political and social pages of history.[54] In this, he was successful.

In the process of eliminating the Oinwars from the historical record, the *gotra* of the royal family became matrimonially isolated. This resulted from the fact that there was a preference for giving daughters to slightly higher-ranking families in Mithila. Over time, this preference tended to promote the collapse of the hierarchy. Very early in the Khandavala Dynasty's history, as a consequence of a serious reduction in the number of Srotriyas, the royal family found it difficult to arrange marriages that were not considered, by definition and rule, incestuous. The family was finding it difficult to find spouses who they were not technically related to within the category of pure-blooded Srotriyas. This predicament was resolved when Maharaja Chhatra Singh Bahadur (*c.* 1787-1839) ascended to the throne in 1808. He was the first prince to have been scandalously tainted by a non-Srotriya bloodline. His father, Madho Singh (1776-1807) had married a Yogya woman, thus tainting the royal bloodline.[55] Almost immediately, yet another round of reforms was undertaken among the Maithil Brahmanas to resolve this genealogical impasse. The solution was to create a new set of lineage titles known as *laukits*. This was followed by yet another 'overhaul' of the system, resulting in the creation of still more classes within each *laukit*. These were known as *shrenis*.

Now, every Maithil Brahmana can identify himself by *shakha*, *gotra*, *pravara*, *mula*, *grama*, *laukit*, and *shreni*, and each must be taken into account when marriages are being arranged.[56] Every Maithil Brahmana is *expected* to know his or her *shakha*, *gotra*, *pravara*, *mula*, *grama*, *laukit*, and *shreni*. Even if all this data was to be computerized, instead of being originally maintained on specially prepared palm leaves, it is doubtful that errors would not be made by the *panjikars*. Further, the system is inherently self-destructive and subject to entropy. Brown notes that: 'The inevitable result is that the whole society is gradually falling in rank; in 1904 there were 115 first shreni Srotriya men; in 1909 there were 76; in 1975 there were 18; and . . . in 1980 there were only six first shreni men living, and none had passed it on to their children.'[57]

The Maithil Brahmanas' rules to prevent ritual and closely consanguineous marriages are such that along with the tainting of bloodlines and the rules of right conduct (*karmakanda*), the pool of eligible marital partners will decline, generation by generation, until either the system is again reorganized or there are no long any eligible marriage partners. It is already one of the most complex matrimonial systems ever devised.

In addition to their unique position within the Srotriya lineage system, the maharajas also played a unique and functional role in the *panji* system itself. The maharajas supported the system as much out of necessity as bowing to the Srotriya community's unending threat of withdrawal from the system itself. The maharaja enforced the system through his personal, centralized control of all marriages among Srotriyas. This control was exerted through the agency of the *Raj Panjikar*. No Srotriya marriage could be authorized until all the parties consulted with the *Raj Panjikar*, who examined the bloodlines of both the bride and groom, on behalf of the maharaja, to determine if any of the 29 forbidden connections had been violated. A report was then submitted to the maharaja, who either granted or denied the issuance of a *parmangee*, a formal permission to marry. Any marriage between Maithil Brahmanas, but especially the Srotriyas, without a *parmangee* resulted in the outcasting of both the bride's and groom's families.[58] The net effect of such outcasting was to exclude both families, and all future generations, from participation in the *panjis* and the Maithil Brahmanas' marriage system and network.

Through his participation in the *panjikar* process, the maharajas received both ritual and secular legitimacy and authority above and beyond their political standing. These attributes, in addition to a certain amount of political, economic, and social adroitness, extended and multiplied their overall authority and power. Further, the position of the maharaja could also be used to change individual *shrenis*. Brown records that the last maharaja, Kameshwar Singh, was only a second *shreni* when he came to the throne but that seemed inappropriate and, as a consequence, his *laukit* was changed, which permitted his postion to be raised to first *shreni*. Likewise, the same process was used to 'upgrade' the wives of Kameshwar's brother, Bishveshwar Singh; and had he ascended to the throne, his *laukit* would have been changed also, promoting him to the status of first *shreni*.[59]

Maharajadhiraja Kameshwar Singh lost his temporal powers as the prince of the Darbhanga Raj in 1947, becoming a simple citizen of India. However, he retained his position as the head of the Maithil Brahmana community. When he died in 1962, confusion developed over the future of the Srotriyas' system of centralized control of marriage. Kameshwar Singh left no heirs. There was no one to assume control over communal affairs, since he had not made a formal nomination. Until his will was read and made public, there was no one who could perform the duties of *parmangee*. The will, when finally read, did not nominate a successor to the maharajaship nor the duties of *parmangee*. Eventually, one of his nephews, Subheshwar Singh assumed the maharajaship, becoming known as Maharajadhiraja Subheshwar Singh Bahadur and assumed the responsibilities as the head of the Srotriya Brahmanas and, therefore, became the leader of the Maithil Brahmanas.[60]

Subheshwar Singh was not well-educated and, apparently, had no desire to continue his studies. Soon, it was recognized that he was incapable of performing his *parmangee* duties. Additionally, the society of Srotriyas found him unacceptable. Even before his decision to renounce his duties of *parmangee*, the Srotriyas had become divided over who should be the head of the community. Apparently, a large number of Srotriyas wanted Babu Chandradhari Singh of Ranti Deorhia (a collateral from the same dynasty) to take over the leadership of the community.[61]

Before the community could take formal action, in 1975, Subheshwar Singh Bahadur renounced his authority as head of the Maithil community, simultaneously announcing that all differences between the Srotriya and the other Maithil Brahmana gotras were thereafter eliminated. By this time, however, the importance of the *parmangee* had become moot for many.

Most of the Srotriya rejected the abolition of their exalted status. The Yogyas and Jaibars accepted the wisdom of the announcement. The threat of excommunication by the conservative Srotriya largely fell on deaf ears and since 1975, marriages between the Srotriyas,

Yogya, Bans, and Panjibaddha have become frequent and where breaches of protocol have occurred, they have gone largely 'unpunished'. No one seems to care. Likewise, the annual marriage fair, the Saurath Sabha or Sabha Gachchi, has become increasingly unimportant and is all but a memory now, with only a few prospective brides and grooms attending, where, only twenty years earlier, a lakh of prospective brides and grooms attended. Nevertheless, the more orthodox continue to consult with the *panjikars*, because unless he issues the *Swajan Virjan Adhikar Patra*, popularly known as the *Sidhanta*, no sanctioned marriage can take place. Some traditions continue while others fade, becoming nothing more than memories or historical footnotes.

In the Aftermath of Independence

Shortly after Independence, attempts were made to disenfranchise the zamindars and establish progressive direct tax relationships with the *ryots* through land reforms. Bihar was the first state to legislate and implement a broad range of land reforms. These enactments, however, were more for reasons of political economy than as a genuine attempt to remove the zamindars or reorganize Bihar's agriculture or rural society.

Land reforms in Bihar failed miserably because many of the politicians and bureaucrats who were responsible for the implementation of these new regulations came from the zamindari class, thus ensuring that the reforms would never be strictly implemented. The strict enforcement of land reforms would have meant the passing of power, property, and status from one group to another by legislative decree. In the politically, socially, and economically hidebound context of Bihar, the elimination of the zamindars would have meant the complete overhaul of Bihar society. That simply was not an option.

For the politicians and the zamindars, it was much more prudent to give the illusion that something monumental and substantive was being done, rather than actually doing it. Once the zamindars had exhausted all legal avenues in their resistance to the implementation of land reform legislation, they resorted to subterfuge to retain ownership of their lands and the power that such ownership provided. In the end, only the very largest zamindars felt the pinch of land reforms anywhere in India. The group that was most easily targeted was that of zamindars with revenues in excess of Rs 500,000.[62] The remainder 'resumed' the cultivation of their lands under the guise of *bakast* (self tilled).

The largest zamindaris were easy targets for the governments. Among the largest in Bihar were those of the Bettiah, Hathwa, Dumraon, Ramgarh families and the Darbhanga Raj. These zamindaris had created efficient revenue collecting organizations and were only interested in revenue collection, not the direct management of the land. Thus, they could not justifiably nor legally claim *bakast*. The smaller zamindars, however, were much more involved in the direct management of their holdings and could, at least superficially, claim the bulk of their holdings as self-tilled. As a consequence, within these smaller zamindaris the tradition of subinfeudation remained intact and the system of multiple tenancies has remained a salient feature of Bihar agriculture, past and present.

Tejakar Jha, a nephew and travelling companion of the Maharaniadhirani Kam Sundari Devi of Darbhanga, and historian, responded to a question from the author concerning the maharaja in the early post-Independence era, especially with regard to the maharaja's views on zamindars' participation in development and his resistance to zamindari abolition. Tejakar stated:

> The Maharaja of Darbhanga was in a class by himself, just as his holdings were. He felt that tenant and landless labourers must be made equal partners in production, along with the zamindars. He felt that both classes should care for one another. Further, he felt that the government should suspend revenue payments so that the zamindars could waive rents in times of calamity. In turn, the zamindars should develop irrigation systems and the government should care for the transport system.
>
> The Maharaja had a number of sugar, jute, cotton and paper mills in the region. All were supported by the agricultural produce of the region and gave a market to the farmers and employment to landless labourers in the region.
>
> He fought to save his zamindari, not for the sake of money but based on that principle that a government could not selectively take over private property. He won his case in the Supreme Court of India. After the promulgation of the nation's new Constitution, he pressed his case in the courts. Again, the Government was looking at defeat. Prime Minister Nehru

personally came to Patna and appealed to the Maharaja to give up his zamindari, for the sake of democracy. The Maharaja [ultimately] gave up his zamindari in 1950 without taking a single penny as compensation.

The people of Mithila were, until 1965, three years after the Maharaja's death, in good economic condition. The farmers had enough money and great purchasing power. Slowly the government took over all the industrial units run by the Darbhanga Raj. Within a decade, all of these units were closed due to mismanagement. The economy of the region went down. The people became impoverished.

How could we say that the economy (industrial and agrarian) developed only in the regions and era where there was no zamindari.[63]

There is no doubt that there is a certain bias in Jha's comments but, in general, they reflect the realities faced by the residents of Mithila. The maharaja's factories failed. Poverty increased. The economy in Bihar declined precipitously. Was the prosperity of Mithila truly a function of the Darbhanga Raj? In all likelihood, no. However, the Raj did control – politically, socially, and economically – much of the area known as Mithila. And once the maharaja had abdicated, everything does seem to have deteriorated, falling into a form of limited anarchy, which was accompanied by a similar state-wide malaise, a state from which Bihar is only possibly beginning to recover.

The Maharaja's Impact on the Indian Constitution

Shortly after Independence, a Constituent Assembly was convened to frame India's new constitution. The Maharaja of Darbhanga was one of its charter members. Among the major issues facing the Assembly was the right of property. At the time the leaders of the triumphant Congress party were inclined to eliminate all the zamindars without compensation and put into effect a 'socialist' industrial policy that gave the State the dominant role in the control of both private and public industry through a planning process that, in effect, pre-empted the rights of private citizens.

The new constitution, when finally adopted in 1950, contained a property clause that consisted of two parts – Article 19(1)(f) and Article 31.[64] Article 19 specifically guaranteed to all citizens the right to acquire, hold and dispose of property. Article 31 provided that 'no person shall be deprived of his property save by authority of law'. It also provided that compensation would be paid to a person whose property has been taken for public purposes.

Nehru believed that these provisions would not stand in the way of his 'socialist' programmes. He also believed that compensation, provided for in Article 31, would be limited to petty compulsory acquisitions but not so for large-scale acquisitions that would benefit the whole country. For such large-scale acquisitions, Nehru suggested that compensation should be equitable from the perspective of society rather than that of the individual property owner.[65] The courts, however, did not agree. For the next twenty-five years, Nehru's philosophy and land policy would conflict with the judiciary. Ultimately, the 'property clause' was removed from the Indian Bill of Rights.

Three early cases almost immediately brought the Centre's rights and those of the individual and landowners into conflict. One of the first of these case filings was on behalf of the Maharaja of Darbhanga. The courts struck down Bihar's land reform laws for being *ultra vires* (beyond the power or scope of the state legislature) and, therefore, they were deemed unconstitutional.

Surprisingly, these early acts were struck down not on the grounds of personal property rights but because of the inequality clause of Article 14 and the reasonableness provisions of Article 19 of the Constitution. Nehru's allies viewed the court's decisions as reactionary, anti-reform, and counter-productive. At the same time, Maharaja Kameshwar Singh's suit was still pending.[66] Fearing that the maharaja might be vindicated in the face of Bihar's land reforms, the Constituent Assembly introduced the constitution's First Amendment Act (1951). This amendment excluded state acquisitions of 'estates' or rights in 'estates' and similar forms of land tenure from being declared invalid on the basis of Articles 14, 16, or 31. These articles specifically spoke about the guarantees of equality, reasonableness, and property, respectively. Changing the impact of these articles cleared the way for the elimination of those kinds of land rights that the Bihar land reforms legislation had been specifically designed to avoid, that is, the rights of large zamindars. In effect, the First Amendment barred judicial review of certain land reform enactments.[67]

When the maharaja's appeal was finally heard by the Supreme Court, it found that the amendment did indeed protect the land reform legislation from judicial review, but the court unexpectedly declared that the amount of compensation was not barred from review nor was the issue of public purpose. Based on this interpretation, the court struck down two sections of the reform law for being inconsistent with the requirement that the legislation's intent was for a higher public purpose. As van der Walt suggests, 'This decision [was] regarded as a sign of defiance against the reformist intentions of the legislature'.[68]

In a series of subsequent decisions handed down between 1952 and 1956, the courts' decisions focused on the property clause, disregarding the issue of equality. Most of the previous decisions had been based on the adequacy of compensation. In the case of *State of West Bengal* v. *Subodh Gopal Bose*,[69] the Supreme Court took the position that Article 31 must be read as a unit and could not be used sectionally or divisibly. In so doing, both acquisition [Article 31(2)] and deprivations of property [Article 31(1)] required compensation. The court's position restricted the states' ability to introduce such legislation that did not guarantee the owner of lands being confiscated, for whatever reason, fair and equitable compensation. This, in turn, prevented deprivations of property.

Prem Chandra Thakur writes concerning the maharaja's efforts to protect his ancestral estate from confiscation without compensation: 'Thus, Raj Darbhanga indirectly contributed to the abolition of the right of property in India.'[70] Although correct, it sounds very much like an indictment, when it should not. The maharaja's suits and appeals, as well as those of numerous other landowners, reflected legitimate concerns. The British had debated long and hard over the importance and benefits of private property. Permanent Settlement conferred the right of private property on a variety of landholders in the belief that property ownership was a fundamental human right. It was this fundamental right that was initially guaranteed by the Indian Constitution under Articles 19 and 31. '[The Maharaja of Darbhanga] never fought to retain his zamindari for the sake of money. It was just a matter of principle that he argued; how could a government selectively takeover the private property [of any citizen].'[71]

The provisions relating to the right to property were changed a number of times. The Forty-Fourth Amendment of 1978 deleted the right to property from the list of fundamental rights.[72] Another provision, Article 300-A, was added providing that 'no person shall be deprived of his property save by authority of law'. Thus if a legislature makes a law that deprives a person of his property, there would be no obligation on the part of the State to pay anything as compensation. The aggrieved person shall have no right to move the Court under Article 32. Thus, the right to property is no longer a fundamental right, though it is still a constitutional right. If the government appears to have acted unfairly, the action of the State can be challenged in a Court of Law by citizens.

In 2009, the Supreme Court sent a notice to the government questioning why the right to property should not be brought back as a fundamental right. The Court suggested that the right to property had been relegated to a mere statutory right and was no longer relevant since the intent of the 1978 enactment was specifically designed to abolish large landholdings owned by zamindars; and having achieved that purpose, the government should initiate measures to restore the right to property as a fundamental right, subject to a pending public interest (PIL) filing before the Court.[73] Then, in 2010 the court rejected the PIL.[74] The justices stated that the word 'socialist' by having been placed into the Preamble of the Constitution had preemptive authority over all subsequent contraindicative language in the Articles that followed. Further, to reinstate the right to property as a fundamental right would necessitate the reversal of earlier judgements on property rights. The court, therefore, was unwilling to contemplate or consider any further challenges to the existing property rights guarantees. Property would continue to be a legal right but not a fundamental right. This had the effect of closing the debate.[75]

* * *

The fate of the Maharaja of Darbhanga and the Darbhanga Raj was preordained when Nehru and his vision of a socialistic society became the driving force behind the Indian Constitution as implemented through State planning for the greater welfare of the Indian State and its people. However, to realize the goal of a fully Social State, where everyone was guaranteed equality, certain people were required to relinquish their rights for what was believed to be the greater good. The maharaja, as a citizen, had the obligation under the law and the Indian Constitution to challenge government actions he deemed unfair and unconstitutional. It took more than twenty-five years for the Government of India to completely erase the right to property as a fundamental right. The maharaja's efforts to retain his estates was a legal battle over individual and fundamental rights, equality, reasonableness, and equity. His efforts, and those of others like him, prevented the State from blatantly ignoring guaranteed rights even when they conflicted with the aim of national government. For this, he should be recognized and applauded. He was a citizen and a patriot.

Had the Maharaja of Darbhanga been interested only in the monetary value of his estates, he would not have refused to accept compensation for his zamindari. His personal wealth and net worth were already things people dream of but cannot imagine. He had campaigned tirelessly against land reform and he pressed his and other zamindars' cases on the elected officials. The Congress party controlled most of the state legislatures, and despite the maharaja's best efforts land reform legislation was enacted, although its implementation was repeatedly postponed by litigation and was not declared valid until 1952.

Congress leaders believed that land reforms, and especially zamindari abolition, was an important part of the process of transforming India's feudal and semi-feudal society into a modern socio-capitalist state. It was believed that land reforms would serve as the catalyst, eliminating old classes and permitting new classes to emerge, and simultaneously, economic, political and social power would be redistributed. This was the same line of thinking the British had used in creating landowning zamindars in 1793. With the emergence of the new classes, agricultural production would also change. Land reforms were seen as the 'magic wand' that would transform India.

LAND REFORM LEGISLATION IN BIHAR

The Bihar Abolition of Zamindari Bill (1947) was the first post-Independence bill passed, designed to abolish the zamindari system. It had been preceded by Bihar State Acquisition of Zamindari Bill earlier in the same year, but had failed to obtain Congress' approval. The new Bill was simultaneously offered to the Governor-General pursuant to the Government of India Act, 1935, and Congress Parliamentary Committee for review. It was returned to the Bihar legislature accompanied by suggestions. An amended Bill was approved by the Governor-General on 6 June 1949 and published as the Bihar Abolition of Zamindari Act, 1948 (Bihar Act XVIII of 1949). Immediately, the constitutionality of the Act was challenged in the courts and injunctions were issued blocking the implementation and enforcement of the Act's provisions.

Recognizing flaws in the original Act, the 1948 Act was repealed and an even more comprehensive Act was drafted. The new Act, known as the Bihar Land Reforms Bill, 1949, was introduced and passed in 1950 by the Bihar legislature.[76] It was then given to the President of India for consideration, pursuant to Article 31(4) of the Constitution of India. It received the assent of the President and was published as the Bihar Land Reforms Act, 1950 (Bihar Act XXX of 1950). Again, the Act was challenged in the courts. It was contravened pursuant to the equality and equal protection portions of Article 14 of the Indian Constitution. The government responded with the First Amendment Act, which had the effect of validating the Bihar Land Reforms Act. Again, the zamindars appealed to the Supreme Court. In 1952, the Supreme Court validated the Bihar Land Reforms Act, 1950.

The zamindars, individually and collectively, utilizing every avenue open to them sought to delay or dilute the legislation and its intent. Letters and memoranda, long and short, were prepared and delivered to every conceivable official in government, including President Rajendra Prasad, with the power or authority to defeat the Act. Unanimously, their appeals were rejected. The Revenue Minister of Bihar, Krishna Ballabha Sahay who had been the driving force behind the Zamindari Abolition Act in Bihar, was prepared to press the issue, even if it meant confrontation. President Prasad wrote to Sahay on 27 April 1947:

> Any hope that you may have of giving satisfaction to tenants by simply getting rid of the zamindars is doomed to failure unless it is accompanied by some positive steps for the betterment of the tenants' lot, but I gathered . . . that you were not thinking of the next step and that for the present you would be satisfied if you can remove the zamindars . . . I have never been able to understand the justice or fairness of depriving a man of the management of his property. I can understand abolition of zamindari. The

Congress has sanctioned that, but I do not think there is any sanction in the Congress Resolution for forcibly dispossessing people of their property before they have been compensated for it.[77]

Elsewhere in the same letter, Prasad cautioned Sahay that the proposed legislation would 'affect the entire economic life of the Province'. Sahay was neither repentant nor chastened by Prasad's letter. As if to confirm his position vis-à-vis the President, Sahay replied attaching a printed copy of the Bihar State Acquisition of Zamindari Bill, 1947.

Sahay, largely because of his almost obsessive desire to see the Act become Law, was the target of the zamindars and the sympathetic press. An editorial appeared in *The Indian Nation*, Bihar's premier English language newspaper.[78]

The fire of power politics is consuming his whole being. The Revenue Minister is evidently insensible to the fact that the bill when enacted will upset the rural economy. The Revenue Minister is either one-eyed or wilfully blind. Bihar is screeching under the stewardship of an aggressive politician who has no vision and faith, but who is obstinate and petty. He is impatient to see Zamindars out; he is anxious to favour men with countless jobs in the event of the abolition of the Zamindari system; he is shaking with joy that he will be able to reward his followers and purchase his critics . . . We plead for rational, cool, and calm thinking on this great issue.[79]

The position of Sahay and that of *The Indian Nation* seemed to be almost vitriolic. There was little subtlety in either's position. However, shortly after Sahay's defeat in the bitterly contested 1957 election, the same newspaper praised him for his patriotism, his service and sacrifice. However, the editorial on 20 March 1957, also anticipated the bitter political, group, and caste infighting that was brewing in Bihar and continues to this day. This is not to suggest that relations between the various political parties, groups, or castes were ever bucolic but under the aegis of the zamindars, much of this dissention was carried out at the local level, never making its way to the state level. And, at least for the Maithil Brahmanas, as long as the maharaja of Darbhanga was able to assert his influence, strife and dissention was limited in scope and intensity. Once his leadership was gone, the politics of northern Bihar, Mithila, became increasingly strident and self-serving.

OBSERVATIONS

The last maharajadhiraja, Kameshwar Singh, finally transferred ownership of his estates to the state of Bihar in 1950. He was permitted to retain certain buildings and lands under the terms of the agreement with the state of Bihar.

Had it not been for a personal plea made by Nehru to the maharaja to relinquish his properties in the name of democracy, it is entirely possible that the maharaja's pending appeal before the Supreme Court – challenging the right of the state to confiscate private property with or without compensation – would have been heard and in all likelihood would have been successful. Had he not withdrawn his petition, the Khandavala family's unique status and the nature of its holdings might well have been exempted from compliance with the land reform laws. Instead, Kameshwar Singh simply transferred his vast estate to the Government of Bihar and, figuratively, walked away a national hero.

* * *

Neither Kameshwar, nor any of his predecessors were intimately involved in the management of the their estates, which were scattered throughout numerous districts. The management of the estates was left to a large and loyal corporate-like management system. Although the system could not be compared to modern-day asset management firms, with their systems of oversight and accounting checks and balances, it was by the standards of the day, efficient.

The loyalty of the Raj's upper- and mid-level managers was not typical of such management organizations within other large zamindaris, in other provinces. Unlike the *amla* attached to other zamindaris, specifically in Bengal, many of whom were disloyal, corrupt, and self-serving, the Raj's managers, by and large, were trustworthy.[80]

The primary flaw in the Raj's management organization lay with the village- and circle-level *patwaris* and *jeth ryots* – the personnel who had the most direct contact with the village-level elites and *ryots*. Often, it was difficult to determine to whom they owed their allegiance, the village leaders or the maharaja. The failure or inability of the Raj to monitor the day-to-day activities of the *patwaris* and *jeth ryots* provided opportunities for these petty officials to marginally plunder the revenue destined for the Raj's treasury.

Further, because of the maharaja's detachment, no thought was given to reinvesting a portion of the profits in an effort to increase agricultural production and simultaneously to improve the lives of his *ryots*. The Raj's bureaucracy was not designed nor intended to be a mechanism or agency for rural development.

Under the circumstances, one has to question the source of the loyalty demonstrated by the maharaja's managers and the majority of his petty, village-level officials. The loyalty extended to the maharajas was largely the result of the traditional authority they commanded in what many observers would deem an economic backwater, then and now.

* * *

The leaders of the Maithili and Mithila movements looked to the maharaja for support and leadership. In fact, the Maharaja was generally seen as the ruler of Mithila, providing leadership well beyond the bounds of his own personal estate. He became the living embodiment of Mithila's independence and unique culture, as well as the pre-eminent head of the Maithil Brahmanas and the Maithil Mahasabha, the caste association of Maithil Brahmanas and Kayasthas.[81] Additionally, the maharajas were ardent supporters of orthodox Hindu practices in both caste and religion, as well as instrumental in their support of the Sanskrit tradition.[82]

On the national level, the maharajas, while remaining loyal to the British, also contributed financially to the Indian National Congress. Further, the maharajas, especially Kameshwar Singh, played an important part in defending the rights of the large landlords, private property ownership and rights, promoted nationalism, the endowment of centres of learning, and invested heavily in a broad range of businesses and industries, many of which have contributed to the greater well-being of the Indian people.[83]

Following Independence, Kameshwar Singh worked tirelessly for national integration but these efforts took a toll on other projects dear to his heart. He wavered on his support of the Maithili language, and began to support the cause of a single national language – Hindi. This was seen as a great contribution to national integration but a loss for Mithila.[84]

Kameshwar Singh's popularity, in all likelihood, was due to his vision for the new state of India, as well as the fact that he and his social intimates were elites with few ties to the people and the land. Since Kameshwar Singh's death, the Darbhanga Raj has remained officially heirless, which has resulted in a long-term contest between his surviving relatives over the titles and inheritances associated with the estate. If Paul Brass is correct, the hangers-on and aspiring relatives of the Darbhanga Raj do not enjoy much popularity among the elites of Darbhanga.[85]

Nevertheless, the Darbhanga Raj and its maharajas for centuries were at the centre of Mithila's cultural, historical, and regional or national identity. Furthermore, they were unique, serving as the regional elite of the Maithil Brahmanas who collectively have served as the carriers of a distinct regional culture and defined the symbols that define Mithila and Maithili culture even today.

NOTES

1. In 1860, the Raj was without an adult heir and fell under the control of the Court of Wards. It was returned to the adult heir to the estate, Lakshmishwar Singh, nineteen years later. When returned to the rightful heir, it was larger and financially stronger than before it had been taken over by the court.
2. Meaning king of kings.
3. *Shrauta* traditions are conservative ritualistic traditions of the historical Vedic religion of Hinduism, placing more emphasis on the performance of rituals than a specific set of beliefs.
4. See, Shyam Narayan Singh, *History of Tirhut: From the Earliest Times to the End of the Nineteenth Century*, vol. 2, ed. Hetukar Jha, Darbhanga: Maharajadhiraja Kameshwar Singh Kalyani Foundation, Maharajadhiraja Kameshwar Singh Bihar Heritage Series - 16, 2012, pp. 1-3.
5. From the sixth- to the ninth-centuries the Pala Dynasty ruled over Mithila. In the ninth century, the Pala Dynasty was defeated by Adishur Samant Sen, and the Sena Dynasty ruled until the eleventh century. In the eleventh century, Nanya Deva defeated the last king of the Sena Dynasty and became the King of Bengal and Mithila. Nanya Deva established the Karnataka/Deva Dynasty.

A priest lived at the court of the last King of the Karnataka/Deva Dynasty. And it was this priest, Kameshwar Thakur, who was later appointed the King of Mithila by Firoz Shah Tughlaq in 1326.

6. Adapted from George A. Grierson, *Bihar Peasant Life, Being a Discursive Catalogue of the Surroundings of the People of that Province,* Calcutta: Bengal Secretariat Press, 1885, map opposite title page. Compare Grierson's depiction with that of Shyam Narayan Singh, *History of Tirhut: From Earliest Times to the End of the Nineteenth Century,* Kameshwar Singh Bihar Heritage Series, no. 16, Series Editor Hetukar Jha, Darbhanga: Maharajadhiraja Kameshwar Singh Kaylani Foundation, 2012, map at the end of the volume.
7. Carolyn Henning Brown, 'Substance and Structure Among the Maithil Brahmans', *Eastern Anthropologist,* vol. 36, no. 3, 1983, pp. 199-200; and Rabindra Ray, *Project Report No. 29: Indianization of the Maithils,* Allahabad: Govind Ballabh Pant Social Science Institute, 1987, p. 34.
8. Makhan Jha, *Anthropology of Ancient Hindu Kingdoms: A Study in Civilizational Perspective,* New Delhi: M.D. Publications, 1997, p. 60.
9. Pradeep Jha, 'Land Reforms in Bihar: Need for a Far-reaching Approach', *CPIML-Liberation Page,* July 1997, http://www.cpiml.org/liberation/year_1997/july/article3.htm, accessed 2 October 2012.
10. From all indications, the name of the dynasty initiated by Mahesh Thakur is derived from the native phrase for 'the richest landlord'. Tejakar Jha suggests that the dynastic name – Khandavala – is derived from the fact that 'Someone from this dynasty got lands and villages in grants at Khandva, in Madhya Pradesh, ... One section of the family settled there and the rest returned to Mithila. Mahamahopadhyaya Mahesh Thakur, who lived at Khandva, [was granted] the Sirkar Tirhut and returned to Mithila and established this dynasty. Hence it also came to be known as Khandavala, meaning people from Khandva' (personal e-mail communication 13 February 2013).
11. Since the Indian Constitution does not recognize titles [Article 18 (1-2)], the title of 'maharaja' ceases to have any legitimate importance. However, the descendants of the maharajas still fight bitterly for the right to use such titles.
12. Paul R. Brass, 'Language, Religion and Politics in North Bihar', Lincoln, NE: iUniverse, 2005, pp. 58-9 suggests that the *Sarkar* of Tirhut, corresponded to the present districts of Darbhanga and Muzaffarpur and that 'the Sarkar of Tirhut was practically an independent kingdom by the eighteenth century. However, after the conquest of Bengal and Bihar by the British, the Raja of Tirhut or Darbhanga was recognized in the Permanent Settlement only as a zamindar'. See also, Jnanendra Nath Kumar, *The Genealogical History of India,* pt. II, Calcutta: Jnanendra Nath Kumar, 1933, pp. 10-13.

13. It has been suggested that the districts 'belonging' to the Maharaja of Darbhanga were ceded to the Company by the King of Nepal, as part of the Segauli Treaty of 1815-16.
14. See, Stephen Henningham, *A Great Estate and Its Landlords in Colonial India: Darbhanga 1860-1942,* Delhi: Oxford University Press, 1990; Carolyn Henning Brown, 'Raja and Rank in North Bihar', *Modern Asian Studies,* vol. 22, no. 4, 1988, p. 758. In a website maintained by the Anthropology Department of Chico State University, the area of the Darbhanga Raj is put at 4,400 sq miles, or 11,396 sq km which is closer to the figure the author arrived at through the interpolation of the information depicted in Map 9-2. See, Carolyn Brown Heinz, 'The Maithil Brahmans: An Online Ethnography', 1999, http://www.csuchico.edu/anth/mithila/index.htm, accessed 4 November 2012, Genealogies: Rank, Gender, and Patriarchy, Changes in Political Control of Mithila, Item 4.
15. Surprisingly, even after consulting with other authorities, like Sirajul Islam and Stephen Henningham, there appears to be no extant documentation or maps that provide detailed information regarding the Darbhanga Raj's actual landholdings. These documents may still exist but, as Henningham and Islam suggest, they are probably lying among the piles of documents yet uncataloged and mouldering in some dark, dank storage room [personal e-mail communications]. Further, it is readily acknowledged that the maharaja did not own every village and acre of land within the depicted boundary. However, without the benefit of documentary evidence, we are only left with conjecture. The figure of 6,200 sq km is, however, in the author's opinion, probably significantly understated. See, also, n. 6, above. Shortly before this volume was completed, the author was informed by Tejakar Jha that the administrative circles map of the Darbhanga Raj, mentioned by Henningham and believed to have been lost, was recently discovered in the archives of the Raj in Darbhanga.
16. This map is based, at least in part, on a map that appears in George A. Grierson, *Bihar Peasant Life, Being a Discursive Catalogue of the Surroundings of the People of that Province,* 1885, opposite the title page of the book. It suggests that the Raj had once controlled property in Nepal. Paschim and Purba Champaran districts have been excluded from inclusion in the Darbhanga Raj, despite the fact that they fall within the territorial definition of Tirhut. These districts were largely under the control of the Bettiah Raj. Likewise, all or parts of Saran, Siwan, and Gopalganj districts have been excluded since they fall to the Hathwa Raj. It is the author's personal opinion that, in reality, it is doubtful that the Raj, even at its peak, ever encompassed the area shown on the map. Cf., Shyam Narayan Singh, *History of Tirhut: From the Earliest Times to the End of the Nineteenth Century,* Darbhanga:

Maharajadhiraja Kameshwar Singh Kalyani Foundation, Kameshwar Singh Bihar Heritage Series, No. 16, 2012, see especially the foldout map of Tribhukti at the end of the volume.

17. Bhojpuri culture is largely identified by the use of the Bhojpuri language in northern Bihar, as opposed to the use of the Maithili language. The Bhojpuri language is part of the Eastern Hindi complex of languages using the Devanagari script, while Maithili is a more direct off-shoot of the Indo-Aryan complex of languages and traditionally used the Mithilakshar or Tirhuta script, although, due to its lack of recognition for many years by the Bihari government, many Maithili speakers now use Devanagari script.
18. Following the bifurcation of Bihar into the states of Bihar and Jharkhand, Bihar was left with only 38 districts. Should the State of Mithila become a reality, conceivably, Bihar could be reduced to only 14 districts.
19. Two dates have been given for the end date of the Raj. This reflects the end of the Darbhanga Raj zamindari, which succumbed to land reforms shortly after Independence. The second date represents the death of the last legitimate Maharaja, Kameshwar Singh Bahadur, thus officially or effectively ending the Khandavala Dynasty. The honorific title of 'Maharaja' has been used by Kameshwar Singh's heirs but it is no longer officially recognized by the Indian government.
20. Qeyam Uddin Ahmad, 'Origin and Growth of the Darbhanga Raj (1574-1666), Based on Some Contemporary and Unpublished Documents', *Indian Historical Records Commission Proceedings,* vol. 36, pt. II, 1961, pp. 96-7.
21. The greatest possible estate in land, wherein the owner has the right to use it, exclusively possess it, dispose of it by deed or will, and take its fruits. A fee simply represents absolute ownership of land, and the owner may do whatever he or she chooses with the land (J. Lehman and S. Phelps, *West's Encyclopedia of American Law,* vol. 2, Detroit: Thomson/Gale, 2005, p. 40).
22. Qeyam Uddin Ahmad, 'Origin and Growth of the Darbhanga Raj (1574-1666), 1961, p. 97; Makhan Jha, *Anthropology of Ancient Hindu Kingdoms: A Study in Civilizational Perspective,* 1997, p. 35, n. 39; S.V. Shiny, 'Notes on the Revenue History of Darbhanga Raj', *Journal of the Bihar Research Society,* vol. 48, 1962, especially p. 106; and Jogendra Nath Bhattacharya, *Hindu Castes and Sects,* Calcutta: Thacker, Spink & Co., 1896:

    The head of the Maithil Brahmans is the Maharaja of Darbhanga. The founder of the family, Mahesh Thākoor, bore a Brahmanical surname . . . his descendants at present use the Kshatriya surname of Singh. The transformation is exactly the opposite of what has taken place in many Kshatriya families, though the ambition of the Rajput to be elevated from the rank of a Singh (lion) to that of Thākoor (god) is certainly more intelligible, than the desire on the part of any royal family to be degraded from the rank of a god to that of a lion (pt. III, p. 47).

23. See, Laksman Jha, *Mithila: A Union Republic,* Darbhanga: Mithila Mandal, 1952, pp. 57-8.
24. Tanistry – a rule of succession by which the heir or successor of a chief or king is appointed during the lifetime of the reigning chief. It is not necessarily his oldest son, but is generally the worthiest and wisest of the male relatives of the chief. *Kulachar* – a Muslim variation of tanistry-based system of inheritance and succession law based on primogeniture, as opposed to the Hindu system of inheritance where all male heirs share equally in their father's estate
25. The last Maharaja, Kameshwar Singh Bahadur, died in 1962 without any heirs, a vague will, and without naming a successor. Thus, officially, the Khandavala Dynasty came to an end. The sons of his younger brother, Raja Bahadur (Raja Bishweshwar Singh), have claimed their right to the title. Their suit remains unresolved today. However, since the Indian Constitution does not recognize the title of 'maharaja', Kameshwar Singh Bhadur was, technically, the last Maharaja of Darbhanga. See, Henry Soszynski, *Indian Princely States - Darbhanga,* 23 May 2007, http://archiver.rootsweb.ancestry.com/th/read/INDIA-ROYALTY/2007-05/1179883554, accessed 21 August 2012. All but a few honorary titles were abolished shortly after Independence by Article 18 of the Indian Constitution.
26. Bettiah Raj was recognized as the second largest zamindari in Bihar, occupying approximately 1,800 sq miles, but possibly the oldest with its roots dating back to mid-1200s. See, Anand A. Yang, *Bazaar India: Markets, Society, and the Colonial State in Bihar,* Berkeley: University of California Press, 1999, p. 69.
27. The question arises, if the Sarkar of Tirhut had already been awarded to Mahesh Thakur by Akbar nearly a century earlier, why would Alivardi Khan's offer of a *mukarari* lease of Tirhut have any appeasement value for Raghu Singh? Is it a simple matter of terminology or was there a genuine benefit to be realized by the new raja?
28. See, L.S.S. O'Malley, *Bengal District Gazetteers: Champaran,* vol. 10, Calcutta: The Bengal Secretariat Book Depot, 1907, pp. 143-4.
29. Roper Lethbridge, *The Golden Book of India,* London: Macmillan & Co., 1893, p. 107.
30. While what happened does not seem to be historically disputed, the players and the timeline seem to become muddled, depending upon the authorities one consults. On the one side were the Rajas of Darbhanga – Raghu Singh (ruled 1700-36), Vishnu Singh (1736-40), and Narendra Singh (1740-60). On the other was Nawab Alivardi Khan. The reason that there is some dispute is that Raghu Singh died in 1736, four years before Alivardi Khan [also referred from time to time by his honorific names – *Shujaul-Mulk* (Hero of the Country), *Hashim ud-Daula* (Sword of the State), and *Mahabat*

Jang] assumed the office of Nawab of Bengal. However, Alivardi Khan was the Naib Nazim (Deputy Subahdar) of Behar during this period (1733). So, some of the confusion may be due to misuse of titles in the sources.

31. O'Malley, *Bengal District Gazetteers: Champaran,* vol. 10, 1907, p. 144.
32. Jata Shankar Jha, *Biography of an Indian Patriot: Maharaja Lakshmishwar Singh of Darbhanga,* Patna: Maharaja Lakshmishwar Singh Smarak Samiti, 1972, pp. 3-4.
33. Radhakrishna Choudhary, *History of Bihar.* Patna: Motilal Banarsidass, 1958, p. 202.
34. L.S.S. O'Malley, *Bengal District Gazetteers: Purnea,* vol. 25, Calcutta: Bengal Secretariat Book Depot, 1911, p. 151.
35. Stephen Henningham, *A Great Estate and Its Landlords in Colonial India: Darbhanga 1860-1942,* 1990, p. 23.
36. Secretary, Board of Revenue to Government of Bengal, 13 January 1866, *Bengal Revenue Proceedings.* Bundles, February 1866, no. 52. As cited by Anand A. Yang, *The Limited Raj: Agrarian Relations in Colonial India, Saran District, 1793-1920,* Berkeley: University of California Press, 1989, fn. 70, p. 84.
37. See, Jata Shanker Jha, 'History of Darbhanga Raj', *Journal of Bihar Research Society,* vol. 48, 1962, p. 81.
38. Very little work has been done regarding the actual internal management and organization of the zamindaris, with the exception of Stephen Henningham, *A Great Estate and Its Landlords in Colonial India: Darbhanga 1860-1942,* 1990; Stephen Henningham, 'Bureaucracy and Control in India's Great Landed Estates: The Raj Darbhanga of Bihar, 1879 to 1950', *Modern Asian Studies,* vol. 17, no. 1, February 1983; S.V. Sohini, 'Notes on the Revenue History of Darbhanga Raj', 1962; and Jata Shanker Jha, 'History of Darbhanga Raj', 1962. Of these, Henningham's works are possibly the most detailed and will be used here extensively.
39. Stephen Henningham, *A Great Estate and Its Landlords in Colonial India: Darbhanga 1860-1942,* 1990, p. 47. In a private communication with Tejakar Jha, the nephew of Maharaniadhirani Kam Sundari Devi, the widow of Maharajadhiraja Kameshwar Singh, the last reigning Maharaja of Darbhanga, and the webmaster for the Rani's Maharajadhiraja Kameshwar Singh Kalyani Foundation (http://www.kalyanifoundation.org/aboutus.htm), the extent of the Raj exceeded 2,400 sq miles (6,216 sq km.), consisted of 18 circles, and included 4,497 villages (personal communication from Tejakar Jha, 6 January 2008).
40. Later, as the Raj expanded, the number of circles was increased to eighteen.
41. *Raj Darbhanga Directory,* 1941 (Darbhanga: Raj Press, 1941) as cited by

Stephen Henningham, *A Great Estate and Its Landlords in Colonial India: Darbhanga 1860-1942,* 1990, fn. 1, p. 47. Tejakar Jha suggests that the Raj's administration employed 7,000 (personal communication from Tejakar Jha, 6 January 2008). The author is inclined to accept Jha's figure regarding the number of people employed by the Raj based on simple mathematics. Assuming the Raj commanded 4,497 villages, and accepting Henningham's statement that each *jeth ryot* collected rents from 1 or 2 *mauzas,* the Raj would have employed a full 2,209 *jeth ryots* alone. If you add the *patwaris, barahils, tahsildars,* circle managers and their staff, chief manager and his staff, plus solicitors and barristers, Henningham's figure of 2,000 personnel in the Raj's administration is simply too low.

42. Stephen Henningham, *A Great Estate and Its Landlords in Colonial India: Darbhanga 1860-1942,* 1990, p. 48.
43. Ibid., p. 53, and fn. 12, p. 53.
44. Ibid., citing Sunder, confidential notes, fn. 13, p. 53.
45. Ibid., p. 54.
46. Ibid., p. 57, quoting: 16D2, C. Jhanjharpur, G 1941-2.
47. Ibid., p. 581 quoting from Raj documents: Parihar AAR 1349 F, f 16D2, 1942-3; and Nishankpur AAR 1349 F, f 16D1, G 1942-3.
48. Ibid., p. 161.
49. Among the companies that the maharaja either owned or was a partial owner in, were:
    - Newspaper & Publications Pvt. Ltd., published two newspapers from Patna, Bihar. *The Indian Nation* was an English daily newspaper while the *Aryavarta* was a Hindi daily newspaper. It also published *Mithila Mihir,* a periodical in the Maithili language, and *The Dove*, a monthly magazine in English. In addition, the maharaja held a major share in two British home newspapers, the *Pioneer* and the *London Mail* (then the *Associate Press*) (personal communication, Tejakar Jha, 24 August 2012).
    - Walford, a chain of automobile dealerships.
    - Darbhanga Aviations, a commercial airline with a fleet of DC-3s and airstrips at Darbhanga and Madhubani.
    - Ashok Paper Mills, manufacturers of newsprint.
    - Sakri Sugar Factory and Pandaul Sugar Factory.
    - Rameshwar Jute Mills, sold to the Birlas in 1960.
    - British India Corporation.
    - Octavius Steel.
    - Thacker Spink & Co. (P) Ltd.
    - Darbhanga Investments Private Ltd., the investment arm of Raj Darbhanga held shares of various companies, including companies of the Tata Group.
    - Darbhanga Dairy Farm (P) Ltd.

- Darbhanga Marketing, now a part of KK Birla Group.
- Tirhoot State Railway.

50. Carolyn Henning Brown, 'Raja and Rank in North Bihar', 1988, p. 758.
51. Makhan Jha, *Anthropology of Ancient Hindu Kingdoms: A Study in Civilizational Perspective,* 1997, p. 153. Around 1324, Hari Singh Deva sought sanctuary in Nepal in an attempt to avoid the first of the Muslim invasions of Mithila. There his family established the Karnataka/Deva Dynasty that lasted nearly a century.
52. *Gautamsmruti*, 10.9, 10 and *Yajnyavalkyasmruti*, 3.44.
53. Carolyn Henning Brown, 'Raja and Rank in North Bihar', 1988, p. 768.
54. Ibid., p. 765.
55. The Maithil Brahmanas are divided into three major groups: the Jaibar, the lowest level Brahmanas, comprising the vast majority are found throughout Mithila. The Yogya, the mid-level Brahmanas, are mostly consolidated in villages around Madhubani. The Srotriyas, the highest ranking Brahmanas and are mostly consolidated in 36 villages slightly north-east of Darbhanga, in an area known as Sotipura.
56. See, Carolyn Henning Brown, 'Raja and Rank in North Bihar', 1988, for a comprehensive discussion of the Maithil Brahmanas' lineage system.
57. Ibid., p. 767.
58. Ibid., p. 768.
59. Ibid., p. 769.
60. In a private communication with Tejakar Jha, dated 24 November 2012, the nephew of the Maharaniadhirani Kam Sundari Devi – the widow of Maharajadhiraja Kemeshwar Singh – the will only provided a formula for the distribution of the Raja's wealth, naming his two surviving wives and nephews and their children. Subheshwar Singh was acknowledged as the virtual successor, in spite of the fact that, at the time, he was only twelve-thirteen years old.
61. Personal communication from Tejakar Jha, 24 November 2012.
62. Rajendra Prasad, the first President of India, made the distinction between those zamindars with revenues over Rs 5 lakhs and with revenues under 5 lakhs. It is unclear why, or how, this distinction was arrived at but for Prasad it seemed a benchmark when discussing zamindars.
63. Personal e-mail communication, dated 20 December 2007.
64. Article 19(1)(f), among other things, provides the fundamental right of all citizens to acquire, hold, and dispose of property. Article 19(5) allowed for reasonable restrictions to be placed on this right of ownership. Article 31(1) provided that no person shall be deprived of property save by authority of law, and Article 31(2) provided that no property shall be dispossessed or acquired for public purposes unless the law in question provides for

compensation. Article 31(5) provided for a number of exclusions from the compensation guarantee.

65. M. Chaskalson, 'The Problem with Property: Thoughts on the Constitutional Protection of Property in the United States and the Commonwealth', *South African Journal on Human Rights (SAJHR),* vol. 9, 1993, p. 390.
66. *Kameshwar Singh* v. *State of Bihar,* AIR (38) 1951, Pat 91 (FB).
67. See, V.N. Shukla, *The Constitution of India,* vol. 5, Lucknow: Eastern Book Co., 1969.
68. Andre van der Walt, 'The Constitutional Property Clause: Striking a Balance Between Guarantee and Limitation', in *Property and the Constitution*, ed. Janet McLean, 276. Oxford: Hart Publishing, 1999, p. 119.
69. *The State of West Bengal* vs. *Subodh Gopal Bose and Others* on 17 December 1953, 1954, AIR 92, 1954 SCR 587, Bench: Sastri, M. Patanjali.
70. Prem Chandra Thakur, 'Darbhanga Raj', *The International Journal's Research Journal of Social Sciences and Management,* vol. 2, no. 2, June 2012, p. 10.
71. Personal e-mail communication from Tejakar Jha, 20 December 2007.
72. The Forty-fourth Amendment to the Indian Constitution clearly states that:

    [Paragraph] 3. In view of the special position sought to be given to fundamental rights, the right to property, which has been the occasion for more than one amendment of the Constitution, would cease to be a fundamental right and become only a legal right. Necessary amendments for this purpose are being made to Article 19 and Article 31 is being deleted. It would, however, be ensured that the removal of property from the list of fundamental rights would not affect the right of minorities to establish and administer educational institutions of their choice.

    [Paragraph] 5. Property, while ceasing to be a fundamental right, would, however, be given express recognition as a legal right, provision being made that no person shall be deprived of his property save in accordance with law.
73. The PIL was filed by Sanjiv Kumar Agarwal on behalf of the NGO, Good Governance India Foundation.
74. See, Dhananjay Mahapatra, 'Should Right to Property Return'? 28 February 2009, http://articles.timesofindia.indiatimes.com/2009-02-28/india/28016971.public-purpose-poor-farmers-property, accessed 21 August 2012; and J. Venkatesan, 'Court Rejects Plea to Make Property a Fundamental Right', 19 October 2010, http://www.thehindu.com/news/national/article836599.ece, accessed 21 August 2012.
75. See, also, R. Rajesh Babu, 'Constitutional Right to Property in Changing Times: The Indian Experience', *Vienna Journal on International Constitutional Law,* vol. 6, no. 2, 13 September 2012, pp. 213-47.
76. H.D. Malaviya, *Land Reforms in India,* vol. 2, New Delhi: Economic and

Political Research Department, All India Congress Committee, 1955, pp. 205-6.

77. As quoted by F. Thomasson Jannuzi, *Agrarian Crisis in India: The Case of Bihar,* Austin: University of Texas Press, 1974, pp. 15-16.
78. It must be noted that Maharaja Kameshwar Singh of Darbhanga, who fought so strenuously against land reforms and particularly against zamindari abolition, owned both *The Indian Nation*, and its sister newspaper, a Hindi daily known as *Aryavarta.*
79. F. Thomasson Jannuzi, *Agrarian Crisis in India: The Case of Bihar,* 1974, p. 17.
80. It must be noted that even at the time of Permanent Settlement, the Company's revenue officials recognized a significant difference between the zamindars of Bengal and those in Bihar, and it was this difference that permitted the settlement in Bihar well before that in Bengal. The primary difference was that almost all the zamindars in Bihar were, by tradition, much more like absentee landowning landlords than the zamindars of Bengal. In some ways, it is this difference that made them more vulnerable and served to disqualify them from assuming *bakast* or self-tilled lands, since they were never involved in the day-to-day management of any of their agricultural lands. Their only right in the land was one of ownership and the right to collect revenue, and nothing more.
81. Jnanendra Nath Kumar, *The Genealogical History of India,* pt. II, 1933, p. 78; Laksman Jha, *Mithila: A Union Republic,* 1952, p. 58.
82. Ibid., pp. 28-9, 31-2, 34, 38, 41, 61, 64-5, 71 and 77.
83. See n. 39, above.
84. See the comment by the Secretary of the Maithil Mahasaha in Paul R. Brass, 'Language, Religion and Politics in North Bihar', 2005, p. 60.
85. Ibid.

CHAPTER 7

Pulling the Threads Together

INTRODUCTION

Throughout the previous chapters, we have examined both the history of development and elements of the history of South Asia. We have explored a broad range of topics that begin to form a framework for understanding the alarming concentration of backward districts in Bihar, more specifically, northern Bihar. The question before us now: How or why have all these historical, as well as the socio-economic, cultural, and political institutions, come together with such a negative impact in Mithila?[1]

Admittedly, there is no single, readily identifiable cause for Mithila's 'backwardness'. There is no one thing that we can point to, producing one of those 'a-ha' moments when everything becomes clear; everything just falls into place. If there was, policies and programmes would have already been put in place to effect the necessary change(s). After all, it has been 65-plus years since the independent government of India came into existence, with its multiple development plans.

Instead, it is a constellation of nearly invisible practices and attitudes that individually are more or less benign but when they come together, when they amalgamate, reinforcing and multiplying the effects of one another, their collective influence becomes almost palpable. Most of these practices and ideas have very long historical roots, which demonstrates their cultural importance, thus ensuring their retention and durability. These are the gossamer threads of backwardness. These threads have been, to use a familiar phrase, 'hiding in plain sight' for decades.

Some of these threads, while acknowledged, have been ignored, largely because of the prevailing political and social mandate for India, as a nation, to be politically correct, mixed together with a generous dose of political economy. Being politically correct sometimes permits politicians to 'ignore the elephant in the room'. 'If we ignore him, he will simply go away.' This solution to any problem, while a convenient political tool, does little to resolve problems. It only postpones them and some cannot or at least should not be postponed. The Government of India has attempted to ignore the problems or consequences of multiple languages, multiple cultures, communalism, regionalism, religion, and casteism, wishfully thinking (but not necessarily believing) that one day India will miraculously discover a new national identity that will somehow transcend its many divisive differences. This has not and, in all likelihood, will never happen. But this is the vision politicians continue to cling to.

Isabel Paterson probably stated the underlying truth about political correctness and political economy when she said: 'Most of the harm in the world is done by good people, and not by accident, lapse, or omission. It is the result of their deliberate actions, long persevered in, which they hold to be motivated by high ideals toward various ends.'[2]

* * *

Assuming that these gossamer threads are the source of Mithila's backwardness, it leaves us with possibly an equally difficult problem. Who in government or the foreign development agencies is in a position to say the people of Mithila should 'become more modern'? Is there no room for the possibility that, under certain circumstances, people should just be left alone to pursue their own cultural path, even if this results in happy poverty or differs from the abstract vision India's politicians and planners have for the country?

Aside from language, do all the citizens of India need to be homogenized, becoming someone's idealized version of what an 'Indian' should be? Is there not sufficient tolerance to permit communal or cultural choice when it comes to development? The Government of India already tolerates the proliferation of states based on language and culture. Repeatedly, the Centre perpetuates, even encourages national divisiveness by carving linguistic and cultural states from existing states, just to satisfy or ensnare vote banks, appear politically correct, and create political capital, which in no way furthers national unity, cohesiveness, or strengthens the idea of a single national identity.

Would it not be permissible for a group of people, tied together by language and culture, who reject the notion of development, to have their own state – Mithila? Does everyone need to attain some predetermined level of human or economic development, if it means discarding cultural practices that have served certain groups adequately for, possibly, millennia?[3]

The search for the root causes of Mithila's apparent backwardness is a valid enterprise, despite the real possibility that it could easily result in myriad and more perplexing ethical questions later. Underlying these questions is yet another historical question: Has Indian society changed its basic value set? It seems modern man has developed the sense that change is being imposed upon him whereas prior to the nineteenth century, many believed they created change for themselves, through their own choices and actions. Is this change in thinking a function of a growing global culture?[4] Development is being imposed on people, not just in India but around the world. From an economic standpoint, this is understandable but ethically, is it right?

Amartya Sen in the late 1980s began to lecture on the importance of ethics and economics. He indicated that somewhere during its evolution, economics had become separated from ethics, despite the fact that modern economics was originally an off-shoot of ethics, and now the two needed to be reunited.[5] In many respects, Sen's clarion call, made more than twenty-five years ago, has gone largely unheeded. As Mozaffar Qizilbash has pointed out, 'recent work at the borderlines of ethics and economics' has been undertaken, but little has been done to extend it to development economics; and this is where it is most sorely needed.[6] Sen's belief in the importance of re-engaging economics and ethics resulted in the creation of 'quality of life' indices like the Human Development Index and the Oxford Multidimensional Poverty Index. However, gauging human development is an objective response to a need to compare. These indices do not, however, answer the fundamental question: Is development always necessary or desirable?

HISTORICAL ROOTS

'Aryans', 'Hinduism', and Tradition[7]

Over the last few decades, the veracity of the terms 'Aryans' and 'Hinduism' has been increasingly called into question. It has been suggested that both terms were invented or imagined by British scholars and colonial administrators in the nineteenth century and neither existed in any meaningful sense before then.[8] It is not our intent to dive headlong into these debates but rather, to look at the role of Hinduism as one of several building blocks in constructing an understanding of the backwardness in Mithila.

Even raising the spectre of Hinduism as an ingredient in our explanation of backwardness will surely raise eyebrows and, possibly ire. Here you will not find an indictment of Hinduism as a religion but some of its day-to-day consequences may be called into question. It may be politically incorrect to even mention Hinduism within this context but we cannot ignore a reality to satisfy an ideology. Philosophical and liturgical concerns seldom manifest themselves as backwardness.

Hinduism theologically and devotionally was based on certain early texts such as the Vedas, the Upanishads, and other philosophical commentaries, practices and beliefs, and as a 'religion' was firmly established well before British hegemony.[9] Yet, to refer to Hinduism as a 'religion' within the Western sense of the term may well be a misnomer. The philosophical and religious umbrella of Hinduism is far broader than for, say, Presbyterianism or even Catholicism.

Language and Literature

Until the Aryans arrival on the subcontinent, their language, known generically as Proto-Indo-European (PIE), remained unwritten but nevertheless, it had already developed a rich oral literary tradition. In India, a written language now known as Vedic Sanskrit was developed that culminated in the creation of the oldest formal, written Sanskrit literature and the oldest scripture of Hinduism, the Vedas. The Vedas represent four canonical collections of metrical material of which the first three are related to the performance of sacrifices in the historic Vedic religion. The fourth is a collection of spells and incantations, apostrophic charms and speculative hymns. For both the Vedic religion and the Vedas, an oral tradition predominated until *c.* 1000 CE.[10] Until the advent of Sanskrit, tens of thousands of verses were transmitted orally and verbatim, generation to generation, teacher to disciple, with the help of elaborate mnemonic techniques, a tradition that continues to be practiced in parts of modern India.

The Vedas as the most ancient of the world's scriptures contain hymns or chants that must be performed in a precise form if they are to propitiate or be properly received by the gods. Thus, their sound and presentation are profoundly important and have become ritualized, preserved as a part of the Shrauta tradition of Vedic chanting. The static, unchanging nature of Vedic Sanskrit defies the natural evolutionary tendencies of most languages as to content, style, and usage.

Modern Sanskrit is a different language from Vedic Sanskrit, the latter having remained unchanged due to the Vedas themselves. The reason for its stasis lies in the sound aspect of the Vedic hymns. The metre of the verses when chanted properly have a completeness all their own and any mutation or distortion of the words would alter their sound aspect and meaning, and it is this sound aspect that has prevented the alteration of Vedic Sanskrit.[11] Classical Sanskrit, on the other hand, dating back to the fourth century BCE, emerged as the language of science, scholarship, and debate based on the detailed grammatical rules set forth by Panini.[12]

Rammohun Roy described Sanskrit in his Letter on Education, as follows:

> The Sanscrit language, so difficult that almost a lifetime is necessary for its acquisition, is well known to have been for ages a lamentable check to the diffusion of knowledge, and the learning concealed under this almost impervious veil is far from sufficient to reward the labour of acquiring it.
>
> In the same manner the Sanscrit system of education would be the best calculated to keep this country in darkness, if such had been the policy of the British legislature.[13]

It is clear that Rammohun Roy viewed the study of Sanskrit as counterproductive to the needs of his countrymen. Could the preoccupation with Sanskrit, both as a language and a literature, have contributed to Mithila's failure to progress?

Hinduism

Much of modern, mainstream Hinduism remains connected to the Vedic texts as well as Vedic thought and philosophy. But unlike most of the other universal religions of the world, Hinduism is the only major religion that lacks a self-defining origin; that is, it does not contain within its texts accounts of its origin. Christianity has the *Bible*, Islam the *Koran* and *Hadith*, and Judaism the *Torah* or *Pentateuch*. Each in its own way provides a history of its origin but not so with the Vedas. Either this aspect was never recorded or formalized, and never handed down to the scribes of the Vedas; or they never contained this kind of historical content. Either way, the sacred texts of Hinduism contain virtually no narrative history.

The Vedas are deemed to be *apauruseya* (not of human agency).[14] The Vedas were verbally revealed by the god(s) and were handed down in their full and completed form, and thus they are called *śruti* (that which is heard),[15] as distinguishing them from other religious texts, which are called *Smriti* (that which is remembered).

No texts exist before 1500 BCE and the texts after 1200 BCE contain no information regarding the beginnings or evolution of the religion. Scholars are able to piece together the earliest phases of Hinduism only through archaeology, clues in later texts, and by extrapolating from existing traditions. Reconstructing the ancient history of any civilization is, at best, tentative and all such efforts are little more than educated speculation.

The Vedas are universally considered the foundational scriptures of Hinduism. They represent a rich and colourful 'theo-mythology' – a religious mythology that weaves myth, theology, and history together to achieve a story-like religious root. They lay down the concept of God, nature, and deities without losing sight of the importance of human intention and action, and the principles upon which much of subsequent Indian religious tradition and society have been based.[16]

Although Hinduism currently exhibits many philosophical and religious traditions and encompasses a broad range of religious doctrines and practices that have some common characteristics, it lacks definiteness, a unified system of beliefs and practices. This polymorphic description is entirely consistent with the view that Hinduism, rather than following a linear evolutionary path, emerged in its current form(s) as a series of reformation movements intended to return Indian society to some idealized, pre-stress state, particularly following the rise of Buddhism and Jainism.[17] Nevertheless, in modern Hinduism, some of the traditional Vedic rituals, specifically, animal sacrifice, were replaced due to the acceptance of the doctrine of *ahimsa* – non-injury to others, human as well as animals, and an outgrowth of Jainism. Thus, while Hinduism may have evolved as a form of reformation, at the same time, it has incorporated much of what it intended to resist.

The earliest form of Hinduism is represented by early Brahmanism, the religion of priests who performed the Vedic sacrifices. These priests served as mediums between the gods, the cosmos, and mankind. The Vedas represent the liturgy and interpretation of these sacrifices.

Hinduism, even from Vedic times, was a religion built on a literature that was pre-eminently priestly and religious. Beginning with the first of the Vedas to the last Purāna, religion was either the subject matter, or as with the epics, the basis of didactic interpolations that are peculiarly theological in character.[18] In addition, in early Indian literature, history and oratory are virtually unknown. Early poetry consists entirely of hymns. The early prose focuses on liturgies, linguistics, law, theology, sacred legends, and other works, which all appear to be designed to supplement the knowledge of the Vedas, explain ceremonies, or reinforce one or more religious principles. As Deward Hopkins suggests:

> . . . in all this great mass, till that time which Mueller has called the Renaissance – that is to say, till after the Hindus were come into close contact with foreign nations, notably the Greeks, from which has been borrowed, perhaps, the classical Hindu drama – there is no real literature that was not religious originally, or, at least, so apt for priestly use as to become chiefly moral and theosophic; while the most popular works of modern times are sectarian tracts, Purānas, Tantras and remodelled worldly poetry. The sources, then, from which is to be drawn the knowledge of Hindu religions are the best possible – the original texts.[19]

For some of the more puritanical followers of Hinduism, a heavy reliance is placed on the rigid performance of Vedic rituals, in terms of action, form, and strict adherence to the recitation of incantations. Among the most parochial adherents of this strict observance of Vedic rituals are the Maithil Brahmanas.

Varna and Caste

The caste system, believed to be one of the fundamental components of Hindu society and religion, finds its initial conception scattered throughout the sacred texts. Its origin is often traced to the Vedas, specifically the poem, '*Purusha Sukta*', in the tenth book of the *Rig-Veda*. In the '*Purusha Sukta*', the four chief *varnas* – the Brahmin, Ksahtriya, Vaishya, and Shudra – are pictured as having come from the Lord's mouth, arms, middle and feet, respectively. If the poem is simply read as presenting four labour classes within society, with each providing an indispensable function, instead of any implicit or explicit hierarchy, *varna* takes on a much less onerous connotation, as functioning parts of a body, none is superior to the other.

Vedic society was largely, if not completely, egalitarian and the four-fold caste system had not yet evolved. The warrior category, then known as the Rajanyas, was the most superior in society. The priests, who performed rituals and sacrifices, occupied a secondary position. Later, however, this apparently egalitarian social system began to change as a consequence of the increased importance placed on the strict performance of rituals and sacrifices, thus increasing the importance of the Brahmins, who emerged as the preeminent social class within Vedic society. As the rituals became increasingly complex, a professional, specialized priesthood evolved, with those in charge of the invocations and litanies (the *Hotr*); the *Adhvaryu* those who were in charge of the physical details of the rituals and sacrifice; the *Udgātr*, the chanters of hymns; and the Brahmins, who were the superintendents over the entire performance and who were also responsible for correcting any mistakes in the liturgy. Of the four classes of priests, the Brahmins became the most exalted since they were the only ones able to perform the sacrifices properly, making corrective alterations as needed to insure the efficacy of the rite. The intended beneficiary of the rite had little or no direct involvement in the actual ceremony. In Vedic times, the beneficiary was only the sponsor, with the *Hotr* or Brahmin standing in his stead during the performance of the ritual.

As the ritual importance of the Brahmins increased, so did their social position within Vedic society. The goals of these sacrifices, offerings, and rituals were to obtain beneficence or blessings from the gods in the form of good crops, cattle, good weather, progeny, good health, happiness of any kind, etc. The Vedic scriptures from the very outset mandated that sacrifice was essential if man wished the Gods' favour. Later, Vedic ritual changed, with an emphasis being placed on the human supplicant rather than on the external expression of the ritual in the form of elaborate, detailed performances that could only be performed or officiated over by a qualified priest. During this period of change, knowledge came to be seen as the equivalent of ritual sacrifice. It is this change from external ritual to the internalization of knowledge that commemorates the leap from Vedic religion to an early form of Hinduism, a form that would be recognizable within the context of modern Hindu society and contributed to a functioning Hindu identity devoid of colonial influence.

While the *Rigveda* enumerates the four *varnas* and their functions within society, there is no indication that one's *varna* was believed to be hereditary or hierarchical. The *Rigveda*'s conception of *varna* is little more than a simple device for characterizing labour divisions within Vedic society. As such, *varna* and caste can be viewed as two separate institutions.

If the *Purusha Sukta* is read as a simple acknowledgment of labour categories without any negative hereditary connotations and without any clear-cut impediment to social mobility, it is clearly unlike the later manifestations of caste. It is only the alignment of *varna* with hereditary types of employment that converts it into the caste system and becomes the real source of abuse. It is this hereditary component that betrays the intent of the scriptural character of the *Rigveda*.

Further, if the original intent of the *varnas* is accepted, and it was not until the time of Buddha and Mahavira that caste was found to be offensive, we can infer that the change from *varna* to caste took place sometime in the early first millennium BCE. The transformation of *varna* into caste brought with it inequality, hereditary hierarchy, separation, as well as the division of labour, and the reinforcement of social distance through ritual practices and religious principles.

At least a part of the problem with caste and casteism is, in fact, directly attributable to colonial influences.[20] The British in their attempt to rule India more efficiently, prepared lists of Indian communities. They used two terms to describe Indian communities – Castes and Tribes – with the word caste denoting both *varna* and *jati*.[21] These lists, in turn, sharpened and expanded the norms and conventions of the then existing caste system, and was important in further institutionalizing and perpetuating a more caste-conscious society.

The British saw the caste system as a hierarchical and inflexible means of perpetuating a Brahmin-centered value system. From this perspective, it can be argued that the caste system was as much British as it was Indian in origin. These lists of castes and tribes later became part of the Indian government's system for the enumeration of its population during the decennial census, continuing and institutionalizing them even further.

For the British, caste was a means to bridge many boundaries such as faith, region and economic status but it was also used as a tool to exclude, subjugate and disempower. This was done in order for certain groups to gain an advantage over others. With hundreds of different cultures and languages, caste could be used to bring the nation together; it could also be used to gain political and economic advantage. In the colonial quest for monetary exploitation, caste was used to create political allegiances and undermine and prevent coordinated opposition.

The leaders of independent India, however, determined that India would be democratic, socialist, and secular. As a secular state, discriminating against a person based on his caste was forbidden but the government was permitted to practice 'reverse discrimination' when it came to the depressed classes. Concomitant with the advent of the secular state, the caste system became more flexible, with the urban population less likely to observe strict caste rules and protocols. In the rural areas, however, caste continued and continues to play an important role in social, economic, and political affairs and serves as one of the primary rallying points for political alliances, especially in Bihar. As a consequence, the continued paramountcy of caste in Bihar has led to unbridled caste tensions and inter-caste violence. Dr. Anupama Rao, with a background in anthropology and history, began her speech on the campus of the University of Central Florida with the following statement: 'In order to understand India's democracy, we have to understand caste.'[22] It is a fact of life. As a result, India responds to the idea of equality differently, because caste and Hinduism are important components of Indian culture.

Traditionalism

P.T. Raju, writing in the early 1950s, suggested that all our thoughts and actions are controlled by our thought and behaviour mechanisms and both are rooted in tradition.[23] Traditions are society's formulae for dealing with life's challenges. They are tried and true, and in general, they work. Change is society's admission that traditions are not infallible and there is potentially a 'better' alternative. These alternatives are realized through borrowing and invention. Each addition or replacement is accommodated through the process of attaching meaning to these new items as they are integrated into the culture. A perfect integration is never fully achieved because, if there was complete integration, the perceived problem would no longer exist and there would be no further need for change. Since human and physical environments are never in a state of complete stasis, change is an on-going need and adaptive process. However, cultures cannot be changed or preserved at will. There is persistence, a durability within every culture. They have their own unique internal dynamics and cohesiveness. How else can we explain the continued existence of cultural diversity all around the world well after the end of the classical period of colonization and the advent of the globalization?

Everett Hagen once described the world view of most traditional societies as follows:

> The image of the world of the simple folk and elite classes alike includes a perception of uncontrollable forces around them that restrict and dominate their lives. . . . The lines of dependence extend upward to the spiritual powers, to whom the members of the society appeal for protection against the physical forces. . . . Each individual finds his place in the authoritarian

hierarchy of human relationships . . . the simple folk find satisfaction in both submissiveness and domination; their personalities as well as those of the elite are authoritarian. . . . In these societies, except for struggles within the class of elite itself, class relationships are fixed.[24]

This type of world view inhibits both economic growth and social development. In such societies, behaviour is governed more by custom than law, the social structure is hierarchical, and both economic and agricultural production tends to be low.[25] These conditions while describing the attributes of traditional societies also serves to describe backwardness. In Mithila, it is not just custom nor the hierarchical nature of rural society that thwarts development but it is the re-inforcement of these social characteristics through fundamental, orthodox religious practices that shapes the philosophical and practical world view of Maithili society. The interlocking character of the caste system, priest-craft, ancestor worship, social and ceremonial rules, sacrifices, marriage prohibitions, etc., results in the creation of a unique form of Indian culture that C.S.P. Sinha once referred to as the simultaneity of ancient, medieval and modern traditions co-existing, side by side, in the cities and villages of rural India.[26]

* * *

While there were no 'social scientists' in Mithila to explore the nature of society in thirteenth century Mithila, there were social observers in the form of writers and bureaucrats. Therefore, we must look elsewhere for the sources of Maithili culture. The historian, Irfan Habib has pointed out that we need to scrutinize literary sources more closely for descriptions of rural life, society and peasantry.[27]

Of the various Maithili authors of the time, one stands out, Vidyāpati, a poet, writer, storyteller, composer, and courtier in Mithila (approximately 1353-1448). As Radhakrishna Chaudhary points out, many of Vidyāpati's works were saved, almost single-handedly, through the efforts of George Grierson, the Irish linguist and folklorist.[28] Vidyāpati, in addition to his literary accomplishments, was recognized as an authority on *Smriti*.[29] Collectively, *Smriti* writers concerned themselves with social and domestic life, digests, and the rules and regulations of conduct, *dharma*.

The consequences of the development and growth of *Smriti*, as well as its persistence into the present, according to Chaudhary, were that: 'While the whole of northern India was convulsed by religious and social upheavals, Mithila remained unaffected, deeply engrossed in the details of Karmakānda and technicalities of rituals. This obsessive dedication to Vedic tradition served to hamper the growth, or need for critical and liberal education.'[30]

The stasis that exists in Mithila, reinforced by *Smrti*, was made all the more durable by Mithila itself. Agricultural productivity was traditionally high due to the benefits of reliable rainfall and the annual floods that restored the soil's fertility with a rich layer of silt. Consequently, the peasants were not slaves to their land. The land produced sufficiently with a minimum of labour, providing the food and a surplus that satisfied the rulers' demand for revenue.

Its comparative geographic isolation, due to its labyrinth of rivers, streams, and swamps, tended to exclude all but the most dedicated travellers or invaders. In their isolation, the rulers and peasantry of Mithila grew in complacency and were prideful of their accomplishments. Security and comfort were sometimes substituted for freedom.[31] The comforts of Mithila, as well as her isolation, permitted its population to thrive economically and intellectually, and spawned the development of a unique form of socio-economic and political parochialism, a form of on-going cultural stasis.

Although a bit hyperbolic, P. C. Roy Chaudhury describes Mithila as:

> The geographical situation has given an almost unbroken continuity of life and pattern of culture since time immemorial and at the same time it accounts for the insularity and exclusiveness for which the Maithilas are well known. Darbhanga district is a typical example of the influence of geography on history and culture of a land. The innumerable rivers and rivulets of the [area], the alluvial soil and the usual monsoon rains make the tract one of the most important productive centres of Bihar and the area has rightly been described as the granary of north India. . . .
>
> It was as a result of this assured security on account of geographical features that traditions could grow unhampered and the literary pursuits in different directions continued unabated through the ages. The climate . . . is responsible for the characteristic ease-loving complacent attitude and excessively talkative character of the people. Naturally, therefore, the

philosophic discussions and erotic poems found a fertile soil in the [region] where people are allergic to hard work.[32]

When the Muslims initially swept down the Ganges, all the way to Bengal, they bypassed the ancient core area of Mithila. In so doing, Mithila remained for centuries an isolated outpost and centre of Brahmanic and Sanskrit scholarship – a tradition begun before 1000 BC.[33] Here, in comparative isolation, Hindu scholars were able to protect the purity of their ideals and traditions. Even today, Mithila has been able to preserve her interest and love of traditional, Sanskritic learning and debate.[34] Throughout Mithila, in *Tols* or *Catispsāihī-s*, pundits continue to impart education along traditional lines in both Sanskrit and Maithili.[35]

Jayakanta Mishra in his paper on the influence of Sanskrit on the Maithili language and literature notes that within Mithila, a number of unique customs and ceremonies, which have their roots in Vedic traditions, continue to be practiced. He goes so far to say:

Most of the customs and practices of Mithila are also remnants [of tradition]. For example, a peculiar custom mentioned in the *Satapatha Brāhmana* (IV. iv. Iii. 19) is still observed in Mithila in its original form. . . . On the day after the Sukharātri festival (corresponding to the Diwali festival) a pig is tied to a post or tree outside the village where all domestic animals, such as the cows, buffaloes and bullocks, are brought by every farmer. Then these animals are given a chance to play with the pig, strike it with their horns and, it is believed, the more the pig cries the better are the fruits and harvests of the people. . . .[36]

This custom harkens back to Vedic animal sacrifice long before the institutionalization and incorporation of the concept of *ahimsa* in modern Hinduism. While the animal is possibly 'tortured' by the other animals, it is not physically sacrificed.

The cumulative effect of such extraordinary devotion to Sanskrit learning, Vedic ceremonies, and a variety of intellectual games played by adults and students alike, has served to maintain Mithila as a centre of Vedic scholarship and culture down through the centuries, and is responsible for the extraordinary orthodoxy and conservativeness that are found there today. Consequently, the land north of the Ganga has remained a stronghold of Sanatana Dharma, Vedic orthodoxy.[37] The people of Mithila have traditionally viewed everything that runs counter to these ancient traditions with extreme suspicion. Likewise, while the use of Hindi throughout northern India has become commonplace, Maithili continues to be spoken, often exclusively within many villages; but only recently was it accorded the status of a recognized national language, allowing it to be used in the schools of Bihar.

The Legacy of British Imperial Institutions

If we assume that history does matter, because it is history that shapes institutions, and institutions shape economies, is there any basis for the belief that we can change Mithila's current development course? We have assumed for over sixty-five years that if there is either a political or social will, institutions can be changed. We have blindly accepted the proposition that institutions are manipulable. The question now is, how long does it take before the effects of such manipulations are observable? The persistence or effects of an institution, even after it has been changed, is referred to as institutional overhang, or less pretentiously, simply social inertia.[38] Is Mithila simply 'suffering' from social inertia?

Well before the British became a *bona fide* player in the game of thrones in India, they possessed certain ideas based on their uniquely British mind-set – a mind-set that grew out of a common Indo-European linguistic tradition but, at the same time, evolved quite differently from that which prevailed on the subcontinent. That mind-set did not, however, have a genuine impact on Indian society, economics or politics until the mid-eighteenth century with the 'conquest' of Bengal and the emergence of the East India Company as a political power, initially disguised as a shadow government for the Mughal emperor as the Diwan of Bengal – a government in the guise of a merchant. Until 1757, the British had been satisfied to maintain trading footholds throughout India and had shown little interest in participating in Indian society or conquest. The acceptance of the *diwani* of Bengal, however, thrust the British into what Karl deSchweinitz called 'the cockpit of Indian continental political struggles'.[39]

Within fifty-five years from its foothold in Bengal and the assumption of the *diwani* of Bengal, the British established hegemonic control throughout much of South Asia. Concomitant with this political and administrative control came the British 'civilizing missions', as both an excuse and apology for its imperialism. The civilizing mission sought to recast Indian society through the implementation of British social, economic, and political institutions. This was a complete turnaround for the heretofore detached, aloof and isolated gentlemen traders of the East India Company.

As long as imperialism could be justified on purely economic grounds there was no pressing need for the development of a grand plan or guiding ideology to coordinate empire-building. Consequently, early British imperialism was seen as little more than an adventure and was largely guided by classical liberalism and economics. Later, however, issues of legitimacy and sovereignty arose, which spurred liberal debate in metropolitan London. It was these debates, on the streets of London as well as in the halls of Parliament, that gave rise to what might be called Britain's imperial policy; and it ultimately altered how Britons saw their rapidly growing empire and themselves.

British political thinkers genuinely struggled with the idea of British rule in India. From the beginning, British rule was deemed strange and anomalous. Thomas Babington Macaulay observed in 1833:

> It is true that the power of the Company is an anomaly in politics. . . . But what constitution can we give to our Indian Empire which shall not be strange, which shall not be anomalous? That Empire is itself the strangest of all political anomalies. . . . Reason is confounded. We interrogate the past in vain. General rules are useless where the whole is one vast exception. The Company is an anomaly; but it is part of a system where everything is anomaly. It is the strangest of all governments; but it is designed for the strangest of all empires.[40]

Henry Sumner Maine characterized Britain's Indian possessions as a 'most extraordinary experiment involving the virtually despotic government of a dependency by a free people'.[41] Out of these debates came models for the creation of an imperial government that had the goals of stemming the natural inclination of semi-autonomous representative-adventurers-traders who had already begun to fall prey to the lure of money, corruption, and despotism and, at the same time, provide beneficial government for the subject peoples. The leaders of the various 'schools of thought' included Edmund Burke, James Mill, and John Stuart Mill. Each in his own way sought to frame the government of imperial India in ethical terms, with Parliament serving as the moral arbiter over a civilized administrative bureaucracy thousands of miles from home. Out of this heated debate came the Empire's model of liberal imperialism, a more or less coherent ideology that included both a self-serving justification for its existence and governing strategies that centered on a duty to reform the indigenous population.[42] Only later did liberal imperialism give way to political pragmatism and, in so doing, as Karuna Mantena suggests, the imperial government in India operated from a position that required much less justification and became more of an 'alibi for the *fait accompli* of Empire'.[43]

* * *

Beginning in the mid-eighteenth century, due to emancipation, nationalism, and imperialism, an ideology of racism began to emerge in Europe; and soon British urbanity and enlightenment gave way to arrogance and censoriousness. The roots of this growing ethnocentrism were the result of:

- The English, Scottish, and Welsh people grappling with their new 'British' identity, instead of being separate communities;
- Nascent colonialism evoked a sense of 'British patriotism';
- Industrialization and overwhelming industrial capacity;
- An evangelical revival; and
- The rise of utilitarian philosophy.[44]

Together, they evoked a belief that England should assist in advancing 'backward peoples' towards greater refinement, just as the Romans had done in England. This mission was given even greater impetus with the successful conquest of Ireland.[45]

Of these influences, it was undoubtedly industrialization that resulted in the greatest disparity between England and the rest of the world, fostering among Britons contempt for all those who had not experienced it. Out of their economic superiority came a uniquely British arrogance and this resulted in cultural aggression, inspiring a passion to 'improve' those deemed less culturally and economically fortunate; culminating in what Rudyard Kipling and Cecil Rhodes were to refer to as the 'White Man's Burden'.

Although couched in humanitarian terms, the superiority of the British system demanded that the British 'raise up' the lesser heathens. The nations of Western Europe justified their imperialism with rationalization. Imperialism was visualized as an attempt to spread civilization, to spread Christianity, and to introduce progress to the 'less fortunate'. The subjugation of people of colour was considered the inevitable consequence of the superiority of the white man and Western culture.

The utilitarians found much to criticize in India – its religions, its culture, its philosophy, its social and political structures. They were regarded as corrupt, barbarous, and despotic. Ultimately, it were the utilitarians – James and John Stuart Mill – who dominated the liberal debate in London. Initially, at the centre of this debate was the issue of how to justify or legitimize British rule over foreign peoples. Although never resolved to everyone's satisfaction, the liberal policy in India became one of reform – reshaping India and its people into Britons, both politically and culturally, through legal reform and education. The clash between Victorian liberalism and conservatism resulted in 'Britain's role in India as being that of a benevolent and reforming conqueror, or the embodiment of the old Mughal regime. Ultimately it was a combination of both imperial visions that defined the liberal empire in India'.[46]

* * *

Having been acculturated within a highly hierarchical society, the British immediately sought to arrange all that they encountered into discrete and 'logical' groupings. This propensity either created or formalized existing social, religious, cultural, economic, or political groupings; and resulted in the evaluation of everything that was not European or British. Every aspect of a culture was gauged or measured by British standards which were, above all, deemed accurate, universal, valid, and more importantly, indisputable. Thus, every other culture was subject to being weighed and measured, and almost always judged to be universally wanting.

Through the British system(s) of administration, uniquely British institutions were thrust upon India. Two of these institutions in particular – the concept of private property and an English-styled system of justice – had the most profound impact on the native population.

Private Property

Before the British takeover, land rights in India were typically informal, complex, overlapping, and locally defined by tradition and village leaders. The British attempted to introduce impersonal and bureaucratic – modern – forms of property rights. In part, this was understandable, but why did they go to such lengths, when India already had a system that had adequately fulfilled the administrative and revenue requirements of its rulers for centuries?

It was not until the acceptance of the position of Diwan of Bengal that most servants of the Company took any more than a casual interest in either Indian agriculture or its land systems. Some within the Company, for purely personal reasons, immersed themselves in Indian history, culture, religion, and linguistics – largely out of curiosity or as a way to idle away the time. The prosaic studies of agriculture and land relations were much less attractive topics of study.

Diwani, however, thrust the Company headlong into the world of estimating crop production, cadastre, and India's intricate system of land relations – endeavours for which the Company's personnel were completely untrained or prepared for. Individually and collectively, they did not possess sufficient command of the local language(s), an understanding of rural social, economic, or political structures, an understanding of centuries old land tenure types and land relations, or Indian agricultural methods. Nothing these servants encountered had counterparts or equivalencies in their native systems of reference. As a consequence, they found direct involvement in the performance of their revenue duties impossible, and were forced to rely on indigenous intermediaries to fulfil their administrative duties. It would take decades before a fully functioning cadre of English revenue officers was prepared for their administrative responsibilities; however, the only way they could direct or 'takeover' their revenue responsibilities was by first dismantling and recasting the existing Mughal land revenue system and the traditional land tenure and land relations apparatus. They were never able, or possibly more accurately, willing to come to grips with the complexities and nuances of the native systems of land tenure and revenue collection.

* * *

For the Mughals, the form of landownership held little importance. Their only concern was the amount of land rent, taxes, or revenue that could be extracted from the cultivators. The British took a broader view. They saw private property as the mechanism for increasing agricultural production and accelerating economic development, and at the same time, it would permit them to raise tax revenue for their governments, at home and in India.[47]

The fundamental difference between the Mughal and English conceptions of land lay in how it was seen as either an inanimate source of rent or as a dynamic factor of production. For the Mughals, it was the cultivator that produced the value to be taxed. Land was seen as a passive factor of production. For the English, however, in addition to its productive value, land also had a market value, a concept unfathomable by either the Mughals or Indian society since the sale of land was virtually unknown. One could sell, mortgage, and transfer rights in a piece of land but not the land itself. The Indian conception of land did not include the concept of property, something that can be owned.[48]

From 1765 to 1793, the government of India, in the form of the East India Company, struggled and experimented with ways to more efficiently collect the land revenues of greater Bengal. Much of the experimentation reflected differing philosophies and views regarding the form of land ownership and with whom to make the revenue settlement. Within the top echelons of the Company, the primary philosophical debates pitted mercantilism against the thinking of the physiocrats.

Despite their philosophical differences, both groups agreed that private property rights were essential to the revitalization or development of the rural economy of Bengal. The principles of mercantilism had permitted the Company to use its share of the land revenue from Bengal to finance the purchase of spices, cotton and silk from India and sell them at huge profits to the burgeoning consumer markets in Britain and Europe. The Bengali land revenues stemmed the flow of bullion from Britain. India was now financing its own economic exploitation. For the Company, the primary objective became the maximization of its share of the land revenue which ultimately became the Company's main source of income.

The mercantilists manoeuvred the Company into a perfect position to exploit India. It was self-sufficient, no longer requiring the infusion of capital from home to maintain its trading or security operations. However, as the Company's profits soared, the support and patronage it had enjoyed at home began to wane upon reports of egregious corruption and mismanagement. Changing priorities and sensibilities in metropolitan England brought the Company's profitability and its mercantilist regime into question and brought upon itself intense scrutiny. In the end, the Company lost both its trading monopoly in India and its authority to govern its territorial possessions.

* * *

The physiocrats, on the other hand, saw the true wealth of a nation as a function of net agricultural surplus, that is, the amount of agricultural production above and beyond the cost of producing the crop. Other forms of economic production were derived from and made possible only by using surplus agricultural production to feed the workers who produced other goods and services. And because the suppliers of these goods and services were unable to 'feed themselves', they were deemed to be 'sterile' producers, a drain on the wealth of the nation.

The physiocrats opposed mercantilism on the grounds that the emphasis on the exchange of goods between countries was a drain on the agricultural surplus produced by the peasantry. Mercantilism advocated a policy of promoting greater exports than imports paid for in gold and silver in order to use the funds generated to subsidize the protection of export-oriented commerce and industry. The balance of trade, in the form of an increase of gold and silver, is the most visible form of a national surplus in value, and what brings it about, directly speaking, is export-related commerce and industry. In the case of commerce, as long as equivalents are exchanged, no surplus profit can be generated, while in the case where non-equivalents are exchanged, the gain on one side is a loss on the other.

The physiocrats believed that none of the theories concerning the value of land could work in the absence of privately owned property. Private property and a strong sense of individualism were critical components in the physiocrats' philosophy. They were interested in the accumulation of capital within agriculture and the interests of capitalist agricultural entrepreneurs. Quesnay, the founder of physiocracy wrote: 'That the ownership of the landed properties and the mobile wealth be assured to those who are their legitimate possessors; for the security of property is the essential fundamental of the economic order of society.'[49] Schlatter paraphrases la Riviere, one of Quesnay's staunchest supporters and a member of his inner circle, as follows:

> It is from the right of property, maintained in all its natural and primitive fullness, that all the institutions which make up the essential form of society necessarily flow: you can think of the right of property as a tree, and all the institutions of society are the branches which it shoots forth, which it nourishes, and which perish when they are detached from it.[50]

The capitalistic essence of the physiocratic school is also manifested in the two main policies it advocated: (1) a single tax on rent (*impêt unique*) and (2) and a *laissez-faire* economic approach. Emphasis upon private property as a means rather than something given or ordained pervades the writings of the physiocrats' in two contexts. First, it was believed that the harmony of interests was accomplished through the institution of private property. It was believed that individual and social interests were best served and secured by private property. This concern, at least superficially, fulfilled the British self-imposed civilizing mandate.

Private property rights were defended as instrumental in securing private interests and in attaining the harmony of interests – '. . . the unity of social interests and its conformity with the law of justice . . . (Letrosne)'.[51] Thus, 'Individual interest is the primary bond of society, which will be the more solid in proportion as private interest is secure',[52] is the basis for holding that 'freedom in exchange, an absolutely unshackled use of the wealth of individuals, could not be dissociated from the full enjoyment of the rights of private property'.[53]

Second, private property rights were justified on the equally utilitarian grounds that it stimulates and facilitates the production and accumulation of wealth. Private property, then, becomes the foundation of the natural order, because it is a fundamental asset.[54]

* * *

While the members of the Supreme Council in Calcutta were divided philosophically, mercantilists versus physiocrats, and they had varied personal agendas, they all agreed that the future of India was predicated on the institution of private property, and they would endeavour to see that it became a part of the Indian socio-economic fabric. Further, philosophical differences aside, by imposing private property rights a number of potential difficulties were, at least theoretically, resolved. Among these were: first, the confusion that surrounded traditional Indian property rights. The English mind simply could not, or possibly did not wish to entertain a land system based on customary, simultaneous, overlapping and undocumented rights in land.[55] Second, the absence of an absolute 'owner' of the land – someone who was legally responsible to the government for the payment of land revenue – was anathema to the British world view.

The simple and arbitrary act of creating private property rights in India had a profound impact on rural India's social, political, and economic institutions. The fabric of Indian rural life was irreparably altered by the seemingly simple word: 'private'. India had been a social and economic system where the concept of 'private' was virtually meaningless. Individuals may possess or inherit things but they were shared with the family, one's caste, the village, and the state. Others always had rights in or to the possessions of others.

Cornwallis observed: 'There is every ground to expect that the large capitals possessed by many of the natives will be applied to the purchase of landed property as the tenure is declared to be secure, and they are capable of estimating what profit they will be certain of deriving from it, by the public tax upon it being unalterably fixed.'[56]

Once the decision to re-engineer the Indian land system had been made, the only questions remaining were, who should the Company appoint as the legal owners of the land and how much could be exacted from these new owners. There were only two real alternatives to the first question. The first and possibly the most appropriate choice would be the *ryots* who cultivated the land. Second, the zamindars who, for centuries, had served as the revenue collectors under license from the Mughal state. Either choice had its advantages and disadvantages. If the *ryots* were made the owners of the land, there were thousands upon thousands of individuals with whom settlements would have to be negotiated and from whom the land rent would have to be collected. For the Company, this was potentially a logistical nightmare. The Company simply did not have the necessary manpower to negotiate and collect the land rent from the individual *ryots*. For this reason, and possibly this reason alone, the Company decided to make their settlements with the zamindars. In the end, fewer than 100 large zamindars in Bengal were made the legal owners and proprietors of the lands they had once serviced only as revenue collectors. Cornwallis believed that a great agrarian revolution would begin with making the zamindars the owners of the land and it would be they who would be the principal beneficiaries of the anticipated agricultural revolution in Bengal.

The establishment of private ownership of the land created, for the first time, a land market in Bengal and Bihar where none had existed before. Since land, with the stroke of a pen, became a private possession, with all its incumbent rights, it immediately became a commodity that could be bought and sold. The land market became a harbinger of a radical change in the conception of property and property rights in India, as well as changes to come in Indian rural society, rural economics, and most definitely in the operation of rural politics.[57]

It also struck at the heart of orthodox Hinduism as practiced by the people of Mithila and especially among the 'land owning' Brahmins – the Maithil Brahmanas. While, on the one hand, opposing the concept of private property, they, nevertheless, exploited it to their social, political, and economic advantage. Yet, the orthodox practices of the Srotriyas continued to set the spiritual tone for the people of Mithila, and it is at least their superficial rejection of worldly wealth that set the pattern for what is deemed 'the good life' – happy poverty.

British Law

Pre-colonial India was characterized by pluralistic and fragmented cultural, religious, political, and legal structures. There was no single authority governing everyone, except in the person of the Mughal emperor. Castes, tribes, sects, and families crossed both religious and political lines; and each community was subject to variations in legal custom, the law, and its application and implementation. Due to the customary nature of law, with adjudication shared and separated by communal divisions, many Westerners, accustomed to a single 'common law', were left with the impression that India lacked what might be deemed a system of law.[58]

When the Company acquired the Diwani of Bengal, it immediately became apparent that a new political and legal system would be required to administer its newly-acquired domains and the people who occupied them.[59] Warren Hastings was the first to assert that the Company's government had the right to interfere with the native administration of law. Through political bargaining, over a span of years, the colonial governors generally ceded authority in family law to the customary religious or canonical courts, leaving pre-colonial jurisdictions largely unaffected. This system of law was largely a matter of religious prescriptions and philosophical discourse, emanating from the Vedas, the Upanishads, the Laws of Manu, other religious texts, and the *Institutes* of law-givers like, Yajnavalkya, Brihaspati, and Narada.

The codification of law in India continued through the time of the Mughal Emperor Aurangzib, with the *Fatawa-i-Almagiri* being the most durable of Aurangzib's reign. From the British perspective, Asiatic governments, including the Mughals, were in form and function more tax-taking enterprises than law-making governments.[60] Inasmuch as the Mughal state was governed by *Sharia* law, the sovereign needed no law-making power and there was no need for a law-making body. From this perspective, the British observation that the Mughal system of government was not a law-making institution has some merit but, in reality, there were a number of 'schools of thought' regarding the application of *Sharia* law, and it were these traditions that governed the Muslim courts; all of which originated outside India. However, *Sharia* law had one drawback within the context of India – it was only applicable to Muslims, a minority population. Therefore, another system of law was required for the Hindus, thus creating a dual system of jurisprudence, but both were forms of customary law, not law developed by judges based on prior decisions or precedence.

This dual system of justice was a contentious issue for the British who were accustomed to 'one law for all'. Until the reissue of the Charter to the East India Company in 1726, Company employees were subject to British Common and Criminal Law through the agency of the Company, and were either tried in India for minor offences or returned to England for trial for more grievous acts, largely against other Europeans but not against the native population.[61] The 1726 Charter presaged the establishment of Crown's courts in India. The charter permitted the creation of 'Mayor's Courts' which were not Company courts but courts of the King of England located within the confines of the Company's urban outposts, and superseded all existing courts of the Company. These Mayor's Courts administered English law and their jurisdiction was restricted to the inhabitants of the individual British settlements, and was applied to all, irrespective of nationality.

The Regulating Act of 1773 created a Supreme Court in Calcutta but its jurisdiction was limited to British subjects in the provinces of Bengal, Bihar, and Orissa. The Charter of 1774 established the Supreme Court but did not define its jurisdictions. Edmund Burke, commented on this oversight in the charter as follows: '. . . that no Rule was laid down, either in the Act or the Charter, by which the Court was to judge. No Description of Offenders or Species of Delinquency, were properly ascertained according to the Nature of the Place or the prevalent Mode of Abuse'.[62]

Especially significant was that the power and jurisdiction of the Court over natives was unclear. The Act of Settlement of 1781 remedied many of the defects of the Charter Act and removed the

Court's application of English law to Hindus and Muslims. Communal law was reinstated for the native population. It remained obvious, however, that this dual system of justice within British-controlled territories was growing increasingly time consuming and lacked both uniformity as well as impartiality. The apparent lack of uniformity and impartiality of native law and its prescription galled the British sense of propriety. It became incumbent upon the British to right this obvious and grievous misapplication of justice.

* * *

It was not until America achieved its independence from Britain in 1776 that serious debate began regarding the role of the Crown and Parliament in British colonies. Likewise, heretofore, there was little or no debate over the jural and legal institutions that would prevail. They would be English. However, in the wake of American independence, in both London and India, the role of the Crown, Parliament, the nature of the state and society, sovereignty, and the legal system(s) as they applied to India became bitterly contested. In large measure, this was due to the fact that British colonialism had exceeded all prior colonial experience. The American Revolution had stunned the British. There was no longer any imperial or colonial precedent to draw upon.

Everyone associated with India recognized that India had its own system of state. It had its own systems of jurisprudence. India had a history of high civilization. It was also recognized that the existing British system of governance was not up to the imperial task at hand following the Battle of Plassey. The East India Company had acquired many of the trappings of a state following the Treaty of Allahabad, which had given it financial control over the Mughal Empire's richest province, Bengal. It could wage war, raise an army, make peace, raise taxes, and administer justice to its employees and an indigenous population that outnumbered that of Great Britain itself. The Company found itself in the position of being a sovereign. Between 1760 and 1785, a middling approach to colonial rule in India was ultimately implemented. The Company could administer its territories to the benefit of its stockholders, subject to Parliamentary regulations and review. Once the Company's position vis-à-vis the Crown and Parliament had been adequately resolved, the Company's leadership set about reforming India through the implementation of a complex, hybrid system of British and Indian laws.

Warren Hastings and William Jones, based on their study of traditional native legal systems, believed that basic Hindu and Muslim law was sufficient to resolve most legal disputes in India; therefore, native law should be preserved inviolate, with British law serving only as a check on native interpretations. Such a hybrid system of law, they suggested, would provide checks and balances (a British legal ideal), would require little disruption of the people's lives, and simultaneously provide satisfaction and security to the native populations, the government, and fulfil the goals of the British civilizing mission, without incurring unnecessary financial outlays. Unfortunately, British legal scholars and Parliamentarians in London did not agree; and it was they who would ultimately determine the fate of the law in India.

Jones endeavoured to translate and catalogue the ancient Sanskrit materials relating to Hindu law. However, he died in 1794 before the work was completed. Jones' great Sanskrit enterprise fell to Henry Thomas Colebrooke to complete. Jones' work was finally completed and published in 1801 as the *Digest of Hindu Law on Contracts and Successions*.[63]

Hastings' efforts to implement a native constitution failed because law in India was deemed to be 'somehow different' from Western law and much of Indian law was based on the will of the Emperor, not codified law. Mughal law was seen as absolute, arbitrary, and unchecked. Justice was not based on a rule of law but on the rule of men who could be influenced by money, status, and intimidation. This was counter to the British system of law that was believed to be impartial and immune to outside influences.

In the absence of an impartial system of justice, it was suggested that a British system of law should be introduced. Hastings railed against this proposal, taking his case to both the Company's Court of Directors and Parliament. He suggested that the British system of law was too technical, too complicated, and did not 'fit' the circumstances as they prevailed in India.

In the end, Jones' and Colebrooke's *Digest* did not satisfy the courts. They never attained a level of completeness required for the administration of Hindu law in British courts. Part of the problem with the *Digest* was that the sources of Hindu law could not be identified with absolute certainty as to authorship or chronology. Nevertheless, a unique form of Hindu case law was created; and this evolved into a type of English case law for use by the courts in colonial India. 'What had started with Warren Hastings and Sir William Jones as a search for the "ancient Indian constitution" ended up with what they had so much wanted to avoid – with English law as the law of India.'[64] Nevertheless, it was this collection that became the foundation material for the Cornwallis Code of 1793 – that comprehensive body of rules dealing with every department of the state, including the reform of the Indian legal system.

* * *

Before the introduction of his now-famous Cornwallis Code, Cornwallis introduced a system of circuit courts with a superior court in Calcutta in 1790. This was the first step in remodelling the courts and legal systems of India. Over the next three years, until his departure in 1793, Cornwallis sought to harmonize the legal codes of India. Cornwallis' Code of 1793 was designed to separate government's basic administrative, commercial, and judicial responsibilities and jurisdictions. It also served to define a workable system of justice in India. The most profound effects of the Cornwallis Code were the reformation of criminal law and the creation of a venue (courts) for cases involving property based on laws and regulations, not custom. Cornwallis maintained that the Company had not only the right but the obligation to reform Indian law. The Muslims immediately objected. For Muslims, all law, but especially criminal law was divinely ordained and, as such, was not deemed within the purview of British infidels. Nevertheless, Cornwallis introduced changes in the criminal law between 1790 and 1793 which eliminated certain Muslim practices such as grants of pardon by the family or relatives of victims of murder or the demand of compensation in money as a blood price. Likewise, amputation was replaced with imprisonment and hard labour, according to the circumstances of the case. Further, the new regulations denied the restrictions on non-Muslims testifying against

Muslims. While hotly contested, the will of the government was not to be denied, and the criminal reforms were promulgated and implemented.

* * *

While the reformation of administrative, commercial and criminal law was deemed profound, even more profound was the change in Indian land and property law, which had the effect of demolishing centuries old customary and institutional land relations. The concept of private property was introduced in India in 1793 through the implementation of the Permanent Settlement of Bengal. British liberals believed that by introducing private property in India, the parasitic intermediaries of communal property would be eliminated. Further, by vesting all property rights in one landowner, and securing those rights through the agency of British Common Law, maintained by a Western system of law and courts, would alter traditional modes of land tenure and the fabric of traditional Indian society.[65]

At the apex of this traditional social system were the zamindars, the revenue collectors of the Mughal emperor. These non-proprietary 'landholders' were transformed into a new class of landowning gentry. As proprietary landowners, a gift from the Company, the zamindars, for the first time, had the right to transfer their land freely by way of sale, mortgage, gift or inheritance. By conferring proprietary property rights on the zamindars, except in unusual circumstances, property rights were denied to the *ryots*, the tillers of the soil. The *ryots* could, however, hold hereditary land rights subject to the payment of rent.

To retain their estates, the zamindars were required only to pay the government their revenue demand with absolute punctuality. The zamindars had been informed and warned that failure to make their revenue payments in a timely manner would result in, 'a sale (in auction) of the whole of the lands of the defaulter, or such portion of them as may be sufficient to make good the arrears, will positively and invariably take place'.[66] This provision of automatic sale to recover revenue in arrears was colloquially referred to as the Sunset Law. The Mughal tradition or practice of allowing revenue remissions during times of poor harvests, bad weather or calamity, or peasant unrest was abolished. The government steadfastly and mechanically expected all revenue payments to be made, without exception, at the appointed time. Failure to do so automatically resulted in the sale of land.

It was also the impartial implementation and application of British land and property law that ultimately deprived many of the zamindars of their grand estates. Initially, not comprehending the blind application of British revenue law by the government, many zamindars faced the forced sale of their estates for failing to pay their land revenue as set forth in their settlement agreements. By the time the zamindars realized just how efficient, ruthless and indifferent the collectors were with regard to the enforcement of the Sunset provisions of the Permanent Settlement agreement, all or parts of the largest estates had been sold to competing zamindars and new aspiring zamindars.

Zamindars

The zamindars had been a recognizable social, economic, and political class of functionaries, appearing soon after the first arrival of the Muslims, beginning in the twelfth to thirteenth centuries. However, it was not until the accession of the Mughals as emperors that the role of zamindars grew and, as a class, they became increasingly powerful. Their power emerged from the exploitation of the pre-Mughal *bhuiyan* or *bhupati* land tenure system, within which the zamindar was seen as a hereditary landholder but not as the owner of the land he administered. Even under the Mughals, and later after Akbar's administrative reforms, the zamindars continued to lack a uniform identity or purpose. In Bengal, the term zamindar could be applied broadly, encompassing many people with different kinds of landholdings and rights that ranged from autonomous or semi-independent chieftains to peasant-proprietors. Many of the larger chieftains became *peshkashi* (tribute-paying) allies of the Mughal regime. The lesser zamindars were mostly *mal-wajibi* (land revenue paying), whose primary function was to collect revenue for the Mughals. However, for the *peshkashi*, their duties extended to various other administrative responsibilities and the administration of justice.

While the revenue demanded of the zamindars was fixed, the amount the zamindars extracted from the *ryots*, or paying cultivators, was set by the zamindars. Initially, the zamindars could not afford to be oppressive, for there remained un-cleared arable land. If a zamindar became too overbearing, his *ryot*-tenants could, and often did, abandon their lands, taking refuge in wastelands. It was, therefore, in the best interests of the zamindar to protect the rights and traditional privileges of the *ryots*. As population density rose, however, and the demand for land increased, the zamindars could pit *ryots* against one another in a bidding war for the right to cultivate the zamindar's land. This competition permitted the escalation of rent rates, often above customary levels or *pargana nirikh*.

Each zamindar developed his own system of management, and often lived in a state of unrepentant luxury. During the pre-British period, there were few absentee zamindars. Thus, their lives and authority were confined to their personal 'kingdoms'. Until their elevation to the position of proprietary landowners under Permanent Settlement (1793), zamindars were little more than public functionaries. The actual collection of revenue was frequently delegated to underlings, lesser zamindars, often referred to as *jotedars*.

As their power and authority grew, conflict with the acknowledged political authorities, Mughal or British, was inevitable. The only leverage the Mughals held over the zamindars was the fact that their position, at least in terms of legitimacy, was dependent upon the continuation of their *sanads* – a charter of inviolable rights and responsibilities on the part of the zamindar given by the government. Later, as zamindaris became increasingly inheritable positions, the retention of one's zamindari rights was as much through the show of force as it was through the issuance of *sanads*. In fact, many zamindars fought wars with other zamindars in an endeavour to increase their holdings. The Mughals tolerated such inter-zamindar wars as long as they did not threaten the flow of revenue to the emperor's treasury or foment rebellion. They also had the effect of consolidating the land among fewer landholders, thus streamlining the revenue-collection process.[67] The British were not quite so accommodating.

Under the Mughals, zamindari estates were never divisible nor transferable. They were not inheritable. The only way a relative or kinsman could obtain an estate of a deceased family member or kinsman was through the issuance of a new *sanad* from the government;

and the government always reserved the right to cancel or forfeit *sanads* at any time. A zamindar continued his status through good conduct, not through any right. A failure of revenue payment punctually did not, however, lead automatically to the loss of zamindari rights unless it was deliberately done out of malice or some conspiratorial motive. A zamindar could seek relief from the government when his *ryots* failed to pay their revenue. This custom of relief, later, under the British, was abolished but many zamindars continued the practice only to find that failure to make their revenue payments according to the government's schedule resulted in the loss of property. For the government, there was no 'grace period' with regard to the payment of revenue.

Cornwallis concluded the Permanent Settlement with zamindars in March 1793. The status of zamindars and their roles were very different under Permanent Settlement. Landholders of all categories were declared proprietors of the land. As proprietors, zamindars were to pay government revenue without any alteration for all time to come. The zamindari property, like any other property, under English law, could be freely transferred or mortgaged without the necessity of such transfers or indentures being sanctioned by the authorities. The zamindari right was also inheritable among the successors of zamindars according to Hindu and Muslim laws of succession. In return for these rights and privileges, zamindars were only required to pay revenue to the government with unalterable punctuality according to their contract with the government, otherwise, their lands were subject to public auction (sale) for the non- or under-payment of revenue.

Zamindars were formally stripped of all the state powers and privileges they had enjoyed traditionally as local potentates. Traditional zamindari *adalat* (courts) were banned. The zamindari right to *sayer* collection was abolished and all *sayer mahals* (*hats*, bazaars, *ganjes*, *octrois,* fisheries) were resumed and brought under direct rule of the district collector. In the eyes of law, zamindars and *ryots* were made equal.[68]

Predictably, the zamindars responded to the Permanent Settlement vociferously. They accepted the settlement because there was no alternative before them. They were asked to either accept the settlement or to surrender their rights in the land in lieu of an annuity. Zamindars by and large acquiesced to the Permanent Settlement because they quickly recognized that those who resisted were ruthlessly suppressed.

The framers of the Permanent Settlement could not ignore the social, political, and economic influence of the old zamindari class, nor could they simply disenfranchise them without raising the spectre of rebellion. What was needed, however, was a new, enterprising class of zamindars. The Sunset Sale law provided the mechanism for the transfer of power from the old to a new class of zamindars. They had hoped that the regulations of the Permanent Settlement, when implemented, would create a competitive land market that would eliminate the weak and incapable zamindars and infuse new blood into land ownership. It was anticipated that these new men of capital and enterprise would, in time, acquire land in the burgeoning land market and would serve as catalysts for change in the agrarian landscape.

Unfortunately, the new zamindars, most of whom came from zamindari service, government jobs and trade and commerce, were fundamentally no different than their predecessors. While the traditional zamindars tended to show indolence and a lack of motivation, the newcomers were found to be more eager to enhance their income by increasing rents without making any capital investment in their lands. As a consequence, the relationship between zamindars and *ryots* deteriorated progressively in the early part of the nineteenth-century. The conflict between the two classes mainly stemmed from zamindari attempts to enhance the established rent rates. The pressure of the Permanent Settlement, decline in zamindari income through the rise in prices, litigation, family feuds and fragmentation of the parent estates among successors prompted zamindars to raise the rents of *ryots*. But the *ryots* steadfastly resisted such attempts on the grounds that zamindars had no right to change the *pargana nirikh* or established rent rates. The zamindars refused to accept such arguments and asserted that as the absolute proprietors of the land they had the right to revise the rate of rent according to the fluctuation of prices and value of land. As a consequence, peasant unrest and occasional uprisings occurred. The unrest ultimately led to the great anti-zamindari peasant uprisings in the 1870s.

These peasant movements only indicated that there was considerable awareness developing among the peasantry. They sought to assert their rights which zamindars refused to accept and about which courts were giving contradictory verdicts. The customary rights of peasants were vaguely recognized in the Cornwallis Code but these were never expressly defined. The widespread peasant discontent in the countryside led the government to study the zamindar-*ryot* problem and subsequently took action to establish peace.

Another problem was the creation of hierarchic intermediate classes in land control. Most zamindars, particularly of the eastern Bengal districts, had created permanent intermediate tenures called *madhyasvatvas*, which had effectively isolated and insulated the superior zamindars from their *ryots*. Numerous intermediary layers developed between the zamindars and the *ryots*, with several degrees of interests one upon another, with each drawing its rental income from the same plot of land and from the same *ryot*. Overburdened *ryots* responded to such conditions by desertion or organized resistance.

Try as the government might, the conflicts between the zamindars and *ryots* continued unabated into the twentieth-century and the pent up antagonism between these two groups was skilfully exploited and manipulated by the Indian nationalist leadership, especially by Mahatma Gandhi. The importance of the peasantry to the successful achievement of independence resulted in the Congress party's commitment to the abolition of the zamindari system as early as 1937.

Within five years of independence, the Congress party fulfilled its commitment to the peasantry. In almost every state, zamindari, tenancy, and land reform legislation was passed with varying success as to its implementation and enforcement. Bihar was one of the earliest states to pass zamindari abolition and other land reforms but while this legislation remained firmly entrenched in the law, it was only half-heartedly implemented and even more casually enforced.

The only enduring and effective portion of the zamindari abolition laws dealt with the elimination of the *madhyasvatvas* or intermediary tenures, thus eliminating thousands of rent-absorbing, unproductive collectors. This had three consequences. First, without the *madhyasvatvas*, rents accrued directly to the zamindars. Second, without the intervention of the intermediaries, the amount of rent received by the superior zamindars increased. Finally, the primary land-owning zamindars were forced to 'assume the cultivation of their lands', placing the day-to-day management of their lands in the hands of far fewer 'managers'.

Except for a change in nomenclature, from 'zamindar' to 'landowner', little has actually changed in terms of land ownership patterns in Bihar or Mithila since independence. The new landowners have effectively blocked, evaded, or ignored all existing land reform legislation. In part, this is explained by the simple fact that until the mid-1990s, Bihar's politics was overseen by the Hindu-dominated Congress party, upper castes and particularly the Brahmins, who were the dominant land-owning class/caste and they had no reason to want to see such legislation implemented or enforced.

It is only with the recent emergence of the political alliances between the Backward and Other Backward Castes that any pressure has been placed on the land-owning castes. While Lalu depended on the non-landowning castes as part of his political vote bank, Nitish's success can be pinned to his ability to lull the lower castes and, at the same time, maintain the tacit support of the upper caste landowners.

What is in a Name?

Traditionally, the title 'zamindar' carried with it responsibilities and obligations – secular, communal, economic, and religious. This relationship has frequently been referred to as the *jajmani* system.[69] The title 'landlord' or even better, simply 'landowner', carries with it few responsibilities or obligations. For the large, landowning castes in Mithila, it is politically safer to be referred to as a landowner than to continue calling oneself a zamindar with all the negative and collateral baggage that such a title represents and carries with it. This is the current situation for modern-day Bihari zamindars. Now, for the most part, they are content to live their lives as large landowners, without the notoriety, responsibilities, obligations, and worries that plagued them before. And yet, they continue to possess the social, political, and economic currency their positions had previously carried.

The feudal nature of Bihar's rural landscape continues. The Lalu

Prasad Yadav era has been replaced by that of Nitish Kumar, both with firm footings in the OBC communities, but Nitish also maintains a 'quiet alliance' with the landed upper castes. Since Kumar's election as chief minister, new private caste armies have emerged in the state, ostensibly, against the Maoists. In addition, many of the earlier *senas* continue to operate, most notably the Ranvir Sena. The most (in) famous among the newer senas is the Kaimur Shanti Sena, a Yadav-led private army in central Bihar.

Most progressive peasant movements in Bihar failed to give rise to an upsurge against both landlordism and Brahmanism. During the 1980s and the early part of the 1990s, a conflict between the traditional ruling classes and the 'nouveau elite' from the backward castes began to emerge. During the mid-1990s, however, there was a process of reconciliation resulting in unstable alliances on social, economic and political issues.

The politics in Bihar remains a challenge not because the state has become a model of neoliberal developmentalism, but because it raises new questions about class and caste as it relates to the regime of Nitish Kumar. Nitish has become the passive beneficiary of previous Dalit and other exploited class mobilizations. In fact, on closer examination, it would not be an exaggeration to suggest that under Nitish's leadership, there has been a certain amount of disenfranchisement among Dalits and the return of a type of landed class hegemony. The Dalit political space has been almost completely eliminated by Nitish, both discursively as well as politically. It would seem that it is Nitish's intention to stabilize the existing class balance in a state where the traditional elites and emerging petty-bourgeois classes play a dominant role. This can be accomplished by simply invoking a protracted discourse over development and Bihari pride, which will serve to distract all parties from the other more substantive questions of equity, welfare, and representation.

It would be political suicide and ideologically defeating for Nitish to take a firm stand against either the dominant landlords or the Ranvir Sena. Nitish has repeatedly shown what he stands for within the so-called developmentalist framework. It is clear that Nitish's government does not want to send any mixed signals to its rural electorates. What he has done is to try and substitute a superficial discourse of 'governance' for justice and genuine socio-economic progress. All historical wrongs are, at least theoretically, to be corrected through 'schemes'. This situation reflects upon the stronghold of conservative castes and the dominant peasant ideology in the new era of governance in Bihar. It is, again, the blending of the old and traditional with the new, liberal, and the profession of faith in the ideal of development.

Is this new regime substantially more different than any of the past in Bihar? If one scrapes away the layers of political posturing and idealism, and analyzes the fundamental workings of the newest in a long line of political leaders, one will undoubtedly find a hardened political pragmatist, not unlike every 'politico' who has occupied the office of chief minister. But one thing is certain; whatever the new regime accomplishes it will not be achieved without the real or tacit support of the upper castes, the landed aristocracy (zamindars) who, while sitting out of the limelight of day-to-day politics, still 'pull the strings' of those who parade around like peacocks on Bihar's political stage.

Caste Politics

Caste politics in Bihar reached a breaking point in the 1990s. The decade marked the complete breakdown of the Congress system in the state which was concomitant with a shift in the balance of social and political power. It has been suggested that the decline and demise of the Congress party was the direct consequence of the party's failure to provide for the participation of the backward castes. The Congress party which had been dominated by upper castes and the reluctance of the party's leadership to share power with the numerically stronger backward castes precipitated the defection of its backward caste members. In the wake of the 1990 elections, politics has largely been the politics of reassertion and reaffirmation of old caste cleavages. People now tend to vote more for identity (of caste) than for non-parochial issues such as good governance, improvement in the material conditions of people, betterment of and universal access to health and educational facilities and universal provision of basic amenities or human rights.

Bihar is a state of villages, having the lowest level of urbanization of any state in India. The vast majority of the people of Bihar are illiterate. Almost 90 per cent of the population is dependent upon agriculture for their livelihood; and the agricultural sector is non-competitive, with low yields both in terms of per acre and per capita. Agriculture has stagnated. Nevertheless, land remains the most important measure of a family's prestige, social and political standing. Bihar continues to rank high in terms of population below the poverty line, with more than 42 per cent of the population living below that line in 2004-5.

Caste, above all, remains the most durable source of social and political identity. Upper or forward-caste Hindus were estimated to constitute 21.50 per cent of the population of Bihar in 2001.[70] Backward castes constitute the largest portion of Bihar's population, accounting for approximately 51 per cent of the total population.[71] While the upper castes are numerically small, they have traditionally dominated the social, economic, and political life of Bihar. Not only were they the most powerful castes/class in Bihar society, they also were the largest landowners, dominated the bureaucracy, academia, big business and until quite recently occupied or controlled most of the state's ministerial offices.[72]

Much of this upper caste socio-cultural domination has been based on what Pandey termed 'upper-caste racism', not with regard to biological claims or even racial purity but racism based on cultural unity and allegiance to Hindu symbols of identity.[73] These were the tactics developed, refined and used by the Indian National Congress party (Congress). This form of nationalism, however, wore thin for the backward classes, and they began mobilizing around topics and symbols that were more in tune with their own socio-economic needs, erupting in the demise of the Congress as both the peoples' party and as the dominant political organization in Bihar just prior to the 1990 elections, although the decline of Congress had begun in the mid- to late-1960s.

From 1947 to 1967, the Congress was the dominant political party in Bihar. It had been the leading party during the freedom struggle and transformed its popularity into political prominence. This is not to say that there were no opposition parties in Bihar but they were unable to consolidate popular support. In the absence of political rivals, Congress occupied every major political position in the state, thus monopolizing political power.

At this time, the party was dominated by the upper castes – Brahmins, Rajputs, Bhumihars, other recognized landowning castes (the Kshatriya), and landed aristocrats. The OBCs were loyal to the Congress, in large measure, due to the party's leadership as personified by Gandhi who had successfully manipulated both high and low castes for reasons of political economy. As a consequence of Congress's leadership during the independence movement, there really was no other viable political alternative. Additionally, Congress appeared to embody the reformist spirit that had been used by Gandhi to maintain the support of both the upper and lower castes during the fight for independence. This image continued but, at least in Bihar, it was illusory.

Through political sleight of hand, Congress orchestrated the passage of land reform legislation. Even after its initial enactment, zamindari abolition had little effect. The 1953-4 NSSO recorded that the top 10 per cent of rural households owned over 52 per cent of the land and the bottom 40 per cent owned only 1.25 per cent of the land.[74] Intentional loopholes in the legislation insured that the zamindars and largest landowners would not lose control of their lands. The zamindars were able to exploit these legal exemptions because 'the state itself – as represented by legislature and bureaucracy – was overwhelmingly dominated by zamindars themselves'.[75]

Even within the Congress-dominated government, tensions arose as the zamindars effectively avoided both the letter and spirit of land reform. In an attempt to appease the national government, and simultaneously satisfy the dissidents within the party, the Congress- and landlord-dominated government passed a series of land reform acts in 1961, designed to place ceilings on holdings. Although the government obtained title to 22 per cent of the agricultural land in the state, the former zamindars, through intrigue and fraud, were able to retain control over large portions of their previous holdings.[76] Typically, the largest landowner in each village exerted almost unlimited authority over the everyday lives of the villagers. Custom mandated that the villagers consult the landowner concerning the issue of wages and land rights, thus, making it possible for the landowners to effectively, socially and economically, exploit the people under them. In effect, the villagers were forced to relinquish their freedom in exchange for the security of employment.[77] This pattern is little changed today; only the methods of intimidation have become more subtle or sophisticated, and less obvious.

The land that was obtained and distributed by the government as a consequence of land reform legislation went primarily to the Yadavs, Koeris, and Kurmis, who utilized their newfound importance as landowners to leverage their demand for a larger share of the political power. Surprisingly, however, the upper landowning castes and the newly landed Yadavs united against the lower OBCs and Backward Castes.[78] Further, the new landowners began to consolidate and began demanding more change but the forward castes within Congress were either unwilling or unprepared to share power with the emerging OBCs. This unwillingness fostered a sense of greater urgency among the new Yadav landowners to mobilize both the landed and un-landed Yadavs against the recalcitrant landowning upper castes within the Congress. This divisiveness, ultimately, undermined the strength of the Congress as a legitimate and formidable force in Bihar politics. Further, over the subsequent years, the backward castes began to realize that they could control the state's political system through sheer numbers if they were only able to mobilize their constituencies.

The 'game of thrones' that transpired subsequently left the Congress party largely impotent but the various coalitions that were required to form each state government only brought less stability and uncertainty until 1990, when the Janata Dal under the leadership of Lalu Prasad Yadav swept into the Bihar Vidhan Sabha. The Janata Dal assumed control but, even so, internal squabbles between the ambitious champions of the backward castes resulted in a schism, splitting the party in two. On the one hand was Lalu Prasad Yadav's Janata Dal. On the other was the Samata Party, led by Nitish Kumar.

Nevertheless, when all the caste and political rhetoric is swept aside, neither the mobilization of the OBCs nor the election of their candidates to seats within the Vidhan Sabha produced any significant change on the ground. The only changes at this level were the enhancement of voting rights and choices for the OBCs, and the landed elites, now working behind the scenes as power brokers, who continued to control the rural landscape. As long as they were able to enjoy their practical and political safety, out of the political limelight, and were able to control, or at least manipulate or manage the ebb and flow of Bihar politics, there was no need for costly personal investments in the political arena. They can appear to sit safely on the political sidelines, reaping all the practical benefits of political suzerainty without the liability of personal exposure.

As Carolyn Heinz so succinctly summarizes it:

> The persistence of caste consciousness is attributed to [the] failure of modern institutions to take hold: there is a lack of economic growth and social development to provide incentives to shed caste controls and build cross-caste friendships and partnerships; politicians exploit caste anxieties about changing power valences and reinforce caste solidarity as voting blocs; with a dysfunctional state apparatus, castes provide some security against encroaching interests of other groups. These points are real enough, yet they resemble explanations for the persistence of religion solely by its functions in intergroup conflict. Castes are also social and cultural systems that provide connectedness and meaning much as religion does. It may seem odd, years after anthropologists turned their attention away from caste (as if all had already been said), to suggest it is time to take another look. We should ask how particular local jatis construct their bonds of community such that they appear given, natural, and immutable, the only constant in a world of change.[79]

DRAWING THE THREADS TOGETHER

In the final analysis, to understand the current district-level backwardness of Mithila, it is necessary to look beyond traditional categories of analysis. No one component, neither historical, political, religious, economic, social, cultural, nor institutional, is capable of adequately explaining the unique pattern we find. It is the fine blending of these categories or institutions that has resulted in the concentration of district-level backwardness.

At the heart of Mithila's backwardness is the persistence of a socio-economic and political structure created by the British in the eighteenth century. The feudal structure that preceded the British takeover was only solidified and legitimized by the implementation of the Permanent Settlement through the institution of formal land rights. Where rights to and in the land had been based on long-standing traditions, the imposition of British concepts of land ownership and an English system of law had the effect of disenfranchising the *ryots* while, at the same time, legitimizing the position and role of the zamindars. This set in motion a disequilibrium that has never been corrected, at least not in Bihar.

The zamindars under the British became the large landowners of modern Bihar. The same feudal system that had existed before independence continues to operate today, if only with more finesse. Land reforms have had little or no significant impact on the patterns of land ownership. There still remains a landed aristocracy, an aristocracy that, when the Congress party dominated state politics, was composed of upper caste Hindus. The Congress party, at least as a tenable political party in Bihar, no longer exists. It served its primary purpose – to organize and coordinate the push for independence. It was the rallying point for both the landed elite and the *ryot/kisans* of Bihar. After independence, however, that role and purpose expired. Congress could no longer encompass the economic and social diversity that existed in the state and her politics.

Lower caste mobilization and activism only created a schism among the constituent parts of the old Congress. The landed aristocracy's needs were diametrically opposed to those of the aspiring, awakening, and power-hungry lower castes. For these lower castes, it was a time for restitution, making long overdue wrongs, right. The awakening of the lower castes and the recognition of their numerical political superiority did not, however, happen overnight. It took over forty years for the political scales in Bihar to tip; and in 1990, the lower castes achieved their long-sought, and one might say, rightful democratic, representative place in Bihar politics.

Neither the implementation of land reforms nor the rise of the lower castes changed the land patterns in Bihar appreciably, nor did they extinguish the political, economic, and social power of the existing landed aristocracy. While they no longer rule or lead from the front they control and manipulate from what American political observers might call a 'smoke-filled room' – a cabal of powerful or well-connected men meeting privately to make decisions without regard for the will of the public; at the same time their social, financial and political support contributes immeasurably to the success of those in search of power. Current leaders, of any party, cannot survive politically without the tacit support of these 'behind the scenes' powerbrokers. As a consequence, and in recognition of this fact, the leadership of any successful party in Bihar is dependent upon the support of this landed aristocracy.

This is particularly important as parties joust for political and ideological support among the highly fragmented lower castes. It is becoming increasingly difficult for any one party to take control of the Vidhan Sabha without resorting to the creation of tenuous political coalitions.

For the leaders of the lower caste parties and coalitions, the support of the landed castes comes at a cost. There have been a series of court judgments in recent years that have strengthened the perception that the present regime is being held hostage by upper-caste economic and social interests. For example, the Amir Das Commission was convened to determine if there were any links between Bihar's political parties and the Ranvir Sena. The Nitish Kumar government abruptly disbanded the commission in 2006, just before it was to submit its report. Some have suggested that the commission's findings were going to demonstrate firm links between the Ranvir Sena, Nitish's JD(U), the BJP, and NDA.[80]

The Nitish government appointed the Bihar Land Reform Commission in 2006. It submitted its report in April 2008. The commission made important recommendations suggesting that sharecroppers' cultivating rights be made more secure and making available surplus land for distribution to the landless by implementing a ceiling on land holdings. Nitish's government has been largely silent on the commission's findings, thus reinforcing the idea that the government will *never* take any action against the interests of the landed castes.

Never may be too strong a word. 'When the time is right', may represent the government's true timeline. However, if Nitish wishes to remain in office, he must find some way to appease his constituencies, the lower castes, as well as the upper, landed castes. As one Bhumihar MP from Munger, Rajeev Ranjan Singh commented on the suggestion that the Nitish government might implement a new law to protect sharecroppers: 'there would be civil war in the state on the issue'. A similar sentiment was voiced by Prabhunath Singh, a JD(U) upper caste MP: '. . . you [Nitish] would be simply betraying the faith, trust and aspirations of the people who voted you to power and made you the chief minister'.[81]

Nitish, at a meeting of landowners in Patna, addressed the audience suggesting that no sharecropper's (*bataidari*) bill was currently on the table and it was only: 'Those who do not want social peace [that] are trying to create a rift and sow seeds of hatred and discontent . . . They tell landholders "Nitishwa will take away your land" and then say to landless farm labourers that the government will not implement "bataidari" law.'[82]

Nitish further reminded his audience that there already existed a Bihar Tenancy Act and that it provided for sharecroppers' occupancy rights. He continued: 'I am taking all sections into confidence and working for them. If this is a crime, I am definitely a culprit. Whether I remain in power or not, I will continue to do this.'[83]

There is no doubt that the landed upper castes, and in the case of Mithila, this includes a large number of upper-caste Brahmins, especially Maithil Brahmanas, continue to control virtually every aspect of rural life. The methods and tactics used to maintain control may be more subtle in India's secular democracy, but caste and land continue to define one's place within the agriculturally-dominated rural society of Bihar. The landowners (landlords/zamindars) continue to control the land, credit, and wages. The only thing, it would seem, they cannot control is how their tenants and sharecroppers vote, and given the opportunity, they would control this too.

The landed aristocracy of Mithila continues to wield the same types of feudal power and authority that the rajas of Darbhanga once did. The interplay of religious tradition, orthodoxy (religious and social), a complex social structure, blatant casteism, reactionary caste politics, economic opportunity (or lack thereof), increased competition for land (the result of spiralling population), the failure of the elected government to implement and enforce land reforms, and a history and tradition of landed elites has conditioned the people of Mithila to a lifestyle characterized by unrepentant poverty that has resulted in the most comprehensive and abject form of social inertia imaginable.

The upper, landed castes will relinquish neither their control nor their authority without a fight. They successfully fended off the British attempts to dominate them. They will not allow a lower-caste dominated state government to dictate how they must live. These are resourceful people with much to lose. They have proven their resourcefulness and resilience time and again.

The failure of the government, its development agencies, or development programmes to effectively address the social, political and economic inequities allows the people of northern Bihar to wallow in a continuous state of poverty. In the absence of gainful employment, the able bodied workers of Bihar are forced to seek employment in other states or even abroad, leaving behind the aged and dependent. The best and brightest are lured away to educational opportunities in other states, most never returning. The tales of Biharis employed in the Delhi area and throughout western India are legendary. In the absence of opportunities in Bihar, Bihar society is being drained of its human resources.

Recent economic advancements, attributed to the government of Nitish, have done little to promote significant economic development in rural Bihar. The economic benefits of the capital-infrastructural construction projects have fallen to the urban areas and among the middle and upper metropolitan classes – the contractors, suppliers, and businessmen.

Rakesh Ankit stated:

> For nearly a half-century, Bihar has been consistent in one respect: poor ranking on almost all major social and economic indices. Education remains, simply put, a dead loss. With great schools and colleges of the past having lost all strength and credibility, anyone who can afford it sends their charges to Delhi, Calcutta or elsewhere, as long as it is outside of Bihar. With young Bihari men and women clearing the country's most prestigious entry-level service exams year after year, it is obvious that the problems of Bihar lie not with its people.
>
> The rotten state of Bihar's roads provides a window into the state's abysmal physical infrastructure. The lack of productive employment pushes unorganized labour to the metropolises in western India, Delhi and Calcutta, while organized labour within the state is used as cannon-fodder by the various political parties. The professional class in Patna is skeletal, with the best and the brightest having evacuated. A heavily compromised bureaucracy and judiciary are used to uphold the status quo. Faced with such a wall of inadequacy in governmental institutions, the people have decided to tune out and live their lives as best they can – in the manner of their ancestors, who similarly did not expect help from the state.[84]

At one time, Bihar was the shining star of India. Its political activism was legendary and preceded much of the rest of the country. The people, from the lowest *kisans* to the *babus* were politically aware. Many of the earliest agrarian movements began or had their roots in Bihar. Its government was one to be emulated. Its agricultural productivity was legendary. Major political reform movements, like that of Jayaprakash Narayan in the 1970s, began in Bihar, only to unravel later. Nonetheless, the movement left its imprint on Indian politics. Now, all that has changed.

The people of Bihar have simply given up. They have resigned themselves to fate, seeing no way out. It is not that their land is not as fertile as the land in Punjab or Haryana. It is not because the modern agricultural inputs are unavailable. It may well be that they are no longer able to conceive of a life of prosperity. Being unable to visualize an alternative to their current situation, they are unable to achieve it. Additionally, they have incorporated the karmic belief that this is their lot in life and that there is little in *this life* they can do, so they do not try. There is a natural order of things (*rta*), a certain justice, social harmony and human happiness, and these require that human beings live in a manner appropriate to the requirements of that order.

Due to competition between and within castes for land control, there has been an unprecedented increase in casteism. As a consequence, casteism is tearing at the very fabric of rural Bihar. Caste and casteism are crushing the life out of the people. Valuable time and resources are diverted from useful programmes of upliftment and used to support reactionary political gamesmanship and even armed, private armies that appear to be little more than strong-arm gangsters.

In many other areas of India, rural societies have participated in large-scale social reform programmes. This has not happened in much of Bihar. Caste in Bihar, maybe more so than in other regions, has become the essential political ingredient. Most of the leaders of the leading political parties are also the leaders of their castes. Since caste tends to be one of the primary components of modern Bihar, a break between the castes means a break in Bihari society. It is this break, the politicization of caste, that has immobilized Bihar's politics and government, and this immobility prevents or constrains social and economic development. A further consequence of this extreme casteism is the loss of what might be termed a 'Bihari identity'. There is nothing to hold the Biharis together for the common good.

There is no sense of Bihari nationalism. The emergence of electoral politics and creation of new political identities during British rule in India has placed the pursuance of sectional interests above national interests. At present, a large number of political leaders/groups/political parties are vocal about sectional interests as it garners votes and creates vote banks for them.

Ashok Jha suggests that there are two types of identities among Biharis – Indian and caste.[85] When a Bihari is asked to identify himself, he will typically respond he is of a certain caste from Bihar. The fact that he is a Bihari is deemed comparatively unimportant. Caste affiliation is deemed far more relevant than one's state citizenship. Thus, Bihar has no sub-national identify, and what identity Biharis have seems to be largely negative, at least as viewed by outsiders. In the absence of a unique Bihar identity, there is no one to speak for Bihar. There are numerous caste spokesmen but few spokesmen for Bihar. As a result, Bihar seems to have no voice in national affairs. Without a voice, it is easily ignored. This may be changing under the leadership of Nitish but only time will tell.

* * *

Part of the failure of Bihar to thrive is its cultural tendency to resist change. This refusal to change has not always been a part of the Bihari make-up. Saibal Gupta suggests that Mithila's developmental resistance didn't surface until the beginning of the nineteenth century, becoming more acute and strident after the First War of Liberation in 1857. Because a large number of Biharis were involved in the rebellion, the British retaliated, singling out the people of Bihar for retribution. In response, the Biharis turned against almost everything Western, and as a consequence, they did not follow the same path to social, economic and political modernity that others did in many other parts of India. Western ideas, including the concept of progress, were rejected and lost.[86]

While agreeing with Dr. Gupta's thesis that the people of Mithila seem resistant to change, the author believes this social trait or behaviour began long before the First War of Liberation. Whether due to or aided by Mithila's physical geography, it has had a very long tradition of reactionary social, intellectual and physical isolation. This extreme conservatism is easily traced back to Vedic times and the enduring importance of Vedic traditions. This is nowhere more evident than among the landowning, ranking Brahmanas of Mithila, who continue to practice a strict form of orthodox *karma kanda* – that part of the *Śruti* (Vedic) writings which relate to ceremonial acts and sacrificial rites. These pious, orthodox Hindus believe that the ultimate truth in matters of religion is to be found in the Vedas or *Śruti* revelation. While the six orthodox systems of philosophy all claim Vedic origin and authority, those whose religious practices are based on *Śruti* constitute the most primitive, primal form of orthodox Hinduism, and it would not be too far afield to say Vedic Brahmanism, with an emphasis on traditional Sanskrit chants, rituals, rites, and fire sacrifices, continues to influence the behaviour of the Maithil Brahmanas and Mithila.[87]

Representative of this cultural tradition, Mithila continues to remain a centre for Sanskrit studies, education, research, manuscript conservation, publication, and philosophical debate. And here you find the state-sponsored Mithila Institute of Post Graduate Studies and Research in Sanskrit Learning, established by the state of Bihar in 1951 and the Kameshwar Singh Darbhanga Sanskrit University on what were once the grounds of the Maharaja of Darbhanga's Anand Bagh Palace (aka Lakshmivilas Palace) in Darbhanga city.

* * *

Usha Alexander's words continue to ring true:

> It is the sense of futility, of a widespread hopelessness, as if the mindset and the expectations of the people have slipped to meet the level of their condition. There is little sense of dignity, little stirring of curiosity, little energy for ambition. Never before have I so realized the power and value of hope as a necessary tool or ingredient for the upliftment of people. But how to jump-start a sense of hope from futility and powerlessness?[88]

When a people have nothing and are prevented from having anything, no social or economic insulation against the next wave of stress, trauma, or catastrophe, the will to live erodes. The people of Bihar, in general, and Mithila, in particular, have been numbed by environmental problems – floods and droughts, crop failures, and the destruction of their homes and infrastructure. Their work conditions are abysmal. When their wages often barely cover the necessities of life, and there is little or no opportunity to accumulate sufficient capital to fend off the next catastrophe, people simply lose hope. More importantly, there is no one in government prepared to help. The government doles out compensation for losses and relief but makes no effort to protect its rural population and what protective efforts are instituted often only result in the exacerbation of the problems. Under these circumstances, no help is often deemed better.

Considering all the almost invisible forces that govern and control the lives of Bihar's rural population, each crushing the life out of already impoverished, hungry *ryots* and agricultural workers, is it any wonder that there is little emotional, financial, or social capital left to invest in the future? Under the circumstances, there is little to suggest that these people possess either the will or the means to achieve even 'happy poverty'. Even that seems well beyond their grasp.

NOTES

1. As an aside, the author will admit that the use of the word 'negative' is potentially pejorative but it is not intended as such. It was used only to reflect the current institutional/developmental view of the socio-economic conditions prevailing within these districts.
2. Isabel Paterson, *God of the Machine*, 8th printing, New Brunswick: Transaction Publishers, 2009, p. 235.
3. There is an entire literature devoted to globalization, culture change, and cultural homogenization, just as a sampling: Michael Amaladoss, 'Global Homogenization: Can Local Cultures Survive?' *East Asian Pastoral Review*, vol. 36, no. 4, 1999, http://eapi.admu.edu.ph/content/global-homogenization-can-local-cultures-survive; Ian Angus, 'The Anxiety Concerning Cultural Homogenization', Burnaby: Simon Fraser University, Department of Humanities, n.d.; Nigel Hollis, Millward Brown's 'POV – Culture Clash: Globalization Does Not Imply Homogenization', n.d., May 2009; John Tomlinson, *Globalization and Culture*, Chicago: University of Chicago Press, 1999; Callum Martin, 'Do Global Communications Inevitably Lead to Cultural Homogenization?' *E-International Relations Students*, 1 February 2013, http://www.e-ir.info/2013/02/01/does-the-development-of-global-communications-inevitably-lead-to-cultural-homogenization/; Vandana Desai and Robert B. Potter, *The Companion to Development Studies*, London:

Routledge, 2008; and Michael Kearney, 'The Local and the Global: The Anthropology of Globalization and Transnationalism', *Annual Review of Anthropology*, vol. 24, 1995, pp. 547-65.

4. See, Philip McMichael, *Development and Social Change: A Global Perspective*, 5th edn., Los Angeles: Sage, Sociology for a New Century Series, 2012.
5. See, Amartya Sen, *On Ethics and Economics: The Royer Lectures*, Oxford: Blackwell, 1987, p. 2. See, also, as examples: Mozaffar Qizilbash, 'On Ethics and the Economics of Development', *The Journal of Philosophical Economics*, vol. 1, no. 1, 2007, pp. 54-73; James L. Alvey, *Ethics and Economics, Today and in the Past*, Palmerston North, NZ: School of Economics and Finance, Massey University, 2011, http://economics-finance.massey.ac.nz/publications/discuss/2011/DP1106.pdf; M.S. Swaminathan, 'Ethics of Economic Development', a paper prepared for the Regional Meeting on Ethics of Science and Technology, 5-7 November 2003, Bangkok: UNESCO; and Des Gasper, 'Development Ethics and Human Development', *HDR Networks*, Issue 24, January 2009.
6. Qizilbash, 'On Ethics and the Economics of Development', 2007, p. 55.
7. I will admit, I could not have started this discussion with a topic, or topics that are either more disputed or complicated but. . . .
8. Edwin Bryant, *The Quest of the Origins of Vedic Culture: The Indo-Aryan Migration Debate*, Oxford: Oxford University Press, 2001; and Edwin Francis Bryant and Laurie L. Patton, *The Indo-Aryan Controversy: Evidence and Inference in Indian History*, London: Routledge, 2005 provides a thorough review of the two opposing theories with regard to the Aryans. Here is no place to enter into this discussion or debate. That will be left to those more learned on the subject. Whether the origins of the Aryans are ultimately found to be endogenous or exogenous, is in large measure immaterial to our discussion here. What the Aryans did, however, is.
9. David Neal Lorenzen, *Who Invented Hinduism: Essays on Religion in History*, Delhi: Yoda Press, New Perspectives on Indian Pasts Series, 2006, provides a serviceable survey of some of the issues surrounding the Aryans and Hinduism. See, in particular, chapter I, pp. 1-36. Today, any debate over who first called Hinduism, Hinduism, seems rather pedantic, erudite, and comparatively unimportant. Furthermore, in deference to racial nationalists, the imprecision of the term 'Aryan' as a racial or ethnic classification is understood and, as used here, 'Aryan' is nothing more than a convenient heuristic device. Finally, there is a growing and somewhat unnerving tendency among many modern Indian historians to adopt a strangely pre-colonial, colonial, or post-colonial mind-set or paradigm when it comes to the emergence of 'Indian institutions'.
10. Burjor Avari, *India: The Ancient Past: A History of the Indian Sub-Continent from c. 7000 BC to AD 1200,* London: Routledge, 2007, p. 76.
11. G. Venkataraman, 'The Vedas: Their Evolution and Significance', 2010,

http://www.tamilbrahmins.com/general-discussions/3871-evolution-significance-vedas.html.

12. See, George Cardona, *Recent Research in Paninian Studies,* 2nd, revd. edn., Motilal Banarsidass, 2004; and Arthur A. MacDonell, *A Sanskrit Grammar for Students,* 3rd edn., rpt. Delhi: Motilal Banarsidass, 1974/2003. See, George Cardona, *Panini: A Survey of Research,* 1st Indian edition, rpt. Delhi: Motilal Banarsidass, 1998. It must be admitted that the archaeological record for a written language prior to the *Rigveda* is largely non-existent but does this mean there was no prior written language? There is practically no evidence of writing from the centuries between the abandonment of the Harappan cities and the Maurya Empire. Does this prove that writing was absent from India, and that the grammarians including Panini had to do their research without a literary corpus or written notes? Of course not. The inability of archaeologists to find physical evidence to 'prove' the existence of a literate Indian civilization simply proves that the archaeological record in India falls short of the historical. In the case of artefacts, this may be due to the use of organic, perishable materials to write on. Organic materials simply decay and disappear in India's damp heat. See, Koenraad Elst, *Update on the Aryan Invasion Debate,* Delhi: Aditya Prakashan, 1999, chapter 4.4.2: 'The Absence of Horse Remains'.
13. As quoted by William Theodore de Bary, *Sources of Indian Tradition*, 2 vols., 6th printing (2nd printing of text edition in 2 vols.), New York: Columbia University Press, 1966, vol. II, pp. 42-3.
14. Kamakoti.org, *Sound and Creation,* 9 September 2013, http://www.kamakoti.org/hindudharma/part5/chap7.htm; S. Chandrasekharendra and Bharatiya Vidya Bhavan, *The Vedas,* Mumbai: Bharatiya Vidya Bhavan, Sudakshina Trust, 2009, pp. 3-7.
15. Vaman Shivram Apte, *The Practical Sanskrit-English Dictionary,* 4th enlrg. edn., Delhi: Motilal Banarsidass, 1965, p. 887; and Friedrich Max Müller, *Chips from a German Workshop,* vol. 1, New York: Charles Scribner's Sons, 1891, pp. 17-18.
16. Although it is commonly held that the roots of modern Hinduism and caste are to be found in the Vedas, some, like Dr. Jose Kuruvachira, a lecturer at the Pontifical Salesian University (UPS) in Rome, do not agree. See his paper: 'Is Hinduism a Continuation of the Vedic Religion?'; and J. Kuruvachira, *Is Hinduism a Continuation of the Vedic Religion?* Rome: UPS, 2010.
17. It must be noted that, viewed as a reformation, and in response to Buddhist and Jainism's discarding of basic Hindu tenants, specifically the role of an entrenched priesthood and caste, Hinduism does appear to be part reformation and in part, a return to a prior Golden Age.
18. Deward Washburn Hopkins, *The Religions of India,* Boston: Ginn & Co., 1895, p. 2.

19. Ibid.
20. Similarly, the term Hinduism does not appear in the Vedas or subsequent religious texts but was given to the people of the Indus or Sindhu region by foreigners who arrived in the region thousands of years ago.
21. *Jati* – a distinctive social group that traditionally often included the exclusive occupation of its male members and often, through usage, seems to be synonymous with *varna* or caste.
22. UCF Today, 'The Question of Caste in Modern India', 12 November 2012, http://today.ucf.edu/the-question-of-caste-in-modern-india/. Dr. Rao, is an Associate Professor of South Asian History at Columbia University.
23. Pulla Rirupati Raju, *Idealistic Thought of India*, London: Routledge, Routledge Library Editions: Buddhism, 1953 [2009], p. 399.
24. Everett Hagen, *On the Theory of Social Change*, Homewood: Dorsey Press, 1962, pp. 83-4.
25. Ibid., pp. 55-6.
26. C.S.P. Sinha, 'Tradition and Development: The Context of Education', pp. 179-88, in *Tradition and Development*, Sachchidananda, B.B. Mandal, K.K. Verma and R.P. Sinha (eds.), Delhi: Concept Publishing Co., 1988, p. 179.
27. Irfan Habib, 'The Peasant in Indian History', *Social Scientist*, vol. 11, no. 3, 1983, pp. 21-64.
28. Radhakrishna Chaudhary, *Mithilā in the Age of Vidyāpati*, Varanasi: Chaukhambha Orientalia, 1973, p. 6.
29. *Smriti* – a body of Hindu religious scripture – a codification of Hindu customary law.
30. Chaudhary, *Mithilā in the Age of Vidyāpati*, 1973, p. 7.
31. Ibid., p. 27.
32. P.C. Roy Chaudhury, *Bihar District Gazetteers: Darbhanga*, Patna: Superintendent, Secretariat Press, 1964, p. 24.
33. Jayakanta Mishra, 'Influence of Sanskrit on Maithili Language and Literature', *Proceedings of the First International Sanskrit Conference, Papers of Section Two,* pt. 1, pp. 133-9, New Delhi: Government of India, Ministry of Education and Social Welfare, 1975, pp. 133-4.
34. Ibid., pp. 133-4.
35. *Tols* are private schools, typically with a single pundit, teaching classical subjects. A *Catispsāihī-s* is similar in concept to a *Tol*, only with several pundits teaching a common philosophy. Personal e-mail communication from Tejakar Jha, 30 March 2014.
36. Ibid, p.135.
37. Bechan Jha, 'Influence of Sanskrit on the Maithili Literature', *Proceedings of the First International Sanskrit Conference, Papers of Section Two,* pt. 1, New Delhi: Government of India, Ministry of Education and Social Welfare, 1975, pp. 140-3.

38. Cf., S.L. Engerman and K.L. Solokoff, 'Factor Endowments, Institutions, and Differential Paths of Growth Among New World Economies: A View from the Economic History of the United States', in S. Faber (ed.), *How Latin America Fell Behind: Essays on the Economic Histories of Brazil and Mexico, 1800-1915*, Stanford: Stanford University Press, 1997, pp. 260-304.
39. Karl de Schweinitz, *The Rise and Fall of British India: Imperialism as Inequality*, New York: Methuen, 1983, p. 99.
40. Thomas Babington Macaulay, 'Government of India', 10 July 1833, in Thomas Babington Macaulay, *Prose and Poetry*, Cambridge: Cambridge University Press, 1970, pp. 695-6.
41. Henry Sumner Maine, 'The Effect of Observation of India on European Thought', in *Village Communities in the East and West*, the Rede Lecture of 1875, London: John Murray, 1876, p. 233.
42. See Robert Koebner and Helmut Dan Schmidt, *Imperialism: The Story and Significance of a Political Word, 1840-1960*, Cambridge: Cambridge University Press, 1964.
43. Karuna Mantena, 'The Crisis of Liberal Imperialism', *Histoire@Politique, Politique, culture, société*, vol. 11, no. 2, 2010. The souce material used here is from a condensed version of a chapter of the same title in Mantena's book, *Alibis of Empire: Henry Maine and the Ends of Liberal Imperialism,* Princeton: Princeton University Press, 2010.
44. Ronald Hyam, *Britain's Imperial Century, 1815-1914: A Study of Empire and Expansion,* 2nd edn., ed. D.A. Low, New York: Palgrave Publishers, Cambridge Commonwealth Series, 1993, p. 74.
45. Thomas R. Metcalf, *The New Cambridge History of India: Ideologies of the Raj*, vol. III, 4, Cambridge: Cambridge University Press, 1994, pp. 2-3.
46. Michael Chiarello, 'An Empire of Good Intentions? Liberalism and the Justification of Britain's Empire in India, *c.* 1820-1905', Senior Paper, HIS4397B_Essay.pdf, Academia.edu, 2012, https://www.academia.edu/1545698/An_Empire_of_Good_Intentions_Liberalism_and_the_Justification_of_Britains_Empire_in_India_c.1820-1905, p. 3.
47. From the time of the award of Diwani, the British experimented with a variety of schemes for the collection of land revenue until they settled on the system known as the Permanent Settlement.
48. There are two types of property – real property and personal property. For most of the world, the legal concepts and rules associated with both types of property are derived from English Common Law. In general, property is something that is owned or possessed. Property may be real (land), personal, tangible (touchable), or intangible (such as the interest in a play or other creative work).
49. François Quesnay and August Oncken, *Œuvres économiques et philosophiques de F. Quesnay, fondateur du système physiocratique; accompagnées des éloges et*

d'autres travaux biographiques sur Quesnay par différents auteur, ed. Auguste Oncken, Paris: Joseph Baer, 1888, p. 331.

50. Richard Schlatter, *Private Property: The History of an Idea,* New Brunswick: Rutgers University Press, 1951, p. 217. Pierre-Paul Le Mercier de La Rivière was a French administrator who shared physiocratic views.
51. Robert Harry Inglis Palgrave (ed.), *Dictionary of Political Economy,* vol. 2, London: Macmillan, 1915, p. 598.
52. Ibid., vol. 3, 1915, p. 105.
53. Ibid., vol. 2, 1915, p. 148.
54. Warren J. Samuels, 'The Physiocratic Theory of Property and State', *Quarterly Journal of Economics,* vol. 75, no. 1, February 1961, pp. 96-111.
55. Ironically, it can be argued that with time the Collectors would have come to grips with the amorphous character of traditional Indian land relations as a necessity. However, there is one feature of this system that, even then, would have frustrated the English mind. By imposing the concept of private property, it both simplified and provided a mechanism for the documentation of rights. It was the act of documentation that was of utmost importance for the Company's bureaucracy.
56. Letter of 6 March 1793, Paragraph 22, *General Letters to the Court of Directors,* Revenue Department, vol. 7.
57. Christopher J. Baker, 'Tamilnad Estates in the Twentieth Century', *Indian Economic and Social History Review,* vol. 13, no. 1, 1976, pp. 1-44; B.B. Chaudhari, 'The Land Market in Eastern India, 1793-1940: Part I: The Movement of Land Prices', *Indian Economic and Social History Review,* vol. 12, no. 1, 1975, pp. 1-42; and Walter C. Neale, *Economic Change in Rural India: Land Tenure and Reform in Uttar Pradesh, 1800-1955,* New Haven: Yale University Press, 1962.
58. W.H. Rattigan, 'Customary Law in India', *Law Magazine and Law Review,* vol. 10, nos. 1, 3-4, 5th Series, 1884-5.
59. Janaki Nair, *Women and Law in Colonial India: A Social History*, Delhi: Kali for Women in collaboration with the National Law School of India University, 1996, p. 19.
60. Henry Maine, *The Early History of Institutions*, London: John Murray, 1890, pp. 383-4.
61. Elizabeth Kolsky, *Colonial Justice in British India: White Violence and the Rule of Law*, Cambridge: Cambridge University Press, Cambridge Studies in Indian History and Society, no. 17, 2010 provides, possibly a one-sided recounting of the misapplication of justice in crimes against the Indian population prior to the Cornwallis Code.
62. Great Britain, Parliament, House of Commons, *Reports from Committees of the House of Commons: Re-printed by Order of the House*, vol. 6, East Indies -1783, London: n.d., 1806, p. 48.

63. Jagannatha Tarkapanchanana and Henry Thomas Colebrooke, *A Digest of Hindu Law, on Contracts and Successions: With a Commentary,* Cacutta: Printed at the Honourable Co.'s Press, 1801.
64. Bernard S. Cohn, *Colonialism and Its Forms of Knowledge: The British in India*, Delhi: Oxford University Press, 1996, p. 75. See, also, his entire chapter 3: 'Law and the Colonial State in India', pp. 57-75.
65. Asma Barlas, *Democracy, Nationalism, and Communalism: The Colonial Legacy in South Asia*, Boulder: Westview Press, 1995, p. 49.
66. Section 7, Regulation 1 of the Permanent Settlement of 1793.
67. R. Ray, 'The Bengal Zamindars: Local Magnates and the State Before the Permanent Settlement', *Indian Economic & Social History Review*, vol. 12, no. 3, 1975, pp. 267-9.
68. *Sayer* – internal taxes and duties.
69. In its simplest form, the *jajmani* system is a traditional, mutually obligatory socio-economic system between upper and lower castes, where lower castes perform various functions for the upper castes and, in turn, are provided for and protected by the upper castes – a system of traditional linkages between the landowning high castes and the occupational lower castes within agriculturally dominated rural societies and provides for the guaranteed distribution of food, goods, and services.
70. Sanjay Kumar, Mohammad Sanjeer Alam and Dhananjai Joshi, 'Caste Dynamics and Political Process in Bihar', *Journal of Indian School of Political Economy,* vol. 20, nos. 1 and 2, January-June 2008, pp. 1-32. See fn. 7, p. 30, for discussion on how the percentage of upper and forward-caste Hindus was arrived at.
71. NSSO, *Employment and Unemployment Situation Among Social Groups, 1999-2000, 55th Round, Report No. 469,* National Sample Survey Organization (NSSO), New Delhi: Government of India, Ministry of Planning and Statistics, 2000. It must be noted that during the time that this survey was taken, Bihar and Jharkhand were bifurcated and adjustments were made to account for OBC differences between present-day Bihar and Jharkhand. The figure reported for the combined state was 54 per cent. That number was reduced for our purposes due to the higher percentage of OBCs in Jharkhand.
72. See, Harry W. Blair, 'Rising Kulaks and Backward Classes in Bihar: Social Change in the Late 1970s', *Economic and Political Weekly,* vol. 15, no. 2, January 1980, pp. 64-74; and Christophe Jaffrelot, *India's Silent Revolution: The Rise of the Lower Castes in North India,* New York: Columbia University Press, 2003.
73. See, Gyanendra Pandey, 'Which of Us are Hindus?', in *Hindus and Others: The Question of Identity in India Today*, ed. G. Pandey, Delhi: Viking, 1993.
74. NSSO, *Report on Landholdings, 1953-54, 8th Round, Report No. 74,* National

Sample Survey Organization (NSSO), New Delhi: Government of India, Ministry of Planning and Statistics, 1954; and Pradhan H. Prasad, 'Agrarian Violence in Bihar', *Economic and Political Weekly,* vol. 22, no. 22, May 1987, pp. 847-52.

75. Arun Sinha, 'Legal Loopholes: To Landlord's Rescue', *Economic and Political Weekly,* vol. 3, no. 42, October 1987, p. 1759.
76. Ibid., pp. 1758-60; and Jose J. Nedumpara, *Political Economy and Class Contradictions,* Delhi: Anmol Publications, 2004.
77. Pradhan H. Prasad, 'Agrarian Unrest and Economic Change in Rural Bihar: The Three Case Studies', *Economic and Political Weekly,* vol. 10, no. 24, June 1975, pp. 931 and 933-7; and Arun Sinha, 'Legal Loopholes: To Landlord's Rescue', *Economic and Political Weekly*, October 1987, pp. 1758-60.
78. Sanjay Kumar, Mohammad Sanjeer Alam, and Dhananjai Joshi, 'Caste Dynamics and Political Process in Bihar', January-June 2008, p. 7.
79. From Carolyn Brown Heinz, 'Bihar: Caste, Class, and Violence', in the *Modern Anthropology of India: Ethnography, Themes and Theory*, chapter 3, pp. 29-45, New York: Routledge, 2013, p. 33.
80. Jamal Kidwai, 'The Return of the Dead', 7 June 2012, http://www.telegraphindia.com/1120607/jsp/bihar/story_15580035.jsp. The Janata Dal (United) it is a constituent of the Bharatiya Janata Party (BJP)-led National Democratic Alliance (NDA).
81. Imran Khan, 'Farm Tenants' Rights, Caste Issues on Test in Bihar Poll', 31 October 2010, http://twocircles.net/2010oct31/farm_tenants_rights_caste_issues_test_bihar_poll.html. See, also, *Deccan Herald,* 'Nitish Kumar Threatened for Wanting to Protect Sharecroppers', 19 February 2012, http://www.deccanherald.com/content/53604/content/196937/ipl-2012.html.
82. Faizan Ahmad, 'Where is Bataidari Bill? Asks Nitish'. 21 February 2010, http://articles.timesofindia.indiatimes.com/2010-02-21/patna/28129160_1_nitish-kumar-bataidari-bill-sections.
83. Ibid.
84. Rakesh Ankit, 'Analysis: Modern Zamindari', *Himal Southasian,* vol. 18, no. 2, November-December 2005, p. 91.
85. Ashok K. Jha, 'Why Bihar Failed to Develop?', 6 November 2007, http://www.americanchronicle.com/articles/view/42328.
86. Saibal Gupta, 'The Rediff Interview/Dr. Shaibal Gupta', 16 February 2005, http://www.rediff.com/election/2005/feb/16inter2.htm. Also, personal e-mail communication with Dr. Gupta, 26 April 2014.
87. The six orthodox schools of philosophy are examined in William Theodore de Bary, *Sources of Indian Tradition,* 1966. These are: *Yoga, Sankhya, Vedanta, Vaisheshika, Nyaya,* and *Mimansa.*
88. Usha Alexander, 'Bihar', 28 November 2002, http://blog.shunya.net/shunyas_blog/2007/11/bihar.html. Used by permission.

CHAPTER 8

Some Final Thoughts and Observations

THE TROUBLE WITH DEVELOPMENT

It was 1949 before the word 'development' was intellectually and programatically connected to the word 'underdevelopment' within their current contexts. According to Gilbert Rist, the self-proclaimed Swiss gatekeeper of the history of development, the idea of national development versus underdevelopment began as a 'public relations gimmick . . . by a professional speech-writer'.[1] Incumbent, President-elect Harry S. Truman wanted a fourth point for his inaugural address and development *versus* underdevelopment became that point. No one, in all likelihood, including Truman himself, really knew what was meant by development and underdevelopment at the time, and no one could have anticipated what the impact of those simple words would have on the United States and the world. At the time, they simply sounded new and original; somehow charged with anticipation.

Truman's words took on a life of their own, constantly being re-defined, reinvented, and moulded to the needs of those using them. Development and its associated buzzwords gained legitimacy through their vagueness and euphemistic qualities, their capacity to embrace a multitude of possible meanings, and their normative resonance, but even more important is that these words, by connotation or inference, contain a sense of worthiness that is inherently beyond reproach.

The words development and underdevelopment became fashionable and an entirely new industry developed around them, although the idea and intent was already in operation with the formation of Oxfam in 1942 and The World Bank Group in 1944, culminating in such organizations as the US Agency for International Development (USAID), 1961; the Organization for Economic Cooperation and Development (OECD), 1961; the United Nations Development

Programme (UNDP), 1965; and the Third World Network (TWN), 1984, to name but a few.[2]

DEVELOPMENT TODAY

After more than sixty-five years of use, 'development' continues to represent one of the most difficult and elusive concepts known to mankind. The advocates of development seem to fall into two main camps – those that embrace the idea that development is largely a reflection of the global extension of the marketplace; and those that strive to make the lives of the 'backward folk' better which, in the final analysis, is simply a form of political economy, or possibly less politically correct, cultural or ethnocentric chauvinism. Neither approach is inherently wrong but, at the same time, neither is entirely correct. Most observers are struck by the visible, let alone the economic gap between the so-called Haves and Have-nots. Somewhere inside most of us is a yearning to see everyone happy, safe, adequately fed and housed, and healthy. But, if history is any indicator, the gap between the Haves and Have-nots continues to exist and despite our best efforts, seems to be getting wider.[3]

Naturally, striving to better the welfare of our fellow man is laudable but if we continue to operate under the current conceptions of what development and underdevelopment are, we will simply continue to repeat the failures of the past. In general, much of our 'development activity' has been in vain. The world has somehow fallen prey to or been lulled into believing that 'development' will cure all the social, political, and economic ills of mankind when, in fact, history has shown that it has only had the effect of increasing social inequality and accentuated economic vulnerabilities.

Globalization has become the mechanism for the spread of technological capacity and information and has fostered a despair that has grown so profound that zealots have been able to pervert religious canons and indoctrinate followers into believing that their lives, and the lives of others, have lost all importance and meaning. The result is terrorism and suicide bombers.[4] If 'development' continues along the same trajectory it has followed since the beginning of the Industrial Revolution, it is conceivable that the despair that has prompted the current state of global terrorism, intra-national uprisings, and revolutions will only serve to generate even greater cynicism between the Haves and Have-nots of the world.

Part of the problem with 'development' and 'backwardness' lies not in the philosophical question of whether or not they are good or bad, or right or wrong. Instead,

> . . . for centuries no one – or virtually no one – took it into their head to relieve the misery of others by structural measures, especially when they lived in different continents. What is the origin of this collective task which, though constantly criticized for its lack of success, appears to be justified beyond all dispute. What sense can we make of the numerous debates which, for nearly fifty years, have offered a solution to the problems that majority destitution poses in the face of minority opulence? How are we to explain this whole phenomenon, which mobilizes not only the hope of millions but also sizeable financial resources, while appearing to recede like the horizon just as you think you are approaching it?[5]

Development and backwardness must be seen as historical processes. They are the culmination of social, cultural, political, and economic processes that originate exogenously and endogenously but, in general, are only observable by outsiders. Those deemed to be underdeveloped or backward typically do not perceive themselves as such. These are labels placed on them by outsiders. Thus, underdevelopment and backwardness are conditions based on one's observational perspective, superior versus inferior, and are typically based on technological superiority.

Since the advent of the Industrial Revolution, and even possibly dating back to medieval European ecclesiastical doctrines, the concept of progress has been a key component of Western thinking and ideology. It occupies an important place in the core of the West's most fundamental belief system. It was not until the nineteenth-century that the superiority of the West was finally proclaimed and ratified and allowed to flourish. As evidence of its superiority, Western Civilization needed only to point to its productiveness, the role of reason in deciding all things, and its explosive growth in science and technology.

Progress, or development, as conceptualized by Westerners, at least in the nineteenth and early twentieth centuries became the prophetic 'blueprint' for all societies. In time, everyone could achieve the same mastery of the world around them. Progress was envisioned as destiny, an inevitability if the backward societies only applied themselves.

Realistically, however, the world's finite resources preclude everyone achieving the same high level of consumption of goods and resources within the context of current technology. Nevertheless, the concept of growth appears to be more important to the idea of development than reality itself. As a consequence, we ignore the reality that growth and development cannot continue indefinitely or for everyone. It is the West's inability to recognize this simple fact that distinguishes it from every other culture. In every endeavour, whether economic, military or technological, the West continues to look ahead blindly to a future that continues to improve, making everything better. It is this unrealistic belief in the future that has become the mantra of every politician, economist, and businessman everywhere, even while logic tells us it is technically impossible.

The idea of progress ends in the simple yet complex term 'modernity'. Modernity, in turn, represents advancement, or an evolution toward a higher level of technological and socio-economic capacity, and inherently represents a transition from a more primitive state to a more advanced one. The problem with these concepts is that each is so infused with European intellectual and cultural bias as to have little meaning almost anywhere else. For this reason, it is probably inappropriate to subscribe to development paradigms formulated in the West with the expectation that they will have applicability elsewhere. Even such simplistic schema as Rostow's classic stages of economic growth have little validity outside the sphere of European culture.[6]

Until very recently, the industrialized countries of the world have served as the model or template for other nations, and developmentalists would have us believe that eventually every nation will become industrialized and homogenized. Isn't this what globalization is all about – the homogenization of the world – one world, one economy, one culture, one language, one race? Is this what we want for the world or is it an inevitability?

The West has become the standard by which all less-developed nations are gauged. Even the 'ecumenical' UNDP gauges and classifies national development using largely Western evaluation tools and measures while, at the same time, acknowledging the fact that every nation must strive towards and forge its own definition of and path to development. Each nation intuitively must occupy a position along the continuum between the least and most developed countries. The variance of one country's position along this line, when compared to the industrialized countries, represents its degree of backwardness.

Development should manifest itself differently within each culture complex but, in reality, to aspire to or achieve a state or form of development that is not shared or appreciated by the developed nations of the world means that such development will be unappreciated, negatively evaluated, and deemed backward. Part of this situation stems from the assumption that all societies that share similar goals share similar beliefs; and yet, history has taught us, time and again, that similarly generalized goals frequently come from very different systems of belief. Likewise, very different sub-national systems of belief can exist within individual nations, and these beliefs must be recognized and validated, not systematically derided and condemned.

It is the accommodation of different systems of belief and the acceptance of differences in what constitutes modernity that must become part of national development plans. Harkening back to an old concept, popularized by Robert Redfield decades ago, nations must conceive of themselves as composed of individual folk societies – 'small [sub-regional], isolated, groups that exhibit local cultures [traditions]; they are relatively homogenous with regard to the distribution of knowledge, attitudes, and functions; they demonstrate a strong sense of group solidarity; and knowledge is not explicitly systematized'.[7] It is such groups that development agencies and agents and national political leaders characterize as 'backward'. This description also encompasses the situation as it obtains in much of Mithila and Bihar.

If development is to take place, agents of development must understand and incorporate the 'development trajectories' of national, regional, and sub-regional world views. And where these world views differ from the national vision, governments must permit themselves to acknowledge these differences and celebrate them rather than trying to eradicate them. Traditionalism, within this context, and 'backwardness', need not be viewed as developmental failures but a lower, non-optimized level of success. Traditional groups, while adopting certain modern technologies need not embrace the whole idea of an aspiring, homogenized Western culture.[8]

Further, government policies and institutions shape economic incentives which have a direct impact on economic development. Good policies generally encourage social and economic investment but many developing nations implement policies that discourage investment and maintain institutions that result in the continuation or exacerbation of backwardness. In general, policies that discourage investment are the result of power groups – elites that perceive no long-term benefit arising from equity-based development or reform policies, or the creation of superior institutions and technologies which might reduce their economic, political, and social power. As a consequence, these elites, or power brokers, have no incentive to support broad-spectrum development programmes or reforms. For them, the *status quo* guarantees their position within society. In more politically economic terms: Elites will block economic and institutional changes when they believe that such changes will destabilize the existing socio-economic system and make it more likely that they will lose power.[9]

For rural elites, traditionalism is an effective strategy since it provides a fertile basis for political hegemony of elites who wish to continue to speak on behalf of the rural sector with the state.[10] Elites wish to subvert rural identities and associations, hoping to maintain social, economic, and political control over rural realms.

Nations and national leaders are faced with the difficult task of choosing a development strategy. At least on the surface, this is much like untying the proverbial Gordian Knot. Choosing any one strategy has the potential of fundamentally changing the cultural, social, political, and economic character of the country irretrievably and in unanticipated ways. Once some actions are taken, there is no going back. A safe, middle-ground approach to development would be a sound strategy; however, few developing nations have ever successfully found or navigated this ideal path. Inevitably, as with any development strategy, there will be winners and losers; and sometimes, it is difficult to predict who they will be or even who they are. Development is not a science but rather a game of probability. Any particular development strategy, no matter how well conceived, is a gamble with often unanticipated consequences for both the agents of change and the target population.

Only total revolution – the internal collapse of a state, its institutions, and culture – is capable of displacing the 'old guard' in any society; but with revolution, the result is typically the simple replacement of one set of elites with another, often with disastrous consequences for the average citizen.[11] Most revolutions are 'at the top'. Governments fall and new politicians replace the fallen, with very little change in the life of the peasant toiling in the fields. For the peasant, the political philosophy of the government has very little meaning because of little changes in his day-to-day life or existence. It is simply the exchange of one faceless politician for another. It is when the roots of revolution, or development, alter established rural power structures that the rural peasant begins to take notice.

This, then, leaves the question: if everyone cannot achieve the same level of material satisfaction, given the finite nature of energy and resources, and changes in government typically have no demonstrable effect on the peasantry, should we consider redefining how one achieves, attains, or lives 'the good life'? Obviously, there are numerous ways of defining a 'good life', and it is incumbent upon each of us, or our socio-cultural communities to invent its own definition.

Rist uses the phrase, 'happy poverty' to differentiate between what we have, previously, called the Haves and Have-nots.[12] Is this possible or permissible? The answer, much like so many questions surrounding development, is neither easy nor necessarily neat. Is it possible and permissible to permit segments of the world's population to live in 'happy poverty'?

If Westerners are willing and able to discard the notion that progress and development are natural and inevitable, then, can we permit others to live in happy poverty? However, to discard these twin notions of progress and development would mean exorcising the fundamental articles of Western socio-economic faith from the Western psyche, a job probably more easily contemplated than achieved.

THE UNITED NATIONS AND THE NEED TO GAUGE HUMAN DEVELOPMENT

The UNDP is the world's global development network. It focuses and intercedes on behalf of development's key issues, providing measurement tools, innovative analysis and often controversial policy proposals. It serves as an advocate for change, connecting countries to knowledge, experience and resources, helping them to build a better life. It provides expert advice, training, and grant support to developing countries, using a variety of statistical tools to gauge the success of these programmes. Among the most important of these tools are the Human Development Index (HDI) and, more recently, the Oxford Multidimensional Poverty Index (MPI or OPHI).

Together, these provide quantitative or qualitative information on all the major areas of the lives of people in the majority of recognized national states in regular reports that can then be used for comparative purposes. Among the areas examined are economic and social development, living conditions, health, education, and the environment. These data are then converted into tables, graphs or maps and provide decision makers with statistics to be used in the formulation of policy.

The problem with the UNDP, its purpose, its activities, and its development statistics is that they are all predicated on the Western notion of progress. The UNDP describes its activities as 'partnering with people at all levels of society to help build nations that can withstand crisis and drive and sustain the kind of growth that improves the quality of life for everyone', thus, promoting a form of socio-economic development that will result in some higher, less demeaning state of existence. If this statement of purpose sounds idyllic and slightly out of touch with reality, you are beginning to get a feel for what the UNDP, and possibly every other United Nation's sponsored programme is all about.

The UN was organized and founded by idealists of the 1940s who saw a need for a legitimate world government. Today's UN, as well as the upper echelon leadership in every branch of every agency or programme centre of the UN, is populated by equally idealistic do-gooders. The problem is that doing good has somehow become a very expensive proposition – missions out of touch with reality with very large budgets. If the notions of progress and development are philosophically and intrinsically impossible to achieve, are not the UNDP and its development statistics simply perpetuating a myth – the unachievable?

Yet, day after day, HDIs and OPHIs are consulted, policy decisions are made, and development programmes are formulated to raise the backward and under-developed nations, their people, or subsets thereof. If these statistics are based on a fallacious premise and are used to compare nations and their populations, do they serve a valid or legitimate purpose?

Obviously, if the goal is to achieve equality between the people of the planet in terms of socio-economic development, then, such statistics and their use are being used to perpetuate a myth. Inherent in development statistics is the notion that equality is achievable. There can be no equality within the context of the world's current resource inventories and their consumption and the current economic, military, and political power structures. At best, equilibrium can be achieved but this will not curb national nor individual aspirations to have a larger portion of the economic pie.

Possibly a more realistic assessment of official statistics use is providing a 'yardstick' by which the Haves measure their success against the Have-nots. Since the majority of the Haves are Western, industrialized nations, most development statistics represent self-patronizing and self-serving proofs of the West's innate superiority. Thus, development statistics simply serve to legitimize the West's image of itself.

SUSTAINABILITY

The unfounded belief that progress and development can continue unabated and indefinitely seems to have infected the thinking of everyone: governments, public officials, and the majority of the world's population. How else can one explain the unending search for more development? There are those within the international development community who have doubts, but either they voice their scepticism in private, away from the cameras and microphones of the media, or they just remain silent. After all, development is their occupation, their *raison d'être*. Even with the spectre of failure, well established and documented, these same Doubting Thomases continue to perpetuate the myth. Maybe one or more of the fixed variables will miraculously change and the myth will be proven right. Minor, transitory successes here and there only serve to reinforce the myth and its perpetuation. Abject failures are explained away by rising interest rates, civil unrest, famine, unanticipated unemployment, war, or malgovernance, but never by the impossibility of the proposition that development or progress are achievable goals, if only some time in the future. The goal never dies; only the means of achieving it becomes less and less clear and increasingly elusive.

Nevertheless, the premier development agencies – the UNDP and the World Bank – continue to advocate the benefits of development, recognizing that development means different things to different people and that different countries have different priorities. They recognize that, to compare development levels, one needs to determine what development means and what it is supposed to achieve. Is the goal to increase national wealth or something more subtle? Improving the well-being of the majority of the population? Ensuring people's freedom? Increasing economic and food security?

UN documents emphasize human development, using measures of life expectancy, adult literacy, access to education, as well as people's average income, which is a prerequisite for freedom of choice. More recently, the UN has added happiness to its mix of variables; yet another index of well-being.

The Happiness approach to development incorporates all aspects of an individual's well-being, from their health status to their economic and political freedom. Thus, economic development becomes the means for the attainment of overall human development. However, history has shown that economic growth is not always followed by similar progress in human development. Instead, economic growth has frequently resulted in greater inequality, higher unemployment, weakened democracy, loss of cultural identity, or the ruinous over-consumption of natural resources. This type of development is 'unsustainable', with sustainability becoming the newest in a long list of catch words for developmentalists.

Sustainable development is a term that only recently has come to be used by politicians. It lacks a uniform definition or interpretation but sounds somehow politically correct. The UN World Commission on Environment and Development suggests that development is sustainable if it 'meets the needs of the present without compromising the ability of future generations to meet their own needs'.[13] At best, such a statement represents an unrealistic goal and at worst is inherently meaningless. It is based on the assumption that future development can be both equitable and balanced, that for development to continue indefinitely, it would balance the interests of different people within the same generation and among generations yet to come. Sustainable development, then, would require equality of opportunities for people's well-being as well as the conservation of finite resources. Current technology and existing social organizations simply are not capable of juggling so many diverse objectives with any reasonable expectation of success. Such an agenda is little more than politically correct word play or politicians' legerdemain, a form of verbal double-speak. It cannot be done but it sounds good.

DEVELOPMENT'S BUZZWORDS

Wolfgang Sachs suggests that 'development is much more than just a socio-economic endeavour; it is a perception which models reality, a myth which comforts societies, and a fantasy which unleashes passions'.[14] It is these myths, models, and passions that are sustained by development's buzzwords. Sustainable development is one of the more recent additions to the lexicon of buzzwords used by development's spokesmen.

Why are buzzwords so important? Because language plays a very important part in defining what development is and what it does. Development's buzzwords are crucial to successful fundraising, influence, and legitimacy. They are the important telltale markers of the development profession. These words get their 'buzz' by becoming in-words, words that define what is currently in vogue, and like all buzzwords, their durability is based on their ability and effectiveness as response-evoking terms. Some are, therefore, short-lived, while others go out of vogue only to be resurrected from time to time often bearing new or modified meanings.

New and possibly even more potent words began to be added to the development lexicon. One of the first was 'poverty'. The word 'poverty', even more than the word 'development', is possibly one of the most powerful and compelling words used by developmentalists today. The mere mention of poverty evokes a normative, gut-level, visceral response. The word does not even need to be intellectually processed to elicit a response. It is autonomic. When one speaks of 'poverty reduction', there is an automatic and immediate sense of obviousness to whatever follows. The phrase is one of those unique combinations that needs absolutely no explanation or justification. Who could criticize or challenge the philosophical validity or need to reduce poverty? Poverty reduction is axiomatic. It is a universally righteous virtue for which there can be no legitimate basis for criticism or question.

Other buzzwords are frequently seen as jargon and unintelligible to those outside the development community. They are part of the language of development professionals. They sound intellectual, academic, and scientific and beyond the ken of the lay person. Most do, in fact, have their origin in academic circles but once incorporated into the vocabulary of the development specialist they somehow metamorphose or completely lose their original meaning. Only the term remains but with a new meaning and having a new feel about it, until it falls from grace only to be reborn again at some later date.

Equally important is the fact that while these buzzwords gain universal acceptance, they are rarely translatable into other languages conceptually and most find their roots in English. As a consequence, other languages adopt these terms as loan-words. While they gain universal use they do not possess universality as words or concepts. For example, Gilbert Rist writes: 'I eventually decided to write this article in English, for the simple reason that "buzzword" is just impossible to translate into French. It comes under what we call "la langue de bois", whose translation into English does not exactly convey the same meaning.'[15]

Andrea Cornwall suggests that *la langue de bois* is best translated as the 'language of evasion', and this captures one of the functions of development's buzzwords.[16] Buzzwords cloud meanings, and this may be, in fact, one of their most important attributes.

The language of development, along with its concomitant buzzwords, has a life of its own. It has become a hybrid language – not a language of the social sciences but a language dedicated to the mediation of political consensus and camouflaging the ideological and practical inconsistencies inherent in development's principles and rhetoric. Thus, the language of development is infused with ambiguity that is necessary to create a following and which depends on individual interpretation to bridge the gap between theory, policy, and reality; and it insulates the proponent of development from having to make a definitive commitment to any particular strategy, policy, or idea. In political-speak, the imprecise nature of the language of development provides everyone with an exit strategy – 'plausible deniability'. The political spin doctors need only reply: 'obviously, you misunderstood'.

Different words, different interpretations, different contexts and different strategies are needed, depending on the situation, to resolve different problems. In some ways, the language of development is a game of cat and mouse but with real people suffering the consequences. The words, by design, are slippery for, after all, development is most frequently a national or regional problem addressed by international agencies. It uses a language, a form similar to that used in diplomacy, with all its imprecision, jargon, and politically correct gibberish. Without its imprecision, jargon, and gibberish, the agencies and individuals who command and commit billions in scarce funds to unproductive development studies and programmes would have a difficult time explaining the continued misuse and misappropriation of vast amounts of money and other resources.

FOREIGN AID AND DEVELOPMENT

In 2006, US $103.6 billion in foreign aid flowed to developing countries. Over the last fifty years, the amount of foreign aid dispersed totals over US $2.3 trillion.[17] Together with this rather large amount of money, equally large quantities of time and other resources were also pumped into development assistance programmes. All the more disconcerting is the fact that all the scarce resources were consumed in the absence of a theoretical consensus regarding the effectiveness of foreign aid and no ultimate assurance there would be a positive outcome!

More importantly, recent studies suggest that foreign aid has no effect on growth nor any of the other indicators of poverty.[18] Peter Leeson suggests, however, that most developing countries have weak institutions and ineffective policies which promote poverty. Where aid is needed, it will not help because the necessary institutions are lacking. Where it could benefit the people, in those countries with good policies and institutions, it is not needed.[19]

Repeatedly, foreign aid is offered and accepted by the governments of developing nations, and both the providers and recipients are aware that research has shown that it has little effect on target populations. When foreign aid's goals are compared with its achievements, the results have consistently proven to be disappointing.

The only real benefit of foreign aid accrues to the ruling governments, the politicians in the recipient nations, and those in the donor agencies. The funds are simply swallowed up by the machinery that oversees its distribution and it disappears since the recipient governments have no real incentive to promote their efficient use; there is little or no accountability, and special interest groups and individuals readily benefit from such funding. Corrupt governments are acutely aware that the donor countries have little incentive to monitor how aid is allocated once it is in the hands of their government. Further, the recipient governments are equally aware that they will not be held accountable even if nothing is achieved, since there are no institutional sanctions for the misuse of such funds or lack of success. Time and again, the current system of top-down, central planning and aid distribution has proven ineffective; and we should not be surprised when foreign aid does not achieve its intended goals. Nevertheless, top-down development funding continues unabated in the absence of any other reasonable alternative.

Theodore Dalrymple of *The Telegraph* recently asked what, at first, seems to be an outlandish question: India has just announced that it will send a space probe to Mars and now possesses more technological prowess than Britain, then why is it still poor?

The former Indian Finance Minister Pranab Mukherjee (now the President), said that India did not need British aid which, he added, was 'peanuts' anyway. He was right on both accounts, but oddly enough, his pronouncement – no more than the most obvious truth –

was met by almost grovelling British requests to continue aid to India. Why?[20]

Dalrymple's question is simple, straightforward, and to the point. Why does the West continue to export absolutely huge quantities of scarce financial resources to so many developing nations?

If we accept the premises that: (a) development is based on a Western myth, (b) there is no theoretical or practical agreement on what development really is, (c) it is relentlessly funded by Western nations, who have no way of either accounting for nor controlling how their development funds are being used or misused, and (d) neither the donor nor the recipient nations have any incentive but to continue dispersing massive amounts of money among ineffective programmes, is there any wonder there is no substantive improvement?

Development programmes and foreign aid are, however, comprehensible if you simply take out the expectation that their intent is to improve the welfare of the underdeveloped. If viewed as a form of economic penance – reparations paid by the West to the developing nations of the world, because the West has become socio-economically and politically successful – the continued funding of development makes sense. Even so, to spend billions of dollars, year after year, with no expectation that anything will change, qualitatively or quantitatively, defies logic. It is simple patronization. Development funding and foreign aid do not help poor countries; it just corrupts their governments. It definitely does not buy allegiance nor promote lasting friendship for the donor nations.

THE CURRENT STATUS OF BIHAR

Bihar is unique in many respects. It has a long history of intellectualism and as A.L. Basham characterized it, 'intellectual' ferment. Bihar was a place that 'not only produced philosophers and ascetics, but also merchant princes and men of action'.[21] The roots of three of the world's greatest religions can be traced to Bihar, and specifically northern Bihar. Northern Bihar, from Vedic times onward, has been politically volatile, with successions of kingdoms ebbing and flowing, changing the political map of northeastern South Asia.

In more modern times, Bihar was one of the most important strongholds of India's struggle for independence. Gandhi's first Satyagraha was launched in West Champaran in 1917.[22] Bihar was among the most progressive states in the newly established independent Republic of India. In the 1950s, Bihar was the third most prosperous state in India. It was an example of political activism and inspired broad-based political involvement. In the 1960s, Bihar began to falter. By 2004, writers for *The Economist* offered the following description:

> Bihar has become a byword for the worst of India, of widespread and inescapable poverty, of corrupt politicians indistinguishable from mafia-dons they patronise, caste-ridden social order that has retained the worst feudal cruelties. . . . an area of darkness where many Indians are being left behind, [where] chronic misrule . . . has led to crumbling infrastructure, collapsing education and health systems and evaporating law and order, and . . . [where the State's] biggest growth industry is kidnapping for ransom.[23]

At least on the surface, again, things seem to be changing. Nitish Kumar, Bihar's latest chief minister, has spent the last eight to nine years fixing the state's roads and building other infrastructure. Crime has decreased due to his no-nonsense approach to justice. He has set up a system of fast-track courts that has convicted nearly 66,000 criminals – including some Members of Parliament.[24] Now, he is targeting official corruption, which has elicited a debate over whether corruption is an unavoidable lubricant in the country's rush to prosperity.

Nitish, who until recently was often mentioned as a possible future prime minister, believes that justice need not be sacrificed to achieve growth, and that Bihar can show the way for the rest of India. When he made his first run for the post of chief minister, he was a single-issue candidate. His primary message was to re-establish the rule of law. While he promised law and order, his opponents' speeches promised what every politician before him had promised – jobs, state subsidies, empowerment of the lower castes. They were reluctant to condemn lawlessness. After all, much of recent political power in Bihar has been the result of orchestrated violence.

Once elected, Nitish filled thousands of vacant police posts with retired military personnel and ended political interference in law enforcement, the haven for many political powerbrokers. His policies had broad appeal; as security improved, growth followed, much of which has been based on large scale public-works of projects financed by New Delhi or the Asian Development Bank.

Yet, while violent crime declined during his tenure as chief minister, the recent political assassination of Brahmeshwar Singh, a wealthy landlord and the *de facto* leader of the Ranvir Sena, the most powerful of Bihar's numerous private militias, calls into question Nitish's real ability to control the gangs of Bihar. It has long been recognized that Bihar's overall power structure rests on the use of violence, shared between racketeers, landlords, contractors, politicians, and ward bosses who bring out the voters and suppress the opposition at election time. At the same time, he has shied away from substantive land reforms, which are both complex and deeply unnerving to the upper-caste landowners who are an important part of his political coalition.

Hulas Pandey (the prime suspect in Brahmeshwar Singh's assassination) and other members of the Ranvir Sena are all part of Nitish's political support structure – landlords of the Bhumihar and Rajput castes. When the head of Bihar's state police was asked about the killing of Brahmeshwar Singh, the arrest of Pandey, and the subsequent lawlessness that attended Singh's funeral, 'he implied what everyone knew: politics had tied his hands'.[25] Politics still plays an important role in Bihar's system of justice.

Bihar was backward and recognized for its lawlessness when Nitish took power. Seven years later, all indications are that it still is. This is not to say that Nitish has not made substantive statistical improvements in the state's economic growth, but his compromised past still remains with him – his power continues to be based on traditional sources of power. Kumar 'rode a tiger' to unseat Bihar's incumbent government in 2005, a ruling party man told the Kolkata *Telegraph*, and 'now he is afraid [or unable] to dismount.'[26] The epigram by Jean-Baptiste Alphonse Karr: *Plus ça change, plus c'est la même chose* [The more things change, the more they stay the same] seems to apply to Bihar's recent political past and present. One can neither ignore nor discard one's past obligations in Bihar.

THE ROOTS OF BIHAR'S BACKWARDNESS

Modern, pre-bifurcation Bihar is the home to nearly 93 per cent (13 of 14) of the most consistently enumerated backward districts in India.[27] Only one of the fourteen backward districts falls outside modern Bihar/Jharkhand/Mithila. This lone backward district is Barabanki in Uttar Pradesh. Districts deemed to be backward were found in 22 of India's 28 states, representing 251 of 636 districts. Some states like Goa, Kerala, Mizoram, Tamil Nadu, and Tripura had no enumerated backward districts.[28] See, Map I.1, Master Study Map, located in the pocket at the end of the book.

Of the twelve backward districts found in residual Bihar (post-bifurcation), eleven fall in the area commonly referred to as Mithila. Of the backward districts in Bihar, only one of the twelve – Nawada – falls south of the Ganga (see Map 8.1).

All fourteen backward districts fall in what Banerjee and Iyer termed landlord land revenue areas.[29] All fell under the terms of the original Permanent Settlement (1793) or its subsequent applications.

We have discussed at length the factors that have contributed to modern-day Bihar's socio-economic backwardness. While the principles and patterns of backwardness are substantially the same in every one of the backward districts, those in Mithila exhibit a certain uniqueness. That uniqueness stems from a socio-religious influence that literally can be traced back to Vedic times, has been reinforced again and again through Mithila's very long history, and has been cemented and formalized through the agency of the Darbhanga Raj and *'Asabiyya*.

From the Vedic period to the present, at the grassroots level of Maithili society, tradition and traditionalism have systematically and repeatedly resisted the inroads of modernization. Paraphrasing Heinz:

> The persistence of caste consciousness and influence, especially among Bihar's Brahmins, is attributed to the failure of modern institutions to take hold. In the absence of substantive economic growth and social development in rural Bihar, the typical incentives to shed caste controls and build cross-caste friendships and partnerships languish. Politicians consistently and unabashedly exploit caste anxieties about changing power structures which only serves to reinforce caste solidarity as voting blocks. And due to the dysfunctional nature of Bihar's state apparatus, castes, at least, provide some security against encroaching interests of other groups.[30]

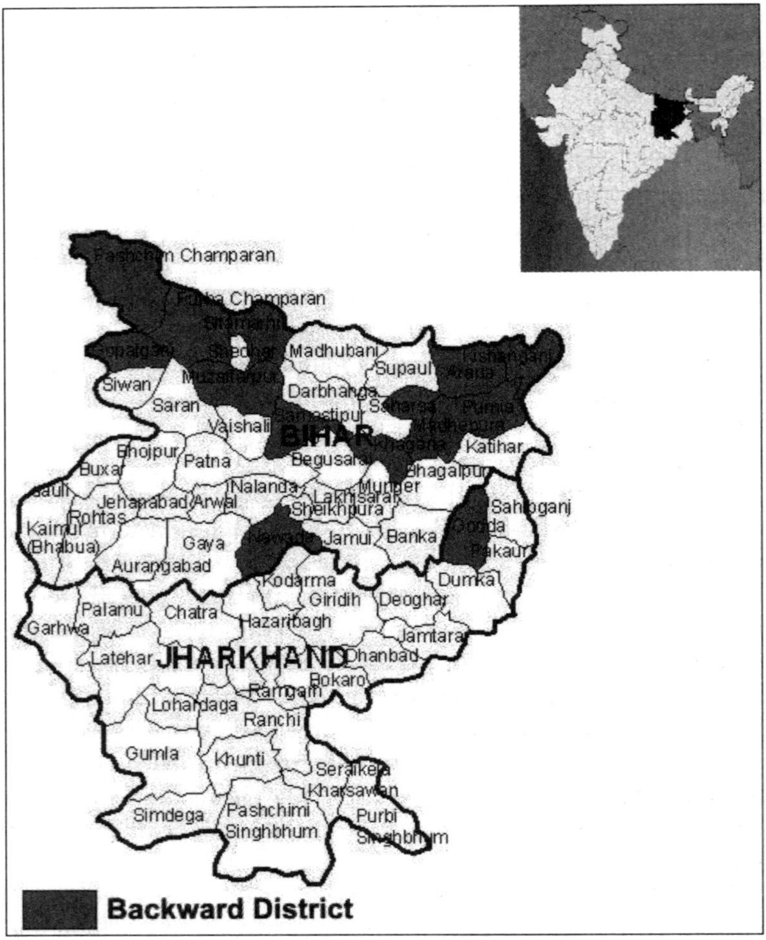

MAP 8.1: BACKWARD DISTRICTS OF MODERN BIHAR AND JHARKHAND

The inspriational source of this traditionalism can be traced to one small group, the Srotriyas – the most traditional of the Maithil Brahmanas. Their influence overlays Brahmin and non-Brahmin castes alike. They set the ideal for all those below them ritually and socially. Their influence, and that of the erstwhile Darbhanga Raj, continues to hold sway throughout Mithila. Unlike much of southern Bihar, with its lawlessness, kidnappings, rapes, murders, massacres, *sena*-based gangsterism and Naxalism, in Mithila, there has been a tranquillity and by comparision, little open violence.

This tranquilly, to be sure, is relative but, nonetheless, perceptible. The lawlessness and all its associated manifestations in southern Bihar can be seen as a society attempting to reconcile the past with new social and political opportunities – change. Society and its sub-sets of classes and castes, in southern Bihar, unlike in Mithila, have been wrestling with the stresses of modernization, increased communication, and increasing social, economic, and political aspirations and opportunities.

When aspirations go unmet and opportunities do not materialize, there is unrest which often manifests itself in the form of violence. The more downtrodden any individual or group feels, the greater the group's felt or real disenfranchisement, insufficient or unequal opportunities, or legacy of violence, the greater the likelihood of spontaneous or coordinated violence. At the same time, violence can also be seen as proactive rather than reactive. The senas of Bihar are both reactive and reactionary, responding to the challenges of traditional opponents and competitors for scarce economic and political resources. Both sides see the other as a competitor and they react accordingly. In the case of the upper castes, there is a reactionary component, the preservation of prior privileges and power.

This growing and pent up class and caste violence has been aided by the diffusion of increasingly powerful technologies of violence. As technological change makes it easier to kill people, groups that have been locked in a perpetual cycle of conflict find it easier to resort to violence than queue up and wait for their chance to exploit political and economic development opportunities. Violence simultaneously reduces the opportunities for democratic dialogue and seriously impedes the process of real institutional and political reform. Thus, violence is, ultimately, unproductive, but it nevertheless, is frequently viewed by some as easy or their only first choice.

* * *

In Mithila, one is left with the 'feeling' that despite the destitution it is somehow tolerable or, if one draws upon Hindu belief, it is just *karma* at work and it is inevitable. It is futile to fight. Accept the inevitable and make the best of it in this life. Is this Rist's 'happy poverty'?

There is an orderliness to Mithila. Is this the institutional overhang of the Darbhanga Raj, the legacy of the Maithil Brahmanas, the Srotriyas, or the prolonged legacy of the area's intellectual and cultural isolation? In some areas, it almost feels like one is stepping back in time, where the meanings, values, and paraphernalia of twenty-first century society are left behind but one continues to be reminded that it is the twenty-first century by computers, internet, cell phones, radios, televisions, and futures reported by the Chicago Board of Trade. One sees professionals with traditional *tilakas* running between courtrooms in their flowing robes, files and a laptop under one arm, and a briefcase in the other hand.

The study of Sanskrit and Vedic Sanskrit continues. University names still extol the importance of Sanskrit. Small groups – men and women – sit animatedly discussing philosophical matters drawing upon the Vedas, Upanishads, Puranas, the *Ramayana* or *Bhagavad Gita*, and a host of other lesser known texts.

In the villages, the orthodox Brahmanas rise before sunrise, enter their courtyards, and begin several hours of worship defined by Vedic tradition. All major life-cycle rites, known as *samskaras*, are conducted in the courtyard. The four-house compound of a typical rural village with the *mandap* – a covered raised platform whose primary function is to protect the Vedic fire – at the centre. One observes the deference shown to the Srotriyas in everyday life.

Unlike central and southern Bihar, Mithila has remained comparatively immune to largescale inter-caste violence. There are no senas and few organized, armed gangs, and only recently have the Maoists, who have been the primary target of nefarious *senas* in central and southern Bihar, begun to organize in those districts of northern Bihar bordering on Nepal. Seeking safe bases from which to operate, Indian Maoists have linked up with their counterparts in Nepal. Further, the porosity of the India-Nepal border affords both sides refuge when government officials from either side begin their routine manhunts. However, while the Indian Maoists utilize bases in the border districts with Nepal, most of their military expeditions continue to focus on targets south of the Ganga, leaving Mithila largely untouched and uninvolved.

While the people of Mithila are backward, when one uses almost any one of the numerous indices of development, indices developed by Westerners and used to measure social and economic well-being in Western terms, they do not see themselves as backward. They are poor, illiterate, lacking in western-defined amenities, including infrastructure, communication, and health services. No one asks if they are content. Are they happy? We assume, because they do not possess the same quantities and kinds of things used by the evaluation gurus to measure well-being, that they are automatically and inherently backward.[31] Western standards are being applied in non-Western situations. It is human nature to want more, to have the 'good life'. However, the good life is relative. It is not a universal condition shared or desired by everyone.

The continued use of international development criteria by domestic development agencies ignores the cultural values of indigenous populations. The wants and needs of people are conditioned by culture and, therefore, differ greatly from society to society. There may be certain essentials that all human beings, as biological organisms, require but beyond those essentials, culture and opportunity define the difference between a want and a need. Most development programmes and evaluation criteria ignore this difference.

We need to ignore Western-driven schemes for the evaluation of socio-economic development and define and tailor development programmes around what the subject population wants, not what the development agents want for them. If we ask the target population what they want, and provide them with the means of acquiring it, the primary goal of development will have been achieved. People are not 'cookie cutter' clones. This recognition may play havoc with international development goals, criteria, evaluation measures, and comparisons, but the recognition that not everyone wants or needs the same things will get us much closer to the ideal of providing what they do want, and the word 'backward' will no longer have any real meaning. The point of development should be to give people opportunities and freedoms to change and improve their lives, if that is what *they* want.

THE GOSSAMER THREADS – SOCIAL DEVELOPMENT, SOCIAL INERTIA, RELIGION, AND *'ASABIYYA*

Rural development, underdevelopment, and backwardness in rural India, and specifically in rural Mithila, are collectively and individually a function of what we have labelled 'gossamer threads of history' – interconnections of individuals and groups, even nations, as well as social structures, religious beliefs, social and political ideologies, culture, and practical and theoretical economic constructs. The words, ideas, and actions of specific historical figures and groups have collectively contributed to either the emergence of the British Empire, the independence of modern India, or the backwardness that continues to prevail in Mithila. Each left a mark. Each left behind a legacy – a legacy that can still be seen in rural Bihar in the twenty-first century, if one is able and willing to 'connect the historical dots'.

Social Development

Ian Morris, in his critically acclaimed book *Why the West Rules for Now: The Patterns of History and What They Reveal about the Future* suggests that societies and cultures thrive or decline based on a concept he calls 'social development'. As used by Morris, social development

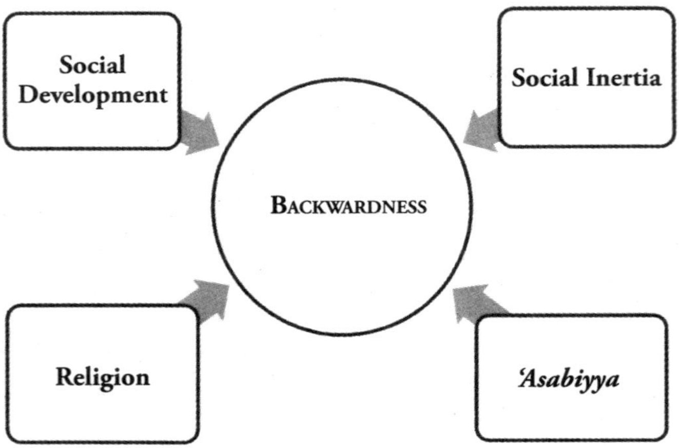

FIGURE 8.1: A FACTORAL, GRAPHIC REPRESENTATION OF BACKWARDNESS IN MITHILA

represents society's ability to get things done – its ability to shape its physical, economic, social, and intellectual environments to its own ends.[32] In general, the changes in these environments fall under the umbrella term, 'development', which is unquestionably good, at least within Western cultures.

The term development has became synonymous with the concept of progress – progress toward some ill-defined utopian society, affluence, or God. Each and all of these goals is deemed reasonable and satisfactory life goals and, therefore, worth pursuing. Not even in the West, however, were these goals universally accepted. It is an individual choice of which goal is to be pursued. Of the three broad general classifications of what one sought to pursue, affluence was the most dominant in the West; and it was affluence that permitted the West to explore, expropriate, and dominate much of the planet's geography and population by the mid-eighteenth century. Utopian societies and Godliness were little more than 'also rans' in the grand scheme of things.

Morris further posits what he refers to as the Morris Theorem: 'Change is caused by lazy, greedy, frightened people looking for easier, more profitable, and safer ways to do things. And they rarely know what they're doing.'[33]

Since it is difficult to accomplish each of these ends simultaneously, in most cases, the Morris Theorem might be slightly adjusted to read: greedy, lazy frightened people seek an equilibrium between being comfortable (satisfied), working as little as possible, and being safe (socially, politically, and economically). It might be one thing to make such a statement but history has shown that achieving the desired end result balancing out the forces, needs, and wants of the individuals within a society is a monumentally complicated process, often generating as many new problems as old problems are resolved or become manageable.

Typically, those who are the most flexible in their thinking will be viewed by history as most successful and adaptive. Those would be considered to be the most advanced in their social development. Those that hang back, or are unable to resolve the most pressing social, political, economic, or environmental challenges will lag behind and become known as 'backward'. It is the acceptance of the challenge, their resolution, and adaptability that fosters social development. Traditionalism, whether in one's social, political, or economic life, or the minimization of environmental problems will result in social developmental backwardness.

The people of Mithila are located in one of the most densely populated parts of the 'Hindu heartland' and have been unsuccessful in mitigating or resolving the problems that have confronted them. Traditionally, Bihar's rural poverty has been associated with limited access to land, poor education, poor health care, and the absence of well-paying jobs and social status. The rural poor tend to be dependent upon agricultural wages or casual non-farm labour; a large percentage of the rural population is landless or near-landless. Likewise, social or caste characteristics have served to severely limit both social and economic opportunities.

Socially, the people of Mithila are subject to a complex, rigidly stratified social structure which prevents effective communication and problem-solving within and between groups and communities. Politically, caste dominates and factionalizes the political process, undermining meaningful and efficient governance, as well as undermining individual and collective initiative and security. Economically, affluence has eluded the people of Mithila; and environmentally, the challenges of uncontrolled and uncontrollable flooding and drought remain unresolved. Equally important is the fact that Bihar's government, even today, has been dependent upon programmatic allocations from the Central Government but has been unable to fully or efficiently utilize these grants; and over time, the state has become increasingly dependent on these transfers to finance every aspect of state government. It has been estimated that the state forfeited (returned) one-fifth of its programmatic funding to the Centre, failing to use the funds provided between 1997 and 2000.[34]

In large measure, the inability of the people of Mithila to resolve the challenges before them are influenced by their socio-religious practices, the hidebound strength of tradition, and the resistance to any change that would serve to undermine the existing social, political, and economic hierarchies. Many of the people of Mithila are ardent practitioners of a traditional form of Hinduism with direct links to Vedic Brahmanism. The existing caste structure fosters traditional, *jajmani*-like social and economic dependencies. The existing pattern of land ownership tends to cement and solidify a traditional form of social, political, and economic behaviour and perpetuates a form of feudal or semi-feudal *status quo*. Every socio-economic system in Mithila either condones or fosters traditional patterns of behaviour and it is these behaviours that have impeded 'development'.

However, while they have successfully fended off change, the social and economic elites have perpetuated a form of security that was once deemed to be within the province of caste; but the politicization of caste in Bihar has only served to fragment castes for political purposes, thereby increasing insecurity. All this developmental resistance would not have been possible without a focal point, someone or something to focus on or organize around. That focal point came in the person of the Maharaja of Darbhanga, the Darbhanga Raj and the recognition of the Srotriya of the Maithil Brahmanas as the region's preeminent spiritual and ritual leaders.

The Role of Social Inertia – Overhang

Throughout rural India, rights in land traditionally have been the basis of many social relationships and cultural values, and a source of prestige and power. The resulting social networks that are built up within specific social and cultural groups are a very important asset in ensuring the very livelihood of many rural households. The nature of land rights goes a long way toward explaining the persistence of certain social behaviours among rural householders.

The 1290 *Statute of Quia Emptores* formally abolished the manorial, feudal system of land tenure in England, however, many of the habits and institutions that were the foundation of that system lingered on for centuries, due to what may be referred to as social inertia or overhang – resistance to change simply due to habit. Resistance to change results when people perceive change as a threat. The key words here are 'perceive' and 'threat'. The threat need not be real nor large to create fear.

While agents of change would suggest that resistance is counter-productive, in its defence, resistance simply represents all the forces which contribute to stability in a social system. The tendencies for individuals as well as larger social units to achieve, preserve, and return to a state of equilibrium is both salutatory and natural. In other words, human nature. Together, they permit the duration of character, intelligent actions, institutions, civilization and culture.[35]

Change typically triggers fear of the unknown. Most people prefer what they know, even if it is not in their best interests because it is something in this world that they can 'depend' on. It provides a false sense of security; people would rather suffer through something not in their best interests than take a chance with the unknown. Resistance to change, therefore, is not necessarily an irrational and dysfunctional reaction.

It is, however, viewed as irrational and dysfunctional, in most cases, by the agents of change. The preponderance of change studies suggest that those seeking to bring about change are doing the right and proper things while change recipients, on the other hand, respond with what are perceived to be unreasonable obstacles or barriers.[36] Change agents are typically portrayed as undeserving victims of the irrational responses of change recipients. This view assumes that resistance is: (a) an accurate report by unbiased observers and (b) is an objective and true representation of the facts. Most often both assumptions are inaccurate.[37] In most instances, resistance to change is a tenable alternate survival strategy within the rural landscape, and can be used equally by many of society's powerbrokers.

Resistance to change *must* be considered to be a rational response under certain circumstances, especially if the change being proffered is deemed to be threatening to the individual or a collection of individuals, such as a family, village, tribe, or ethnic group, and especially to traditional elites. Within this context, there is a certain inner logic to social inertia.

Only recently have developmental economists begun to use the concept of social inertia as an explanation or tool for either the non-adoption of innovations or developmental backwardness.[38] It may not be a universal explanation nor applicable everywhere but, likewise, it should not be ignored just because 'newer and more sophisticated' explanations have become fashionable. Often these 'new' explanations blind us to reality. Academic pressures play a role in focusing research. It must be based on the most current theoretical constructs and sophisticated techniques of analysis if it is to be recognized by either one's colleagues or publishers. Nevertheless, some old concepts have a place in contemporary research efforts, especially if they apply.

Religion and Development

Religion is always a popular topic of discussion but it is also a political mine field filled with ideological pitfalls. To ascribe a causal relationship between it and development has become a 'hands off' issue or, more correctly, politically incorrect; especially in developing nations like India. In large measure, this is due to the desire of most developing nations to be seen not as religious or spiritual states, but rather as secular.

The idea of *laïcité* is possibly a better term than secular within the context of India. The French word *laïcité* is difficult to translate directly into English. In essence *laïcité* means the strict separation of State from Church – in other words to have no state religion. It does not mean the rejection of religion nor does it mean that religion or religious principles do not influence state decisions. The author likes the French term here because one cannot statutorily eliminate religion from influencing individual decision-making, just as it is impossible to eliminate racism, sexism, prejudice, or discrimination from a person's mind. You can only create penalties for overt racial, sexual, or discriminatory actions or behaviour. However, stopping the behaviours does not necessarily alter the thinking since in most instances, these ideas and behaviours are the result of perceived, real or imagined, loss of power, ignorance, and fear, which is fed by privilege and power.

Under *laïcité*, a state officially regards religion as a private affair; and if this is what is meant by secularism, fine and good. However, to attempt to eliminate all religious influence, beliefs, or considerations from state affairs is naïve and particularly so within the context of India.

Part of the problem with the idea of India being viewed as a secular state stems from the fact that, at least from a Western perspective, Hinduism is both more than and less than a religion. To label Hinduism, using a typically Western definition of what a religion is, or 'should be', leaves what Thomas Kuhn would refer to as anomalies – facts that are difficult to explain within the context of an existing paradigm, theory, or definition.[39] While these anomalies are often resolved, in some cases they simply accumulate until a new paradigm or definition is devised to encompass both the core beliefs and the anomalies.

Hinduism still remains well beyond the scope of an acceptable Western definition of a religion. It continues to be a collection of doctrines, principles, beliefs, rites, and rituals that simply cannot be stuffed into one simple, neat Webster-like dictionary pigeon-hole. If Hinduism is not a religion, it has to be something else, making it impossible for India to be a Hindu religious state.

While this may seem like a play on words or naiveté, it is neither. Hinduism is far more than a simple religion. It is a way of life that expresses itself in almost an unimaginable number of ways. That is the beauty of Hinduism. It is whatever the individual follower wishes it to be. It is limitless and thus defies easy definition.

Hindu and Muslim symbols are to be found everywhere on the Indian landscape. They adorn buildings throughout the country. Even national treasures, like the Taj Mahal, are representative of Islam. The Muktesvara Temple in Bhubaneswar, Odisha, the Sri Ranganathaswamy Temple in Srirangam, Tamil Nadu, the Harmandir Sahib in Amritsar, Punjab, or the Great Stupa of Sanchi in Madhya Pradesh are all religious, historical, and national landmarks. Does their existence violate the separation of 'Church and State'? Does the wearing of a *hijab*, *pagri* or a *tilaka* in Parliament or the courts create confusion? Is it not more important that everyone lives in an intelligent, thoughtful, historically-literate society which is capable of recognizing the difference between the promotion of religion and religion itself as an institution? Recognizing what is or is not a religion is not the same as promoting it.

* * *

Canada has resolved this problem by the institutional acceptance of a policy built on doctrine, parliamentary statutes, and cultimating in the *Charter of Rights and Freedoms*. The *Charter* is a bill of rights entrenched in the Constitution of Canada and guarantees certain political and civil rights for everyone. It is designed to unify Canadians around a set of principles that embody those rights and the defense and interpretation of those rights have become the bedrock of Canadian society. Among the fundamental freedoms protected by the *Charter* are freedom of conscience, freedom of religion, freedom of thought, freedom of belief, and freedom of expression, among others. The protection of these fundamental rights and their enforcement has permitted religious freedom without infringing on the secular nature of the constitutional state. This, combined with a liberal policy of multiculturalism, has fostered societal peace in an otherwise divisive socio-political environment. India could learn from the Canadian experience.

* * *

India, however, is a uniquely singular place where religion cannot be easily separated from everyday life or decision-making. On any day, one need only walk down a street, dirt path, or alleyway, whether in a city or some remote village, and hear a line from the Epics being quoted as part of everyday conversation. These are not holy men, men of letters or high education. These are simple, common, everyday people. Their religion is more than a religion in the Western sense. It is an integral part of their lives, their being.

This phenomenon – quoting from the primary religious texts – is not limited to Hindus. Lines and passages from the Qur'an are also frequently part of everyday conversations among Muslims. Among the most frequent comments heard are: 'Glory to Allah', 'All praise belongs to Allah', 'Allah is the Greatest', 'Peace be on you and the mercy and blessings of Allah', 'As Allah wills'.

Should such statements or quotations be prohibited because the people of India live in a secular state? If they were abolished, India would not be the rich cultural tapestry it is and should remain. The profession of one's faith, by word, deed, or appearance, according to the concept of *laïcité* is simply a private matter and should not be governed or controlled by government, except to protect the individual's right to practice his or her religious beliefs.

While religion is not or should not be the subject of government in a secular or *laïcité* state, it does in fact have an impact on the lives of the people who practice religion. We must remember that secularism is a Western concept that grew out of the Enlightenment. According to the anthropologist, Talal Asad, European secularism presupposes a specific post-Reformation concept of 'religion' and a very specific post-Enlightenment concept of 'the state', as well as a notion of secular citizenship that owes much to the notion of individual agency developed in Protestant theology. 'The secular,' he argues, 'is a concept that brings together certain behaviors, knowledges, and sensibilities in modern life.'[40]

European secularism and religion are defined primarily based on the beliefs of its adherents. Likewise, the secular 'state' is understood to be the modern nation state operating on capitalistic principles. Out of the European concept of religion and state the concept of citizenship emerges. Secular citizenship was supposed to rise above individual identities that, heretofore, have been predicated on class, gender, and religion. Secular citizens were conceived to be individuals unencumbered by ties to any other social groups and who are responsible for the consequences of their own actions. This concept of agency is absolutely crucial to the successful functioning of democratic government and the capitalist market, and is itself the product of Protestant theology. In the religious context, independent, self-motivating individuals are responsible before God; in their role as citizens of a liberal secular state, they are individually responsible before the law.[41]

With secularism as a political doctrine intimately tied to the uniquely European forms of religion, politics, and economics, it would seem difficult to find it applicable in non-Western settings or cultures that do not share similar types of historical influence or development. This is particularly true within non-Western states that are rooted in religious orthopraxy, or correct religious practices.[42] These types of practices are especially important to Muslims and segments of the Hindu faith, and make it difficult for the followers of such faiths to integrate themselves into larger 'secular' societies. Ultra-orthodox religious sects have always found it difficult to participate or exist in otherwise secular states, whether they be Jewish, Muslim, or Hindu.

These secular states find it easier to recognize one's ethnicity or cultural origin than to recognize the people's need to be incorporated into their religious communities, which is based more on patterns of obedience than citizenship. This is particularly true for Muslims immigrating to Western Europe and North America. In most Western societies, special privileges and religious practices are abolished and as a consequence, orthopraxic practices conflict with this hard-won socio-political principles. The survival of secular states, then, is predicated on the assimilation or incorporation of all its citizenry into a functioning, orthodox system of social beliefs. However, the Western concept of political correctness and the recognition of individual rights and freedoms now finds itself simultaneously in conflict with and allied to the practitioners of orthopraxic religions; and ultimately, this could undermine democracy itself in the West and elsewhere, as we know it.

* * *

Developmental economists are very careful in even suggesting religion plays a role in development, economic variables and processes. However, turning a blind eye to its importance is equally short-sighted. Religion affects society and demography in very important sociological and psychological ways since religion is frequently the primary source of a society's most basic beliefs, norms, values, morals, and culture.[43] Max Weber argued that Hinduism was 'other-worldly' or 'world-rejecting' advocating escape from and not mastery over the material world.[44] The problem with Weber's analysis stems from the fact that unlike most mainstream religions like Christianity, Hinduism lacks a hard and fast set of core principles but, at the same time, its influences are capable of shaping social behaviour. Of particular importance is Hinduism's emphasis on ritual law and performance of rituals.

While the West takes pride in its separation of 'Church and State', the role of religion is no less evident or profound in 'the secular West'. The rise of the concept of progress and the need for development were incorporated into the philosophy of the West through the agency of the Catholic Church. In the medieval period, it was the Church that encouraged the clearing of the forests of Europe, under the pretense that it was part of Man's duty to 'finish the Creation'.[45]

Wonsub Eum suggests that having different religions within a society may serve to 'disturb' economic growth.[46] On the face of it, with the persistence of religious violence throughout India, between Muslims and Hindus, Eum's thesis bears consideration; however, within the context of Mithila, the divisions causing much of Bihar's political problems and violence are due more to the politicization of caste and caste dynamics than religious differences. Surprisingly, the contentiousness of Muslim-Hindu relations in Mithila is comparatively unimportant. There is more enmity between castes than religions.

Robert Barro and Rachel McCleary studied the effects of religiosity on economic development, finding that one's preoccupation with religion and religious activities tends to reduce economic growth.[47] Using Barro and McCleary's finding as a basis, we can extrapolate that the higher the daily commitment made to religious activity, as a substitute for 'church attendance', one would expect lower levels of economic development.

Among the Maithil Brahmanas, the strict observance of daily ceremonial activities, responsibilities and obligations can be quite easily seen as the equivalent of Barro and McCleary's 'religiosity' variable, and this commitment to religious orthodoxy and orthopraxy has had an effect on overall economic development. Further, the demand of daily religious ceremonies and sacrifices tends to depress growth because it signifies an increased use of both economic resources and time by the religious sector. The use of these resources for religious purposes makes them unavailable for other economic activities.

Viewed alternatively, for the Maithil Brahmanas, the continued commitment to the strict observance of Vedic sacrifices and ceremony might also serve to increase one's 'social capital' within the community. In other words, religious orthodoxy for the Maithil Brahmanas increases their stature and influence within the community. Their strict religious behaviour, then, serves as an example for others to emulate. Likewise, their orthopraxic observance of Vedic rites further enhances their religious authority and legitimacy within the Brahmin community. Cumulatively, orthodoxy, while raising social capital, results in the diminishment of real world capital through the diversion of tangible resources for religious purposes but possibly more importantly, it reduces one's 'productive' time.

'ASABIYYA

'Asabiyya is an Arabic term that refers to a form of social solidarity with an emphasis on unity, a group consciousness and sense of shared purpose – a form of social cohesion. It was a well understood term within the Arab community even before the advent of Islam. The resurrection of *'Asabiyya* in modern social research stems from the fact that Ibn Khaldun, writing in 1377, was able to describe a process that was concise, explanatory and universal.[48] While later paradigms became more fashionable, *'Asabiyya* never lost its legitimacy, only its popularity.

In the *Muqaddimah*, literally the introduction to Ibn Khaldun's monumental opus, a premodern Islamic history of the world, he begins by saying:

> It should be known that history, in matter of fact, is information about human social organization, which itself is identical with world civilization. It deals with such conditions affecting the nature of civilization as, for instance, savagery and sociability, group feelings, and the different ways by which one group of human beings achieves superiority over another. It deals with royal authority and the dynasties that result (in this manner) and with the various ranks that exist within them. (It further deals) with the different kinds of gainful occupations and ways of making a living, with the sciences and crafts that human beings pursue as part of their activities and efforts, and with all the other institutions that originate in civilization through its very nature. . . .
>
> (The subject) is in a way an independent science. (This science) has its own peculiar object, that is, human civilization and social organization. It also has its own peculiar problems, that is, explaining the conditions that attach themselves to the essence of civilization, one after the other. Thus, the situation is the same with this science as it is with any other science, whether it be a conventional or an intellectual one.[49]

Ibn Khaldun's exposition was clearly ahead of its time. His approach to history and his assessment of the historical processes that propelled human organization and civilization were prophetic; it anticipated the yet-to-be-evolved science that one science fiction writer called psychohistory.[50] A contemporary writer, reflecting on Ibn Khaldun's masterpiece suggests ' . . . Ibn Khaldun was setting himself up to be the Hari Seldon of medieval Islam. And he did a pretty good job!'[51]

Other modern thinkers and academics believe that the *Muqaddimah,* the source of Ibn Khaldun's concept of *'Asabiyya,* is the first work dealing with the philosophy of history or equal parts of modern sociology, demography, historiography, cultural history, and economics.[52]

* * *

Ibn Khaldun describes *'Asabiyya* as the fundamental bond of human society and the basic motive force of history, a spirit of kinship within a tribe or family, or as Franz Rosenthal interprets it, a 'group feeling' wherein religion plays a crucial role in binding the members of the group together.[53] Nevertheless, Muhammad condemned *'Asabiyya* as being contrary to the spirit of Islam.

In the modern period, the term is generally analogous to solidarity. However, the term is often perceived negatively because it has been used frequently to suggest loyalty to one's group regardless of the circumstances.[54] One writer suggests that *'Asabiyya* means supporting one's group or people, whether they are right, wrong, the oppressors or the oppressed.[55] It is the support of the group rather than the faith of Islam that Muhammad found offensive and pernicious, since group loyalties tend to create hierarchies, when all Muslims were deemed equal, at least in the eyes of Allah.

The cohesiveness of *'Asabiyya* is spontaneous, especially in small groupings like tribes, and can be intensified or solidified by religious ideology or orthodoxy. The stronger the orthodoxy and orthopraxy, the stronger the group's cohesiveness, which permits the small social group to expand territorially, carrying with it the same fervour or commitment contained within the smaller social unit, until it can expand no more. The limit of expansion is determined by the strength of the orthodoxy, and the psychological, sociological, economic, and political integrity of the group's core beliefs and principles. At its territorial limit, the group either wilts and is taken over, or it remains resistant but can expand no further.

Such is the case of the Maithil Brahmanas and their supporting religious, social, political, and economic universe. It is the Maithil Brahmanas' spiritual and philosophical orthodoxy and dedication to *karmakanda*, *śrúti*, and *smriti* that separates them, and their retinue, from those following less demanding ritualistic Hindu traditions.[56]

THE GOSSAMER THREADS IN A NUTSHELL

Morris' theorem – lazy, greedy, frightened people look for easier, more profitable, and safer ways to do things – is nowhere more applicable than in northern Bihar. The modern-day landlords, formerly known as zamindars, have sought to retain centuries old control of their lands. At one time, it was achieved through *sanads*. *Sanads* were superseded by British law and property rights, stemming from the Permanent Settlement of 1793. When their property rights came under attack by the government of independent India, these former zamindars, property owners, sought refuge and power in the form of political involvement, occupying many of the positions of power within Bihar's system of government, both at the state and national levels. Their direct involvement in the state political system evaporated as the Congress party collapsed, the BC and OBC, who had been politicized in the 1990s, assumed political control in Bihar. These former zamindars further retreated to the safety of their rural estates. From the safety of their estates, through the economic and social control that obtained from land ownership, they continue to influence the politics of the state in the form of a 'shadow government'; as political powerbrokers, not having to endure the day-to-day tribulations that come from the occupation of ministerial seats. Patronage insures their prominence, and they thus avoid the vitriolic assaults that stem from occupying high-profile ministerial positions.

All the while, they avoid or obstruct all legislation that would jeopardize their landholdings and their ancestral source of economic power. While modern 'secular' India continues to search for social and political legitimacy over a caste- and class-riven nation, the zamindars of Bihar have perfected a social and economic system of domination, one not so very different from the feudal system that existed well before the British arrival in India. Although less able to control the voting habits of their tenants, sharecroppers, and labourers as in times past, remnants of the old jajmani system – one based on economic dependency – continue to operate as the mechanism of economic control. By controlling who has access to land and work, these zamindars control the countryside. For the peasantry, clinging to the last bit of dignity that they can muster, they work the fields and pay their rents. To press too hard for change would mean a form of social and economic suicide, and without access to land or wage labour, there is only one alternative. Life might be difficult under the zamindars, but life is better than the alternative for poorly educated, skilless manual labourers in the outside world.

While land alone could serve as the means of their domination, at least in northern Bihar and Mithila, these modern-day zamindars exploit their unique advantage stemming from a historical permutation where Brahmins became the primary landowners and hereditary rulers from the thirteenth and fourteenth centuries onward. Through a fluke of history, the Brahmins of Mithila replaced the Kshatriyas and Rajputs as the primary landowning and ruling class/caste, culminating in the establishment of the Darbhanga Raj.

Social, economic, and political control were further reinforced by the position the Maithil Brahmanas held in the system of caste hierarchies. Their ritual superiority, combined with practical land politics and traditional systems of authority, set the social and economic tone for the people of Mithila. Thus, the power and influence of the landowners of Northern Bihar was constructed on a long history of religious, social, and economic ties that either undermined or served to sabotage all efforts to effect Western-styled socio-economic development. The zamindars were able to avoid the pressure to change by adapting but these adaptations were always built upon and driven by centuries old ties and obligations. The zamindars have effectively fulfilled Morris' theorem.[57] By nature, they were lazy, greedy and frightened, and through the manipulation of traditional religious, social, and economic systems, they have made their lives easier, more profitable, and safer.

Had they, as a group, become fragmented by bitter rivalries, they might well have succumbed to the pressures of modern governance. However, the Rajputs, Bhumihars, and Maithil Brahmanas have stood together, not allowing differences in caste to factionalize them. Land and landownership served as their primary, common bond, and this was sufficient to weather the political storms resulting from the mobilization and politicization of the tenant, sharecropper, and labourer castes, the BC and OBC, that were so effectively exploited by Lalu Prasad Yadav in the 1990s and into the twenty-first century. Land and control was reinforced through that almost intangible adhesive Ibn Khaldun called *'Asabiyya.*

* * *

While social inertia is the outward manifestation of choices by the people of Mithila, it is the product of the Maithil Brahmanas' acceptance, perpetuation, and commitment to orthodox Vedic religious, social, and economic patterns of behaviour. It is their *'Asabiyya,* their cohesiveness that has withstood the relentless onslaughts of modernity. The persistence of the Maithil Brahmanas' caste consciousness and influence obtains from their ability to resist the lure of modern institutions. As a consequence, economic growth and social development have been routinely rejected by both the Brahmanas and those reliant upon them. There exists within the Brahmanas a solidarity of purpose that extends out and is felt by all those who see themselves as beneficiaries. As landlords (zamindars), the Brahmanas possess undisputed social and economic status; and tradition serves to reinforce their position within the rural economy and political hierarchy. Likewise, tradition, much like caste itself, provides a certain amount of security and it is the security of the known and the fear of the unknown that serves to perpetuate the Brahmanas' socio-economic control over Mithila.

From the outside, Mithila appears to be largely backward but alternately, viewed by the Brahmanas and their dependents, social inertia provides social and economic benefits – security. It is this sense of unchanging security that may well be exactly what Rist had in mind when he spoke of 'happy poverty'.

The current economic state of Mithila superficially reflects a society whose social development might appear to have failed when, in reality, it continues to serve the leaders' needs admirably. The social leadership finds sanctuary in its ability to stop further development. This is their solution to an overwhelmingly hostile or confrontational socio-economic landscape; one in which they could be swallowed up if they did not defend themselves in the only way that, for them, is most effective – control. They have psychologically retreated into the past, taking much of Bihar with them, refusing to be pulled into the future. It has been stated that the Indian outlook is generally more historical than ideological. This observation is no more evident than in Mithila and especially so among the Maithil Brahmanas. They cultivate the past in order to persevere and manage the present, using all the symbols of power and control available to them. Men of all times have been influenced as much by beliefs as by facts; and beliefs are frequently deemed more profound and powerful than facts. It is beliefs and traditions that the people of Mithila have placed above fact and development.

* * *

Development, at least as viewed by Westerners, means progress, to move toward increased material affluence. In the West, this is the goal of life. It is not, however, necessarily the goal in all societies. If one has all that one needs, or if a society's leaders can convince their followers that what they have is all they need (in this life) why pursue more? This difference is possibly the root of much of the West's problems – wanting more than is required: more money, more power, more things, more recognition.

Mithila has simply rejected development or progress. Its resistance reflects choices that are simply at odds with those of the agents of change. It is neither necessarily dysfunctional nor irrational. It is a tenable alternate survival strategy. It is a defence mechanism that provides frightened people with an acceptable balance between being satisfied, working as little as possible, and being safe.[58] It is a sociological response to change (history) within a unique geographic environment; and it is the interplay of society and history, within this unique setting, that has resulted in the persistence of district-level backwardness in Mithila.

Resistance to change *must* be considered to be a rational response under certain circumstances, especially if the change being offered is deemed to be threatening. There is a certain metaphysics, an inner logic or underlying design to socio-economic resistance and social inertia. At least for the Maithil Brahmanas, it has served to keep them in a position of power for nearly 600 years.

Progress or development is an integrated process with multiple interconnections and influences. It is not a simple linear process but it almost always is equated with materialism where the physical world is the only one worth acknowledging. This is not India and it is not Mithila.

The objective of progress, and therefore change, is to accomplish something better, more quickly, more efficiently, more thoroughly, or more cheaply. Again, this is not India; or at least it is not rural India.

Is change always progress? Not according to H.L. Mencken; but progress requires change and it is change that the Maithil Brahmanas seek to avoid, for social, political, or economic change would alter their culture and power.[59] Progress has many dimensions. Progress generally involves the extension of freedom, longer lives, better education and literacy, health, and the command over resources. The Maithil Brahmanas want to maintain the *status quo*, where they retain their control over their lands and maintain their cultural, social, political, and economic monopoly, even if this means denying others more freedom, longer lives, better education and literacy, health, and access to resources. To date that strategy has proven successful. Whether it will continue remains to be seen. The power and lure of progress, even if it is a Western conception, is powerful and addictive.

In Bihar we have seen much change but without progress. Many of the changes we have witnessed in Bihar and Mithila have had negative impacts – unorganized social and political mobilizations, social stratifications, caste divisiveness, corruption, malgovernance, criminality, economic and moral destitution, poverty, the breakdown of infrastructure, and the erosion of the people's will and ability to cope. Will Nitish Kumar's programme of development and law be sufficient to carry Bihar through to a new stage in its development? Only time will tell.

As for development in Mithila, little will change as long as the will of the Maithil Brahmanas continues to predominate. Progress means change and it is change that the Brahmanas must resist if they are to remain in their current position of power. Their social authority comes from their orthodoxy and orthopraxy and Brahmin status. Their economic power and authority is derived from their ownership of land. Together, social and economic power insures their survival.

NOTES

1. Gilbert Rist, 'Development as a Buzzword', *Development in Practice,* vol. 17, nos. 4-5, August 2007, p. 485.
2. President Harry S. Truman proposed an international development assistance programme in his 1949 inaugural address. The 1950 Point Four Programme focused on two goals: creating markets for the United States by reducing poverty and increasing production in developing countries, and diminishing the threat of communism by helping countries prosper under capitalism. From 1952 to 1961, programmes supporting technical assistance and capital projects continued as the primary form of US aid, and were recognized as a key component of US foreign policy. On 4 September 1961, Congress passed the Foreign Assistance Act which mandated the creation of an agency to promote long-term assistance for economic and social development – the US Agency for International Development (USAID).
3. In July 2011 the UN General Assembly passed a historic resolution. It invited all member nations to measure the happiness of their people and to use this to help guide their public policies. The first 'Happiness Report' appeared in 2012, J.F. Helliwell, R. Layard and J. Sachs (eds.), *World Happiness Report,* New York: Earth Institute, Columbia University, 2012. The second instalment appeared in September 2013, John Helliwell, Richard Layard and Jeffrey Sachs (eds.), *World Happiness Report, 2013,* New York: UN Sustainable Development Solutions Network, 2013. The three main life evaluations are the Cantril ladder of life, life satisfaction, and happiness with life as a whole. Together, these three types of reports constitute the primary measures of subjective well-being. See, E. Diener, J.F. Helliwell and D. Kahneman, *International Differences in Well-being,* Oxford: Oxford University Press, 2010 for discussion of the concept of 'well-being'.
4. For many, suicide bombers represent a form of lunacy but that implies the 'us' and 'them' construction so often used in the West, and releases us from the need to understand what is obviously a complex process. Possibly more accurate is to see suicide bombers as an outgrowth of certain societies' world views, rules, and rituals. Once a society settles on a set of values and accepted ways of obtaining them, society's members are compelled to follow certain paths. Within this context, suicide bombers, especially religiously motivated, represent true believers that are simply following a long tradition of socially-sanctioned brutal rituals; and one of the strongest motivations is revenge for

real or imagined personal loss. Further, research has shown that the group dynamic can and often does override the individual's own, personal, 'normal', psychological disposition. This phenomenon, alone, explains why there is virtually no recorded case of a suicide bomber acting alone. Suicide bombers may kill themselves and their targets as individual bomb carriers but, generally they first need to be recruited, guided, and indoctrinated to the point where they develop a brotherhood mentality toward one another, encouraged by a common cause and sense of loyalty. Equally important is the glamorization of martyrdom, especially as a mechanism for the achievement of rewards in the afterlife. Combined, these factors represent a fairly intoxicating environment and undermines the individual's personal survival instincts. One is dying for a higher cause.

5. Gilbert Rist, *The History of Development: From Western Origins to Global Faith,* 3rd edn., 2nd Impression, tr. Patrick Camiller, London: Zed Books, 2010, p. 1.
6. Walter Rostow, *The Stages of Economic Growth*, London: Cambridge University Press, 1960.
7. Robert Redfield, 'The Folk Society', *American Journal of Sociology*, vol. 52, no. 4, 1947, pp. 282-308. Redfield was drawing upon A.A. Goldenweiser, *Early Civilization*, New York, Alfred A. Knopf, 1922, pp. 117-18.
8. Nick Stein, 'Development – A Fight Between Modernity and Traditionalism?', 25 February 2013, http://www.hiidunia.com/2013/02/development-a-fight-between-modernity-and-traditionalism/, p. 6.
9. See, Daron Acemoglu and James Robinson, *Economic Backwardness in Political Perspective,* Cambridge: National Bureau of Economic Research, NBER Working Paper No. 8831, December 2002, p. 2.
10. Tom Brass, 'The Politics of Gender, Nature and Nation in the Discourse of the New Farmers' Movement', in *New Farmers' Movement in India*, London: Frank Cass & Co., 1995 pp. 27-71; and Subir Sinha, Shubhra Gururani, Brian Greenberg, 'The "New Traditionalist" Discourse of Indian Environmentalism', *Journal of Peasant Studies*, vol. 24, no. 3, 1997, p. 89.
11. Immediately, the Russian, Chinese, and Cuban revolutions spring to mind as examples of potentially bad revolutions, while the American and Mexican revolutions seem to have been 'good' revolutions. The real key to the success of a revolution lies in the degree to which institutions have been carried over and whether or not the general population is successfully stabilized and is hopeful about the future. Long-term anarchy and retribution are not signs of successful revolutions.
12. Ibid., p. 137.
13. United Nations General Assembly, *Report 42/187 of the World Commission on Environment and Development,* Transmitted to the General Assembly as an Annex to Document A/42/427 - Development and International Co-operation: Environment, New York: United Nations, 1987.

14. Wolfgang Sachs, *The Development Dictionary: A Guide to Knowledge as Power,* London: Zed Books, 1992, p. 1.
15. Andrea Cornwall, 'Buzzwords and Fuzzwords: Deconstructing Development Discourse', *Development in Practice,* vol. 17, nos. 4-5, August 2007, quoting Rist, pp. 473-4.
16. Ibid., p. 474.
17. William Easterly, *The White Man's Burden: Why the West's Efforts to Aid the Rest Have Done so Much Ill and so Little Good,* New York: Penguin Press, 2006, p. 4.
18. Cf., Peter Boone and the National Bureau of Economic Research, *Politics and the Effectiveness of Foreign Aid,* Cambridge: National Bureau of Economic Research, Working Paper No. 5308, 1995; J. Svensson, 'Aid, Growth and Democracy', *Economics and Politics,* vol. 11, no. 3, 1999, pp. 275-97; J. Svensson, 'Foreign Aid and Rent-seeking', *Journal of International Economics,* vol. 51, no. 2, 2000, pp. 437-61; S. Knack, 'Aid Dependence and the Quality of Governance: Cross-country Empirical Tests', *Southern Economic Journal,* vol. 68, no. 2, 2001, pp. 310-29; H.J. Brumm, 'Aid, Policies, and Growth: Bauer was Right', *Cato Journal,* vol. 23, no. 2, 2003, pp. 167-74; T. Ovaska, 'The Failure of Development Aid', *Cato Journal,* vol. 23, no. 2, 2003, pp. 174-88; William R. Easterly, R. Levine and D. Roodman et al., *New Data, New Doubts: A Comment on Burnside and Dollar's Aid, Policies, and Growth,* National Bureau of Economic Research, Working Paper No. 9846, 2003; S. Djankov, J.G. Montalvo and M. Reynal-Querol, 'Does Foreign Aid Help?' *Cato Journal,* vol. 26, no. 1, 2006, pp. 1-28; William Easterly, *The White Man's Burden: Why the West's Efforts to Aid the Rest Have Done so Much Ill and so Little Good,* 2006; Benjamin Powell and M.E. Ryan, 'Does Development Aid Lead to Economic Freedom?' *Journal of Private Enterprise,* vol. 22, no. 1, Fall 2006, pp. 1-21; Claudia R. Williamson, 'Foreign Aid and Human Development: The Impact of Foreign Aid to the Health Sector', *Southern Economic Journal,* vol. 75, no. 1, 2008, pp. 188-207; and Claudia R. Williamson, 'Exploring the Failure of Foreign Aid: The Role of Incentives and Information', *Review of Austrian Economics,* vol. 23, no. 1, March 2010, pp. 17-33.
19. Peter T. Leeson, 'Escaping Poverty: Foreign Aid, Private Property, and Economic Development', *Journal of Private Enterprise,* vol. 23, no. 2, 2008, p. 48.
20. Theodore Dalrymple, 'India is Heading for Mars: It Doesn't Need British Aid Money to Pay the Bills', 16 August 2012, http://www.telegraph.co.uk/news/worldnews/asia/india/9480279/India-is-heading-for-Mars-it-doesnt-need-British-aid-money-to-pay-the-bills.html.
21. A.L. Basham, *The Wonder That Was India,* 8th printing, New York: Grove Press, 1959, p. 45.

22. Gandhi launched two Satyagrahas between 1917 and 1918, the first was in West Champaran but the term 'Satyagraha' was not officially applied to this agitation until later but its principles and strategies were the foundation of the Champaran campaign.
23. Press Trust of India, 'Bihar a Byword for Worst of India', *The Economist,* 25 February 2004, http://www.expressindia.com/news/fullstory.php?newsid=28789.
24. Zoaib, 'Breaking Free: How Nitish Kumar Turned Bihar into a Model of Indian Reform', 18 May 2012, http://www.siasat.pk/forum/showthread.php?112370-Nitish-Kumar-The-Chief-Minister-who-changed-Bihar.
25. Dan Morrison, 'The Dark Side of India's "Mr. Clean"', *Al Jazeera,* August 2012, http://www.aljazeera.com/indepth/opinion/2012/08/2012869281872518.
26. Ibid.
27. Mentioned or enumerated in each of the five 'backward district' studies consulted.
28. Jammu and Kashmir were generally excluded from each of the studies for political reasons. It is assumed that most of these districts would have been included if enumerated.
29. Abhijit Banerjee and Lakshmi Iyer, 'History, Institutions, and Economic Performance: The Legacy of Colonial Land Tenure Systems in India', *The American Economic Review,* vol. 95, no. 4, 2005, pp. 1190-1213.
30. Carolyn Brown Heinz, 'Bihar: Caste, Class, and Violence', in *The Modern Anthropology of India: Ethnography, Themes and Theory,* ed. Peter Berger and Frank Heidemann, New York: Routledge, 2013, pp. 29-45, esp. p. 33.
31. With the UN's push to add 'happiness' as a variable in well-being evaluations, who knows, may be the Government of India will focus more on making its people happy than being developed.
32. Ian Morris, *Why the West Rules for Now: The Patterns of History and What They Reveal about the Future,* London: Profile Books, 2010, p. 24.
33. Ibid., p. 28.
34. World Bank, *Bihar – Towards a Development Strategy,* Washington, DC: World Bank, 2006, p. 2 of Executive Summary.
35. G. Watson, 'Resistance to Change', in D.G.W. Warner Burke, *Organization Change: A Comprehensive Reader,* San Francisco: Jossey-Bass/John Wiley & Sons, 2009, pp. 364-76.
36. See, Jeffrey D. Ford, Laurie W. Ford and Angelo D'Amelio, 'Resistance to Change: The Rest of the Story', *Academy of Management Review,* vol. 33, no. 2, 2008, p. 362
37. See, J. Svensson, 'Foreign Aid and Rent-seeking', 2000, pp. 437-61; Karl E. Weick, *Sensemaking in Organizations,* Thousand Oaks: Foundations for Organizational Science, Sage, 1995; Karl E. Weick, *The Social Psychology of*

Organizing, 2nd edn., New York: McGraw-Hill, 1979; and Peter L. Berger and Thomas Luckmann, *The Social Construction of Reality: A Treatise in the Sociology of Knowledge*, Garden City: Doubleday, 1966.

38. See, Jean Drèze and Haris Gazdar, 'Uttar Pradesh: The Burden of Inertia', in Jean Drèze and Amartya Sen (eds.), *Studies in Development Economics – Indian Development: Selected Regional Perspectives*, Delhi: Oxford University Press, 1997; Jean Drèze, and Amartya Sen, *India: Development and Participation,* New York: Oxford University Press, 1995a; and Jean Drèze and Amartya Sen, *India: Economic Development and Social Opportunity,* Delhi: Oxford University Press, 1995b.
39. Thomas S. Kuhn, *The Structure of Scientific Revolutions,* 50th anniversary edition, 2012, Chicago: University of Chicago Press, 1962.
40. Talal Asad, *Formations of the Secular: Christianity, Islam, Modernity,* Palo Alto: Stanford University Press, 2003, p. 25.
41. Ibid.
42. Orthopraxy focuses primarily on the idea of correct practice rather than correct belief, which distinguishes it from orthodoxy.
43. Laurence R. Iannacone, 'Introduction to Economics of Religion', *Journal of Economic Literature*, vol. 36, no. 3, September 1998, pp. 1465-95.
44. See, Detlef Kantowsky, *Recent Research on Max Weber's Studies of Hinduism: Papers Submitted to a Conference Held in New Delhi, 1-3.3, 1984,* München: Weltforum Verlag, 1986, pp. 86-8; and Maya Warrier, *Hindu Shelves in a Modern World: Guru Faith in the Mata Amritanandamayi Mission,* London: Routledge Curzon, 2004, p. 16.
45. See the discussion in J. Albert Rorabacher, 'Geo-Historical Approaches to Environment: The Evolution of Environmental Thought in Western Civilization', *Journal of Geography,* vol. 72, no. 4, April 1973, pp. 31-41.
46. Wonsub Eum, *Religion and Economic Development: A Study on Religious Variables Influencing GDP Growth Over Countries,* Berkeley: University of Califorinia, 29 April 2011, p. 1. See, also, E. de Jong, *Religious Values and Economic Growth: A Review and Assessment of Recent Studies,* Nijmegen, The Netherlands: Nijmegen Center for Economics (NiCE), Working Paper 08-111, November 2008.
47. Robert J. Barro and Rachel M. McCleary, *Religion and Economic Growth,* Cambridge: National Bureau of Economic Research, Working Paper 9682, 2003's variable for determining the influence of religion of economic development was increased church attendance, p. 37 of PDF version.
48. Abd Ar Rahman bin Muhammed ibn Khaldun, *Muqaddimah,* tr. Franz Rosenthal, 1967.
49. Ibid., pp. 5 and 8.
50. Psychohistory is a fictional science in Isaac Asimov's *Foundation* universe

which combines history, sociology, etc., and mathematical statistics to make general predictions about the future behaviour of very large groups of people. Ibn Khaldun was clearly searching for or beginning to construct his own medieval Islamic version of psychohistory.

51. Paul Krugman, *Ibn Khaldun, Psychohistorian,* vol. 25, August 2013, http://krugman.blogs.nytimes.com/2013/08/25/ibn-khaldun-psychohistorian/?_r=0.
52. See, Sayyid Wahid Akhtar, 'The Islamic Concept of Knowledge', *Al-Tawhid: A Quarterly Journal of Islamic Thought and Culture,* vol. 12, no. 3, 1997; Akbar Ahmed, 'Ibn Khaldun's Understanding of Civilizations and the Dilemmas of Islam and the West Today', *Middle East Journal,* vol. 56, no. 1, January 2002, pp. 20-45; H. Mowlana, 'Information in the Arab World', *Cooperation South Journal,* 2001; Warren E. Gates, 'The Spread of Ibn Khaldun's Ideas on Climate and Culture', *Journal of the History of Ideas,* vol. 28, no. 3, July-September 1967, pp. 415-22; S.H. Alatas, 'The Autonomous, the Universal and the Future of Sociology', *Current Sociology,* vol. 54, 2006, pp. 7-23; Salahuddin Ahmed, *A Dictionary of Muslim Names,* New York: C. Hurst & Co., 1999; and Mohamad Abdalla, 'Ibn Khaldun on the Fate of Islamic Sciences after the 11th Century', *Islam & Society,* vol. 5, no. 1, Summer 2007, pp. 61-70.
53. Abd Ar Rahman bin Muhammed ibn Khaldun, *Muqaddimah,* tr. Franz Rosenthal, 1967, *passim.* Yves Lacoste, *Ibn Khaldun: The Birth of History and the Past of the Third World,* London: Verso Editions, 1984 concurs with Rosenthal's translation of 'Asabiyya as group feeling. See, also, Asyiqin Abdul Halim, Mohd Roslan Mohd Nor, Ahmad Zaki Berahim Ibrahim, and Faisal Ahmad Faisal Abdul Hamid, 'Ibn Khaldun's Theory of 'Asabiyyah and its Application in Modern Muslim Society', *Middle-East Journal of Scientific Research,* vol. 11, no. 9, 2012, p. 1234.
54. Shelagh Weir, *The Tribal Order: Politics and Law in the Mountains of Yemen,* Austin: University of Texas Press, Modern Middle East Series, no. 23, 2007, p. 191.
55. drkjke. 'Asabiyyah or Nationalism and Why Islam Prohibits it, and Pakistans Poor Condition'. 2 September 2010, http://www.siasat.pk/forum/showthread.php?35450-The-Cloak-of-Nationalism-is-the-Burial-Shroud-of-Islam.
56. *Karmakanda* – the ritualistic portion of the Samhitā segment of the Vedas, which defines and prescribes various rituals and sacrificial acts to be performed unalterably for the attainment of specific ends. *Śruti* – that body of sacred texts comprising the central canons of Hinduism and one of the three main sources of dharma. *Smriti* – refers to a specific body of Hindu religious scripture, and is a codified component of Hindu customary law, behaviour, and ritual.

57. See, Ian Morris, *Why the West Rules for Now: The Patterns of History and What They Mean About the Future,* London: Profile Books, 2010, p. 24, for his view of social development.
58. See, Ibid.; and P.C. Roy Chaudhury, *Bihar District Gazetteers: Darbhanga,* Patna: Superintendent, Secretariat Press, 1964 wrote: 'The climate . . . is responsible for the characteristic ease-loving complacent attitude and excessively talkative character of the people', p. 24. He did not call the people of Mithila 'lazy' but rather, 'ease-loving'.
59. H.L. Mencken, as quoted in 'H.L. Mencken Quotes', *Great Quotes.com,* retrieved 7 December 2014, from http://www.great-quotes.com/quotes/author/H.L./Mencken/pg/12. No original source provided.

CHAPTER 9

Postscript[1]

The 2014 Lok Sabha Elections in Bihar: What Happened and What it Means?

INTRODUCTION

Any discussion of Indian politics is fraught with certain problems and becomes almost incomprehensible for the average Western observer. The principles of an operational democracy are seldom in question; but what makes the Indian political scene appear so chaotic or incomprehensible is the extent to which the political drama is acted out and the overriding influence of religion, caste, class, and culture. This confusion stems largely from the sheer number of political parties, the number of regional parties operating within each state, the rapidity with which individuals break away from one party and

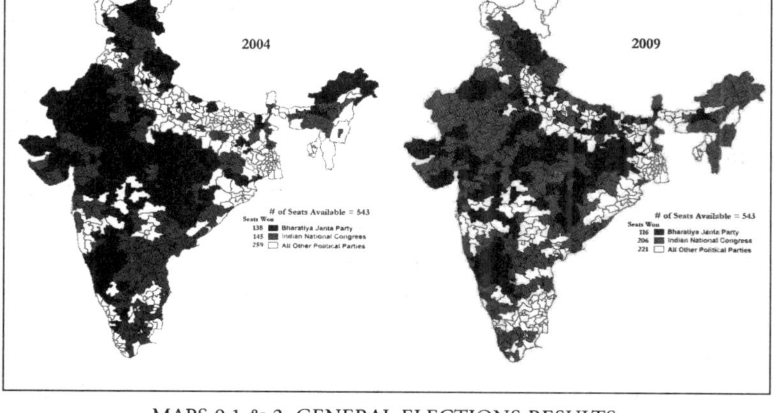

MAPS 9.1 & 2: GENERAL ELECTIONS RESULTS, 2004 AND 2009: WINNERS BY PARTY[2]

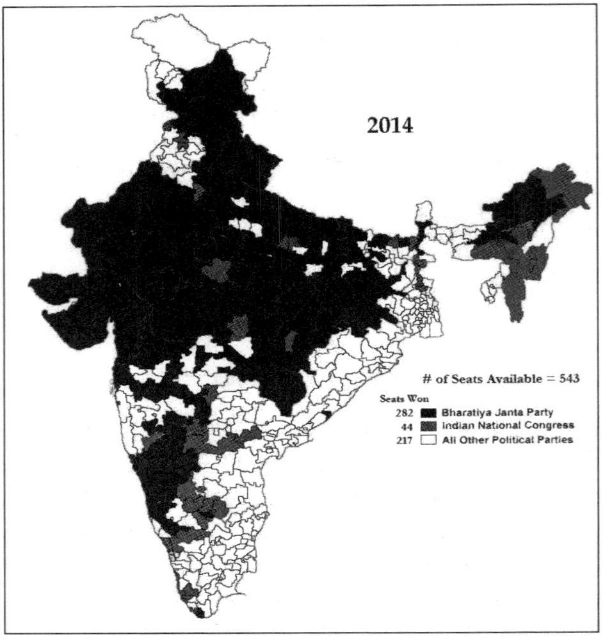

MAP 9.3: GENERAL ELECTIONS RESULTS, 2014:
WINNERS BY PARTY

join or form other parties, or the frequency with which parties form short- and long-term alliances.

In the West, in most congressional or parliamentary political systems, there are two or three major political parties, and there may be additional special interest political parties with little or no real influence. In India, as of 12 March 2014, there were 1,616 registered political parties – 6 national parties, 47 state parties, and 1,563 so-called 'unrecognized' or regional parties.[3] In Bihar, three national parties contested the latest elections and nine regional parties had candidates. Because there are so many parties and their names are often long, it is common practice to simply refer to them by their acronyms for the sake of brevity. Even the plethora of acronyms seems at times overwhelming.

Each political party is typically the product of a single politician with a different point of view. Most party leaders start out as members of other parties, then, for political or personal reasons, they break away, forming their own separate party. This process goes on, *ad infinitum*. The consequence is that the differences between many of the unrecognized, regional parties represents little more than minute nuanced differences in platform, policy, or position and, as such, most of these splinter parties are difficult to characterize, categorize, or legitimately differentiate but each has its cadre of followers.

Maps 9.1 through 3, provide a type of time-lapse image of the changing pattern of legislative constituency winners during the general elections of 2004, 2009, and 2014. From election to election, there has been an ebb and flow of party success, with one or the three major national political parties gaining here, losing there but in the most recent election, that patter of shifting allegiances changed most dramatically.

Except for the Indian National Congress (1885) and the Communist Party of India (1925), no national political party predates Independence. The other national parties – the Bharatiya Janata Party (BJP) (1980), Communist Party of India (Marxist) (1964), National Congress Party (1999), and Bahujan Samaj Party (BSP) (1984) – were all formed between the mid-1960s and late 1990s. Most of the unrecognized state, and regional political parties have been formed and reformed within the last twenty years in response to changes in the national party platforms and ideological shifts.

When observing Maps 9.1 through 3, one pattern is clearly evident. Over the last decade, the Indian National Congress (INC) has lost the support and allegiance of the Indian electorate. At one time, Congress was the premier political party and an integral part of Indian public life. From 1951 with the seating of the first Lok Sabha to the 16th Lok Sabha in 2014, the Indian National Congress party (Congress) has controlled the Lok Sabha 11 times in 16 elections, with the highest percentages of seats won between 1951 and 1984, ranging between 75.10 and 37.24 per cent. From 1989 onward, until Narendra Modi led the BJP to victory in 2014, no party approached the 'landslide' victories of Congress. Since 1984, coalitions and alliances dominated the Indian political scene (see Table 9.1).

The pre-1989 Congress party political victories can be seen, in large measure, as the country's reward for the statesmanship of

TABLE 9.1: LOK SABHA MAJORITY PARTY VICTORIES, NUMBER OF SEATS WON, 1951-2014

Year	Lok Sabha				
	Election	Seats Available	Seats Won	Majority Party	% of Seats
1951-2	1	489	364	INC	74.44
1957	2	494	371	INC	75.10
1962	3	494	261	INC	52.83
1967	4	520	283	INC	54.42
1971	5	518	352	INC	67.95
1977	6	542	295	BLD	54.43
1980	7	529	351	INC	66.35
1984	8	541	404	INC	74.68
1989	9	529	197	INC	37.24
1991	10	521	232	INC	44.53
1996	11	543	161	BJP	29.65
1998	12	543	182	BJP	33.52
1999	13	543	182	BJP	33.52
2004	14	543	145	INC	26.70
2009	15	543	206	INC	37.94
2014	16	543	282	BJP	51.93

Source: Wikipedia, from http://en.wikipedia.org/wiki/Elections_in_India, 29 December 2014.

Mahatma Gandhi and Jawaharlal Nehru in their search for independence. During this protracted political struggle, Gandhi and Nehru deftly manipulated the various vote banks available to them, often pitting one group against the other to achieve their long-term political goal – *kisans* against landowners, tenants against landless labourers, industrialists against politicians, etc. Eventually, the combustible and explosive character of the various alliances that Congress had forged began to unravel and fracture. Over time, large and small vote banks fled the umbrella-like Congress party. In the end, it was only history and tradition that inspired the party and the people's allegiance to the Gandhi-Nehru legacy. Ultimately, there was not, in and of itself, sufficient political capital to maintain the people's trust and the party succumbed to the natural processes of decay and spoilage.

Although the steady decline of Congress took more than thirty years, it has been variously attributed to the strong-arm political tactics of Indira Gandhi and the inexperienced and ineffective leadership of her sons, and later, Sonia Gandhi, the wife of Indira Gandhi's assassinated son Rajiv. Some have characterized the Congress-Gandhi system of leadership as similar to a type of kingdom where sons and daughters inherit the political throne, having begun with Jawaharlal Nehru. In large measure, Congress has lost its ability to bind together the disparate social, political, and economic components of modern Indian society. That said, the primary cause of Congress's decline has been relentless allegations of internal corruption, scandal, and economic calamities that are so often caused by a system of dynastic rule in its final throes of usefulness or legitimacy. The country has outgrown its 65-year love affair with the daughter, grandsons, in-laws, and great-grandsons of Jawaharlal Nehru. These problems and their consequences have gnawed away at the people's confidence in Congress and diminished its vote banks.

On the other hand, despite ups and downs, the BJP has become the single most dominant force in Indian politics. The reason for the BJP's success? The people of India have grown weary – weary of relentless and rampant corruption at the highest levels of government; they are tired of soaring food prices and mass unemployment; they yearn for inspired leadership and development; and they may well be rejecting Indian secularism in favour of Narendra Modi's charismatic form of Hindu nationalism (*Hindutva*).

The next few years will be pivotal for India and Modi. Drawing upon the opening lines of Dickens' classic, *A Tale of Two Cities*:

> It was the best of times, it was the worst of times, it was the age of wisdom, it was the age of foolishness, it was the epoch of belief, it was the epoch of incredulity, it was the season of Light, it was the season of Darkness, it was the spring of hope, it was the winter of despair, we had everything before us, we had nothing before us, we were all going direct to Heaven, we were all going direct the other way—in short, the period was so far like the present period, that some of its noisiest authorities insisted on its being received, for good or for evil, in the superlative degree of comparison only.

Only time will tell what kind of times Narendra Modi will bring to India.

BIHAR – THE 2014 GENERAL ELECTIONS

Bihar's recent past successes and future plans have been intimately tied to Nitish Kumar as the state's chief minister. His political successes were largely due to the downfall of Lalu Prasad Yadav and his skilful manipulation of Bihar's political milieu. Likewise, he tapped into readily available development funding from the Centre and the Asian Development Bank (ADB), which was used to underwrite much needed infrastructural construction – highways, roads, and bridges. The funds spurred Bihar's lagging economy, pushing the state's economic growth rate to unprecedented levels.

This economic development, however, went hand-in-hand with Nitish's re-establishment of the rule of law and order to end street-level crime, and police and political corruption; and, for a time the state and the nation responded to this new Bihar. The 'honeymoon' between Nitish, the people of Bihar, and the nation was short-lived, however. While street-level crime declined after decades of chaos, giving everyone the impression that the streets of Bihar had become safe, bureaucratic recalcitrance, inaction, and indifference quickly quelled the enthusiasm of potential outside investors, who were perceived to be the keystones of Bihar's long-term development plans. Nevertheless, Centre and ADB funding was sufficient to give the impression that Bihar had, somehow, turned the corner and was on its way to becoming internally a fully functioning state and a full-fledged participant within the community of Indian states.

Nitish's political successes were largely dependent upon his ties with Narendra Modi's BJP within a coalition known as the National Democratic Alliance (NDA). Modi, as the chief minister of Gujarat had set his eye on the position of prime minister, which he achieved on 26 May 2014, following the Lok Sabha elections, but this was accomplished without the assistance of Nitish.

In 2013, Nitish's economic successes in Bihar were beginning to rival those of Modi in Gujarat, and there was 'talk' of Nitish as a possible challenger for the position of prime minister. Nitish caught the attention of Nobel laureate Amartya Sen in 2010. Sen then suggested that Nitish should be considered as a tenable candidate for the nation's prime ministerial office based on his economic growth successes and secular credentials. For Sen, Modi and Nitish were on par in terms of developmental success but, for Sen, Modi's record on secularism and equality among Hindus and Muslims was unsatisfying.[4]

If Nitish wanted to become prime minister, however, it was apparent he could not do it as a member of the NDA run by Modi; nor could he legitimately seek the assistance of other parties, especially the Indian National Congress party (Congress), as long as he and his Janata Dal United Party [JD(U)] were members of the NDA. In June 2013, Nitish broke with the NDA, taking his JD(U) out of the alliance, presumably as a gesture to Congress and as a prelude to the creation of a new Congress-JD(U) alliance in Bihar.

In late 2013, however, before a formal alliance could be formed between Nitish, his JD(U), and Congress, another old player, Lalu Prasad Yadav [and his Rashtriya Janata Dal Party (RJD)], re-entered the political arena. Despite Lalu's 3 October conviction and five-year sentence for his part in the decades old 'Fodder Scam', he reappeared on the political stage in Bihar, electioneering on behalf of RJD candidates throughout the state.[5] After serving only two-and-a-half months in the Birsa Munda Central Jail, Ranchi, Lalu had been released on bail, pending the appeal of his conviction. For Lalu, however, his conviction was sufficient to result in the immediate loss of his seat in Parliament pursuant to a recent Supreme Court ruling banning convicted politicians from holding office and effectively barring him from running for re-election until and unless his conviction was later overturned.

Upon his release, Lalu said: 'I will go around the country to strengthen the secular forces, and Narendra Modi or BJP or RSS (Rashtriya Swayamsevak Sangh) will not be allowed to fulfil their dreams.'[6] While Lalu sought to derail the BJP's dominance in Bihar, he was largely unsuccessful. Thirty-one of Bihar's forty seats in the Lok Sabha were ultimately won by BJP/NDA candidates.[7] Lalu's participation in the elections only served to splinter the anti-BJP opposition. The RJD party only won four seats. Only two JD(U) candidates won in the Lok Sabha. Graph 9.1 shows the percentage of contest winners by party.

The success of the BJP was largely aided by: (a) The BJP-JD(U) alliance at one time had a strong cross-class and caste, secular following but the defection of Nitish's JD(U) only served to push more and more electors into the BJP camp. Together, the BJP and JD(U) had proclaimed good governance, law and order, and development. For an aspiring Bihari population, the BJP-JD(U) message was appealing and even more importantly, for a while, those aspirations were being met. Nitish's break with the more powerful BJP was really a breakaway move by him to get out from under the shadow of Modi and his communal policies; but he left without having a sufficiently large enough personal vote bank that he could depend on. He had believed he would continue to have the support of the Muslims and his caste members, the Kurmis. Neither was realized.

Nitish had aspired to become prime minister, believing his own propaganda and national importance as a consequence of 'his' state's economic success. He misjudged his personal popularity. Congress, sensing Nitish's lack of personal political support in Bihar, never fully extended its hand in support.

(b) Lalu misjudged the RJD's ground-level support. While local personality cults, like those that surrounded Lalu and Nitish, generated political vote banks, now, larger national issues, national aspirations concerning development, inflation, unemployment, corruption, good

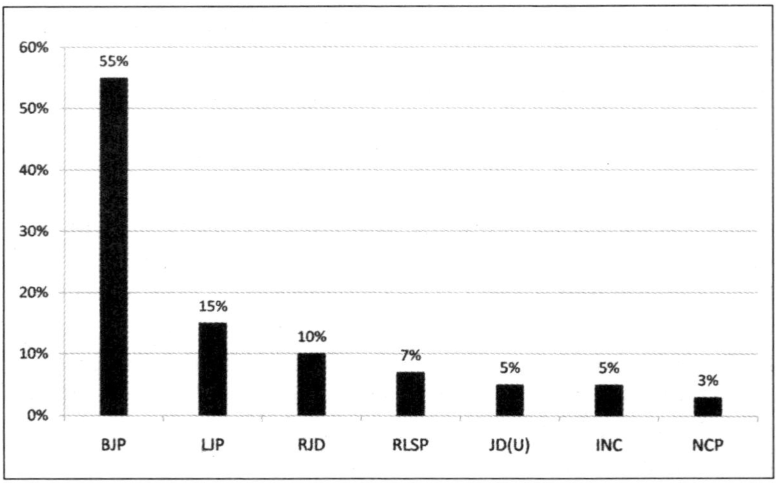

GRAPH 9.1: BIHAR 2014 GENERAL ELECTIONS RESULTS BY PARTY WINNER[8]

governance, and equality had become more important. Voters, it seems, saw support for the now-convicted Lalu as regressive and no one wanted a return to that state of anarchy or another 'Jungle Raj' in Bihar that resulted under Lalu's direct or indirect leadership.

(c) Congress, much like the JD(U) was able to secure only two seats in Bihar in the Lok Sabha election of 2014. Congress's popularity in Bihar declined precipitously in the mid- to late-1990s, having outlived its political connections with the people there. It was no longer able to placate or bind the rapidly growing class and ideological differences between Bihar's politically aware population, especially between the upper castes, the BC, and OBC. Congress, subsequently, all but collapsed in Bihar.

(d) The BJP, under the leadership of Modi, was quick to cultivate support for itself after the defection of Nitish in 2013. Modi's visits to Bihar seemed to polarize the Bihar electorate. There were those who wanted to see Modi as prime minister, and those who did not. For many of the disadvantaged in Bihar, Modi was seen as a successful kindred spirit from the ranks of the OBC, who understood the plight of the Biharis, an image Modi cultivated with finesse.

When the ballots were finally counted, Nitish became a political cipher. Although elections to the state's Assembly are scheduled in late 2015 and Nitish could have remained chief minister, he resigned his position on 17 May 2014, recognizing and accepting responsibility for his party's abysmal showing in the polls. A day later, Jitan Ram Manjhi was appointed Bihar's newest chief minister.

The question, now is, why has Nitish Kumar fallen from being an aspirant to the office of prime minister to being a *former* chief minister? The answer does not necessarily lie in what Nitish did or did not do; but what three men and a state did to one another – the state, Bihar, the men, Nitish Kumar, Lalu Prasad Yadav, and Narendra Modi.

The Players

NITISH KUMAR

At heart, Nitish is a pragmatic opportunist. His personal star did not begin to shine, however, until he left Lalu Prasad Yadav's RJD in

1994. Even after his breakaway, he again found himself eclipsed by Sharad Yadav and George Fernandes. Yadav, formerly the leader of the Janata Dal, forged a union between his faction within the JD and the Lokshakti and Samata parties, forming the JD(U) Party in 2003. Fernandes and Nitish had been the leaders of the Samata Party. The only common bond between these parties, however, was their opposition to Lalu and the RJD. The JD(U) allied with BJP and defeated the RJD-led United Progressive Alliance in Bihar in 2005. Nitish emerged from the shadows of Fernandes and Yadav, when they both lost their seats in Parliament.

On 24 November 2005 after the Assembly elections, Nitish was elected chief minister, filling the office that had been vacant following nearly eight months of President's Rule. He remained chief minister for nearly two full terms, which ended on 20 May 2014, when Jitan Ram Manjhi was sworn in as the new chief minister after Nitish's resignation.

Nitish's second term catapulted him to national prominence as a consequence of dramatic increases in the state's economic growth, good governance, the return to law and order, improved healthcare, the resurrection of Bihar's educational system, and his campaign against corruption in government. These developments prompted rising expectations among the people of Bihar and simultaneously inflated Nitish's own self-image. And it may have been these aspirations and his own sense of worth that brought his downfall.

In Indian politics, and especially in Bihar, traditionally there are two things that matter to people: (i) identity in terms of religion, caste, sub-caste, and class; and (ii) Concerns involving development and security. Nitish's downfall can be attributed to two mistakes predicated on social identities and development and security.

POLITICAL MISCALCULATIONS

Beginning with Lalu, Bihar voters began dividing themselves politically along a fault line between forward and backward classes. The forward castes – Brahmins, Bhumihars, Rajputs, and Kayasthas – deserted the Congress party and aligned themselves with the BJP. The Yadavs, Kurmis, Koeris, Other Backward Castes, and Muslims aligned with the RJD until 2005. The JD(U)-BJP alliance, under the banner of the NDA, allowed the alliance to rout the RJD giving Nitish the opportunity to become chief minister.

In June 2013, Nitish and his JD(U) broke with the BJP. In so doing, the bulk of Bihari voters realigned with the larger and more powerful national BJP. Nitish was left with only a loose coalition of Kurmis, Koeris, Muslims, and Extremely Backward Classes with comparatively little political clout.

Further, a concerted campaign by Modi characterized Nitish as having rejected the mandate of the people and branded him a 'back-stabber'. This characterization found fertile ground among many of Nitish's former supporters at all levels and among all classes, and his political vote banks virtually disappeared.

FAILED PROMISES AND EXPECTATIONS

All that Nitish had left was his claims of good governance, unprecedented economic growth, his law and order platform, and the rising expectations of the people. During his first five years as chief minister, all went well. He dragged Bihar out of a state of RJD-inspired chaos, and replaced it with safety and growth. In his second term, expectations were even higher. The people had seen what *could* be achieved. Now, they wanted more but they wanted to see the benefits of a rising GDP at the Everyman level, not just in the hands of the development and political elites. Nitish could not replicate his prior feats and the benefits of development were still not trickling down and into the hands and pockets of the Everyman.

One indicator of the public's dissatisfaction was the rise in communal unrest and violence. Whereas Bihar had not seen a single reportable communal clash in the first seven-and-a-half years of Nitish's rule, between June and December 2013, after his break with the BJP, there were 87 major and minor communal conflicts. Incidences of crime also began to rise on a monthly basis.

Development failures, the rise of corruption in government, increased crime and crime rates, failure to deliver on political and social promises all led to the fall of Nitish Kumar. It was only the casting of the votes in the 2014 general election that sounded Nitish's political death knell and it ended in a form of political suicide, the resignation of a defeated man.

Had he been willing to play 'second fiddle' to Narendra Modi, and had he remained allied with the BJP, would Nitish have found himself in the position of a defeated man on 17 May 2014? That is a question for historical revisionists. Or, just possibly, Nitish will find a way to rise from the ashes yet again. However, at present, political mismanagement and miscalculations have left him on the political sidelines but possibly holding the reins of political control through his puppet appointee, Jitan Ram Manjhi, a practice learned from Lalu.

However, recently, Manjhi seems to have found his own footing as chief minister, and is beginning to show signs that he is, in fact, his own man. A NDTV news commentary suggested that Manjhi 'is better' than his predecessor Nitish.[9] At the same time, Manjhi is on the receiving end of criticism for comments made regarding the upper castes. While speaking at a function in Bettiah, he stated: 'The upper caste people are foreigners and descendants of the Aryan race . . . they have come here from foreign countries. Only tribals and Dalits are indigenous people.'[10] This comment, whether made intentionally or extemporaneously and spontaneously, has only served to anger the upper caste constituencies within Bihar, who perceived it to be both racist and divisive. This gaffe, apparently one of several, may represent a politician who is out of his element or beginning to flounder under the pressure of the office.[11] On the face of it, Nitish's selection of Manjhi to replace him as chief minister can be seen as the appointment of someone Nitish felt he could later easily defeat or just another miscalculation on Nitish's part.

Lalu Prasad Yadav

Lalu Prasad Yadav ruled Bihar for nearly fifteen years from 1990 to 2005, first as chief minister and, later, through the agency of his wife, Rabri Devi. His RJD party repeatedly fended off Congress, the BJP, and the socialist splinter parties who attempted to dislodge him. In 2005, however, a coalition of parties, including the BJP and Nitish

Kumar's JD(U) routed both Lalu and his RJD from the Bihar Assembly, with Nitish becoming chief minister.

For the next nine years, the RJD was defeated both in the Lok Sabha and the Bihar Assembly. At least in part, Lalu was distracted from his party's day-to-day political problems as a result of his involvement in the Fodder Scam, which was coming to a head after decades of on-again, off-again prosecution by the centre and state governments.

The year 2014 was a watershed year for Lalu and his RJD. A year before the elections, Nitish and his JD(U) party severed their ties with the BJP, believing they were strong enough to 'go it alone' in Bihar, believing they had the support from segments of the upper-castes, backward castes, a sizeable share of the Dalit and Muslim vote, which comprised approximately a third of the state's electorate. Nitish was of the opinion that he had commandeered and controlled a significant share of the BJP's rank and file voters. At the same time, Lalu anticipated that the BJP-JD(U) split would make both vulnerable. Lalu believed that without a strong showing among the upper castes for the JD(U) it could not win. Likewise, without the backward castes support, Dalits, and Muslims, which the JD(U) had brought to the NDA, the BJP would find itself disadvantaged. Thus, Lalu saw the 2014 elections as a three-way race of near equals – the RJD, BJP, and JD(U). In addition, Lalu believed that his fellow Yadavs would defect to the RJD along with the Muslims. To further entice the upper castes to join the RJD, Lalu became apologetic for his nearly forty years of incessant anti-upper caste politicking and bashing, ignoring the fact that it was he who was responsible for the ouster of the upper castes from nearly every important position within the government of Bihar. The Bihar electorate had never been as vulnerable or factionalized as it was immediately prior to the 2014 elections, or that is what the political pundits would have us believe. For most outsiders, the elections would represent a political free-for-all, and it was anybody's guess who would come out on top.

The problem that Lalu faced was the people's memory of the state's government in the hands of the RJD. Few believed that Lalu was capable of providing good leadership or good governance. Everyone could recall Lalu's tenure of misrule, lawlessness, and corruption. For many, the idea of Lalu returning to power made them blanch.

In the end, Lalu's presence held little sway in the 2014 elections. The anticipated defections to the cause of the RJD never materialized and the RJD was successful in taking only four seats in the Lok Sabha. Lalu's future, much like that of Nitish, is becoming less and less relevant.

Narendra Modi

Although formed in 1980, it was nearly 20 years before the BJP became a force in Bihar politics. In 1991, the BJP did not win a single seat in what would later become residual Bihar. It did, however, win five seats in what was to become Jharkhand. In subsequent Lok Sabha and Bihar Assembly elections, the BJP fared unimpressively until 2005. Only through an alliance between the BJP and JD(U) did the BJP 'get its foot in the door' in Bihar, and together they took the Bihar Assembly and Nitish became chief minister for the first time.

The rise of the BJP in Bihar in the 2014 general elections was largely a result of the efforts of one man – Narendra Modi, the BJP's leader. Modi's leadership would possibly have not been enough had it not been for a rapidly growing anti-incumbency attitude toward Nitish Kumar and his government over unfulfilled expectations and promises, ground-level anti-Congress feelings among voters, and inconsistency and marginalization of the RJD. Inside Bihar, political workers were quick to point out that the rapid economic development that the state had experienced since 2005 – large-scale highway construction projects and development monies – was overseen by BJP ministers, not those of the JD(U).

CHANGING ALLIANCES AND VOTE BANKS IN BIHAR

Nitish's dream of a *Naya Bihar* had become 'a fiction of his fancies' according to one political correspondent.[12] Nitish's fiction included the idea that he, Nitish, had single-handedly created a new Bihari identity that encompassed all castes and creeds and development had become the people's common purpose. That idea had grown thin with the ground-level electorate, who personally had not shared in Bihar's developing economy. Nitish found himself floundering, losing legitimacy because, on his own, he had no history of winning a mandate from the people. He always relied on alliances to keep him in power. Elsewhere, development and good governance might garner votes but not in Bihar, where it was believed that the political system had yet to rise above *biradaris* (caste and creed). No one had ever won an election in Bihar without resorting to cold, calculated caste and class arithmetic.

To achieve any kind of success in Bihar, one must have a good showing among either the OBC or BC and one of the other major constituencies. The victory of the BJP alliance (accounting for 31 of 40 seats in the Lok Sabha), the poor performance of the RJD-Congress alliance (7 seats), and the dismal outcome for the JD(U) (2 seats) is remarkable and no one could have predicted the final outcome before the elections began. What had changed, or depending upon one's perspective, what had gone wrong?

Two things had changed in Bihar between 2005 and 2014. First, the aspirations of the people exceeded the seated government's ability to deliver. Rhetoric and promises of better times to come began to fall on deaf ears, as the benefits of nearly a decade of positive economic growth failed to find its way into the hands of the ground-level voters – the rural and urban poor. Second, the voters of Bihar began

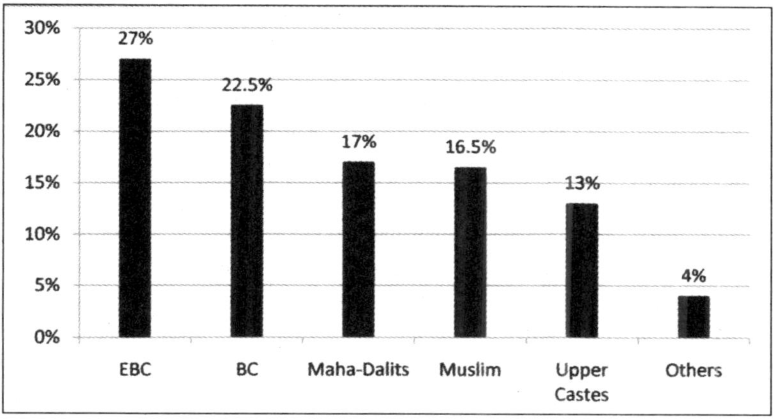

GRAPH 9.2: BIHAR, VOTER COMPOSITION, 2014, AS PER CENT OF TOTAL VOTER POPULATION[13]

looking outside the state, for possibly the first time, for change. This apparent change in the Bihari worldview could be either temporary or long-termed, and it remains unclear which until the time of the elections for the state Assembly in a little over a year 2015.

If the Assembly elections follow the pattern observed in the 2014 general elections, Biharis may well be looking beyond traditional parochial politics in their search for change. If, however, the Assembly elections are quantitatively different from the 2014 Lok Sabha elections, it could signal a return to 'politics as usual' in Bihar. The 2014 elections could also mean that the voters of Bihar are finally recognizing and becoming part of the greater Indian political system, finally differentiating between state and national political agendas, goals, and aspirations.

The BJP's alliance with the Ram Vilas Paswan-led Lok Jan Shakti Party (LJSP) and Upendra Kushwaha's Rashtriya Lok Samta Party (RLSP) represents, for the first time, the formation of a coalition between segments of the upper castes, Dalits, and sections of the OBC. This alliance would not have been possible without the leadership of Narendra Modi, a successful chief minister in Gujarat and backward caste member; and in a largely backward class and caste dominated state like Bihar, his caste credentials provided him with legitimacy and gave him a significant amount of political capital. Further, capitalizing on his humble roots, Modi had visited Bihar numerous times preaching traditional Hindu values at meetings designed to attract Dalits, backward classes and EBC, the one segment of Bihar's electorate that the BJP had not attracted during its alliance with the JD(U). It was the JD(U) and Nitish who had brought the lower class voters into the BJP-JD(U) fold in 2005.

When the final vote tally had been completed it was apparent that the BJP had reaped far more votes than had been projected by the political pundits. Graph 9.3 shows the percentage of selected castes voting for BJP candidates. Surprisingly, over three-quarters of the upper castes chose to vote for BJP candidates. Likewise, unanticipated numbers of lower OBCs and other Dalit castes voted for the BJP. Never before had Bihar voters from the upper castes and Dalits joined in support of the same candidates. Historically, these two groups were and are presumed to have insurmountable political differences. The alliance with the RLSP, however, helped consolidate a sizeable segment of the Koeris and Kurmis, two of the dominant OBC castes, who voted BJP. These two castes, in particular, had been expected to vote for the JD(U).

During Lalu's heyday, he had successfully inverted the traditional political pyramid in Bihar, cultivating the large Yadav vote and combining it with the Muslim vote. This Yadav-Muslim combination gave Lalu nearly a third of the Bihar vote bank; and within the context of Bihar's political divisiveness, one-third of the vote generally means political control in the Bihar Assembly. The BJP-JD(U) coalition in 2005, through the agency of the JD(U), brought in the Muslim vote.

Now, the question was, could Nitish, alone, control the Muslim vote. All that seemed to be necessary was to continue to use Modi as a political hate figure to consolidate the Muslim voters. If the Muslims were to defect, aligning themselves with any other party, a large segment of Nitish's political vote bank would disappear. In the end, two-thirds of the Yadavs and Muslims voted for RJD-Congress candidates. Nitish could not mobilize even his core constituencies, the Kurmis and Muslims. The Kurmis' defection stunned Nitish, a Kurmi himself. His own caste had abandoned him. The BJP had not anticipated a strong turnout from the Muslims in light of Modi's long history of anti-Muslim rhetoric, although he did attempt to reconcile with the Muslims during his visits to Bihar during pre-election electioneering.

* * *

The 2014 general elections in Bihar has had the effect of: (1) representing a type of referendum for Narendra Modi. Nitish Kumar had been an aspirant to the position of prime minister, building on his successes in Bihar. This placed him in a head-to-head contest with Modi for the office of prime minister. Believing he could defeat Modi, based on his nearly ten years as chief minister in Bihar, he elected to sever his ties with Modi's BJP approximately a year prior to the 2014 general elections. This removed him from the ever-growing shadow of Modi, who was seen as the front-runner in the national race for prime minister. Immediately, the folly of that decision became apparent. Nitish's political support, both in Bihar and elsewhere, began to crumble and the 2014 Lok Sabha elections only saw his political capital dissolve and disappear. His JD(U) candidates were only able to win two of the forty seats in the Lok Sabha. By a large margin, Modi and his BJP-alliance candidates swept the election. It was a clear-cut indication that Nitish no longer had a tenable political base even in his home state and even among his own caste. Modi was the people's preferred choice for prime minister. Modi built his reputation on the development of Gujarat and voters all over India believed he was the man to develop India.

For the first time in generations, Modi and his BJP successfully overcame Bihar's long-standing, convoluted system of caste and class politics. If the bottleneck of caste and class politics has been irretrievably broken, Bihar may, once and for all, be entering a new era of cooperation. Even if the caste/class system of politics in Bihar has not been completely redefined, at least it has been shown that cooperation, rather than obstructionism, can lead to long-term benefits for everyone.

(2) The election was also a referendum for Modi the man, in the sense that, in addition to eliminating his competition for the position of prime minister, it was a vote over his personality, secularism, and

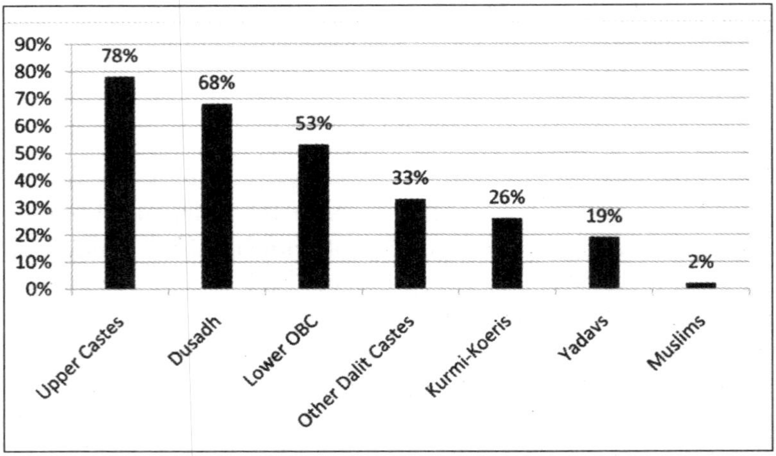

GRAPH 9.3: BJP VOTES BY CASTE, 2014 BIHAR GENERAL ELECTION[14]

communalism. To many, Modi's style is viewed as rough and tumble, not that of a statesman, an attribute many equate with the office of prime minister. His speeches, normally laced with folksy humour, over the course of the campaign, had grown increasingly harsh and laden with invective toward anyone who opposed him. This phenomenon has left a tinge of fear and discomfort among even his followers. Is it possible this is a man to be feared more than applauded? As one commentator stated: 'The line between mockery and rudeness, between affectionate jibes and healthy leg-pulling on the one hand and baldly insulting commentary on the other is a thin one. Once that line is crossed there rises a perennial wall between speaker and listener.'[15] Modi's tone often speaks louder than his words. He often comes across as unnecessarily crude and strident instead of rustically colourful. As a leader of a nation, is it possible that his demeanour belies his intent rather than his words? In a patriarchal society one yearns for a strong leader. If this is a true assessment, India will have the leader and government it needs and deserves.[16] If the assessment that India has gone 'rudderless' for a decade under Congress-led coalitions is true, where growth has fallen by half, reforms have gone undone, roads and electricity unavailable, people lack healthcare, children go uneducated, and corruption is a way of life, Modi represents a possible solution to the problems of leadership or, equally possible, much worse. Only time will tell.

Nevertheless, Modi walked into Bihar and talked about the need to rise above caste politics. He proclaimed poverty has no religion, words no Indian politician has ever used in Bihar before. He suggested that to dream of reviving Bihar's growth prospects, to talk about jobs, to tap into the people's restlessness and need to do things was not wishful thinking. He became the embodiment of the idea of change. He spoke to Biharis as equals, as citizens of a greater India.

Modi has been criticized for not stepping in to quell communal riots in Gujarat in 2002. In the minds of many political analysts, a vote for the BJP and every seat taken by the BJP was a vote for communalism. Repeatedly, Modi spoke of Hindu nationalism in the form of the ideology of Hindutva. This has only served to fan tensions between Hindus and Muslims. In India, violence between the two communities is never far from the surface. By refusing to put Muslim fears to rest, Modi, either intentionally or unintentionally, fed those fears. Sooner or later, he will have to face the realities of sectarian bloodshed or a crisis with Pakistan. At present, no one knows what he will do when faced with such monumental challenges. He is a man of action and decision but the wrong decision could well inflame long-festering communal violence. Even among his critics, those who continued to beat the drum of massacre in Gujarat in 2002, many have begun to proclaim it is time to wipe the slate clean, forget about the past, and honour the choice of the electorate.[17]

(3) Demonstrating the people's desire for change, especially the alleviation of abject poverty, urban and rural. That hope caused the people of Bihar to abandon the Congress, when it was clear that it could no longer bridge the caste and class differences that existed in the state. Lalu Prasad Yadav offered caste upliftment, but with it, came corruption, crime, low levels of economic development, becoming what is now known as the 'Jungle Raj' in Bihar, as he toppled the old political structure within the state. Nitish brought hope and the idea of good governance and economic development to Bihar. For a time, Bihar enjoyed good government and economic growth, but the widespread poverty remained largely unchanged. His failure to extend the benefits of the state's economic growth to all levels of Bihar society resulted in disenchantment with Nitish and his government.

The scale of Modi's victory casts him as an Indian strongman capable of doing things in an unprecedented fashion. Even without its allies, the BJP has enough seats in the Lok Sabha to govern on its own terms. The BJP, alone, holds 282 of 543 seats. The National Democratic Alliance commands the Lok Sabha, with 330 seats. As a consequence, the BJP need not cater to the demands of any other party. Map 9.3, depicts the extent of the BJP's win.

Although the implementation of economic programmes is dependent upon the cooperation of state legislatures, Modi's BJP victory will most likely force the states to comply with the demands of the Centre, thus forcing even recalcitrant states to participate in economic programmes that, in all likelihood, will reflect the patterns, principles, and designs that were found to be most successful in Gujarat. Likewise, other collateral and supporting programmes will be rolled out and implemented. Never before has any party other than the Congress been handed as profound a mandate as has been handed to Narendra Modi and the BJP. It is now only a matter of wait and see.

Before the elections, it was believed that within Bihar, the rural and urban poor, Muslim communities and peasants from the Other Backward Castes, were mobilising against Modi. In the past, caste and class factionalism has dominated Bihar politics. Achieving a majority in the State Assembly was always a process that represented equal amounts of skilful statesmanship, illusion, and legerdemain; and, at best, such coalitions or alliances were tenuous. Consequently, more time was often spent in maintaining the coalitions than focusing on genuine problems of good government.

For the first time, questions of land distribution, resources, the absolute necessity of meaningful democracy in people-oriented development, and not caste or class have become the focus and driving force behind Bihar's electoral process. Even so, Modi's message – one of Hindu nationalism – has alienated Muslims; and despite his own personal backward-caste origins, he has been successful in mobilizing the upper castes, which can only breed hostility toward the lower castes, thus nurturing the traditional split between the upper and lower castes and classes.

Further, it has been suggested that the defeat of Nitish and his JD(U) and Lalu Prasad Yadav's RJD in the polls has forced the two leaders to open discussions with one another for the first time in nearly two decades. It would seem, they have seen 'the writing on the wall'. These bitter political rivals, if they are to remain relevant to Bihar politics, may find it necessary to reconcile their differences and join forces if either or both men, and their parties are to survive the BJP onslaught.

Their discussions, and their tacit agreement to work together paid off in the Bihar bypolls held in August 2014. A RJD-JDU-Congress alliance won six of ten available seats in the Bihar Assembly.[18]

More recently, a meeting between Nitish Kumar, Lalu Prasad Yadav, Mulayam Singh Yadav, and others, resulted in an announcement that the 'Janata Parivar' 'could come together to form a party in the future'.[18] In the wake of many of the smaller party defeats during the 2014 elections, the meeting is seen as an attempt to revitalize parties made irrelevant by the overwheling BJP landslide. Each of these smaller parties, at one time or another, had played an important role in propping up minority governments led by BJP and Congress over the years.[19] A month later, Lalu Prasad Yadav announced that the merger of the 'Janata Parivar' parties was now a permanent alliance.[20] The occassion upon which Lalu made his announcement 'coincided' with the pre-engagement ceremony of his daughter to the Samajwadi Party chief Mulayam Singh's grand-nephew. [In many respects, the engagement and the announcement of the formation of a permanent alliance between the Janata Parivar constellation of parties very much resembles a medieval alliance of kingdoms through marriage.] Together, these smaller parties may be able to influence both state and national policies, become tenable political opponents for BJP candidates, and revitalize the political careers of Lalu Prasad Yadav and Nitish Kumar, both of whom were sidlined by either legal problems or political inadequacy during the Lok Sahba elections earlier in the year.

The BJP landslide redefined the social and political landscape of Bihar, *possibly* fusing together political factions that, in the past, have long been traditional enemies. And in so doing, a more democratic and just social and political map will emerge in Bihar. The days of the highly local, small political parties may be numbered as they find themselves permanently sidelined by the larger and more powerful national parties and alliances – a process not unlike that experienced in Western Europe and North America.

For Nitish Kumar, it is not only a question of political survival, but a matter of personalities. As long as Nitish was in an alliance with the BJP, he never allowed the Gujarat strongman to enter Bihar for political campaigning, fearing a Muslim backlash. He never shared a good personal relationship with Modi; however, under the current circumstances, the architect of the 'new Bihar' is looking for any political life preserver just to survive; and if Modi has his way, neither Nitish or Lalu will ever step foot on the political stage again.

NARENDRA MODI, PRIME MINISTER

After eight months in office, one of the most commonly heard descriptions of his tenure as prime minister is that he has taken the reins of government and is in command of the most powerful prime minister's office since Indira Gandhi. He appears to be combining the needs of modern India with deft touches of Hindutva politics, which was the basis of his platform from the very beginning. Much of his short-term success appears to be based on his decisiveness and his ability to micro-manage the government of the world's largest democracy.

He has effectively centralized all authority in his hands, much like his late predecessor, Indira Gandhi, did before her assassination in 1984. Since then, the politics of India, and its centre leadership, has suffered from indecisiveness with little strong leadership at the top; the nation often appearing almost rudderless. The downside of strong central leadership is that too much centralization '. . . can discourage ministries from taking their own initiatives', according to Prabhat Kumar, a former cabinet secretary.[21]

It has been suggested that his government is heavily influenced by the agenda of the RSS, the BJP's ideological fountainhead. As a consequence of Modi's strong-arm style of rule, it has been suggested, although undoubtedly hyperbolically, there is almost no corruption now at the top level of government.

While domestic issues remain largely topics of discussion and announcement, Modi has demonstrated greater success in the area of international diplomacy. He has strengthened India's relationship with some of its neighbours and has forged personal ties with leaders like Shinzo Abe of Japan and Tony Abott of Australia. In general, Modi has focused his diplomatic efforts on placing India squarely in the middle of the global economy debates. Likewise, ties with the US, which have been tenuous and cool for decades, seem to be thawing, with President Obama attending the Republic Day festivities in January 2015.[22]

Less success was achieved by Modi with regard to relations with Pakistan and China. The key to solving the relationship problems between India and China and Pakistan is largely one of trust. Past governments' waffling did little to strengthen ties between the countries. Modi's real test will come when he is required to move against or resist Pakistan, especially in light of his prior communal policies in Gujarat.

Nevertheless, Modi has not forgotten domestic economic issues. While the new government would like to accept credit for the recent dip in the inflation rate in India, it, undoubtedly, has more to do with the decline in prices in the global marketplace, led by declines in petroleum prices. Whatever the source, after years of price escalations for essential foodstuffs, prices are showing signs of levelling off, with the possibility of their easing.

Little or no progress has been made on the overall domestic economic front, which is to be expected. Moving the Indian national economy forward, away from low industrial output levels and exports, may take years to achieve and it is far too early to even begin to assess where Modi's model of economics will take the nation over the next few years.

One has to ask, are the people expecting too much of Narendra Modi? On the heels of his landslide victory, everyone had high expecations. Everyone wants change and they want it now. The question is, how long does it take to change a country and how do we measure it? Since his election to the office of prime minister, one cannot genuinely expect one man, one party to turn a nation of 1.3 billion into a new version of itself overnight. To even think of applying the usual metrics used to assess progress would be a grand mistake at this juncture. At this point, talk is about all that one can genuinely expect from a newly seated prime minister. If Modi is moving in the right direction, in the next year or so, we should be able to apply our regualr metrics. Until then . . .

* * *

What will the general elections results of 2014 mean for the people of Bihar? It is far too early to begin making long-term predictions but things will change. They have already changed. One of the most startling consequences of the elections is the nature of voter alliances, bringing together, for the first time, heretofore caste and class enemies. These groups put aside their traditional caste and class enmity finding, in the person of Narendra Modi, a leader who could galvanize what were believed to be completely polar political and social aspirations. People who could not even be in the same room without resulting in rancorous exchanges now are voting for the same candidates. In Bihar, this is progress. If cross-caste and -class dialogues can be maintained, the political and social face of Bihar will change forever. No one will be able to describe Bihar as socially stratified, economically backward, or politically fractured, resulting in the absence of economic equality and equity, and social disenfranchisement. How this will change the equitable distribution of future economic growth and development remains to be seen. However, simply having traditional enemies voting for the same candidates represents a promising beginning for a second *Naya Bihar*.

NOTES

1. The manuscript for this volume was largely completed in late 2012 and revised throughout 2013 and 2014. Since its completion, and especially during the latter half of 2014, the political milieu of Bihar and India has undergone a significant change. This change will or could possibly have a direct impact on Bihar's and Mithila's development. Therefore, the author felt it necessary to address some of these changes.
2. The boundaries of the Assembly and Lok Sabha constituencies have not changed since 2002. Based on the Delimitation Commission of India's most recent report, which is based on the 2001 census, the constituencies will not be changed until the first census after 2026, as per the provisions of the Delimitation Act of 2002.
3. Wikipedia, 'List of Political Parties in India', retrieved from: http://en.wikipedia.org/wiki/List_of_political_parties_in_India, 3 June 2014.
4. See, for example, *Tehelka Daily*, 'I Don't Want Modi as My PM – Amartya Sen', retrieved from: http://www.tehelka.com/i-dont-want- modi-as-my-pm-amartya-sen/, July 2013; and Lalita Panicker and Gaurav Choudhury, 'Nitish Kumar is Amaryta's Nominee for Prime Minister', retrieved from *Hindustan Times* (Kolkata), from: http://paper.hindustantimes.com/epaper/viewer.aspx, 3 May 2014.
5. The so-called 'Fodder Scam' spanned several decades prior to the case being made public in 1996. The case involved the supposed purchase of food, medicine, and livestock equipment for fictitious cattle herds in Bihar. Lalu was among more than 500 people charged in 53 separate indictments. Lalu narrowly avoided conviction on all but one – the last – indictment against him.
6. Agency PTI, 'Lalu Prasad Yadav Released from Jail', retrieved from DNA, from http://www.dnaindia.com/india/report-lalu-prasad-yadav-released-from-jail-1936089, 16 December 2013.

7. The NDA – National Democratic Alliance – is a centre right political coalition composed of the BJP, LJP, and RLSP in Bihar. BJP candidates won 22 seats, LJP candidates won 6 seats, and RLSP candidates won 3 seats for a total of 31 seats for the NDA.
8. Data obtained from 'Elections India, Bihar Lok Sabha Election Summary 2014', retrieved from Elections.IN from: Http://www.elections.in/bihar/, 30 May 2014. Parties noted:

JD(U)	Janata Dal-United – Secular/centre-left party primarily in Bihar.
BJP	Bharatiya Janata Party – Right wing national party.
RJD	Rashtriya Janata Dal – Secular/Socialist/conservative party, primarily in Bihar.
LJP	Lok Janshakti Party – Secular/Socialist party, primarily in Bihar.
RLSP	Rashtriya Lok Samata Party – Socialist party, primarily in Bihar.
INC	Indian National Congress – Modern, liberal, national party.
NCP	Nationalist Congress Party – Centre left party primarily in Maharashtra.

9. See, All India Press Trust of India, 'Jitan Ram Manjhi a Better Chief Minister than Nitish Kumar, Says Ram Vilas Paswan', *NDTV*, retrieved from http://www.ndtv.com/article/india/jitan-ram-manjhi-a-better-chief-minister-than-nitish-kumar-says-ram-vilas-paswan-628467, 1 December 2014.
10. Abhinav Bhatt, 'Upper Caste People are Foreigners, Says Bihar Chief Minister Jitan Ram Manjhi', *NDTV*, retrieved 21 December 2014, from http://www.ndtv.com/article/india/upper-caste-people-are-foreigners-says-bihar-chief-minister-jitan-ram-manjhi-620148, 13 November 2014.
11. While Manjhi tried to retract this statement it appears to be only one in a series of missteps. In the past, he has said he supports bribery, has endorsed corruption and black marketing and has said that his married son cannot be faulted for having a girlfriend, though the alleged companion also turned out to be married and an employee of the Bihar government.
12. Sankarshan Thakur, 'ABCD of Elections in Bihar', retrieved from *The Telegraph*, from http://www.telegraphindia.com/1140420/jsp/nation/story_18259296.jsp, 20 April 2014.
13. Data from: *HT* Correspondent, 'The Caste Factor While Casting Votes in Indian Elections', retrieved from *Hindustan Times – On-line* from http://www.hindustantimes.com/elections2014/the-big-story/is-the-die-caste-for-may-16-mandate/article1-1205899.aspx, 9 April 2014.
14. Sanjay Kumar, 'Bihar: Interpreting the Massive Mandate', retrieved from *The Hindu – Online*, from http://www.thehindu.com/opinion/op-ed/bihar-interpreting-the-massive-mandate/article6037680.ece, 23 May 2014.
15. Rajan Alexander, 'Raja or Rage: Why is Narendra Modi So Angry?' Retrieved from Exit & Opinion Polls India, from http://exitopinionpollsindia.blogspot.ca/2014/04/raja-of-rage-why-is-narendra-modi-so.html, 30 April 2014.

16. Joseph de Maistre, and later Walter Lippmann, voiced the opinion that: 'In a democracy, people get the government they deserve' or 'In a democracy people get the leaders they deserve'. The assumption behind these two statements seems to be, where the public is charged with the choosing of its leaders, representatives, or government, it is important that everyone eligible participates; and the majority will prevail, right or wrong. Those who choose not to participate have no basis for criticism. Even the majority may vote for the wrong person for any office, that is simply human nature. However, in a democracy, probability generally tends to result in the right person occupying every office.
17. Quoting Tunku Varadarajan, in 'After US Hegemony, Modi, An Indian Caesar? Or, How Not to Interpret the Indian Election Results', retrieved from https://rpalat.wordpress.com/2014/05/19/modi-an-indian-caesar-or-how-not-to-interpret-the-indian-election-results/, 19 May 2014.
18. IBNLive, 'Bihar Bypoll Results: Nitish-Lalu Formula Works as RJD-JDU-Congress Alliance Wins 6 out of 10 seats', *IBNLive*, retrieved 7 December 2014, from http://ibnlive.in.com/news/bihar-bypoll-results-nitishlalu-formula-works-as-rjdjducongress-alliance-wins-6-out-of-10-seats/494100-3-232.html, 25 August 2014.
19. Rahul Shrivastava, 'Nitish Kumar Hints at "One Single Party" after Meeting Mulayam, Lalu', *NDTV*, retrieved 7 December 2014, from http://www.ndtv.com/article/india/nitish-kumar-hints-at-one-single-party-after-meeting-mulayam-lalu-617014, 6 November 2014.
20. These smaller parties include: SP, Janata Dal (Secular), RJD, Janata Dal (United), Indian National Lok Dal and Samajwadi Janata Party.
21. Press Trust India, 'Merger of "Janata Parivar" Parties a Permanent Alliance, Says RJD Chief Lalu Prasad Yadav', *NDTV*, retrieved 7 December 2014, from http://www.ndtv.com/article/india/merger-of-janata-parivar-parties-a-permanent-alliance-says-rjd-chief-lalu-prasad-yadav-631179?ndtv_related, 7 December 2014.
22. See, for example, Harsh V. Pant, 'Modi's Diplomatic Chutzpah', *The Diplomat*, retrieved 26 November 2014, from http://thediplomat.com/2014/11/modis-diplomatic-chutzpah/; Shannon Tiezzi, 'Modi Remakes India-China Relations', *The Diplomat*, retrieved 27 May 2015, from http://thediplomat.com/2015/05/modi-remakes-india-china-relations/; and Michael Schuman, 'Why India's Modi and Japan's Abe Need Each Other – Badly', *Time*, retrieved 15 September 2014, from http://time.com/3255880/japan-india-narendra-modi-shinzo-abe-business-economy-trade-china/.

Bibliography

Abdalla, M. (Summer 2007). 'Ibn Khaldun on the Fate of Islamic Sciences after the 11th Century'. *Islam & Society, 5*(1), 61-70.

Acemoglu, D. and J. Robinson (2008). *The Role of Institutions in Growth and Development.* Washington, D.C.: The World Bank, Commission on Growth and Development.

——— (December 2002). *Economic Backwardness in Political Perspective.* Cambridge: National Bureau of Economic Research, NBER Working Paper No. 8831.

Acemoglu, D., S. Johnson and J. Robinson (2001). 'The Colonial Origins of Comparative Development: An Empirical Investigation'. *American Economic Review, 91*(5), 1369-1401.

——— (2002). 'Reversal of Fortune: Geography and Institutions in the Making of the Modern World Income Distribution'. *Quarterly Journal of Economics, 117*(4), 1231-94.

Adams, M. and P. Hanna (1 August 2012). 'Your Past is Not Their Present: Time, the Other and Ethnocentrism in Cross-cultural Personality Psychology'. *Theory and Psychology, 22*(4), 436-51.

Adams, R.M. (2005). *The Evolution of Urban Society: Early Mesopotamia and Prehispanic Mexico.* New Brunswick: Aldine Transactions.

Agency PTI (16 December 2013). 'Lalu Prasad Yadav Released from Jail'. Retrieved from DNA Analysis, from http://www.dnaindia.com/india/report-lalu-prasad-yadav-released-from-jail-1936089.

Agravāla, P.K. (2010). *Land Reforms in States and Union Territories in India.* Delhi: Concept Publishing.

Ahmad, F. (21 February 2010). 'Where is Bataidari Bill? Asks Nitish'. Retrieved 1 December 2012, from *The Times of India:* http://articles.timesofindia.indiatimes.com/2010-02-21/patna/28129160_1_nitish-kumar-bataidari-bill-sections.

——— (23 February 2011). 'Bihar Ranks Poorest Despite Giant Strides'. Retrieved from *The Times of India*. Patna: http://articles.timesofindia.indiatimes.com/2011-02-23/patna/28626349_1_lakh-tonnes-economic-survey-capita-income.

——— (6 March 2013). 'Fearing Jail, Lalu Prasad the Father in Hurry'. Retrieved from *The Times of India.* Patna: http://articles.timesofindia.indiatimes.com/2012-05-06/india/31596780_1_lalu-and-rabri-lalu-prasad-lalu-confidant.

Ahmad, Q.U. (1961). 'Origin and Growth of the Darbhanga Raj (1574-1666), based on Some Contemporary and Unpublished Documents'. *Indian Historical Records Commission Proceedings,* vol. 36, pt. II.

Ahmed, A. (1 January 2002). 'Ibn Khaldun's Understanding of Civilizations and the Dilemmas of Islam and the West Today'. *Middle East Journal, 56*(1), 20-45.

Ahmed, A.F. (1965). *Social Ideas and Social Change in Bengal, 1818-1835.* Leiden: E.J. Brill.

Ahmed, S. (1999). *A Dictionary of Muslim Names.* New York: C. Hurst & Co.

——— (25 January 2012). 'Loss of Innocence: School-children Used as Tool to Loot Money in Bihar'. Retrieved from Zakat Foundation of India/ TwoCircles.net: http://twocircles.net/2012jan25/loss_innocence_schoolchildren_used_tool_loot_money_bihar.html.

——— (10 March 2012). 'Beyond Bihar'. Retrieved 2 October 2012, from *The Telegraph.* Online: http://www.telegraphindia.com/1110310/jsp/opinion/story_13690337.jsp.

——— (30 September 2012). 'From Ranvir Sena to Ranvir Yadav: Nitish's Yatra to Disrepute'. Retrieved 3 October 2012, from *Daily Bhasker.* Online: http://daily.bhaskar.com/article/BIH-from-ranvir-sena-to-ranvir-yadav-nitishs-yatra-to-disrepute-3855701.html.

Akhtar, S.W. (1997). 'The Islamic Concept of Knowledge'. *Al-Tawhid: A Quarterly Journal of Islamic Thought and Culture, 12*(3). Retrieved from http://www.al-islam.org/al-tawhid/islam-know-conc.htm.

Alatas, S.H. (2006). 'The Autonomous, the Universal and the Future of Sociology'. *Current Sociology, 54,* 7-23. doi:10.1177/0011392106058831.

Alavi, S. (ed.) (2002). *The Eighteenth Century in India.* Delhi: Oxford University Press.

Alexander, R. (30 April 2014). 'Raja or Rage: Why is Narendra Modi so Angry'? Retrieved from Exit & Opinion Polls India, from http://exitopinionpollsindia.blogspot.ca/2014/04/raja-of-rage-why-is-narendra-modi-so.html.

Alexander, U. (28 November 2002). 'Bihar'. Retrieved 22 September 2012, from Shunya's Notes: http://blog.shunya.net/shunyas_blog/2007/11/bihar.html,

Alkire, S. and E.M. Santos (July 2010). 'Acute Multidimensional Poverty: A New Index for Developing Countries'. Oxford Poverty & Human Development Initiative (OPHI). Retrieved 13 June 2013, from http://www.ophi.org.uk/acute-multidimensional-poverty-a-new-index-for-developing-countries/.

——— (July 2010). *Multidimensional Poverty Index Research Brief.* Oxford: Oxford Poverty & Human Development Initiative.

Allen, T. and A. Thomas (eds.) (1992). *Poverty and Development in the 1990s.* Oxford: Oxford University in association with the Open University.

Retrieved from http://books.google.ca/books?id=y0heAAAAIAAJ&q=definition.

Almond, I. (2007). *The New Orientalists: Postmodern Representations of Islam from Foucault to Baudrillard.* London: I.B. Tauris.

Alvey, J.E. (2011). 'Ethics and Economics, Today and in the Past'. Palmerston North, New Zealand: Massey University, School of Economics and Finance. Retrieved from http://economics-finance.massey.ac.nz/publications/discuss/2011/DP1106.pdf.

Amaladoss, M. (1999). 'Global Homogenization: Can Local Cultures Survive?' *East Asian Pastoral Review, 36*(4). Retrieved from http://eapi.admu.edu.ph/content/global-homogenization-can-local-cultures-survive.

American Association of Pastoral Counselors (AAPC) (October 1993). 'The Bihari of India: Still Unreached with the Gospel'. *International Journal of Frontier Missions, 10*(4), 201-2.

Amurt Deutschland, e.V. (1998-2012). 'Bihar – Kosi River'. Retrieved from Amurt Deutschland, e.V.: http://www.amurt.eu/node/21.

Angel Commodities (June 2013). *Monsoon Report.* Mumbai: Angel Commodities Brokering.

Angus, I. (n.d.). *The Anxiety Concerning Cultural Homogenization.* Simon Fraser University, Department of Humanities.

Ankit, R. (November-December 2005). 'Analysis: Modern Zamindari'. *Himal Southasian, 18*(2), 91-3.

Apte, V.S. (1965). *The Practical Sanskrit-English Dictionary* (4th and enlrgd. edn.). Delhi: Motilal Banarsidass. Retrieved from http://books.google.ca/books?id=viCLcBdaPAEC&printsec=frontcover#v=onepage&q&f=false.

Asad, T. (2003). 'Formations of the Secular: Christianity, Islam, Modernity'. Palo Alto: Stanford University Press. Retrieved from http://books.google.ca/books?id=CeJ85XwCPxQC&printsec=frontcover#v=onepage&q&f=false.

Athrady, A. (10 March 2014). 'India's Ground Water Table to Dry up in 15 Years'. Retrieved from *Deccan Herald:* http://www.deccanherald.com/content/56673/indias-ground-water-table-dry.html.

Aullet, A. (n.d.). 'Private Property: Should Everything in the World be Owned?' Retrieved from http://www.ted.com/conversations/7712/private_property_should_every.html.

Avari, B. (2007). *India: The Ancient Past: A History of the Indian Sub-Continent from c. 7000 BC to AD 1200.* London: Routledge.

Baber, Z. (March 2000). 'Religious Nationalism, Violence and the Hindutva Movement in India'. *Dialectical Anthropology, 25*(1), 61-76.

Babu, R.R. (13 September 2012). 'Constitutional Right to Property in Changing Times: The Indian Experience'. *Vienna Journal on International Constitutional Law, 6*(2), 213-47.

Baden-Powell, B.H. (1974 rpt.). *The Land-Systems of British India.* Delhi: Oriental Publishers.

Baker, C.J. (1976). 'Tamilnad Estates in the Twentieth Century'. *Indian Economic and Social History Review, 13*(1), 1-44.

Baker, J.L. (2000). *Evaluating the Impact of Development Projects on Poverty: A Handbook for Practitioners.* Washington, DC: World Bank.

Balagangadhara, S.N. (1994). *"The Heathen in His Blindness" – Asia, the West and the Dynamic of Religion.* Leiden: E.J. Brill, Studies in the History of Religions, no. 64.

Bandhopadhyay, D. (14 July 2007). 'A Trickster Extraordinaire: Sordid Tale of the Hathua Raj'. Retrieved 17 November 2011, from Mainstream, vol. XLV, no. 30: http://www.mainstreamweekly.net/article214.html.

Banerjee, A.V., P.J. Gertler and M. Ghatak (2002). 'Empowerment and Efficiency: Tenancy Reform in West Bengal'. *Journal of Political Economy, 110*(2), 239-80.

Banerjee, A. and L. Iyer (2005). History, Institutions and Economic Performance: The Legacy of Colonial Land Tenure Systems in India. *The American Economic Review, 95*(4), 1190-1213.

Banerjee, A. and L. Iyer (March 2002). *History, Institutions and Economic Performance: The Legacy of Colonial Land Tenure Systems in India.* Princeton: MIT, Department of Economics.

Banerjee, P.K., Registrar General and Census Commissioner (14-16 April 2014). *Management of Statistical Information in Socio Economic and Canste Census – India,* New Delhi: Office of the Registrar General and Census Commissioner, India.

Banerjee, S. (21 May 2010). '12 Districts in Bihar Identified as "Highly Food Insecure"'. Retrieved from *The Hindu,* National: http://www.thehindu.com/news/national/other-states/12-districts-of-bihar-identified-as-highly-food-insecure/article435263.ece.

Bansil, P.C. (2011). *Bihar Agriculture: A Perspective.* Delhi: Concept Publishing. Retrieved from http://books.google.ca/books?id=WUlVKM4aZDcC&printsec=frontcover#v=onepage&q&f=false.

Bardhan, P. and D. Mookherjee (2005). *Working Paper: Political Economy of Land Reforms in West Bengal, 1978-98.* Berkeley and Boston: University of California; Boston University.

Barik, R.K. (2006). *Land and Caste Politics in Bihar.* Delhi: Shipra Publications.

Barlas, A. (1995). *Democracy, Nationalism and Communalism.* Boulder: Westview Press.

Barman, A. (27 March 2013). 'A Special Curse for Nitish'. Retrieved from *The Economic Times:* http://blogs.economictimes.indiatimes.com/folk-theorem/entry/a-special-curse-for-nitish.

Barro, R.J. and R.M. McCleary (2003). *Religion and Economic Growth.*

Cambridge: National Bureau of Economic Research, Working Paper 9682. Retrieved from http://www.nber.org/papers/w9682.

Basham, A.L. (1959). *The Wonder That Was India* (8th edn.). New York: Grove Press.

Battacharya, J.N. (1896). *Hindu Castes and Sects.* Calcutta: Thacker, Spink & Co. Retrieved from http://archive.org/stream/hinducastesands00bhatgoog#page/n8/mode/1up.

Bayly, C.A. (2012). *Recovering Liberties: Indian Thought in the Age of Liberalism and Empire: The Wiles Lectures Given at the Queen's University of Belfast, 2007.* Cambridge: Cambridge University Press, Ideas in Context Series, 100.

Bayly, S. (2001). *Caste, Society and Politics in India from the Eighteenth Century to the Modern Age* (1st Paperback edn.). Cambridge: Cambridge University Press, New Cambridge History of India, IV, 3. Retrieved from http://books.google.ca/books/about/Caste_Society_and_Politics_in_India_from.html?id=HbAjKR_iHogC&redir_esc=y.

BBC News - Online (5 April 2000). 'Laloo Prasad Taken into Custody'. Retrieved 1 October 2012, from BBC News: http://news.bbc.co.uk/2/hi/south_asia/701186.stm.

Berger, P.L. (1990). *Sacred Canopy: Elements of a Sociological Theory of Religion* (rpt.). New York: Anchor Books.

Berger, P.L. and T. Luckmann (1966). *The Social Construction of Reality: A Treatise in the Sociology of Knowledge.* Garden City: Doubleday.

Bergunder, M. (2004). 'Contested Past: Anti-Brahmanical and Hindu Nationalist Reconstructions of Indian Prehistory'. *Historiographia Linguistica, 31*(1), 59-104.

Bernstein, H. (ed.) (1973). *Underdevelopment and Development: The Third World Today: Selected Readings.* Harmondsworth: Penguin Books.

Berry, B.J. (1966). *Essays on Commodity Flows and the Spatial Structure of the Indian Economy.* Chicago: University of Chicago Press.

Besley, T. and R. Burgess (May 2000). 'Land Reform, Poverty Reduction and Growth: Evidence from India'. *Quarterly Journal of Economics, 115*(2), 389-430.

Bétille, A. (21 February 2012). 'India's Destiny not Caste in Stone'. Retrieved from *The Hindu.* On-line: http://www.thehindu.com/todays-paper/tp-opinion/indias-destiny-not-caste-in-stone/article2914365.ece.

Bhagavad Gita: The Song of God, Introduction by Aldous Huxley. (1947). (tr. S. Prabhavananda and C. Isherwood). London: Phoenix House.

Bhatia, B.M. (3 December 1992). 'Back to Mandal'. *The Hindustan Times.*

Bhattacharyya, K. (1998). *Applied Geomorphological Study in a Controlled Tropical River: The Case of the Damodar Between Panchet Reservoir and Falta.* Burdwan: The University of Burdwan.

Bhatt, A. (13 November 2014), 'Upper Caste People are Foreigners, Says Bihar Chief Minister Jitan Ram Manjhi', *NDTV*. Retrieved 21 December 2014, from http://www.ndtv.com/article/india/upper-caste-people-are-foreigners-says-bihar-chief-minister-jitan-ram-manjhi-620148.

Bhattacharyya, K. (2011). *The Lower Damodar River, India: Understanding the Human Role in Changing Fluvial Environment.* Dordrecht: Springer. Retrieved from http://books.google.ca/books?id=V892MENKn2kC&printsec=frontcover#v=onepage&q=Lamplugh&f=false.

Bhunia, A. (6 August 2013). 'Nitish Shows the Way: Bihar's Enviable Story'. Retrieved from *The Herald of India:* http://www.heraldofindia.com/article.php?id=457.

Bihar Agricultural Management & Extension Training Institute (2008). 'Status of Agriculture in Bihar', in Bemati.Org, *Bihar State Profile.* Government of Bihar. Retrieved from http://www.bameti.org/pdf/state_profile.pdf.

Bihar Inter Agency Group; US Aid; Project Concern International; Global Forum for Disaster Reduction (2010). *Bihar State Forum for Disaster Risk Reduction (BSFDRR).* Patna: BIAG; US Aid; PCI/India; GFDR.

Bihar Lok Manch (2004). *Mithila, The Cultural Region*. Retrieved 15 November 2012, from Bihar Lok Manch: http://biharlokmanch.tripod.com/id2.html.

Bihar State Pollution Control Board; Department of Environment and Forest, GoI (2007). *State of Environment Report, Bihar.* Patna: Bihar State Pollution Control Board; Department of Environment and Forest, GoI.

BiharDiary.Com (5 October 2012). 'Bihar People'. Retrieved 5 October 2012, from BiharDiary.com: http://bihardiary.com/bihar/people.asp.

Bilal, S.M. and T. Sarwar (2008). 'Effect of Tube Well Drainage on Water Logging and Salinity in Kafur Dheri Unit Pesawar'. *Sarhad Journal of Agriculture, 24*(1), 49-58.

Blair, H.W. (12 January 1980). 'Rising Kulaks and Backward Classes in Bihar: Social Change in the Late 1970s'. *Economic and Political Weekly*, 15(2), 64-74.

Boone, Peter; National Bureau of Economic Research (1995). *Politics and the Effectiveness of Foreign Aid.* Cambridge: National Bureau of Economic Research, Working Paper No. 5308.

Borooah, V.K. and A. Dubey (December 2007). 'Measuring Regional Backwardness: Poverty, Gender and Children in the Districts of India'. *Journal of Applied Economic Research, 1*(4), 403-40.

Borooah, V., K. Amaresh and D. Amaresh (2007 [Posted 25 December 2009]). 'Measuring Regional Backwardness: Poverty, Gender and Children in the Districts of India'. Munich: Munich Personal RePEc Archive.

Brass, P.R. (2005). 'Language, Religion and Politics in North Bihar'. Lincoln, NE: iUniverse. Retrieved from http://books.google.ca/books?id=SylBHS8IJAUC&printsec=frontcover#v=onepage&q&f=false.

Brass, T. (1995). 'The Politics of Gender, Nature and Nation in the Discourse of the New Farmers' Movement', in T. Brass (ed.), *New Farmers' Movement in India* (pp. 27-71). London: Frank Cass & Co. Retrieved from http://books.google.ca/books?id=9IcjA67sdrsC&printsec=frontcover#v=onepage&q&f=false.

Brodbeck, M. (ed.) (1968). *Readings in the Philosophy of the Social Sciences.* New York: The Macmillan Co.

Brouwer, C. and K. Prins (1989). *Training Manual No. 4: Irrigation Water Management: Irrigation Scheduling.* Rome: Food and Agricultural Organization of the United Nations.

Brown, C.H. (1983). 'Substance and Structure Among the Maithil Brahmans'. *Eastern Anthropologist, 36*(3), 197-210.

———. 'The Gift of a Girl: Hierarchical Exchange in North Bihar'. *Ethnology: An International Journal of Cultural and Social Anthropology, 22*(1), 43-62.

——— (1988). 'Raja and Rank in North Bihar'. *Modern Asian Studies, 22*(4), 757-82.

Brumm, H. J. (2003). 'Aid, Policies and Growth: Bauer was Right'. *Cato Journal, 23*(2), 167-74.

Bryant, E. (2001). *Vedic Culture: The Indo-Aryan Migration Debate.* Oxford: Oxford University Press. Retrieved from http://books.google.ca/books?id=-Grpz1tmcSMC&printsec=frontcover#v=onepage&q&f=false.

Bryant, E.F. and L.L. Patton (2005). *The Indo-Aryan Controversy: Evidence and Inference in Indian History.* London: Routledge.

Buckley, R.B. (1905). *The Irrigation Works of India* (2 edn.). London: E. and F.N. Spon. Retrieved from http://archive.org/stream/irrigationworks00buckgoog#page/n6/mode/2up.

Bureau Report (11 April 2012). 'Starving in India: The Forgotten Problem'. Retrieved 3 November 2012, from ZeeNews.Com - On-line: http://zeenews.india.com/exclusive/starving-in-india-the-forgotten-problem_5168.html.

Buruma, I. and A. Margalit (2004). *Occidentalism: The West in the Eyes of Its Enemies.* New York: Penguin.

Carbonnier, G. (April 2013). *Religion and Development : Reconsidering Secularism as the Norm.* doi:10.4000/poldev.1351.

Cardona, G. (1998). *Panini: A Survey of Research* (1st Indian edition). Delhi: Motilal Banarsidass.

Cardona, G. (2004). *Recent Research in Paninian Studies* (2nd, revd. edn.). Motilal Banarsidass.

Chakravarti, U. (2003). *Gendering Caste: Through a Feminist Lens.* Calcutta: Stree.

Chamberlain, G. (14 September 2010). 'Hunger in India: The Real Cause is Lack of Political Will'. Retrieved 15 October 2012, from The Guardian - Global Development: http://www.guardian.co.uk/environment/2010/sep/14/hunger-india-actionaid.

Chandrasekharendra, S. and Bharatiya Vidya Bhavan (2009). *The Vedas.* Mumbai: Bharatiya Vidya Bhavan, Sudakshina Trust.

Chaskalson, M. (1993). 'The Problem with Property: Thoughts on the Constitutional Protection of Property in the United States and the Commonwealth'. *South African Journal on Human Rights (SAJHR), 9*, 388-411.

Chatterji, A. (13 September 2008). 'Hindutva's Violent History'. Retrieved 28 August 2013, from *Tehelka Magazine*, vol. 5, no. 36: http://archive.tehelka.com/story_main40.asp?filename=Ne130908HindutvasViolentHistory.asp.

Chaturvedi, S. and S.K. Mohanty (October 2008). *Assessing the Market Openness Effects of Regulation in India: An Overview of Emerging Trends and Policy Issues.* Macao Regional Knowledge Hub (Markhub) - Working Papers, no. 7. United Nations Economic and Social Commission for Asia and the Pacific (ESCAP).

Chaudhari, B.B. (1975). 'The Land Market in Eastern India, 1793-1940: Part I: The Movement of Land Prices'. *Indian Economic and Social History Review, 12*(1), 1-42.

Chaudhary, R. (1973). *Mithila in the Age of Vidyāpati.* Varanasi: Chaukhambha Orientalia.

——— (2010). *A Survey of Maithili Literature.* Delhi: Shruti Publication.

Roy Chaudhury, P.C. (1964). *Bihar District Gazetteers – Darbhanga*, Patna: Superintendent, Secretariat Press.

Chiarello, M. (2012). 'An Empire of Good Intentions? Liberalism and the Justification of Britain's Empire in India, c. 1820-1905', *Paper HIS4397B_Essay.pdf.* University of Ottawa. Academia.edu. Retrieved from https://www.academia.edu/1545698/An_Empire_of_Good_Intentions_Liberalism_and_the_Justification_of_Britains_Empire_in_India_c.1820-1905.

Choi, C. (28 May 2012). 'Huge Ancient Civilization's Collapse Explained'. Retrieved 13 September 2012, from Live Science: http://www.livescience.com/20614-collapse-mythical-river-civilization.html.

Chopra, A. (1 July 2010). 'The Great Leap Forward?' *Caravan Magazine - Online.* Retrieved 16 July 2013, from http://caravanmagazine.in/reportage/great-leap-forward.

Choudhary, R. (1958). *History of Bihar.* Patna: Motilal Banarsidass.

Clarke, J. J. (1997). *Oriental Enlightenment.* London: Routledge. Retrieved from http://www.worldcat.org/title/oriental-enlightenment-the-encounter-between-asian-and-western-thought/oclc/52219015/viewport.

Clarke, M. (2014). 'Understanding the Nexus Between Region and Development', in M. Clarke (ed.), *Handbook of Research on Development and Religion* (pp. 1-16). Glos: Edward Elgar Publishing.

CNBC-TV 18. (29 July 2013). Retrieved from Moneycontrol.com: http://www.moneycontrol.com/news/economy/credit-nitish-for-focusgrowth-qualitylife-sen_922732.html.

Cohn, B.S. (1961). 'From Indian Status to British Contract'. *Journal of Economic History, 21*(4), 613-28.

——— (1996). *Colonialism and Its Forms of Knowledge: The British in India.* Princeton: Princeton University Press. Retrieved from http://books.google.ca/books?id=uIalYaenrTkC&printsec=frontcover#v=onepage&q&f=false.

Comby, J. (1990). *L'impossible propriété absolue.* Paris: Association des études foncières (ADEF).

——— (2002). Les avatars de la propriété. *de la Revue Etudes foncières, no. 100*, 1-4.

Communist Party of India (June 2012). 'Rising Injustice, Crime and Repression in Nitish's Bihar: Cover Feature'. Retrieved from Communist Party of India - Online: http://www.cpiml.org/liberation/year_2012/june_2012/cover_feature.html.

Conning, J.H. and J.A. Robinson (2007). 'Property Rights and the Political Organization of Agriculture'. *Journal of Development Economics,* 82, 416-47.

Copson, A. (27 June 2013). 'Comment: Religion is in Decline – So Why are People So Well Behaved?' Retrieved from Politics.co.uk: http://www.politics.co.uk/comment-analysis/2013/06/27/comment-religion-is-in-decline-so-why-are-people-so-well-beh.

Cordaid (December 2013). 'Bihar Floods 2013'. Retrieved from Disaster-Response 2013, India: http://www.cordaid.org/en/projects/bihar-floods-2013/110243/.

Cornwall, A. (August 2007). 'Buzzwords and Fuzzwords: Deconstructing Development Discourse'. *Development in Practice, 17*(4-5), 471-84.

Covault, J.A. (2011). 'Submarine Fans and Canyon-Channel Systems: A Review of Processes, Products and Models'. *Nature Education Knowledge, 3*(10), 4. Retrieved from http://www.nature.com/scitable/knowledge/library/submarine-fans-and-canyon-channel-systems-a-24178428.

Cowen, M.P. and R.W. Shenton (1 October 1991). 'Bankers, Peasants and Land in British West Africa, 1905-1937'. *Journal of Peasant Studies, 19*(1), 26-58.

——— (1996). *Doctrines of Development.* New York: Routledge. Retrieved from http://books.google.ca/books?id=P2PpVvVnLiYC&printsec=frontcover#v=onepage&q&f=false.

Cristaller, W. (1933). *Die zentralen Orte in Suddeutschland.* Jena: Gustav Fischer.

Daines, S.R. and J.R. Pawar (1987). *Economic Returns to Irrigation in India: A Report Prepared for the U.S. Agency for International Development Mission to India.* New Delhi: SDR Research Groups Inc. & Development Group Inc.

Dalrymple, T. (16 August 2012). 'India is Heading for Mars: It Doesn't Need British Aid Money to Pay the Bills'. Retrieved 29 October 2012, from *The Telegraph* - On Line: http://www.telegraph.co.uk/news/worldnews/asia/india/9480279/India-is-heading-for-Mars-it-doesnt-need-British-aid-money-to-pay-the-bills.html.

Danish, M., P. Gupta, J. Alam and M. Muzammil (12 April 2013). 'River Kosi, Sorrow of India: An Overview', *Paper-CV-111.* 2nd International Conference on Emerging Trends in Engineering & Technology, 12-13 April.

Dasgupta, S. (28 November 2012). 'In Nitish's Bihar, A Village's Power Cut has Lasted 17 Years'. Retrieved from *NDTV*: http://www.ndtv.com/article/india/in-nitish-s-bihar-a-village-s-power-cut-has-lasted-17-years-298262.

de Bary, William T. (1958 [5th printing (in 2 vols.) 1964]). *Sources of Indian Tradition.* New York: Columbia University Press.

de Jong, E. (November 2008). *Religious Values and Economic Growth: A Review and Assessment of Recent Studies.* Nijmegen, The Netherlands: Nijmegen Center for Economics (NiCE), Working Paper 08-111.

De, U.S., R.K. Dube and G.S. Rao (July 2005). 'Extreme Weather Events over India in the last 100 Years'. *Journal of the Indian Geophysical Union, 9*(3), 173-87.

Debroy, B and L. Bhandari (2003). *District-Level Deprivation in the New Millennium* (D. Debroy and L. Bhandari, eds.). Delhi: Konark Publishers.

Deccan Herald (19 February 2012). 'Nitish Kumar Threatened for Wanting to Protect Sharecroppers'. Retrieved 29 November 2012, from *Deccan Herald:* http://www.deccanherald.com/content/53604/content/196937/ipl-2012.html.

Delhi High Court PR Wire (19 July 2013). 'Delhi High Court Dismisses Reopening CBI Report in Nitish Sleeper Scam'. Retrieved from India News Co.: http://politics-indianews.rhcloud.com/news/delhi-high-court-dismisses-reopening-cbi-report-nitish-sleeper-scam-6917042.

Department of Agriculture (20 September 2012). 'Online Reporting'. Retrieved 20 September 2012, from Department of Agriculture, Government of Bihar: http://krishi.bih.nic.in/.

Desai, D. and R.B. Potter (2008). *The Companion to Development Studies.* London: Routledge. Retrieved from http://books.google.ca/books?id=UO3vCiWw-xwC&printsec=frontcover#v=onepage&q&f=false.

DeSchweinitz, K. (1983). *The Rise and Fall of British India: Imperialism and Inequality.* London: Methuen.

Dickens, C. (1990). *Hard Times.* Champaign: Project Gutenberg, no. 786.

Diener, E., J.F. Helliwell and D. Kahneman (2010). *International Differences in Well-being.* Oxford: Oxford University Press.

Diwakar, R.R. (ed.). (1958/9). *Bihar Through the Ages.* Bombay: Orient Longman.

Diwanji, A.K. (9 February 2005). 'Lalu's a Rascal, but Will Vote for Him'. Retrieved 1 October 2012, from Rediff Elections: http://in.rediff.com/election/2005/feb/09spec5.htm.

Dixit, A. (7 February 2009). 'Kosi Embankment Breach in Nepal: Need for a Paradigm Shift in Responding to Floods'. *Economic and Political Weekly, 44*(6), 70-8.

Djankov, S., J.G. Montalvo and M. Reynal-Querol (2006). Does Foreign Aid Help? *Cato Journal, 26*(1), 1-28.

DNA (1 June 2012). 'Ranvir Sena Chief Killing: Nitish Kumar Asks People to Maintain Calm'. Retrieved 3 October 2012, from DNA - Daily News & Analysis - Online: http://www.dnaindia.com/india/report_ranvir-sena-chief-killing-nitish-kumar-asks-people-to-maintain-calm_1696801.

——— (11 June 2012). 'Nitish Kumar Evades Questions on Ranvir Sena'. Retrieved 3 October 2012, from *DNA* - Daily News & Analysis - Online: http://www.dnaindia.com/india/report_nitish-kumar-evades-questions-on-ranvir-sena_1700948.

Donkin, R.A. (1998). 'Beyond Price: Pearls and Pearl-fishing: Origins to the Age of Discoveries', *Memoirs of the American Philosophical Society*, vol. 224.

Dow, A. (1812). *The History of Hindostan: Translated from the Persian* (new edn.). tr. A. Dow. London: J. Walker. Retrieved from http://books.google.ca/books?id=tHDUAAAAMAAJ&printsec=frontcover#v=onepage&q&f=false.

Down To Earth (30 September 1999). 'Engineered Chaos'. Retrieved from Down To Earth: http://www.downtoearth.org.in/node/20456.

Dowson, J. (1888). *A Classical Dictionary of Hindu Mythology and Religion, Geography, History and Literature* (2nd edn.). London: Trubner & Co.

Drèze, J. and H. Gazdar (1997). 'Uttar Pradesh: The Burden of Inertia', in J. Dreze and A. Sen (eds.), *Studies in Development Economics Indian Development: Selected Regional Perspectives.* Delhi: Oxford University Press.

Drèze, J. and A. Sen (1995a). *India: Development and Participation.* New York: Oxford University Press.

——— (1995b). *India: Economic Development and Social Opportunity.* Delhi: Oxford University Press.

——— (1997). *Indian Development: Selected Regional Perspectives.* Delhi: Oxford University Press, Studies in Development Economics. Retrieved 2 June 2013, from http://books.google.ca/books?id=E82zY2iOuQ8C&printsec=frontcover#v=onepage&q&f=false.

drkjke. 'Asabiyyah or Nationalism and Why Islam Prohibits it, and Pakistans Poor Condition'. 2 September 2010, http://www.siasat.pk/forum/showthread.php?35450-The-Cloak-of-Nationalism-is-the-Burial-Shroud-of-Islam.

DWIDP (July 2007). *Disaster Review 2006, Series XIV.* Kathmandu: Department of Water Induced Disaster Prevention (DWIDP).

Easterly, W. (2006). *The White Man's Burden: Why the West's Efforts to Aid the Rest Have Done so Much Ill and so Little Good.* New York: Penguin Press. Retrieved from http://www.worldcat.org/title/white-mans-burden-why-the-wests-efforts-to-aid-the-rest-have-done-so-much-ill-and-so-little-good/oclc/62326881/viewport.

——— (3 April 2006). *Why Doesn't Aid Work?* Retrieved 4 November 2012, from Cato Unbound: http://www.cato-unbound.org/2006/04/03/william-easterly/why-doesnt-aid-work/.

Easterly, W. and R. Levine (January 2003). 'Tropics, Germs and Crops: The Role of Endowments in Economic Development'. *Journal of Monetary Economics, 50*(1), 3-39.

Easterly, W. and S. Radelet (1 December 2006). 'The Effectiveness of Foreign Aid'. Retrieved 23 December 2011, from Council on Foreign Relations: http://www.cfr.org/foreign-aid/effectiveness-foreign-aid/p12077.

Easterly, William R. et al. (2003). *New Data, New Doubts: A Comment on Burnside and Dollar's Aid, Policies, and Growth.* National Bureau of Economic Research, Working Paper, no. 9846.

Elections India (30 May 2014). 'Bihar Lok Sabha Election Summary 2014'. Retrieved from Elections.IN from: Http://www.elections.in/bihar/.

Elst, K. (1999). *Update on the Aryan Invasion Debate.* Delhi: Aditya Prakashan. Retrieved from http://www.voiceofdharma.com/books/ait/index.htm.

Embree, A.T. (ed.) (1971). *Alberuni's India* (Abridged edn.) E.C. Sachan. New York: W.W. Norton & Co.

Emmott, B. and V. Shiva (2000). *Is Development Good for the Third World? The Ecologist*, vol. 30(2), pp. 22-5.

Energypedia (25 June 2013). 'Bihar Energy Situation'. Retrieved from Energypedia: https://energypedia.info/wiki/Bihar_Energy_Situation.

Engerman, S.L. and K.L. Solokoff (1997). 'Factor Endowments, Institutions and Differential Paths of Growth Among New World Economies: A View from the Economic History of the United States', in S. Faber (ed.), *How Latin America Fell Behind: Essays on the Economic Histories of Brazil and Mexico, 1800-1915.* Stanford: Stanford University Press, pp. 260-304.

Ernst & Young, FIDS (2013). *Bribery and Corruption: Ground Reality in India: A Survey by Fraud Investigation and Dispute Services.* Kolkata: Ernst & Young LLP/FICCI.

ET Bureau (19 February 2014). 'Implementing Food Security Law to Cost Government Rs 88,500 Crore', Retrieved from *The Times of India.* On-line, http://timesofindia.indiatimes.com/business/india-business/implementing-food-security-law-to-cost-government-rs-88500-crore/articleshow/30665108.cms.

Etzioni, A. (1991). 'The Socio-Economics of Property', in F.W. Rudmin (ed.), *To Have Possessions: A Handbook on Ownership and Property* [*Special Issue of the Journal of Social Benaviour and Personality* (vol. 6, no. 6, pp. 465-8)].

Eum, W. (29 April 2011). *Religion and Economic Development: A Study on Religious Variables Influencing GDP Growth over Countries.* Berkeley: University of California.

Express News Service (1 March 2011). 'Politics Keeping Caste System Alive'.

Retrieved from *Indian Express* – Journalism of Courage Archive: http://archive.indianexpress.com/news/-politics-keeping-caste-system-alive-/756166/.

Eze, E.C., ed. (1997). *Race and the Enlightenment: A Reader.* Cambridge, MA: Blackwell.

Fan, S., P.B. Hazell and S.S. Thorat (1999). *Linkages between Government Spending, Growth and Poverty in Rural India.* Washington, DC: International Food Policy Research Institute.

Fisher, M.H. (2004). *Counterflows to Colonialism: Indian Travellers and Settlers in Britain, 1600-1857.* Delhi: Permanent Black.

——— (2007). *Visions of Mughal India: An Anthology of European Travel Writing.* London: I.B. Tauris.

Ford, J.D., L.W. Ford and A. D'Amelio (2008). 'Resistance to Change: The Rest of the Story'. *Academy of Management Review, 33*(2), 362-77.

Foucault, M. (2009). *Discipline and Punish: The Birth of the Prison.* New York: Vintage.

Frey, B.S. and F. Schneider (1986). 'Competing Models of International Lending Activity'. *Journal of Development Economics, 20*(2), pp. 225-45.

Fukuda-Parr, S. (2003). 'The Human Development Paradigm: Operationalizing Sen's Ideas on Capabilities'. *Feminist Economics, 9*(2-3), 301-17. doi:10.1080/1354570022000077980.

Fukuyama, F. (1989). *The 'End of History?'.* Washington, DC: US Institute of Peace, no. 11.

Furber, H. (n.d.). 'The History of East India Companies: General Problems', in M. Mollat (ed.). *Sociétés et Compagnies de Commerce en Orient et dans l'Océan Indien; actes du huitième Colloque international d'histoire maritime (Beyrouth, 5-10 septembre 1966).* Paris: S.E.V.P.E.N., Bibliothèque générale de l'École pratique des hautes études., Sciences économiques et sociales, pp. 415-18.

Galay, V.J. (1987). *Erosion and Sedimentation in the Nepal Himalayas: An Assessment of River Processes.* Kathmandu: His Majesty's Government of Nepal, Water and Energy Commission Secretariat, Ministry of Water Resources.

Galy, Valier et al. (15 November 2007). 'Efficient Organic Carbon Burial in the Bengal Fan Sustained by the Himalayan Erosional System'. *Nature*, 450, 407-10.

Garde, R.J. and K.G. Raju (1985). *Mechanics of Sediment Transportation and Alluvial Stream Problem.* New York: Wiley.

Gates, W.E. (July-September 1967). 'The Spread of Ibn Khaldun's Ideas on Climate and Culture'. *Journal of the History of Ideas, 28*(3), 415-22. doi:10.2307/2708627.

Geosynthetic Materials Association. (2012). *Geosynthetics.* Retrieved 18 September

2012, from Canal Lining with Geosynthetics: http://geosyntheticsmagazine.com/articles/wp5_canal.html.

Gerschenkron, A. (1966). *Economic Backwardness in Historical Perspective: A Book of Essays*. Cambridge: Belknap Press of Harvard University Press.

Ghose, T. (8 August 2013). 'Genetic Study Reveals Origin of India's Caste System'. Retrieved from Live Science: http://www.livescience.com/38751-genetic-study-reveals-caste-system-origins.html.

Glacken, C. (1967). 'Traces on the Rhodian Shore: Nature and Culture in Western Thought from Ancient Times to the End of the Eighteenth Century'. Berkeley: University of California Press.

Glencorse, B. (December 2011). 'Analysis: Building on Bihar'. Retrieved from *Himal*: http://www.himalmag.com/component/content/article/4836-building-on-bihar.html.

GoI Monitor Desk (25 August 2012). 'Watering the Future Disaster'. Retrieved 17 September 2012, from GoI Monitor: http://www.goimonitor.com/story/watering-future-disaster.

Goldenweiser, A.A. (1922). *Early Civilization*. New York: Alfred A. Knopf.

Gole, C.V. and S.V. Chitale (1966). 'Inland Delta Building Activity of Kosi River'. *Journal of Hydraulics Division, American Society of Civil Engineers, 92*(2), 111-26.

Golwalkar, M.S. (1939). *We, or, Our Nationhood Defined*. Nagpur: Bharat Publications. Retrieved from http://www.scribd.com/doc/95053816/We-or-Our-Nationhood-Defined-Shri-M-S-Golwalkar-Guruji-1#.

Gopal, L. and V.C. Srivastav (eds.) (2008). *History of Agriculture in India, Up to c. 1200 A.D.* (vol. 5: *Agriculture in India*). Delhi: CSC and Concept Publishing Co., Project of History of Indian Science, Philosophy and Culture in Indian Civilization. Retrieved from http://books.google.ca/books?id=FvjZVwYVmNcC&printsec=frontcover#v=onepage&q&f=false.

Goulet, D. (1 August 1980). 'Development Experts: The One-eyed Giants'. *World Development, 8*(7-8), 481-9.

Government of Bihar; World Bank (2010). *Bihar Kosi Flood (2008) Needs Assessment Report*. Global Facility for Disaster Reduction & Recovery.

Government of India, Planning Commission (August 1966). *Implementation of Land Reforms: A Review by the Land Reforms Implementation Committee of the National Development Council*. New Delhi: Government of India. Retrieved from http://planningcommission.nic.in/reports/publications/pub1966land.pdf.

Government of India (2005a). *Backward Districts Initiative – Rashtriya Sam Vikas Yojana – The Scheme and Guidelines for Preparation of District Plans*. New Delhi: Government of India, Planning Commission, MLP Division.

——— (2005b). *Report of the Inter-Ministry Task Group on Redressing Growing Regional Imbalances*. New Delhi: Planning Commission.

——— (4 November 2009). 'Backward Region Grant Fund'. Retrieved from Ministry of Panchayati Raj: http://epanchayat.gov.in/mopr/viewPortalPage.do?cToken=null.

——— (2011a). *Census of India 2011, Provisional Population Totals*. Patna: Office of the Director of Census Operations, Bihar.

——— (2011b). *Census of India 2011, Final Provisional Population Totals*. New Delhi.

Gramsci, A. (1998). *Prison Notebooks: Selection* (new edn.). London: Lawrence & Wishart.

Gray, H. (September 1962). 'The 1962 General Election in a Rural District of Andhra'. *Asian Survey, 2*(7), 25-35.

Great Britain, Parliament, House of Commons (1806). *Reports from Committees of the House of Commons: Re-printed by Order of the House* (vol. 6: *East Indies - 1783*). London: n.d. Retrieved from http://books.google.ca/books?id=nPKf8RhmzZIC&pg=PA48&lpg=PA48&dq=rule+was+laid+down+either+in+the+Act+or+the+Charter+by+which+the+Court+was+to+judge.+No+description+of+offenders+or+species+of+delinquency+was+properly+ascertained+according+to+the+nature+of.

Grierson, G.A. (1885). *Bihar Peasant Life: Being a Discursive Catalogue of the Surroundings of the People of that Province*. Calcutta: Bengal Secretariat Press.

——— (1903-28/1967 rpt.). *Linguistic Survey of India*. Delhi: Motilal Banarasidas.

——— (1909). *An Introduction to the Maithili Dialect of the Bihari Language as Spoken in North Bihar*. Calcutta: Asiatic Society.

Guha, Ramchandra (4 December 2005). 'The Wisest Man in India'. Retrieved from *The Hindu* - On-line: http://www.hindu.com/mag/2005/12/04/stories/2005120400480300.htm.

Guha, R. (1996). *A Rule of Property for Bengal: An Essay on the Idea of Permanent Settlement*, Durham: Duke University Press.

Guha, R., P. Chatterjee, D. Arnold and G. Bhadra (2008). *Subaltern Studies: Writings on South Asian History and Society* (vol. 9) (ed. R. Guha). Delhi: Oxford University Press.

Gupta, S. (16 February 2005). 'The Rediff Interview, Dr. Shaibal Gupta'. Retrieved from http://www.rediff.com/election/2005/feb/16inter2.htm.

——— (15 May 2012). 'Bihar on the Wings of Progress'. Retrieved from The Times of India - Patna: http://articles.timesofindia.indiatimes.com/2012-05-15/patna/31711061_1_bad-roads-pratyaya-amrit-governance.

Habib, I. (1983). 'The Peasant in Indian History'. *Social Scientist, 11*(3), 21-64. Retrieved 23 February 2013, from http://dsal.uchicago.edu/books/socialscientist/pager.html?issue=118&objectid=HN681.S597_118_023.gif.

Hagen, E. (1962). 'On the Theory of Social Change'. Homewood: Dorsey Press.

Halbfass, W. (1988). *India and Europe: An Essay in Understanding*. Albany: State

University of New York Press. Retrieved from http://books.google.ca/books?id=su7rAAAAIAAJ&q=Hegel.

Halim, A.A., M.R. Nor, A.Z. Ibrahim and F.A. Hamid (2012). 'Ibn Khaldun's Theory of 'Asabiyyah and its Application in Modern Muslim Society'. *Middle-East Journal of Scientific Research, 11*(9), 1232-7. Retrieved from http://www.academia.edu/3019741/Ibn_Khalduns_Theory_of_Asabiyyah_and_its_Application_in_Modern_Muslim_Society.

Hall, R.E. and C.I. Jones (1999). 'Why do Some Countries Produce so Much More Output Per Worker?' *Quarterly Journal of Economics, 114*(1), 83-116.

Hamilton, Francis, Ananta Prasad Banerji-Sastri, Bihar Research Society (1939). *An Account of the District of Bhagalpur in 1810-11* (ed. A. Banerji-Sastri) Patna: Rai Bahadur Radha Krishna Jalan.

Hardin, G. (13 December 1968). 'The Tragedy of the Commons'. *Science, 162*(3859), 1243-8. Retrieved from http://links.jstor.org/sici?sici=0036-8075%2819681213%293%3A162%3A3859%3C1243%3ATTOTC%3E2.0.CO%3B2-N.

Harding, A. (1 August 2013). 'World Systems, Cores and Peripheries in Prehistoric Europe'. *European Journal of Archaeology, 16*(3), 378-400. doi: 10.1179/1461957113Y.0000000032.

Harris, M. (1968). *The Rise of Anthropological Theory: A History of Theories of Culture.* New York: Thomas Y. Crowell Co.

Harris Polls. (16 December 2013). 'Americans' Belief in God, Miracles and Heaven Declines'. Retrieved from Harris: A Nielsen Company On-line: http://www.harrisinteractive.com/NewsRoom/HarrisPolls/tabid/447/ctl/ReadCustom%20Default/mid/1508/ArticleId/1353/Default.aspx.

Harrison, H.L. (1875). *The Bengal Embankment Manual: Containing an Account of the Action of the Government in Dealing with Embankments and Water-courses since the Permanent Settlement*, Calcutta: Bengal Secretariat Press.

Harrison, P. (1990). *'Religion' and the Religions in the British Enlightenment.* Cambridge: Cambridge University Press.

Hassan, F.A. (1 January 2010). 'Climate Change, Nile Floods and Riparia - English Translation'. *Bar International Series, 2066*, 131-52.

Heider, F. (1958). *The Psychology of Interpersonal Relations.* Hillsdale: Lawrence Erlbaum Associates. Retrieved from http://books.google.ca/books?id=Zh6TDmayL0AC&printsec=frontcover#v=onepage&q&f=false.

Heinz, C.B. (1999). 'The Maithil Brahmans: An Online Ethnography'. Retrieved 4 November 2012, from Anthropology Department, Ethnographic Lab: http://www.csuchico.edu/anth/mithila/index.htm.

——— (2013). 'Bihar: Caste, Class and Violence', in P. Berger and F. Heidemann (eds.), *The Modern Anthropology of India: Ethnography, Themes and Theory* (pp. 29-45). New York: Routledge. Retrieved from http://books.google.ca/books?id=sBgLb8XIGR8C&printsec=frontcover#v=onepage&q&f=false.

Helliwell, J.F., R. Layard and J. Sachs (eds.) (2012). *World Happiness Report.* New York: Earth Institute, Columbia University.

Helliwell, John, Richard Layard, Jeffrey Sachs (eds.) (2013). *World Happiness Report, 2013.* New York: UN Sustainable Development Solutions Network.

Henningham S. (February 1983). 'Bureaucracy and Control in India's Great Landed Estates: The Raj Darbhanga of Bihar, 1879 to 1950'. *Modern Asian Studies, 17*(1), 35-57.

——— (1990). *A Great Estate and Its Landlords in Colonial India: Darbhanga 1860-1942.* Delhi: Oxford University Press.

Herodotus (1890). *The History of Herodotus* (tr. G.C. Macaulay). London: MacMillan & Co.

Hira, G.S., S.K. Jalota and V.K. Arora (2004). *Efficient Management of Water Resources for Sustainable Cropping in Punjab.* Ludhiana: Department of Soils, Punjab Agricultural University.

Hodkinson, J., J. Walker, S. Mazumdar and J. Feichtinger (eds.) (2013). *Deploying Orientalism in Culture and History: From Germany to Central and Eastern Europe.* Rochester: Camden House.

Hollis, N. (May 2009). *Millward Brown's POV – Culture Clash: Globalization Does Not Imply Homogenization.* New York: MillwardBrown. Corporate Blog and PDF Publication.

Hooning, E. (October 2011). 'Flooding and Sediment Management on the Kosi Alluvial Fan, Nepal': A M.Sc. thesis. Delft, Netherlands: Delft University of Technology, Department of Civil Engineering and Geosciences, Hydraulic Engineering.

Hopkins, D.W. (1895). *The Religions of India.* Boston: Ginn & Co.

Horo, P.C. (1976). 'Christian Missions and Communities in Bihar', in Z.K. Datta and J. Jha (eds.), *The Comprehensive History of Bihar* (vol. III, pt. II, pp. 109-292). Patna: Kashi Prasad Jayaswal Research Institute.

Hoyt, S.F. (1912). 'The Etymology of Religion'. *Journal of the American Oriental Society, 32*(2), 126-9. doi:10.2307/3087765.

HT Correspondent (9 April 2014). 'The Caste Factor While Casting Votes in Indian Elections'. Retrieved from Hindustantimes – On-line from http://www.hindustantimes.com/elections2014/the-big-story/is-the-die-caste-for-may-16-mandate/article1-1205899.aspx.

Human Rights Watch (March 1999). *IV.* 'The Pattern of Abuse: Rural Violence in Bihar and the State's Response'. Retrieved 24 October 2012, from Human Rights Watch: http://www.hrw.org/reports/1999/india/India994-06.htm.

Hyam, R. (1993). 'Britain's Imperial Century, 1815-1914: A Study of Empire and Expansion' (2nd edn.) (ed. D.A. Low). New York: Palgrave Publishers, Cambridge Commonwealth Series.

Iannacone, L.R. (September 1998). 'Introduction to Economics of Religion'. *Journal of Economic Literature, 36*(3), 1465-95.

IANS (1 May 2009). 'Nitish Kumar's Development Agenda Makes Waves in Bihar'. Retrieved 2 October 2012, from *India Today* - Online: http://indiatoday.intoday.in/story/Nitish+Kumar%27s+development+agenda+makes+waves+in+Bihar/1/39785.html.

——— (24 November 2010). 'Jailed Criminal from Nitish's Camp Wins'. Retrieved from *HindustanTimes*. Online: http://www.hindustantimes.com/India-news/Bihar/Jailed-criminal-from-Nitish-s-camp-wins/Article1-630552.aspx.

——— 25 November 2014. 'Narendra Modi Rule: Six Months of New Style Governance with Iron Hand'. Retrieved on 9 December 2014, *MF Monitor*: http://www.microfinancemonitor.com/2014/11/25/narendra-modi-rule-six-months-of-new-style-of-governance-with-iron-hand/.

Ibn Battuta (1990). *Travels in Asia and Africa, 1325-1354* (tr. H.A. Gibb). Delhi: Saeed International.

IBNLive (25 August 2014). 'Bihar Bypoll Results: Nitish-Lalu Formula Works as RJD-JDU-Congress Alliance Wins 6 out of 10 Seats', *IBNLive*. Retrieved 7 December 2014, from http://ibnlive.in.com/news/bihar-bypoll-results-nitishlalu-formula-works-as-rjdjducongress-alliance-wins-6-out-of-10-seats/494100-3-232.html.

IBNS (3 September 2012). 'Bihar Lagging Behind in Healthcare: Govt'. Retrieved from Sify News: http://www.sify.com/news/bihar-lagging-behind-in-healthcare-govt-news-health-mjdlHfgdbjc.html.

IMD&WMO (n.d.). *Average Rainfall for India in June* (India Meteorological Department and World Meteorological Organization). Retrieved from Current Results: http://www.currentresults.com/Weather/India/precipitation-june.php.

India Today (3 July 2012). 'Bihar: Fear of Drought Looms Large'. Retrieved 12 September 2012, from *India Today* Online: http://indiatoday.intoday.in/story/bihar-drought-monsoon/1/203520.html.

——— (9 May 2013). 'Two Woman Legislators of JDU at Loggerheads over Murder in Bihar'. Retrieved from India Today.IN: http://m.newshunt.com/India+Today/East/21359123/993.

India Today.IN. (25 September 2011). 'A Wedding Gift for Bihar Strongman's Wife'. Retrieved from India Today.IN: http://indiatoday.intoday.in/story/assembly-polls-wife-of-bihar-strongman-bags-jdu-ticket/1/152604.html.

India TV. (23 September 2012). 'Electricity to all Villages in Bihar by 2015, Promises Nitish'. Retrieved from India TV: http://www.indiatvnews.com/politics/national/electricity-to-all-villages-in-bihar-by-2015-promises-nitish-5449.html.

Indiafacts (20 July 2011). 'Urban and Rural Population of India 2011'. Retrieved from Indiafacts.in:http://indiafacts.in/india-census-2011/urban-rural-population-o-india/.

Indian Express (8 June 2012). 'Bardhan Says Nitish Took Ranvir Sena Help to

Dethrone Lalu Yadav'. Retrieved 3 October 2012, from *The Indian Express*. Online: http://www.indianexpress.com/news/bardhan-says-nitish-took-ranvir-sena-help-to-dethrone-lalu-yadav/959570/.

Indiaonlinepages.com. (8 August 2013). 'India's Population 2013'. Retrieved from Indiaonlinepages.com: http://www.indiaonlinepages.com/population/india-current-population.html.

Inglis, J. (1892). *Tent Life in Tiger Land; and Sport and Work on the Nepaul Frontier.* London: Sampson Low, Marston, & Co.

Institute for Studies in Global Prosperity (2010). *Science, Religion, and Development: Promoting a Discourse in India, Brazil, and Uganda - Occasional Papers on Insight and Practice 1.* New York: Institute of Studies in Global Prosperity.

Islam, S. (1979). *The Permanent Settlement in Bengal: A Study of Its Operation, 1790-1819* (1st edn.). Dacca: Bangla Academy.

Iversen, V., R. Palmer-Jones and K. Sen (2012). *On the Colonial Origins of Agricultural Development in India: A Re-examination of Banerjee and Iyer, 'History, Institutions and Economic Performance'.* Manchester: Brooks World Poverty Institute, BWPI Working Paper 174.

Jacobsen, T. (1978). *The Treasures of Darkness: A History of Mesopotamian Religion.* New Haven: Yale University Press.

Jacoby, H.G. (1 July 2000). 'Access to Rural Markets and the Benefits of Rural Roads'. *The Economic Journal, 110*(465), 713-37.

Jafferlot, C. (2003). *India's Silent Revolution: The Rise of the Lower Castes in North India.* New York: Columbia University Press.

Jagran Post (5 June 2012). 'Nitish Kumar Refuses to Comment on Ranvir Sena's Chief's Murder'. Retrieved 3 October 2012, from Jagran Post - Online: http://post.jagran.com/nitish-kumar-refuses-to-comment-on-ranvir-sena-chiefs-murder-1338903749.

Jain, A.K. and R. Kumar (2009). *Water Management Issues – Punjab.* Ludhiana: Punjab Agricultural University. Retrieved from http://akicb.ifas.ufl.edu/powerpoints/Tuesday/watermanagement-issues-punjab.pdf.

Jaiswal, S. (2008). 'Caste, Gender and Ideology in the Making of India'. *Social Scientist, 36*(1 & 2), 3-39.

Jannuzi, F. T. (1974). *Agrarian Crisis in India: The Case of Bihar.* Austin: University of Texas Press.

——— (1977). 'An Account of the Failure of Agrarian Reforms and the Growth of Agrarian Tensions in Bihar: 1949-1970', in R.E. Frykenberg (ed.), *Land Tenure and Peasant in South Asia.* New Delhi: Orient Longman, pp. 211-12.

Jaoul, N. (2009). 'Naxalism in Bihar: From Bullet to Ballot', in L. Gayer and C. Jaffrelot (eds.), *Armed Militias of South Asia: Fundamentalists, Maoists and Separatists.* New Delhi: Foundation Books, pp. 19-43.

Jebaraj, P. (21 September 2012). 'Bhoodan Land at Centre of Unparalleled Scam, says Ramesh'. Retrieved 3 October 2012, from *The Hindu* - Online - News - Editorial: http://www.thehindu.com/news/national/article3919255.ece.

Jha, A.K. (6 November 2007). 'Why Bihar Failed to Develop?' Retrieved 30 November 2012, from American Chronicle: http://www.americanchronicle.com/articles/view/42328.

Jha, B. (1975). 'Influence of Sanskrit on the Maithili Literature', in V. Ragjavam (ed.), *Proceedings of the First International Sanskrit Conference, Papers of Section Two, Part 1*. New Delhi: Ministry of Education and Social Welfare, Government of India, pp. 140-3.

Jha, C.S. (25 November 2006). 'Saurath Sabha Only Part of Folklore'. Retrieved 30 September 2012, from *Times of India* - India - Online: http://articles.timesofindia.indiatimes.com/2006-11-25/india/27830846_1_saurath-sabha-gachhi-marriage-mithila.

——— (9 March 2008). 'Saurath Sabha Goes Unnoticed'. Retrieved 31 September 2012, from Times of India - Patna - Online: http://articles.timesofindia.indiatimes.com/2008-03-09/patna/27766671_1_saurath-sabha-gachhi-groom-marriage-season.

Jha, D. (n.d.). *Land Reforms in India.* Chennai: Madras School of Economics.

Jha, G. (8 June 2012). '"Slain Ranvir Sena Chief was Gandhian": Nitish Minister Praises Mukhiya for Dedicating his life to Farmers' Causes'. Retrieved 3 October 2012, from Daily Mail Online India: http://www.dailymail.co.uk/indiahome/indianews/article-2156542/Slain-Ranvir-Sena-chief-Gandhian-Nitish-minister-praises-Mukhiya-dedicating-life-farmers-causes.html.

——— (28 October 2012). 'Lawless in Bihar: Ex-JD(U) MLA Makes Extortion Calls in the Name of Nitish's Rally While Still in Jail'. Retrieved from India Today.IN: http://indiatoday.intoday.in/story/bihar-munna-shukla-extortion-nitishs-rally/1/226612.html.

Jha, J.S. (1962). 'History of Darbhanga Raj'. *Journal of Bihar Research Society, 48*, 1-91.

——— (1972). *Biography of an Indian Patriot: Maharaja Lakshmishwar Singh of Darbhanga.* Patna: Maharaja Lakshmishwar Singh Smarak Samiti.

Jha, L. (1952). *Mithila: A Union Republic.* Darbhanga: Mithila Mandal.

Jha, M. (1997). *Anthropology of Ancient Hindu Kingdoms: A Study in Civilizational Perspective.* New Delhi: M.D. Publications. Retrieved from http://books.google.ca/books?id=A0i94Z5C8HMC&printsec=frontcover#v=onepage&q&f=false.

Jha, M.K. and Pushpendra (March 2012). *Governing Caste and Managing Conflicts Bihar, 1990-2011: Policies and Practices, Report No. 48.* Kolkata: Mahanirban Calcutta Research Group.

Jha, P. (July 1997). 'Land Reforms in Bihar: Need for a Far-reaching Approach'. Retrieved 2 October 2012, from CPIML-Liberation Page: http://www.cpiml.org/liberation/year_1997/july/article3.htm.

Jha, S.N. (14 February 1970). 'Caste in Bihar Politics'. *Economic and Political Weekly, 5*(7), 341 and 343-4.

Jha, T.N. and K.U. Viswanathan (1999). 'Problems and Prospects of Agricultural Development in Bihar: Occasional Paper 10'. Mumbai: National Bank for Agriculture and Rural Development.

Kahle, S. (1993). 'Orientalism i Sverige' in the Preface, in E. Said, *Orientalism*. Stockholm: Ordfront, pp. 7-62.

Kahlown, M.A., M. Iqbal, G.V. Skogerboe and S. Rehman (1998). *Waterlogging, Alinity and Crop Yield Relationships*. Mona Reclamation Experimental Project; International Irrigation Management Institute.

Kale, V.S. (1997). 'Flood Studies in India: A Brief Review'. *Journal of the Geological Society of India, 49*(4), 359-70.

——— (December 2008). 'Catastrophe that Engulfed North Bihar'. *Journal of the Geological Society of India,* 72, 713-19.

Kamakoti.org. (9 September 2013). 'Sound and Creation'. Retrieved 9 September 2013, from Kamakoti.org: http://www.kamakoti.org/hindudharma/part5/chap7.htm.

Kamali, M. (n.d.). 'Conceptualizing the "Other", Institutionalized Discrimination and Cultural Racism'. Miscellaneous E-publication, University of Uppsala, Department of Sociology, Uppsala. Retrieved from ftp://ftp.cordis.europa.eu/pub/.../docs/ser_racism_kamali_session2.pdf.

Kamara, A.B. (June 2004). 'The Impact of Market Access on Input Use and Agricultural Productivity: Evidence from Machakos District, Kenya'. *Agrekon, 43*(2), 202-16.

Kangle, R.P. (2010, 7th rpt.). *The Kautiliya Arthasastra* (vol. II). Delhi: Motilal Banarsidass.

Kantowsky, D. (1986). 'Recent Research on Max Weber's Studies of Hinduism', Papers Submitted to a Conference held in New Delhi, 1.-3.3. 1984. München: Weltforum Verlag.

Kapur, S. and S. Kim (October 2006). 'British Colonial Institutions and Economic Development in India'. Cambridge: National Bureau of Economic Research, NBER Working Paper No. 12613.

Karlan, D., D.S. Karlan and J. Appel (2011). *More Than Good Intentions: How a New Economics is Helping Solve Global Poverty*. New York: Penguin Books.

Karunakaran, N. (10 September 2004). 'Living With Floods'. Retrieved 1 September 2012, from Counter Currents.Org: http://www.countercurrents.org/en-naren100904.htm.

Kearney, M. (1995). 'The Local and the Global: The Anthropology of Globalization and Transnationalism'. *Annual Review of Anthropology, 24*, 547-65.

Keay, J. (2000). *India: A History*. New York: Grove Press.

Keller, C.A. (1978). 'Mystical Literature', in S. Katz (ed.), *Mysticism and Philosophical Analysis*. New York: Oxford University Press, pp. 75-100.

Kesavan, N. (5 June 2012). 'Bihar's Caste Curse'. Retrieved 22 September 2012, from *The Hindu* - Opinion Editorial: http://www.thehindu.com/opinion/editorial/article3490670.ece.

Khaldun, A.A. (1967). *Muqaddimah* (tr. F. Rosenthal). Retrieved from http://www.scribd.com/doc/60030982/The-Muqaddimah.

Khan, I. (31 October 2010). 'Farm Tenants' Rights, Caste Issues on Test in Bihar Poll'. Retrieved 29 November 2012, from TwoCircles.net: http://twocircles.net/2010oct31/farm_tenants_rights_caste_issues_test_bihar_poll.html.

Khan, M.S. (9 March 2007). 'Building Infrastructure in Bihar: Roads Need Urgent Attention'. Retrieved from The Bihar Times: http://www.bihartimes.in/articles/msrabbkhan/roads.html.

Khazanov, A.M. (1984). *Nomads and the Outside World.* Madison: University of Wisconsin Press. Retrieved from http://books.google.ca/books?id=PPumUjpp--UC&printsec=frontcover#v=onepage&q&f=false.

Kidwai, J. (7 June 2012). 'The Return of the Dead'. Retrieved 29 November 2012, from The Telegraph – On-line: http://www.telegraphindia.com/1120607/jsp/bihar/story_15580035.jsp.

King, R. (1999). *Orientalism and Religion: Postcolonial Theory, India and 'the Mystic East'.* London: Routledge.

Kinsley, D.R. (1993). *Hinduism: A Cultural Perspective*, 2nd edn. Englewood Cliffs: Prentice-Hall.

Kishen, R. (12 September 2012). 'India's Poor Starve as Politicians Steal Their Food'. Retrieved 19 December 2012, from BloombergBusinessweek - Global Economics: http://www.businessweek.com/articles/2012-09-06/indias-poor-starve-as-politicians-steal-their-food.

Kishore, A. (31 July-6 August 2004). 'Understanding Agrarian Impasse in Bihar'. *Economic and Political Weekly, 39*(31), 3484-91.

Knack, S. (2001). 'Aid Dependence and the Quality of Governance: Cross-country Empirical Tests'. *Southern Economic Journal, 68*(2), 310-29.

Knoema, 2015, 'GDP per Capita by Country 1980-2014', based on International Monetary Fund data. Retrieved from *Knoema.com*, on 5 May 2015, from: http://knoema.com/pjeqzh/gdp-per-capita-by-country-1980-2014#India.

Koebner, R. and H.D. Schmidt (1964). *Imperialism: The Story and Significance of a Political Word, 1840-1960*, Cambridge, Cambridge University Press.

Koestler, A. (1960). *The Lotus and the Robot.* New York: Macmillan.

Kolsky, E. (2010). *Colonial Justice in British India: White Violence and the Rule of Law.* Cambridge: Cambridge University Press, Cambridge Studies in Indian History and Society, no. 17.

Kosambi, D.D. (1965). *Ancient India: A History of Its Culture and Civilization.* New York: Pantheon Books.

Kostman, C.J. (Fall-Winter 1995). 'The Demise of Utopia: Contexts of

Civilizational Collapse in the Bronze Age Indus Valley'. *Journal of the Association of Graduates in Near Eastern Studies, 6*(1).

Kramers, J.H. (1931). 'Geography and Commerce. in T.W. Arnold and A. Guillaaume (eds.), *The Legacy of Islam*. Oxford: The Clarendon Press, pp. 79-107.

Krishibhoomi (4 July 2012). 'Drought Situation to Emerge in Bihar with Delayed Monsoons'. Retrieved 11 September 2012, from Krishibhoomi: National Agricultural News Portal: http://www.krishibhoomi.in/detailnews.aspx?Dept=weatherwatch&SID=41.

Krishnakumar, R. (September-October 1999). 'Flood Management: The Kosi Untamed'. Retrieved 1 September 2012, from *Frontline:* India's National Magazine, vol. 20, no. 16: http://www.frontlineonnet.com/fl1620/16200650.htm.

Krugman, P. (25 August 2013). 'Ibn Khaldun, Psychohistorian'. Retrieved 8 October 2013, from *The New York Times* – The Opinion Pages - The Conscience of a Liberal: http://krugman.blogs.nytimes.com/2013/08/25/ibn-khaldun-psychohistorian/?_r=0.

Kümmel, C. (2001). Frühe Weltsysteme: Zentrumund Peripherie-Modelle in der Archäologie. *Tübinger Texte, Materialien zur Ur- undFrühgeschichtlichen Archäologie, 4.*

Kuhn, T.S. (1962). *The Structure of Scientific Revolutions* (50th Anniversary Edition, 2012 edn.). Chicago: University of Chicago Press.

Kuhnen, F. (1986-7). 'Causes of Underdevelopment and Concepts for Development: An Introduction to Development Theories'. *The Journal of Development Studies, 8*, pp. 11-25.

Kumar, A. (25 January 2005). 'Bhumihars Rooted to the Ground in Caste Politics'. Retrieved 25 October 2012, from *Times of India*, Patna: http://articles.timesofindia.indiatimes.com/2005-01-25/patna/27831627_1_bhumihars-caste-politics.

——— (11 July 2009). 'A Class Analysis of the "Bihari Menace"'. *Economic and Political Weekly, XLIV*(28), 124-7.

Kumar, A. and S. Bhattacharya (4 August 2013). 'The Fall of an Icon'. Retrieved from *The New Indian Express:* http://newindianexpress.com/magazine/The-fall-of-an-icon/2013/08/04/article1712213.ece.

Kumar, D. (24 April 2014). 'RJD Bouncing Back in Bihar, but Lalu Prasad Remains Grounded'. Retrieved 2 May 2014 from NDTV-India Votes 2014: http://www.ndtv.com/elections/article/election-news/rjd-bouncing-back-in-bihar-but-lalu-prasad-remains-grounded-513494.

——— (ed.). (1989). *The Cambridge Economic History of India: c. 1757-c. 1970* (vol. 2). Cambridge: Cambridge University Press.

——— (2005). *Millennium Strategy for the Kosi.* Patna: Allied Publishers.

Kumar, D. and M. Kumar (22 April 2014). 'Nitish Kumar Admits Outcome of General Election will Impact his Government's Survival'. Retrieved 2 May 2014 from NDTV - India Votes 2014: http://www.ndtv.com/elections/article/election-2014/nitish-kumar-admits-outcome-of-general-election-will-impact-his-government-s-survival-512208.

Kumar, J.N. (1933). *The Genealogical History of India,* pt. II. Calcutta: Jnanendra Nath Kumar.

Kumar, M. (29 September 2012). 'JD(U) MLA's Husband Snatched Police Carbine at Khagaria'. Retrieved from *The Times of India,* Patna: http://articles.timesofindia.indiatimes.com/2012-09-29/patna/34162804_1_khagaria-elections-ljp-candidate.

Kumar, S. (23 May 2014). 'Bihar: Interpreting the Massive Mandate'. Retrieved from *The Hindu* – Online, from http://www.thehindu.com/opinion/op-ed/bihar-interpreting-the-massive-mandate/article6037680.ece.

Kumar, S., M.S Alam and D. Joshi (January-June 2008). 'Caste Dynamics and Political Process in Bihar'. *Journal of Indian School of Political Economy, 20*(1 & 2), 1-32.

Kurian, N.J. (2001). *Regional Disparities in India.* New Delhi: Planning Commission of India. Retrieved from http://planningcommission.nic.in/reports/sereport/ser/vision2025/regdsprty.pdf.

——— (October 2007). 'Review Article: Widening Economic & Social Disparities: Implications for India'. *Indian Journal of Medical Research, 126*(4), pp. 374-80.

——— (n.d.). 'Widening Regional Disparities in India'. Retrieved 21 December 2012, from http://planningcommission.nic.in/reports/articles/ncsxna/art_wide.pdf.

Kuruvachira, J. (2010). *Is Hinduism a Continuation of the Vedic Religion?* Rome: Pontifical Salesian University (UPS).

Lacoste, Y. (1984). *Ibn Khaldun: The Birth of History and the Past of the Third World.* London: Verso Editions.

Lal, C.K. (13 July 2006). 'Cultural Flows Across a Blurred Boundary'. Retrieved 5 October 2012, from Madhesi - United We Stand: http://madhesi.wordpress.com/2006/07/13/cultural-flows-across-a-blurred-boundary/.

Lamplugh, G.W. (1914). 'Physiographical Notes. II. On the Taming of Streams (Continued)'. *Geographical Journal,* 43(6), 651-6. Retrieved from http://www.jstor.org/discover/10.2307/1779149?uid=3739448&uid=2129&uid=2&uid=70&uid=3737720&uid=4&sid=21101168423811.

Lanman, C.R. (1912). *A Sanskrit Reader: With Vocabulary and Notes* 1st edn., 6th issue. Ginn & Co. doi:http://archive.org/stream/asanskritreader01lanmgoog#page/n10/mode/2up.

LaPorta, R., F. Lopez-de-Silanes and A. Shleifer (2008). 'The Economic Consequences of Legal Origins'. *Journal of Economic Literature, 46*(2), 285-332.

LaPorta, R., F. Lopez-de-Silanes, A. Shleifer and R.W. Vishny (1998a). 'Law and Finance'. *Journal of Political Economy, 106*(6), 1113-55.

LaPorta, R., F., Lopez-de-Silanes, A. Shliefer and R.W. Visny (April 1999). 'The Quality of Government'. *Journal of Law, Economics, and Organization, 15*(1), 222-79.

LaPorta, R., F.L. Silanen, A. Sheifer and R. Vishney (1998b). 'Quality of Government'. *Journal of Law, Economics and Organization, 15*(1-2), 3-27.

Lashari, B.K. and S.M. Kori (2010). 'Drainage Scavenger Tube Wells Can Sustain Rural Livelihoods: Evidence from Sindh Pakistan'. *Proceedings of IWRM2010*. Nanjing: IAHS, pp. 316-23.

Leeson, P.T. (2008). 'Escaping Poverty: Foreign Aid, Private Property and Economic Development'. *Journal of Private Enterprise, 23*(2), 39-64.

LeFevre, R. (1980). 'Ownership of Land', in *The Philosophy of Ownership*. Auburn: Ludwig von Mises Institute, pp. 46-53. Retrieved 17 November 2012, from http://books.google.ca/books?id=wm_QGgpzVi0C&printsec=frontcover#v=onepage&q&f=false.

Lehman, J. and S. Phelps (2005). *West's Encyclopedia of American Law* (2nd edn.). Detroit: Thomson/Gale.

Leibniz, G. (1999). 'Some Aspects of Indo-European Agriculture', in M.H.D. Disterheft (ed.), *Studies in Honor of Jaan Puhvel, Part I, Ancient Languages and Philology*. Washington, D.C.: Institute for the Study of Man, Monograph No. 20, pp. 221-40.

Lemon, R. (2011). *Imperial Messages : Orientalism as Self-critique in the Habsburg Fin de Siècle.* Rochester: Camden House.

Lethbridge, R. (1893). *The Golden Book of India.* London: Macmillan & Co.

Lewis, B. (1993). *Islam and the West.* New York: Oxford University Press.

Leys, C. (1996). *The Rise and Fall of Development Theory.* Oxford: James Currey.

Lindsay, R. (15 March 2011). 'The Aryan Migration Theory: Last Word'. Retrieved from https://robertlindsay.wordpress.com/2011/03/15/the-aryan-migration-theory-last-word/.

Live Mint (11 August 2013). 'Fodder Scam Trial: SC Reserves Verdict on Lalu Prasad's Plea'. Retrieved from Live Mint & The Wall Street Journal: http://www.livemint.com/Politics/Hdt5TvicWCOoNO4IDfzEAK/SC-reserves-verdict-on-Lalus-plea-to-transfer-fodder-scam-t.html.

Lorenzen, D.N. (2006). *Who Invented Hinduism: Essays on Religion in History.* Delhi: Yoda Press, New Perspectives on Indian Pasts Series. Retrieved from http://books.google.ca/books?id=SO-YmMWpcVEC&printsec=frontcover#v=onepage&q&f=false.

Louis, P. (2002). *People Power: The Naxalite Movement in Central Bihar.* Delhi: Wordsmiths.

Ludden, D.E. (2005). *Making India Hindu: Religion, Community, and the Politics of Democracy in India* (2nd edn.). Delhi: Oxford University Press.

Lyon, P. (2008). *Conflict Between India and Pakistan: An Encyclopedia.* Santa

Barbara: ABC-CLIO. Retrieved from http://books.google.ca/books?id=vLwOck15eboC&printsec=frontcover#v=onepage&q&f=false.

Macaulay, T.B. (1970). 'Government of India', 10 July 1833, in Thomas Babington Macaulay, *Prose and Poetry*, Cambridge: Cambridge University Press, 1970.

MacDonell, A.A. (1974/2003). *A Sanskrit Grammar for Students* (3rd rpt. edn.). Delhi: Motilal Banarsidass.

Macpherson, T.S. (1908). *Final Report on the Operations for the Preparation of a Record of Rights in Pargana Porahat, District Singhbhum, 1905-1907.* Calcutta: Bengal Secretariat Book Depot.

Mahadevan, R. (December 2003). 'Productivity Growth in Indian Agriculture: The Role of Globalization and Economic Reform'. *Asia-Pacific Development Journal, 10*(2), 57-72.

Mahapatra, D. (28 February 2009). 'Should Right to Property Return?' Retrieved 21 August 2012, from *The Times of India:* http://articles.timesofindia.indiatimes.com/2009-02-28/india/28001697_1_public-purpose-poor-farmers-property.

Maine, H.S. (1876). 'The Effect of Observation of India on European Thought', in *Village Communities in the East and West*, the Rede Lecture of 1875, London: John Murray.

——— (1890). *Lectures on the Early History of Institutions.* London: John Murray.

Majumdar, R.C. (2003). *Ancient India* (8th rpt. edn.). Delhi: Motilal Banarsidass. Retrieved from http://books.google.ca/books?id=XNxiN5tzKOgC&printsec=frontcover#v=onepage&q&f=false.

Malaviya, H.D. (1955). *Land Reforms in India* (2nd edn.). Delhi: Economic and Political Research Department, All India Congress Committee.

Mantena, K. (2010). 'The Crisis of Liberal Imperialism', *Histoire@Politique. Politique, culture, société*, 11(2).

Marchand, S.L. (2010). *German Orientalism in the Age of Empire: Religion, Race, and Scholarship.* Cambridge: German Historical Institute & Cambridge University Press.

Marshall, K. (1998). 'Development and Religion: A Different Lens on Development Debates'. *Peabody Journal of Education, 76*(3-4), 339-75.

Marshall, K and L. Keough (2004). *Mind, Heart, and Soul in the Fight against Poverty.* Washington, DC: World Bank.

Martin, C. (1 February 2013). 'Do Global Communications Inevitably Lead to Cultural Homogenization?' E-International Relations. Retrieved from http://www.e-ir.info/2013/02/01/does-the-development-of-global-communications-inevitably-lead-to-cultural-homogenization/.

Marx, K. (7 and 10 February 1844). 'A Contribution to the Critique of Hegel's Philosophy of Right'. *Deutsch-Französische Jahrbücher, Proofed and corrected by Andy Blunden and corrected by Matthew Carmody, 2005 & 2009.*

Masih, A. (24 May 2013). 'Has Change Really Come to Bihar?' Retrieved from Rediff News: http://www.rediff.com/news/report/what-change-is-really-like-in-nitish-kumars-bihar/20130523.htm.

Maxwell, S. (February 1999). *The Meaning and Measurement of Poverty - ODI Poverty Briefings Issue 3*. Retrieved 3 January 2011, from ODI - Shaping Policy for Development: http://www.odi.org.uk/publications/2277-meaning-measurement-poverty.

Mayotte, J.A. (Summer-Fall 1998). 'Religion and Global Affairs: The Role of Religion in Development'. *SAIS Review, 18*(2), 65-9.

McMichael, P. (2012). *Development and Social Change: A Global Perspective* (5th edn.). Los Angeles: Sage, Sociology for a New Century Series. Retrieved from http://www.worldcat.org/title/development-and-social-change-a-global-perspective/oclc/810433569/viewport.

McNeill, W.H. (1963/1991). *The Rise of the West: A History of the Human Community.* Chicago: University of Chicago Press.

MDM [Michael Dennis Mooney]. (13 April 2011). 'Thou Shalt Not Sit with Statisticians Nor Commit a Social Science'. Retrieved 5 June 2013, from The Fine-Wrought Figure: http://lightneasy.wordpress.com/2011/04/13/the-hermetic-decalogue-by-w-h-auden/.

Meadows, D.H. (1972). *The Limits to Growth: A Report for the Club of Rome's Project on the Predicament of Mankind.* New York: Universe Books, Potomac Association Books Series.

Meinzen-Dick, R.S. (1984). *Local Management of Tank Irrigation in South India: Organization and Operation.* Ithaca: Cornell University - Cornell Studies in Irrigation, no. 3.

Menon, M. (19 March 2010). 'The Nowhere People'. Retrieved from *The Hindu* On-line: http://www.thehindu.com/todays-paper/tp-opinion/the-nowhere-people/article731085.ece.

Merchant, M. (1 August 2013). 'Gujarat *vs.* Bihar: Which Development Model Works Best?' Retrieved from The Economic Times: http://blogs.economictimes.indiatimes.com/headon/entry/gujarat-vs-bihar-which-model-works-best.

Metcalf, B.D. and T.R. Metcalf (2001, 2006). *A Concise History of Modern India* (2nd edn.). Cambridge: Cambridge University Press.

Metcalf, T.R. (1994). *The New Cambridge History of India: Ideologies of the Raj,* vol. III, 4. Cambridge: Cambridge University Press.

Mikic, M. (2011). 'Preferential Market Access Issues', in *Studies in Trade and Investment 76.* New York: United Nations Economic and Social Commission for Asia and the Pacific (ESCAP), pp. 25-37.

Miller, E. (29 April 1970). 'Is "Development" Good For The Third World? (Vandana Shiva)'. Retrieved 5 December 2012, from America.org: http://www.amerika.org/texts/is-development-good-for-the-third-world-vandana-shiva/.

Ministry of Environment & Forests, Government of India (2014). 'Status of Surface and Groundwater in Bihar'. Retrieved from Bihar Envis Centre - State of Environment: http://bhenvis.nic.in/intro_water.html.

Ministry of Rural Development (2011). *Socio-Economic and Caste Census, 2011-Rural: Instruction Manual for Enumerators.* New Delhi: Government of India.

Ministry of Rural Development (25 July 2011). *Socio Economic & Caste Census, 2001, in Rural India.* Delhi: Government of India.

Ministry of Water Resources (2009). *Ground Water Resources Estimation Methodology.* New Delhi: Government of India, Ground Water Resource Estimation Committee.

Mishra, D. (15 November 2001). 'Bihar Feels the Pinch of Bifurcation'. Retrieved from *The Times of India* – Patna: http://articles.timesofindia.indiatimes.com/2001-11-15/patna/27259995_1_bihar-bifurcation-economist-saibal-gupta.

——— (12 December 2009). 'BPL Population of Bihar 55%, says Report'. Retrieved from *The Times of India*, Patna: http://articles.timesofindia.indiatimes.com/2009-12-12/patna/28109823_1_bpl-families-bpl-population-bpl-list.

Mishra, D.K. (30 August 1997). 'Special Articles: The Bihar Flood Story'. *Economic and Political Weekly, XXXII*(35), 2206-17.

——— (1 January 1997). 'The Bihar Flood Story'. *Economic and Political Weekly, 32*(35), 2206.

——— (August 2004). 'Harvesting Flood Relief'. Retrieved 11 August 2012, from India Together: http://www.indiatogether.org/2004/aug/opi-floods.htm.

——— (7 August 2009). 'The Kosi is Back to Its Permanent Clientele'. Retrieved 20 September 2012, from d-Sector.org: d-sector, http://www.d-sector.org/article-detailCon.asp?id=12.

——— (March 2011). 'The People *vs* the Environment'. Retrieved 2 September 2012, from Himal Southasian: http://www.himalmag.com/component/content/article/4288-the-people-vs-the-environment.html.

——— (April 2012). 'Managing Embankments to Manage Disasters'. *South Asia Network on Dams, Rivers and People*, 1-4. Retrieved from http://sandrp.in/floods/Managing_Embankments_to_Manage_Disasters.pdf.

Mishra, J. (1975). 'Influence of Sanskrit on Maithili Language and Literature', in V. Raghavan (ed.), *Proceedings of the First International Sanskrit Conference, Papers of Section Two, Part 1.* New Delhi: Government of India, Ministry of Education and Social Welfare, pp. 133-9.

Mishra, S. (22 March 2013). *A Tricky Lesson for Bihar.* Retrieved from Business Standard: http://www.business-standard.com/article/beyond-business/a-tricky-lesson-for-bihar-113032200484_1.html.

Mishra, S.G. (2000). *Democracy in India.* New Delhi: Sanbun Publishers. Retrieved from http://books.google.ca/books?id=cFs0YSkA4ckC&pg=PA19&lpg=PA19&dq=Licchavis,+democracy&source=bl&ots=z-GGu5mZrP&sig=r3fNAClGw6UjRL0ygY1YbJhoeYg&hl=en&sa=X&ei=xoQcUf3OEaO42gX4q4DwCA&ved=0CDsQ6AEwAg#v=onepage&q=Licchavis%2C%20democracy&f=false.

Mishra, V. (2005). 'The Heroes have Finally Arrived on the Stage! - Exerpts from the Report from the Flaming Fields of Bihar'. Retrieved 22 September 2012, from CPIML.Org: http://www.cpiml.org/liberation/year_2005/january/remembering_vm.htm.

Mitra, A. (1965-6). *Census of India, 1961: Levels of Regional Development in India, Vol. I, Part 1-A (I & II).* New Delhi: Registrar General of India.

Mitra, M. (1976). 'A Review of the Role of Zamindars in Bihar vis-à-vis the Agrarian Economy'. *Proceedings of the Indian History Congress, 37th Session.* Calicut: Indian History Congress, pp. 114-239.

Monchuk, D., K. Deninger and H. Nagarajan (2010). *Does Land Fragmentation Reduce Efficiency? Micro Evidence from India.* Denver: Agricultural and Applied Economics Association (AAEA), CAES and WAEA Joint Annual Meeting, 25-6 July.

Morrell, D. (January-February 2011). 'Who is Poor?' Retrieved 3 November 2011, from Harvard Magazine - On-line: http://harvardmagazine.com/2011/01/who-is-poor.

Morris, B. (1987). *Anthropological Studies of Religion: An Introductory Text* (14th Printing, 2003 edn.). Cambridge: Cambridge University Press.

Morris, I. (2010). *Why the West Rules for Now: The Patterns of History and What They Reveal about the Future.* London: Profile Books.

Morrison, D. (8 August 2012). 'The Dark Side of India's "Mr. Clean"'. Retrieved 30 October 2012, from Aljazeera - On line: http://www.aljazeera.com/indepth/opinion/2012/08/2012869281872518.

Mosley, P. (1985). 'The Political Economy of Foreign Aid: A Model of the Market for a Public Good'. *Economic Development and Cultural Change, 33*(2), pp. 373-93.

Mowlana, H. (2001). 'Information in the Arab World'. *Cooperation South Journal.*

Müller, F.M. (1888). *Biographies of Words and the Home of the Aryas.* London: Longmans, Green. Retrieved from http://books.google.ca/books?id=9GUSAAAAYAAJ&printsec=frontcover#v=onepage&q&f=false.

——— (1891). *Chips from a German Workshop* (vol. 1). New York: Charles Scribner's Sons. Retrieved from http://books.google.ca/books?id=J8Zo_rtoWAEC&printsec=frontcover#v=onepage&q&f=false.

Muesse, M.W. (2011). *The Hindu Traditions: A Concise Introduction.* Minneapolis: Fortress Press. Retrieved 25 August 2013, from http://books.google.ca/books?id=VlQBfbwk7CwC&printsec=frontcover#v=onepage&q&f=false.

Mukherjee, S. (4 August 2013). 'For Now, Bihar Likely to get just a "Backward" Boost'. Retrieved from *Business Standard:* http://www.business-standard.com/article/economy-policy/for-now-bihar-likely-to-get-just-a-backward-boost-113032600438_1.html.

Mukherji, A. and A. Mukherji (2012). *Bihar: What Went Wrong? And What Changed?* New Delhi: National Institute of Public Finance and Policy, Working Paper No. 12/107.

Nagaraj, R. (4 March 2010). 'How Real is Bihar's Growth Story?' Retrieved from Rediff Business: http://www.rediff.com/money/column/guest-how-real-is-bihars-growth-story/20100304.htm.

Nair, J. (1996). *Women and Law in Colonial India: A Social History.* New Delhi: Kali for Women in collaboration with the National Law School of India University. Retrieved from http://books.google.ca/books?id=XUsqAAAAYAAJ&focus=searchwithinvolume&q=dominions.

Nair, K. (1961). *Blossoms in the Dust: The Human Factor in Indian Development* (7th edn.). New York: Frederick A. Praeger.

Nakazato, N. (1994). *Agrarian System in Eastern Bengal: 1870-1910.* Calcutta: K.P. Bagchi & Co. Retrieved from http://books.google.ca/books/about/Agrarian_system_in_eastern_Bengal_c_1870.html?id=VDWFAAAAIAAJ&redir_esc=y.

Nanda, R. (10 April 2010). 'It's Official: 37 pc Live Below Poverty Line'. Retrieved from IBN Live - India: http://ibnlive.in.com/news/its-official-37-live-below-poverty-line/113522-3.html.

Nandy, A. (18 February 1991). *Hinduism versus Hindutva: The Inevitability of a Confrontation*. Retrieved from Manas, Originally taken from *The Times of India:* http://www.sscnet.ucla.edu/southasia/Socissues/hindutva.html.

Narayan, D., R. Patel, K. Schafft, A. Rademacher and S. Koch-Schulte (2000). *Voices of the Poor: Can Anyone Hear Us?* New York: World Bank & Oxford University Press.

Narayan, S. (8 April 2011). 'India's Battle Against Hunger'. Retrieved 3 November 2012, from *The Guardian* - On-line: http://www.guardian.co.uk/global-development/poverty-matters/2011/apr/08/india-battle-against-hunger.

Narayanan, M.G. (October 1975). 'Historical Perspectives on Ancient India'. *Social Scientist, 4*(3), 3-11.

Nath, S. (November 2007). 'Religion and Economic Growth and Development'. Munich Personal RePEc Archive, Paper No. 8181. Retrieved from http://mpra.ub.uni-muenchen.de/8181/.

National Highways Authority of India, M.O. (August 2013). 'Indian Road Network.' Retrieved from Indian Road Network: http://www.nhai.org/roadnetwork.htm.

National Informatics Centre (2011). 'The Changing Face of Urban Bihar'. New Delhi: National Informatics Centre. Retrieved 21 July 2013, from urban.bih.nic.in/docs/changing-face-of-urban-bihar-in-english.pdf.

Nayyar, R. (2004). 'Planning for the Development of Backward Districts'. New Delhi: Planning Commission, Government of India. Retrieved from http://www.dfid.gov.uk/r4d/PDF/Outputs/ChronicPoverty_RC/chap-23.pdf.

Neale, W.C. (1962). *Economic Change in Rural India: Land Tenure and Reform in Uttar Pradesh, 1800-1955.* New Haven: Yale University Press.

Nedumpara, J.J. (2004). *Political Economy and Class Contradictions.* New Delhi: Anmol Publications.

NIC (n.d.). 'Chapter III: *Performance Audit – Performance Review* on Tubewell Project in Bihar'. Retrieved 18 September 2012, from http://ag.bih.nic.in/AuditReports/2006-07/Civil/05-Chapter-3.pdf.

No Bribe (9 November 2009). 'Changing Bihar, Slowly'. Retrieved from No Bribe - Corruption Free India: http://www.nobribe.org/changing-bihar-slowly.

North, D.C. (1990). *Institutions, Institutional Change and Economic Performance.* Cambridge: Cambridge University Press.

NSSO (1954). *Report on Landholdings, 1953-54, 8th Round, Report No. 74.* National Sample Survey Organization (NSSO). New Delhi: Government of India, Ministry of Planning and Statistics.

——— (2000). *Employment and Unemployment Situation Among Social Groups, 1999-2000, 55th Round, Report No. 469.* National Sample Survey Organization (NSSO). New Delhi: Government of India, Ministry of Planning and Statistics.

Ocken, J.R. (30 September 2008). 'Enabling Analysis' (ed. D. Ganse), *Synygy, 4*, 19-21.

Office of National Statistics (2012). *Religion in England and Wales 2011.* London: Government of Great Britain.

Ojha, G. (1977?). *Land Problems and Land Reforms: A Study with Reference to Bihar.* New Delhi: Sultan Chand & Sons.

Oldmeadow, H. (2004). 'The Debate about "Orientalism"', in H. Oldmeadow, *Journeys East: 20th Century Western Encounters with Eastern Religious Traditions* (pp. 3-19). Bloomington, IN: World Wisdom. Retrieved from Journey East: 20th Century Western Encounters with Eastern Religions: http://books.google.ca/books?id=vC1qAj6RbRQC&printsec=frontcover#v=onepage&q&f=false.

O'Malley, L.S. (1907). *Bengal District Gazetteers: Champaran.* Calcutta: Bengal Secretariat Book Depot. Retrieved from http://www.dli.gov.in/scripts/FullindexDefault.htm?path1=/data_copy/upload/0076/008&first=1&last=214&barcode=6010010076003.

——— (1911). *Bengal District Gazetteers: Purnea* (vol. 25). Calcutta: Bengal Secretariat Book Depot.

O'Malley, L.S. and M. Chakravarti (1909). *Bengal District Gazetteers, Howrah* (vol. 18). Calcutta: Bengal Secretariat Book Depot. Retrieved from http://books.google.ca/books?id=40_RAAAAMAAJ&q=embankments# search_anchor.

Oman, J.C. (1899). *The Stories of the Ramayana and the Mahabharata.* London: George Bell & Sons.

Ong, W. (1982). *Orality and Literacy: The Technologizing of the Word.* London: Methuen.

Open Science Collaboration (2013). 'The Reproducibility Project: A Model of Large-scale Collaboration for Empirical Research on Reproducibility: Open Science Collaboration'. Open Science Collaboration (OSC). Retrieved 1 July 2013.

Open Science Framework (2011-12). *About Open Science Framework.* Retrieved 1 July 2013, from OpenScienceFramework.org: http://openscienceframework.org/about/.

Outlook India.com. (2002). *A Brief Outline of the Hindutva Movement.* Retrieved 26 August 2013, from Outlook India.com: http://www.outlookindia.com/articlefullwidth.aspx?217966.

Ovaska, T. (2003). 'The Failure of Development Aid'. *Cato Journal, 23*(2), 174-88.

Overdorf, J. (16 July 2012). *India: Food Rots as People Starve.* Retrieved 4 November 2012, from Global-Post: http://www.globalpost.com/dispatch/news/regions/asia-pacific/india/120712/food-security-hunger-starvation-wheat-prices.

Palanisami, K. and P. Paramasivam (2007). *Irrigation Sector in India: Trends, Issues, and Prospects.* Coimbatore: Tamil Nadu Agricultural University.

Palgrave, R.H. (ed.), (1915). *Dictionary of Political Economy* (vol. 2). London: Macmillan.

Pandey, G. (1993). 'Which of Us are Hindus?', in G. Pandey (ed.), *Hindus and Others: The Question of Identity in India Today.* New Delhi: Viking.

Lalita Panicker, L. and G. Choudhury (3 May 2014). 'Nitish Kumar is Amaryta's Nominee for Prime Minister'. Retrieved from *Hindstan Times* (Kolkata), from: http://paper.hindustantimes.com/epaper/viewer.aspx.

Panikkar, Avanish K. (Content Source: FAO). (19 March 2012). 'Water Profile of India'. Retrieved 18 September 2012, from The Encyclopedia of Earth: Environmental Information Coalition, National Council for Science and the Environment: http://www.eoearth.org/article/Water_profile_of_India.

Pant, Harsh V. (26 November 2014). 'Modi's Diplomatic Chutzpah', *The Diplomat.* Retrieved from http://thediplomat.com/2014/11/modis-diplomatic-chutzpah/.

Pant, N. and R.K. Verma (2010). *Tanks in Eastern India: A Study in Exploration.* Hyderabad and Lucknow: IWMI-Tata Policy Research Program and Centre for Development Studies. doi:10.5337/2010.228.

Parameshwarappa, K.G. (2009). *Climate Change and Perspectives for Indian Agriculture,* n.p.: IOP Conference Series: Earth and Environmental Science 6: Climate Change: Global Risks, Challenges and Decisions.

Paterson, I. (2009). *God of the Machine* (8th edn.). New Brunswick: Transactional Publishers. Retrieved from http://books.google.ca/books?id=Bgw2nKffTXMC&printsec=frontcover#v=onepage&q&f=false.

Patna Bureau (4 January 2007). *The Great Job Swap.* Retrieved 30 October 2012, from *The Economist* - On line: http://www.economist.com/node/8498853?zid=306&ah=1b164dbd43b0cb27ba0d4c3b12a5e227.

Pew Forum on Religion and Public Life (February 2008). *U.S. Religious Landscape Survey: Religious Affiliations: Diverse and Dynamic.* Washington, DC: The Pew Forum on Religion & Public Life. Retrieved from Pew Research Religion & Public Life Project.

Pierce, J.L. and I. Jussila (2011). *Psychological Ownership and the Organizational Context: Theory, Research Evidence, and Application.* Northampton: Edward Elgar Publishing, New Horizons in Management Series. Retrieved from http://books.google.ca/books?id=g3Z7QC01oowC&printsec=frontcover#v=onepage&q&f=false.

Pierce, J.L., T. Kostova and K.T. Dirks (2003). 'The State of Psychological Ownership: Integrating and Extending a Century of Research'. *Review of General Psychology: Journal of Division 1, of the American Psychological Association*, 84-107.

Planning Commission (1997). *Report of the Committee to Identify 100 Most Backward & Poorest Districts in the Country [aka Sarma Committee Report].* New Delhi: Government of India, Ministry of Rural Areas and Employment.

——— (2003). *Task Force on "Identification of Districts for Wage and Self Employment Programmes".* New Delhi: Planning Commission, Government of India.

——— (April 2008). *Bihar's Agriculture Development: Opportunities & Challenges, Report of the Planning Commission Special Task Force on Bihar.* New Delhi: Government of India.

——— (November 1981). *Report on General Issues Relating to Backward Area Development.* New Delhi: Government of India, National Committee on the Development of Backward Areas.

Polgreen, L. (10 April 2010). 'Turnaround in India's State Could Serve as a Model'. Retrieved 16 July 2013, from *The New York Times* - On-line: http://www.nytimes.com/2010/04/11/world/asia/11bihar.html?_r=0.

Pollock, S. (2006). *The Language of the Gods in the World of Men: Sanskrit, Culture, and Power in Premodern India,* Berkeley: University of California Press, Retrieved from http://books.google.ca/books?id=0UCh7r2TjQIC&printsec=frontcover#v=onepage&q&f=false.

PolyEyes Staff (2 May 2013). 'Bihar Economy Statistics: Infrastructure and Communications'. Retrieved 4 August 2013, from PolyEyes: http://www.polyeyes.com/Article/Bihar-Economy-Statistics-Infrastructure-and-Communications.

Ponraj, S.D. (Spring 2009). 'Graveyard to Vineyard: Transformation in Bihar'. Retrieved 15 November 2012, from New Wineskins Missionary Network: http://www.newwineskins.org/content/graveyard-vineyard-transformation-bihar.

Powell, B. and M.E. Ryan (Fall 2006). 'Does Development Aid Lead to Economic Freedom?' *Journal of Private Enterprise, 22*(1), 1-21. Retrieved from http://journal.apee.org/index.php?title=Fall2006_1.

Prakash, G. (1 January 1990). 'Writing Post-Orientalist Histories of the Third World: Perspectives from Indian Historiography'. *Comparative Studies in Society and History: An International Quarterly,* 32, 383-408.

Prasad, E. (2003). *Bihar's Flood Survival Mechanism.* Retrieved 2 September 2012, from India Water Portal.Org: http://www.indiawaterportal.org/sites/indiawaterportal.org/files/floodissuecore11-30.pdf.

Prasad, G. (1997). *History of Irrigation in Bihar* (2nd edn.). Patna: Water & Land Management Institute.

Prasad, P.H. (14 June 1975). 'Agrarian Unrest and Economic Change in Rural Bihar: The Three Case Studies'. *Economic and Political Weekly, 10*(24), 931, 933-7.

——— (30 May 1987). 'Agrarian Violence in Bihar'. *Economic and Political Weekly, 22*(22), 847-52.

Pratyaya. (18 July 2013). 'Bihar Tragedy: The State of Education and Healthcare Infrastructure'. Retrieved from Pratyaya - Indian Education Policy: http://pratyaya.nationalinterest.in/2013/07/18/bihar-tragedy-a-reflection-on-the-state-of-education-and-healthcare-infrastructure/.

Press Trust of India (29 September 2012b). 'No Case Against Ranvir Yadav: Police'. Retrieved from ZeeNews.com: http://zeenews.india.com/news/bihar/no-case-against-ranvir-yadav-police_802760.html.

——— (25 February 2004). 'Bihar a Byword for Worst of India: The Economist'. Retrieved 27 October 2012, from ExpressIndia.Com: http://www.expressindia.com/news/fullstory.php?newsid=28789.

——— (20 September 2012a). 'Sharad Yadav Gives Cleat Chit to Gun-totting JD(U) Leader Ranveer Yadav'. Retrieved from NDTV: http://www.ndtv.com/article/india/sharad-yadav-gives-clean-chit-to-gun-totting-jd-u-leader-ranveer-yadav-273945.

——— (10 August 2013). 'Telephone Boom in Bihar Most Visible Sigh of Economic Growth'. Retrieved from *Business Standard:* http://www.business-standard.com/article/economy-policy/telephone-boom-in-bihar-most-visible-sign-of-economic-growth-113022400147_1.html.

——— (1 December 2014). 'Jitan Ram Manjhi a Better Chief Minister than Nitish Kumar, Says Ram Vilas Paswan', *NDTV,* Retrieved 21 December 2014, from http://www.ndtv.com/article/india/jitan-ram-manjhi-a-better-chief-minister-than-nitish-kumar-says-ram-vilas-paswan-628467.

——— (7 December 2014). 'Merger of "Janata Parivar" Parties a Permanent Alliance, Says RJD Chief Lalu Prasad Yadav', *NDTV*, Retrieved 7 December 2014, from http://www.ndtv.com/article/india/merger-of-janata-parivar-parties-a-permanent-alliance-says-rjd-chief-lalu-prasad-yadav-631179?ndtv_related.

——— (2 March 2013a). 'Bihar CM Worried over Population Growth Rate'. Retrieved 3 August 2013, from The Hindu Business Line: http://www.thehindubusinessline.com/news/states/bihar-cm-worried-over-population-growth-rate/article4469147.ece.

——— (31 July 2013b). '150 Students Fall Ill after Midday Meal in Bihar'. Retrieved from DNA: http://www.dnaindia.com/india/1868262/report-150-students-fall-ill-after-midday-meal-in-bihar.

——— (2 August 2013c). 'BJP Alleges Return of "Jungle Raj" in Bihar'. Retrieved from *The Hindu - Business Line:* http://www.thehindubusinessline.com/news/states/bjp-alleges-return-of-jungle-raj-in-bihar/article4981845.ece.

——— (9 August 2013d). 'Fodder Scam: Supreme Court Reserve Order on Lalu's Plea to Change Judge'. Retrieved from *The Economic Times:* http://articles.economictimes.indiatimes.com/2013-08-06/news/41131972_1_fodder-scam-shanti-bhushan-plea-seeking-transfer.

Pryor, J.H. (1992). *Geography, Technology, and War: Studies in the History of the Mediterranean, 649-1571.* Cambridge: Cambridge University Press.

Qizilbash, M. (2007). 'On Ethics and the Economics of Development'. *The Journal of Philosophical Economics, 1*(1), 54-73.

Quesnay, F. and A. Oncken (1888). *Œuvres économiques et philosophiques de F. Quesnay, fondateur du système physiocratique; accompagnées des éloges et d'autres travaux biographiques sur Quesnay par différents auteurs* (A. Oncken, ed.) Paris: Joseph Baer.

Radcliffe-Brown, A.R. (1952). 'Structure and Function in Primitive Society: Essays and Addresses'. Glencoe: The Free Press.

Radhakrishnan, S. (1980). *The Hindu View of Life.* London: Unwin Paperbacks.

Raghavan, A. (2014). *British Orientalism in India: Nature and Impact on Indian Society (A Historiographical Survey); Critically Analyze the Nature of Orientalism and its Impact on Indian History with an Emphasis on Edward Said's Arguments.* Retrieved from Academia.edu, Paper 2565126: http://www.academia.edu/2565126/British_Orientalism_in_India_Nature_and_Impact_on_Indian_Society_A_Historiographical_Survey.

Rahmatian, A. (19 November 2008). 'Psychological Aspects of Property and Ownership'. *Liverpool Law Review, 29*(3), 287-308. doi:10.1007/s10991-008-9046-5.

Rai, L. (1917). *England's Debt to India: A Historical Narrative of Britain's Fiscal Policy in India.* New York: B.W. Huebsch.

Rai, P. (2012). 'The Great MNREGA Robbery: Wretched of Bihar Robbed of

Nearly Rs. 6000 Crore'. New Delhi: HIVOS and Centre for Environment and Food Security.

Rajalakshmi, T.K. (October-November 2001). 'Land Rights and Wrongs in Bihar'. Retrieved 3 October 2012, from *Frontline*, vol. 18, issue 22: http://www.frontlineonnet.com/fl1822/18220460.htm.

Raju, P.R. (1953 [2009]). *Idealistic Thought of India.* London: Routledge, Routledge Library Editions: Buddhism. Retrieved from http://books.google.ca/books?id=LY5TAQAAQBAJ&printsec=frontcover#v=onepage&q&f=false.

Ram, B. (1997). *Land and Society in India: Agrarian Relations in Colonial North Bihar.* New Delhi: Orient Longman Ltd. Retrieved from http://books.google.ca/books?id=2b_j0mNe2FwC&printsec=frontcover#v=onepage&q&f=false.

Ramoo (25 February 2012). 'Punjab: Declining Water Table Reduce Area Under Paddy, Water Board Tells Govt'. Retrieved 17 September 2012, from Indian Agrarian Crisis: http://agrariancrisis.in/2012/02/25/punjab-declining-water-table-reduce-area-under-paddy-water-board-tells-govt/.

Rapson, E.J. (1995). *Ancient India: From the Earliest Times to the First Century A.D.*, 3rd edn., New Delhi: Asian Educational Services.

Rapson, E.J. (ed.). (1968). *The Cambridge History of India: Ancient India* (3rd Indian Reprint edn., vol. I). Delhi: S. Chand & Co.

Rattigan, W.H. (1884-5). 'Customary Law in India'. *Law Magazine and Law Review, 10*(1, 3 & 4, 5th Series).

Rawlinson, H.G. (1937 [3rd printing, 1965]). *India: A Short Cultural History.* New York: Frederick A. Praeger.

Ray, R. (1975). 'The Bengal Zamindars: Local Magnates and the State Before the Permanent Settlement'. *Indian Economic and Social History Review, 12*(3), 263-92.

——— (1987). *Project Report No. 29: Indianization of the Maithils.* Allahabad: Govind Ballabh Pant Socieal Science Institute.

Raychaudhuri, H. (2009). *Political History of Ancient India, from the Accession of Parikshit to the Extinction of the Gupta Dynasty* (8th edn.). Delhi: Oxford University Press.

Reddy, M.V. (2009). 'User Organizations as a Demand Management Option: Potentials, Problems and Prospects', in R.M. Saleth (ed.), *Strategic Analyses of the National River Linking Project (NRLP) of India, Series 3 – Promoting Irrigation Demand Management in India; Potentials, Problems and Prospects.* Colombo: International Water Management Institute, pp. 147-70. Retrieved from http://books.google.ca/books?id=LCtg4vYhQQ0C&printsec=frontcover#v=onepage&q=Table%201&f=false.

Redfield, R. (1947). 'The Folk Society'. *American Journal of Sociology, 52*(4), 292-308.

Rediff India Abroad (25 February 2004). *Bihar a 'Byword' for India's Worst: The Economist.* Retrieved 15 January 2012, from Rediff India Abroad - Business: http://www.rediff.com/money/2004/feb/25shining1.htm.

Rediff News (12 January 2012a). 'Bihar: Govt-run Schools have More Than 3,000 Fake Students'. Retrieved from Redif.com News: http://www.rediff.com/news/report/bihar-govt-run-schools-have-more-than-3000-fake-students/20120112.htm.

——— (7 October 2010). 'Crime and Politics go Hand-in-hand in Bihar Polls'. Retrieved from Rediff News: http://www.rediff.com/news/slide-show/slide-show-1-criminals-politics-go-hand-in-hand-in-bihar/20101007.htm.

——— (10 May 2012b). '15 Lakh "Fake" Students Enrolled in Bihar Schools!' Retrieved from Rediff.com News: http://www.rediff.com/news/report/lakh-15-fake-students-enrolled-in-bihar-schools/20120510.htm.

——— (26 November 2012c). 'Bihar Govt to Probe in Misuse of Rs 5,900 Cr NREGA Funds'. Retrieved from Redif.Com News: http://www.rediff.com/news/report/bihar-govt-orders-probe-in-misuse-of-rs-5/20121126.htm.

Reserve Bank of India (n.d.). 'Real Sector, National Income, Annualized Data'. Retrieved from Database on Indian Economy - RBI's Data Warehouse: http://dbie.rbi.org.in/DBIE/dbie.rbi?site=statistics.

Reuters (9 April 2009). 'Caste Calculations Still Dictate Bihar Politics'. Retrieved 2 October 2012, from *The Indian Express.* Online: http://www.indianexpress.com/news/caste-calculations-still-dictate-bihar-politics/445052/.

Rise Up. (30 August 2008). 'Bihar Flood: The Disaster Widens'. Retrieved 7 September 2012, from Rise up India Weblog: http://riseupindia.wordpress.com/2008/08/30/bihar-flood-the-disaster-widens/.

Rist, G. (2002). *The History of Development* (2nd edn., 3rd rpt.). (tr. P. Camiller). London: Zed Books.

——— (August 2007). 'Development as a Buzzword'. *Development in Practice, 17*(4-5), 485-91.

——— (2010). 'Development as a Buzzword', in A. Cornwall & D. Eade (eds.), *Deconstructing Development Discourse: Buzzwords and Fuzzwords.* Rugby, Warwickshire, U.K.: Practical Action Publishing in association with Oxfam, GB, pp. 19-27. Retrieved from http://www.scribd.com/doc/52829823/Deconstructing-Development-Discourse-Buzzwords-and-Fuzzwords.

——— (2010). *The History of Development: From Western Origins to Global Faith* (3rd edn., 2nd impression). (tr. P. Camiller). London: Zed Books. Retrieved from http://books.google.ca/books?id=NpV64yAbBvQC&printsec=frontcover#v=onepage&q&f=false.

Robb, P. (1997). *Ancient Rights and Future Comforts: Bihar, The Bengal Tenancy Act of 1885, and British Rule in India.* London: Curzon Press, London Studies on South Asia Studies, no. 13.

——— (2002). *A History of India.* New York: Palgrave.

Robb, P.G. (2007). *Peasants, Political Economy, and Law: Empire, Identity, and India.* New Delhi: Oxford University Press. Retrieved from http://books.google.ca/books?id=LuLsAAAAMAAJ&q=Bhumihars#search_anchor.

Robin, C. (2012). 'Bihar: The New Stronghold of OBC Politics', in C. Jaffrelot and S. Kumar (eds.), *Rise of the Plebeians?: The Changing Face of the Indian Legislative Assemblies.* Hoboken: Taylor & Francis, pp. 65-102.

Rocher, R. (1993). 'British Orientalism in the Eighteenth Century: The Dialectics of Knowledge and Government', in C.A. Breckenridge and P. v. Veer, *Orientalism and the Postcolonial Predicament: Perspectives on South Asia.* Philadelphia: University of Pennsylvania Press, pp. 215-49.

Roeck, T. (19 February 2014). *Oxford Professor Emeritus Charts Human Development.* Retrieved 26 February 2014, from The Observer: http://ndsmcobserver.com/2014/02/oxford-professor-emeritus-charts-human-development/.

Rogers, E.M. (1983). *Diffusion of Innovations.* New York: Free Press.

Rorabacher, J.A. (April 1973). 'Geo-Historical Approaches to Environment: The Evolution of Environmental Thought in Western Civilization'. *Journal of Geography, 72*(4), 31-41.

——— (2010). *Hunger and Poverty in South Asia.* Delhi: Gyan Publishing.

——— (2014). *Property, Land, Revenue, and Policy: The East India Company, 1757-1825.* Delhi: Manohar.

Rostow, W.W. (1960). *The Stages of Economic Growth.* London: Cambridge University Press.

Rousseau, J.-J. (2008). *The Social Contract* ([Originally published in 1762]). New York: Cosimo. Retrieved from http://books.google.ca/books?id=CyiOSafbzUYC&printsec=frontcover#v=onepage&q&f=false.

Roy, S. (2 August 2013). 'Mr Lalu Prasad at his Wily Worst in Fodder Scam'. Retrieved from Governance Now: http://www.governancenow.com/news/regular-story/mr-lalu-prasad-his-wily-worst-fodder-scam.

RT Question More (11 August 2010). *Indian Poor Starve While Grain Rots in Depots.* Retrieved 12 August 2012, from RT Question More: http://rt.com/news/india-hunger-grain-depot/.

Rudolph, L.I. and S.H. Rudolph (1984). *The Modernity of Tradition: Political Development in India.* Hyderabad: Orient Longman. Retrieved from http://books.google.ca/books?id=7guY1ut-0lwC&printsec=frontcover#v=onepage&q&f=false.

Rudra, K. (2012). *Atlas of Changing River Courses in West Bengal, 1767-2010.* Kolkata: Sea Explorers' Institute.

Sachs, W. (1992). *The Development Dictionary: A Guide to Knowledge as Power.* London: Zed Books. Retrieved 27 October 2012, from http://www.worldcat.org/title/development-dictionary-a-guide-to-knowledge-as-power/oclc/25597945/viewport?bib_key=ISBN:1856490440.

Safi, L.M. (2001). *Islam and the Secular State*. Retrieved from Islam Awareness: http://www.islamawareness.net/Secularism/secular.html.

Sahalan, A.W. (2014). 'Travellers to Ancient India'. Retrieved from ReoCities.com: http://www.reocities.com/rezuj/ati.html

Said, E.W. (1978, 2001). *Orientalism*. Delhi: Penguin Books. Retrieved from http://books.google.ca/books?id=66sIHa2VTmoC&printsec=frontcover#v=onepage&q&f=false.

Salama, M. (2011). *Islam, Orientalism, and Intellectual History: Moderniry and the Politics of Exclusion since Ibn Khaldun*. London: I.B. Tauris.

Samaj Pragati Sahayog (December 2011). 'Leveraging MGNREGA for Flood Control: A Case for Policy Reform in Bihar'. National Consortium of Civil Society Organizations on MGNREGA.

Samuels, W.J. (February 1961). 'The Physiocratic Theory of Property and State'. *Quarterly Journal of Economics, 75*(1), 96-111. Retrieved 18 November 2012, from http://members.shaw.ca/compilerpress1/Anno%20Samuels%20Property.htm.

Santayana, G. (1980). *Reason in Common Sense* (vol. 1). New York: Dover Publications.

Satapathy, A. (June 2012). 'The Idea of England in Eighteenth-century Indian Travel Writing'. (M. Ramanan and T. Mukherjee, eds.) *CLCWeb: Comparative Literature and Culture - Thematic Issue New Work in Comparative Indian Literatures and Cultures, 14*(2), Article 3: 1-8.

Savarkar, V.D. (1989 [1923]). *Hindutva: Who is a Hindu?* (6th edn.), New Delhi: Bharti Sahitya Sadan.

Schaff, P. (1890). *NPNF1-02. St. Augustin's City of God and Christian Doctrine*. New York: Christian Literature Publishing.

Schlatter, R. (1951). *Private Property: The History of an Idea*. New Brunswick: Rutgers University Press. Retrieved 18 November 2012, from http://books.google.ca/books?id=mwFeAAAAIAAJ&q=fullness.

Schuman, Michael. (2 September 2014). 'Why India's Modi and Japan's Abe Need Each Other – Badly', *Time*, retrieved 15 September 2014, from http://time.com/3255880/japan-india-narendra-modi-shinzo-abe-business-economy-trade-china/.

Schwartzberg, J.E. (1969). *Census of India, 1961: Occupational Structure and Level of Economic Development in India: A Regional Analysis* (vols. Monograph Series, Monograph no. 4). New Delhi: Office of the Registrar General.

Schwartzberg, J.E. (ed.) (1978). *A Historical Atlas of South Asia* (1st edn.). Chicago: University of Chicago Press.

Scott, F.R. (August-September 1952). 'Canada et Canada français', *Esprit* (Paris), nos. 193-4.

Sèfèriadès, M.L. (1995). 'Spondylus and Long-Distance Trade in Prehistoric Europe' (A.G. Brown, tr., and ed.), 178-89. Paris: Centre National de la

Recherche Scientifique (CNRS). Retrieved from http://www.nyu.edu/isaw/exhibitions/oldeurope/sites/all/themes/isaw/Spondylus.pdf.

Sekhri, S. (2012). *Sustaining Groundwater: Role of Policy Reforms in Promoting Conservation in India.* Washington, D.C.: National Council of Applied Economic Research, Indian Policy Forum 2012 - Brookings Institution.

Sen, A. (1981/2011). *Poverty and Famines: An Essay on Entitlement and Deprivation* (16th edn.), Delhi: Oxford University Press.

Sen, A. K. (1987). *On Ethics and Economics: The Royer Lectures.* Oxford: Blackwell.

Shah, T. (2011). *Past, Present and the Future of Canal Irrigation in India.* Colombo: International Water Management Institute.

Sharma, G. (1994). 'Contributions of the Socialists to the Kisan Movement in Bihar, 1931-1950', in K.M. Naidu (ed.), *Peasant Movements in India.* New Delhi: Reliance Publishing House, pp. 71-89.

Sharma, K. (2006). *Land Rights.* Development Alternatives, Pricewaterhouse Coopers, Ltd., Department for International Development, UK. Empowerpoor.org.

Sharma, S. (August 2008). 'Missing the River for the Dam'. Retrieved 11 September 2012, from Infochange-Environment: http://infochangeindia.org/environment/analysis/missing-the-river-for-the-dam.html.

Shewale, M.P. and S. Kumar (2005). *Climatological Features of Drought Incidences in India.* Pune: India Meteorological Department.

Shrivastava, R. (6 November 2014). 'Nitish Kumar Hints at "One Single Party" after Meeting Mulayam, Lalu', *NDTV*, Retrieved 7 December 2014, from http://www.ndtv.com/article/india/nitish-kumar-hints-at-one-single-party-after-meeting-mulayam-lalu-617014.

Shukla, V.N.; Government of India. (1969). *The Constitution of India* (5 edn.). Lucknow: Eastern Book Co.

Sidhu, H.S. (Fall 2005). 'Production Conditions in Contemporary Punjab Agriculture'. *Journal of Punjab Studies, 112*(2), 197-217.

Sidhu, R.S. and K. Vatta (2010). *Degradation and Management of Groundwater Resources in Indian Punjab.* Ludhiana: Department of Economic and Sociology, Punjab Agricultural University.

Singh, K. (2006). *Fall in Water Table in Central Punjab: How Serious.* Chandigarh: The Punjab State Farmers Commission, Government of Punjab.

——— (2008). 'Water Table Behaviour in Punjab: Issues and Policy Options'. (C.P. International Water Management Institute, Producer). Retrieved 12 September 2012, from Ideas - Research Division of the Federal Reserve Bank of St. Louis: http://ideas.repec.org/p/iwt/conppr/h042912.html; http://publications.iwmi.org/pdf/H042912.pdf.

Singh, L. (2012). *Popular Translations of Nationalism, Bihar 1920-1922.* Delhi: Primus Books. Retrieved from http://books.google.ca/books?id=J8jCrDbHtIMC&pg=PA5&lpg=PA5&dq=how+did+the+bihar+zamindars+differ+

from+the+bengal+zamindars&source=bl&ots=6xZiwMli48&sig=bqA2maX9mIf6ND4PFVaD7Jby7y8&hl=en&sa=X&ei=WuAsUvD5EI6kqwGWs4HYBw&ved=0CDoQ6AEwAzgU#v=onepage&q=how%20d.

Singh, P. (1 June 2008). 'Colonial State, Zamindars and the Politics of Flood Control in North Bihar (1850-1954)'. *Indian Economic and Social History Review, 45*(2), 239-59.

Singh, P., N. Ghose, N. Chaudhary and R. Hansda (2009). *Life in the Shadow of Embankments: Turning Lost Lands into Assets in the Kosi Basin of Bihar, India.* Kathmandu: International Centre for Integrated Mountain Development (ICIMOD).

Singh, R.K.P. (11 August 2011). 'Changing Face of Agriculture in Bihar'. Retrieved 14 September 2012, from *The Bihar Times: A Passage to Bihar*, http://www.bihartimes.in/articles/RKP/Agriculture.html.

Singh, S.N. (2012). *History of Tirhut: From the Earliest Times to the End of the Nineteenth Century* (2nd edn.). (H. Jha, ed.). Darbhanga: Maharajadhiraja Kameshwar Singh Kalyani Foundation, Maharajadhiraja Kameshwar Singh Bihar Heritage Series - 16.

Singh, S.R. (2005). *Land Reforms and Farm Diversity.* Delhi: APH Publishing.

Singh, S. and V.A. Kumar (2012). *Politics and Public Policies: Politics of Human Development in Uttar Pradesh, India.* Bangalore: The Institute for Social and Economic Change. Retrieved 29 June 2012.

Singh, V., J. Dhillon, S. Basu and G. Shanmugavel (2010). *Longman History & Civics, ICSE 9.* Noida, U.P.: Dorling Kindersley. Retrieved from http://books.google.ca/books?id=EXPouL4BYTMC&printsec=frontcover#v=onepage&q&f=false.

Singh, Y. (1973). *Modernization of Indian Tradition* (1977 rpt. edn.). Faridabad: Thomson Press.

Sinha, C.P. (June 2011). 'Climate Change and its Impact on the Wetlands of North Bihar', *Lakes & Reservoirs: Research & Management*, vol. 16, no. 2, pp. 109-11.

Sinha, C.S. (1988). 'Tradition and Development: The Context of Education', in Sachchidananda, B.B. Mandal, K.K. Verma and R.P. Sinha (eds.), *Tradition and Development.* New Delhi: Concept Publishing Co., pp. 179-88.

Sinha, R. (January 2009). 'Dynamics of a River System - The Case of the Kosi River in North Bihar'. *e-Journal Earth Science India, 2*(1), 33-45. Retrieved from http://www.earthscienceindia.info/.

Sinha, R. and P.F. Friend (1994). 'River Systems and their Sediment Flux, Indo-Gangetic Plains, Northern Bihar, India'. *Sedimentology, 41*(4), 825-45.

Sinha, S., S. Gururani and B. Greenberg (1 January 1997). 'The "New Traditionalist" Discourse of Indian Environmentalism'. *Journal of Peasant Studies, 24*(3), 65-99.

Siskin, W. (11 April 2010). 'Trip to Bhutan: Road Conditions in Bihar'. Retrieved from Welkinizer: Everything that Welkin's Gotta Say!: http://welkinizer.wordpress.com/category/trip-to-bhutan/.

Smith, G. (2008). *A Short History of Secularism.* London: I.B. Tauris.

Smolin, L. (2006/2007). *The Trouble with Physics.* Boston: Houghton Mifflin Co./A Mariner Book.

Sohini, S.V. (1962). 'Notes on the Revenue History of Darbhanga Raj'. *Journal of the Bihar Research Society,* 48, 105-41.

Sokoloff, K.L. and S.L. Engerman (Summer 2000). 'History Lessons: Institutions, Factor Endowments and Paths of Development in the New World'. *Journal of Economic Perspectives, 14*(3), 217-32.

Soszynski, H. (23 May 2007). 'Indian Princely States - Darbhanga'. Retrieved 21 August 2012, from India-Royalty Archives: http://archiver.rootsweb.ancestry.com/th/read/INDIA-ROYALTY/2007-05/1179883554.

Soubbotina, T. P. (2004). *Beyond Economic Growth: An Introduction to Sustainable Development* (2nd edn.). Washington, D.C.: The World Bank, WBI Learning Resources Series.

Spate, O.H. and A.T. Learmonth (1967). *India and Pakistan: A General and Regional Geography.* Suffolk: Methuen.

Special Task Force on Bihar. (2008). *Bihar's Agriculture Development: Opportunities & Challenges.* New Delhi: Government of India.

Srinivas, M.M. (1995/2005). *Social Change in Modern India* (rpt. edn.). Hyderabad: Orient Longman. Retrieved from http://books.google.ca/books?id=ZrJB-MsbWvoC&printsec=frontcover#v=onepage&q=Sanskritization&f=false.

Srivastava, A. (17 April 2009). 'Kitchen Instinct'. Retrieved 1 October 2012, from *India Today* - Election News: http://indiatoday.intoday.in/story/Kitchen+instinct/1/37184.html.

——— (1 July 2013a). 'Nitish's Most Favoured Dons'. Retrieved from India Today.in:http://indiatoday.intoday.in/story/nitish-kumar-bihar-chief-minister-tainted-cabinet-ministers-criminal-records/1/284623.html.

——— (15 July 2013b). 'Why Lalu is Laughing'. Retrieved from India Today.in:http://indiatoday.intoday.in/story/lalu-yadav-rjd-bihar-political-prospects/1/287101.html.

Srivastava, M. and A. MacAskill (29 August 2012). 'Poor in India Starve as Politicians Steal $14.5 Billion of Food'. Retrieved 5 November 2012, from Bloombersg.Com: http://www.bloomberg.com/news/2012-08-28/poor-in-india-starve-as-politicians-steal-14-5-billion-of-food.html.

Staff Reporter (28 June 2013). 'Fodder Scam: Jharkhand HC to Decide on Lalu's Transfer Plea'. Retrieved from *The Hindu*. Online: http://www.thehindu.com/news/national/other-states/fodder-scam-jharkhand-hc-to-decide-on-lalus-transfer-plea/article4860469.ece.

Stanbury, W.T. (August 1998). 'Canadian Content Regulations: The Intrusive State at Work', *Fraser Forum*, Special Issue.

Stein, N. (25 February 2013). 'Development: A Fight Between Modernity and Traditionalism?' Retrieved from hiiDunia: http://www.hiidunia.com/2013/02/development-a-fight-between-modernity-and-traditionalism/.

Sudhir-Yadav, et al. (2010). 'Water Balance in Dry Seeded and Puddle Transplanted Rice in Punjab, India'. *Soil Solutions for a Changing World.* Brisbane: 19th World Congress of Social Science, pp. 43-6.

Sukel, K. (26 February 2013). 'Replicate This'. Retrieved 6 June 2013, from Mission & State – Pacific Standard: http://www.psmag.com/magazines/march-april-2013/reproducibility-project-science-53141/.

Sullivan, B.M. (1999). *Seer of the Fifth Veda: Krsna Dvaipayana Vyasa in the Mahabharata.* Delhi: Motilal Banarsidass. Retrieved from http://books.google.co.in/books?id=8XO3Im3OMi8C&pg=PA86&dq=brahma+created+vedas&hl=en&sa=X&ei=W_MZUt71GMXJrAecvoCoCg&ved=0CC0Q6AEwAA#v=onepage&q&f=false.

Sun, G. (1989). *History of Navigation in Ancient China.* Beijing: Ocean Press.

Super Admin EMDAT (2014). [Université Catholique de Louvain, Brussels (Belgium)] Retrieved 27 February 2014, from The OFDA/CRED International Disaster Database: http://www.emdat.be/natural-disasters-trends.

Suryawanshi, S., R. Bhasha and S. Swarup (2010). *Principles of Pumps and Pumping Installation.* Nasik: Institution of Railway Electrical Engineers.

Svensson, J. (1999). 'Aid, Growth and Democracy'. *Economics and Politics, 11*(3), 275-97.

——— (2000). 'Foreign Aid and Rent-seeking'. *Journal of International Economics, 51*(2), 437-61.

Sweetman, W. (December 2004). 'The Prehistory of Orientalism: Colonialism and the Textual Basis for Bartholomaus Ziegenbalg's Account of Hinduism'. *New Zealand Journal of Asian Studies,* 6(2), 12-38.

Taddei, M. (1970). *The Ancient Civilization Series: India* (tr. J. Hogarth). London: Barrie & Jenkins.

Talling, P.J., J. Hunt and I. Harding (2014). *How Efficient is Organic Carbon* Brial and Eequestration *by Large-Scale Sediment Flows in the Deep Ocean, and what are the Implications for Global Carbon Cycle?* Retrieved from National Oceanography Centre - From Coast to Deep Ocean: http://noc.ac.uk/gsnocs/project/how-efficient-organic-carbon-burial-sequestration-large-scale-sediment-flows-deep-oce.

Tehelka Daily (July 2013). 'I Don't Want Modi as My PM – Amartya Sen'. Retrieved from: http://www.tehelka.com/i-dont-want-modi-as-my-pm-amartya-sen/.

Ter Haar, G. (2005). 'Religion: Source of Conflict or Resource for Peace?' in G.T. Haar and J.J. Busuttil (eds.), *Bridge or Barrier: Religion, Violence and Visions for Peace*. Leiden and Boston: Brill, pp. 3-34.

Ter Haar, G. and S. Ellis (September 2006). 'The Role of Religion in Development: Towards a New Relationship between the European Union and Africa'. *The European Journal of Development Research, 18*(3), 351-367. doi:10.1080/09578810600893403.

Thakur, P.C. (June 2012). 'Darbhanga Raj'. *The International Journal's Research Journal of Social Sciences and Management, 2*(2), 1-11. Retrieved from http://api.ning.com/files/08dJCY*3QrLpxKbPzk63O0w4H8MeK868Rg2Co5PiVsbGgkTufyve8WPOL2lK55pV1FZ3x8befHC4PGzDInq3XnKYrwUhzUOq/84426151PB1.pdf.

Thakur, S. (20 April 2014). *ABCD of Elections in Bihar*. Retrieved from *The Telegraph*, from http://www.telegraphindia.com/1140420/jsp/nation/story_18259296.jsp.

Thapar, R. (1966). *A History of India* (vol. I). Baltimore: Penguin Books.

——— (1981). 'Ideology and the Interpretation of Early Indian History'. *Social Science Information,* 20(2), 239-58.

The Contempt Theme (n.d.). 'What is Hindutva'. Retrieved 28 August 2013, from The Hindutva Movement: Examining Hindu Extremism in India: http://hinduextremism.wordpress.com/about/.

The Economic Times (11 April 2011). 'Bihar's Decadal Population Growth Rate Dips'. Retrieved 3 August 2013, from *The Economic Times - Politics and Nation*. Online: http://articles.economictimes.indiatimes.com/2011-04-11/news/29406296_1_literacy-rate-males-growth-rate.

The Economist (28 January 2010). 'The Bihari Enlightenment'. Retrieved from The Economist - Development: http://www.economist.com/node/15393980.

The Extinction Protocol (12 July 2013). 'Northern India Hit by Worst Flooding in 50 Years: 100 Villages Swamped in Bihar'. Retrieved from *The Extinction Protocol:* http://theextinctionprotocol.wordpress.com/2013/07/12/northern-india-hit-by-worst-flooding-in-50-years-100-villages-swamped-in-bihar/.

The Irish Times (3 July 2012). 'India's Children Starving to Death While Grain Rots in Fields'. Retrieved 3 November 2012, from *IrishTimes.Com.* On-line: http://www.irishtimes.com/newspaper/world/2012/0703/1224319264513.html.

The Telegraph (11 July 2013). 'Bihar at a Glance: Scam'. Retrieved from *The Telegraph.* Online: http://www.telegraphindia.com/1130711/jsp/bihar/story_17102824.jsp.

The Times of India (29 October 2012). 'Popular Articles About Munna Shukla'. Retrieved from *The Times of India.* Online: http://articles.timesofindia.indiatimes.com/keyword/munna-shukla.

Thomas, W.L. (ed.). (1956/1971). *Man's Role in Changing the Face of the Earth.* Chicago: University of Chicago Press.

Tiezzi, Shannon. (27 May 2015). 'Modi Remakes India-China Relations', *The Diplomat,* retrieved 27 May 2015, from http://thediplomat.com/2015/05/modi-remakes-india-china-relations/.

Tiffin, C. and A. Lawson (eds.) (1994). *Describing Empire: Post-colonialism and Textuality.* Routledge: London.

Times of India, Patna (29 March 2012a). *13362 Per Capita Income in Bihar.* Retrieved from *The Times of India,* Patna. Online: http://timesofindia.indiatimes.com/city/patna/13362-per-capita-income-in-Bihar/articleshow/12448422.cms.

Times of India, Patna (1 June 2012b). 'MLA's Husband Awadhesh Mandal Arrested'. Retrieved from *The Times of India,* Patna: http://timesofindia.indiatimes.com/city/patna/MLAs-husband-Awadhesh-Mandal-arrested/articleshow/13694674.cms.

Tomlinson, J. (1999). *Globalization and Culture.* Chicago: University of Chicago Press.

Tripathi, P. K. and K. Jamal (26 March 2011). 'Groundwater Crisis Runs Deep'. Retrieved from *The Telegraph.* On-line: http://www.telegraphindia.com/1110326/jsp/bihar/story_13743985.jsp.

Tripp, C. (1 January 2009). 'All (Muslim) Politics Is Local', Gilles Kepel and Ali A. Allawi explore the troubled relationship between power and Islam and conclude, each in his own way, that Muslims who seek to shape the world according to their religious values often confront an obd. *Foreign Affairs, Review Essays, 88*(5), 124-9. Retrieved from http://www.foreignaffairs.com/articles/65229/charles-tripp/all-muslim-politics-is-local.

Truman, H.S. (2012). 'Harry S. Truman, Inaugural Address, Thursday, January 20, 1949'. Retrieved 8 December 2012, from Bartleby.com - Inaugural Addresses of the Presidents: http://www.bartleby.com/124/pres53.html.

Trumbull, W. N. and H. J. Wall (1994). 'Estimating Aid-allocation Criteria with Panel Data'. *The Economic Journal, 104*(425), pp. 876-82.

Tullock, G. (Spring 2001). A Comment on Daniel Klein's 'A Plea to Economists Who Favor Liberty'. *Eastern Economic Journal,* 27(2), 203-7. Retrieved 4 June 2013.

Tyndale, W. (2001a). 'Poverty and Development: Has Religion a Contribution to Make?'. *Commentary: International Movement for a Just World, 1*(2), 1-5.

——— (2001b). 'Towards Sustainable Development: A Shift in Values'. *Commentary: International Movement for a Just World, 1*(8), 1-4.

UN (United Nations) (2014). 'The Universal Declaration of Human Rights', Retrieved 2 May 2014, from http://www.un.org/en/documents/udhr/index.shtml#a11.

UCF Today (12 November 2012). 'The Question of Caste in Modern India'.

Retrieved 12 November 2012, from *Community - UCF Today:* http://today.ucf.edu/the-question-of-caste-in-modern-india/.

UNDP (2009). 'Kosi Floods 2008: How We Coped! What We Need – Perception Survey on Impact and Recovery Strategies'. New Delhi: United Nations Development Programme.

——— (2001). *South Asia: State of the Environment 2001.* Pathumthani: United Nations Environment Programme/Regional Resource Centre for Asia and the Pacific.

UNICEF (n.d.). 'Bihar Drought'. Retrieved 13 September 2012, from India: http://www.unicef.org/india/media_2645.htm.

United Nations General Assembly (1987). *Report 42/187 of the World Commission on Environment and Development.* New York: United Nations. Retrieved 26 October 2012, from http://www.un.org/documents/ga/res/42/ares42-187.htm.

United Nations Press Release (3 May 2011). *World Population to Reach 10 Billion by 2100 if Fertility in all Countries Converges to Replacement Level.* New York: United Nations.

United Nations World Food Programme; Institute for Human Development. (2008). *Food Security Atlas for Rural Jharkhand.* New Delhi: Institute for Human Development.

van der Walt, A.V. (1999). 'The Constitutional Property Clause: Striking a Balance Between Guarantee and Limitation', in J. McLean (ed.), *Property and the Constitution.* Oxford: Hart Publishing, p. 276. Retrieved from http://books.google.ca/books?id=UkINeBpxESIC&pg=PA118&lpg=PA118&dq=Kameshwar+Singh+v.+State+of+Bihar,+AIR+(38)+1951+Pat+91+(FB).&source=bl&ots=k3IR6p2HwF&sig=hMfFEFZ8SAISh-jAFPzAQeikhSA&hl=en#v=onepage&q=Kameshwar%20Singh%20v.%20State%20of%20Bihar%2C%20AI.

Varadarajarn, T. (19 May 2014). 'After Us Hegemony, Modi, Indian Caesar? Or, How Not to Interpret the Indian Election Results'. Retrieved from https://rpalat.wordpress.com/2014/05/19/modi-an-indian-caesar-or-how-not-to-interpret-the-indian-election-results/.

Venkataraman, G. (2010). 'The Vedas: Their Evolution and Significance'. Retrieved 11 November 2012, from *Tamil Brahmins:* http://www.tamilbrahmins.com/general-discussions/3871-evolution-significance-vedas.html.

Venkatesan, J. (19 October 2010). 'Court Rejects Plea to Make Property a Fundamental Right'. Retrieved 21 August 2012, from *The Hindu:* http://www.thehindu.com/news/national/article836599.ece.

Verma, P. (6 June 2012). 'Ranvir Sena Chief Brahmeshwar Singh's Murder a Ploy to Corner Nitish Kumar'. Retrieved 3 October 2012, from *IBN Live - Online:* http://ibnlive.in.com/news/brahmeshwar-killing-a-ploy-to-corner-nitish/264670-37-64.html.

Visram, R. (2002). *Asians in Britain: 400 Years of History.* London: Pluto.

von Braun, J., M.S. Swaminathan and M.W. Rosegrant (2004). *Agriculture, Food Security, Nutrition and the Millennium Development Goals.* Washington, DC: International Food Policy Research Institute.

von Oppen, M. (1978). *The Effect of Interregional Trade and Market Infrastructure on Aggregate Productivity.* Pantacheru, India: International Crop Research Institute for Semi-Arid Tropics, Economic Program.

von Oppen, M., B.K. Njehia and A. Ijaimi (1997). 'Policy Arena: The Impact of Market Access on Agricultural Productivity: Lessons from India, Kenya and Sudan'. *Journal of International Development, 9*(1), 117-31.

Wajihuddin, M. (31 July 2010). 'Decline of Brahmin Dulha Bazaar in Bihar'. Retrieved 30 September 2012, from *Times of India* - Online: http://articles.timesofindia.indiatimes.com/2010-07-31/india/28281912_1_saurath-sabha-maithil-brahmins-marriage.

Waldman, A. (2 December 2002). 'India's Poor Starve as Wheat Rots'. Retrieved 3 January 2011, from *The New York Times* -- Asia Pacific -- On-line: http://www.nytimes.com/2002/12/02/international/asia/02FARM.html?pagewanted=all.

Warnholz, J. (October 2007). 'Poverty Reduction for Profit? A Critical Examination of Business Opportunities at the Bottom of the Pyramid, AEH Working Paper Series QEHWPS 160'. Oxford: Queen Elizabeth House Working Papers Series.

Warrick, R. A. (1975). *Drought Hazards in the United States: A Research Assessment, Monograph # 4.* Boulder: Institute of Behavioral Science, University of Colorado.

Warrier, M. (2004). *Hindu Shelves in a Modern World: Guru Faith in the Mata Amritanandamayi Mission.* London: Routledge Curzon. Retrieved from http://books.google.ca/books?id=foMbmT6KZOgC&pg=PA16&lpg=PA16&dq=Max+Weber,+hinduism,+other-worldly&source=bl&ots=ylIqd_EbNm&sig=0TaZjoqqV90qq0UWZnjin0jcSsY&hl=en&sa=X&ei=JIszUvOWBcKj2QX2uICwBQ&ved=0CGEQ6AEwCA#v=onepage&q=Max%20Weber%2C%20hinduism%2C%20ot.

Waskey, A. J. (2007). 'The Political Theory of Theocracy'. *National Sociial Science Journal, 28*(1), 116-29. Retrieved from National Social Science Association: http://www.nssa.us/journals/2007-28-1/2007-28-1-16.htm.

Watson, G. (2009). 'Resistance to Change', in D.G. Burke, *Organization Change: A Comprehensive Reader.* San Francisco: Jossey-Bass/John Wiley & Sons, pp. 364-76.

Weick, K.E. (1979). *The Social Psychology of Organizing* (2nd edn.). New York: McGraw-Hill.

——— (1995). *Sensemaking in Organizations.* Thousand Oaks: Foundations for Organizational Science, Sage.

Weir, S. (2007). *The Tribal Order: Politics and Law in the Mountains of Yemen.*

Austin: University of Texas Press, Modern Middle East Series, no. 23. Retrieved from http://books.google.ca/books?id=4W3o6bUwCYEC&printsec=frontcover#v=onepage&q&f=false.

Wejnert, B. (2002). 'Integrating Models of Diffusion of Innovations: A Conceptual Framework'. *Annual Review of Sociology,* 28 *(Annual Reviews),* 297-306. doi:10.1146/annurev.soc. doi: 28.110601.141051.

Whitcombe, E. (2005). 'Irrigation', in K. Kumar and M. Desai (eds.), *The Cambridge Economic History of India, c. 1757-1970* (vol. 2, pp. 677-737). Hyderabad: Orient Longman.

Whitfield, S. (1999). *Life Along the Silk Road.* Berkeley: University of California Press.

Whitfield, S. and U. Sims-Williams (eds.) (2004). *The Silk Route: Trade, Travel, War and Faith.* London: British Library.

Wiki Commons (13 November 2005). *River Levee Cross Section Figure.png.* Retrieved 3 March 2014, from Wikipedia: http://commons.wikimedia.org/wiki/File:River_Levee_Cross_Section_Figure.png.

Wikipedia (20 June 2012). 'Climate of Bihar'. Retrieved 15 September 2012, from http://en.wikipedia.org/wiki/Climate_of_Bihar#Precipitation.

——— (3 June 2014). 'List of Political Parties in India'. Retrieved from: http://en.wikipedia.org/wiki/List_of_political_parties_in_India.

Willcocks, W. (1928 [1984]). *Ancient System of Irrigation in Bengal and its Application to Modern Problems.* Delhi: B.R. Publishing.

Willett, M. (17 December 2013). 'A Fascinating New Poll Shows That Americans are Losing Faith in God'. Retrieved from *Business Insider:* http://www.businessinsider.com/new-harris-poll-on-religion-in-america-2013-12.

Williams, M. (14 April 2009). *Bihar: After the "Jungle Raj".* Retrieved 1 October 2012, from *Reuters.* Online India Insight: http://blogs.reuters.com/india/2009/04/14/bihar-after-the-jungle-raj/.

Williamson, C.R. (2008). 'Foreign Aid and Human Development: The Impact of Foreign Aid to the Health Sector'. *Southern Economic Journal, 75*(1), 188-207.

——— (10 March 2010). 'Exploring the Failure of Foreign Aid: The Role of Incentives and Information'. *Review of Austrian Economics, 23*(1), 17-33.

Winerman, L. (February 2013). 'Interesting Results: Can They be Replicated?' Retrieved 1 July 2013, from American Psychological Association: http://www.apa.org/monitor/2013/02/results.aspx.

Witsoe, J. (2011). 'Corruption as Power: Caste and Political Imagination of the Postcolonial State'. *American Ethnologist, 38*(1), 73-85.

Wittfogel, K. (1981). *Oriental Despotism: A Comparative Study of Total Power.* New York: Vintage Books.

Witzel, M. (2006). 'Rama's Realm: Indocentric Rewritings of Early South Asian History', in G.G. Fagan, *Archeological Fantasies: How Pseudoarchaeology*

Misrepresents the Past and Misleads the Public. London: Routledge, pp. 203-32. Retrieved from http://www.worldcat.org/title/archaeological-fantasies-how-pseudoarchaeology-misrepresents-the-past-and-misleads-the-public/oclc/58456268/viewport.

World Bank (2005). *India's Water Economy: Bracing for a Turbulent Future.* Washington, DC: The International Bank for Reconstruction and Development/The World Bank.

——— (2006?). *Bihar – Towards a Development Strategy.* Washington, DC: World Bank.

——— (2010). *Deep Wells and Prudence: Towards Pragmatic Action for Addressing Groundwater Overexploitation in India.* Washington, DC: The International Bank for Reconstruction and Development/The World Bank.

World Food Programme and Institute for Human Development (2009). *Food Security Atlas of Rural Bihar.* New Delhi: Institute for Human Development.

Wrenn, E. (28 May 2012). 'Climate Change Wiped Out One of the World's First, Great Civilizations More than 4,000 Years Ago'. Retrieved 12 September 2012, from Daily Mail Online: http://www.dailymail.co.uk/sciencetech/article-2151143/Climate-change-wiped-worlds-great-civilisations-4-000-years-ago.html.

Writer at Large (9 September 2008). *Killer Kosi Could Leave Bihar Barren.* Retrieved 7 September 2012, from Writer at Large: http://rovingwriter.blogspot.ca/2008/09/killer-kosi-could-leave-bihar-barren.html.

Yadav, C.P., B.S. Gupta and S. Kumar (2000). 'Export Potential of Agriculture', in J. Prasad (ed.), *Export Potential of Indian Agriculture: Bihar – Perspective and Issues*. New Delhi: Mittal Publications, pp. 113-22.

Yadav, P. (29 June 2012). *Ground Water Level Declining, Contamination Rising in Punjab*. Retrieved 17 September 2012, from *The Times of India*: http://articles.timesofindia.indiatimes.com/2012-06-29/india/32472235_1_ground-water-nitrate-water-table.

Yang, A.A. (1989). *The Limited Raj: Agrarian Relations in Colonial India, Saran District, 1793-1920.* Berkeley: University of California Press. Retrieved from http://books.google.ca/books?id=Ck4jmD7H34UC&printsec=frontcover#v=onepage&q&f=false.

——— (1999). *Bazaar India: Markets, Society, and the Colonial State in Bihar.* Berkeley: University of California Press.

Yardley, J. (8 August 2010). *India Asks, Should Food Be a Right for the Poor?* Retrieved 14 December 2012, from *The New York Times* - Asia Pacific: http://www.nytimes.com/2010/08/09/world/asia/09food.html?pagewanted=all&_r=0.

Young, G.K. (2001). *Rome's Eastern Trade.* London: Routledge.

Zedong, M. (1964). *Quotations from Chairman Mao (The Little Red Book).* Peking: Foreign Languages Press.

Zee Media Bureau (6 July 2013a). 'Nitish Kumar Will be Taught Lesson for Betraying BJP: Narendra Modi'. Retrieved from Zeenews.com: http://zeenews.india.com/news/nation/nitish-kumar-will-be-taught-lesson-for-betraying-bjp-narendra-modi_860316.html.

——— (13 August 2013b). 'Nitish Kumar is Secular, Have Always Sought Support from Right-minded People: PM'. Retrieved from *Z News:* http://zeenews.india.com/news/nation/nitish-kumar-is-secular-have-always-sought-support-from-right-minded-people-pm_855637.html.

Zee News (25 November 2010). 'Politicians with Criminal Backgrounds Make it to Bihar House'. Retrieved from *Zee News:* http://zeenews.india.com/news/bihar/politicians-with-criminal-background-make-it-to-bihar-house_670318.html.

Zeebiz.com (11 March 2014). 'Pushing Food Security at WTO is a Challenge: India', Retrieved from, http://zeenews.india.com/business/news/economy/pushing-food-security-at-wto-is-a-challenge-india_96013.html.

Zoaib (18 May 2012). 'Breaking Free: How Nitish Kumar Turned Bihar into a Model of Indian Reform'. Retrieved 30 October 2012, from Sissat.pk - On line: http://www.siasat.pk/forum/showthread.php?112370-Nitish-Kumar-The-Chief-Minister-who-changed-Bihar.

Index